D1246843

Contemporary Labor Economics: Issues, Analysis, and Policies

Juanita M. Kreps
Duke University
Gerald G. Somers
University of Wisconsin at Madison
Richard Perlman
University of Wisconsin at Milwaukee

Wadsworth Publishing Company, Inc.
Belmont, California

Designer: Russell K. Leong

Editor: Kevin Gleason

Technical Illustrator: Mark Schroeder

ISBN 0-534-00303-6
L. C. Cat. Card No. 73-83273
Printed in the United States of America

1 2 3 4 5 6 7 8 9 10—77 76 75 74 73

Preface

The past decade has witnessed notable changes in the focus of labor problems and the policies adopted to solve them. Manpower policies and programs for the disadvantaged—programs that were not in existence until 1960—have become an integral part of our national attack on unemployment.

Textbooks in the labor field can become dated quickly. Although such issues as unemployment, inflation, work, and welfare have long been with us, their configuration and relevance have changed in the last few years. The Manpower Development and Training Act (MDTA) of 1962 was aimed at members in the main stream of the work force who were unemployed or potentially unemployed because of technological change. By the middle of the 1960s, the MDTA's emphasis had shifted to the disadvantaged. By the end of the decade, the earlier reliance on institutional training in vocational schools had been replaced by a growing stress on the subsidization of private employers. However, the initial success of on-the-job training rested on an expanding economy; and by the early 1970s, with relatively high rates of national unemployment, attention was shifting from the subsidization of private employers to the creation of jobs in the public service. Whereas manpower policies had been the solution to unemployment in the 1960s, now there is growing interest in the potential effect of these programs on inflation and on shifting persons from welfare to work.

This volume covers the most recent issues in the labor market and describes and evaluates the most recent policies enacted or proposed as solutions to labor market problems. In addition, the fundamental forces at work in the labor market are described and analyzed, both to help us understand the causes of current problems and to predict the changes that lie ahead. The analytical sections include the most recent research in labor force participation, internal and dual labor markets, wage-price relationships, income maintenance experiments, and investments in human capital. Trade unionism, collective bargaining, and social security are integrated with the discussions of wage determination, wage-price relationships, and income-maintenance programs to provide a new perspective on the traditional institutions and concepts.

Thus, the volume strives to achieve currency without neglecting traditional labor market analyses and institutional developments necessary for understanding the modern issues. The presentation is kept at an introductory level for those who may be unacquainted with labor economics and employment policy.

Contents

Part One   Introduction

Chapter One

Labor Economics: An Overview

Introduction

This volume is concerned primarily with current issues and policies in the labor market. The key issues are the relationship of unemployment to wages and inflation, and the relationship of work and welfare. As is noted in Parts Five and Six, these issues are by no means new. The difficulties of achieving full employment while maintaining price stability were recognized in the writings of economists during World War II and in the post-war years; some economists stressed that union wage pressures bring about cost-push inflation in an economy moving toward full employment. Similarly, since the 1930s there have been expressions of concern with rising welfare rolls: controversies have centered on the ability of welfare recipients to take gainful employment and the extent to which public welfare payments might create disincentives for work.

Even though these problems have been with us for some time, they have recently become matters of urgent national concern. The coexistence of relatively high rates of both unemployment and price increases in the early 1970s has led to the first imposition of wage and price controls in our peacetime economy. The unemployment–inflation dilemma has profound implications for the role of collective bargaining in a free society; and has brought renewed attention to manpower policies—such as training and mobility programs—as a substitute for tax and spending policies which have traditionally been the most useful measures for dealing with national unemployment and inflation.

The long-standing issue of work and welfare has come to the fore not only because the welfare rolls have grown exceptionally in recent years but also because in the past decade the nation has concentrated on the problems of poverty in America. As the American economy has become more affluent, the remaining pockets of poverty in rural areas and urban ghettos have been more glaringly revealed. The work versus welfare issue has assumed added importance because it is related to discrimination in the labor market against racial minorities and women. Thus, income-maintenance programs have been accompanied by antidiscrimination measures and manpower policies to further the employment of the disadvantaged.

Apart from the issues, evaluation of recently enacted labor-market policies is a central purpose of this volume, for the problems they have been designed to combat are fundamental and persistent. However, we cannot evaluate such policies without a full understanding of the forces that have given rise to current labor-market problems. Thus, the discussion of issues and policies in the final two parts of this volume is preceded by an analysis of the structure, institutions, and functioning of the labor market.

The labor market

Framework of the labor market

In a "perfect" labor market, without the institutional factors that intervene in the free flow of labor, employers would compete freely in the hiring of labor, and workers would be allocated in accordance with market demand with frictionless mobility. The decisions of employers and workers, motivated by economic principles, would lead to an efficient allocation of labor, the elimination of wage differentials for similar work, and compensation reflecting the worker's productivity. However, the labor market departs significantly from this "perfect" model. As is discussed in Chapter 2, labor is not a commodity to be bought and sold like securities on a stock exchange. Workers are not homogeneous productive units, uniform in ability and application, and neither workers nor employers have the information about alternatives which would permit "full economic rationality" in their labor-market choices.

Equally important, labor unions, management, and government affect the allocation of labor and the workings of the labor market. There are actually labor markets within labor markets, the boundaries of which are defined by institutional forces as well as worker preferences. Each business establishment constitutes an "internal" labor market, with a complex set of interconnections with the "external" labor market outside the plant or firm. Most workers who have acquired some seniority in a particular plant move much more readily within the establishment than between establishments. And even within the internal labor market, rules established by management and collective bargaining agreements often confine mobility to within particular occupations. The boundaries of these labor submarkets within an establishment will be shaped by provisions for training and promotion.

Like the internal labor market, the external labor market (outside a plant or firm) is actually a series of labor submarkets. For although there is substantial migration from region to region and state to state, workers move much more readily from one job to another in a particular locality. Moreover, even in a single community there is often a dual labor market for blacks and whites, for men and women, for skilled and unskilled. A disadvantaged worker with an eighth-grade education and no vocational skills can expect to move repeatedly from one low-paying, dead-end job to another. He may never enter the labor market enjoyed by most workers—a market with some permanency of job tenure and some chance for advancement to more remunerative and pleasing work.

It is these labor submarkets, which result from frictions or imperfections in the mobility of labor, that explain why wages vary between occupational groupings within business establishments, between employers in the same community, and between regions of the country. Although the long-run forces of the market might promote equal pay for equal qualifications and equal work, short-run impediments and imperfections persistently interfere with the accomplishment of this long-run goal.

Supply and demand

Efficiency of the labor market becomes significantly impeded when there are fundamental shifts in labor demand and supply: problems arise because changes in demand are not always met by changes in supply, and new entrants to the labor force cannot quickly respond to new labor market needs.

Changing demand   Such far-reaching changes in the U. S. labor market in the last fifty years help to explain the problems that are the focus of our inquiry. As our living standards rise we shift from coal heating to gas. This change in tastes forces coal miners into unemployment. As airlines, automobiles, and buses become our primary means of transportation, railroad workers fall from their former positions at the pinnacle of American labor and many become redundant.

As is noted in Chapter 4, these marked declines have occurred in primary industries, in which workers extract minerals from the land or harvest the fruits of the land. Within secondary industries (manufacturing), changing consumer demands have also forced substantial shifts in labor, with autos, aluminum products, and electronics absorbing ever larger segments of the workforce, moving from declining products no longer in favor. The government's demand attracted large numbers into aerospace and defense production in the '40s and '50s, but by the early '70s this demand had declined.

Demand for labor has expanded most in the area of services—especially government services. In this tertiary sector the affluent society has its greatest impact; as we move beyond the basic requirements of food, shelter, and clothing, increasing incomes and wealth permit us to devote more of our time and resources to education, entertainment, and the public services which improve the amenities of life. As is indicated in greater detail in later chapters, much of the growth of employment in the United States in recent years has come in the public rather than in the private sector. The federal government has had its principal impact on labor demand through the explosion of military expenditures in this century of wars. But the greatest growth in the demand for labor services in the public sector has been at state and local levels, reflecting the requirements of education, welfare, and roads.

The other major influence on the demand for labor is technological change. Since the industrial revolution improvements in the methods and organization of production have been characteristic of the economic development of Western nations. There is some evidence that the pace of this advance has quickened sharply in the past 50 years, and changing methods of production have always been an unsettling force in the labor market. The full impact of technology on labor is discussed in detail in Chapter 19.

The declines noted above in labor demand in primary industries are as much due to technological change as to shifts in the tastes of consumers. Coal miners are made redundant not only by consumer preference for gas heating but, just as important, by the introduction of continuous-mining machines which have increased the tonnage per man-day tenfold during the past 50 years. When declines in consumer demand are accompanied by production changes which permit fewer men to satisfy that declining need, there result the prolonged, extensive pockets of unemployment characteristic of coal mining areas. Dieselization has had a similar compounding effect, along with changing preferences in transportation, in reducing labor requirements on the railroads. And, most notable of all, the cumulative spread of mechanization on the farms has done more than any other factor in changing our workforce from predominantly agricultural to predominantly urban.

The quickening pace of technological change in the last couple of decades has come to be labeled automation—a term that strikes terror in the hearts of some and bountiful joy in others. Automation embodies the mechanization of the eighteenth century, the mass-production principle of the present century and the automatic, electronic controls of the post–World-War II period. Heralded by some as the prime mover in a new era of boundless abundance and efficiency, automation has been feared by others as the harbinger of manless factories, unemployment, and want. Although these far-reaching predictions have not come to pass, there can be little doubt about the unbalancing effect of recent technological advance on labor demand in particular sectors of the economy.

The price of technological advance is loss of employment opportunity for some. And this has always been so. For the craftsman who produced hand-blown glassware or hand-rolled cigars, the loss of employment due to mechanization of these functions 50 years ago was no less serious than the loss of employment in automated factories today. Indeed, those who study the impact of automation on the demand for labor might well borrow Dickens' words that it is the best of times and it is the worst of times. Like mechanization and mass production of an earlier period, automation leaves in its wake a network of contrasts, contradictions, and imbalances in the labor market; and the technological revolution makes necessary a revolution in corrective manpower policy.

The rapid changes in labor demand have been especially troublesome because of their cumulative impact on particular workers in particular occupations, industries, and geographic regions. The growing literature on plant shutdowns is replete with unfortunate repercussions of changing demand on workers in the local area. When the combination of consumer shifts and technological change has forced the closing of a coal mine, a railroad center, a meatpacking plant, a papermill, or an aerospace plant, the labor market and the entire economy of the area surrounding the closure frequently become depressed. Many communities are dominated by a single mine, mill, or factory, especially in those industries that have been most seriously affected by declining demand for labor.

Thus, depressed industries frequently cause depressed areas. It is no coincidence that the most persistent pockets of unemployment and poverty in the United States are in the Appalachian coalfields, in former railroad centers, in marginal farming regions, and in former lumbering areas.

The workers hardest hit by these shifts in the demand for labor are those who are least transferable to other occupations, industries, or areas: the old, the uneducated, the unskilled, and those with skills highly specialized to the defunct industry or occupation. Is it any wonder, then, that the Appalachian coal miner, laid off after fifty years in the mines, sits idly and forlornly in the former company town, hoping against hope that some miracle will reopen the only employment that he has known and for which he has a skill that could command a respectable wage?

While the losers bemoan their fate, those who gain from consumer demand and technological change favor the manpower revolution. The technician who helped design a continuous-mining machine in a California factory may find his services in great demand in the very period in which the West Virginia coal miner has been laid off by use of the more productive machine. Less directly, technicians, skilled craftsmen, and some service workers greatly benefit from the shifts of labor demand characteristic of an affluent society and advanced technology. Professional vacancies and skill shortages exist side by side with pools of persistent unemployment among the unskilled. The white-collar worker, especially at higher levels of education and training, may find budding employment opportunities at the very time the most disadvantaged of the blue-collar workers are reduced to an ever-shrinking labor market.

Changing supply   As is discussed in further detail in Chapter 3, shifts in demand for labor cannot be disassociated from shifts in supply. As supply changes and affects factor prices, demand responds; and in turn many shifts in supply are a result of changes in demand.

When demand for labor diminishes, older men, often less educated and less skilled than their younger counterparts, find themselves unwanted and because of improved social security benefits and private pension plans are able to retire earlier. Thus, in recent decades the labor-force participation rate of males over 65, the ratio of workers in this age–sex group to the total number in the group, has declined sharply. Likewise, the labor-force participation rate of young male workers has been sharply reduced: the growing need for highly educated technical and skilled personnel has prompted many younger people to remain longer in school. They have been aided by the growing affluence of our society which permits such increased investments in human beings.

However, these very forces of industrial and occupational change have much benefited young, better educated women. Just as technological advance has reduced their household chores, it has increased the opportunities for their employment in offices, service establishments, and factories. Clearly women have not to any significant degree directly displaced older and younger men. (One need only think of the elderly male office clerks featured in the writings of Dickens to appreciate that even a direct displacement is not completely fanciful.) However, most often women have taken new jobs created by technology, whereas older men have been displaced from the declining primary sectors of industry.

Labor supply has been redistributed largely in response to changing labor demand, but there have also been exogenous changes in labor supply (not called forth by demand changes), with significant impact on the labor market. Population-growth and birth rates since World War II have produced in recent years a great influx of young workers into the labor market. Those among them who failed to complete high school found themselves at a growing disadvantage in the competition for desirable jobs. Thus, the mere change in numbers in certain age–sex categories of the labor force, unrelated to labor demand, has intensified the imbalances and employment problems for younger members of the labor force.

These imbalances are reflected in the chronically high unemployment rates for the young: since 1948 the rates for teenagers are practically at depression depths, are increasing, and are becoming especially high for girls. As the discussion in Part IV indicates, the combination of youth and racial minority status has given rise to the most intractable problems of unemployment. Many of the labor-market policies of the 1960s and '70s have been geared to ameliorate these problems.

Labor-market institutions

Unions and collective bargaining come into being in response to such problems as unemployment and income insecurity. In their efforts to protect workers against these ills, however, unions give rise to a new set of labor-market issues and policies. Government intervention in the labor market stems from the perceived need to regulate union–management relations. The government also intervenes directly through passage and enforcement of such labor legislation as that regulating minimum wages and maximum hours, the Employment Service, and the protection of occupational health and safety. Since collective bargaining and government regulations affect labor supply and demand, the price of labor, and the cost of production, they have a significant impact on the functioning of the labor market.

Part Three is concerned with the factors which give rise to unions and to the establishment of union–management collective-bargaining agreements. It is seen that by collective bargaining unions strive to raise the income of workers, and that through strike activity and through provisions governing the layoff and promotion of employees they can affect supply and allocation of labor. The effects of unions on wages and employment in the labor market are more fully analyzed in Chapter 13 of Part Four.

Although unionism and collective bargaining are still strongest in the private sector, especially in manufacturing, mining, and transportation, the greatest recent expansion has been in federal, state, and local public employment. As is noted in Chapter 8, many of the policies and procedures developed in private collective bargaining are now being extended to negotiations between government agencies and their employees. Wage bargaining and job-security provisions for government workers are found not only in blue-collar negotiations but also in a growing number of white-collar and professional unions and associations. Though the government labor market differs from that of the private sector, they share many factors of supply, demand, and mobility. Expanding unionism in public services is likely to have as profound an impact on government labor markets as it has long had in private employment.

Among the early acts of government intervention in the labor market was the effort to regulate union–management relations. The Labor-Management Relations Act (Wagner Act) of 1935 coincided with the great upsurge of unionism in that decade. With the Taft-Hartley Act of 1947 and the Landrum-Griffin Act of 1959, public regulation of collective bargaining and internal union affairs became more extensive and detailed. In recent years there have been no further extensions of such general regulation of union-management activities, in spite of a number of Congressional and Executive proposals for such regulation.

The principal concern with unions and collective bargaining has focused on the effects of strikes and the possible inflationary impact of wage negotiations. Strikes and wage pressures are deemed by many legislators to significantly affect the labor-market process and the cost of goods and services. Although efforts have failed to further regulate strikes that may imperil the national health and safety, the passage of wage and price controls in 1971 reflects government concern with the inflationary impact of collective bargaining (see the discussions in Chapters 9, 13, and 20).

Though related to collective bargaining, wage and price controls are also part of a lengthy tradition of direct government intervention in the functioning of the labor market. Since passage of the Fair Labor Standards Act in 1938, the federal government has set minimum wages and maximum hours (prior to the payment of overtime premiums) for the bulk of American workers. Most states have set similar wages-and-hours legislation for certain groups not covered by the federal act. Minimum wages have risen progressively in the succeeding years, and they are likely to rise further, especially against a background of inflationary wage–price increases in the economy as a whole. As is noted in Part IV, government establishment of a minimum wage may have significant implications for employment and unemployment. Whereas opponents of such legislation are alarmed by the cost effects of minimum wages in marginal firms, those who favor expansions in the level and coverage of the minimum-wage law see it as an important contribution to the reduction of poverty.

The public Employment Service established by the Wagner-Peyser Act of 1933 was one of the first measures enacted in Franklin Roosevelt's New Deal. Like private employment agencies, the system of public employment offices is designed to make the labor market more efficient by matching job seekers with available job opportunities. Since the Employment Service has been given increasing responsibilities for the management of manpower policies, it plays an important role in the labor market—and is discussed in further detail in connection with government labor-market policies.

A third example of government control over private employment decisions is found in the Occupational Safety and Health Act of 1970. The act was designed to protect workers against industrial health and safety hazards from air contaminants and physical agents as well as from such traditional dangers as unguarded machines. The act notes that it is the policy of the government "to assure as far as possible every working man and woman in the nation safe and healthful working conditions." However, though the goal is commendable, it has been noted that detailed enforcement of the act might significantly increase production costs; and union officials have deplored the lack of enforcement of the new legislation.[1]

---

[1] See the discussion on the initial experience with this recent legislation in *Proceedings of the Industrial Relations Research Association* (Madison, Wisconsin: September 1972).

Like other institutional influences in the labor market, the government's laudable desire to provide protection to workers through O.S.H.A. has aroused controversy because of the resulting departures from what might be considered a competitive model of the labor market.

Unemployment and poverty

Determinants of employment and income

A person's decision to seek work may be independent of the business cycle or the demand for labor, but who actually finds work is essentially determined by the complex of competitive and institutional labor-market factors discussed in the previous section. As the analytical chapters in Part IV indicate, these factors influence the amount of employment and wages paid in the firm, in the labor market, and in the economy as a whole.

How many are to be employed is linked to how much they are to be paid, especially in the long run. And both employment and wages are crucially influenced by worker productivity, the contribution of their service to output. For shorter periods of time, collective bargaining and managerial and government policies may temporarily separate the close links between employment, productivity, and money income. But if money wages are established at levels significantly above value productivity, the contribution of labor services to the value of output, in the long run, the quantity of employment in particular firms is likely to suffer; and in the total economy, product prices are likely to rise, thereby reducing the workers' real income, money income corrected for the price change.

Aggregate demand for goods, services, and labor

Since the demand for labor is derived from the demand for goods and services, rising nationwide unemployment has traditionally been linked to insufficient total demand for goods and services. The Gross National Product —that is, the value of all goods and services produced in the economy—has frequently been inadequate to sustain full employment. As is discussed in detail in Chapters 14 and 20, demand was deficient in the Great Depression of the 1930s and has been in more recent periods of recession. When there are more job seekers than job openings almost everywhere in the country, employment must be restored first through stimulation of total demand for goods and services.

Demand for labor is influenced by productivity and technology as well as by total monetary demand. As noted in the preceding sections and in fuller detail in Chapter 19, technology has had a profound impact on the quantity and quality of work. Indeed, some have feared that automation is drying up the total number of jobs in the economy; they urge a shift from training for work to the training of workers for leisure.

These dire predictions notwithstanding, a mere listing of the job requirements for today or five years hence belies the myth of the disappearance of work. When the National Planning Association a decade ago prepared estimates of the costs of attaining various national goals, it discovered that the first-priority needs far exceeded our productive capacity. And these were quite modest goals: a limited attack on the housing, health, transportation, and education needs then confronting the nation. Yet the Gross National Product by 1975 was expected to fall $150 billion short of the volume needed for their attainment.

Since that time our needs have grown, and each goal seems more urgent than heretofore. For example, consider the human resources needed to make American cities habitable: manpower must be deployed to build housing, to construct urban transportation networks, to devise antipollution schemes for air and water, and to conduct the business and financial arrangements under which orderly growth can take place. Even if military commitments were reduced to a minimum, it would still be necessary to scale down our aspirations because we simply cannot do all the jobs that need doing. As the National Planning Association study concluded:

> *We could rebuild our cities or abolish poverty; or replace all the obsolete plant and equipment in private industry; or we could begin to develop the hardware to get us to Mars and back before the year 2000. We could make some progress on all the goals, perhaps substantial progress on many; but we cannot achieve all our objectives at the same time.*[2]

One must distinguish between the work of producing automobiles, which can be largely done by machines, and the work of producing ideas, rendering services, and meeting the demands of a new and very complex society. Education and manpower training must transform the industrial worker into a computer programmer or an engineer—or where this is not possible, must direct the new generation into the emerging jobs. In the transition from automobiles to electronics, many workers lose jobs and some do not find new ones. The skill levels of the old jobs and the new may not be comparable, geographical locations may be different, the timing may not be such as to smooth the transfer.

Such structural difficulties are not to be confused, however, with an actual drying-up of jobs as some are automated out of existence but new ones are not created. The generation of new jobs, which depends on the final

---

[2]Leonard H. Lecht, *The Dollar Cost of Our National Goals* (National Planning Association, 1965), p. 5.

demand for goods and services, is a function of the rate of economic growth. If the economy is growing rapidly, with real GNP rising each year by 4 or 5 percent, it is capable of absorbing most of the workers displaced through technological change. By contrast, recession years always bring with them significant unemployment; displaced workers find no demand for their services, even if they undergo retraining.

The requisites for high employment are thus twofold: a growing demand for goods and services, and a well-trained labor force. Even though jobs are being eliminated (many of them quite rapidly), the workless society seems to recede farther into the future, for man's material wants still far outstrip his capacity to produce. Until he has made much greater progress in the pursuit of his private wants and social goals, toil seems inevitable.

Whether the jobs of the future will be "what is commonly reckoned as work" is an interesting question. Is an assembly-line job work and executive decision-making leisure? Is carrying on laboratory experiments play? What of exploration and space travel? How does one classify continued study in one's professional field long after formal education is complete—work or leisure? The merging of one's work with his other activities seems much more likely, as work itself becomes more appealing. For work, then, we may need a more elegant word, one that is less suggestive of the factory and more descriptive of today's job content. But as technological advance and skill development permit us to raise the quality of work, policies to satisfy society's unmet needs will be required to maintain the quantity of work at the full employment level.

Structural and personal factors   In the euphoria of the prosperous years that followed World War II, some said that the United States had moved from "mass" unemployment to "class" unemployment. Although there were at least as many job vacancies as job seekers in the economy as a whole, pockets of unemployment remained because of structural imbalances or personal characteristics. Some areas, industries, and occupations would be depressed for the reasons discussed in preceding sections (and in more detail in Chapter 16); and some groups of workers would be unemployed because they were too distant or too little skilled to fill the job vacancies, or because employers would discriminate against them because of their race, religion, or sex.

In more recent years we have come to recognize that a combination of inadequate total demand, structural labor-market imbalances, and personal characteristics of workers can keep national unemployment rates high. This view is buttressed by the coexistence of high unemployment and inflation, for rising prices have traditionally been associated with high total demand (see Chapter 20).

Table 1/1 and Figure 1/1 show the impact of the various causes of unemployment on the differential unemployment rates for young and old, men and women, black and white. In periods of inadequate total demand, such as 1958–61 and 1970–72, unemployment rates rise for all workers. However, the rates are much higher for young workers, women, and nonwhites than they are for adult white men. In 1972, the average unemployment for the total male labor force had risen to 4.9 percent; but for all women the rate was 6.6 percent; for young men of 16–17 years it was 18.2 percent; and for young women in this age category the rate was 18.8 percent. Whereas the unemployment rate for all white workers, male and female, rose from 4.5 to 5.0 percent between 1970 and 1972, the rise for nonwhite workers was from 8.2 to 10.0 percent.

In a period of high unemployment, age, sex, and race combine to produce even more startling contrasts. For black teenagers the unemployment rate in 1972 was 33.5 percent, more than double the rate for white teenagers (14.2 percent). For adult blacks, the unemployment rate for men in 1972 was 6.8 percent and for women 8.7 percent.

Similar disparities in unemployment are found in various geographic areas, although our statistical data on area unemployment are not as reliable or accurate as those for population categories, that is, the characteristics of a population. Some chronically depressed areas in Appalachia and New England have had average unemployment rates of over 10 percent for many years, and they go even higher in a national recession. And although the average unemployment rates in most large urban areas do not exceed the national average, they can be as high as 30 percent in the ghettos of central cities. For black teenagers in these areas, the rates in 1970–72 were estimated to be even higher.

Thus, structural and personal factors cause our most pressing, persistent unemployment problems. And these problems become especially crucial in a period of total deficiency in aggregate demand. We may be able to "live with" a national unemployment rate of 5-6 percent, but we must recall that it is likely to be two to five times that rate for certain subgroups and labor submarkets.

Income distribution and poverty

Minority groups in the labor force suffer from more than a paucity of jobs. As is indicated in Chapter 21, even those who find employment are likely to be in the lowest occupations. Thus, families headed by blacks, women, and older people are much more likely to be classed among "the working poor" than those headed by white adult males.

Nineteenth-century and twentieth-century appraisals of poverty are almost identical. Both focus first on the material progress of the era—progress which confers on society as a whole a dramatic improvement in living levels.

Figure 1/1.   Unemployment rates for black and white
workers, 1969-1972

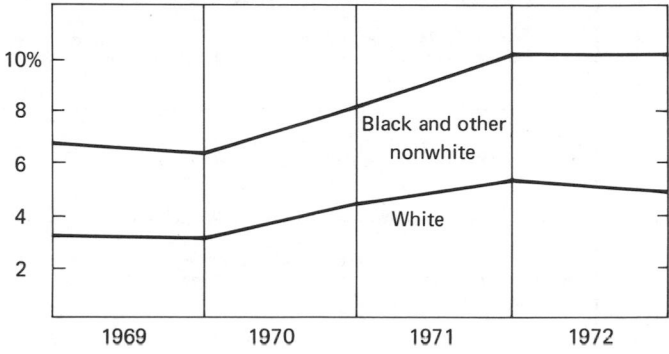

Source: Manpower Report of the President, 1973

Moreover, both appraisals emphasize that the rapid economic growth of the period widens the gap between rich and poor. By implication, the poor grow poorer, not because their absolute standards decline, but because they stand still while other families move up the economic scale.

This relative deprivation explains much of the current concern with the problem of poverty. For poverty is a relative term which, like "affluent," "wealthy," and even "middle-class," has a meaning only in comparison with other incomes in the population, or with populations of other countries or other times. References to the economic status of American society as a whole —the affluent society that John Kenneth Galbraith so vividly portrayed in the book with that title—serve merely to project a national image. It is not inconsistent that an economy be affluent while yet containing many pockets of poverty; in fact, Galbraith, among others, has pointed up this poverty-in-the-midst-of-plenty dilemma.

"Some cultures and subcultures breed poverty as surely as a waterfront breeds rats," Kenneth Boulding has commented. "Other societies and subcultures pursue unremittingly the long, hard climb out of poverty."[3] Which identity fits American society? What are its pathways to progress for the individual? To what degree are opportunities free and equal? How great are the barriers to individual economic advance? These are questions of importance to labor economists, who are interested primarily in the relation of work

---

[3]Kenneth E. Boulding, "Reflections on Poverty," *The Social Welfare Forum: 1961* (New York: Columbia University Press, 1961), pp. 45–58.

Table 1/1. Unemployed persons 16 years and over and unemployment rates, by sex and age: annual averages, 1947-72

Sex and year	Total, 16 years and over	16 and 17 years	18 and 19 years	20 to 24 years	25 to 34 years	35 to 44 years	45 to 54 years	55 to 64 years	65 years and over	14 and 15 years
				Unemployment rate						
Male										
1947	4.0	10.3	11.3	8.5	3.4	2.6	2.6	2.9	2.8	4.8
1948	3.6	10.1	9.6	6.9	2.8	2.4	2.5	3.1	3.4	5.4
1949	5.9	13.7	14.6	10.4	5.2	4.3	4.3	5.4	5.1	5.2
1950	5.1	13.3	12.3	8.1	4.4	3.6	4.0	4.9	4.8	6.6
1951	2.8	9.4	7.0	3.9	2.3	2.0	2.4	2.8	3.5	4.7
1952	2.8	10.5	7.4	4.6	2.2	1.9	2.2	2.4	3.0	5.5
1953	2.8	8.8	7.2	5.0	2.2	2.0	2.3	2.8	2.4	4.6
1954	5.3	13.9	13.2	10.7	4.8	4.1	4.3	4.5	4.4	4.9
1955	4.2	12.5	10.8	7.7	3.3	3.1	3.2	4.3	4.0	6.2
1956	3.8	11.7	10.4	6.9	3.3	2.6	3.0	3.5	3.5	6.9
1957	4.1	12.4	12.3	7.8	3.3	2.8	3.3	3.5	3.4	7.6
1958	6.8	16.3	17.8	12.7	6.5	5.1	5.3	5.5	5.2	8.4
1959	5.3	15.8	14.9	8.7	4.7	3.7	4.1	4.5	4.8	7.8
1960	5.4	15.5	15.0	8.9	4.8	3.8	4.1	4.6	4.2	8.6
1961	6.4	18.3	16.3	10.7	5.7	4.6	4.9	5.7	5.5	8.7
1962	5.2	15.9	13.8	8.9	4.5	3.6	3.9	4.6	4.6	8.3
1963	5.2	18.8	15.9	8.8	4.5	3.5	3.6	4.3	4.5	8.8
1964	4.6	17.1	14.6	8.1	3.5	2.9	3.2	3.9	4.0	9.0
1965	4.0	16.1	12.4	6.3	3.0	2.6	2.5	3.3	3.5	8.6
1966	3.2	13.7	10.2	4.6	2.4	2.0	2.0	2.6	3.1	8.9
1967	3.1	14.5	10.5	4.7	2.1	1.7	1.9	2.4	2.8	10.5
1968	2.9	13.9	9.7	5.1	1.9	1.6	1.6	1.9	2.9	10.3
1969	2.8	13.8	9.4	5.1	1.9	1.5	1.5	1.8	2.2	9.8
1970	4.4	16.9	13.4	8.4	3.4	2.4	2.4	2.8	3.3	12.2
1971	5.3	18.6	15.0	19.3	4.4	3.1	3.0	3.3	3.4	12.8

Table 1/1. (continued)

Sex and year	Total, 16 years and over	16 and 17 years	18 and 19 years	20 to 24 years	25 to 34 years	35 to 44 years	45 to 54 years	55 to 64 years	65 years and over	14 and 15 years
Female										
1947	3.7	9.8	6.8	4.6	3.6	2.7	2.6	2.6	2.2	7.8
1948	4.1	9.8	7.4	4.9	4.3	3.0	3.0	3.1	2.3	7.3
1949	6.0	14.4	11.2	7.3	5.9	4.7	4.0	4.4	3.8	7.4
1950	5.7	14.2	9.8	6.9	5.7	4.4	4.5	4.5	3.4	9.0
1951	4.4	10.0	7.2	4.4	4.5	3.8	3.5	4.0	2.9	6.6
1952	3.6	9.1	7.3	4.5	3.6	3.0	2.5	2.5	2.2	7.0
1953	3.3	8.5	6.4	4.3	3.4	2.5	2.3	2.5	1.4	4.2
1954	6.0	12.7	10.5	7.3	6.6	5.3	4.6	4.6	3.0	7.5
1955	4.9	12.0	9.1	6.1	5.3	4.0	3.6	3.8	2.3	7.0
1956	4.8	13.2	9.9	6.3	4.8	3.9	3.6	3.6	2.3	8.9
1957	4.7	12.6	9.4	6.0	5.3	3.8	3.2	3.0	3.4	7.5
1958	6.8	16.6	12.9	8.9	7.3	6.2	4.9	4.5	3.8	6.6
1959	5.9	14.4	12.9	8.1	5.9	5.1	4.2	4.1	2.8	5.7
1960	5.9	15.4	13.0	8.3	6.3	4.8	4.2	3.4	2.8	7.9
1961	7.2	18.3	15.1	9.8	7.3	6.3	5.1	4.5	3.9	6.2
1962	6.2	16.8	13.5	9.1	6.5	5.2	4.1	3.5	4.1	6.7
1963	6.5	20.3	15.2	8.9	6.9	5.1	4.2	3.6	3.2	7.6
1964	6.2	18.8	15.1	8.6	6.3	5.0	3.9	3.5	3.4	5.9
1965	5.5	17.2	14.8	7.3	5.5	4.6	3.2	2.8	2.8	5.7
1966	4.8	16.6	12.6	6.3	4.5	3.6	2.9	2.3	2.8	6.3
1967	5.2	14.8	12.7	7.0	5.4	4.0	3.1	2.4	2.7	7.2
1968	4.8	15.9	12.9	6.7	4.7	3.4	2.4	2.2	2.7	7.0
1969	4.7	15.5	11.8	6.3	4.6	3.4	2.6	2.2	2.3	7.5
1970	5.9	17.4	14.4	7.9	5.7	4.4	3.5	2.7	3.1	9.3
1971	6.9	18.7	16.2	9.6	7.0	5.2	4.0	3.3	3.6	10.2
1972	6.6	18.8	15.2	9.3	6.2	4.9	3.6	3.3	3.5	10.8

Source: Manpower Report of the President, 1973.

to income. Our study of labor markets will focus on the relationship of poverty, work, and income-maintenance payments. These issues are raised again in the policy discussions in the next section; and the extent of poverty as well as antipoverty policy alternatives are discussed in full detail in the four chapters of Part V.

Labor-market policies

Problems of labor immobility, unemployment, and poverty have long been a concern of public policy here and abroad. A number of government measures enacted to meet these problems during the New Deal era of the 1930s—such as the Employment Service, unemployment compensation, social security, and minimum wages—remain important measures today. The Employment Act of 1946, committing the country to a policy of "maximum employment, production and purchasing power," is still a goad to our economic conscience if not a direct guide to our macroeconomic policies.

However, some measures aimed at specific groups of unemployed and poverty-stricken workers in the '30s, such as the make-work programs, were products of the Depression and passed with the coming of full employment in the '40s. It was not until the high unemployment rates of the late 1950s persisted into the next decade that the U.S. government once again turned to structural labor-market policies and antipoverty measures on a large scale. Continuation of many of these policies even after unemployment was reduced in 1966–68 gave some reason to believe that structural policies had become part of a more durable package of economic measures affecting the labor market.

The scope of labor-market policies

Labor-market policies may be placed in three major categories:

1. Policies related to the general economy, such as aggregate monetary–fiscal measures to attain full employment, wage–price controls to combat inflation, public service employment, and area redevelopment policies to reduce geographic disparities in income and employment. These policies are discussed in Chapters 20 and 25 against the background of the descriptive and analytical discussions of the chapters in Part IV.

2. Policies related to income-maintenance programs for nonworkers, the unemployed, and the working poor. These include social security, welfare payments, unemployment compensation, minimum wages, and proposals for minimum incomes. All are discussed in the four chapters in Part V.

3.   Manpower programs and other investments in human resources, such as training, career-oriented education, job counseling, relocation, the job-matching employment service, and antidiscrimination legislation. These policies are discussed in Chapters 21-25.

Full employment, anti-inflation, and manpower policy

Before turning to more detailed discussions of issues touched briefly in this chapter, it is useful to conclude the overview of manpower and labor economics with a reminder that the problems, issues, and policies covered in this book are all interrelated.

Efforts to achieve full employment without inflation through "Keynesian" monetary–fiscal measures may be thwarted by structural imbalances in the labor market and by union-management policies. Thus, government units increasingly rely on such direct labor-market measures as wage–price controls and manpower policies. But because manpower programs can do little to reduce unemployment or stem inflationary pressures unless enrollees can find jobs after completion, manpower programs are linked to job creation through public-service employment and area-redevelopment policies. And both the need for such microeconomic employment policies and their success are influenced by whether the macroeconomic policies achieve full employment.

Antipoverty programs, income maintenance, and manpower policy

A similarly complex interaction is found between antipoverty programs and manpower programs. American workers enjoy high real wages based on high productivity. In most American industries a heavy endowment of capital equipment and advanced technology combined with substantial investments in human resources enable the worker to produce more in a day than his foreign counterpart. These circumstances are not incompatible with a high incidence of poverty, because there are wide disparities in income and we set our poverty threshold at a level that reflects our high standards of living.

A full-time job in one of the better-paying industries insures a comfortable—though not affluent—standard of living. This level of comfort becomes, then, the standard that all workers aspire to. But jobs in many areas of the economy are much less remunerative, and workers in the less productive industries feel deprived. Moreover, the family without a wage earner usually has no income at all, and between the highly productive worker and the unemployed, the aged, or the handicapped the differences in income are especially acute. The poor might find it easier to live in a nation with less extreme variations in income levels.

In a laissez-faire economy, extremes in income are endorsed by the belief that the promise of higher pay provides an incentive for work, and work in turn produces the goods and services of which real incomes consist. Income distribution in a society that relies on the pricing mechanism is bound to be skewed. Moreover, as long as income is considered a necessary incentive for work, there is likely to be a strong bias against providing any income guarantees, lest such measures discourage output. Certain questions nevertheless arise: How much income is required in order to motivate people to perform? Have the wage differentials been too wide?

Until recently, proposals for minimum income guarantees have not been seriously supported in this country, except for groups who could not work. Hence, incomes for the aged, the disabled, mothers of dependent children, and the temporarily unemployed worker are acceptable. But a guaranteed income for the "able-bodied worker," i. e., the male of working age, has not been considered the obligation of society. Alternatively, the proposal for guaranteed jobs—the government as an employer of last resort—is frequently made.

Reliance on work as a means of eliminating poverty is understandable, given the wide range of jobs that need to be done in the public sector and the current shortage of workers in much of the private economy. Yet an income guarantee does not preclude employment and earnings, which would then be an addition to the minimum income available to all. A noncategorical approach to income support may yet be in the making, if public expenditures on defense and related items are curtailed, and if the economy's current inflationary bias abates. There seems little likelihood of an early move in this direction, though, given the President's decision not to press again for income-maintenance legislation, and Congressional defeat of these proposals in the early 1970s.

But how willing and able potentially productive workers may be incorporated in the workforce will depend not only on the level of nonworking income guarantee they might receive, but also—and crucially—on the success of job creation through macroeconomic monetary–fiscal policies, public-service employment, and area redevelopment. It will also depend upon the skills and mobility they possess or can attain—that is, on the manpower policies that emerged in the 1960s, to be modified in the early 1970s.

Thus, once again we come full circle. The interdependence and interaction of the issues and policies of labor economics run through this volume. We return to this question in the final chapter, following the descriptions and analyses that provide a foundation for greater understanding of the problems and their possible solutions.

Part Two

The Labor Market

Chapter Two

Framework of the Labor Market

In strict economic terms, the market for labor is like any other market. It serves as a mechanism by which labor is bought and sold, and in the process it allocates labor according to market demand in various occupations, industries, and geographic areas. The market also sets the price of labor, and the price in turn influences the allocative mechanism. This chapter discusses the basic structure and functioning of labor markets.

A model of the perfect market

For analysis of the framework and functioning of active labor markets, it is helpful to compare them with a conceptually perfect market. Perhaps the best example of such a market in the real world is a securities market, in which there is perfect knowledge and perfect exchange of information about those who wish to buy and sell specific quantities at specified prices. There is a clear definition of the goods being bought and sold, and all of those interested in the purchase and sale of the securities are in direct and immediate contact with each other. At the same time the number of buyers and sellers is too great to permit monopolistic or monopsonistic collusion among sellers or buyers; and surpluses or shortages are quickly eliminated through rapid movements in price.

If a labor market met the requirements of this perfect model, its key characteristic would be complete knowledge and immediate exchange of information concerning all workers available for jobs and all employers seeking workers. The reservation or asking wage of the workers would be known to all potential employers, just as the wage and other conditions of the job openings would be known to all job seekers in the labor market. Furthermore, the boundaries of a particular labor market for workers of the same occupation, each with identical productive capacity, would be clearly defined, and the area within these boundaries would be of such size that the conditions of perfect knowledge and perfect information could prevail. Employers would compete freely in hiring labor, and workers would engage in frictionless mobility in response to the economic and noneconomic advantages of alternative job opportunities. There would be too many employers to allow collusion on hiring practices and wage rates, and there would be no organization of workers to force up wages unduly or to prevent them from falling with market demand. This free competition of employers and free movement of workers would be likely to eliminate wage differentials for comparable workers in comparable employment. Needless to say, the employers and workers in the perfect market would be essentially "economic men," motivated by maximization of their wages and income.

Imperfections in labor markets

Essential differences between labor and commodities

The mere listing of these rigorous requirements for a perfect labor market makes it clear that real labor markets depart from the model in significant degree. Imperfection in the labor market derives from the fact that labor is not a commodity. Many people dislike the notion that labor should be considered a good like a pound of cheese or sack of grain. But the economic differences between labor and commodities are significant enough without appealing to philosophical attitudes to reject the comparison.

In fact the very bases of labor economics as a special study—that workers cannot be separated from their services and that work takes time and effort—also explain the inherent imperfection in labor markets. Perfectly competitive markets require large numbers of buyers and sellers of a homogeneous product. These conditions fit neither the buyer (employer) nor seller (worker) in the labor market for a particular occupation.

Consider a skilled mechanic: from his point of view firms differ not only in rates of pay (about the only element that compares clearly with a product-market characteristic—price) but in working conditions, location, company prestige, chance for promotion, seniority rules, friendliness of co-workers, etc. Each mechanic gives different weights to these factors. In effect, then, the individual mechanic faces a number of differentiated potential purchasers of his services.

Employers see an equal lack of product homogeneity: workers differ in attitudes, motivation, stability, to say nothing of skill. It is only a moderate exaggeration to say that the firm does not face a supply of mechanics but separate minimarkets for individual mechanics.

In short, buyer differentiation among firms, from the workers' point of view, and product differentiation among workers, from the employer's position, explain the dissimilarities and the imperfection in the labor market. This imperfection, in turn, explains the elusiveness of a market price (wage) even for a particular grade of labor.

How far the market is from perfection is often obscured by confusion over labor-market boundaries. If a labor market is defined as an area in which employers recruit workers and workers move to employment, where knowledge of applicants and openings is relatively widespread, then it is obvious that the boundaries of a labor market will differ for different types of workers and different occupations and industries.

Labor-market boundaries

For most relatively unskilled manual workers the labor market is local. If they are unwilling to move to take a new job, the maximum commuting distance from home to work might be considered the radius of their labor market. Knowing they could not induce workers to move from outside of this area to their factories, employers would also be constrained by this boundary to the labor market. On the other hand, skilled blue-collar craftsmen (especially in the building trades) learn about job opportunities in their trade over a wide geographic area; and they are frequently willing to travel the great distances required to obtain such employment. Aware of this potential mobility, employers in the construction industry seek and obtain workers from considerable distances by means of the union information network.

Labor market boundaries may be national or even international for many professional workers—certainly for engineers and scientists. Many academicians who obtain their doctorates expect to do their graduate work away from their home community, and expect their first and future jobs to be far from where they received their graduate training. Although labor market information for such professionals is far from perfect, it is frequently national in scope, and potential employers and job applicants are aware of the terms and conditions which must be met for a successful "sale of labor" at many scattered points throughout the country.

External and internal labor markets

The foregoing discussion of labor-market boundaries assumes that employers fill their job openings through recruitment from outside the plant. It also assumes that workers already employed are actively interested in improving their positions by moving to alternative employment opportunities. However, many employers and most workers are really not in the external labor market at all. Employers may be primarily concerned with filling job openings through promotion of employees already on their payroll. And workers in these establishments may be equally interested in moving to other jobs in the plant, especially to more highly rated jobs, rather than in moving to another firm even in the same locality. These employers and workers are concerned with the internal labor market, their hopes and ambitions for the efficient allocation of labor and for the advancement of economic welfare lie within the boundaries of their existing establishment.[1]

For most firms and workers the internal and external labor markets are linked. Even though employers may fill almost all of their job openings by means of internal transfer and promotion, for any internal employment expansion they must hire some workers from the lowest labor grades through the external market at the plant gate. Similarly, if particular job openings call for skills that are internally unavailable, employers must search the external labor market. Workers, too, might feel that their mobility was best confined within the walls of their existing establishment, but if the differential in wages or improvement of conditions in an external job opportunity were sufficiently marked, these workers might be induced to move to another firm. Just as workers may enter a plant at a relatively unskilled level through the common-labor "port of entry," workers may enter a specific department in the plant through a particular occupational route and then decide to make that department their own little internal labor market—a market from which they desire to have no exit.

Thus, if the boundaries of a labor market are to be defined by workers' propensity to move to alternative jobs within that market, the size of the labor market for particular workers in particular occupations may vary from a single department in a plant to the nation as a whole and, indeed, even to other continents.

Interest in the internal labor market in recent years is partially related to the growth of on-the-job training and union–management institutional rules governing promotion, transfers, and other forms of in-plant mobility. Training within industry has assumed greater importance with the growing complexity of modern technology. With a work force that has received a good amount of general schooling, the firm can graft on specialized skills required for its production more easily than it could in the past when its work force had little experience with schooling and educational techniques. The tasks in modern production often require specialized knowledge that is not even obtainable in vocational schools.

The firm is willing to pay the costs of this specialized training, which includes instructional expenses and the cost of low output or inferior products during the training period. The firm also reduces the risk of turnover to the degree that the new skills the workers acquire through training are specific to the firm and are not transferable to other firms. Even though the firm pays all the training costs, it may pay the trained workers a higher wage than before, even if the worker cannot market his skills elsewhere. For one thing, the higher wage maintains the morale of a worker who is now performing

---

[1]Peter Doeringer and Michael Piore, *Internal Labor Markets and Manpower Analysis* (Lexington, Mass.: D. C. Heath, 1971), present a detailed analysis of the operation of the internal labor market and of dual labor markets (see "Dual labor markets," below).

more demanding and responsible tasks. For another, the higher wage serves as an inducement for the worker to undergo training in the first place.

Information in the labor market

Contrary to the premise of the perfect-labor-market model, surveys indicate that most workers have only the haziest idea of alternative employment opportunities, even in their local community; they know even less about the wages, working conditions, and possibilities of promotion in job openings elsewhere; and even those workers who do state wage rates in other establishments are often grossly wrong in their estimates.

There are many reasons for these failures in information and communication. Many workers, content in their current positions, have no desire to learn about the economic and noneconomic conditions of alternative job opportunities. Employers seldom have an incentive to give widespread information on the monetary aspects of their job openings, preferring to compete on the basis of noneconomic factors. Since only a small percentage of jobs are listed at the public employment exchange, there is seldom a central place where workers can learn about job openings and the wages and other conditions of employment in alternative jobs.

Even if such objective information as the existence of job openings and wages were public knowledge widely distributed in the labor market, workers would still have little basis for a direct comparison between jobs because of the difficulty in appraising noneconomic advantages and disadvantages. If wage information is imperfect, how much more difficult is it for a worker to know about the personalities of foremen, the friendliness of his fellow workers, and the pleasantness of the work surroundings? Can he be sure of the promotional possibilities and job security? These uncertainties are likely to preclude mobility.

As is noted in a later chapter, efforts to improve labor-market information constitute an important form of investment in human capital. Some feel that it is one investment in human beings which may have a higher rate of return than many other kinds of investment that have received considerably greater publicity.

Dual labor markets

Recently concern and the literature about the existence of a dual labor market have grown. Especially within large cities, it has been posited that there are two separate labor markets, and there is mobility within each market but none between the two. Movement between the two labor markets even within the same community is inhibited by the nature of the job opportunities and of the individuals within each market.

The primary market, in the mainstream of the labor force, is populated by the relatively privileged workers. Their primary attachment is to an internal labor market, within a business establishment and an occupational classification characterized by high pay, attractive working conditions, job security, and upward mobility toward even better conditions and earnings.

In the secondary sector in the "dual economy" of the large urban area jobs are far less attractive: low pay, insecure employment, below standard working conditions, and high turnover rates.

The workers who fill the jobs in these two labor markets are quite different. Those in the primary sector enter with relatively high levels of education and skill and manifest characteristics of reliability, responsibility, and educability through further training and instruction. Their tendency to stay with the firm warrants the firm's investment in their skill development. In the secondary labor market, the characteristics of the workers reflect the low-level nature of the job. Their rates of turnover are likely to be high and they are likely to lack the habits of work discipline, stability, and reliability. The characteristics of workers and jobs in the secondary labor market bear a close resemblance to the "culture of poverty" which sociologists and economists have stressed in their recent analyses of urban problems.

Although this "dual labor market theory" is clearly overdrawn, there are obvious truths in some aspects of this formulation. It helps to explain such labor market phenomena as the coexistence of high and low wages in the same community, differential rates of mobility between workers at different skill levels, and the concentration and perpetuation of poverty within certain geographic areas and within certain minority groups.

Institutional market forces

A number of employer and union practices militate against the efficiency of the labor market as an allocative mechanism; the tendency of employers to operate in an internal labor market has already been noted. The discussion below is concerned with "anticompetitive" policies in the external market.

Recruitment policies

Most employers are reluctant to recruit and interview job applicants who are already employed in another establishment in the local labor market. These "antipirating" agreements are widespread, and employers who launch a vigorous campaign to attract workers from a neighboring plant may be ostracized socially and face mounting antagonism in the employers' associations of the local community.

If an employed worker in search of a job change shows up at the plant gate of another employer in the community, the personnel recruiter is likely to turn him away unless he can obtain the approval of the job applicant's present employer. Or many employers will insist that the job applicant quit his present job before being considered for a position in the new company —a demand that produces insecurity that may discourage the worker from further labor-market search.

Other employers will treat each such job application on its individual merits. If the applicant appears to be promising and offers persuasive reasons for wanting to leave his current employer, the personnel manager who interviews him may rationalize: "Well, he would quit anyway, and if I don't take him some other firm will." More likely he will try to persuade the job applicant's current employer that he does not want an unhappy worker and should be quite willing to let the employee go with his blessing. Even so, a worker who knows that his present employer will be contacted concerning his job search elsewhere may think twice before showing up at the personnel office of a competing firm when that firm has not made a specific job offer.

Another widespread recruitment practice of employers similarly restricts job openings to a relatively small number of potential applicants: preference in recruitment is given to the friends and relatives of present employees, whom many employers use as the primary channel by which information concerning job openings is transmitted to workers outside of the plant. Although this policy may have some advantages for the employer and raise the morale of present employees, it limits the role of the labor market as a competitive mechanism for matching job openings with the best applicants available on a competitive basis.

Thus, typical employer recruitment policies restrict the availability of jobs and information about those that are available. Frequently, only the unemployed or new entrants into the labor market can expect to be given consideration in hiring. And even these are likely to learn about the job opportunity through informal contacts with friends, relatives, and neighbors rather than through any formal information network.

Unions and job placement

The building trades unions and a few other unions serve as an active employment exchange for their members. They undoubtedly increase the amount of job information available to their members and thereby increase mobility and the effectiveness of the labor market as an allocative mechanism. However, few unions assume such a labor exchange responsibility.

It is generally agreed by the scholars of the field that, taken as a whole, collective bargaining reduces the mobility of workers between establishments in the labor market. There are a number of reasons for this.

1.   Most union contracts have a posting and bidding procedure for filling job vacancies. Present employees must be given notification and first preference in filling vacancies before outside hiring occurs. Thus, the external labor market is slighted in favor of internal movement.

2.   Seniority provisions, stressed in most collective bargaining agreements, reduce the motives and incentives for workers to move to another establishment. Besides its contribution to longevity wage increases, length of service is becoming increasingly advantageous for promotions, pensions, length of vacation, and layoffs. A worker's seniority rights are a precious possession, and they are not lightly foregone, as they would have to be if the worker began a new job in a new establishment.

3.   By providing the union member with a grievance procedure, especially one that protects him against arbitrary discharge, the collective bargaining agreement provides security and may further the morale of the employees. Workers have less reason to quit because of real or fancied wrongs at the hands of management; and management thinks twice before discharging an employee. Thus, simply by removing causes of discontent, unions may discourage the mobility of workers from one establishment to another.

The role of the employment service

It is the appointed task of private and public employment exchanges to further the efficiency of the labor market as an allocative mechanism. They are to do this by providing information about job openings for job seekers and by giving information about job applicants to employers in search of manpower. In addition to providing information, the Employment Service is supposed to match workers and job openings through listings of vacancies, recruitment, interviews, and tests of job applicants. Thus, the Employment Service has considerable potential as an offset to the obstacles to mobility found in the practices of employers, unions, and workers themselves.

The Employment Service has not always lived up to this promise—chiefly because of the complex problems of the job market. But employers and job seekers also add to placement and mobility difficulties: only a small proportion of employers (ranging generally from 10 to 20 percent) use the public employment offices to fill job openings; and, perhaps as a consequence, relatively few workers use the offices to obtain jobs or improve their job positions.

There are hopes, however, that the Employment Service can come to be used. Data on job vacancies are likely to be improved by current surveys and statistical series being developed by the Service in cooperation with the Bureau of Labor Statistics. Improved data come along at an opportune time to be fed into the growing number of computerized job banks now being developed in employment offices across the country. Such developments may encourage greater numbers of employers to list their job openings with the Employment Service, and this in turn will induce workers to come more readily to local employment offices in search of job opportunities. A recent survey indicates that the Public Employment Service is the second most used method in job search. But Figure 2/1 shows that direct application to firms is used more than twice as often.

Figure 2/1.   Percent of jobseekers using various job-search methods, 1971

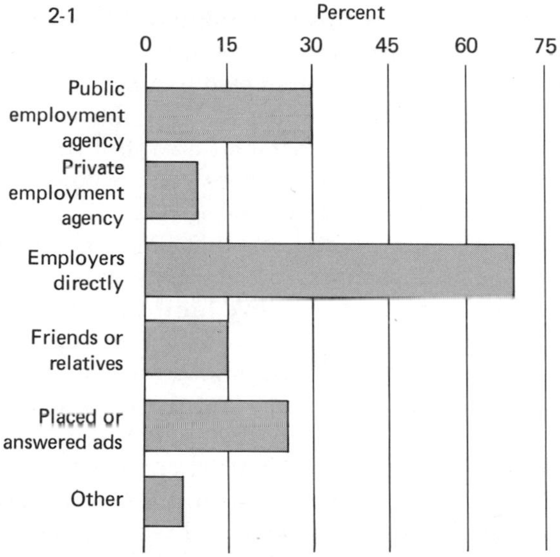

2-1

Source: "Jobseeking Methods Used by Unemployed Workers," Monthly Labor Review (February 1973). Note: Percentages exceed 100 because jobseekers often report more than one source.

Characteristics of labor mobility

If the labor market were functioning in accordance with the perfect model, one could expect substantial mobility between firms, industries, occupations, and geographic regions, designed to improve the worker's economic and noneconomic positions. The discussion above leads to the conclusion that in actual labor markets inhibiting factors reduce the movement of workers below the optimal level.

Types and patterns of mobility

There have been numerous attempts to measure the extent and patterns
of labor mobility in the United States, especially since World War II. Although some important tentative conclusions have emerged, efforts have
been hampered by conceptual problems as well as by lack of adequate data.
The conceptual problems are concerned with the meaning of "mobility" as
well as with the types of mobility. Frequently "mobility" is used to mean the
"propensity" of a worker to move, that is his motivation or willingness to
change jobs. Such propensities can have important effects on wages as well
as on other aspects of the welfare of employees and employers, even if no
actual movement occurs. However, mobility customarily means an actual
movement of workers; and it is this meaning which is almost always employed in efforts to measure patterns of mobility.

A number of field surveys have attempted to ascertain the propensity of
workers to move by asking such questions as, "Would you move from your
present job to Firm (or industry or geographic area) B if the wages in B were
$25 (or $50 or $10) per week higher than those you are now receiving?" Even
though such surveys have produced interesting responses, there is a general
feeling among survey research investigators that such "iffy" questions do not
provide consistently reliable responses. Some surveys have shown that many
workers who indicate a propensity to move (in their answers to one of the
conditional questions) do not actually move when an opportunity arises.

Actual movement of a worker between jobs reflects not only his desire
or *propensity*, but also his *ability* to move and the *opportunity* to move. Although the best research on this topic has attempted to distinguish among the
complexities of motivation, incentives, abilities, propensities, and opportunities for mobility, efforts have seldom met with full success, and the interaction of these factors as they affect mobility still remains somewhat obscure.

The following types of mobility have been distinguished:

1.   Intraplant mobility: *movement between occupational classifications in the
plant; usually by promotion (i.e., the internal labor market).*

2.   Intrafirm mobility: *movement between plants of multiple-plant firms; usually by company-directed transfers.*

3.   Interfirm mobility or labor turnover: *movement of workers from one firm
or establishment to another without necessarily changing occupational classifications. Labor turnover is customarily measured on this concept of mobility.*

4.   Interindustry mobility: *crossing industry lines—for example, from coal
mining to automobile manufacturing—as the worker moves from one firm to*

another, either in the same occupation (e.g., mechanic) or in a different one (e.g., from coal loader to assembly-line worker).

5.   Interoccupation mobility: *a move to another job classification (e.g., from utility labor to machinist), either within the same firm and industry or because of a change of firms and/or industries.*

6.   Geographic or interarea mobility: *a change in jobs of firms requiring relocation from one local labor market to another or from one region of the country to another, often involving a rural-to-urban movement.*

7.   Employment–unemployment mobility: *movement of workers from the employed to the unemployed ranks, or vice versa.*

8.   Labor force mobility: *movement in and out of the labor force, primarily by such so-called secondary workers as students or married women who sometimes work to supplement family income.*

In practice, a number of these types of mobility are often combined in a single move: when a coal loader laid off in the mines of West Virginia moves to an assembly-line job in an auto plant in Detroit, he has clearly combined several of the forms of the mobility listed above. If his wife, who was unable to find employment in the coal area, can now take an office job in Detroit, mobility into the labor force has also been accomplished through the miner's move.

How much mobility is there in the United States? Studies made in recent years indicate that approximately one-fourth of the total labor force changes jobs each year. One survey conducted by the Bureau of the Census in the latter half of the 1950s revealed that about one-tenth of all workers made at least one change of employers during the year. At the same time, there is considerable employment stability. It was found that in the 1960s more than one-third of those employed had been with their current employer or in self-employment for at least a ten-year period.

Who moves? All of the surveys revealed that mobility is concentrated among a relatively small proportion of the labor force (as is implied in the figures on mobility and stability cited above). There is a distinct inverse correlation between age and mobility: the younger the worker the greater is his propensity to move and the more likely he is to engage in job movement. Studies reveal that young entrants into the labor market shop around for jobs, sometimes derogatorily called "job-hopping" by employers. It is only after the new entrants have sampled several jobs within a one- to two-year period that they settle down, acquire seniority, and probably join the ranks of the stable, nonmobile employees. The difficulties workers have in discovering job opportunities and in comparing jobs make this sampling procedure by young workers seem rational; experience in a variety of job situations provides many young workers with the only basis for comparison, especially of noneconomic employment conditions. Familiarity, inertia, and seniority inhibit the mobility of workers as they grow older and acquire lengthier tenure in a particular establishment.

Another important reason for the greater mobility of young workers is their lack of security and low earnings in their current jobs. They have little to give up in moving to another job. We speak of restless and ambitious youth, but in addition to physical and psychological factors, there is a strong economic basis for this willingness to change among the young: they have plenty of room for economic improvement. Shakespeare put it best: "Lowliness is young ambition's ladder."

A worker's occupation affects his mobility propensities and patterns. Mobility rates generally decrease as the level of skill rises, so that managerial and professional workers show considerably less mobility than unskilled labor. However, certain skilled craftsmen, such as in the building trades, show considerable mobility, partly because their work is seasonal and short-term and partly because they wish to remain within the skilled and high-paid classification wherever the job opportunities may lead. Although the overall rates of mobility for professional, technical, and managerial personnel are below those of manual workers, geographic mobility rates are higher for the more skilled classifications. Whereas most workers have a strong sentimental attachment to their home locality (stronger than their attachment to their industry or occupation), professional and technical workers have less of a regional or geographic attachment than manual workers.

The highly skilled will move longer distances for job changes than the unskilled because as skills become more specialized and narrower, the local labor market for the worker's services becomes thinner. The highly trained worker may have skills that fit only a few firms in the whole country, and a job change for a better position may require a long-distance move.

Also, movement to a distant state involves considerable expense, not closely related to the worker's pay, so that it is easier for high-wage (highly skilled) workers to make such moves. Similarly, the employer who underwrites moving costs will more likely finance those workers who will individually contribute most to production, again the highly skilled. Recently available 1970 census data substantiate these tendencies, although mobility differences by age, with declines in mobility rate for every subsequent age group after 17, are more pronounced than those by occupation. Table 2/1 does show slightly lower overall geographic mobility for professionals than for the unskilled, but a stronger tendency for the former to move long distances, at least to different states.

Table 2/1. Mobility rates by age and occupation, 1968 to 1969

Percent distribution Age — Occupation	Total: 14 years old and over			14 to 17 years old			18 to 24 years old			25 to 34 years old			35 to 44 years old			45 to 64 years old			65 years old and over		
	Same county	Same state*	Different state	Same county	Same state*	Different state	Same county	Same state*	Different state	Same county	Same state*	Different state	Same county	Same state*	Different state	Same county	Same state*	Different state	Same county	Same state*	Different state
Total employed	12.4	3.3	3.2	8.3	1.8	1.9	25.2	6.5	7.7	18.8	5.3	5.0	10.6	2.8	2.7	6.5	1.5	1.2	3.1	1.0	0.7
White-collar workers	11.4	3.9	3.8	4.8	0.7	1.1	24.2	7.4	10.1	11.4	6.4	6.2	8.6	3.5	3.0	6.0	1.8	1.4	2.5	1.7	1.0
Professional, technical, and kindred workers	13.2	5.4	5.4	B	B	B	28.1	11.0	11.9	19.5	8.0	7.9	8.2	3.8	4.3	6.4	2.1	1.8	2.4	3.4	0.6
Managers, officials, and proprietors	9.8	3.0	2.6	B	B	B	31.8	8.2	8.8	19.5	5.5	4.4	8.3	3.2	2.9	6.0	1.7	1.4	1.4	1.8	1.3
Clerical and kindred workers	11.4	3.4	3.6	9.0	1.2	1.0	20.2	5.3	10.5	16.3	5.0	4.3	10.7	3.6	0.4	3.9	1.6	0.8	4.7	1.0	1.7
Sales workers	10.9	2.6	3.0	2.7	0.3	1.2	18.8	3.4	6.4	18.4	4.2	6.3	9.0	3.4	2.0	7.9	1.9	1.0	3.1	—	—
Manual workers	14.0	3.0	3.0	9.3	1.7	2.4	27.7	6.5	6.5	20.0	4.4	4.3	10.9	2.2	2.5	6.9	1.4	1.1	3.2	0.6	0.6
Craftsmen, foremen, and kindred workers	12.1	2.9	2.6	B	B	B	30.5	6.6	7.5	18.8	4.5	3.9	9.8	2.6	2.4	6.1	1.4	1.0	3.3	0.4	0.9
Operatives and kindred workers	15.3	3.2	3.2	10.5	1.3	3.5	28.2	6.6	6.1	20.7	4.3	4.3	11.1	2.2	2.4	7.3	1.3	1.1	2.5	0.6	06
Laborers	15.3	3.1	3.7	8.2	2.2	1.8	23.4	5.9	6.5	22.3	4.4	5.6	14.3	0.9	3.5	9.1	1.9	1.7	4.1	1.0	—
Service workers	12.6	2.9	2.8	10.6	2.5	1.5	17.6	4.9	7.7	21.0	3.6	3.3	11.3	3.0	2.7	9.0	2.1	1.1	4.5	0.6	0.5
Private household	B	B	B	B	B	B	B	B	B	B	B	B	—	—	—	B	B	B	B	B	B
Other service workers	12.6	3.0	2.8	10.6	2.6	1.6	17.4	5.0	7.5	21.2	3.7	3.4	11.3	3.0	2.7	9.0	2.1	1.0	4.7	0.6	0.5
Farm workers	8.8	1.6	1.4	8.2	3.0	2.5	13.1	2.6	4.0	14.2	5.0	2.3	8.1	1.7	1.4	4.3	0.4	0.8	1.8	0.6	0.3
Farmers and farm managers	4.2	0.9	0.8	B	B	B	B	B	B	9.2	2.2	2.1	5.0	1.1	1.6	3.1	0.4	0.3	1.3	0.7	—
Farm laborers and farm foremen	11.3	2.7	2.4	8.4	3.1	2.6	11.1	1.8	3.2	20.4	8.4	2.6	15.2	2.9	1.0	8.8	0.1	2.4	B	B	B

*Different county in the same state.

B - Base less than 75,000 - Represents zero or rounds to zero.

Source: U.S. Bureau of the census. "Mobility of the Population of the United States, March 1968 to March 1969." Current Population Reports, P-20. No. 193, December 26, 1969.

Wage differentials and allocation

Are wages as important in labor allocation as competitive economic theory, or the perfect model, would lead us to believe? Surveys indicate that workers give many noneconomic reasons for their mobility. However, as a trigger for mobility, wage differentials become more important both in the long run and according to the size of the differential. Even though many workers move for noneconomic reasons, the number of workers who move in search of higher wages seems to give credence to the economic theory underlying the functioning of labor markets.

That studies show workers more often move for nonmonetary than for monetary reasons does not indicate that pay is not important to workers comparing jobs. One could logically argue just the opposite: pay is so important a consideration that firms usually take wages "out of competition." Wage differences certainly exist, but firms are careful to keep their pay scale in line with the competition for labor, especially in tight labor-market conditions and among firms with a strong interest in minimizing turnover.

Rural–urban mobility as a prototype

The migration of workers from depressed rural areas to the cities provides an interesting test of mobility analysis. Government efforts to subsidize such movement offer a further opportunity for understanding mobility motivation.

Rural–urban mobility must be viewed in the context of income-differentials. Close to fourteen million rural Americans are poor. According to the report of the President's National Advisory Commission on Rural Poverty, there is relatively more rural than urban poverty. In metropolitan areas, one person in eight is poor, in the suburbs one in fifteen, but in rural areas one in four persons is poor. Rural areas house some 30 percent of our total population but 40 percent of the nation's poor. Most of the rural poor live in small towns and villages rather than on farms; only one poor rural family in four lives on a farm. Although three out of five rural nonwhite families are poor, most of the rural poor (eleven million out of the fourteen million) are white. Poor nonwhites are concentrated in the poorest counties, whereas poor whites are more widely scattered.

Rural poverty is heavily concentrated in the South, and within the South in such areas as Appalachia, the Coastal Plains, the Ozarks, the Old South and the Southern border. There are also heavy concentrations of rural poverty on Indian reservations in the Southwest and the upper Great Plains and other concentrations of rural poor in New England and the upper Great Lakes. In 1969, 49.1 percent of the poor lived in nonmetropolitan areas while 31.9 percent lived in the central cities and 19.1 percent in suburbs.

In addition to low incomes and few employment opportunities, areas of rural poverty are characterized by little formal education, dilapidated housing, many children and old people dependent on those of working age, and low levels of labor-force participation. These symptoms of poverty perpetuate poverty, for high rates of out-migration create an age distribution in rural counties that reduces opportunities for further economic growth.

Migration from rural areas   If the rate of outward migration is viewed as a measure of the poverty of opportunity in rural areas, there have been some surprising improvements in the past decade. Rural counties retained their population growth much better in the 1960s than they did in the 50s. The change has been most dramatic in the East south-central states—Kentucky, Tennessee, Mississippi, and Alabama. These four states "exported" a net of 1.5 million migrants per year from their rural areas in the 1950s, but only 164,000 per year from 1960 to 1966. The West north-central states—Minnesota, Iowa, Missouri, the Dakotas, Nebraska, and Kansas— have not done as well since 1960. However, as is noted below, a change in the pattern of migration may reflect changes in labor demand outside of depressed areas as much as changes in economic conditions within rural areas. The Southern states continue to have the most extensive concentration of rural poverty.

We must understand the natural flows of populations, those not directed by special programs, from rural areas if we are to fully assess how income differentials create an incentive for mobility. This assessment is important for public policy as well as for economic theory. In the last few years, mobility proponents who once simply encouraged rural out-migration have now changed their emphasis to redirecting rural out-migrants from the largest cities to smaller ones. The Watts riots in Los Angeles (1965) may have marked the turning point in our concern over rural–urban migration. It is clear that this concern is more for nonwhite migrants to the central cities than for white migrants. Therefore, our background discussion of the natural population flows must stress rural–urban shifts of minority groups and recent changes in these transfers.

The data on migratory flows are somewhat sketchy. We know in very general terms that 18 percent of the U. S. population changed residence between 1968 and 1969, but only 3.4 percent moved between states. Though there are no annual estimates of migration from rural to urban areas, the figure is probably around 200,000 people each year. Figures from 1967 show that blacks are represented according to their proportion in the population among those who, since their sixteenth birthday, had moved from rural to urban areas (11 percent). For those who moved from urban to rural areas, however, blacks numbered only 4 percent.

The data on rural out-migration must be disaggregated if we are to understand the processes at work. The first notable fact is that the peak of farm-related out-migration has passed. The net annual average of persons leaving farms dropped from 1.0 million in the 1950s to approximately 600,000 in the period 1965–69. Since farm residents are now only one-fifth of the rural population, future out-migration is likely to be dominated by the nonfarm rural sector.

Second, total rural migration to urban areas has shown signs of decline. Preliminary estimates from 1970 census data, for instance, show that the number of urban counties with net in-migration rates greater than 30 percent of its base-year population was 119 for 1960–1970, whereas for the decade 1950–1960 the number was 171. The pattern, of course, differs among rural regions of the country.

Third, the patterns of minority-group migration from rural to urban areas differ sharply from those of most whites. However, the migration of (a) rural blacks from the South, (b) Mexican-Americans from the Southwest, and (c) American Indians is similar to that of (d) whites from Southern Appalachia. But these four groups differ from other white rural migrants, such as those from the farms of Iowa, Utah, or upstate New York, and though they comprised less than 20 percent of U. S. rural population in 1950, they contributed about 50 percent of the net migration out of rural counties into predominantly urban counties in the 1950–60 decade. The four groups have much higher birthrates than the average of other rural populations or of the nation as a whole, and, thus, will provide a ready supply of potential migrants whenever conditions encourage rural–urban transfers. Because of their patterns of out-migration and their high birthrates, these four groups have a significantly lower median age than other rural populations. Rural blacks are much more likely to migrate to cities of over 500,000 in size than are whites from rural areas. It has been estimated that a rural black is seven times more likely to end up in a city of over 500,000 than is a white born in the same rural area. Southern blacks have not only moved to large metropolitan areas, they have moved along three major streams to the largest cities—one up the Eastern Seaboard, another up the Mississippi River to Ohio and Michigan, and a third westward to California. The pattern for rural whites is much more diffuse.

A study by Michigan's Survey Research Center has also disclosed important differences between blacks' and whites' sociopsychological attitudes toward mobility which produce differences in behavior. Fear of discrimination, emotional or family ties to a particular locality, and uneasiness about unfamiliar surroundings are the principal barriers to black mobility and explain a lower overall rate of black mobility than white mobility. The tie to family and friends discourages some blacks from leaving rural areas, but others are prone to join earlier leavers in the concentrated centers of large urban areas.

Fourth, black migration to the cities has declined notably in recent years. According to the figures given to the House Subcommittee on Urban Growth by the Census Bureau, black migration to the cities dropped to about 110,000 a year from 1966–68, in contrast with the average of 370,000 a year in the previous six years. At the same time, however, because of a relatively high birthrate among blacks and because whites have been leaving the central cities three times as fast in the past two years (compared with the previous six years), the percentage of blacks living in predominantly black neighborhoods in fifteen large cities over the last eight years has increased. Thus, the recent decline in black migration to large cities has not reduced their heavy concentration in urban ghettos; and the continuing high birthrate of rural blacks provides a potential for a reversal of the recent decline in migration if socioeconomic circumstances should change in the future.

Finally, there appears to be a notable difference in the rate of return migration between whites and blacks. A very large proportion of migrants from the farms return to the farms, but blacks are much less likely to do so. Whereas the South gained about as many whites as they lost through migration between 1955 and 1960, there was only about one nonwhite in-migrant for every three out-migrants. Blacks who migrate from Southern rural areas to the North are much more likely than whites to remain in the North.

Mobility and economic gain   Blacks apparently derive greater economic gain than whites from their migration to urban areas. In spite of the congestion and social problems of large cities, there is evidence that rural migrants moving to large cities are likely to enjoy a greater gain in income than those who move to smaller cities. Since blacks move primarily to large cities they benefit from this differential gain: their median family income outside the South is much higher than in the South; and their level of income relative to that of whites is much more favorable outside of the South than in the South. Since the differentials are not as great for whites and since their migration patterns are more diffused (including considerable movement to other rural areas), rural whites have less clear cut gains to expect from migration than blacks have.

Pilot mobility projects   The effects of reducing the economic costs of mobility from rural areas can be appraised in recent federal mobility projects. Under authorization of the Manpower Development and Training Act, as amended in 1963, a total of thirty-seven pilot mobility projects had been conducted through 1968. Approximately 14,000 workers were relocated through these experimental programs. Over half of the projects were concentrated on rural areas, primarily in the South. Most of the moves were in-state or for relatively short distances to neighboring states, and all but 10 percent were to communities outside of the major metropolitan areas (population over a million). Most of those relocated had suffered lengthy periods of joblessness or underemployment. Project costs averaged less than $800 a move, with nearly half going for financial assistance to the relocating family. Those relocated were given differing packages of assistance in the various projects, including moving allowances, job interview allowances, payment for the temporary maintenance of two households, job development, and counseling.

The U. S. Department of Labor judged the mobility projects useful. Although not all of the projects were equally successful, on the whole they induced some mobility out of depressed rural areas that might not have otherwise occurred, they encouraged a more rational migration to known job opportunities, and the economic benefits derived from the resulting relocation exceeded the costs of the government programs.

Although there seems to be ample evidence that those relocated by these projects improved their economic status, more extensive experience with assisted relocation and more detailed research evaluation will be required to substantiate the durable value of this type of government policy. Further detailed research is required to determine whether any of those relocated might not have moved even without assistance, whether they were persuaded to move to small cities rather than large cities because of the project, and whether the high rate of return migration (30 percent for rural migrants) seriously reduces the benefits derived from the projects. Additional experience and research can demonstrate whether mobility-assistance projects can reduce the sociopsychological costs of moving and whether they can serve to reduce the congestion of minority groups in the ghettos of large urban areas. These questions are discussed further in the concluding chapters of this volume.

Regional economic development and mobility   Regional economic development is a partial alternative to the dual specters of depressed rural areas and movement to congested urban ghettos. To the extent that regional economic development policies are successful, they can reduce the rural-to-urban mobility discussed above.

Earlier regional economic development involved a widespread scattering of economic assistance over extensive geographic areas of the country; this approach has been replaced by a concentration on infrastructure and on economic development in concentrated areas of major economic potential. Very little economic gain could be demonstrated under the earlier approach, but it is still too early to derive inferences of important economic expansion under the current policies.

There are three possible alternatives ·in a more concentrated approach: suburban development; new towns; or growth centers in the most promising sections of depressed rural regions. Among these alternatives, most government officials now favor the development of growth centers because they believe that suburban development would be too costly and that the experience with new towns has been unfavorable.

Although the growth-center approach has many attractions and is being widely espoused in Western Europe as well as in the United States, there are still few success stories. Experience indicates that the growth center must have at least 25,000 to 50,000 people to be economically viable as a center of spreading economic expansion. Industrial employment opportunities must be developed in these centers at the same time as residential sections. Economics and politics frequently obstruct such developments, and large gray areas can threaten to develop in the territory surrounding the growth center if population is drained off from the rural areas as a whole to a few major concentrations. Nonetheless, the growth-center approach appears to be much more promising than the earlier attack through a multitude of so-called "development areas."

Because there is little favorable experience with new towns in Europe and in this country, it is notable that the National Committee on Urban Growth has recently proposed the building of one hundred new cities to accommodate at least 100,000 population each and ten cities for at least 1,000,000 each. The Committee's stricture that the new cities "should have gainful, varied, and satisfying employment for low and moderate income persons" is, unfortunately, contrary to the experience with the "new towns" developed in this country to date.

These plans for regional economic development, if carried out, would have a significant impact on labor mobility and on the structure of local, regional, and national labor markets.

Education, training, and mobility   The relatively low levels of formal education and the lack of vocational training facilities in poor rural areas exacerbate and perpetuate the economic problems of such areas stemming from an unskilled work force. Rural high schools are often too small to provide meaningful vocational training; and industrial facilities are too few to serve as a source of on-the-job training and work experience. Area vocational schools and new programs for the disadvantaged, established under the Vocational Education Acts of 1963 and 1968, may provide a greater opportunity for vocational instruction in depressed rural areas. Unfortunately, there has been little assessment of these developments to date.

The Manpower Development and Training Act could play an important role in rural areas. Between 1963 and 1968, 20 percent (some 200,000) of all

MDTA trainees were in rural areas. The Concerted Services approach adopted through the Employment Service and the MDTA in Arkansas, Minnesota, and New Mexico offers further hope of meaningful education and training programs for rural workers. In addition, the Job Corps has enrolled approximately 25 percent of its members from rural areas. Operation Mainstream is also primarily for rural adults. The Concentrated Employment Program, begun in 1967 to coordinate manpower services in rural poverty areas (as well as in city slums), was redesigned in 1969 to correct earlier deficiencies and improve the program's effectiveness.

Depending on the nature of the training, either MDTA and other types of courses can help retain older workers in local service industries and government agencies in rural areas, or courses geared to distant opportunities for younger workers can encourage outward migration. Vocational training courses must be properly mixed to accommodate the composition of the local work force and the patterns of local and distant employment opportunities. Thus, training in rural areas can serve either to retain the local work force in such areas or to encourage mobility between labor markets. Studies have shown both of these effects. Training is likely to enhance the income of migrants and of stationary workers as well.

Conclusion

The typical labor market is seen, then, as a substantial departure from the perfect model exemplified by a securities exchange. The very nature of the participants precludes a perfectly competitive labor market. Furthermore, knowledge and information are imperfect. None of the actors who play a role in the labor market carry out their parts as one would expect in a perfect labor market: employers do not compete freely for labor and workers do not compete freely for jobs; and the Employment Service suffers serious limitations as a disseminator of labor-market information and as a labor-market broker.

It is seen, however, that in spite of these imperfections and limitations, there is considerable mobility in local and national labor markets. Even though much of this movement may be "irrational" from an economic standpoint, there is still considerable movement in search of improved economic opportunity and social welfare—especially by those who find themselves most disadvantaged in areas of severely depressed employment opportunities. The rural-to-urban movement in this country generally accords with the tenets of the "rational economic" labor market model, for it has been movement toward economic gain. Recent changes in this mobility—toward smaller urban centers—may also reflect a rational blending of economic and social considerations.

Readings

Blau, Peter and Otis D. Duncan. *The American Occupational Structure.* New York: John Wiley and Sons, 1967.

Burton, John F., Jr., et al., eds. *Readings in Labor Market Analysis.* New York: Holt, Rinehart and Winston, 1971.

Doeringer, Peter, and Michael Piore. *Internal Labor Markets and Manpower Analysis.* Lexington, Mass.: D. C. Heath, 1971.

Fleisher, Belton M. *Labor Economics: Theory and Evidence.* Englewood Cliffs, N. J.: Prentice-Hall, 1970.

Lansing, John B., and Eva Mueller. *The Geographic Mobility of Labor.* Ann Arbor: Survey Research Center, University of Michigan, 1967.

Lipset, Seymour, and R. Bendix. *Social Mobility in Industrial Society.* Berkeley and Los Angeles: University of California Press, 1960.

Parnes, Herbert S. *Research on Labor Mobility, Bulletin 65.* Social Science Research Council, 1955.

Perlman, Richard. *Labor Theory.* New York: John Wiley and Sons, 1969.

Reynolds, Lloyd G. *The Structure of Labor Markets.* New York: Harper and Row, 1951.

Sheppard, Harold L., and A. Harvey Belitsky. *The Job Hunt.* Baltimore, Md.: Johns Hopkins Press, 1966.

"The Returns to Geographic Mobility: A Symposium," *Journal of Human Resources* (Fall 1967).

Chapter Three   The Labor Force

Introduction: definition of the
labor force

The *labor force* includes all persons who are employed or who are unemployed but looking for work; it excludes those who are unwilling or unable to work. (Accurate statistical measurement requires that precise definitions be followed.) The portion of the labor force classified as *employed* includes all noninstitutional persons 16 years or older who hold a job during the week of enumeration, even if they are temporarily absent from work due to illness, vacation, etc. The *unemployed* classification includes all noninstitutionalized persons 16 years or older who are not at work but who are actively seeking employment during the week of enumeration. The unemployed pose special problems to the economy and, therefore, merit further discussion.

Since official unemployment statistics require that a worker actively seek work to be included in the unemployed count, they do not always serve as a good guide to the extent of economic misery. During bad times many jobseekers leave the labor force, that is, discouraged by their failure to find work they quit looking for nonexistent jobs. By doing this they become part of the *hidden unemployed,* those who would work if jobs were available but who do not actively seek work. Many secondary family workers—those other than the principal breadwinner, especially wives, who do not seek work when the job search is difficult and usually unsuccessful in bad times but who take easily available jobs in good times—fit the hidden unemployed category.

Many critics of official unemployment statistics think they should be changed to include the hidden unemployed so that the official figures would not longer understate the actual number who would work given adequate job opportunities. But it would be very difficult to count those who would fill the jobs if they became available; such persons are quite different from those actively seeking work and are much more numerous.

There is danger, too, in indiscriminate counting of the labor reserve in labor-force and unemployment figures. Some of the hidden unemployed have the thinnest of ties to the labor force. Typical would be a housewife of a high-income husband: she might be dissatisified with her nonwork activities, and would work if the "right" job came along, one suitable to her interests, to her training of perhaps twenty years ago, and to what she considers her station in life. If she were counted as unemployed the unemployment rate would certainly exaggerate the degree of weakness in the economy. To overstate the problem of unemployment would reduce the chance of measuring the success of full-employment programs and policies, even if they were really effective in strengthening the economy enough to employ all primary workers.

Unemployment and underemployment

Although the primary problem discussed in this chapter is to find enough workers to do all the jobs we want done, it should be noted that at times there seem to be too many job seekers. Unemployment is a social problem as well as an economic one; during periods of high unemployment many persons suffer from loss of income, businesses lose their customers, and the economy's output is only a fraction of its potential. The unemployed are usually not responsible for their failure to have jobs—a lesson we learned during the acute Depression of the 1930s. It was in that era that the federal government initiated a system of unemployment insurance which enabled the unemployed to support their families, albeit meagerly, while seeking employment.

Even during the recent decades of prosperity unemployment has remained a problem. In the past, economists have attributed unemployment to various causes: frictional effects, seasonal changes, technology, business cycle fluctuations, structural barriers. But regardless of the cause, unemployment usually affects certain groups of workers more than others. Most susceptible to unemployment are teenagers and nonwhites, who are often the last to be hired and the first to be dismissed. Women usually experience a higher unemployment rate than do men: white females in the lowest and highest age groups have an unemployment rate similar to that of white males in those age groups, while in the middle years their rate is much higher than that of the males. However, for nonwhite females, a different pattern appears: they are subject to heavier unemployment than nonwhite males during the younger years, but in their older worklives the rates are reversed.

Characteristically, the overall rate for nonwhites (which for all practical statistical purposes can be considered blacks, since blacks comprise over 90 percent of the nonwhite group) is about twice the white rate. Charts 3/1, 3/2, 3/3 and Table 3/1 show that this pattern holds for both males and females, with the variations as noted between age groups. The interracial rate difference narrows in very good times and widens from the customary 2.1 ratio in bad times, a reflection of the last-in–first-out employment experience of blacks. By occupational breakdown, white-collar workers experience the

Figure 3/1.   Unemployment rates by color

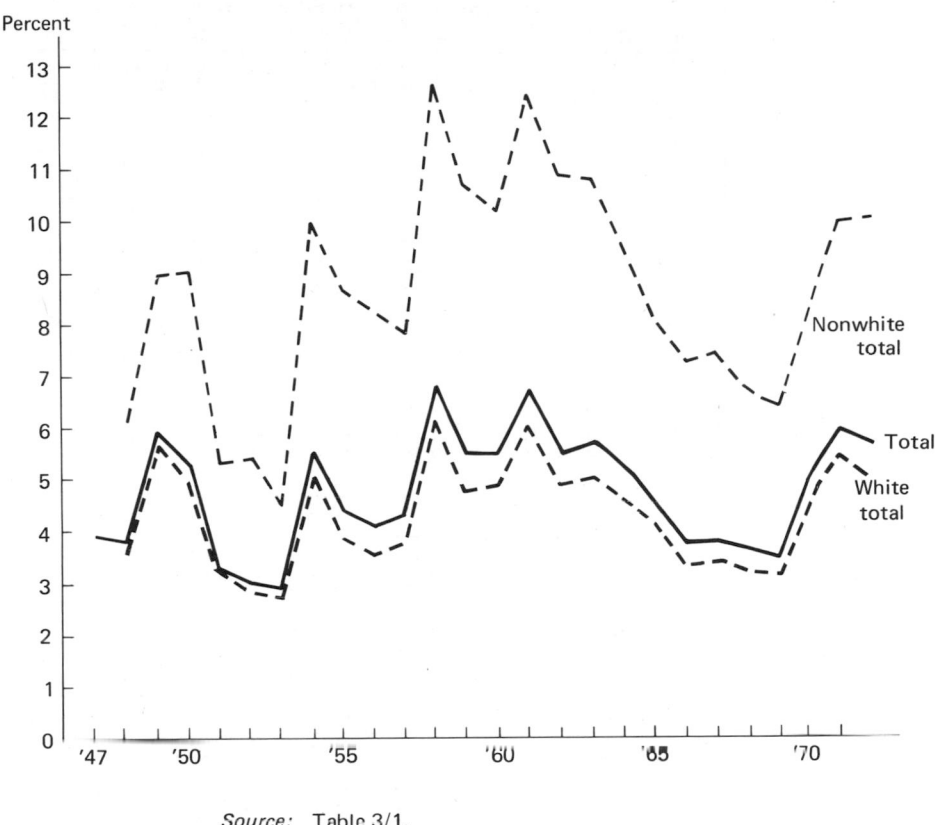

Source: Table 3/1.

least unemployment, blue-collar workers the most. By far, the group hardest hit by unemployment is the unskilled nonfarm laborer.

Underemployment is employment of persons in jobs that do not use their full capabilities (this is not to be confused with part-time employment): for example, an architect performing the job of a draftsman is underemployed. Although not easily quantified, underemployment of any portion of the labor force results in a level of output smaller than the economy's potential. Underemployment, therefore, has the same effect as unemployment on the nation's output. Underutilization of the skills of some groups of workers is commonplace; employees are overeducated for their positions, and are held in those jobs by lack of alternative opportunities, lack of mobility or entry into the higher-level jobs they could competently handle.

Underemployment arises in bad times because of downward mobility of the labor force. As jobs become scarce for all labor classes, the highly trained

Table 3/1. Unemployment rates, by sex and color: annual averages, 1947-72

Number unemployed (thousands)

Year	Total	Male	Female	White Total	White Male	White Female	Negro and other races Total	Negro and other races Male	Negro and other races Female
1947	2,311	1,692	619	(¹)	(¹)	(¹)	(¹)	(¹)	(¹)
1948	2,276	1,559	717	(¹)	(¹)	(¹)	(¹)	(¹)	(¹)
1949	3,637	2,572	1,065	(¹)	(¹)	(¹)	(¹)	(¹)	(¹)
1950	3,288	2,239	1,049	(¹)	(¹)	(¹)	(¹)	(¹)	(¹)
1951	2,055	1,221	834	(¹)	(¹)	(¹)	(¹)	(¹)	(¹)
1952	1,883	1,185	698	(¹)	(¹)	(¹)	(¹)	(¹)	(¹)
1953	1,834	1,202	632	(¹)	(¹)	(¹)	(¹)	(¹)	(¹)
1954	3,532	2,344	1,188	2,860	1,913	947	674	431	243
1955	2,852	1,854	998	2,248	1,475	773	601	376	225
1956	2,750	1,711	1,039	2,162	1,368	794	592	345	247
1957	2,859	1,841	1,018	2,289	1,478	811	569	363	206
1958	4,602	3,098	1,504	3,679	2,488	1,191	925	611	314
1959	3,740	2,420	1,320	2,947	1,904	1,044	794	518	276
1960	3,852	2,486	1,366	3,063	1,987	1,076	787	497	290
1961	4,714	2,997	1,717	3,742	2,398	1,344	970	599	371
1962	3,911	2,423	1,488	3,052	1,915	1,137	859	508	351
1963	4,070	2,472	1,598	3,208	1,976	1,232	864	496	368
1964	3,786	2,205	1,581	2,999	1,779	1,220	786	426	360
1965	3,366	1,914	1,452	2,691	1,556	1,135	676	359	317
1966	2,875	1,551	1,324	2,253	1,240	1,013	621	311	310
1967	2,975	1,508	1,468	2,338	1,208	1,130	638	299	338

Unemployment rate

Year	Total	Male	Female	White Total	White Male	White Female	Negro and other races Total	Negro and other races Male	Negro and other races Female
1947	3.9	4.0	3.7	(¹)	(¹)	(¹)	(¹)	(¹)	(¹)
1948	3.8	3.6	4.1	3.5	3.4	3.8	5.9	5.8	6.1
1949	5.9	5.9	6.0	5.6	5.6	5.7	8.9	9.6	7.9
1950	5.3	5.1	5.7	4.9	4.7	5.3	9.0	9.4	8.4
1951	3.3	2.8	4.4	3.1	2.6	4.2	5.3	4.9	6.1
1952	3.0	2.8	3.6	2.8	2.5	3.3	5.4	5.2	5.7
1953	2.9	2.8	3.3	2.7	2.5	3.1	4.5	4.8	4.1
1954	5.5	5.3	6.0	5.0	4.8	5.6	9.9	10.3	9.3
1955	4.4	4.2	4.9	3.9	3.7	4.3	8.7	8.8	8.4
1956	4.1	3.8	4.8	3.6	3.4	4.2	8.3	7.9	8.9
1957	4.3	4.1	4.7	3.8	3.6	4.3	7.9	8.3	7.3
1958	6.8	6.8	6.8	6.1	6.1	6.2	12.6	13.8	10.8
1959	5.5	5.3	5.9	4.8	4.6	5.3	10.7	11.5	9.4
1960	5.5	5.4	5.9	4.9	4.8	5.3	10.2	10.7	9.4
1961	6.7	6.4	7.2	6.0	5.7	6.5	12.4	12.8	11.8
1962	5.5	5.2	6.2	4.9	4.6	5.5	10.9	10.9	11.0
1963	5.7	5.2	6.5	5.0	4.7	5.8	10.8	10.5	11.2
1964	5.2	4.6	6.2	4.6	4.1	5.5	9.6	8.9	10.6
1965	4.5	4.0	5.5	4.1	3.6	5.0	8.1	7.4	9.2
1966	3.8	3.2	4.8	3.3	2.8	4.3	7.3	6.3	8.6
1967	3.8	3.1	5.2	3.4	2.7	4.6	7.4	6.0	9.1

Table 3/1. (continued)

Year	Number unemployed (thousands)									Unemployment rate								
	Total			White			Negro and other races			Total			White			Negro and other races		
	Total	Male	Female	Total	Male	Female	Total	Male	Female	Total	Male	Female	Total	Male	Female	Total	Male	Female
1968	2,817	1,419	1,397	2,226	1,142	1,084	590	277	313	3.6	2.9	4.8	3.2	2.6	4.3	6.7	5.6	8.3
1969	2,831	1,403	1,428	2,261	1,137	1,124	570	266	304	3.5	2.8	4.7	3.1	2.5	4.2	6.4	5.3	7.8
1970	4,088	2,235	1,853	3,337	1,856	1,480	752	379	373	4.9	4.4	5.9	4.5	4.0	5.4	8.2	7.3	9.3
1971	4,993	2,776	2,217	4,074	2,302	1,772	919	474	445	5.9	5.3	6.9	5.4	4.9	6.3	9.9	9.1	10.8
1972	4,840	2,635	2,205	3,884	2,160	1,724	956	475	482	5.6	4.9	6.6	5.0	4.5	5.9	10.0	8.9	11.3

[1] Absolute numbers by color are not available prior to 1954 because of the absence of population controls by color, and rates by color are not available for 1947.

Source: *Manpower Report of the President*, 1973.

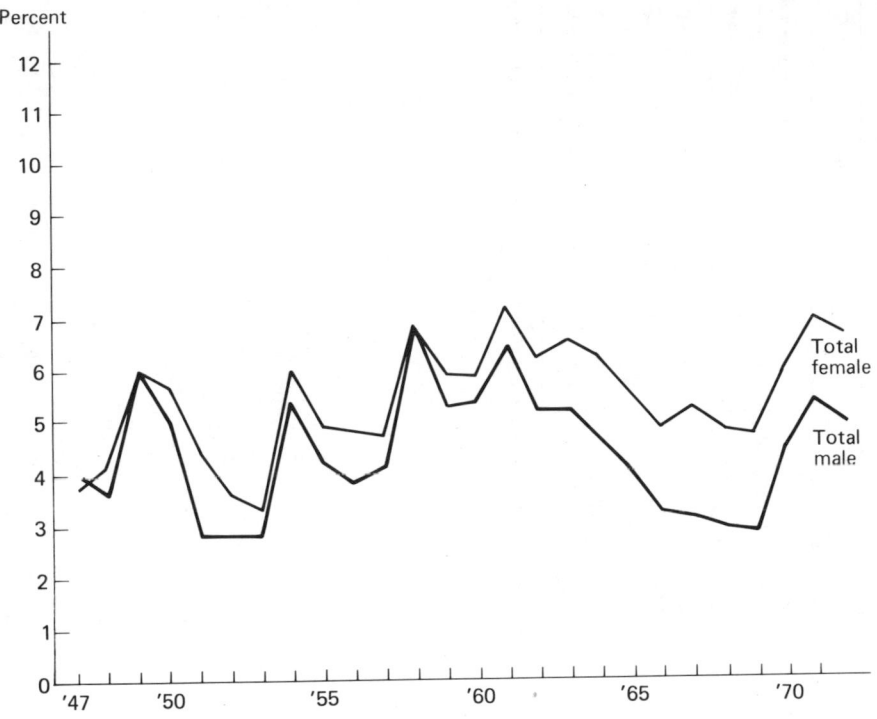

Figure 3/2.   Unemployment rates by sex

Source: Table 3/1.

unemployed can enter the lesser-skilled job market to compete for positions with those who normally supply their labor services in this market. To the extent they find jobs below their skill potential, the highly trained do keep employed, but at a cost of lower income, and morale reduced by performing duties below their capabilities.

Besides underutilizing their skills in weak economic periods, workers can also underutilize their time when they become involuntary part-time workers in slack labor markets. Unemployment statistics do not capture the unsatisfied supply of man-hours represented by workers who are employed fewer hours than they wish. Again, there is a loss in worker income and national production.

Neither do unemployment data record the underutilized work time and effort of the self-employed. In bad times the self-employed are still counted as employed, and fully so, even if they have few customers, clients, patients,

Figure 3/3. *Unemployment rates by sex and color*

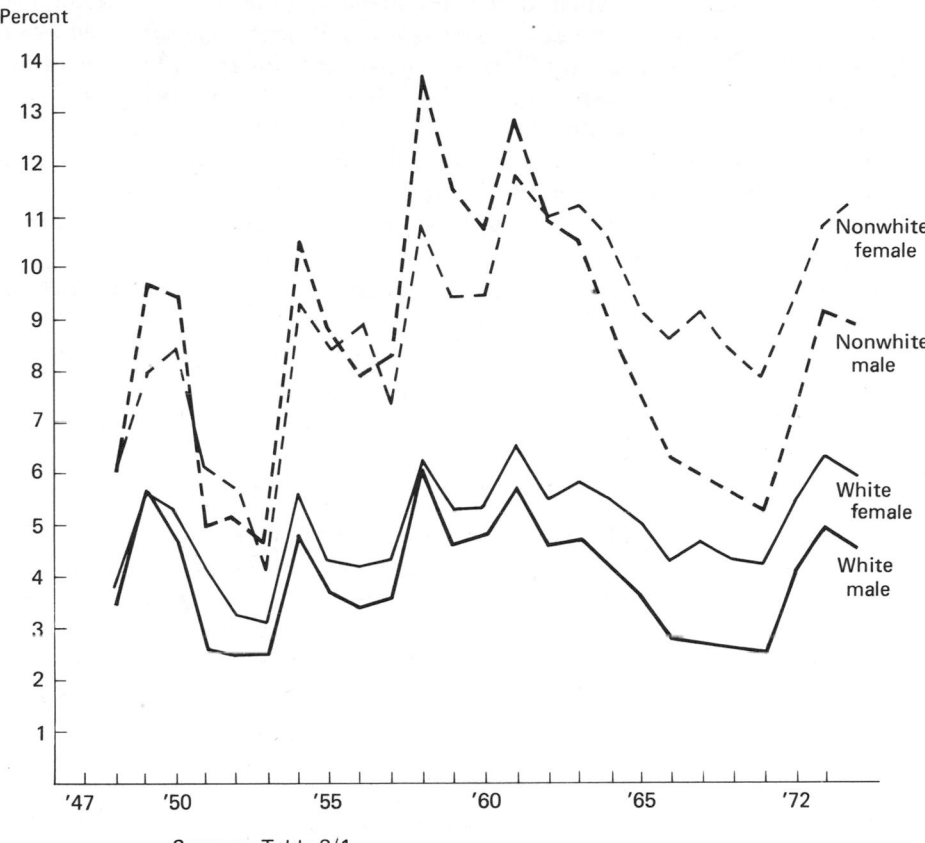

Source: Table 3/1.

etc. Once more, unemployment figures serve as a poor guide to loss of individual income and national production.

The labor force and economic growth

Productive resources are classified as land, labor, and capital. The total output of the economy is constrained by the amount available and the quality of these resources. With a given amount of capital and land and a given state of technology (none of which vary in the short run), the level of production will be determined by the size and quality of the labor force and by how fully it is utilized. A growing labor force enhances economic growth by increasing output, with no change in the labor-force participation rate. The combination of more labor and more labor productivity brings about a higher rate of economic growth, even when there is no increase in the volume or quality of the other productive resources. Of course, *per capita* growth is not raised when increased output results only from an increased labor force, but per capita growth can take place even with a stable labor force if the worker's productive efficiency improves. Within a population of a given size, the size of the labor force is set by the participation rates of working-age persons. The productivity of labor is determined primarily by the amount of capital available to combine with labor, and by the state of technology. Long-run investments in capital goods, or in the education and training of the labor force— that is, in human capital—raise the productivity of labor and the rate of economic growth.

The potential supply of labor

Population size

Population size is affected not only by the natural rate of growth but also by immigration and emigration. In turn, the potential supply of labor from any given population size is affected by its age composition. Population estimates show that the 1960 and 1970 age structures differ. Although the percent of population over 16 years of age remained approximately the same, subgroups changed at different rates. The 16-to-24 age group increased from 12.1 percent of the total population in 1960 to 15.6 percent in 1970, while the 25-to-44 age group declined from 26.1 percent of total population to 23.3 percent. These shifts in age composition are important because the highest labor force participation rates occur among the 25 to 44 year-olds. Thus, a drop in the relative proportion of this age group—a reflection of the low birth rate during the 1930s—will be reversed during the '70s by the large number of marriages and births following the Second World War.

Immigration can affect the total population and the labor supply. Immigration measured as a percent of population has not been great during the twentieth century. For example, in 1960 immigration as a percent of population was only 0.1 percent, (Table 3/2). During periods when the natural rate of population growth provides an inadequate supply of labor, as during the colonial and industrializing eras in the United States, immigration is critical to the expanding economy. However, during periods of labor excess, when unemployment is high, heavy immigration only aggravates the situation. The threat of unemployment thus underlies immigration policies that require aliens to obtain work certificates, which are issued only to persons with skills in demand in this country.

Emigration from the United States has never been sizable enough to be important. But emigration can have a great impact upon smaller and less-

Table 3/2.   Immigration to the United States,
1900–1960

	Number of immigrants	Percent of United States population
1900	448,572	0.6
1910	1,041,570	1.1
1920	430,001	0.4
1930	241,700	0.2
1940	70,756	0.05
1950	249,187	0.2
1960	265,398	0.1

Source: *Historical Statistics of the United States Colonial Times to 1957*, 1960, R56; 1960 figure from *Statistical Abstract of the United States, 1971*, U. S. Department of Commerce, p. 91.

developed countries. Cuba experienced a great stream of emigration during the early years of Fidel Castro's rule, when many middle-class persons left. As a result, Cuba faced an extreme shortage of labor, especially skilled and professional. Many of the developing nations lose educated labor to the United States when their nationals who study here are attracted to the better-paying jobs available in this country.

Population trends and projections

By 1970, the United States population had grown to approximately 2¾ its size at the beginning of the century. The growth has been irregular, with a high 21 percent from 1900 to 1919, and a low 7 percent increase from 1930 to 1940. An expected 17 percent increase in the decade of the seventies will raise the 1980 population to 243 million, or over 3 times the 1900 total. The number of persons of prime working ages (25–64 years) in 1970 was close to 90 million, and by 1980 will reach 106 million, for an increase of almost 18 percent in the decade of the '70s. Between 1960 and 1970, this age group grew by only 8 percent. The nation thus faces a decade of challenge, for it may prove quite difficult to sufficiently stimulate the demand for labor to maintain a low rate of unemployment. Table 3/3 shows the population by age groups from 1900 through 1970 and projected to 1980.

Labor-force participation

The labor-force participation rate is that proportion of the population 16 years of age or older that is active in the labor force, either as workers or as jobseekers. For example, in 1960 the total population 16 years of age or older

Table 3/3. Total population of the United States, 1900 to 1970 and projected to 1980, by age group
(in thousands)

Age	1900	1910	1920	1930	1940	1950	1960	1970	1980
Total	76,094	92,407	106,466	123,077	132,122	152,271	180,684	207,326	243,291
Under 16 yrs.*	24,581	27,806	31,756	33,638	30,521	43,131	58,868	65,300	76,737
16 yrs. & over**	51,513	64,601	74,710	89,439	101,601	109,141	121,814	142,025	166,552
16 to 24***	16,514	20,024	20,858	24,852	26,454	20,222	21,814	32,347	37,937
25 to 44	21,433	27,037	31,800	36,309	39,868	45,673	47,134	48,276	62,373
45 to 64	10,466	13,555	17,123	21,573	26,249	30,849	36,208	41,817	43,179
65 yrs. +	3,100	3,985	4,929	6,706	9,031	12,397	16,658	19,585	23,063

Notes: *The figures for 1900–1940 are for under 14 years.
         **The figures for 1900–1940 are for 14 years and over.
        ***The figures for 1900–1940 are for 14 to 24.

Sources: 1900–1950 Historical Statistics of the United States, Colonial Times to 1957, 1960,
p. 11; 1960–1980, Statistics on Manpower, 1969, p. 77.

was 121,814,000 and the total labor force numbered 72,104,000 or 59.2 percent of that age group; thus, in that year about 3 out of 5 persons aged 16 and over were members of the labor force. The labor-force participation rate and total population (the base to which the rate is applicable) are the relevant components of the supply of labor. Neither variable changes swiftly; the size and age composition of the population shift only from one generation to another, and participation in the work force is also slow to change.

The labor-force participation rate is affected by various factors that in this country have tended to have offsetting influences on its size during this century. The labor-force participation rate of women, which was discussed in Chapter 2 with particular reference to its steady growth, is affected by the husband's income, age of children, place of residence, educational level, and society's attitude toward women working outside the home. There is an inverse relationship between the husband's income and the labor-force participation rate of a married woman—hardly surprising, since married women work primarily to increase the family income. However, in recent years, women's work has reflected higher career aspirations. The industrial mix and job availability in the area around a woman's place of residence clearly influence her decision whether to work or stay in the home. Urban areas offer more job opportunities than rural areas, and service industries demand more white-collar workers—hence more women—than manufacturing industries. The positive correlation between years of education and labor-force participation of women is also a reflection of the greater range of employment opportunities enjoyed by educated women.

During prosperity, when jobs are plentiful, women, teenagers, and older persons join the labor force. But during depressions, conflicting forces operate. When the family head loses his job, members of the family not usually in the labor force may seek work in order to maintain family income. But on the other hand some workers who become discouraged when they lose their jobs drop out of the labor force altogether. Other factors such as child-labor laws, discriminatory practices, and retirement arrangements affect the labor-force participation rate of segments of the population.

Those who enter the labor force in good times in response to greater job availability are called members of the secondary work force. They have a looser attachment to work as a way of life than permanent, or primary, workers, but they have an important effect on economic policies, especially those designed to attain full employment. When they enter the job market in good times they retard the movement to full employment. Similarly, as the economy loses some of its vigor, when they leave the work force they dampen the growth in unemployment. In effect, then, the secondary work force acts to reduce swings in unemployment. As noted in the beginning of this chapter though, this effect applies only to official unemployment figures. When secondary members leave the official work force in bad times they enter the ranks of the hidden unemployed.

It is interesting to note that the secondary work force has grown in recent years even though fewer youths and older men are working and more women have joined the primary force. This means that women have been increasing their labor-force participation both as primary and as secondary workers.

Trends in labor-force participation

In keeping with the traditional American view of the family structure, males and females in this country exhibit different rates of labor-force activity. However, in recent decades significant changes have occurred in both rates. During the twentieth century, for males of all ages the labor-force participation rate has declined from almost 86 percent in 1900 to 80 percent in 1970. (These rates are not strictly comparable; prior to 1950, the percentage applied to all males aged 14 and over, whereas the 1960 and subsequent rates included only 16-and-over men. See Table 3/4). For females, the rate has increased markedly since the beginning of the century—from 20.0 percent in 1900 to an estimated 40.5 percent in 1970. These changes in the rates have brought about concomitant change in the sex composition of the labor force. For while in 1900 almost 82 percent of the labor force was male and 18 percent was female, the present division is approximately two-thirds male and one-third female.

As indicated earlier, marital status affects the work activity of both males and females. Married men usually have higher labor-force participation rates than single men, whereas single women have higher rates than married women. Labor-force participation by single women has changed negligibly; it is married women whose propensity to work outside the home has grown. Since 1947, as noted above, the labor-force participation rate of married women has risen from 20 percent to the 1970 rate of over 40 percent.

Table 3/4 shows the long-term trends for the sex and age composition of the work force. Projections for 1980 predict a leveling off of the trends. Male participation for different ages is expected to be more or less constant, except for the continued departure of older men from the work force. All of the slight gain in overall participation is anticipated from women: substantial increases are forecast for middle-aged women, but the expected stagnation in rates for the much larger younger groups will severely retard the overall female expansion.

Nonwhite females have a higher labor-force participation rate than white females in all age categories except the 16-to-19-year-old group. Nonwhite males have a somewhat lower rate than white males, however; in addition, most nonwhite men have low-paying jobs. Economic necessity therefore drives nonwhite females into the labor market.

Table 3/5 shows the labor-force participation pattern by race, sex, and age. Of particular interest is the low rate of black prime work-force males in

Table 3/4. Labor-force* participation rates, by sex and age group, 1900–1980

	1900	1920	1930	1940	1950	1960	1970	1980
Total 16 yrs. and over	53.7%	54.3%	53.2%	55.3%	57.7%	59.2%	59.7%	60.4%
Males								
16 yrs. +	85.7	84.6	82.1	82.6	83.2	82.4	80.3	80.3
16 – 19	62.0	51.5	40.1	44.0	52.7	58.6	56.4	56.7
20 – 24	90.6	89.9	88.8	95.2	88.0	88.9	86.6	87.2
25 – 34)	94.7)	95.6)	95.8)	96.7)	95.5	96.4	96.2	96.2
35 – 44)						96.4	96.7	96.7
45 – 54)	90.3)	90.7)	91.0)	90.4)	90.4	94.3	95.0	95.0
55 – 64)						85.2	84.3	83.7
65 +	63.1	55.6	54.0	44.2	44.7	32.2	25.1	21.8
Females								
16 yrs. +	20.0	22.7	23.6	27.9	32.8	37.1	40.5	41.9
16 – 19	26.8	28.4	22.8	23.1	31.3	39.1	39.4	40.0
20 – 24	31.7	37.5	41.8	49.1	45.9	46.1	50.3	52.6
25 – 34)	17.5)	21.7)	24.6)	32.1)	36.2	35.8	38.6	40.3
35 – 44)						43.1	47.5	50.0
45 – 54)	13.6)	16.5)	18.0)	21.7)	32.9	49.3	55.3	59.5
55 – 64)						36.7	43.8	47.3
65 +	8.3	7.3	7.3	7.2	9.5	10.5	9.8	9.9

Note:* Labor Force prior to 1950 includes all persons 14 years or older; figures for 1960 and afterward include all persons 16 years or older.
Sources: 1900–1950 *Historical Statistics of the United States, Colonial Times to 1957*, 1960, p. 11; 1960–1980, *Statistics on Manpower*, 1969, p. 77.

the age groups 25 to 54. The overall difference between white and black males of this age (about 4 percent: 97 for white and 93 for blacks) might not seem significant, but in this age group nonparticipation is rare.

It is reasonable to assume that many black males fit the discouraged worker description. With jobs scarce for them because they are poorly trained and/or discriminated against, black men quit the work force in despair of finding jobs. The relatively low unemployment rate for black men in these age groups, low even if it is double the white level (see Table 3/1), obscures their lack of job opportunity; discouraged workers are not counted in the labor force and thus do not appear in the unemployment figures.

Nonparticipants in the labor force

In recent decades attention has been directed to those adults who are outside the labor force, and why. A large pool of potential labor supply—an estimated 57 million persons in 1970—suggests a possible expansion in total

Table 3/5. Civilian labor force participation rates[1] for persons 16 years and over, by color, sex, and age: annual averages, 1948–72

Item	Total, 16 years and over	16 and 17 years	18 and 19 years	20 to 24 years	25 to 34 years	35 to 44 years	45 to 54 years	55 to 64 years	65 years and over	14 and 15 years
White										
Male										
1948	86.5	51.2	76.2	84.4	96.0	98.0	95.9	89.6	46.5	26.1
1949	86.4	50.1	74.8	86.5	95.9	98.0	95.6	87.6	46.6	26.3
1950	86.4	50.5	75.5	87.5	96.4	97.7	95.9	87.3	45.8	27.6
1951	86.5	52.7	74.2	88.4	97.0	97.6	96.0	87.4	44.5	26.9
1952	86.2	51.9	72.7	87.6	97.6	97.9	96.3	87.7	42.5	25.3
1953	86.1	49.8	72.8	87.4	97.5	97.9	96.4	87.7	41.3	23.6
1954	85.6	47.1	70.4	86.4	97.5	98.2	96.8	89.2	40.4	24.5
1955	85.4	48.0	71.7	85.6	97.8	98.3	96.7	88.4	39.5	23.5
1956	85.6	51.3	71.9	87.6	97.4	98.1	96.8	88.9	40.0	26.7
1957	84.8	49.6	71.6	86.7	97.2	98.0	96.6	88.0	37.7	25.1
1958	84.3	46.8	69.4	86.7	97.2	98.0	96.6	88.2	35.7	24.1
1959	83.8	45.4	70.3	87.3	97.5	98.0	96.3	87.9	34.3	24.2
1960	83.4	46.0	69.0	87.8	97.7	97.9	96.1	87.2	33.3	22.2
1961	83.0	44.3	66.2	87.6	97.7	97.9	95.9	87.8	31.9	22.2
1962	82.1	42.9	66.4	86.5	97.4	97.9	96.0	86.7	30.6	22.3
1963	81.5	42.4	67.8	85.8	97.4	97.8	96.2	86.6	28.4	21.4
1964	81.1	43.5	66.6	85.7	97.5	97.6	96.1	86.1	27.9	21.2
1965	80.8	44.6	65.8	85.3	97.4	97.7	95.9	85.2	27.9	21.7
1966	80.6	47.1	65.4	84.4	97.5	97.6	95.8	84.9	27.2	22.3
1967	80.7	47.9	66.1	84.0	97.5	97.7	95.6	84.9	27.1	22.6
1968	80.4	47.7	65.7	82.4	97.2	97.6	95.4	84.7	27.3	22.7
1969	80.2	48.8	66.3	82.6	97.0	97.4	95.1	83.9	27.3	23.0
1970	80.0	48.9	67.4	83.3	96.7	97.3	94.9	83.3	26.7	23.0
1971	79.6	49.2	67.8	83.2	96.3	97.0	94.7	82.6	25.6	23.7
1972	79.6	50.2	71.1	84.3	96.0	97.0	94.0	81.2	24.4	23.5
Female										
1948	31.3	31.7	53.5	45.1	31.3	35.1	33.3	23.3	8.6	11.1
1949	31.8	31.4	54.0	44.4	31.7	36.1	34.3	24.2	9.1	10.3
1950	32.6	30.1	52.6	45.9	32.1	37.2	36.3	26.0	9.2	11.5
1951	33.4	32.4	54.1	46.7	33.6	38.0	38.0	26.5	8.5	11.2
1952	33.6	34.1	52.0	44.8	33.8	38.8	38.8	27.6	8.7	10.2
1953	33.4	31.2	51.9	44.1	31.7	38.8	38.7	28.5	9.4	9.9
1954	33.3	29.3	52.1	44.4	32.5	39.4	39.8	29.1	9.1	10.5
1955	34.5	29.9	52.0	45.8	32.8	39.9	42.7	31.8	10.5	11.2
1956	35.7	33.5	53.0	46.5	33.2	41.5	44.4	34.0	10.6	12.7
1957	35.7	32.1	52.6	45.8	33.6	41.5	45.4	33.7	10.2	12.5
1958	35.8	28.8	52.3	46.1	33.4	41.4	45.4	34.5	10.1	12.2
1959	36.0	29.9	50.8	44.5	33.4	41.4	46.5	34.5	10.2	13.0
1960	36.5	30.0	51.9	44.5	34.1	41.5	47.8	35.7	10.6	12.5
1961	36.9	29.4	51.9	46.9	34.3	41.8	48.6	36.2	10.5	13.5
1962	36.7	27.9	51.6	47.1	34.1	42.2	48.9	37.2	9.8	13.7
1963	37.2	27.9	51.3	47.3	34.8	43.1	49.5	38.0	9.4	12.2
1964	37.5	28.5	49.6	48.8	35.0	43.3	50.2	38.9	9.9	12.7
1965	38.1	28.7	50.6	49.2	36.3	44.3	49.9	39.4	9.7	12.9
1966	39.2	31.8	53.1	51.0	37.7	45.0	50.6	40.3	9.4	14.5
1967	40.1	32.3	52.7	53.1	39.7	46.4	50.9	41.1	9.3	15.4
1968	40.7	33.0	53.3	54.0	40.6	47.5	51.5	41.9	9.4	16.0
1969	41.8	35.2	54.6	56.4	41.7	48.6	53.0	42.0	9.7	16.1
1970	42.6	36.6	55.0	57.7	43.2	49.9	53.7	42.6	9.5	17.3
1971	42.6	36.4	55.0	57.9	43.6	50.2	53.7	42.6	9.3	17.2
1972	43.2	39.3	57.4	59.4	45.8	50.7	53.4	42.0	9.0	17.7

Table 3/5. (continued)

Negro and other races

Male										
1948	87.3	59.8	77.8	85.6	95.3	97.2	94.7	88.6	50.3	39.3
1949	87.0	60.4	80.8	89.7	94.1	97.3	95.6	86.0	51.4	36.6
1950	85.9	57.4	78.2	91.4	92.6	96.2	95.1	81.9	45.5	37.7
1951	86.3	54.7	80.8	88.7	95.7	96.4	95.1	84.6	49.5	34.6
1952	86.8	52.3	79.1	92.8	96.2	97.2	95.0	85.7	43.3	30.5
1953	86.2	53.0	76.7	92.3	96.7	97.3	93.9	86.7	41.1	27.8
1954	85.2	46.7	78.4	91.1	96.2	96.6	93.2	83.0	41.2	27.2
1955	85.0	48.2	75.7	89.7	95.8	96.2	94.2	83.1	40.0	27.1
1956	85.1	49.6	76.4	88.9	96.2	96.2	94.4	83.9	39.8	25.5
1957	84.3	47.5	72.0	89.6	96.1	96.5	93.5	82.4	35.9	24.7
1958	84.0	45.1	71.7	88.7	96.3	96.4	93.9	83.3	34.5	21.3
1959	83.4	41.7	72.0	90.8	96.2	95.8	92.8	82.5	33.5	23.9
1960	83.0	45.6	71.2	90.4	95.9	95.5	92.3	82.5	31.2	23.3
1961	82.2	42.5	70.5	89.7	95.3	94.8	92.3	81.6	29.4	19.2
1962	80.8	40.2	68.8	89.3	94.9	94.5	92.2	81.5	27.2	16.5
1963	80.2	37.2	69.1	88.6	95.9	94.9	91.1	82.5	27.6	17.2
1964	80.0	37.3	67.2	89.4	95.7	94.4	91.6	80.6	29.6	18.7
1965	79.6	39.3	66.7	89.8	95.5	94.2	92.0	78.8	27.9	18.9
1966	79.0	41.1	63.7	89.9	95.5	91.1	90.7	81.1	25.6	17.3
1967	78.5	41.2	62.7	87.2	95.0	93.6	91.3	79.3	27.2	18.3
1968	77.6	37.9	63.3	85.0	94.4	93.4	90.1	79.6	26.6	18.1
1969	76.9	37.7	63.2	84.4	93.7	92.7	89.5	77.9	26.1	15.8
1970	76.5	34.8	61.8	83.5	92.9	93.2	88.2	79.2	27.4	16.6
1971	74.9	32.4	58.9	81.5	92.7	92.0	86.9	77.8	24.5	15.2
1972	73.7	34.1	60.1	81.5		91.4	86.1	73.6	23.6	14.7

Female										
1948	45.6	29.1	41.2	47.1	50.6	53.3	51.1	37.6	17.5	21.0
1949	46.9	30.1	44.8	49.8	50.9	56.1	52.7	39.6	15.6	23.5
1950	46.9	30.2	40.6	46.9	51.6	55.7	54.3	40.9	16.5	22.0
1951	46.3	30.4	40.2	45.4	51.1	55.8	55.5	39.8	14.0	17.3
1952	45.5	27.4	44.7	43.9	50.1	54.0	52.7	42.3	14.3	18.5
1953	43.6	24.2	37.8	45.1	48.1	54.9	51.0	35.9	11.4	14.9
1954	46.1	24.5	37.7	49.6	49.7	57.5	53.4	41.2	12.2	16.2
1955	46.1	22.7	43.2	46.7	51.3	56.0	54.8	40.7	12.1	11.4
1956	47.3	28.3	44.6	44.9	52.1	57.0	55.3	44.5	14.5	14.4
1957	47.2	24.1	42.8	46.6	50.4	58.7	56.8	44.3	13.6	12.6
1958	48.0	23.2	41.2	48.3	50.8	60.8	59.8	42.8	13.3	11.6
1959	47.7	20.7	36.1	48.8	50.0	60.0	60.0	46.4	12.6	12.6
1960	48.2	22.1	44.3	48.8	49.7	59.8	60.5	47.3	12.8	13.2
1961	48.3	21.6	44.6	47.7	51.2	60.5	61.1	45.2	13.1	11.0
1962	48.0	21.0	45.5	48.6	52.0	59.7	60.5	46.1	12.2	9.7
1963	48.1	21.5	44.9	49.2	53.3	59.4	60.6	47.3	11.8	8.7
1964	48.5	19.5	46.5	53.6	52.8	58.4	62.3	48.4	12.7	8.0
1965	48.6	20.5	40.0	55.2	54.0	59.9	60.2	48.9	12.9	8.1
1966	49.3	23.6	44.0	54.5	54.9	60.9	61.0	49.1	13.0	7.5
1967	49.5	22.8	48.7	54.9	57.5	60.8	59.6	47.1	13.0	9.4
1968	49.3	23.3	46.9	58.4	56.6	59.3	59.8	47.0	11.9	7.2
1969	49.8	24.4	45.4	58.6	57.8	59.5	60.8	47.5	11.9	7.1
1970	49.5	24.3	44.7	57.7	57.6	59.9	60.2	47.1	12.2	9.7
1971	49.2	21.9	41.4	56.0	59.2	61.0	59.4	47.1	11.5	8.3
1972	48.7	21.4	43.9	56.7	60.1	60.7	57.3	43.9	12.8	9.3

[1]Percent of civilian noninstitutional population in the civilian labor force.

Source: Manpower Report of the President, 1973.

output if proper incentives were used to induce them to take jobs. These adult nonmembers include discouraged workers, retired persons, disabled persons, and persons who do not wish to work. A recent survey of nonparticipants showed three major reasons for not entering the labor force: domestic responsibilities, retirement, and school attendance. Domestic responsibilities are the primary reason for nonparticipation by women, particularly mothers of preschool children. Retirement of men and women over age 64 is increasingly common, and there is a growing propensity to retire at younger ages. School attendance is commonly the reason for nonparticipation by teenagers. One other group of nonparticipants is composed of persons who have been in the labor force but have given up looking for jobs and dropped out of the job market, at least temporarily. Not many white males of prime working age are in this group, but females of all ages appear to be vulnerable to this kind of problem. Involuntary nonparticipation is most prevalent among nonwhites, for whom jobs are frequently hard to find or retain. All these nonparticipants comprise the hidden unemployed.

Labor-force size

Changes in any one of the foregoing determinants—population size and composition, participation rates, immigration—will in turn affect the size of the labor force. The effects of changes in labor-force participation rates are less easy to anticipate than those of the other determinants. Long-term trends would seem to indicate a continued growth in the participation rate for married women and a slowly declining participation for men. The net effect is a gradual increase in the overall rate. When combined with the growing population, the rise in the proportion of adults who work necessitates a growing economy in which the aggregate demand for goods, and hence for labor, is sufficient to prevent unemployment and underemployment.

Labor-force growth and trends

From 1900 to 1970 the United States labor force more than tripled its size, while the nation's population grew about 2¾ times. The 1970 labor force of almost 85 million was greater than the total United States population in 1900. The greatest rate of growth came in the labor-force participation of women; their numbers rose from 5 million in 1900 to about 30 million in 1970. In contrast to this six-fold increase, the number of males in the labor force grew by about 2½ times. During the past 20 years the labor force has increased by an average of one million persons each year; however, the growth has not been even. The annual increment has dipped as low as 300,000 and has risen as high as 1.9 million. Table 3/6 shows the size of the labor force from 1900

Table 3/6. Total labor force,* by age group, 1900–1970 and projected to 1980 (in thousands)

	1900	1920	1930	1940	1950	1960	1970	1980
Total, 16 years and over	27,640	40,282	47,404	56,180	64,749	72,104	84,617	99,942
16 – 19	4,064	4,587	4,386	4,970	5,426	5,223	7,188	8,110
20 – 24	4,481	5,865	7,063	8,390	7,905	7,497	11,733	14,444
25 – 34	12,351 ⎫	18,667 ⎫	21,902 ⎫	25,590 ⎫	29,263	15,099	16,957	24,937
35 – 44	⎭	⎭	⎭	⎭		16,779	16,485	18,470
45 – 54	5,630 ⎫	9,600 ⎫	12,015 ⎫	14,950 ⎫	19,119	14,718	17,400	17,024
55 – 64	⎭	⎭	⎭	⎭		9,409	11,655	13,521
65 +	1,114	1,563	2,038	2,280	3,037	3,379	3,199	3,436

*See note, Table 3/3.
Sources: 1900 – 1950, Historical Statistics of the United States, Colonial Times to 1957, 1960, p. 71.
1960 – 1980, Statistics on Manpower, 1969, p. 77
Note: Figures for 1940 forward are annual averages.
1900 – June
1920 – January
1930 – April

to 1970, with the projected figure of almost 100 million for 1980. Note that the average annual increase for the decade of the '70s is 1.5 million.

All growth in the labor force is occurring in the nonagricultural industries. In the last 20 years, not only has employment in agriculture not grown, it has declined by about 4 million, to a low of 3.8 million in 1968. Within the nonagricultural industries, services have been the fastest growing sector, with its employment more than doubling in the two decades.

Labor-force projections

During the 1970s, the expected labor-force growth of 15 million, which will bring the nation's total labor force to almost 100 million in 1980, is based on a population projection of 243 million, and an estimated labor-force participation rate of 60.4 percent. The male labor force is expected to grow about 10 million, to 64 million in 1980; the female labor force to 36 million. Most of this growth is expected in the 25-to-34-year-old age bracket, reflecting the large number of births during the late forties and early fifties. The labor-force participation rate for males in this age category is projected at its 1970 rate of 96.2, whereas females aged 25 to 34 are expected to increase their participation to a rate of 40.3 by 1980.

In addition to assumptions about future labor-force participation rates and population size for the decade, the labor-force projections also assume that unemployment will fall to a low level of about 3 percent, that no catastrophic war or other such event will occur, that college attendance will remain high, as will the numbers of marriages.

Composition of the labor force

For any society the composition of the labor force is a function of the age structure of the population, the labor-force participation rates of various segments of the population, the prevalent retirement arrangements, attitudes toward work for pay, especially as they affect certain groups of the population—married women and teenagers, for example. Further influences include the industrial and occupational needs of the economy, labor legislation affecting hours of work, protection for special groups of workers, possibly minimum wage laws.

If the economy's demand for labor is to be met, appropriate labor-force quality, as well as quantity, must be attained. Workers must acquire those skills in demand by private industry and the public sector or else unemployment may occur, despite a surplus of workers. The market's demand for a particular skill will be felt after some time and training programs and schools will begin to turn out the desired occupational and professional mix. But the number of persons entering a profession or a vocational pursuit increases slowly, particularly in areas requiring high levels of education, and the economy's needs may have shifted by the time the new supply of personnel is available for hire.

The changing needs of industry lead to continuous shifts in labor-force composition. In broad terms, the American economy has been moving from a goods-producing to a service-producing economy. In the present industrial structure 33 percent of all employment is in goods-producing industries, 62 percent is in service-producing industries, and 5 percent is in agriculture. The occupational structure, which is largely dependent on the industrial mix, is demanding greater skill levels, accompanying the shift from blue-collar to white-collar occupations. The present distribution shows that approximately 47 percent of all employed persons are in white-collar positions, with females heavily represented. White-collar employment includes professional and technical persons; managers, officials, and proprietors; clerical workers; and sales workers. The professional and technical is the most rapidly growing classification. Figures 4/2 and 4/3 in the next chapter show the trends in the industrial and occupational composition of the work force.

The labor force is becoming *younger:* over 50 percent of the total labor force is now under 45 years of age; close to 40 percent of the total is 25 to 34 years of age. There are several reasons why the labor force is now concentrated in a few age categories. First, teenage employment is becoming relatively less important because increased educational opportunities encourage young people to extend their education and delay entrance into the labor force. Second, improved social security benefits and other retirement programs are making it possible for workers aged 65 and over to leave the labor force—and many firms require retirement at age 65. Third, the large numbers of post–World War II births have entered the 25 to 34 age group, inflating that segment of the population. Fourth, as noted earlier, females aged 25 to 44 and 45 to 64 have increased their labor-force participation rates.

Women are becoming much more important in the labor force because of their growing numbers. More than half the women in some age groups are in the labor force; the labor-force participation rate for women aged 45 to 54 is now approximately 60 percent. And in turn, about 60 percent of these older working women are entering white-collar positions, mainly clerical jobs. Only about 14 percent of female workers are in professional or technical occupations. Although this represents some increase in numbers, the relative position of women in the professional and technical fields has not improved substantially in the recent past. Of all professional and technical persons in 1958, 36.5 percent were females; in 1968, they were 37.5 percent.

Men dominate such occupations as professional and technical; managers, officials, and proprietors; and the blue-collar occupations. In the shift from blue-collar to white-collar jobs, many women workers have acquired the new white-collar jobs, while men have lost most of the old blue-collar ones. It is clear that the increased demand for white-collar workers has attracted women into the labor force. The percent of the male labor force in white-collar jobs has not increased substantially in recent years; it was 36.5 percent in 1958 and 39.7 percent in 1968.

The *location* of the labor force shifts through time, as does the population. According to 1960 data, the nation's total population was 70 percent urban, 7 percent rural farm, and 23 percent rural nonfarm. But in 1968 only 5 percent of the labor force was agricultural; and two-fifths of the farm dwellers who participated in the labor force were employed in nonfarm industries. Place of residence affects the propensity to participate in the labor force. Men 65 and over who reside on farms have a relatively high labor-force participation rate, since they have a source of work not available to older men elsewhere. Men aged 16 to 19 who live on farms also have a higher labor-force participation rate than small-town or metropolitan-area youths. This reflects the tendency of farm boys to go directly to work rather than into college. Geographic comparisons of industrial compostion reveal that 36 percent of the metropolitan residents in the labor force are employed in goods-producing industries, as compared with 40 percent of the labor-force participants in small towns and 52 percent of those who live on farms. Occupationally, 52 percent of metropolitan resident workers are employed in white-collar jobs, but only 41 percent of small-town residents are, and only 15 percent of farm residents in the labor force are.

Of the 71 million employed workers in 1965, 12 to 13 percent were *part-time employees,* classified as voluntary or economic. Voluntary part-time workers are those who choose to work part-time, economic part-time workers are those for whom full-time work is not available. In addition to the usual, or year-round part-timers, there are such groups as migrant workers, who follow the crop harvesting seasons, beginning in spring in the South. A migrant worker is a farm wage worker who has left his home temporarily (at least overnight) to do farm work for cash wages in another county or state, with the expectation of returning home at the end of the farm-work period. Although migrant workers number only 400,000 to 500,000, deprivation has attracted much attention in recent years.

Summary

1. The most important factor of production, the labor force, has grown in size and improved in quality throughout the nation's history. As population has grown, the numbers of male workers have increased, despite the fact

that young and old male workers have gradually declined as percentages of their respective age groups. Since output per man-hour (and man-year) has grown so rapidly, society has been able to produce the goods for higher and higher levels of living with less and less time at work. Extensions of life-span have been important, also: man lives longer now than in earlier eras, making it possible for him to have a longer work life, as well as more years of education and retirement. Not until the 1950s did the length of work life in this country decline slightly.

2.   Labor-force participation of women has grown during this century, particularly during the Second World War and in the decades since. Married women in their thirties and older whose children are in school or have left home have been the major source of the new supply of female workers. The work life of these women, too, has grown; a woman entering the work force at age 35 can have another 30 years on the job before retirement. Increasingly, this pattern is being adopted. As the participation of women has increased and that of younger and older men declined, the overall labor-force participation rate has changed very little.

3.   The size of the labor force could increase further still from a growth in the proportion of women who work outside their homes. Certainly, the 1970s are likely to see such an expansion. Since labor-force participation correlates directly with educational level, continued improvements in their education will result in continued growth of jobs held by women. Perhaps even more important, the economy-wide shift in types of jobs available— from blue-collar to white-collar, from goods-production to services—is conducive to further increase of women in the labor force.

4.   In the past, a rapidly growing population has usually been applauded because it furnished an expanding supply of labor and a growing market for goods. Except in periods of acute unemployment, the growth in market size was felt to be a major cause of economic growth and economic capability. But in very recent years, population growth in this country has come under severe attack. Crowded conditions in cities; congestion in transportation, schools, and other public areas; shortages of housing; depletion of natural resources —all these problems are worsened by a rapid rate of population growth. Hence, discussions of restricting family size to two children through contraception and abortion are common.

5.   If such restrictions do occur, a generation hence the nation's labor-force potential will be markedly different. The economy will have to adjust to a stable labor force, and to utilize its workers even more efficiently than heretofore. Pressures on the labor force will lead to further mechanization of productive processes, designed to economize on manpower. Progress in this direction has already brought vast gains to the economy in the form of reduced working hours and lengthened vacation periods in accordance with the Greeks' belief that "the goal of war is peace, of work, leisure."

Readings

Becker, Gary S., "An Economic Analysis of Fertility," in *Demographic and Economic Change in Developed Countries,* A Conference of the Universities–National Bureau Committee of Economic Research, Princeton, N. J.: Princeton University Press, 1960.

_____. *Human Capital.* New York: Columbia University Press, 1964.

Bowen, William G., and T. A. Finegan, "Labor Force Participation and Unemployment," in *Employment Policy and the Labor Market,* Arthur M. Ross, ed. Berkeley: University of California Press, 1965.

Cain, Glen. *Married Women in the Labor Force.* Chicago: University of Chicago Press, 1966.

Durand, John D. *The Labor Force in the United States, 1890–1960.* New York: Social Science Research Council, 1948.

Hansen, W. Lee, "The Cyclical Sensitivity of the Labor Supply," *American Economic Review,* 51 (June 1961), 299–309.

Lewis, H. G., "Hours of Work and Hours of Leisure," *Proceedings of the Industrial Relations Research Association,* December 1956, pp. 196–206.

Long, Clarence D. *Labor Force Under Changing Income and Employment.* Princeton, N. J.: Princeton University Press, 1958.

Chapter Four   The Demand for Labor

Introduction

At any given time, producers of goods and services need a certain number of employees of various types who in combination with the other factors of production—land and capital—produce the goods and services demanded by consumers and other businesses. These total manpower needs of all employers, and the wages employers are paying, constitute the demand side of the labor market discussed in Chapter 2. It is important to emphasize the *needs* aspect of manpower demand; these needs for labor are dictated by the economy in which the labor market operates, where quality as well as numbers is specified.

Just as there are various labor markets, there are different levels of demand for labor—local, regional, national (or even international: the occasional importing and exporting of engineers and scientists, for example). In a local market, the demand for labor would be based on the manpower dictates of the industries in the area. This demand may at times exert influence beyond the local market when manpower requirements cannot be met from the local labor supply. Hence, in the *New York Times* one sees advertisements for positions in Berkeley, California.

Remember that this demand for labor exists at a given time; it is a balance-sheet concept of measurement. True, the manpower requirements are likely to be changing continually, although perhaps not noticeably on a day-to-day basis. Over time these changes become apparent, and are reflected in new demand schedules for labor. Five years hence, the economy (or a local labor market) will have a schedule of manpower demand different from the present one. Failure to anticipate future changes in labor-force requirements, in fact, accounts for some of the major problems of both workers and employers.

Measurement of the demand for labor

In the aggregate, the demand schedule for labor consists of the total number of workers employed in the economy at a given time, at their various wage rates or salaries. (Estimates of the employed civilian labor force are reported monthly by the Bureau of Labor Statistics in the *Monthly Labor Review.*) Early in 1970, almost 70 million persons were employed in the nation, more than 65 million of them full-time.

In this chapter demand does not refer to the conventional price–quantity, or in the case of labor, wage–employment relationship. Here demand simply refers to the amount of labor taken off the market by employers at implicit market wages. Separating demand from the price factor is admittedly somewhat artificial; at different wage levels, the numbers employed will vary. But the exposition of this chapter abstracts from wage rates as a determinant of employment. The chapters in the section on analyzing labor supply and demand allow wages their important part in determining the actual level of employment.

Certain types of labor, although extensively used, are less easily quantified, and there is argument as to whether they should be included in the labor force. How should we take account of unpaid workers? Women perform countless household jobs that if performed by a household service worker would be enumerated as part of the aggregate demand for labor, and the remuneration for the services rendered would be included in GNP. But if housewives are to be counted, classification problems arise. Are they full-time housekeepers, or part-time chauffeurs and governesses? In addition to housewives who go uncounted in the demand for labor, there are grandparents and children who perform duties that might otherwise generate a demand for the services of a member of the labor force.

Another difficulty arises in measuring the demand for labor. How should we take account of the unfilled jobs? Attempts have been made to develop job-vacancy time series and some type of job-vacancy reporting system. The Department of Labor and statisticians and economists have expressed interest in this problem: ". . . many problems arise because of the diffusion in responsibility for making decisions on employment, the absence of coordinated and complete statistical records within enterprises or other employers of labor, and the lack of a uniform and explicit definition of a job vacancy."[1] It is clear that job vacancies do reflect both a source of demand for labor, and a shortage of that particular type of labor in the relevant market.

Demand for labor applies to so many levels and qualities of labor that in attempting to measure the demand it is necessary to separate the components

---

[1]John T. Dunlop, "Job Vacancy Measures and Economic Analysis," in *The Measurement and Interpretation of Job Vacancies,* A conference of the National Bureau of Economic Research, 1966, p. 31. See also John G. Myers, "Conceptual and Measurement Problems in Job Vacancies: A Progress Report on the NICB Study," *ibid.* pp. 405–445.

into a series of demand schedules. Just as apples and oranges cannot be summed, physicists and taxicab drivers cannot be summed: they are simply "noncompeting groups." Intricate systems to classify types of labor have been developed by the Bureau of the Census and others, which classify jobs by content and then fit them into general categories such as professionals; technicians; craftsmen; and foremen. Thus, reference to a demand for "professionals" would include medical doctors, attorneys, and professors, for each of which there is a separate demand. In this manner, it is legitimate to speak of the aggregate demand for labor in an economy at a given time, despite the distinct qualitative differences in education, skills, and training among the classifications of labor.

Determinants of demand

Several factors within the economy affect the structure and level of demand for labor. The discussion here will focus on four major determinants:

A.   *the level of economic development;*

B.   *the industrial mix;*

C.   *the level of technology;*

D.   *priorities set for the economy.*

Level of economic development

How far an economy has developed industrially influences the composition of the demand for labor. In the early stages of economic development, a nation is heavily oriented toward primary production—agriculture, mining, fishing, etc.; such labor-intensive industries, which require little capital, are appropriate to the resource base. The labor demanded needs little training or education, being drawn instead from the large pool of unskilled workers.

In the process of industrializing—during which agriculture is mechanized and seed, fertilizers, and cultivation techniques are improved—productivity per man-hour rises and greater total agricultural production is achieved with fewer workers. Thus, a smaller labor force is needed to produce food for the population, and labor is then released to the secondary sector—the production of industrial and consumer goods. Because secondary production demands more craftsmen and skilled and semiskilled workers than the earlier stage, a change from primary to secondary production changes the composition of the labor demanded. During industrialization, the level of technology (discussed below) also affects the composition of demand.

As economic development continues, the economy moves from second-ary to tertiary production—the production of services. This change in empha-sis causes a shift from blue-collar to white-collar occupations in the economy; professionals, managers, and highly trained specialists are required; increased opportunities appear for women, older workers with special knowledge or skills, and for small businessmen. (One example of a new service and its impact on the composition of jobs is that of the computer and the data-processing industry. With the need for software, many young men and women elect to go into programming and systems training, often later to form small data-processing firms that offer programming and systems-analysis services.)

The industrial mix

An economy's industrial mix has important implications for its demand for labor. Its particular combination of primary, secondary, and tertiary pro-duction units determines to a great degree the composition of the labor force, that is, the numbers of unskilled, skilled, and highly trained white-collar workers that are required.

Within secondary production, producing different goods produces differ-ent occupational effects. For example, two manufacturing industry sectors—food and kindred products; and machinery, except electrical—held about the same importance for labor demand in the economy in 1960—2.8 percent of total employment was in food and kindred products and 2.4 percent in ma-chinery, except electrical. However, the occupational structure within the two industries varied radically. Of the total employment in food, 2.6 percent were professional and technical or kindred and 47.1 percent were operatives or kindred workers; for machinery the respective figures were 9.4 percent and 35.0 percent. Within these general groups, for food processing 2.1 percent of the professional group were designers or draftsmen and 30.8 percent of the operatives were truck drivers and deliverymen. The relative importance of these occupations is different in the machinery industry, where 22.2 percent of the professionals were designers or draftsmen and 2.0 percent of the operatives were truck drivers or deliverymen. The implications for derived demand are clearly different for the two industries. The relative importance of designers and draftsmen in the machinery industry will affect the demand for teachers of these skills. That the machinery industry is more important than the food-processing industry to the professional and technical or kin-dred labor market will further affect the demand for instructors of design.

For certain occupational groups, notably scientists, engineers, and some classes of blue-collar employees, defense work is one of the critical areas of employment. As Table 4/1 and Figure 4/1 show, defense-related employ-

Table 4/1. Distribution of employment attributable to defense expenditures, 1970

Occupation	Total	Ordnance	Nonelectrical machinery	Electrical machinery	Aircraft	Department of Defense	Percent of total					
All employees	3,687	203	129	430	445	1,055	100.0	5.5	3.5	10.9	12.1	28.6
Engineers	194	30	5	29	46	56	100.0	15.5	2.6	14.9	23.7	28.9
Aeronautical	31	3			23	4	100.0	9.7			74.1	12.9
Electrical	50	6	1	17	6	15	100.0	12.0	2.0	34.0	12.0	30.0
Mechanical	38	10	2	4	8	9	100.0	26.3	5.3	10.5	21.1	23.7
Technicians	126	12	4	20	19	46	100.0	9.5	3.2	15.9	15.1	36.5
Draftsmen	33	3	3	6	6	5	100.0	9.1	9.1	18.2	18.2	15.2
Natural scientists	36	5		2	4	17	100.0	13.9		5.6	11.1	47.2
Accountants and auditors	37	1	1	4	4	10	100.0	2.7	2.7	10.8	10.8	27.0
Stenographers, typists, and secretaries	208	7	5	19	19	96	100.0	3.4	2.4	9.1	9.1	46.2
Office machine operators	40	1	1	3	2	21	100.0	2.5	2.5	7.5	5.0	52.5
Mechanics and repairmen	213	6	4	12	35	102	100.0	2.8	1.9	5.6	16.4	47.9
Airplane mechanics	56				26	26	100.0				46.4	46.4
Electricians	45	1	1	3	9	21	100.0	2.2	2.2	6.7	20.0	46.7
Machinists	93	11	14	12	24	18	100.0	11.8	15.1	12.9	25.8	19.4
Tool and die makers	30	4	5	5	10	1	100.0	13.3	16.7	16.7	33.3	3.3
Machine tool operators	46	8	8	7	14	3	100.0	17.4	17.4	15.2	30.4	6.5
Foremen	106	8	5	18	22	10	100.0	7.5	4.7	17.0	20.8	9.4
Drivers and deliverymen	117	2	1	2	2	20	100.0	1.7	.9	1.7	1.7	17.1
Inspectors, metalworking	40	5	2	14	11	3	100.0	12.5	5.0	35.0	27.5	7.5
Assemblers, metalworking	110	7	9	50	31	1	100.0	6.4	8.2	45.5	28.2	.9
Welders and flame-cutters	51	5	5	7	6	9	100.0	9.8	9.8	13.7	11.8	17.6
Laborers	172	7	3	8	4	68	100.0	4.1	1.7	4.7	2.3	39.5

Source: Monthly Labor Review, December 1971.

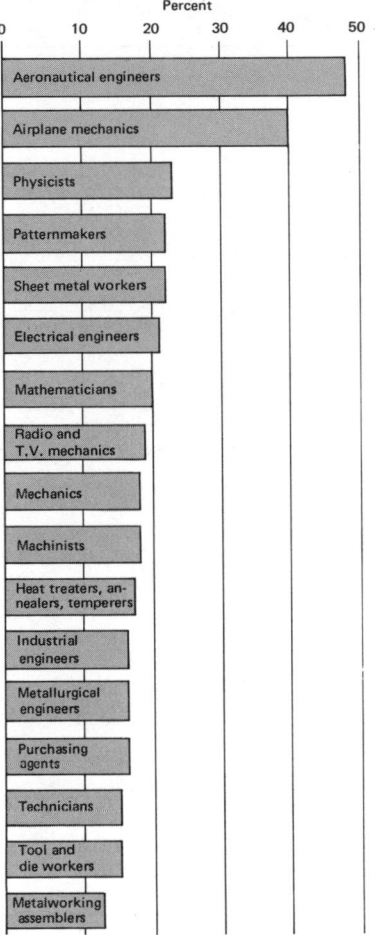

*Figure 4/1.   Proportion of employment resulting
from defense spending, selected
occupations, 1970*

Source: Monthly Labor Review, December 1971.

ment absorbs 40 to 50 percent of the aeronautical engineers and airplane
mechanics; 20 percent or more of the physicists, patternmakers, sheet-metal
workers, electrical engineers, and mathematicians; and 10 to 20 percent of
many other occupational groups. The defense cutbacks in the late 1960s were
particularly severe on these jobs; almost 700,000 defense workers were laid
off in the 1968–70 period, with serious effects on such blue-collar employees
as metal workers, machinists, machine-tool operators, sheet-metal workers,
and assemblers. Among professional workers, engineers and physicists were

especially hard hit. The concentration of defense and aerospace industries in certain areas, especially the West Coast, meant extremely high overall levels of unemployment in those regions.[2]

Changes in industrial mix raise the question of transferability of job skills among industries. It is generally believed that unskilled labor can readily be transferred from one industry to another that maintains the same general job content. Even some skilled occupations, for example, clerical, sales, or secretarial, are easily transferable. Problems are more likely to arise when the demand for a highly trained technical occupation is curtailed; however, even then the problem may have little to do with job content. A study of probable barriers to transferability of skills of missile-production workers concluded that there was a high potential for transferring these skills from defense to nondefense industries; for example, an electrical bench assembler in a missile defense occupation could become a printed-circuit assembler, wire-worker, or electronics assembler in a nondefense plant. The barrier to the shifting of jobs was the wage rate, which is higher for a given job in defense industries than elsewhere.[3]

The level of technology

The level of technology has probably the most important effect on the demand for labor—first, as a direct impact on labor requirements, and second, as a strong influence on the level of economic development and on the industrial mix in the economy. Improved technology enables man to increase productivity per man-hour, develop new products, and improve the quality of life. With advances in the techniques of production, a society gains leisure, higher levels of consumption, and a healthier and more productive population.

The demanded quality of labor—that is, the degree of skill and education required—is always determined by the existing state of technology. As the technology becomes more complex and more productive, by automation or mechanization of a process hitherto performed manually, labor requisites and work patterns must change. Greater output is produced with fewer workers; job content changes; and the skills in demand shift. Often the displaced workers become unemployed and must be retrained for the new jobs, and frequently must move to different parts of the country. The overall effect is to increase the demand for more highly skilled labor and for more highly educated personnel. One of the constraints on development of new technology and its implementation in industry is the pace of qualitative improve-

[2]Richard Dempsey and Douglas Schmude, "Occupational Impact of Defense Expenditures," *Monthly Labor Review*, 94 (December 1971), 12–15.

[3]See John R. Cambern and David A. Newton, "Skill transfers: can defense workers adapt to civilian occupations?" *Monthly Labor Review*, 32, no. 6 (June 1969): 21–25.

ments in the labor component of output. As Victor Fuchs has noted, ". . . the rate at which advances in knowledge affect productivity will depend in part on how fast labor embodying these new advances can be added to the work force."[4]

Technological improvements are aimed at reducing the demand for labor per unit of output, by substituting machine time for human effort. A new, highly automated plant is able to produce at lower costs and to sell the product at a lower price; it therefore pushes the older, more labor-intensive plant out of business. Workers are displaced, as they are when advances in technology have enabled a new and superior product to be developed that substitutes well for an older product. Only expansion in the aggregate demand for goods, which allows displaced workers to be absorbed into the production of new goods and services, can increase or even maintain total employment.

When old products yield to new, the industrial mix of the labor force undergoes significant changes. In this country, rapid technological innovation has diminished the importance of labor in agriculture, mining, and manufacturing, and also in the transportation, communications, and public-utilities industries. Overall, the ratio of production workers to total employment has declined. This long-term shift from blue-collar to white-collar occupations has been an accumulation of gradual shifts, rather than any one sudden switch in labor requirements.

In an economy in which technology is constantly changing, with innovations sometimes becoming obsolete soon after they are implemented, the quantity and quality of labor demanded is also continually shifting. Frequent retraining periods for workers help to minimize the structural problems of such a dynamic state. In order to meet the minimum requirements of the new technology and to avoid unemployment, resources must be devoted to reeducation programs that span the worklife. Education and retraining could absorb much of the leisure time that the mechanization of output creates. Even with nationwide efforts, however, the changing vocational requirements of jobs and employment create barriers to many, especially the older, less mobile labor-force participants.

Priorities set for the economy

Social priorities, whether set consciously or not, influence the level and structure of the demand for labor. In both the public and the private sectors of the economy, the goals pursued dictate the goods and services, hence the types of labor, that are demanded.

---

[4]Victor R. Fuchs. *The Growing Importance of the Service Industries,* Occasional paper 96 (New York: National Bureau of Economic Research, 1965), p. 30.

The public sector influences the demand for labor directly through the vast growth of manpower needs to handle "the business of government." Some government services can be automated, just as in the private sector; for the most part, such automation raises the skills required, as is borne out by the need for highly trained white-collar workers. Despite improved techniques that increase the productivity of the individual government worker, the overall volume of work done by governments has grown rapidly, dramatically increasing government employment in recent years, particularly at the state level. The priorities set by the federal government, as reflected in the composition of its budget, determine the composition of this growing employment sector—for example, whether government employees will be munition workers or social workers. A commitment to full employment may increase public-works programs in periods of unemployment in the private sector. Alternatively, giving a high priority to price stability may allow the unemployment rate to rise, with a resulting impact on the employment prospects for unskilled workers. In a wartime economy, the guns-and-butter trade-off may shift demand for labor from nondefense to defense industries. This type of shift in demand promises future dislocations in the labor market when the war ends.

Just as the public sector can influence labor demand through its priorities and its expenditures to realize them in such fields as education, transportation, environmental control, health, foreign military or nonmilitary relations, so also the private sector directs the allocation of labor through the kinds of goods and services demanded. If businessmen become dedicated to cleaning up pollution, for example, demand will increase for environmentalists and ecologists. The consumer, who ultimately has the decisive voice in the production of consumer goods or services, has the power to influence the ways in which the labor resource is to be utilized. As more people in a population come to enjoy higher education, increased leisure, and more travel, more labor will be diverted into these areas. Regardless of how preferences are expressed —whether in the marketplace or at the polls—the nation's priorities, public or private, have a profound impact on the composition of demand for labor resources.

Other determinants

The short-run demand for labor can be affected primarily by business fluctuations, temporary government or business cutbacks, union–management relationships, financial manipulations that influence public opinion, and political events. Long-run patterns of labor use can be affected by population growth and shifts in the age composition of the population, changes in the level of consumption and in the tastes of consumers, and the evolution of new ideas and attitudes in the society.

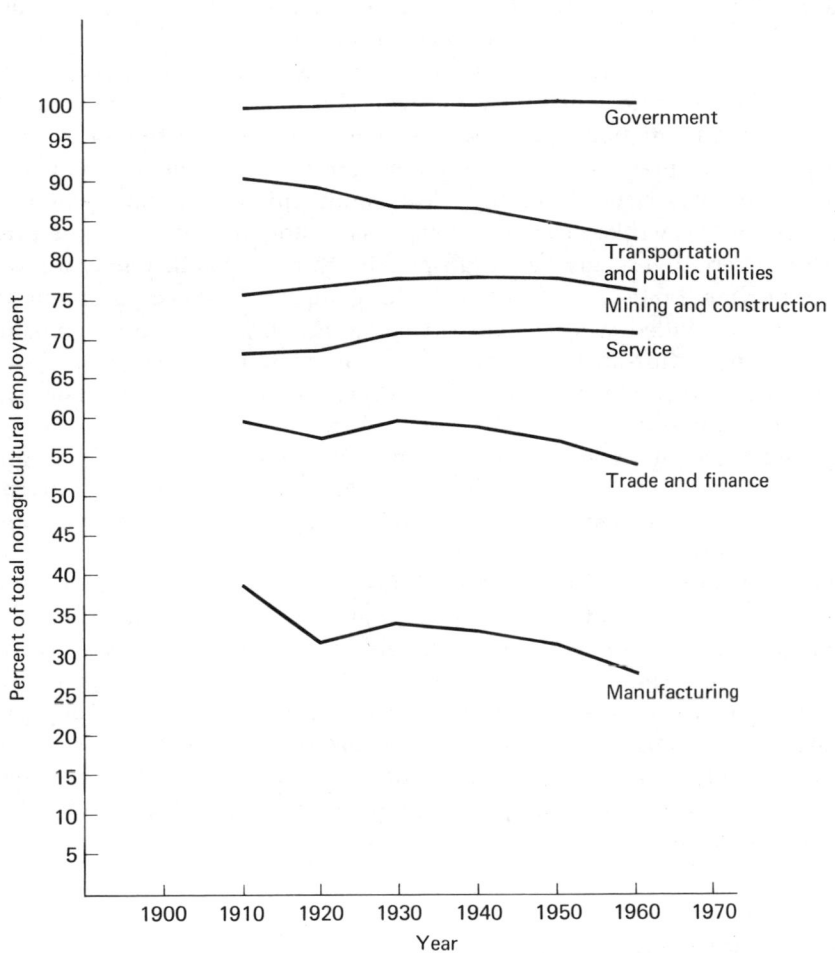

Figure 4/2. Distribution of employment by
nonagricultural industrial sectors,
1920–1970

Source: Handbook of Labor Statistics, 1971, Table 38.

Table 4/2. Employment in nonagricultural industries,
1920–1970 and 1972 (in thousands)

Major industry	1920	1930	1940	1950	1960	1970	% Δ 1920-1970	1972	% Δ 1960-1972
Mining	1,239	1,009	925	901	712	622	−49.7	607	−14.7
Contract construction	848	1,372	1,294	2,333	2,885	3,347	294.7	3,520	22.0
Manufacturing	10,658	9,562	10,985	15,241	16,796	19,393	81.9	18,928	12.7
Transportation and public utilities	3,998	3,685	3,038	4,034	4,004	4,498	12.5	4,495	12.3
Wholesale and retail trade	4,467	5,797	6,750	9,386	11,391	14,950	234.7	15,679	37.6
Finance, insurance, and real estate	1,175	1,475	1,502	1,919	2,669	3,679	213.1	3,926	47.1
Services	2,362	3,376	3,681	5,382	7,423	11,577	390.1	12,309	64.5
Government	2,603	3,148	4,202	6,026	8,353	12,597	383.9	13,287	59.1
Total	27,350	29,424	32,376	45,222	54,234	70,664	158.3	72,750	34.1

Source: Handbook of Labor Statistics, 1971, Table 38 and Manpower Report of the President, 1973.

Labor use in the United States, 1920–1970

During the first half of the twentieth century tremendous increases in productivity per man-hour, especially in agriculture, moved the United States gradually from a primary to a secondary and thence to a tertiary production economy. In the changing industrial mix, shown in Figure 4/2, manufacturing managed to maintain its relative position, while trade and finance and government have become much more important. Table 4/2 shows total employment in nonagricultural industries from 1920 to 1970, (1972 figures in the table are cited in the discussion of short-term changes in the next selection of this chapter); it can be seen that wholesale and retail trade, government, contract construction, and services, made the greatest gains in employment. Wholesale and retail trade rose from 4 1/2 million in 1920 to almost 15 million in 1970; services increased from less than 2 1/2 million to 11.6 million, or 390 percent.

As we noted earlier, technological advance during this period enabled agriculture to support the growing population with drastically reduced manpower. The gains in productivity were greater in the agricultural than in the nonagricultural sector: 2.3 percent average annual change in agriculture, compared with 2.1 percent elsewhere. The greatest agricultural advances were made in the latter part of the period, 1947 to 1970, when productivity rose at an average annual rate of 5.8 percent (Table 4/3).

Changes in the occupational structure of the labor forces paralleled the changes in industrial mix. Along with the shift to the service industries came a shift to nonproduction workers—white-collar personnel. Service industries demand more managers, professionals, and clericals than do goods-producing industries. Moreover, even within the goods-producing industries technological advance has changed the composition of demand for labor; more highly skilled workers are now needed, including substantial proportions of technical employees. Figure 4/3 shows the long-term shift from blue-collar workers in the goods industries to white-collar workers in the service industries. In 1900, white-collar workers accounted for less than 20 percent of the labor force, while in 1970 they made up about 50 percent of the total.

Recent patterns of labor use: the 1960s and early '70s

Workers continued to shift into services throughout the 1960s. Between 1960 and 1970 in the service sector employment grew about 65 percent, while in the goods sector it grew only 26 percent (Table 4/2). In Table 4/5 labor requirements per industry are shown by the distribution pattern for nonagricultural employees in 1960 and 1972 (Table 4/4). In 1972, within the service

Table 4/3.   Indexes of output per man-hour and
related data, private economy,[1] 1947-70

[1967 = 100]

Year	Output per man-hour				Output per employed person			
	Total private	Farm	Non-farm	Man-ufac-tur-ing[2]	Total private	Farm	Non-farm	Man-ufac-tur-ing[2]
1947	51.3	29.2	57.1	54.8	56.5	32.9	61.4	55.2
1948	53.6	34.0	58.8	57.9	58.5	38.0	62.7	57.8
1949	55.3	33.1	61.1	60.0	59.5	36.4	64.4	58.9
1950	59.7	37.7	65.0	64.4	64.4	40.8	68.9	64.8
1951	61.5	37.9	66.3	65.9	66.2	41.4	70.3	66.5
1952	62.7	41.2	66.9	66.2	67.3	44.6	70.9	66.9
1953	65.3	46.7	68.9	68.3	69.7	51.1	72.5	68.8
1954	66.9	49.1	70.5	69.5	70.7	52.8	73.5	68.7
1955	69.9	49.5	73.6	73.7	74.1	52.5	77.2	74.4
1956	70.0	51.6	73.2	72.9	73.6	53.6	76.4	73.2
1957	72.0	54.7	74.8	74.4	74.8	55.4	77.2	73.8
1958	74.3	60.4	76.7	74.4	76.3	60.6	78.4	73.0
1959	76.9	61.5	79.3	78.5	79.5	61.7	81.7	78.6
1960	78.2	64.9	80.3	79.9	80.4	65.6	82.2	79.0
1961	80.9	70.0	82.7	81.8	82.5	69.7	84.1	80.9
1962	84.7	71.7	86.4	86.6	86.6	72.3	88.1	86.4
1963	87.7	78.1	89.1	90.1	89.5	78.1	90.8	90.0
1964	91.1	79.5	92.4	94.5	92.8	79.7	94.0	94.8
1965	94.2	86.9	95.1	98.3	96.2	88.2	96.9	99.5
1966	98.0	90.5	98.4	99.9	99.3	91.3	99.7	101.2
1967	100.0	100.0	100.0	100.0	100.0	100.0	100.0	100.0
1968	102.9	101.4	102.9	104.7	102.5	100.9	102.5	104.9
1969	103.7	107.3	103.2	106.9	102.8	106.3	102.4	106.9
1970	104.6	113.5	103.8	108.1	102.5	110.8	101.9	106.6
Rates of change[3]								
1947-70	3.2	5.8	2.7	2.9	2.7	5.2	2.3	2.9
1957-70	3.2	5.7	2.8	3.2	2.8	5.5	2.5	3.3

[1]Output refers to gross national product in 1958 dollars. Employment includes self-employed and unpaid family workers as well as wage and salary workers.
[2]Information available only for establishment series.
[3]Average annual percent change based on the linear least squares trend of the logarithms of the index numbers.
Source: *Handbook of Labor Statistics, 1971,* Table 8/2.

sector, trade and government were the largest sources of demand for labor, employing 15,950,000 and 13,597,000 respectively. One of the major reasons for such pronounced growth in service-industry employment is the increase in per-capita income: demand for services is somewhat more income-elastic than the demand for goods. In addition, as Victor Fuchs has stressed, there has been a more rapid rate of growth of productivity in the goods industries, and a faster decline in hours worked per man in the service industries, both factors adding to the relative growth of service workers.

Growth in agricultural (as compared with nonfarm) productivity has been greater because there are few service workers in the agricultural work force. Although dramatic improvements in technology that have sharply raised productivity in the making of goods, the expansion of the service sector has had a retarding effect on the rate of growth for overall productivity, making it no more than a slow and steady growth. A continued shift towards services will delay the approach of the workless society, which we dreamed about in Chapter 1. In fact the sequence from improved technology to higher incomes to increased relative demand for personalized services, which have slow growth in productivity, precludes rapid overall productivity growth.

The changes in occupational composition begun earlier in the century also continued throughout the '60s. White-collar workers accounted for 43

Figure 4/3.   The shifting occupational mix of the American labor force

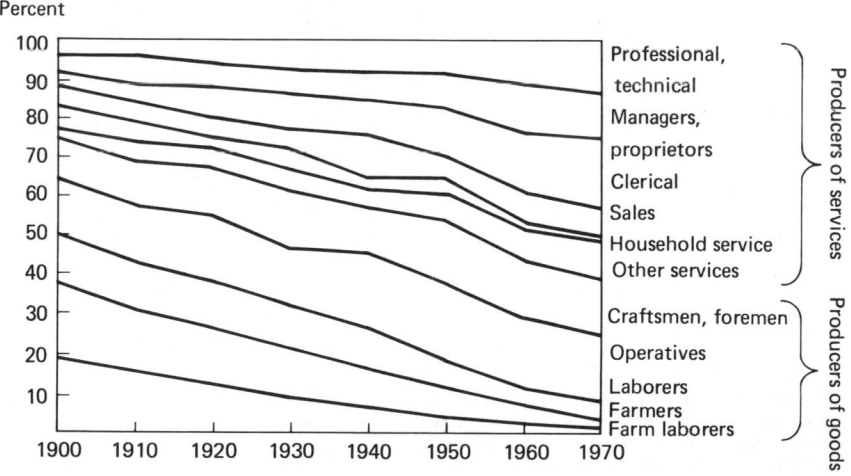

Adapted from: Philip M. Hauser "More from the Census of 1960" *Scientific American,* October 1962, p. 35, and *The Statistical Abstract of the United States, 1971.*

percent of the employed persons in 1960; by 1971 their share had risen to 48.6 percent. The greatest gains were among professional and technical workers and clerical workers (see Table 4/5). These trends reflect the more complex technologies and the corollary manpower requirements for highly educated technicians, and also the increased volume of paper work, which, along with the influx of computers, increased the demand for clerical and technical manpower. Among blue-collar workers, relative gains were seen among craftsmen and foremen and service workers—again, because of the highly technical requirements of the new jobs.

Table 4/4. Percentage of work force in industrial
sectors, 1960 and 1972

Major industry	1960	1972
Agriculture	8.0	5.1
Nonagriculture:		
Mining	1.0	.8
Contract construction	5.0	4.5
Manufacturing	29.0	24.7
Transportation and public utilities	6.0	5.9
Wholesale and retail trade	19.0	20.5
Finance, insurance, and real estate	5.0	5.1
Services	13.0	16.0
Government	14.0	17.4
Total	100.0	99.8

Source: *Manpower Report of the President,* 1973.

Current and future labor-force requirements

The Department of Labor estimates that manpower requirements in 1975 will total about 88.7 million workers (91.4 million overall with a military force of 2.7 million). The projections assume a 3 percent unemployment level. Agricultural manpower needs are expected to decline further, while nonagricultural needs will increase 23 percent between 1966 and 1975, to a manpower requirement of almost 76 million. Within this sector, growth will be greatest in wage and salary employment, although a slight increase (9 percent) is expected in other nonfarm areas (domestics, self-employed, and unpaid family workers).

Service industries will increase their manpower requirements more than will the goods sector. Thus, the labor force is expected to be composed of an even greater proportion of workers in the service industries and in govern-

Table 4/5. Employed persons by occupational group, 1960 to 1971 (in thousands)

Occupation	1960	1969	1971	Percent change 1950-1971
White-collar workers	28,726	36,844	37,988	+ 70
Percent of total	43.1%	47.3%	48.6%	
Professional and technicals	7,475	10,769	11,134	+148
Managers, officials, and proprietors	7,067	7,987	8,590	+ 33
Clerical workers	9,783	13,397	13,236	+ 73
Sales workers	4,401	4,692	5,028	+ 31
Blue-collar workers	24,211	28,237	26,497	+ 13
Craftsmen and foremen	8,560	10,193	9,899	+ 29
Operatives	11,986	14,372	12,707	+ 5
Nonfarm laborers	3,665	3,672	3,891	+ 10
Service workers	8,349	9,528	10,595	+ 62
Farm workers	5,395	3,292	3,123	− 58
Total	66,681	77,902	78,204	+31

Source: *Statistical Abstract of the United States 1971*, p. 222.

Table 4/6. Nonagricultural wage and salary workers, by major industry division, actual 1966 and projected 1975 employment requirements (in thousands)

Industry division	Actual 1966 employment		Projected 1975[1] requirements		Percent change,
	Number	Percent	Number	Percent	1966-75
Total[2]	63,982	100.0	75,900	100.0	18.6
Goods-producing industries	23,103	36.1	24,530	32.3	6.2
Mining	625	1.0	620	0.8	−0.8
Contract construction	3,292	5.1	4,190	5.5	27.3
Manufacturing	19,186	30.0	19,720	26.0	2.8
Service-producing industries	40,880	63.8	51,370	67.7	25.7
Transportation and public utilities	4,151	6.5	4,580	6.0	10.3
Trades	13,211	20.6	16,115	21.2	22.0
Finance, insurance, and real estate	3,102	4.8	3,725	4.9	20.1
Services and miscellaneous	9,545	14.9	12,915	17.0	35.3
Government[3]	10,871	17.0	14,035	18.5	29.1

[1]Based on an assumed national unemployment rate of 3 percent.
[2]Represents wage and salary employment as covered in the BLS monthly establishment survey which excludes self-employed, unpaid family workers, and domestic workers in households.
[3]Data for federal government, included in this series, relate to civilian employment only and exclude the Central Intelligence and National Security Agencies.
Source: *Tomorrow's Manpower Needs*, U.S. Department of Labor Bulletin 1606, Vol. 2, pp. 4–5.

Table 4/7. Employment by major occupational
group,1966 and projected 1975

Occupational group	1966 employment		Projected 1975 requirements		Percent change, 1966–75
	Number (millions)	Percent	Number (millions)	Percent	
Total, 14 years and over	74.1	100.0	88.7	100.0	20
White-collar workers	33.3	45.0	42.6	48.1	28
Professional and technical	9.3	12.6	12.9	14.6	39
Managers, officials, and proprietors	7.4	10.0	9.0	10.2	22
Clerical workers	11.8	16.0	14.8	16.7	25
Sales workers	4.8	6.4	5.9	6.7	24
Blue-collar workers	27.2	36.7	29.9	33.7	10
Craftsmen and foremen	9.6	13.0	11.4	12.8	18
Operatives	13.9	18.7	14.8	16.7	7
Nonfarm laborers	3.7	5.0	3.8	4.3	([1])
Service workers	9.7	13.1	12.7	14.4	31
Farmers and farm workers	3.9	5.2	3.4	3.8	−14

[1]Less than 5 percent.
Note: Projections assume a 3-percent level of unemployment in 1975. Because of rounding, the sum of individual items may not equal totals.
Source: *Tomorrow's Manpower Needs*, U.S. Department of Labor Bulletin 1606, Vol. 3, pp. 4–5.

ment, while the manpower importance of the manufacturing sector will decline substantially. The 1975 projections of nonagricultural wage and salary workers, by major industries, are shown in Table 4/6.

The occupational structure of industry will continue to change as the manpower requirements shift, influenced by technology—new products and processes—and by new corporate structures. Between 1966 and 1975, anticipated occupational needs show a 28 percent increase in demand for white-collar workers (with the greatest growth among professional and technical workers), and only a slight increase in the demand for blue-collar workers (10 percent). However, among blue-collar workers, an 18 percent increase in the numbers of craftsmen and foremen is expected. Of special note is the anticipated 31-percent increase in demand for service workers. The net effect of these changes in manpower needs is a significant shift in the occupational composition of the employed labor force by 1975. Professionals and technical occupations will use close to 14.6 percent of the workers—a gain of 2 percent in 9 years, while operatives will lose 2 percent—a drop from 18.7 percent to 16.7 percent of the workers (Table 4/7). These compositional changes will have profound effects on the educational and vocational training needs in this country.[5]

[5]See the Department of Labor, *Tomorrow's Manpower Needs*, February 1969, Bulletin 1606.

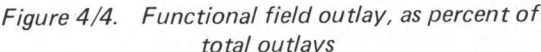

Figure 4/4.   Functional field outlay, as percent of total outlays

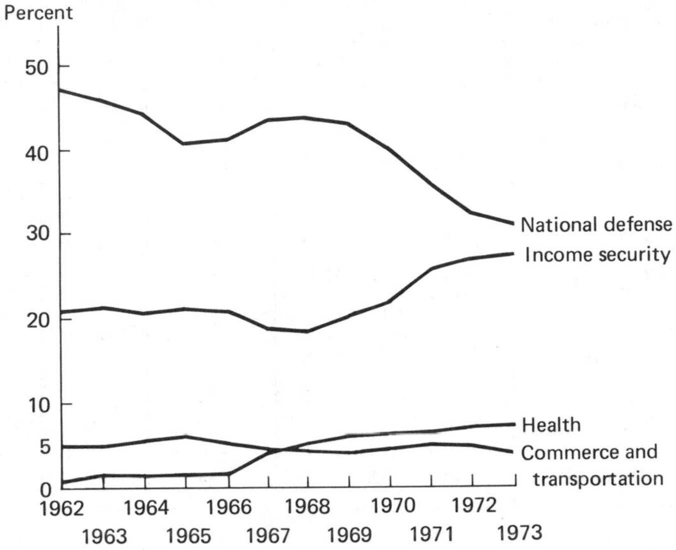

	1962	1963	1964	1965	1966	1967	1968	1969	1970	1971	1972	1973
International affairs and finance	4.2	3.7	3.5	3.7	3.3	2.8	2.6	2.0	1.8	1.4	1.6	1.5
Space research and technology	1.2	2.3	3.5	4.3	4.4	3.4	2.6	2.3	1.9	1.6	1.3	1.3
Agriculture and rural technology	3.8	4.6	4.4	4.0	2.7	2.7	3.3	3.4	3.1	2.4	3.1	2.8
Natural resources and environment	1.5	1.3	1.6	1.7	1.5	1.2	1.0	1.2	1.3	1.3	1.8	.9
Community development and housing	.5	.8	.16	.2	1.9	1.6	2.3	1.1	1.5	1.6	1.7	2.0
Education and manpower	1.3	1.3	1.5	1.9	3.2	3.6	3.8	3.5	3.7	4.0	4.2	4.6
Veteran's benefits and services	5.3	4.9	4.8	4.8	4.4	4.4	3.8	4.1	4.4	4.6	4.7	4.8
Interest	7.8	8.2	8.3	8.8	8.3	7.9	7.7	8.5	9.3	9.2	8.5	8.5
General government	1.5	1.6	1.7	1.8	1.7	1.6	1.4	1.5	1.7	1.9	2.2	2.2
Government revenue sharing											.9	2.0
Allowances											.2	.5
Undistributed government transfers	2.4	2.3	2.4	2.6	2.5	2.5	2.5	2.7	3.2	3.5	3.3	3.5

Changes in priorities and future manpower requirements

In the preceding sections, past and present labor requirements were outlined, showing the changing industrial and occupational structure of the labor

Figure 4/5. Outlays by functional field

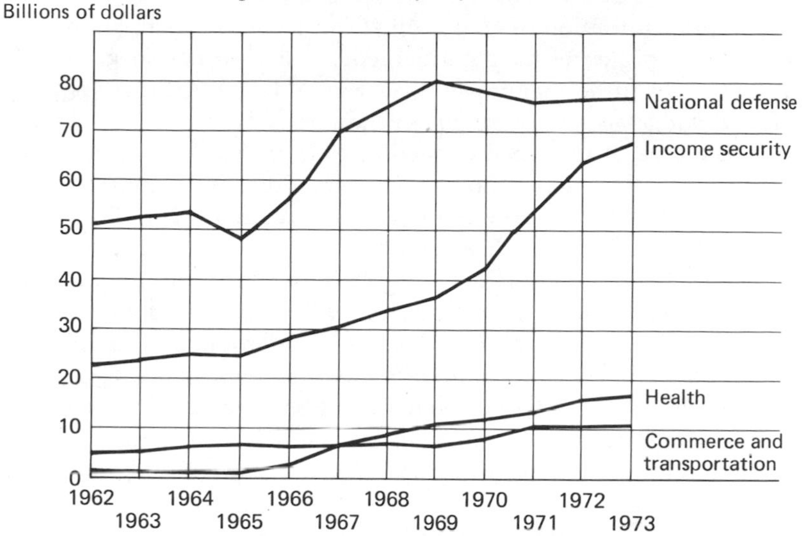

Billions of dollars

	1962	1963	1964	1965	1966	1967	1968	1969	1970	1971	1972	1973	
	4.5	4.1	4.1	4.3	4.5	4.5	4.6	3.8	3.6	3.1	4.0	3.8	International affairs and finance
	1.3	2.6	2.2	5.1	5.9	5.4	4.7	4.2	3.7	3.4	3.2	3.2	Space research and technology
	4.1	5.1	3.2	4.8	3.7	4.4	5.0	6.2	0.2	5.1	7.3	3.5	Agriculture and rural development
	1.7	1.5	2.0	2.1	2.0	1.9	1.7	2.2	2.6	2.7	4.4	2.5	Natural resources and environment
	.6	-.9	-.2	.3	2.6	2.6	4.1	2.0	3.0	3.4	4.0	4.3	Community development and housing
	1.4	1.5	1.8	2.3	4.3	5.9	6.7	6.5	7.3	8.7	10.1	11.3	Education and manpower
	5.6	5.5	5.7	5.7	5.9	6.9	6.9	7.6	8.7	9.8	11.1	11.7	Veteran's benefits and services
	8.3	9.2	9.8	16.4	11.3	12.6	13.7	15.8	18.3	19.6	20.1	21.2	Interest
	1.7	1.8	2.0	2.2	2.3	2.5	2.6	2.9	3.3	4.0	5.3	5.5	General government
											2.3	5.0	General revenue sharing
											.6	1.3	Allowances
	-2.5	-2.6	-2.9	-3.1	-3.4	-3.9	-4.5	-5.1	-6.4	-7.4	-7.9	-8.6	Undistributed intragovernment transactions

Source: Economic Report of the President, 1972, Table B-64.

force under the impact of this century's rapidly improving technology. The effect of public and private priorities on the demand for labor was emphasized. It is important to consider the further shifts in labor-force patterns that may emerge from possible changes in the nation's future goals and priorities.

Now that the Vietnam War has ended, there may be a focus on internal needs that require labor of particular skills. As for the war itself, the manpower effects of its ending have been slight, being a continuation of trends in operation over the past few years. Shrinkage in the Armed Forces has been gradual ever since initiation of the troop withdrawal program, and the cutbacks in the space programs have undoubtedly had a stronger negative effect on demand for scientific manpower than the end of hostilities, especially since defense budgets will not be cut in the near future.

A probable area of increased expenditures in pursuit of future national goals is in improving the environment. The effect of environmental cleanup and control upon the demand for labor is not easily quantified. But it is clear that a commitment of funds to these objectives will cause a shift of personnel into a fairly new field of endeavor. If we reduce our consumption in favor of improving the environment, labor resources will be moved from, say, automobile production to pollution-control equipment production. If we choose not to reduce consumption, but to finance the program by borrowing money that would not have been spent, the effect will be to reduce unemployment by increasing demand for environmentalists, technicians, and garbage collectors, or to generate an inflationary impact—depending on the extent of unemployed labor resources.

Over the next 5 years, billions of dollars are likely to be spent for improving environmental quality. Since the term "environmental quality" covers a broad area, the composition of the labor needed to implement these expenditures is still in question. If conservation of the natural areas for public use is a primary objective, the funds may be spent for land and the building of recreational facilities. If checking the population is of first priority, expenditures will be spent for research and development on contraceptives, dissemination of birth-control literature, and educating the present population on the necessity of no more than two babies per family. Or if our concern is with decreasing air and water pollution, the money will be diverted to building waste-treatment plants and air-pollution control devices.

One obvious way to clean up the environment would be to ban the use of motorized vehicles in cities. Whereas this would succeed in reducing the exhaust fumes into the city air, it would augment the present difficulties of transporting people and goods. Do we gain if the air pollution problem is minimized and the urban transportation problem is worsened? New mass transportation systems would have to be developed. Goods could be moved by forced air through tubes placed underground; this would lead to shifts in the types of occupations in the transportation industry. Truck drivers, bus drivers, and deliverymen would be replaced with skilled mass-transport operators and technicians to supervise the flow of goods through the network of underground tubes.

Summary

In summary, the goals pursued determine the amount and type of labor used in the economy. Other examples can be cited. A slowing of the space program, possibly the decision not to go to Mars, would release men and dollars to be used elsewhere, and the demand for astronauts would decline along with the demand for the technically skilled labor force producing the booster rockets and space ships. A decline in the workweek could lead to a demand for greater recreational facilities—amusements, entertainment, and publishing—thus increasing the demand for manpower in these fields. A commitment to better education increases the demand for educational personnel.

As the American public becomes more alert to the problems of its society, some shifts may occur in the goals pursued. During the sixties, the government and the public became quite health conscious. This awareness is reflected in Figures 4/4 and 4/5, which show that health expenditures rose from about 2 to about 7 percent of the total budget between 1962 and 1971. In dollars, this represented an increase from about $2 billion to over $14 billion during the period. Perhaps with the end of the Vietnam War a decline in the importance of national security will yield to a future rise in the importance of housing, urban rehabilitation, environmental control, and education, even though the immediate postwar budget does not indicate such a trend.

Readings

Bowen, William G., and T. Aldrich Finegan. *The Economics of Labor Force Participation.* Princeton, N. J.: Princeton University Press, 1969.

Crowley, Michael F., "Projected Requirements for Technicians in 1980," *Monthly Labor Review,* 75 (May 1970), 13–17.

Dempsey, Richard, and Douglas Schmude, "Occupational Impact of Defense Expenditures," *Monthly Labor Review,* 94 (December 1971), 12–15.

Fuchs, Victor R. *The Growing Importance of the Service Industries,* Occasional Paper 96. New York: National Bureau of Economic Research, 1965.

Gordon, Robert A., ed. *Toward a Manpower Policy.* New York: John Wiley and Sons, 1967.

Lebergott, Stanley. *Manpower in Economic Growth.* New York: McGraw-Hill Book Co., 1964.

Lecht, Leonard. *Manpower Needs for National Goals in the 1970's.* New York: Praeger Publishers, 1969.

National Commission of Technology, Automation, and Economic Progress. *Technology and the American Economy.* Washington D. C.: U. S. Government Printing Office, 1966.

Travis, Sophia C., "The U. S. Labor Force: Projections to 1985," *Monthly Labor Review,* 75 (May 1970), 3–13.

U. S. Department of Labor. *Tomorrow's Manpower Needs,* Bulletin No. 1606. Washington, D. C.: U. S. Government Printing Office, 1969.

Part Three

Unionism and Collective Bargaining

Introduction

Management views its goals and constraints

> *Context: operation of the free enterprise system*
> > *Economic decisions*
> > *Participants in decision-making*
> *Possible goals: minimum costs, maximum profits*
> *Rationale: decision-making for the common good*

Goals and ideologies of labor organizations

Context: trade union endorsement of free enterprise
Goals: more now
> *Union security*
> *The rationing of jobs*
> *Wages, hours, and working conditions*
> *Grievance procedure*
Rationale: expectations of American workers

Labor and management views on economic policy issues

> *Conflict: when reasonable men differ*
> *Goals: whose welfare?*

Chapter Five

Ideology: American Industry versus the Labor Union

The rights and interests of the laboring man will be protected and cared for, not by the labor agitators, but by the Christian men to whom God in his infinite wisdom has given the control of the property interests of this country.

> *George F. Baer, President of the Philadelphia and Reading Railroad Company, 1902.*

It does not matter that the head of some great corporation may be generous, that he may desire to improve the conditions of the working people. The working people are not satisfied with those gifts and benefactions which are given to them by their employers. What they want is not gifts; they want independence; they want security in their jobs—that reasonable security that makes them feel that they may not be dismissed from their employment without good cause, and that they can not have in the absence of united action.

> *John Mitchell, President of the United Mine Workers of America, 1914.*

I am heartily in favor of those elements of trade unions which are good, and I am equally opposed to those elements of trade unions that are bad . . .

> *Frederick W. Taylor, author of "scientific management," 1912.*

Introduction

The preceding comments typify three stances commonly taken on labor unions: first, that leaders of the labor movement are agitators sent to try the patience of righteous businessmen; second, that workers achieve true progress only through a bargaining position strong enough to guarantee protection from the whims of management; and third, the cliché that unions are separable good from bad. Such indictments of both the troublesome unions and their oppressive opponents abound today, much the same as they did when the first unions were formed more than a century ago.

During their century of growth, labor unions have been blamed for raising the wages of the American worker at the expense of the consuming public—as though these were two completely separate groups of people. They have been charged with crime and violence, presumably without provocation or similar practices on the part of management. They are accused of creating monopolies in restraint of trade and interfering with the freedom of the individual laborer to make his own wage bargain or, worse still, with his right to work.

The bill of indictment against management is equally severe. In its drive for profits, industry has exploited the weakest of the workers, particularly women and children. Wages have been held down, despite productivity increases and rising profit margins. Human labor was regarded as a commodity, and an article of commerce, until legislation specifically set it apart from goods. Concern for the health or well-being of employees, or their welfare outside the workplace—during periods of unemployment, sickness, or old age —was not the responsibility of the employer. Again, only through public action has the worker gained programs which meet some of his needs during periods of dependency.

It is easy to launch criticisms of the tactics of both unions and management. But it is difficult to explain why the two parties chose to observe a pattern of behavior that resulted in such strife, when peaceful negotiations would have served the interests of both groups. Who gains from a long, expensive strike? Why do management and labor condone a seemingly destructive approach to labor relations? Are the motivations for holding the line purely economic? Or does disagreement spring from a power struggle in which both industry and labor feel constantly threatened?

The character of labor unions in the United States differs markedly from that of trade unions in European nations; our business managers, too, are distinctly American. To explain the differences, we will examine the forces that shape institutional behavior, particularly the behavior of the business enterprise vis-à-vis its employees.

Management views its goals and constraints

Labor and management in the United States operate within an economic system that is a curious mixture of free enterprise and government control, competition and monopolistic power, individualistic and socially directed activity. A certain conflict of goals is therefore to be expected. But the major objective of the entrepreneur—that of making profits—is nevertheless sanctioned by one and all; the pursuit of profits is in fact generally credited with creating the highly productive economy that in turn makes high wages possible.

Context: operation of the free enterprise system

An economic system is hard to define and even harder to describe. It may be a loose aggregate of individual businessmen, individual or unionized workers, and individual consumers—each pursuing his own interest, subject to a minimum of government regulation. This description resembles the economic system of the United States, a mixture of private enterprise and central control. Toward the opposite end of the spectrum is the kind of system found in Soviet Russia: an economy that is socialistic, and operates from a government plan that specifies how much of each commodity is to be produced. Between these two extremes are several intermediaries. For example, Sweden has its modified socialism called "the middle way."

Economic decisions   Irrespective of the type of economic system, certain fundamental decisions must be made, either by the system or through its operation. In summary, these decisions have to do with what is produced, how it is produced, and who receives the product. The first question of what is produced would not arise if resources were unlimited in quantity. But in all economies resources are in fact scarcer than human wants would dictate, and scarcity compels us to choose among alternative collections of goods and services. The wartime choice between guns and butter is the most commonly cited example, but in times of peace, too, resources must be allocated in accordance with some set of priorities. We could produce countless combinations of goods and services. We could concentrate on golf clubs, TV spectaculars, chrome-covered cars, and candy bars; or instead on hospitals, classrooms, and museums. Or we could put primary emphasis, as the Soviet Union has, on blast furnaces and rolling mills, hydroelectric dams and copper smelters.

The question of how the preferred bundle of goods is produced must be resolved with care lest the economy use its resources inefficiently and thereby sacrifice some of the goods and services that would otherwise be available. In essence, this decision represents a choice among various combinations of resources that may be used to produce the same output. For example, the foundation of a building may be dug by a steam shovel, by a bulldozer, or by a crew of workmen with hand shovels. Cotton cloth can be woven by a few workers operating huge, mechanized looms, or by many workers operating primitive hand looms. How much capital and how much labor? Every commodity can be produced in different ways; the system must choose a specific combination of resources.

Since resources and hence total output are limited, the third basic decision must be made: who gets the goods and services? Shall we be egalitarian and stipulate that each person receive the same amount? Or shall we be Utopian and say, "From each according to his ability, to each according to his need"?

We may decide that each person gets what he produces; but then some adjustment must be made to provide for people who cannot produce. In any event, the distribution of output (that is, the distribution of income or the command over goods and services) is a critical decision for management and labor. It is in this realm that most of the past conflict between the two groups has arisen; the issue, moreover, is far from being resolved.

Implicit in the choice of what will be produced is the decision as to what proportion of the output is available for immediate consumption and what proportion goes into industrial goods to make possible greater levels of production in the future. Conservation of resources requires a sacrifice of some present consumption: How much oil should be pumped this year? How many acres of land should lie fallow? At what age should people enter the labor force, and how much education should be both free and compulsory?

Participants in decision-making   The scarcity of resources in all economies makes it necessary for choices to be exercised; it is the manner in which these choices are made that gives the economic system its distinctive character. In free-enterprise capitalism, economic decisions are privately made, with the extreme cases of the past—such as the British economy of the late eighteenth and early nineteenth centuries—being examples of almost complete decentralization of economic decision-making. Even today the economies of many western nations have only moderate degrees of government direction and control.

In a capitalistic system consumers decide for the most part what will be produced. Each spending unit (family, or single-member household), faced with a variety of goods and services on which to allocate its limited money income, casts its dollar votes for the commodities most nearly meeting its desires. Note that the economic election is not necessarily a democratic one; each consumer does not have an equal voice in the decision as to what will be produced. The greater one's money income, the greater the number of votes he may cast. Producers are led to turn out those goods consumers demand, since only the goods in demand will sell.

Decisions as to how these goods will be produced are made by businessmen in search of profit, which is to be found in producing goods for which price exceeds cost. For any particular item, the lower the cost, the greater is the profit per unit. Thus, the entrepreneur is motivated to produce the goods that consumers demand, and to adopt those combinations of resources that minimize the cost of production. Efficiency, or least-cost production, is a goal not only of the businessman, but also, and equally, of society. For if least-cost production is achieved for all outputs, society's scarce resources are being used in such a way as to produce the largest possible output of goods and services.

What of the distribution of the output? In a free enterprise system, who decides who gets how much? In a market economy, an individual's income turns on the complex relation of consumer demand to the contribution he makes to meeting that demand. Most people earn incomes by being business-men or by working for businessmen. Employees are hired by business on the expectation that they will contribute to the production of goods and services. Competition among businessmen for the relatively scarce human resources tends to drive wages up until the worker receives a wage or salary roughly commensurate with his contribution to the sale value of the goods he helps to produce.

The drive for greater money income motivates both the businessman and his employee. Incentives to increase production are therefore common to labor and management alike. Given sufficient competition among workers for jobs and among businessmen for workers, the wages of labor and the profits of entrepreneurship tend to reflect their respective contributions to produc-tion. In the final analysis, the incomes of both groups are subject to the whim of the consumer.

But despite these common objectives and pressures, there remains a wide margin for dispute between labor and management. Measures of productivity are rough guides, at best, and a man's individual contribution to the output of a large firm is almost impossible to determine. It is no wonder, therefore, that the worker challenges the right of management to decide his dollar worth. The argument that competition will force industry to pay him his true value is not persuasive, nor is he convinced that it is the consumer who plays the decisive role. To the worker, the company sets its own wage policy, and in the absence of strong, usually collective, action the wage may be some arbitrary figure totally unrelated to his productivity.

The entrepreneur argues that his freedom to make the wage decision is illusory, even in the absence of collective bargaining. He cannot afford to pay workers a rate higher than their output allows; to insist that compensation exceed productivity is to create unemployment. Confronted with the neces-sity for holding costs down, the employer is likely to view any shift in the decision-making balance to the workers as a threat to his business survival. Prices of productive services, including labor services, entrepreneurs argue, should be set in the market by the impersonal forces of demand and supply. Only in this way will the worker receive his just—i.e., his productivity—wage, and society the benefits of the most efficient allocation of resources.

Possible goals: minimum costs, maximum profits

Economists attribute to the business enterprise the primary goal of maxi-mizing profits—or its less pleasant counterpart, minimizing losses. Although there has been some recent dissatisfaction with the profit-maximization model (and a substitution by some writers of alternative business goals, such as revenue maximization subject to some profit constraint), contemporary analysts of business behavior continue to assume that the highest priority goes to the earning of profits.

In the pursuit of this goal, industry has traditionally been free to make the major decisions about which goods it would produce and in what quantities; financial and investment arrangements; plant locations; pricing of the products, etc. But to make these decisions the company must decide how many workers to hire and when to lay off some of them; when to close down a plant altogether; whether to introduce new equipment and methods of production; how to schedule the work to meet production quotas. In many of these latter decisions, the worker's welfare is clearly at stake. The question thus arises: Do such areas of decision-making belong exclusively to management, or are they more appropriately the province of joint labor-management agreement?

Former management prerogatives have eroded with the growth of collective bargaining. Prior to the formation of labor unions, management had the power to set wages which the worker had to accept as a condition of his employment. In 1894, during the government investigation of the riots that accompanied the bitter strike that year against the Pullman Palace Car Company, it was revealed how much autonomy the company had. The following excerpts from the United States Strike Commission hearings are taken from the testimony of Thomas H. Wickes, vice president of the company.

Commissioner Kernan: What is the basis of your objection to the union?

Mr. Wickes: Our objection to that was that we would not treat with our men as members of the American Railway Union, and we would not treat with them as members of any union. We treat with them as individuals and as men. . . .

Commissioner Kernan: You think that you have the right to refuse to recognize a union designed for the purpose of presenting . . . grievances which all complain of or which any complain of?

Mr. Wickes: That is the policy of the company, yes sir. If we were to receive these men as representatives of the unions they could probably force us to pay any wages which they saw fit, and get the Pullman Company in the same shape that some of the railroads are by making concessions which ought not to be made.

Commissioner Kernan: Don't you think that the opposite policy . . . in case you were one who sought to abuse your power, might enable you to pay to the men, on the other hand, just what you saw fit?

Mr. Wickes: Well, of course a man in an official position, if he is arbitrary and unfair, could work a great deal of injustice to the men; no doubt about that. But then it is a man's privilege to go to work somewhere else. [1]

---

[1] The text of this testimony is available in Leon Litwack, *The American Labor Movement* (Englewood Cliffs, N. J.: Prentice Hall, 1962), pp. 64–66.

Note that the company's objection to discussing wages with a union lay in a fear of "getting the Pullman Company in the same shape that some of the railroads are," or in what the official viewed as a poor financial position. Still sometimes in evidence is this fear that once decision-making is removed from management's hands, business failure will surely follow. For the most part the prerogatives that are considered essentially those of management today, however, do not include the setting of wages, hours, and working conditions. Whether or not a union is on the scene, certain rules in these realms have been so established by legislation, by custom, or by the threat of competition or potential union formation, that a firm may have freedom to pay "just what it sees fit."

The province in which management does legitimately exercise exclusive judgment is very hard to define. There is little challenge to the company's right to make the investment, pricing, and size-of-firm decisions it has traditionally made, as long as these commitments do not impinge directly on working arrangements. But beyond this broad generalization, the fine lines of authority remain in doubt. Moreover, attempts to lay down rules covering the gray areas have been fruitless; shifts in authority are inevitable. A labor-management conference concluded two decades ago that "it would be extremely unwise to build a fence around the rights and responsibilities of management on the one hand and unions on the other. The experience of many years shows that. . . . The responsibilities of one of the parties today may well become the joint responsibility of both parties tomorrow."

The high-profit goal of entrepreneurs is seldom challenged, perhaps because of the belief that this goal is compatible with the high-income goal of the worker. As Herbert A. Simon has noted, the ideology that "the way to more pie is to bake a larger one, not to quarrel about the slicing of the smaller one," is widespread in this country. Despite industrial conflict, he concludes, it is easy to make the case that a community of goals exists.[2]

Rationale: decision-making for the common
good

In the evolving labor–management balance, Professor Simon notes further, business, once having realized the "poverty of naked power," has made some concessions to the "authority of approval" and the "authority of confidence," and these concessions may allow the two parties to pursue goals they both find acceptable.

Precisely what are these goals? Are workers agreed that the business objective of maximum profits serves labor's interest along with manage-

---

[2]Herbert A. Simon, "Authority," in Conrad M. Arensberg et al., *Research in Industrial Relations* (New York: Harper & Brothers, 1957). Reprinted in George P. Schultz and John R. Coleman, *Labor Problems: Cases and Readings* (New York: McGraw-Hill, 1959), pp. 120–130.

ment's? And beyond the immediate profit-making goal, what are the common objectives? Consider pricing policy, for example: if business is dedicated to increasing output and lowering prices, thereby passing the fruits of efficiency on to consumers, does labor find this long-run plan compatible with its needs? Or would workers' interests be better served by a policy of raising real wages to absorb the growth in productivity, holding the prices of goods constant? In general, the economy of the nineteenth century reflected the first price policy, while the twentieth century has operated on the second.

Labor's explicit endorsement of the profit motive and the productive efficiency of the free-enterprise system is a commonplace. American trade unions have seldom criticized either income incentives or the business performance they have generated. Disagreement arises over how high profits should be, and how high wages; what responsibility the firm has for the employment security and welfare of its workers; what guarantees are given against discrimination, etc. Beyond these job-related issues that are frequently in dispute, there may be differences of view as to economy-wide goals and their implementation.

Economic goals are necessarily broad in scope, since they are to meet the needs of the whole population, but the attainment of these goals turns largely on business performance. Consider, for example, the national goal of a high rate of growth. Economic growth denotes an annual increase in the output of goods and services, measured either in aggregate or in per capita terms. If the 1972 output is 4 percent higher than the 1971 output (after price increases have been taken into account), people are 4 percent richer in goods by that one year's growth. If this rate is maintained, people's real incomes will double in less than two decades. Although the increased output is not shared evenly on a per-capita basis, the income is certainly not becoming more concentrated; persons at all income levels are therefore sharing in the growth of output.

The rate of growth in the output of goods and services is primarily a result of efficiency in the business sector. Business decisions on the introduction of new techniques, the adoption of technological improvements in production, the development of new products, and the combination of labor and capital in more efficient patterns are therefore critical to the pursuit of our growth objective. The framework within which business makes its decisions, however, is clearly established by government. Public policy that affects rates of interest on loans, for example, may be a major factor in the rate of business expansion and will also influence the level of consumer spending on housing and durables. Tax policy is an even more basic determinant of business behavior.

A high rate of economic growth is one of the goals that are acceptable to both labor and management and applauded by both Republicans and Democrats, as are the goals of price stability and full employment. Again, the decision-making that rests with the individual business firms will largely dictate our progress toward these two goals, and again, the decisions will be made in the cold light of public policy.

Public policy in the areas of taxation and spending, income and employment guarantees, and financial and debt management thus appear to be more critical determinants of labor's welfare than ever before, perhaps more critical than the issues resolved at the bargaining table. Recognizing the interrelationship of business decision-making and governmental decree, labor and management may find it necessary to direct their attention away from each other and toward the third partner in policy formation.

Goals and ideologies of labor organizations

"We believe in the American profit system," George Meany, president of the AFL–CIO, once declared. "We believe in free competition. The American private-enterprise system, despite some defects, has achieved far greater results for wage earners than any other social system in history." In further defense of his thesis, Mr. Meany noted that unions have constantly prodded management to increased efficiency and higher output. And in the process, the scope of collective bargaining has admittedly expanded. Whereas earlier concerns were wages, hours, and working conditions, and a subsequent stage embraced hiring, firing, and promotion, unions now insist on bargaining on issues such as medical care and pensions. The unilateral right of management to set production standards and plant location has also been challenged.

Context: trade union endorsement of free enterprise

Yet, a union's purpose is to protect the worker's interests, Mr. Meany argued, and matters are not challenged that do not affect the worker directly: investment policy, introduction of new products, the building of new plants to serve an expanding market. Only in extreme cases, as when a company refuses to observe union standards "and arbitrarily disrupts the lives of thousands of workers because it may save 7 cents a hat," does the union protest.

Despite some recent inroads on the traditional prerogatives of management, it is clear that the American labor movement has brought little ideological struggle to the scene. In contrast to trade unions in various European countries, American labor's emphasis has been on reform rather than revolution; on the maintenance rather than the overthrow of capitalism; on five cents more per hour in next year's contract rather than pie in the sky by and by. The major goals of union activity have been higher wages, shorter hours, and improved working conditions.

These objectives the unions have sought to achieve more through collective bargaining than through enactment of social legislation. Since the terms of collective agreements apply only to those workers covered, and not to workers in general, the progress made by unions has often been extremely limited. Moreover, because most successful unions were formed by highly skilled craftsmen, the lowest-paid workers have seemingly gained the least from union pressure. This emphasis on practical, immediate goals and the insistence on the collective-bargaining technique combined to give American labor unions an early image that was, in the opinion of some observers, only slightly less conservative than that of American business. According to George Bernard Shaw, trade unionism is the capitalism of the proletariat.

Goals: more now

A better description than Shaw's was offered in 1899 by the President of the Cigar Makers' Union: "Real trade unionists are not pessimists; they are not theorists; they are opportunists. We ameliorate as we journey along to a better industrial system." A brief summary of the goals unions have pursued in the past points up the significance of this philosophy.

Union security   The right, now commonly recognized, to organize and bargain collectively is a merely legal right. This legal sanction may pave the way for the establishment of a union, but the actual strength and success of the union are constantly in question. The security of the union's position must therefore be established before bargaining can occur. From the union's point of view, the ideal union security clause would provide for a *closed shop,* under which the employer could hire only union members. However, because the Taft-Hartley law declared the closed shop illegal, the best security provision the unions can gain is a *union shop,* which allows management to hire anyone it chooses but requires the employee to join the union after a short period of time. A *maintenance-of-membership* clause in the contract requires that all employees who join the union remain members for the duration of that contract. Under *open-shop* arrangements membership in the union is voluntary. Although employers have long argued that only the open shop permits the individual employee freedom of choice, the unions argue that such an arrangement makes it impossible to bargain effectively. Furthermore, the unions argue, any improvement in wage rates, for example, that the union is able to wring from the company then accrues to all employees, irrespective of union status. The free riders therefore receive the benefits of union pressure without sharing any of the risks, trouble, or expense.

A *checkoff* provision often accompanies a union-shop or maintenance-of-membership provision. Under this arrangement management deducts union dues from the member's pay and turns the money over to the union. This saves the union time and effort and guarantees that dues will be paid; employers protest the use of their own facilities in a pro-union cause. The Taft-Hartley law provides that the union member must give the employer written permission to deduct dues.

The rationing of jobs   Workers are constantly faced with the threat of unemployment from business fluctuations, from technological change within particular industries, from seasonal or long-run shifts in demand for products. The union has come to demand a voice in determining which employee is to retain his job longest or how many hours per week each worker may have. The maintenance of *seniority rights* is the best example of union influence on the rationing of job opportunities. In recent years increasing adherence to seniority rule, both in layoffs and in job promotions, has aroused criticism on the grounds that it reduces labor mobility and breeds inefficiency and that it prevents employers from eliminating the less productive employees and rewarding the more productive. In resisting union pressure to promote on the basis of seniority, employers have seldom agreed to use this as the only criterion, but they often agree to consider both length of service and ability in making a promotion. The contract may provide that the senior man be promoted when competent to do the job.

In addition to specifying that preference be given to senior employees, the unions have often sought to share reduced job opportunities by persuading management to reduce all workers' hours, rather than put some workers out of jobs altogether. In irregular or seasonal industries, too, the unions have attempted to work out schemes for sharing the available jobs in some equitable manner.

Wages, hours, and working conditions   Since unions are primarily interested in the economic lot of their members, it is not surprising that the wage rate is usually the most important single issue at the bargaining table. In recent years the move toward wider bargaining—the United Automobile Workers bargaining for all workers in the industry, for example—has given some unions a voice in determining wage rates on a very broad scale. Not only does a single agreement set the wages of most automobile workers, but these wage rates (along with those of steelworkers, also set by industry-wide agreement) have come to serve as a benchmark for wages in general.

Reductions in hours are sometimes demanded by the unions, despite the usual pattern, set by law, of forty hours per week with time and a half for overtime. However, as industry becomes more automated, the issue of hours may become a crucial one. A more important area for negotiation in recent years has been the range of fringe benefits: pension plans, medical care funds, etc. The unions have recognized the value of such benefits to the extent that they sometimes bargain exclusively for concessions in the fringe area, with wage demands being, temporarily at least, not at issue. The past three decades have been characterized by prosperity and rising output, so it has been possible for labor to share in the increased income through both wages and fringe benefits. In a depressed period, it is dubious whether the unions could progress on either front, or in fact whether they would attempt to do more than maintain the status quo.

Grievance procedure   Once a contract has been signed it is binding on both parties, and its rather general terms must be interpreted day-to-day. Disagreement on the exact meaning of the contractual provisions may lead to work stoppages in protest against what a worker views as unjust treatment. Grievance procedures are therefore provided, outlining the steps by which a worker may appeal a decision made by his supervisor on discipline or discharge. In less extreme cases, the employee may simply wish to protest a work assignment, the rate at which he is required to perform, a change in shift work, or some similar condition. The procedure for resolving grievances involves several steps through which agreement may be reached, with arbitration by an outsider usually the final step after all previous attempts have failed.

These practical, immediate goals are typical of the objectives sought by labor unions during their century's growth in this country. Together they make up the bulk of labor's demands both in earlier periods and at today's bargaining tables. The list underscores the truth of the story that when asked what American labor unions wanted, Samuel Gompers once replied: "More. Now."

Gompers had every right to speak for the labor unions. As president of the American Federation of Labor he headed the movement for almost half a century. In fact, the philosophy of trade unionism in this country prior to 1930 was essentially Gompers' philosophy—conservative, pragmatic, devoid of allegiance to any "ism" save capitalism. Only during the depression of the 1930s did unions begin to reshape their image. Labor assumed an active role in political and legislative matters, for example, only in the period after the Second World War, and only after the formation of a new type of union, the Congress of Industrial Organizations.

Rationale: expectations of American workers

Yet it was not Gompers who brought about the formation of unions; he was merely the leader of a movement that workers felt they had to have. In explaining this perceived need, Professors Schultz and Coleman note that once on the job, the American worker has had to realize that for all his heritage of individualism, he needed group action to enable him to achieve his job expectations. Having been told again and again that he could succeed by dint of hard work, he nevertheless one day found himself the victim of discrimination or unemployment. Then he looked for ways to bring about the dream he had always accepted as reality. Labor's group action thus was not due to radicals or agitators, the authors conclude, but to "our educational system, or religious beliefs, and our fundamental faith in democratic rights and duties that planted the seed. Led by all of these things to expect more, the worker was determined to get more."[3]

In their drive to get more, American labor unions today continue to focus most of their attention on their earlier objectives. Economic security remains the primary goal; hence, security of employment and job tenure, an adequate and rising level of wages, and protection against the hazards of disability and old age remain at the top of the unions' list of demands. Acceptable conditions of work and working hours, and a growing participation in the decisions that affect the employee's working life are also high priorities. With some thing less than success, unions have recently turned their attention to the problem of educating their members in their responsibilities as union members and citizens. Finally, the trade unionists have campaigned for the adoption of national and international policies that they believe will further their members' welfare and their conception of the country's welfare.

During the half century of Gompers' domination, the primary means of achieving these goals was negotiation with private employers. In an economy in which employers made almost all the major decisions affecting the worker's welfare, the union could best serve its members by concentrating on the private sphere of influence. But as the government came to play a larger role in the economy, unions found that the attainment of many of their objectives required them to wield an influence on legislation as well as on employers. The political activity of American unions remains essentially an extension of the bargaining process, however; unlike many European labor movements, the main body of American labor has not supported the formation of a labor party. Nor has it given its support altogether to either of the two major political parties. Gompers' dictum that "Labor should reward its friends and punish its enemies without regard to political affiliation" remains a formal tenet of union political philosophy.

---

[3]George P. Schultz and John R. Coleman, *Labor Problems: Cases and Readings, op. cit.,* pp. 5–6.

When confronted with their current widespread support of Democrats, union officials simply respond that they find more friends among the Democrats. They can always point to their support of a few Republicans to substantiate their claim of continued nonpartisanship. The number of Republicans supported by organized labor increases at state and local levels; and in a few national unions, where the top leadership is Republican, political activity is likely to be either limited or divided between the two parties.

When the AFL and CIO merged in the mid-fifties, their political action and education groups joined together to form the Committee on Political Education. COPE carries on a continuing function of presenting political facts and legislative issues to union members in a series of publications. The activities greatly expand during election campaigns, at which time the voting records of competing candidates are publicized and support is urged on the basis of the number of "right" votes as viewed by labor. In cooperation with COPE, local committees are active in seeing that union members are registered and get to the polls on election day.

Since passage of the Taft-Hartley Act, which bars the use of union funds in federal politics, COPE's activities on the national level are financed by voluntary contributions. A number of states also limit the use of union dues in state political campaigns, thus making necessary similar reliance on voluntary support.

Between elections, the AFL–CIO and some national unions maintain lobbyists in Washington. State federations also post legislative representatives in state capitols. These representatives attempt to influence legislation in line with organized labor's conception of union and national interests. Like the criteria by which they judge their friends and enemies, the scope of labor's legislative interests has widened with the passing years. Legislation currently supported or opposed by unions falls into three major categories:

1.   Legislation directed toward organized labor, such as efforts to amend the Taft-Hartley Act and prevent passage of state "right-to-work" laws, which ban the union shop.

2.   Legislation of interest to unorganized as well as organized labor, such as improvement in the minimum-wage laws, social security, unemployment compensation, and full-employment policies.

3.   Legislation affecting all citizens, such as federal aid to education, foreign aid, and other international policies.

In recent years, a candidate is likely to lose labor's support by voting consistently "wrong" in any one of these categories.

Labor and management views on economic policy issues

Because union activity in political and legislative areas has grown, we must examine labor's position on current issues of social policy, as well as its collective-bargaining philosophy. To what extent do labor unions hold views on key legislative proposals that are significantly different from those of business groups? Granted that individual union members may disagree with their union's position (just as a corporation executive may oppose a policy statement of the Chamber of Commerce, the National Association of Manufacturers, or his industry's trade association), there is nevertheless some general agreement on official statements. It is safe to conclude, for example, that most workers are in favor of raising the minimum wage, and that management generally opposes any increase in taxes on business.

Conflict: when reasonable men differ

Political pressure groups were extremely active during the 1968 elections. The campaigns followed all-out lobbying by the various interest groups during the Ninetieth Congress, with major battles being fought over the tax-surcharge bill, open housing, the antiballistic missile (ABM) system, gun control, truth-in-lending, occupational safety, airport development, water-pollution control, and a renewal of the import quota. Between labor and business lobbyists, sharp differences of view arose over the tax-surcharge–spending-cut bill (which business supported and labor opposed), and federal on-the-job safety standards and truth-in-lending (opposed by business and favored by labor). The two groups were united in pressing for import quotas, but they lost the battle to the free-traders.

A quick review of labor and management's rating of the Senators who voted on these or other bills of significance to them is provided by the Congressional Quarterly in Table 5/1. Note that the tally is made for four interest groups: Americans for Democratic Action, formed in 1947 by a group of Democrats "to map a campaign for restoring the influence of liberalism in the national and international policies of the United States"; the AFL–CIO Committee on Political Education, which serves as the political arm of organized labor; National Associated Businessmen, Inc., formed in 1946 "to work toward the longrange objective of getting the government out of competition with taxpaying businesses"; and the Americans for Constitutional Action, formed in 1958 at the request of conservative Senators, for the purpose of electing more "constitutional conservatives" to Congress.

For COPE, the high-scoring Senators were mostly Democrats; 28 Democrats but only seven Republicans scored 100 percent. At the other end of the rating scale, eleven Democrats and eight Republicans scored zero. For the bills

Table 5/1. How special-interest groups rated senators, 1968

	ADA[a]	COPE[b]	NAB[c]	ACA[d]
Alabama				
Hill	7	0	0	48
Sparkman	0	0	0	39
Alaska				
Bartlett	57	75	0	44
Gruening	64	100	75	27
Arizona				
Hayden	7	0	0	43
Fannin	7	0	60	86
Arkansas				
Fulbright	14	33	50	63
McClellan	0	0	40	73
California				
Kuchel	50	100	0	40
Murphy	14	75	60	83
Colorado				
Allott	14	75	80	86
Dominick	29	75	100	83
Connecticut				
Dodd	50	100	0	28
Ribicoff	86	100	25	45
Delaware				
Boggs	43	75	80	63
Williams	21	25	100	96
Florida				
Holland	0	25	33	56
Smathers	7	50	50	67
Georgia				
Russell	0	25	60	86
Talmadge	0	0	25	79
Hawaii				
Inouye	64	100	20	0
Fong	43	75	17	43

	ADA	COPE	NAB	ACA
Louisiana				
Ellender	7	0	50	61
Long	0	0	50	76
Maine				
Muskie	79	67	25	5
Smith	36	25	50	64
Maryland				
Brewster	57	100	33	31
Tydings	86	100	40	12
Massachusetts				
Kennedy	71	100	0	0
Brooke	86	100	60	40
Michigan				
Hart	86	100	40	0
Griffin	43	100	80	47
Minnesota				
McCarthy	21	0	0	0
Mondale	86	100	25	0
Mississippi				
Eastland	0	0	25	75
Stennis	0	0	33	68
Missouri				
Long	50	67	0	38
Symington	64	100	67	44
Montana				
Mansfield	29	100	33	21
Metcalf	79	100	0	9
Nebraska				
Curtis	7	0	80	96
Hruska	7	25	75	100
Nevada				
Bible	14	50	40	67
Cannon	29	100	50	61

	ADA	COPE	NAB	ACA
Ohio				
Lausche	21	100	67	64
Young	93	75	50	18
Oklahoma				
Harris	57	67	0	0
Monroney	21	25	33	32
Oregon				
Morse	79	67	50	21
Hatfield	71	75	75	50
Pennsylvania				
Clark	93	100	50	13
Scott	57	100	40	52
Rhode Island				
Pastore	79	0	67	18
Pell	79	100	33	14
South Carolina				
Hollings	14	75	0	56
Thurmond	0	0	60	92
South Dakota				
McGovern	43	75	80	39
Mundt	0	0	83	95
Tennessee				
Gore	43	100	75	44
Baker	21	50	100	80
Texas				
Yarborough	57	100	40	17
Tower	0	0	50	94
Utah				
Moss	79	100	50	9
Bennet	0	0	67	90
Vermont				
Aiken	43	67	100	48
Prouty	43	75	50	63

Table 5/1. (continued)

State / Senator				
Idaho				
Church	43	75	80	68
Jordan	21	75	83	88
Illinois				
Dirksen	7	67	100	87
Percy	79	100	0	31
Indiana				
Bayh	50	100	40	38
Hartke	50	100	40	41
Iowa				
Hickenlooper	0	0	100	96
Miller	14	25	100	88
Kansas				
Carlson	7	50	0	71
Pearson	21	25	60	72
Kentucky				
Cooper	71	75	80	28
Morton	21	75	100	70
New Hampshire				
McIntyre	50	100	20	23
Cotton	29	75	100	88
New Jersey				
Williams	86	100	33	8
Case	100	100	50	18
New Mexico				
Anderson	21	25	0	25
Montoya	36	100	25	6
New York				
*Goodell**	—	—	—	—
Javits	86	100	40	13
North Carolina				
Ervin	0	33	50	78
Jordan	0	25	40	67
North Dakota				
Burdick	64	75	60	32
Young	0	0	67	80
Virginia				
Byrd, Jr.	0	25	67	83
Spong	29	75	40	41
Washington				
Jackson	57	100	0	12
Magnuson	36	100	0	30
West Virginia				
Byrd	21	0	50	63
Randolph	64	100	40	32
Wisconsin				
Nelson	71	100	40	21
Proxmire	64	50	83	32
Wyoming				
McGee	57	100	0	5
Hansen	7	25	100	89

Democrats in this type; Republicans in italics

ADA—Americans for Democratic Action.
COPE—AFL-CIO Committee on Political Education.
NAB—National Associated Businessmen.
ACA—Americans for Constitutional Action.
* Member did not serve for entire period covered by voting studies.
+ Scores were compiled by Congressional Quarterly from the votes selected by the organization.
a The percentage of the time each Senator voted in accordance with the ADA position on 14 selected votes of 1968. The percentages were compiled by ADA. Failure to vote lowers the scores.
b The percentage of the time each Senator voted in accordance with the COPE position on four selected votes of 1968. Failure to vote does not lower the scores, which were compiled by CQ.
c The percentage of the time each Senator voted in accordance with the NAB position on six selected votes of 1968. Failure to vote does not lower the scores, which were compiled by CQ.
d The percentage of the time each Senator voted in accordance with the ACA position on 25 selected votes of 1968. Failure to vote does not lower the scores, which were compiled by ACA.
Source: Congressional Quarterly Almanac, 1968, p. 872.

of interest to the National Associated Businessmen, ten Republicans (but no Democrats) voted consistently favorably, whereas fifteen Democrats and three Republicans received zero scores. A similar review of action in the House reveals that the line-up was again one primarily of Democrats–COPE versus Republicans–NAB: a total of 138 Representatives (129 Democrats and 9 Republicans) scored 100 percent on COPE's issues, while 168 Representatives (150 Republicans and 18 Democrats) had perfect scores on the bills NAB favored.[4]

Goals: whose welfare?

There is a widespread tendency for each interest group to believe that it represents the public interest. Business groups reason that their capacity to expand the number of jobs and raise wages—which are the most critical determinants of economic progress—depends upon an adequate promise of profit, relative freedom of action in the conduct of their affairs, reasonable tax limits, etc. Labor unions believe that many governmental guarantees are necessary, in the public interest: minimum wages, protection during periods of dependency, consumer protection, adequate expenditures on education and health, etc. Business has consistently battled for less government intervention in the economy, labor (since the 1930s, at least) for more.

Agreement on major goals for the economy—full employment, price stability, high economic growth—does not bring with it any consensus as to how these goals can best be achieved. A particularly pertinent example arises in connection with the attainment of full employment while also maintaining price stability. What constitutes full employment? Or alternatively, how much price inflation is tolerable? There is clearly some trade off, once the level of unemployment reaches about 5 percent. Is the public welfare served by pushing the rate down to 2½ percent, if the rate of spending necessary to achieve this objective generates a price rise of 3 or 4 percent annually?

Even if the terms of the trade off were clearly evident before policy was initiated, there would be a difference of view as to which is less bad: some unemployment or some inflation. The spectre of runaway inflation looms always before business; the ghost of massive unemployment haunts labor. As long as full employment is incompatible with price stability, the difference of view will persist. The only way to remove the source of conflict is to improve the terms of the trade off. For at present both groups are right: unemployment and price inflation are both threats to the general welfare. It is senseless to argue over which constitutes the greater threat.

---

[4]*Congressional Quarterly Almanac,* 1968, pp. 868–887.

Readings

Dunlop, John T., and Derek C. Bok. *Labor and the American Community.* New York: Simon and Schuster, 1970.

Haber, William, ed. *Labor in a Changing America.* New York: Basic Books, 1966.

Kassalow, Everrett. *Trade Unions and Industrial Relations: An International Comparison.* New York: Random House, 1969.

Kerr, Clark; John T. Dunlop; Frederick Harbison; and Charles Myers. *Industrialism and Industrial Man.* Cambridge, Mass.: Harvard University Press, 1960.

Lester, Richard A. *As Unions Mature: An Analysis of the Evolution of American Unionism.* Princeton, N. J.: Princeton University Press, 1958.

Perlman, Selig. *History of Trade Unionism.* New York: The Macmillan Co., 1922.

Ross, Arthur M., and Paul T. Hartman. *Changing Patterns of Industrial Conflict.* New York: John Wiley and Sons, 1960.

Schultz, George P., and John R Coleman. *Labor Problems: Cases and Readings.* New York: McGraw-Hill Book Co., 1959.

Slichter, Sumner, "The Position of Trade Unions in the American Economy," in Michael Harrington and Paul Jacobs, eds. *Labor in a Free Society.* Berkeley: University of California Press, 1959.

Taft, Philip. *Organized Labor in American History.* New York: Harper and Row, 1964.

Chapter Six

Labor Unions in the United States

A certain lassitude has overtaken the trade union movement. . . . Little is left of the proselytizing spirit that created the basic organizations in the building and printing trades in the late nineteenth and early twentieth centuries, the needle trades organizations in the following two decades, and the industrial unions in the thirties. The image of unions as the social conscience of the community has been considerably dimmed.

Solomon Barkin, former director of research for the Textile Workers Union of America, writing in 1961.

Introduction

Labor unions appeared on the American scene much later than in Europe, and throughout their history they have differed markedly from their European counterparts. Many reasons for the slower growth have been advanced: the mobility between classes, which made it possible for American workers to move into the management hierarchy; the existence of westward frontiers, which in earlier times offered factory workers an alternative livelihood; the immigration of workers of different nationalities, for whom unity in any cause was difficult to achieve. One further deterrent was how the American courts interpreted the anti-trust laws; certain actions of labor unions, as well as those of business, have been declared restraints of trade.

Union growth and decline in the United States

Despite their slow beginnings, American labor unions can hardly be considered a recent development; the earliest emerged with the beginnings of our modern industrial system in the eighteenth century. References to labor leaders as *new* men of power are thus difficult to explain, except with reference to the revolutionary growth in union membership in the two decades following the acute depression of the 1930s, and the ever-widening scope of union interests and activities.

The scope of unionism

In 1930 in the United States about 3½ million workers were organized. Some of the most vital industrial areas were almost wholly untouched by unionism. As Figure 6/1 indicates, there has since been more than a six-fold increase in union membership, to almost 20 million workers by 1970. These organized workers constitute about 22 percent of the labor force. But among workers in non-agricultural establishments, where union strength is greatest, the proportion is higher—almost 28 percent (Figure 6/2).

These general figures do not indicate the crucial role of unionism in some industrial sectors of the economy. For example, union membership is high in steel, aluminum, aircraft, electrical machinery, glass, rubber, newspaper, agricultural implements, meatpacking, building construction, railroad, maritime, motion pictures. These are the industries that furnish us with food and shelter; provide basic means of energy, transportation, and communication; and serve as the heart of an industrial civilization in peace and war. In these industries very few decisions affecting the work force can be made without union participation. Moreover, patterns established in the power centers of the union movement influence agreements reached in the remainder of the economy.

Motivations for union growth

In common with men throughout the ages, the American worker has been primarily concerned with the immediate needs of himself and his family for food, shelter, and clothing. As these goals are attained, he seeks to provide the additional comforts and conveniences reflected in higher living standards. And, with the growing satisfaction of current needs, he turns his attention to protecting his future against loss of income caused by illness, disability, unemployment, or old age.

To many employers, the worker's concern with economic security appears to be excessive. But security consciousness is less surprising when we adopt the worker's viewpoint and see the future through his eyes. Few employees have a source of income other than the wages gained from their employment. They are barely able to accumulate sufficient savings to tide them over in any lengthy period without current income. So long as their worklife may include depressions, illness, accidents, and other circumstances that cut off sources of family livelihood, workers are likely to pursue measures which afford them economic security.

Figure 6/1. Membership of national[1] and
international unions 1930–70

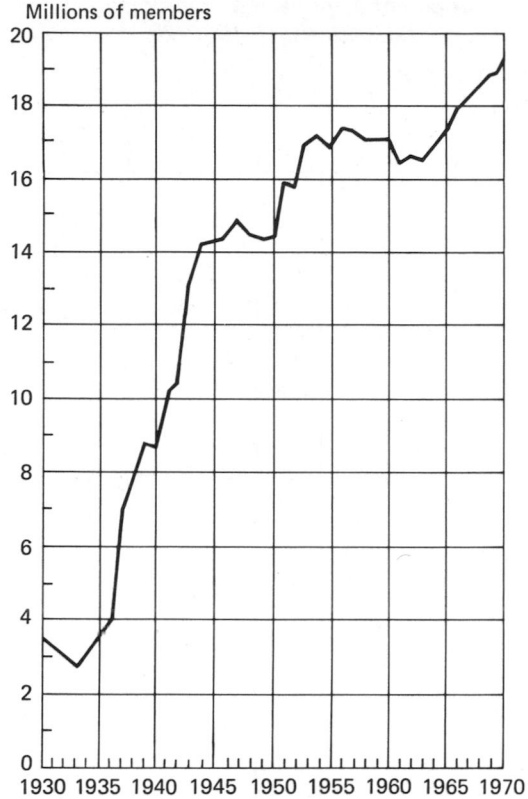

[1] Excludes Canadian membership but includes members in other areas outside the United States. Members of AFL-CIO directly affiliated local unions are also included for the years 1948-52. Midpoints of membership estimates, which were expressed as ranges, were used.

Source: U.S. Bureau of Labor Statistics, *Directory of National and International Labor Unions in the United States, 1967* (Bulletin No. 1596), p. 57; and "Labor Union and Employee Association Membership, 1970," data release of the U.S. Bureau of Labor Statistics, Sept. 13, 1971, p. 4.

From an economic standpoint, unions come into being because individual workers have only limited bargaining power in achieving higher income and security. Bargaining power is basically derived from "withholding power"— the ability to damage the other negotiating party more than you damage yourself by withholding what you have to sell. The average worker who acts

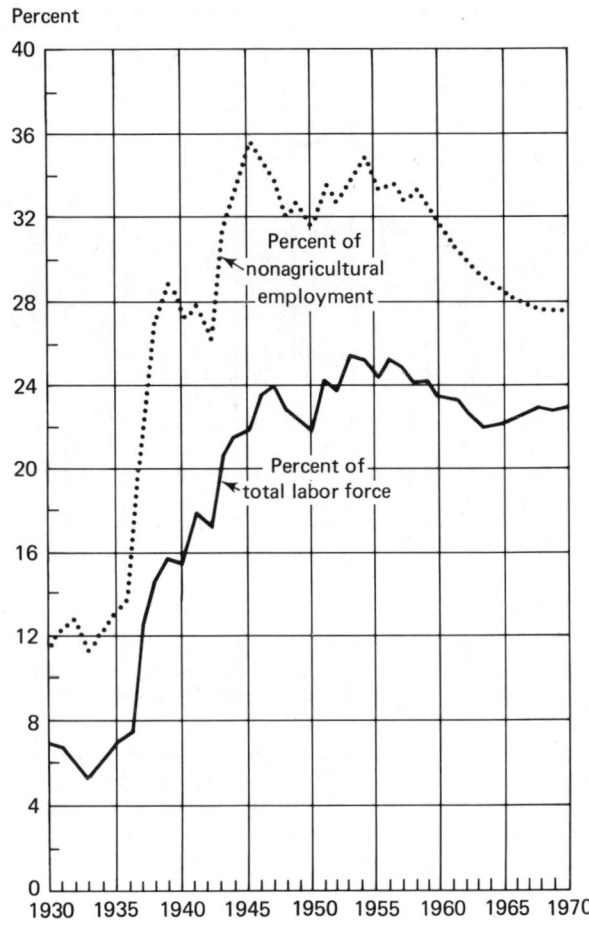

Figure 6/2. Membership[1] as a percent of total labor
force and of employees in nonagricultural
establishments, 1930–70

Percent

Percent of
nonagricultural
employment

Percent of
total labor force

[1] Excludes Canadian membership.

Source: U.S. Bureau of Labor Statistics, *Directory of National and
International Labor Unions in the United States, 1967* (Bulletin No.
1596), p. 57; and "Labor Union and Employee Association Membership, 1970," data release of the U.S. Bureau of Labor Statistics,
Sept. 13, 1971, p. 4.

alone to withhold his labor as a bargaining technique can be readily replaced, but the mass withdrawal of labor during a strike may seriously affect the employer's production; and the bargaining power which results from this collective action will be further strengthened if union strike benefits permit a longer period of withholding.

The effort to gain security through unions must wait upon the development of a working-class outlook. Workers begin to turn to labor organization only when they are convinced that they are likely to remain workers for much of their lives. In the early days of the American economy employee status was generally viewed as only a temporary resting place on the road to independent ownership of a farm or small business. With such social and occupational mobility, the path to economic security was seen to lie not in an organization of workers but in escape from the worker classification. By the end of the eighteenth century, however, an increasing number of workers found their escape route closed and their dependent position more obvious and more permanent. It was then that they began to form organizations based on the acceptance of their worker status, designed to further their economic welfare as workers.

But many workers have formed unions even after their employer has granted above-average wages, working conditions, and supplementary benefits. In these instances, employers learn that union functions go well beyond the economic; workers have to find ways to meet their social needs as well. Basic to these is the need for recognition and acceptance, the need for a sense of belonging and participation. Rank-and-file employees do not readily achieve these satisfactions in the large, modern industrial plant.

Thus, workers may turn to unions for protection against arbitrary treatment at the workplace. Or they may wish to increase their sense of importance or gain a greater feeling of participation in the decisions that affect their working lives. Whereas the employer may consider these activities an encroachment on management rights, the union member is likely to call them the necessary ingredients of industrial democracy.

As union strength increases, various social and institutional pressures develop to force workers into unions. Union members are notably loath to work with nonmembers, the so-called "free-riders" who accept the benefits of collective bargaining without supporting the union. Given the human need for acceptance and a sense of belonging, few workers can tolerate the social rejection resulting from their nonunion status in a predominantly unionized plant.

Limits to unionization

The same factors that explain the initial growth of unions help us to understand the slower rate of union growth in recent years. Prosperity has led many employers to grant high wages and substantial economic security in the absence of unions; moreover, personnel managers have increasingly adopted a "human relations" approach in their dealings with employees, fully recognizing the basic sociopsychological needs of men in a work situation.

In many nonunion firms these practices have been consciously adopted to forestall organization. They are especially effective in small establishments, where close interpersonal relations are more readily achieved. But the approach has also proved to be successful in several large firms in such industries as chemical and steel production.

Several years ago one management official commented on a successful union organizing campaign: "Some employers remind me of the man who hasn't kissed his wife in ten years, yet gets very upset when he finds someone else doing so." Many company executives have taken this admonition to heart. By anticipating and attempting to satisfy the needs a union would fulfill, they have sharply reduced the opportunities for union formation. At the same time these employers have taken full advantage of postwar legislative provisions barring compulsory union membership and granting employers greater discretion to encourage antiunion attitudes among employees.

Whereas a permanent working class was necessary for the historical emergence of labor organization, a current change in occupational structure is hampering further union growth. Labor's great organizational triumphs have been centered in manual worker classifications. Professional and white-collar workers, who are more management-minded, partly because of their briefer tenure as employees, are less amenable than production workers to union-organizing drives. The number of production workers in manufacturing has remained almost stable in recent decades, while there has been a sharp increase in the number of technicians and professional employees.

It is evident that the workers who are most readily organized have already joined the union ranks. Employees in small establishments, in the South, and in the white-collar and professional occupations will present a much more serious challenge to the labor movement. But new fields for organization have appeared among public employees and agricultural workers. As we shall see in the following section, union structure has changed in the past in an effort to meet organizational problems; and the levels of economic activity and government policies have profoundly influenced union growth. Similar institutional changes are likely to play a vital role in the future development of labor organization.

Development of union structure

The first American unions sprang up in the cities of the Eastern seaboard just prior to 1800. For more than a quarter of a century they retained their purely local character, formally unrelated to each other. Today most of the country's sixty- to seventy-thousand locals are joined together in national unions affiliated with a single federation, popularly known as the AFL–CIO, the American Federation of Labor and Congress of Industrial Organizations. The historical development of labor–management relations in the United States is chronicled in the structural changes that occurred during the intervening two centuries.

Local unionism, 1790–1850

The first local unions developed not among the most downtrodden, unskilled labor, but among such skilled craftsmen as shoemakers, blacksmiths, and iron molders. Skilled employees had the potential bargaining power and cohesiveness lacking in the unskilled group; their common craft served as a symbol of unity. But their unity did not extend beyond their own locality, for the means of communication and transportation had not yet advanced to a point which required or facilitated intercommunity combination.

Indeed, it was not until the 1820s that unions in the same locality joined together into city federations. Within such cities as New York, Boston, and Philadelphia, craft unions, with little in common except their members' employee status and their geographic proximity, sought to achieve mutual aid and protection against attacks by the employers and the courts.

Included in these attacks was the "criminal conspiracy doctrine," enunciated by the courts in the early 1800s. This doctrine stated that any combination of labor was a conspiracy punishable by fine or imprisonment. Some relief came in 1842, when the Supreme Court of Massachusetts held that the legality of unions depended on the nature of their objectives rather than the very act of combination.

Nationals and federations, 1850–1886

By the mid-nineteenth century the American economy was ready for a joining of local unions over wider geographic areas. With improvements in transportation and communication, competition in the sale of many products spread westward from the cities on the Atlantic seaboard. Union members moved more frequently from one community to another. Under these circumstances, local unions in the same trade felt a need for a common alliance in order to preserve working standards and retain the strength of their organizations.

The printers formed the first permanent national organization in 1850. They were followed during the same decade by the iron molders and the machinists and blacksmiths. But unions were still bitterly opposed by employers and highly vulnerable to adverse economic fluctuations. The sharp business downturn in 1857 greatly weakened union ranks and obstructed the incipient movement toward nationalization. As in previous depressions, labor's attention was diverted from union organization to a variety of political ventures and activities in the cooperative movement.

It was not until the upswing accompanying the Civil War that national unionism came into its own. As late as 1863, almost two-thirds of all union members were still located in Massachusetts, New York, and Pennsylvania. In the following decade, however, twenty-six national unions were formed, many of which, such as the Carpenters, Bricklayers, and Locomotive Engineers, continue to the present time.

As the number of national unions increased, the way was paved for movement to a still higher organizational stage—a federation of national unions. Two efforts at federation took place in the 1860s: the National Labor Union and the Noble Order of the Knights of Labor. The former lasted only a few years, but the Knights went on to achieve considerable success and reached a membership of 700,000 before its eventual collapse.

The year in which the Knights of Labor reached its peak, 1886, was also the year in which the American Federation of Labor was formed. The decline of the Knights in the following years can best be understood by contrasting its structure and objectives with those of the AFL. The Knights admitted almost anyone to membership; the AFL was initially dominated by skilled craft workers. The Knights were as much concerned with political reform and the cooperative movement as they were with union activity; the AFL concentrated on "business unionism"—collective bargaining over wages, hours, and working conditions.

The comparison is more than a mere academic exercise, for the leaders of the AFL deliberately sought to avoid what they considered to be the errors of the earlier federations, and the rivalry between the Knights and the AFL became a contest between two basically different concepts of labor philosophy.

The AFL, 1886–1935

Since the AFL grew and prospered as the Knights declined, it can be concluded that the structure and goals of the new federation were more in tune with the American environment at the end of the nineteenth century.

"Business unionism"   The AFL unions sought to win acceptance in the hostile American community by avoiding radical political activity and by stressing "businesslike" adherence to the basic principles of American capitalism. As the preceding chapter on union ideology noted, much of the federation's early character was molded by its first president, Samuel Gompers. Gompers had been a socialist in his native England, but he realized that the capitalist society that he found in the United States was too powerful and ascendant to permit the triumph of a radical movement. Accepting the basic tenets of capitalism, he asked only that his skilled unionists be given their rightful share of the proceeds of this prosperous economy. The tight-knit, exclusive unions of the AFL, with their membership of skilled workers, had much greater economic than political bargaining power. The most fruitful path for American organized labor was seen to lie, then, not in political action but in collective bargaining with employers.

Opposition to the AFL   Although the conservatism of the AFL paid off in an initial expansion of membership, the federation soon found itself under attack from two opposed camps. on the one hand, employ ers considered unionism and collective bargaining a threat to the profits and prestige of business; on the other hand, the socialists scored the AFL's emphasis on economic gain for skilled craftsmen.

By the turn of the century, management groups had formed to counter the organization of labor. The National Association of Manufacturers was formed to coordinate the antiunion activities of numerous local employer associations and to lead the campaign for the *open shop* in American industry. While this attack was ostensibly aimed at the unions' *closed shop* (that is, compulsory union membership), it was actually directed toward the elimination of unionism itself. Employers intensified their discrimination against union members and placed discharged union activists on a *blacklist* to prevent their employment elsewhere. In many establishments, workers were forced to sign *yellow dog contracts,* stipulations that they would not join a union. When union organizers sought to persuade such employees to join, they could be legally charged with attempting to induce breach of contract.

In the antiunion environment of the times, employers found willing allies to support their battle against labor organization. The Sherman Antitrust Act, passed in 1890 to prevent business monopoly, was interpreted by the courts to apply to union activities. Charging that strikes were conspiracies to restrain the flow of commerce, employers could readily obtain court injunctions against labor—orders restraining unions from engaging in coercive practices in violation of the antitrust act. Strikes were also defeated through the widespread use of strikebreakers and industrial spies supplied by commercial detective agencies. By means of these devices, bitter strikes were broken in such basic industries as coal mining, steel, and railways in the 1890s.

The socialist indictment of the AFL was centered on the federation's business-union policies and the structure of its affiliated national unions. Most prominent among the critics in the years before World War I was the IWW, the Industrial Workers of the World. An admittedly revolutionary organization dedicated to the forcible overthrow of capitalism, the IWW was especially scornful of the federation's preoccupation with exclusive craft unionism. The Wobblies, as they were called, favored one big union of skilled and unskilled workers alike. But their policies of violence in domestic relations and pacifism in international relations found little acceptance as the United States entered world conflict. By the end of hostilities, the IWW had passed into insignificance, and the business unionism of the AFL continued unshaken.

Loss of strength in the 1920s   Benefiting from wartime prosperity and labor demand, the union movement entered the 1920s with a record level of 5 million members. The national unions had demonstrated their ability to withstand economic depression and employer opposition. But they were weakened in the '20s by their emphasis on craft unionism in the face of far-reaching industrial change and by a new and sophisticated employer attack. Technological change reduced the industrial need for skilled workers at the same time that new mass-production industries, calling for large numbers of semiskilled and unskilled workers, were coming to the forefront. Although the AFL included a few industrial unions in such industries as coal mining and clothing manufacture, in which skilled and unskilled members enjoyed equal status, the federation continued to be dominated by the craft union principle. The AFL's refusal to admit unskilled workers into existing unions or to charter new ones seriously cut total membership.

Employers added to these difficulties by adopting a variety of welfare practices which undermined the unions' appeal to potential members. High wages, pension plans, profit sharing, and improved working conditions were combined with an increasing number of services to win the employee's loyalty. Nor did management abandon its frontal attack on union organization by black-listing, yellow dog contracts, strikebreaking, and company-dominated employee-representation plans. Every AFL effort to get out from under the labor injunction also proved fruitless. As a result of these forces, organized labor entered the debilitating depression of the 1930s already reduced to 3½ million members and hardly in a position to withstand further shock.

New legislation of the 1930s   Ravaged by unemployment and falling wages, the AFL lost an additional half million members by 1932, and the outlook was bleak indeed. It was at this critical hour, however, that the legislative tide turned in labor's favor. The Norris-LaGuardia Act of 1932 severely limited the use of the labor injunction and the yellow dog contract. The National Industrial Recovery Act in 1933 gave workers the right to organize into unions of their own choosing. And the Wagner Act (National Labor Relations Act) of 1935 provided for union recognition through majority election by workers in each bargaining unit. It also declared unlawful such traditional employer practices as company domination of unions and coercion to prevent union organization.

Craft unionism vs. industrial unionism   All was going well for the union movement, except for an issue that had haunted the AFL throughout the '20s and now arose in full force to divide the house of labor: the problem of how best to organize the unskilled workers in the mass-production industries had not yet been solved. It became an even more pressing problem after passage of the Wagner Act, for the probable success of an organizing campaign was now greatly enhanced, and inaction was less excusable. The dominant group of AFL leaders insisted that craft union principles and existing union jurisdictions had to be rigorously observed in approaching the unorganized. The leaders of the few industrial unions in the AFL, such as John L. Lewis of the Mine Workers and Sidney Hillman of the Clothing Workers, pressed for industrial unionism as the only form of organization suited to the conditions of the mass-production industries.

Failing to gain general acceptance of their point of view in the AFL conventions, the industrial union leaders set up their own committee in 1935 to carry out the organization of the unorganized. The Committee for Industrial Organization met with overwhelming success. Sometimes after a struggle, sometimes peacefully, the traditional bastions of antiunionism—steel, autos, rubber, and others—succumbed to the CIO drive. But the craft union leaders looked askance at these activities, called the Committee for Industrial Organization a rival, dual union movement, and, finally, expelled the CIO unions from the AFL.

The AFL and CIO, 1935–1955

Little daunted, Lewis and his colleagues placed the industrial union federation on a permanent footing under the name the Congress of Industrial Organizations. There were now two major branches in the American Labor movement.

Interunion rivalry   In spite of efforts to bring the two federations together, especially in the late '30s, twenty years were to pass before reunification. Still, rather than retard labor's growth in the succeeding two decades, the interunion rivalry may well have increased the rate of organization. The dynamic expansion of the CIO stirred the AFL into renewed activity. Taking full advantage of the Wagner Act and the upturn in the economy, by 1940 the combined labor movement exceeded 8 million members, almost equally divided between the two federations.

The war years   The prosperity and full employment of the war years had the customary expansive effects on union development. The activities and decisions of the National War Labor Board, given responsibility for dispute settlement and wage stabilization during the war years, also served to strengthen the union position. Almost one-fourth of the total labor force was unionized by 1945. The AFL, continuing its departure from a narrow craft basis of organization, matched and even exceeded the CIO's expansion in the newly swollen defense industries.

However, labor's rapid and revolutionary growth was inevitably accompanied by some excesses and internal problems. Much publicity was given to the sit-down strikes and picket-line violence of the 30s. Communists, whose organizational zeal and experience were welcome in the CIO's early expansion, gained entrenched positions in a number of national unions during the wartime alliance with the Soviet Union. They proved to be a growing source of embarrassment to the labor movement as the war came to an end. These developments provided ammunition for those who feared the growing economic and political power of organized labor.

Restrictive legislation   Even before the end of the '30s a number of states revised the Wagner Act philosophy and passed legislation restricting various union activities. And with the prosperity of the following decade, public opinion, which generally had supported efforts to protect the rights of union organization in the depth of the depression, began to veer in the direction of union control. Strikes by the Mine Workers during wartime and the wave of work stoppages that flooded the industrial economy at the end of the war caused an additional loss of public support. With the return of a Republican Congress in 1946, the way was paved for the restrictive legislation which had been threatening. The Taft-Hartley Act was passed in the following year.

The Taft-Hartley Act was based on the premise that the Wagner Act had served the purposes of union protection and expansion too well, that the time had come to restore the balance of power in labor relations. Although union officials bitterly opposed the statute and sought its repeal or substantial amendment, the act remained on the books essentially unchanged for a dozen years. In 1959 a number of significant amendments and additions were enacted. Nonetheless, the Taft-Hartley Act still constitutes the basic law in the national labor relations field.

The AFL–CIO merger, 1955 to present

A number of developments in the postwar years brought the AFL and CIO closer together. First, the craft–industrial-union issue, which had precipitated the initial split, had now become somewhat blurred. Many craft unions in the AFL had increasingly extended their jurisdictional boundaries in the 1940s to include semiskilled and even unskilled workers. The organizational philosophy of a number of the largest AFL unions, such as the Teamsters and the Machinists, was now barely distinguishable from that of many CIO unions.

Second, the two federations also became more similar in political philosophy and activity. The CIO, whose birth and early expansion took place under the aegis of New Deal legislation, was traditionally more active in politics than the AFL. In 1943 the CIO formed its Political Action Committee, while the AFL was still engaged in less formal and less enthusiastic political activity. After passage of the Taft-Hartley Act, however, the AFL established Labor's League for Political Education, and the two federations found that their political goals and programs increasingly coincided. Their similarities became even more obvious with the CIO's expulsion of its communist-dominated unions and its withdrawal in 1949 from the communist-dominated World Federation of Trade Unions.

A third factor impelling unity was the relative decline of the CIO in the postwar years. The expulsion of the communist-dominated unions initially lost the CIO a substantial number of members. The energy spent on this issue, and the resultant internal warfare, diverted the CIO from its campaign of organizing the unorganized. By the early 1950s the CIO had less than half the membership of the AFL and looked with more favor on a reconciliation.

Finally, a change in top leadership of both federations in 1952 provided a strong push toward merger. William Green of the AFL and Phil Murray of the CIO had played major roles in the dramatic split and the subsequent years of bitter vituperation. Their successors, George Meany and Walter Reuther, had been less active in these developments. As in many instances of social transition, a change in personalities permitted institutional developments called forth by a new socioeconomic-political environment.

Current structure and government of unions

When the two rival federations came together in 1955 to form the AFL–CIO, approximately 15 million union members were once again included in a single labor organization.

Structure of unions

Workers are initially represented by some 60,000 to 70,000 local unions; and the locals, in turn, are grouped into approximately 190 national or international unions. Those unions with the word "International" in their names are so designated because of membership in Canada and, occasionally, in Mexico or South American countries. The European ties of American unionists are primarily maintained through the International Confederation of Free Trade Unions, with which the AFL–CIO is affiliated.

Some local unions are directly affiliated with the federation rather than an intermediate national union. In addition to these affiliations, locals are joined together into city and state federations; and these state and local bodies are subordinate to the AFL–CIO. In some trades, locals are also affiliated with area trade councils, designed to further the objectives of closely related unions. Union political action groups are also organized along state lines and, frequently, in affiliation with city federations.

Although national unions are formally federated with the AFL–CIO, they are autonomous in their individual policies and government. The major disciplinary sanction exercised by the AFL–CIO over its affiliated national unions is expulsion from the federation. The federation once expelled a number of unions on corruption charges that were developed in Congressional committee hearings and through the AFL–CIO's own investigations. Earlier, the CIO had expelled unions led by communist-oriented officials; but many of the lost members have since been reabsorbed into other AFL–CIO affiliates.

In addition to the unions expelled from the federation, and those which have voluntarily withdrawn, there are a number of unions that have never been affiliated with it. Most notable among these are three unions of operating railroad employees, an independent telephone alliance, unions of federal government employees, and a large number of small, one-company unions. The total membership in the two largest unaffiliated unions, the Teamsters and the Auto Workers, is slightly over 3½ million.

The relations between the Mine Workers and the federations are especially interesting. In the middle 1930s, the union was the largest in the country and a mainstay of the AFL. In withdrawing from the AFL to form the CIO, the coal union provided the major support for the new federation, and John L. Lewis became its first president. But by 1942, the UMWA had withdrawn from the CIO, and, except for a brief period in 1946–47, when it again joined and withdrew from the AFL, the coal union has since been "independent." It was not included in the formation of the AFL–CIO in 1955. Thus, the union which played so prominent a role in American labor history is now isolated from the main body of labor.

Aside from their independence from the AFL–CIO, the unaffiliated unions are much the same in structure, government, and policies as other national unions. Indeed, unless the federation charters a rival national union, expulsion or withdrawal from the AFL–CIO is likely to have little serious impact on a union's operations. The United Electrical Workers, expelled from the CIO on charges of communist domination, and the Bakery Workers, later expelled from the AFL–CIO on charges of corruption, have suffered substantial membership losses to newly chartered affiliates. But the Mine Workers, the Teamsters, and the Auto Workers have experienced few ill effects from their unaffiliated status.

Trade-union government

With very few exceptions, the constitutions of American unions at local, national, and federation levels provide for democratic procedures in internal government. *Local unions* are usually governed by a president, secretary–treasurer, and executive board elected directly by the rank-and-file members. Membership meetings are held at frequent intervals (usually biweekly or monthly) and are generally characterized by active discussion.

The *national* or *international union* charters the local and provides the constitutional framework for its operation. The national union convention is its final governing authority, and, in most cases, elects the national officers and executive board. In some unions, officers are elected through a referendum. Delegates to the convention are chosen by the local unions on some rough basis of proportional representation. Over half of all national unions schedule conventions either annually or biennially. Almost all of the remainder hold conventions at least every fourth year. Between conventions, leadership authority rests with the elected officers and executive board.

The government of the *AFL–CIO* is similar to that of the national unions. Conventions meet every two years and constitute the supreme governing body of the federation. National unions are entitled to delegates on the basis of membership size. The officers of the federation, consisting of a president, secretary–treasurer, and 27 vice presidents, are elected by the convention and govern between conventions.

Internal issues

As the merged federation of labor began its life, critics made dire predictions of its imminent collapse, while supporters projected rosy pictures of great future accomplishments. In its early years the AFL–CIO has made some progress, but the labor movement has continued to suffer from some serious internal problems of structure and government. These internal issues can best be evaluated in the light of three "Objects and Principles" adopted in Article II of the federation's initial constitution:

1.   To encourage all workers without regard to race, creed, color, national origin or ancestry to share equally in the full benefits of union organization.

2.   . . . to encourage the elimination of conflicting and duplicating organizations and jurisdictions through the process of voluntary agreement or voluntary merger in consultation with appropriate officials of the Federation, [and] to preserve, subject to the foregoing, the organizing jurisdiction of each affiliate.

3.   To protect the labor movement from any and all corrupt influences and from the undermining efforts of communist agencies and all others who are opposed to the basic principles of our democracy and free and democratic unionism.

Restrictions on admission   Since the 1930s the union movement has made considerable progress in reducing admission restrictions based on race, creed, or color. As noted above, the AFL–CIO has taken a strong public stand on this issue; but a number of affiliated craft unions continue to practice discrimination against blacks in their admission or voting procedures. Black leaders inside and outside the federation have been critical of how little pressure has been brought to bear upon the few offending organizations. The Civil Rights Act of 1964 specifically bans racial discrimination, and this Act has spurred compliance even among those unions that had been slow to lower their barriers.

Jurisdictional disputes   As is indicated in the careful wording of the second objective cited above, the AFL–CIO faced a formidable problem in achieving organic integration of separate affiliates of the two merging federations. In industries such as chemicals, meatpacking, and glass manufacturing, AFL unions competed directly with CIO unions. Although there has been some progress in no-raiding agreements and mergers between competing units in recent years, a number of federation affiliates are still in close rivalry within the same industry.

A similar problem, also sidestepped at the time of merger, continues to plague the federation. Even though there were many similarities in the structure of AFL and CIO unions in 1955, the craft–industrial union issue had not been finally laid to rest. After the merger, a number of bitter disputes arose between craft unions (such as metal workers) and industrial unions (such as steel and auto workers) concerning jurisdiction over construction work on industrial sites. At times this issue has threatened to cause a major split in the federation. Although the merger constitution proclaimed the principle that "both craft and industrial unions are appropriate, equal and necessary," it did not prescribe a formula for the resolution of conflict between them. In spite of President Meany's later efforts to provide such a formula and the recent adoption of the arbitration principle as a method of settlement, this troublesome question is likely to be a source of bitterness for many years.

Corrupt influences   Perhaps the most challenging problems to face the AFL–CIO in its early years have arisen from its pledge to "protect the labor movement from any and all corrupt influences." In spite of the federation's codes of ethical and democratic practices, Congressional investigations since the 1950s have disclosed evidence of racketeering and corruption in a number of unions. The disclosures have involved only a few organizations, but one or two large nationals have been affected, and considerable publicity has been given to the findings. The evidence includes alliances between racketeers and union officers; collusion between union officers and employers and insurance companies in the handling of welfare and pension funds; the acceptance of bribes and kickbacks; and the systematic looting of treasuries by union officials.

The AFL–CIO has taken a strong stand against these practices. In addition to the statement of principle described above, the merger constitution established a Committee on Ethical Practices which was to assist the executive council in investigating and, if need be, penalizing any union suspected of corrupt influence. In the following three years the federation adopted four codes of ethical practices defining correct procedure with regard to the granting of local union charters, the administration of union health and welfare funds, the avoidance of conflicts of interest for union leaders, and the belief that "no persons who constitute corrupt influences or practices or who represent or support communist, fascist, or totalitarian agencies should hold office" in labor unions.

In the light of disclosures made by the McClellan Congressional Committee and its own investigating committees, the AFL–CIO expelled three unions accused of corruption in 1957–58. Three other unions were permitted to stay in the federation only after they accepted monitorship. Although the AFL–CIO has been able to recoup some of its losses by chartering competing unions in two of the jurisdictions where expulsions had occurred, it has made no attempt to form a rival for the expelled Teamsters. The loss to the federation goes well beyond the Teamsters' large membership, for the truck drivers' union also plays a strategic role in aiding the organizing and strike efforts of other unions.

By the time of the federation's fourth convention in 1959 it was apparent that expulsion from the AFL–CIO offered no sure road to ethical practices in the labor movement. In that year, the International Longshore Association, which had been expelled by the AFL prior to the merger, was readmitted to the AFL–CIO in spite of a widespread view that its "cleansing" was far from complete. In eliminating remaining pockets of corruption, pressure from within the federation may prove more effective than banishment from the house of labor.

Union democracy   Closely related to the problem of corruption, the basic character of union government has been called into question. Critics have pointed to distinctions between constitutional provisions and day-to-day practices. It is noted, for example, that less than 10 percent of union members attend local meetings; that, in spite of regular elections, most national union officials have lengthy tenure in office; and in four-fifths of presidential elections, the incumbent is unopposed. Moreover, it is claimed that rank-and-file members have only limited facilities for appeal from disciplinary action taken by national executive boards.

Defenders of union government point out that these procedures are not necessarily evidence of lack of democracy. Limited attendance at local meetings may reflect the members' satisfaction with union administration rather than the contrary. Participation greatly increases when important issues are being discussed or elections are being held; and members are kept informed about union business through daily contacts in the shop. Although there are obviously exceptions among the 60,000 to 70,000 locals in this country, local unionism generally meets high standards of democratic administration.

The absence of a "loyal opposition" in national union government (only the typographical union has developed a two-party system) is a more serious obstacle to the attainment of democratic goals. Even here, defenders stress the unions' need to maintain complete unity in the face of attacks by employers, courts, and government. They say that a union, like an army in the midst of a battle, cannot afford a division within its ranks. At any rate, it is pointed out that a union leader becomes so intimately associated with union business that he is often the most logical choice for a succession in office simply judged by qualifications and experience. Nonetheless, the lack of opposition may stem from a fear of retaliation and may permit abuses in union government. Some feel that democratic government cannot be considered complete until a formal opposition is encouraged.

The question of opposition is closely linked to the appeals procedures within unions. It is important that members who are fined or expelled by the union be afforded a rapid and inexpensive means of appeal to impartial tribunals. Almost all union constitutions provide for a system of appeals from the local to district and national officers, culminating in the national convention. But this can be a lengthy process, and impartiality is by no means assured. The Upholsterers Union and the United Automobile Workers earlier established Public Review Boards, composed of eminent outsiders who review union disciplinary actions referred to them.

Although full democracy in union government is a desirable goal, an additional consideration should be borne in mind when evaluating how well the unions are meeting the goal. Unions deal primarily with business enterprises, and these are seldom run on the principle of rank-and-file control. In furthering democracy, union leaders will not wish to undermine the effectiveness and responsibility of control required in their relations with management.

Labor unions today

During the 1960s, labor unions experienced moderate growth. Between 1961 and 1970, union rolls grew by 3 million, reversing the declines of the late 1950s. As noted in Figure 8/1, by 1970 union membership in the United States had increased to a new high, and, in contrast with the early '60s, the downward movement in the proportion of union members to the total labor force had reversed. Despite these increases in membership and in percentage of the total labor force, however, union membership among workers in non-agricultural establishments dropped from 33.4 percent in 1956 to about 28 percent in 1966. The explanation for this drop lies in the faster employment growth rate in trade, services, and government, which have not yet become heavily unionized. Further increases in union strength will depend on active organizing efforts in these new areas of potential membership, and on a continued expansion of employment in industries already organized.

Growth in employment in industries where unionization has been common, such as transportation, contract construction, and metal, machinery, and transportation-equipment manufacturing, has contributed to union gains in recent years. The nation's largest union, the Teamsters, has exhibited significant growth. Membership in the Auto Workers and Steelworkers unions has also increased, although the effects of changes in business activity have been felt to a greater extent. As a result, sharp declines were suffered in the 1957–58 recession. The International Brotherhood of Electrical Workers has registered steady growth for a number of years.

Since the 1957 expulsion of the Teamsters and two smaller affiliates, and the 1968 disaffiliation of the Auto Workers, there has been little change in the strength of the AFL–CIO within the entire union movement.

The size distribution of individual unions has also remained fairly constant during the past several years: the ten largest unions, each with over 400,000 members, represent about 45 percent of the total union membership; and 91 unions, about one-half of all unions, each with fewer than 25,000 members, represent less than 4 percent of total membership. The most significant shift in relative size is that of the American Federation of Government Employees (AFGE), which rose from the forty-third largest union in 1962 to the twenty-third by 1966. Substantial increases in union membership among government employees have resulted from the high growth rate in government employment and were encouraged after 1962, when President Kennedy granted collective-bargaining rights to federal employees.

Although in the past decade union membership has not expanded rapidly in the economy as a whole, in some unions the growth has been substantial. The nation's largest unions, the Automobile Workers and the Teamsters, both currently outside of the principal union federation, the AFL–CIO, have continued to grow rapidly. Each union had well over a million members in 1960, and by 1970 the Auto Workers had almost one-and-one-half-million members and the Teamsters were approaching the two-million mark.

Table 8/1.   Unions that gained 100,000 members or
more, 1960–70

Union	Membership			Increase 1960–70	
	1960	1968	1970	number	percent
Auto Workers (Ind.)	1,136,100	1,472,700	1,485,600	349,500	30.8
Teamsters (Ind.)	1,484,400	1,755,000	1,828,500	344,100	23.2
Retail Clerks	342,000	552,000	605,200	263,200	76.9
Government (AFGE)	70,300	294,700	324,900	254,600	362.2
State, County	210,000	364,500	444,500	234,500	111.7
Service Employees	272,000	389,000	435,000	163,000	59.9
Communications Workers	259,900	357,500	421,600	161,700	62.2
Electrical (IBEW)	771,000	897,100	921,700	150,700	19.5
Teachers	56,200	165,000	205,300	149,100	265.3
Laborers	442,500	553,100	580,000	137,500	31.1
Engineers, Operating	291,000	350,000	392,800	101,800	34.9

Source: "Labor Union and Employee Association Membership, 1970," data release of the U. S. Bureau of Labor Statistics, Sept. 13, 1971, p. 5.

As is seen in Table 8/1, the most phenomenal membership growth has occurred in white-collar and public-employee unions. The American Federation of Government Employees and the State, County and Municipal workers each had exceptionally large percentage increases in membership. The growth of professional unionism can be seen in the 265 percent increase in the membership of the American Federation of Teachers. White-collar union membership as a whole totaled 3.4 million in 1970, an increase of 177,000 during the prior two years.

By occupational group, about 15 percent of union members are white-collar workers and 85 percent are blue-collar workers. While union membership in manufacturing and nonmanufacturing industries has been declining as a proportion of total membership, membership in the public sector has continued to rise. Still, it is estimated that slightly more than half of manufacturing employment is organized, while the figures for nonmanufacturing and government are one-fourth and one-seventh, respectively. More than two-fifths of all union members are found in three major industries: metals and machinery, transportation, and construction. Unions with at least one million members represent other industry groups: in manufacturing, food and tobacco, clothing and leather, and transportation equipment; and in non-manufacturing, retail and wholesale trade and service industries.

About one-fifth of all union members in 1970 were women—4.3 million. Although only about one out of seven females in the labor force is a union member (as compared to one out of four males), the proportion of women union members is slowly rising. Two unions in the apparel industry, the International Ladies Garment Workers and the Amalgamated Clothing Workers, account for almost 18 percent of the female union members.

About one out of three union members are located in the three states with the largest numbers of nonagricultural workers, New York, California, and Pennsylvania. These states, together with Illinois, Ohio, and Michigan, account for more than half of all union members in the United States.

In addition to strength, there are other pressing issues that confront the labor movement. While average wages have continued to rise, the gains have often been achieved at the expense of a higher number of strikes and more worktime lost. Rising prices pose a threat to the real increases reflected in these wage gains. Another union goal, full employment, may suffer with efforts to stabilize prices.

The reasons for labor unrest are not limited to wage negotiation, nor are they confined to industry. Teachers, government workers, nurses, and professional athletes have been party to labor disputes where the issues have gone beyond economic ones. The California grape strike, in attempting to improve the status of the agricultural worker and gain recognition for him, involved political issues. Unions, which at one time faced charges of discrimination, have sometimes seen their role as that of a leader in achieving racial equality. More and better-paying jobs for blacks is not solely an economic issue but a social one as well.

While the public sector offers the greatest potential for union growth, public-service unions have been the center of special controversy over the right of public employees to strike. Unions argue that without the right to strike, workers have no means of pressuring public officials to negotiate in good faith, and that government workers share the needs and interests of all laborers in seeking better working conditions and higher wages. Opponents argue that the essential services of government should not be interrupted and that strikes against a sovereign body, the government, cannot be permitted. The inability to put government out of business through striking and the fact that government will not employ the tactic of the lockout further question the effectiveness of strikes in the public sector. Several alternative solutions to the problem of satisfying the demands of a growing number of public employees without disrupting the operation of government itself have been proposed: laws guaranteeing collective bargaining, creation of special NLRBs in the Federal Service, compulsory arbitration. These issues are discussed further in Chapters 7 and 9.

The mission of unions, with respect to social and political goals and their organizing activities, has caused a split within the union ranks. The break of the UAW from the AFL–CIO in 1968, the first such disaffiliation since the Teamsters Union was expelled in 1957, and the ensuing conflict between Meany's forces and Reuther's UAW followers laid the groundwork for the creation of the Alliance for Labor Action, formed in 1968 by the two disaffiliated unions. The AFL–CIO warned its members that recognition of or support for the rival organization would be grounds for expulsion. With the death of Walter Reuther and the removal of James Hoffa from leadership of the Teamsters, prospects were bright for reconciliation of the AFL–CIO and the two largest national unions in the 1970s.

It is seen, then, that the rapidly changing American scene of the 1970s poses critical challenges for the growth of the trade-union movement. Unions must not only adapt to the shifts in employment and a constantly changing economic environment; they must adjust their political and social goals to the changing outlook and attitudes of their employers.

Readings

Barbash, Jack. *American Unions: Structure, Government and Politics.* New York: Random House, 1967.

Bernstein, Irving. *Turbulent Years: A History of the American Worker 1933–1941.* Boston: Houghton Mifflin, 1970.

Chamberlain, Neil W., and John T. Dunlop. *Frontiers of Collective Bargaining.* New York: Harper & Row, 1967.

Marshall, Ray. *The Negro and Organized Labor.* New York: John Wiley & Sons, 1965.

Perlman, Selig. *History of Trade Unionism.* New York: Macmillan Co., 1922.

Rayback, Joseph G. *A History of American Labor.* New York: Free Press, 1966.

Sultan, Paul E. *The Disenchanted Unionist.* New York: Harper and Row, 1963.

Taft, Philip. *Organized Labor in American History.* New York: Harper and Row, 1964.

Ulman, Lloyd. *The Rise of the National Trade Union.* Cambridge Mass.: Harvard University Press, 1955.

Chapter Seven

Government Regulation of Labor–Management Relations

Introduction

The history of U. S. labor relations, especially since the 1930s, has seen the displacement of common law (court decisions) by legislative enactment as the primary source of public rules affecting unionism and collective bargaining. Government intervention in the labor field has continued to expand in the last three decades, and currently takes the form of a highly complex system of state and federal laws and administrative decisions. The historical impact of legislative changes is noted in Chapter 6. Major provisions can be conveniently summarized under five headings: union administration, compulsory union membership, labor–management relations, political activities, and national emergency disputes.

At the end of this chapter we raise the question: Is more government control needed?

Labor and the courts

Prior to the 1930s, court decisions rather than legislation governed the legal development of unionism and collective bargaining in the United States. In deciding issues presented to them by employers and government units, the courts relied on Anglo-Saxon common law. The first major case involving the right of workers to organize was that of the Philadelphia cordwainers (bootmakers) in 1806. The jury found the union of workers to be an illegal conspiracy and this decision set a precedent for a series of seventeen additional "conspiracy" cases in the following 36 years. Only in 1842 did an equally famous case, *Commonwealth v. Hunt,* provide some basis for organization by insisting that a combination of workers is an illegal conspiracy only if it can be shown to accomplish some criminal or unlawful purpose. However, even with the more liberal attitude provided by *Commonwealth v. Hunt,* unions could hope for only minimal encouragement from the courts for their efforts to organize.

Beginning in the 1880s, there was a growing use of the labor injunction: an employer would file a civil suit in a court of equity, charging that the initiation or continuance of a strike would result in irremediable damages. Upon the employer's request, the court would frequently issue injunctions prohibiting the union action. This device was successfully used to defeat the union in the famous Pullman strike of 1894, and was subsequently used to reduce the effectiveness of union strike power. Up until 1931 over 1,000 labor injunctions had been issued, almost all at the request of employers.

The courts were also used to restrict union power through their interpretation of the Sherman Antitrust Act of 1890. Although designed to eliminate business monopoly, this act was used even more effectively against union organization. In the famous Danbury Hatters Case of 1908, the Supreme Court found that a strike which damaged the employer was illegal under the Sherman Act because it interfered with interstate commerce. In subsequent cases, charges of antitrust violation were combined with court injunctions to prevent or halt boycotts, strikes, and other direct action by unions. As late as 1921, the Supreme Court in *Duplex Printing Press Company v. Deering* demonstrated that unions were still subject to the injunction in spite of an effort to provide some protection against it in the Clayton Act of 1914. The Norris-LaGuardia Act of 1932 when interpreted by the courts in conjunction with the Clayton Act finally provided a significant barrier against court injunctions. In the case of *United States v. Hutcheson* in 1941, the Supreme Court reversed the earlier series of decisions by declaring that neither picketing nor a boycott were enjoinable.

However, the occasional resurrection of court injunctions against union activities indicates that this legal procedure against unions is by no means dead. As indicated below in this chapter ("Should antitrust laws be applied to unions?"), the whole issue of the application of antitrust laws to unions, primarily through court action, is still very much with us.

Areas of government control

Certification and representation

As was noted in the preceding chapter, the National Labor Relations Act of 1935 (popularly known as the Wagner Act after its sponsor, Senator Robert Wagner) established the legal right of workers to form unions of their own choosing. By requiring employers to recognize a union and to bargain with the union in an appropriate unit, the Act gave an important impetus to the growth of the organized labor movement. (The procedures by which bargaining units are determined and representation established are discussed in further detail in Chapter 10). In addition to requiring that employers bargain with unions in good faith, Section 8 of the Wagner Act prohibited discrimination against workers because of their union activity, and the employer was also forbidden to provide financial support to any internal union to prevent outside organization. These company unions, long used by employers to prevent outside organization, were barred. The National Labor Relations Board, established by the Act, was given the responsibility of investigating charges that employers were engaged in such so-called "unfair labor practices."

For many months after passage of the Wagner Act, there was serious question as to whether the Supreme Court would find it constitutional, and many employers ignored its provisions. NLRB rulings can be, and regularly are, appealed to federal courts. In 1937, in the famous case of *National Labor Relations Board v. the Jones and Laughlin Steel Corporation* the Supreme Court upheld the constitutionality of the Wagner Act. Employers were now forced to accept it as the law of the land. They were prone to complain that the Act tilted the balance of power in favor of unions. Union leaders, on the other hand, contended that they needed the protections provided by the Wagner Act to offset the dominant power that employers naturally exercised over their employees. Employers were not only critical of the legislative provisions; they also charged that the NLRB was interpreting those provisions in a manner that favored unions. These charges focused primarily on the insistence that employers bargain in good faith about issues which were previously in the domain of employer discretion. The designation of appropriate bargaining units was also a butt of employer complaints. The unions stressed that the NLRB was simply carrying out its legislative mandate.

The Labor–Management Relations Act of 1947 (the Taft-Hartley Act) was designed by its sponsors to balance the alleged one-sidedness of the Wagner Act. However, it should be noted that, in spite of some concessions to employers and some restrictions on unions, the Wagner Act's basic system of union certification and representation was maintained. Its changes were that employers were given the right to speak out against a union during an organizing campaign; the closed shop was forbidden and states were given the power to legislate against the union shop; a list of unfair union practices was added to parallel the Wagner Act's list of unfair employer practices; and strikes that were determined to imperil the national health and safety could be enjoined for a period of 80 days.

Union leaders were as critical of the Taft-Hartley Act as employers had been of the Wagner Act; and for many years the elimination of the Taft-Hartley Act was a principal goal of labor's political action. However, just as the employers could not prove that the Wagner Act gave an unfair advantage to unions, unions could not demonstrate the damaging effects they attributed to the Taft-Hartley Act. In more recent years, the union's legislative struggle against the Taft-Hartley has been more subdued.

From the standpoint of collective-bargaining procedures, it is important to remember that the pendulum swing from Wagner to Taft-Hartley has left the basic procedures for certification and representation intact. These now appear to be fully accepted as basic institutions in the American collective bargaining system.

Union administration

Although a number of states legislated controls over specific aspects of union government prior to 1947, it was not until the Taft-Hartley Act that national efforts were made to regulate internal union affairs. The Act seeks to protect union members against such abuses as excessive dues and initiation fees, unwarranted expulsion from the union, and restrictions on admission. Officers must file reports on aspects of union finances and other administrative functions with the Secretary of Labor. Reports on the administration of welfare plans were required by the Welfare and Pension Plans Disclosure Act of 1958.

As a result of the McClellan Committee's disclosures of undemocratic and corrupt practices in some unions, the Landrum-Griffin Act (formally titled The Labor–Management Reporting and Disclosure Act) was passed in 1959. Designed to accomplish many of the same objectives as the Taft-Hartley Act in this field, the more recent legislation goes much further in establishing rules for union government:

1.   The act proclaims a "Bill of Rights of Members of Labor Organizations," guaranteeing individual rights of free participation in meetings and elections, as well as safeguards for fairness in cases of union disciplinary action.

2.   The Taft-Hartley reporting requirements are greatly expanded and the reports are to be public information. They must now include information on many constitutional provisions concerned with the union's administration as well as the financial affairs of the union and its officers.

3.   Trusteeships established over a subordinate unit of a union (that is, removal of the subordinate officers and establishment of direct control from the national or district office) must be in accordance with the union's constitution or for other worthy purpose, and must be reported to the Secretary of Labor within 30 days.

4.   The act provides a number of safeguards for the honesty of union elections, including maximum time limits between elections, secret ballots, and regulations governing nominations and candidacy.

5.   Provisions are made for the fiduciary responsibility of union officers, the bonding of officers, court suits against offending officers, and fines and imprisonment for embezzlement.

Compulsory union membership

The most prominent forms of "union security" clauses, involving compulsory union membership, were described earlier. In spite of their widespread adoption, they have come under increasing legislative attack in recent years. The closed shop is banned by the Taft-Hartley Act; and so-called right-to-work laws, which bar all contractual provisions that make union membership a condition of employment, have been passed by 19 states—but none of them except Indiana is a major industrial state, and Indiana later repealed its law. Efforts to enact or repeal these laws, however, have been hotly contested issues in a number of state elections.

Labor–management relations

In spite of many efforts toward its amendment or repeal, the Taft-Hartley Act is still the basic federal labor law. To the Wagner Act's provisions for representation elections and against unfair employer practices, which continue in effect, Taft-Hartley adds a list of unfair union practices, restrictions, and prohibitions. Like employers, unions are now also forbidden the use of coercion or discrimination in organizing campaigns. Severe restrictions are placed on such traditional union weapons as the secondary boycott, sympathy strike, and jurisdictional strike; and strikes which may cause a national emergency can be enjoined for 80 days.

In addition to this federal legislation, many states have labor-relations laws covering workers engaged in intrastate employment. In some cases the statutes are modeled after the federal law, and state labor-relations boards perform functions similar to those of the National Labor Relations Board under the Wagner and Taft-Hartley Acts. On the whole, however, state enactments are more restrictive than federal law on union activities. The Landrum-Griffin Act of 1959 is significant in the labor-relations field in that it gives scope to state jurisdiction over labor activities.

Political activities

The increase in labor's political activity since the 1930s has been noted above. As the political power of unions grew, efforts were made to restrict its scope through legislative enactment. The Taft-Hartley Act provides that union funds must not be used in federal political campaigns. As a result, to finance these political activities unions have been forced to call for voluntary contributions from their members.

A special effort has been made to reduce communist influence in labor affairs. Under the Landrum-Griffin Act, no person who is or has been a member of the Communist Party may hold a union or industrial-relations office within five years of such membership, unless approved by the United States Department of Justice.

National emergency disputes

The significance of strikes and some of the primary procedures for their settlement are discussed in Chapter 9, where we conclude that strikes as a whole are not a major problem for the national interest (whatever their serious effects on individual employers and employees in establishments where strikes occur), although some strikes in essential industries, if prolonged, could seriously endanger the public health, safety, or welfare. Such strikes, whether national or local, have been a focus of government concern and legislative action since the Railway Labor Act and, on a wider basis, since the passage of the Taft-Hartley Act. As a foremost scholar of labor legislation, Benjamin Aaron, has noted, these acts have now been in effect for 37 and 24 years respectively, and for at least the last 20 years there has been persistent criticism of the emergency dispute procedures, accompanied by a regular flow of new bills to repeal, revise, or supplement the existing emergency statutes.[1]

In spite of the many proposals for modification of the Railway Labor Act and of the emergency dispute procedures of the Taft-Hartley Act, Congress has not modified the existing labor-relations law. A primary reason for this legislative inaction appears to be a balance of power between those proposing changes and those opposed to changes in the present law. A continuing series of labor-relations crises on the railroads and serious strikes in such major industries as steel and autos have kept the question of national emergency strikes in the forefront of legislative review. It is likely that proposals for new dispute-settlement procedures will continue to lead the annual list of bills aimed at controlling labor–management relations.

One of the major difficulties in the present statutory provisions is the definition of an emergency dispute, and a number of the proposals for modifications have attempted to clarify this issue. The Railway Labor Act states that an emergency dispute is one that "threatens substantially to interrupt interstate commerce to a degree such as to deprive any section of the country of essential transportation service." Under the Taft-Hartley Act, an emergency dispute is "a threatened or actual strike or lockout affecting an entire industry or substantial part thereof, which will, in the opinion of the President, imperil the national health or safety if permitted to occur or to continue." Even under the Railway Labor Act, it is the President who decides when an emergency dispute exists. Recent legislative proposals have suggested that the President should consult with the Director of the Federal Mediation and Conciliation

---

[1]Benjamin Aaron, "National Emergency Disputes: Some Current Proposals," Spring Proceedings of the Industrial Relations Research Association, 7–8 May 1971.

Service before declaring an emergency, or that an emergency labor-disputes board should be established which would designate the emergency. It has also been proposed that disputes which cause regional emergencies should be designated under new legislation.

Whereas the Railway Labor Act and the Taft-Hartley Act call for a 60-day or an 80-day "cooling off" period, respectively, before a strike is permissible, a number of legislative proposals are designed to prevent emergency disputes from arising in the first place. For example, one recent proposal would establish a seven-member "national special industries commission" of experienced persons appointed by the President. The commission would be authorized to "study and investigate industries (determined by the Secretary of Labor to be particularly vulnerable to national emergency disputes), combinations or groups thereof, and problems relating thereto." The study would include ways and means by which collective bargaining might be improved by revision or supplementation so as to avoid or minimize emergency disputes, and would also evaluate the effectiveness and usefulness of mediation, conciliation, arbitration, and other procedures for supplementing collective bargaining.

Much discontent with the present procedures for handling emergency disputes is created by the strikes that are initiated or resumed after the cooling off period. Many of the new legislative proposals favor giving the President a choice of procedures (an "arsenal of weapons") for handling emergency disputes rather than a single statutory procedure. Before, after, or instead of the present cooling off period, the President might obtain a court injunction, urge Congressional action, appoint a compulsory arbitration tribunal, or even authorize government seizure of the struck plant. The most moderate recent proposals include a simple extension of the current 80-day injunction under the Taft-Hartley Act.

A recently proposed variant of compulsory arbitration is related to the final offers made by the parties: each party would submit two alternative final offers to the Secretary of Labor to be transmitted by the Secretary to the other party; the exchange of offers would be followed by five days of collective bargaining. If no settlement resulted, the parties would have two additional days in which to appoint a three-member, neutral panel to act as the "selector" of the final offer. The panel would be limited to a selection of "the most reasonable of the final offers submitted by the parties."

Benjamin Aaron concludes his analysis of the experience under the national emergency dispute provisions of the Railway Labor Act and the Taft-Hartley Act as follows:

Although there are many obvious shortcomings in our present statutory procedures, the number of disputes causing serious disruptions in operations and services essential to the health and safety of significant numbers of the population has been minimal. Rather than adopt any of the proposals discussed in this paper, I would rather rely on our present emergency procedures and, if necessary, on ad hoc legislation that Congress can always enact to deal with specific disputes that cannot adequately be dealt with in any other way.[2]

Should antitrust laws be applied to unions?

It has frequently been charged that unions are monopolies. Like business monopolies they are contrary to the public interest, and like business monopolies they should be controlled by the antitrust laws. A major difficulty in evaluating these charges is the variety of supporting arguments provided. The arguments are reducible to the contention that unions exercise monopoly power in preventing competition in the labor market, and that they thereby prevent the most efficient allocation of resources and cause unemployment, price increases, or both.

In its crudest form the argument states that unions are monopolistic because by representing workers as a group they prevent individual workers from competing for jobs and wages. Union-shop provisions further this objective, and if union membership is not open to all, workers can thereby be excluded from employment. Strikes and restriction of production reduce the supply of labor output to the firm. Jurisdictional strikes are designed to gain further control over labor supply.

More prevalent current claims that unions are monopolies center on the excessive bargaining power of unions and the uniformity of wages resulting from multiemployer bargaining, pattern bargaining, and national union controls over local bargaining. Uniformity, it is charged, reduces competition among firms, distorts the allocation of labor and other resources, and permits higher wages to be paid by the industry as a whole. These high wages may cause unemployment by pricing labor out of a particular industrial market. If the government succumbs to political pressure from unions to adopt expansionary monetary and fiscal policies, unemployment of this type may not occur; but in this case prices are likely to rise as employers will probably pass along to the public the increase in costs of production resulting from their higher wage bill.

In reply to these charges, defenders of unions state that some abuses such as the closed shop and jurisdictional strikes are already covered by provisions of the Taft-Hartley Act. Few unions are now able to limit the number of employees entering an industry. Although unions may have some effect on the *choice* of specific workers for employment (through seniority provisions, etc.), they have little control over the total supply of labor.

---

[2]Ibid.

Defenders indicate, further, that it has not been proven that the wage level which results from multiemployer bargaining is necessarily higher than that which results from single-plant bargaining. Moreover, there are some economists who contend that in inflationary periods unions have little power to raise wages above what they would be under nonunion conditions. In a tight labor market, employers are eager to raise wages in order to attract and retain a work force.

There is some evidence, however, that there are greater than average wage increases immediately after a plant is first organized; and unions are certainly instrumental in preventing a wage decline in periods of recession. Furthermore, nonunion employers often raise wages to forestall a union organizing campaign, and it is suspected that organized firms may use union wage pressure as a socially justifiable reason for even greater than proportional price increases.

It should be observed, however, that economists are by no means certain about the effects of wage increases on employment and prices.

A wage increase will have very different effects on employment and prices depending on how one or more of the following questions are answered:

1. *Is efficiency increased in response to the wage increase?*

2. *Are employers optimistic or pessimistic about the effect of the wage increase on their operations?*

3. *Is the wage increase financed out of profits or bank borrowing?*

4. *What is the state of the economy and the direction of government monetary-fiscal policy at the time of wage increase?*

This discussion, brief though it is, should make it clear that the relationship of unions to price rises and levels of employment is highly complex, and there are dangers to simple answers concerning the causal nexus. In addition, it is likely that both critics and defenders of unionism tend to place too much emphasis on monetary gain. Scholars in the field are not in agreement concerning the wage advantage accruing to union members. Although unions have played a more positive role in achieving pension plans and other supplementary benefits, many of these too might have been achieved even in the absence of unions.

What, then, is the principal role of unions in our society? It may be that workers gain much more in social, psychological, and political benefits than in economic advantage. The grievance procedure and such protections as seniority give the worker a feeling of security. He would call it industrial democracy. For many workers, it means a great deal to be able to stand up to the boss, secure in the knowledge that they are protected against arbitrary action. In the political realm, unions provide a countervailing force to the influence of business, agriculture, and other pressure groups. Although the primary benefit of union political action accrues to labor, society as a whole may benefit from balance in the political process.

Many of the responses of union defenders provide valid answers to particular indictments of union monopoly. But even the staunchest union defenders cannot deny that it is the purpose of unionism to prevent competition in the labor market. This is the whole rationale of collective bargaining and it has been supported by legislation since 1935. Even earlier the Clayton Act stated that "labor is not a commodity." There are human values which it is public policy to protect against some ill effects of competition.

The term "monopoly," borrowed from the production and sale of commodities, is not suited to the labor market and becomes rather meaningless in this context. Some unions may indulge in abusive practices which the public would want to prevent, but specific legislation aimed at these abuses is preferable to a blunderbuss attack on unions through laws designed to curb business monopoly.

Is more government control needed?

We have seen that by attempting to achieve benefits for their members unions may also create problems for society. The power of organized labor has so grown that it can no longer be held that unions are simply private, voluntary associations which, like clubs and churches, should be free from public intervention. As has been noted above, governing authorities, having taken the view that union actions vitally affect the public interest, have increasingly brought unions within their legislative purview. It remains to be asked whether this process has already gone too far or not far enough. What are the gains and costs of government control over unions and collective bargaining?

The gains to be derived from government intervention often seem apparent. When a strike threatens essential production, when evidence of union corruption is disclosed, when an innocent employer is caught in a jurisdictional dispute, the cry naturally arises for legislative action. But not so apparent as the gains are the costs involved in such intervention.

Foreign students of labor relations viewing the American scene are struck by our attempt to solve all problems by "passing a law." The chief danger of this approach is that it has no logical end. The snowballing effect of government control in the last 35 years has been recounted above. The Wagner Act was "needed" to spell out labor protections, some of which had been introduced in earlier legislation but were not clear or generally applicable. The Taft-Hartley Act was "needed" to restore the balance in labor–management relations by granting protection to employers and the public. The Landrum-Griffin Act was "needed" to strengthen provisions and fill in gaps found in the Taft-Hartley Act.

It is almost axiomatic of legislative control in the labor field that faults can readily be found with existing law, and these are almost invariably to be corrected by more law. Inevitably, the cry for further intervention continues. Demands are now made for an extension of the antitrust laws to unions, for a tightening of restrictions on "national emergency" strikes, and for some means of discouraging wage increases. Other areas for government control can undoubtedly be found.

It is interesting to note that some "rugged individualists" who deplore government intervention in other areas of our economy are eager to see greater intervention in the labor field. But, as recent legislation has disclosed, controls over unions are usually accompanied by controls over management. Wage controls are generally associated with price controls. And government settlement of strikes often involves the dictation of terms to private industry.

Fruitful areas for additional government intervention may well be revealed by the future course of labor relations. But some scholars in the field are now looking toward a reversal of the trend of the last 35 years, toward an era when greater faith is placed in the willingness and ability of the participants in American industrial relations to meet their obligations without undue public action. Although this view runs counter to recent experience, there are also some hopeful signs; and practice in other democratic countries indicates that the growth of union–management relations need not be accompanied by an increasing complex of legislative controls.

Readings

Bok, Derek C., and John T. Dunlop. *Labor and the American Community.* New York: Simon and Schuster, 1970.

Evans, Robert, Jr. *Public Policy Toward Labor.* New York: Harper and Row, 1965.

Fanning, John H., "The Taft-Hartley Act—Twenty Years Later," in *NYU Twentieth Annual Conference on Labor.* New York: Matthew Bender and Co., 1968.

Kassalow, Everett M. *Trade Unions and Industrial Relations: An International Comparison.* New York: Random House, 1969.

Meltzer, Bernard D. "Labor Unions, Collective Bargaining, and the Anti-Trust Laws," *University of Chicago Law Review,* Vol. 32, Summer 1965.

Estey, Martin S., Philip Taft, and Martin Wagner, eds. *Regulating Union Government.* New York: Harper and Row, 1964.

Gregory, Charles. *Labor and the Law.* New York: W. W. Norton and Co., 1961.

Shister, Joseph, Benjamin Aaron, and Clyde W. Summers, eds. *Public Policy and Collective Bargaining.* New York: Harper and Row, 1962.

Chapter Eight

Collective Bargaining: From Private to Public Sectors

Introduction: industrial relations systems

International comparisons

The system of collective bargaining that has developed in North America is a product of the philosophy of workers and management and reflects the economic-legal-political environment in which it operates. This is equally true of other countries and other systems of employer–employee relations.

It must be remembered that unions are not necessarily synonymous with collective bargaining, and collective bargaining does not always imply a system of contractual agreements. In the United States, a formal pattern of collective bargaining contracts accompanied the growth of unionism. In some other countries, collective agreements emerged much more slowly, either because union philosophy opposed them or because employer opposition was strong enough to prevent their development.

Similarly, the content of collective bargaining agreements may differ from country to country. Most notable is how much more union security provisions, such as the closed shop or the union shop, are emphasized in the United States than in European countries. A tradition of worker solidarity, often based on ideological loyalty, makes such provisions less necessary in the eyes of European union leaders. Important components of the package of fringe benefits in the United States, such as health insurance and retirement pensions, are typically covered in Europe by legislation rather than collective bargaining agreements. In countries outside of North America, government is seen to play a much larger role in determining substantive issues between unions and management. In Canada and the United States, although government intervention in collective bargaining has grown consistently, it is still confined primarily to the procedural framework of collective negotiations rather than the content of agreements.

The extent of government intervention in union–management relations is likely to reflect the comparative roles played by the state and private enterprise in the economy as a whole. In countries where the government's role in the economy is greater than it is in the United States, it is not surprising to find its position more dominating in labor–management relations as well. These differences are especially marked when we compare North American collective bargaining with the industrial relations systems of Eastern Europe or with those of many developing nations in Africa and Asia.

The stage of industrialism and technological advance in different countries also affects systems of industrial relations. Unions and collective bargaining have typically lagged in agriculture because of the large number of small farms and family farms. Thus, countries still dominated by an agricultural economy usually have less collective bargaining between unions and management than in most Western nations, and the nature of union–employer relations is bound to differ from that of more technologically advanced economies.

Intersectoral comparisons

These same factors—the philosophy of workers and management, the extent of private competition in product markets, and the state of technology in production—shape differences in collective bargaining systems *within* as well as *among* countries. Although the bargaining procedures and issues in various American industries may appear similar to each other as compared with those of Eastern Europe and Africa, there are important differences among them; for example, the structural arrangements, content, and techniques of bargaining in coal mining differ from those in auto manufacturing or in laundries and dry cleaning. The differences result from the greater militancy and solidarity of coal miners, from the large number of small producing units competing in a national market, from the methods of coal production and the rapid advance of mechanization in recent years. At the same time, the unusual hazards of coal mining have resulted in greater government intervention than in most other American industries. These factors, common to coal production everywhere, have brought about similarities in the *content* of coal-mining agreements in different countries even while contrasting political-economic systems have dictated differences in union–management *procedures*.

The factors that explain collective bargaining differences among nations and among industries are also of basic significance in explaining differences between blue-collar and white-collar employment and between private and public sectors. Unions and collective bargaining have lagged among white-collar workers not only because of a difference in their philosophy and attitudes but also because of contrasts with blue-collar workers in the methods (technology) by which they produce their goods and services. As in the case of industrial workers, the factors interact. Since the "production methods" of white collar workers stress mental rather than manual effort, they often tend to identify with management rather than labor. But these differences in philosophy and attitudes cannot always overcome the basic similarities characteristic of all employees, and white-collar collective bargaining is now increasing. However, as is seen later in this chapter ("Bargaining in the public sector"), collective bargaining among professional employees takes forms significantly different from those of blue-collar workers.

If the role of government is important in explaining differences in collective bargaining among nations and among industries, it is crucial in distinguishing the industrial-relations system in private employment from that of public employment. As an employer, government inhibits the use of the strike, collective bargaining's ultimate sanction. When this inhibition is combined with the negative white-collar attitude toward unions, a lag inevitably occurs in the growth of collective bargaining for such employees as teachers and nurses. And yet, the public is the most rapidly developing sector of collective bargaining. As is noted below, however, when government dominates to the extent of becoming the direct employer, collective bargaining among its employees must differ in important regards from that of private employment.

These differences in collective bargaining among nations, industries, types of workers, and sectors of the economy must be kept in mind in reading this and the succeeding chapter. Although the discussion emphasizes and draws conclusions from the American blue-collar experience, collective bargaining is actually a "many-splendored thing." Only occasional references can be made to the important contrasts with other countries. Greater stress is given to the differences between the blue-collar tradition and white-collar bargaining in public employment.

Bargaining agents and procedures

The process of union recognition

Before a union can bargain on behalf of its members it must gain from the employer recognition of its status as bargaining representative. The history of American labor–management relations is replete with bitter struggles for union recognition. In the 1930s, especially after the formation of the CIO, the issue of union recognition was a principal cause of strikes. In autos, steel, and other major industries, unions attempted to convince employers that they were the legitimate spokesmen for employees in their factories and should therefore be recognized for bargaining on wages and other terms of employment. When employers refused to grant such recognition, the new unions resorted to coercive tactics, such as the sit-down strikes in the auto plants, and violence and bloodshed sometimes followed.

Partly as a result of these violent episodes, the Wagner Act (National Labor Relations Act) of the mid-30s provided a legal procedure for the attainment of union recognition as the collective-bargaining agent. The federal legislation was followed by a number of state laws for employees and unions within their jurisdiction. With passage of the Wagner Act, the customary procedure for obtaining union recognition is that the union file a request with the National Labor Relations Board that it be certified as the collective-bargaining agent. However, since the employer may contest the union's claim to represent a majority of his employees, or since other unions may make such competing claims, an election is customarily conducted by the NLRB in order to determine the views of the employees in the bargaining unit. If a number of unions are competing for representation rights, the employees may be faced with several alternative choices on the election ballot, one for each of the unions seeking to represent them and the alternative, "no union."

· However, before the NLRB can conduct the election, it must determine the appropriate unit to be covered in the election, that is, the appropriate bargaining unit in the particular labor–management situation under consideration. This first step in the process of union recognition and collective bargaining might appear to be a simple one, but it has posed some of the thorniest problems faced by the NLRB. Should the Board select a single craft within a plant as an appropriate bargaining unit and conduct an election to determine which union should represent the members of that craft in negotiating a separate agreement with the employer? Or should the whole plant be designated as the appropriate bargaining unit, thereby permitting all non-supervisory employees to participate in the election, resulting in a single union to represent them all in negotiating a collective-bargaining contract? Or would it be appropriate under some circumstances to have employees in several plants of one company covered by a single collective bargaining agreement? And, to extend the boundaries of an appropriate bargaining unit even further, should the NLRB designate a number of companies or even a whole industry as an entity in which an election would be held, a union be recognized as bargaining representative, and a single collective bargaining contract be negotiated? In practice, the NLRB has made all of these choices under varying environmental circumstances. However, the choice is seldom made without one group or another contending that an alternative choice would have been more valid.

Factors influencing the size of bargaining units   Of the 150,000 union contracts in the United States, the predominant type is the single-company agreement. This is especially true in manufacturing industries. In nonmanufacturing, as well as in some manufacturing industries, most of the collective bargaining agreements cover more than one employer. In some industries, such as in building construction, retailing, and a variety of service industries such as laundries, dry cleaning establishments, and restaurants and hotels, multiemployer collective-bargaining contracts may be restricted to a particular locality. In other industries, the multiemployer agreement may include firms in wide regions of the country, even approaching a national contract; most prominent among such extensive agreements in the nonmanufacturing sector are those in bituminous coal mining and in such transportation industries as trucking, shipping, and railroads. In manufacturing, clothing unions have extensive regional multiemployer contracts, and in glassware manufacturing the collective bargaining agreements approach a national coverage. Employees in bakeries, canneries, breweries, and lumber mills are also frequently covered by a widespread regional collective-bargaining contract.

What explains these widely differing patterns of size in collective bargaining units? A complex network of economic and noneconomic factors may be at work in shaping such decisions. However, the distinguishing causal forces can usually be placed under three broad headings:

a. Competitive forces in the product market   It is almost an axiom in union growth and structural development that employers who compete in the same product market will consistently try to establish some uniformity in wages and other labor costs. If labor costs of one competing employer are forced significantly out of line with those of other firms in the same product market, the competitive disadvantage is likely to result in either bankruptcy or a rejection of the union. An employer who pays high union wages will insist that other employers be brought into line; and workers in low-wage plants are likely to make comparisons with their better-situated brethren in organized plants in order to gain some measure of equal status. As one of the pioneers of labor history, John R. Commons, has noted, the desire to effect some standardization among competing firms gave the initial impetus to the development of national unions, and this factor continues to explain the spread of multi-employer collective-bargaining agreements.

Where product market competition is essentially local, as in retailing, printing, or building construction, the multiemployer bargaining unit is also local. Where employers compete with each other over wide regional areas the multiemployer contracts are also regional, as in clothing or glass manufacturing. The student who knows the geographic spread of product competition can often predict the scope of collective-bargaining units.

In spite of the importance of the area of product competition in determining the extent of multiemployer contracts, it is obvious from the case of automobiles that the intensity of competition is also of crucial importance. Extensive multiemployer contracts are most likely to develop where firm size is small and the intensity of competition among them is great. When the product market is controlled by one or a few firms, the union can often approach the results of a widespread multiemployer contract without actually engaging in multiemployer bargaining. This process is often known as pattern bargaining—a procedure in which a collective agreement is reached with a single major employer, such as General Motors, with other employers in the industry then following the established pattern in essential details. Recent experience in the steel industry has indicated that pattern bargaining may result in a growing cooperation among employers and end up in a species of multiemployer bargaining.

b. Technological factors in production   Methods of production may determine whether a bargaining unit will cover an entire plant or whether separate craft units will be carved out of the larger industrial pie. Differences in production methods in different firms within an industry may also help determine whether multiemployer bargaining will be established and maintained. In the first instance, the NLRB is likely to recognize a separate bargaining unit for skilled craftsmen in an industrial plant if this group of workers is clearly set aside from other workers in the plant by location and skill level, as determined by the technological processes of these firms' operations. Where there are marked differences in productive efficiency among firms in a particular industry, considerable strain might develop within any multiemployer bargaining arrangement because of the resultant differences in labor costs under a common wage contract. Such differences in technological development have hampered the maintenance of a multiemployer contract in the pressed and blown glassware industry.

The nature of technology also helps to determine the relative importance of local versus national issues. In some industries such matters as working conditions and safety—essentially local issues—take on great importance because of the nature of production; and when such local issues predominate over national concerns such as wages, a smaller rather than a larger bargaining unit is likely to result.

c. Power relationships   The size and scope of bargaining units may frequently reflect the relative bargaining power of groups within the union, the power relationships between the union and management, or the relative political power of the parties. A union is not a homogeneous entity. Differences in skill, location, age or a variety of other characteristics may pit one group of union members against another in their preference of bargaining units. Similarly, employers may differ as to the preferred size and scope of a collective bargaining unit because of some of the factors listed above as well as a variety of other professional or personal reasons. The appropriate bargaining unit finally put forth as the preference of unions and management will reflect the relative bargaining power relationships within these units as well as the bargaining power relationships between unions and management in a particular firm or industry.

The size of the bargaining unit becomes in itself an important ingredient of bargaining tactics. If the union feels that more could be gained through a widespread, multiemployer agreement, then it will attempt to persuade the employer and, if necessary, the NLRB, of the virtues of such a bargaining unit. However, if the employer evaluates the situation in the same terms as the union, he might then conclude that a smaller bargaining unit will provide him with the greatest bargaining power in resisting union demands. The resultant decision of the NLRB may well reflect the relative power positions of the two protagonists as well as their powers of persuasion and the "merits" of the case. Governmental policy is itself a result of bargaining power relationships as well as a factor influencing relative bargaining power. Thus, the NLRB moved from a preference for industrial bargaining units in the 1930s to a greater concern for separate craft units under the pressure of AF of L criticism. A further move in this direction occurred when political pressures increased the possibility of separate craft units under the Taft-Hartley Act.

Although government policy in labor–management relations is influenced by the power and political pressures of the groups that government seeks to regulate, the NLRB is not unmindful of the market and technological factors discussed above. Even though there is now a tendency to permit separate craft units when skilled workers insist upon separate representation, companywide bargaining units continue to dominate in many mass-production industries. Here technological factors are of basic importance. It is felt that the continuous, integrated processes of production in such industries as steel, autos, and aluminum dictate the need for large companywide bargaining units, unfragmented by separate craft designations.

Petitions and elections   Within any bargaining unit an election to determine which union will serve as the bargaining agent of the employees in that unit is customarily initiated through a petition filed with the regional office of the National Labor Relations Board. The petition may be filed by employees, a union, or the employer. Having determined that it has proper jurisdiction and that the bargaining unit is an appropriate one, the Board must then determine that the employees or the union forming the petition have a reasonable claim to representation. Specifically, those claiming representation rights must show they are favored by at least 30 percent of the employees in the bargaining unit before an election will be authorized. However, after a petition has been filed by one union, any other union may be placed on the ballot even if it shows it has only one vote, that is, one card signed by an employee in the bargaining unit.

The NLRB will conduct a hearing if the regional director feels that a question of representation affecting interstate commerce exists. The hearing will be conducted for the purpose of discussing the appropriate bargaining unit as well as the appropriateness of an election to determine the bargaining representative. If, after the hearing, it is determined that an election should be held, the Board has the responsibility for overseeing the election and insuring that it is conducted properly.

Having determined the validity of the election procedures, the Board will certify the union that polls the majority of the votes cast as the exclusive bargaining agent of the employees in the unit for a period of at least one year. Once the union is certified as a bargaining agent by the NLRB, the employer is required by law to bargain with it. Failure to do so would constitute an unfair labor practice, and this could result in legal action on behalf of the certified union. However, if the fortunes of the union deteriorate and the employer has reason to feel that the union no longer represents a majority of the employees in the bargaining unit, he may petition the Board for a new election. If a year has passed since the last election, the Board may act favorably on the employer's petition and the election process will be launched again.

This account of the procedural steps for union recognition may tell the reader more than he wants or needs to know about the practical processes of collective bargaining. It is recounted here for two principal purposes: first, these detailed and orderly legal procedures are in sharp contrast with the strikes, and frequently violence, which were associated with the organizing drives of the 1930s. Even though the public may sometimes feel that strikes continue to plague the American collective-bargaining scene, there has clearly been marked progress toward orderly legal procedures in the last three decades.

Secondly, these procedures for union recognition are presented above because they also contrast with the collective-bargaining procedures in a number of other countries. On the one hand, the bargaining in such countries as Sweden and The Netherlands is much more dominated by national considerations and national negotiations. On the other hand, the bargaining in such countries as France is characterized by a notable absence of the detailed legal processes that have emerged since the passage of the Wagner Act in the United States.

The growth of employers' associations

The growth of multiemployer bargaining units presupposes the development of employer bargaining associations. Associations of employers, designed to further a variety of business goals, have existed in the United States for some time. Historical evidence of the existence of master bakers' and master carpenters' associations goes back as far as the mid-eighteenth century. However, it was only toward the beginning of the present century that associations of employers formed in large numbers in order to combat growing union strength. If the formation of unions can be construed as a reaction to unilateral employer activities in the labor field, it is equally true to say that bargaining associations of employers developed in reaction to union strength. A number of the most prominent national associations of employers that formed after 1900 were also among the most belligerent in conducting vigorous antiunion campaigns.

It was only after the Wagner Act of 1935, in which collective bargaining was established as national policy, that most employer associations departed from their public stance of belligerent antiunionism. Although their opposition to unions had not ceased, many associations entered into negotiations with unions, and used their coordinated activities to develop greater bargaining power.

The principal advantages seen by employers in association bargaining are the prevention of "whipsaw" tactics by the union (playing one employer against another) and the pooling of resources in order to employ expert collective-bargaining personnel. These advantages are especially important for small employers in citywide bargaining in such industries as building construction, retailing, and local service trades. In some cities, especially on the West Coast, the employer association goes beyond the negotiation of a master contract. Experts employed by the association also process grievances which arise in the application and administration of the collective-bargaining agreement. The centralization of grievance handling through an employers association not only provides expertise which might not be available in individual small companies, but it also prevents the union from using a favorable grievance settlement in one company to enforce a similar doctrine throughout the multiemployer bargaining unit. A central handling of grievance procedures can guard against the establishment of a precedent that may be unwelcome in other firms.

In addition to increased strength in bargaining negotiations, employer associations provide an opportunity for the pooling of funds in the event of a strike. Relatively weak firms, which might succumb to union demands if forced to withstand a strike alone, may be placed in a better position to wait out the union if supporting funds are forthcoming from affluent firms in the association. Such systems of "strike insurance" can and have been developed by groups of employers even in the absence of a formal association.

In view of the advantages of employer associations in meeting the bargaining power of unions, one might ask not why employer associations have developed in the United States but why they do not exist in all industries where union organization is strong. In the automobile industry, for example, the Auto Workers Union regularly singles out one of the major companies as a target for its intensive negotiations and a possible strike. Frequently, the strategy adopted is one of concentrating on the firm most likely to give in. The agreement reached with the first company is then used as a pattern for negotiations and settlements with other firms in the industry. A similar procedure is followed in the electrical industry, and in the steel industry a group of major producers is used as the pattern-setter in extending the contract provisions to smaller companies in the industry.

In spite of the apparent drawbacks suffered by companies because of their failure to develop formal association bargaining in these pattern-setting procedures, the drawbacks may be more apparent than real. Because the number of firms in these industries is usually small, coordination of employer bargaining procedures may be possible without formal association membership. There may also be a fear of federal antitrust action in the event of formal association activities. In other instances, the formal association of employers may be deemed contrary to the autonomy and independence of employer action which has been widely espoused as a hallmark of the American enterprise system. Under these circumstances, the pattern-setting collective-bargaining arrangement may offer advantages to employers as well as to unions, thereby precluding the need for formal association bargaining.

Negotiating techniques and weapons

Some have likened collective bargaining negotiations to a ritual dance in which both parties act out their assigned roles, knowing full well how it will end. The union negotiators must initially ask for much more than they can ever hope to receive or, as in some recent national negotiations, they must initially leave somewhat unclear exactly what they demand from the employer. The employer must receive the union's initial demands with groans and cries of alarm, and insist that it is not possible to provide much of anything by way of benefits in the contract negotiations this year. Collective bargaining as a stylized game is reflected in the following poetic description of a collective bargaining session:

We wheedled and threatened and blustered,
We ranted and wrangled and roared;
We chided and fretted, we scoffed and we petted,
We snickered and wept and implored;
We groveled and swore and demanded,
We spurned and we fawned and we brayed,
We trampled on data, we tossed ultimata,
We grumped and we stamped and inveighed;
We whimpered and simpered and shouted,
Pretended, defended, and doubted;
We smiled and we jested, reviled and protested,

Debated, orated and scouted;
We fumed and we sneered and we whined,
We flattered, cajoled, and maligned,
Consented, revoked, and declined . . .
And finally the contract was signed![1]

There is undoubtedly much truth in the view of collective bargaining as a ritual. However, one must not exaggerate this aspect of negotiating techniques. The fact that many strikes occur contrary to the desires of both parties is an indication that the roles and tactics of the parties during the negotiations are not preordained, leading to an end known to all.

Negotiations tend to reach higher levels of professionalism as greater expertise is developed in both union and management teams. The degree of expertise and professionalism is often contingent upon the nature of the bargaining unit. In small, one-company bargaining units, the union's bargaining committee is usually elected by the rank and file and often includes the principal officers of the local union. A regional business agent or representative, appointed by the national union, may aid the local bargaining committee in its negotiations. The company will usually be represented in such local bargaining by its top officers, frequently with the aid of an attorney. In larger companies a Labor Relations Director or a vice president in charge of Industrial Relations will head the company's negotiating team. Since he spends full time on labor-relations matters, he develops an expertise matching that of the union's business agent.

The demands prepared by a local bargaining committee for presentation to company negotiators usually emerge from a membership meeting and are then honed and shaped, frequently moderated or eliminated by the local union's bargaining committee. Company negotiators usually prepare by anticipating the union's demands.

In regional or national negotiations the union's negotiating team will customarily be headed by a top national union officer, and the union's initial demands will usually be drafted by the national executive board or a subcommittee drawn from the board. Delegates of local unions must then approve the initial draft before the list is presented to company negotiators. Frequently local unions will give the national negotiators considerable leeway in presenting particular demands, approving broad guidelines for action in particular areas.

In spite of the lengthy preparations which may be carried out by both parties prior to the inception of the negotiations, the parties' positions will usually undergo constant reappraisal after the initial demands of the union

---

[1]Quoted by Henry Mayer, taken from, "Should Politics Make Mediators Expendable?," *Labor Law Journal,* Vol. 4, No. 5 (May 1953), p. 317.

have been presented and the initial reaction of the employer is set forth. Negotiations are often carried on over a period of weeks and even months. Both sides will redraft their versions of contract terms many times before a version emerges which both parties feel they can sign. With each redraft, the union negotiators must report to some broader constituency, either within a local union or, if the negotiations are conducted at a national level, with representatives of a number of local unions. The employers' drafts will be circulated among key company officials, and, sometimes, officials of other companies will be apprised of the changing employer position even if there is no formal employer association. Suppliers of the employers' factors of production, or important consumers of the employers' product, as well as financial institutions which may have provided loans to the employer, may all feel that they have a stake in the course of his negotiations with the union.

As the deadline for contract termination, and a possible strike, comes closer, the parties may no longer be able to afford the luxury of lengthy study, redrafting, and ratification by constituents, and there will be more frequent caucuses during the course of negotiations. Demands and issues which were characterized as precious to both parties at the outset of negotiations, may be dropped, and the union may trade one requested benefit for another. But both parties usually view the contract terms as a "package." Even though they might initial their agreement to particular provisions and temporarily dispose of them as they move on to the next issue, they will not customarily admit to having agreed upon any one item in the new contract until they have agreed upon all of them.

It is frequently part of bargaining tactics to adopt a pose of belligerence or intransigence with regards to any possible concession on particular items. However, the parties must guard against carrying such attitudes too far. On the one hand, the federal law of the land (duplicated in many states) states that the parties must "bargain in good faith." Although there is considerable difference of opinion as to the specific meaning, parties to the negotiations have been charged with an unfair labor practice because they showed a lack of willingness to engage in the customary "give and take" that one expects in collective-bargaining negotiations. On the other hand, belligerence and intransigence carried too far may lead to a real breakdown in negotiations, culminating in a strike that neither party wants. As in any negotiations, it is not always easy to know when your opponent is bluffing or whether your own bluff may be called. Many strikes have been caused by one party's miscalculation of the real motives and intent of the party across the bargaining table.

Among the tactics frequently employed by negotiators is the specification of a constraint on concessions placed by forces beyond the control of the negotiators. Union negotiators may let it be known that even though the negotiators would themselves like to be "quite reasonable" in agreeing with the company position, the membership would "never ratify such an agreement." Company negotiators may let it be known that financial interests or "the stockholders" would "be up in arms" if a proposed issue were settled on the union's terms. In negotiations with public employee unions, employer contentions along these lines may take the more realistic form of asserting that the legislature, the city council, the county board or the school board would never approve a concession which the employer negotiators would be "only too willing to grant."

After sufficient time in negotiations, subcommittees, including representatives from both parties, may be established to tackle issues which appear to be especially intractable or which may be too technical for discussion by large groups in the heated atmosphere of the customary bargaining session. Falling in the latter category may be such issues as time study, job evaluation, or other contractual provisions that may be affected by technological changes in the method of production. Carrying this procedure farther, some have stressed the need for negotiating sessions for the discussion of complex technical issues divorced from the regular contract negotiations. Such "continuous" bargaining was adopted in the steel industry in the early 1960s to deal with such matters as the use of seniority in layoffs and the subcontracting of work outside the steel mills. Although there has been some tendency for this procedure to spread to other industries, internal dissension within the steel union, affecting the outcome of its presidential election, may have served to inhibit the widespread adoption of such continuing contacts between contract negotiations.

One of the reasons why continuous negotiations failed to spread more rapidly is the apparent necessity of a crisis atmosphere for the final settlement of many negotiating issues. Even though weeks of negotiations and the exchange of drafts and redrafts of contract provisions may precede the date of contract termination, relatively few negotiators appear to be able to reach final agreement on the most intractable issues, and therefore on the total "package," until shortly before the date on which the union threatens to strike under the traditional slogan of "no contract, no work." As one veteran negotiator for the Auto Workers Union put it, "The major requirement of a good negotiator in collective bargaining is simply physical stamina. The man who can outlast his opponent across the table during those all-night sessions is the one who will emerge victorious." Although there is some truth in this remark, the contract provisions that are finally embodied in most major collective-bargaining agreements—even though final agreement may be reached only under the pressures of an imminent strike—are usually well considered and more thoroughly constructed than the union official's statement would imply.

Frequently a smaller committee, including representatives of the two parties, will prewrite the contract provisions after an agreement has been reached on them in principle during the last moments of heated negotiations. Such redrafting, which sometimes includes more than simply changes in editorial style, helps to produce a more consistent and unambiguous set of provisions, while not violating the basic intent and understanding of the parties at the negotiating table.

The negotiating parties cannot always escape the Damoclean sword of an imminent strike even after they have reached agreement in their negotiating sessions. The union's threat that certain provisions, which may be agreeable to the union negotiators, will not be ratified by the rank and file membership is sometimes more than an idle bargaining ploy. There is evidence that a growing number of tentative agreements presented to union members by their negotiators are failing to receive membership ratification. Sometimes (although rarely) the union negotiators make a public statement in support of the negotiated package while privately urging the membership not to accept it. The growing failure of membership ratification appears to be part of a general era of protest and opposition to the so-called "establishment." A generation gap exists in some unions as well as in other institutions, and this may be exacerbated by a skill gap and other divisive issues within the union. Some students of such matters have placed the failure rate of membership ratification as high as ten percent of all offered tentative agreements. If the rank and file members refuse to ratify the negotiators' tentative agreement, the parties must return to the bargaining table or contemplate the definite possibility of a strike. A strike may well follow a failure of membership ratification since the management negotiators may feel that they gave their final concessions at the bargaining session that resulted in the tentative agreement.

Ratification is also frequently required for the company's team of negotiators. However, the negotiators on the management team usually have fewer bases to touch, and they can keep in reasonably close touch with their constituents as the negotiations proceed. Consequently, the employer representatives in the negotiations can usually feel much more confident that their agreement at the bargaining table will be acceptable to those they represent.

Issues and content of the agreement

The most pressing issues in contract negotiations will differ according to how long the parties have been engaged in a contractual relationship as well as according to the market forces, the technological conditions, and the power relationships discussed above. However, in spite of the widely varying environmental conditions under which unions and management negotiate, there is much consistency in the types of issues that confront the parties, and most collective bargaining agreements have a similarity in their pattern of provisions. In most blue-collar contract negotiations, the principal issues are wages and fringe benefits and measures for employee protection usually associated with seniority provisions. In most long-standing negotiating relationships the question of union security (check-off of dues, the union shop) has already been settled. Newer unions may still seek such security status, however; and after receiving recognition of the union as bargaining representative and an automatic deduction of union dues from the employee's paycheck, the new union will seek to obtain an agreement on a provision which makes union membership or the payment of union dues a condition of continued employment in the establishment. The former is known as the union shop and the latter is usually termed the "agency shop." (The closed shop, that is, a specific provision that only union members will be hired, is outlawed by federal legislation.)

Unions of long standing have also usually achieved a detailed grievance procedure for handling disputes over interpretation and application of the agreement. In almost all such contracts, final and binding arbitration is included as the last step in the grievance procedure. Efforts are first made to settle the grievance at the level of the employee and his foreman; if this fails, further discussions follow between union and company officials at progressively higher levels. If a neutral arbitrator must be called in, his decision will be final and binding on both parties.

White-collar negotiations, especially those in public employment, are also dominated by discussions of wages and salaries. However, since most of these bargaining relationships are relatively new, disputes over grievance procedures, union security, and arbitration are still frequent. On the other hand, many public employees have for many years enjoyed substantial fringe benefits, such as pension and insurance plans, and these may not loom so large in the negotiations or the collective-bargaining agreement. The peculiar nature of public employment makes it likely that the issue of a "no-strike clause" will also be a central and continuing one.

The following list of topics is indicative of the provisions in a typical union–management agreement:

Wages and Fringe Benefits:
General wage increase
Retroactivity of wage increase
Incentive wage system
Payment for downtime
Daily versus weekly wage computation
Shift bonus
Rate of pay for temporary transfers
Christmas bonus
Overtime pay
Health and welfare plans
Hospitalization plan
Group insurance plans
Pension plans

Hours and Schedules:
Vacations
Holidays
Rest, wash-up, and lunch periods on company time
Leaves of absence
Time off for voting

Working Conditions:
Transfers
Physical examinations
Union–management safety committee

Union Security Provisions:
Union-recognition clause
Union-shop clause
Checkoff of dues

Management Security Provisions:
"No strike" clause
Management prerogatives clause

Employee Security Provisions:
Severance pay
Grievance procedure
Seniority clause
Union stewards
Jobs for older workers

Bargaining in the public sector

Growth of white-collar bargaining

The collective-bargaining procedures, techniques, and issues described above developed from the traditional strength of unions in blue-collar occupations. The collective-bargaining model that emerged in the crafts and skill trades in the early decades of this century proved to be readily transferable to such basic industries as autos, steel, and electrical after the successful organizing drives by industrial unions in the 1930s and '40s. However, by the end of the 1950s a new challenge began to confront unionism and collective bargaining. For the first time the number of white-collar workers began to exceed the number of blue-collar workers in the American labor force. And this occurred at a time when unions had already organized the blue-collar workers who were "easy" targets of the union drives, leaving unorganized those in small firms, very antiunion big firms, and scattered rural firms.

As we moved into the second half of the century, it became clear that great new advances in union organization and collective bargaining would have to come in the most rapidly growing occupations and industries, most especially among white-collar workers, professionals, and those in public employment.

Table 8/1.   White-collar union membership in the
United States, selected years

Year	White-collar union membership (in thousands)	White-collar as percent of total union membership
1956	2,463	13.6
1958	2,184	12.2
1960	2,192	12.2
1962	2,285	13.0
1964	2,585	14.4
1966	2,810	14.7
1968	3,176	15.7
1970	3,353	16.2

Source: Directory of National Employee Association, 1971 (BLS Bulletin #1750, 1972).

Although unionization among white-collar workers has grown in recent years, white-collar union membership is still a small proportion of total union membership in the United States, and has not increased substantially in the past decade. As is seen in Table 8/1, white-collar union members constituted 13.4 percent of total union membership in 1956; by 1966 the percentage had risen to only 14.6. However, the period 1966–70 shows a record addition of 500,000 members, raising the percentage to 16.2. Much of this growth of white-collar unionism has been in the public sector. The growth of unionism among white-collar workers has been much less impressive in private employment. Despite some gained ground in retail trade, in banks, insurance companies, and office work, unionism has grown far less than has total employment in these fields. It must be recalled that, whereas white-collar union members represent only about 16 percent of total union membership in the United States, the white-collar labor force constituted over half of the total U. S. labor force as early as 1956.

The importance of the public sector in the total picture of white-collar unionization is seen in the fact that nearly 42 percent of all union members in public employment are white-collar employees. On the other hand, only 4 percent of all union members in manufacturing and only 22 percent of all union members in nonmanufacturing are white-collar workers.

It should be noted that these figures may understate the true total white-collar union membership in the country. In reporting their membership totals unions do not always clearly distinguish between white-collar and blue-collar employees. Even more important, U. S. membership figures customarily do not include members of staff associations, professional associations, and other organizations which come close to being unions in their activities in such fields as education, health, and public employment. Since the activities of these associations frequently involve a species of collective bargaining, they might well be included among union organizations. It is possible that to include such associations, broadly defined as unions, would increase white-collar union membership by over 2 million. The limited growth of white-collar unionism in the United States contrasts with the rapid expansion of organization among such workers in other countries. It is true that these are countries where blue-collar union membership is also considerably above that of the United States. For example, in Austria and Denmark, where nearly three fourths of nonagricultural blue-collar workers are union members, approximately 60 percent of the white-collar employees are also organized into unions. In Sweden, approximately 80 percent of all nonagricultural blue-collar workers are organized, as are almost 70 percent of the white-collar workers. It is estimated that in France, white-collar union members may actually outnumber blue-collar union members. This experience abroad indicates that white-collar workers can be organized into unions in large numbers, and it raises a question of the obstacles to white-collar union growth in the United States in the past and the possibility of expansion in the future.

Factors influencing white-collar unionization   The most serious obstacle to white-collar union growth in the United States, where individualism and entrepreneurship have been stressed, is that white-collar workers tend to identify more with management than with manual labor. Unions, born and bred in the blue-collar industrial tradition, have not always been able to adjust to the social-psychological environment in which many white-collar workers function. It is being increasingly recognized that a new approach to organization is required if large numbers of white-collar workers are to be added to union ranks, since the methods used to attract blue-collar workers have not been successful in the white-collar field. Stress is given to the union organizer's education and status as well as to his techniques of persuasion. In the technical and professional fields, it has been deemed especially important to employ union organizers who are as educated as the employees they seek to recruit. The AFL–CIO has also made notable public use of the names of movie stars who happen to be members of their unions in the entertainment field.

Given the tendency of white-collar workers to identify with management, organizers in this field tend to stress the respectability and the social acceptability of unionism rather than the earlier emphasis on class struggle and factors that divide worker from management. Protection from arbitrary and inequitable actions by particular supervisors is given greater stress than condemnation of managers as a class. The union is espoused as a vehicle for the promotion of fair treatment and for the avoidance of favoritism rather than as an obstructive force in industrial relations. In professional unions and organizations, a special effort is made to emphasize the professional role of unions. The communication of knowledge about particular skills and techniques, and the participation in planning and advising along managerial lines, are often accorded more weight than some customary economic issues.

In an effort to change the image of unionism, some of the terminology of organization and collective action has also undergone change in the white-collar environment. Thus, some professional associations carefully avoid the use of such terms as "bargaining" or "grievances." For many years the Nurses' Association referred to their version of collective-bargaining activities as their "Economic Security Program." Even the word "union" is often avoided in favor of "association" or "guild" or "federation."

In an effort to give a new and separate image to white-collar union members, a number of industrial unions have established separate white-collar departments—for example, the Technical and Professional Employees Department of the United Auto Workers Union, a traditional labor organization that has spent much time and money organizing white-collar employees in the automobile and aerospace industries. In 1967, 17 AFL–CIO unions created a white-collar professional council called Scientific, Professional and Cultural Employees (SPACE). On behalf of the 400,000 employees in the unions it represents, SPACE performs the following functions:

1. *Preparation and distribution of literature on the benefits of the unions for professionals and white-collar employees;*

2. *Research on problems of white-collar workers common to the member unions;*

3. *Conferences on matters of mutual interest; and*

4. *Promotion of joint action on legislative goals to further white-collar unionization.*

The major opportunity that some union organizers in the white-collar field see lies in changes occurring in white-collar and professional work; it is felt that in large corporations many white-collar workers are subject to the same environmental pressures as blue-collar workers, and the distinction between the two classes of workers is becoming blurred. Contrary to the white-collar worker's dream of individualism and autonomy, he finds that he is controlled by the same "web of rules" as the industrial worker. The white-collar worker may find that the area in which he has discretion concerning his pace of work and the tasks he will perform is constantly shrinking as the hierarchical structure of the modern corporation plays a more dominant role in his life. The established routine and the discipline required in a large office or engineering department may resemble that of a production line.

Even more conducive to organization of white-collar workers is the growing recognition in some white-collar and professional circles that blue-collar workers have been able to achieve substantial gains through exercise of their bargaining power. Quite aside from the gains achieved by industrial unions on behalf of manual workers, many groups in American society are now developing bargaining relationships in order to preserve or further what they consider to be their "equity." Blacks are bargaining with whites; tenants are bargaining with their landlords; welfare recipients are bargaining with their county boards; students are bargaining with college administrations; and even some priests are bargaining with their church. The question raised by some organizers in the white-collar field is whether a particular group of white-collar workers can afford to remain unorganized in a society in which many other groups are advancing their political and economic power and their welfare through collective bargaining. When almost all employees have been organized into pressure groups, the unorganized run the serious risk of being bypassed in the distributive process.

How affluence affects the unionization of white-collar and professional employees is open to debate. On the one hand, we might expect higher living standards to further the traditional tendency of such employees to identify with management rather than with labor. On the other hand, as most workers, including semiskilled and skilled craftsmen, rise well above the levels of economic subsistence, relative standards of economic welfare are stressed more than absolute standards. When white-collar and even some professional employees see skilled craftsmen, organized into unions, with incomes above their own, they may place less value on the fact that their own living standards are substantially above those of their fathers. When affluence suddenly gives way, as in the case of layoffs among engineers and scientists in the aerospace industry when government contracts are dropped, then the contrasts with their former living standards may be a sharper blow to white-collar workers than to blue-collar employees under similar circumstances.

The primary impetus for unionization among blue-collar workers was legislation that enabled and even encouraged collective bargaining. This legislation applies with equal force to the white-collar workers in the private sector. However, there have been serious limitations on unionization and collective bargaining among employees in the public sector, the most rapidly growing sector of white-collar employment. Recent changes in legislative attitudes toward collective bargaining in public employment have undoubtedly been a major influence in the growth of white-collar organization. However, legislative approval has not been nearly as far-reaching as for workers in the private sector, and it has not occurred uniformly on federal, state, and local levels. Whereas the federal government has issued executive orders permitting its employees to organize collectively, less than half the states have passed similar legislation, and a number of municipalities have lagged even further behind. As a reflection of the importance of legislation in encouraging unionization and collective bargaining, it is notable that unionism of federal employees has expanded greatly, while the unionization of state and local employees in recent years has been much less marked.

Federal, state, and local bargaining

Obstacles to the growth of white-collar unionism in the private sector were even more awesome in the public sector. For many years it was held that as an employer government could not legally engage in collective bargaining, for the Constitution and the laws of the land had assigned certain powers to the government which it could not legally delegate to others. Since the strike was construed as a logical extension of the collective bargaining of the private sector, many felt that the development of unions and collective bargaining in public employment would have disastrous implications. It was argued that a strike against the government was intolerable, because it threatened serious danger to the public health, welfare, or safety. Moreover, the contention was made that wages and other conditions of employment could hardly be decided by collective bargaining between managers and organizations of employees because compensation and employment conditions were set by legislation and carried out by the Civil Service Commission through its directives and agency regulations.

As perceived not only by public administrators but by employees as well, these obstacles significantly retarded the growth of public employee unionism prior to the 1960s. Although unions of government employees existed as early as World War I, the phenomenal growth of collective-bargaining organizations among public employees is a very recent development.

As is seen in Table 8/2, in 1956 only 5.1 percent of total membership in unions was in government—915,000 out of the 18.1 million union members in the country. By 1962 union members in government employment rose to 7 percent of total union membership, and by 1970, it had risen to 11.2 percent. During the period 1956–70, government unions scored gains in membership of 153.2 percent while those in private industry gained only 5 percent. It is estimated that, given further advances in public-sector unionism, by mid-1970 there were approximately 2.3 million union members in the public sector.

Unions in the federal service have succeeded in organizing a substantially larger proportion of employees in their jurisdiction than have unions at the

Table 8/2. Union membership by sector, 1956–70
(in thousands)

Year	Total[1]	Manufacturing		Nonmanufacturing		Government	
		Number	Percent	Number	Percent	Number	Percent
1956	18,104	8,839	48.8	8,350	46.1	915	5.1
1958	17,968	8,359	46.5	8,574	47.7	1,035	5.8
1960	18,036	8,591	47.6	8,375	46.4	1,070	5.9
1962	17,564	8,050	45.8	8,289	47.2	1,225	7.0
1964	17,920	8,342	46.6	8,125	45.3	1,453	8.1
1966	19,126	8,769	45.8	8,640	45.2	1,717	9.0
1968	20,210	9,218	45.6	8,837	43.7	2,155	10.7
1970	20,690	9,174	44.3	9,198	44.5	2,317	11.2
Absolute change							
1956–60	−68	−248		−25		155	
1960–68	2,174	627		462		1,085	
1956–68	2,106	379		487		1,240	
1968–70	480	−44		361		162	
Percentage change							
1956–60	−.4	−2.8		−.4		16.9	
1960–68	12.1	7.4		5.5		101.4	
1956–68	11.6	4.3		5.8		135.5	
1968–70	2.4	−.5		4.1		7.5	

[1]Includes membership outside the United States.
Source: Same as Table 8/1.

Table 8/3. Proportion of government employees
organized (numbers in thousands)

Year	Government		Federal government		State and local government	
	Total employment	Percent organized	Total employment	Percent organized	Total employment	Percent organized
1956	7,277	12.6	2,209	------------	5,069	------------
1960	8,353	12.8	2,270	------------	6,083	------------
1964	9.596	15.1	2,348	38.2	7,248	7.7
1966	10,792	15.9	2,564	41.8	8,227	7.8
1968	11,846	18.2	2,737	49.4	9,109	8.8
1970	12,425	18.6	2,723	50.3	9,702	9.7

Note: Dashes indicate data not available.
Source: Same as Table 8/1.

state and local levels. In 1970, one half of all federal employees were union members, while only 9.7 percent of those in state and local government jurisdictions were, giving a total percentage for employees at all government levels of 18.2 percent. (See Table 8/3.) The growth in the percentage organized in the federal government from 1964 to 1968 is especially impressive. However, during the period 1966–68, the rate of expansion of union membership at both the federal and state and local levels was about 25 percent. As is seen in Table 8/3, the absolute increase in union membership at all levels of government since 1956 has been impressive.

There are notable concentrations of union members at both the federal and state levels. In 1968, a large proportion of total federal unionism was concentrated in the Post Office, which was better than 80 percent organized. Union membership in state government agencies varied from a low of 2,000 in Wyoming to a high of 309,000 in New York. Of the total of 2.2 million members at the state level, California, New York, and Illinois accounted for 1 out of every 3 members. These three states, plus Pennsylvania, Michigan, Ohio, Massachusetts, and the Maryland–Washington, D. C., area accounted for over one half of the total union members in state governments. As noted above, there has also been a concentration of government unionism among white-collar workers. Not only do white-collar workers now constitute approximately 42 percent of total government enrollment in unions, but this figure is more than double the 1960 figure.

It should be noted that these figures do not take into account those organizations commonly referred to as "associations" or "near-unions." The National Education Association, with more than 1 million classroom teachers, is a very important source of persons in organizations that frequently engage in collective bargaining. Other associations that have been actively seeking recognition and collective-bargaining rights are found among policemen, social workers, and many other categories of state, county, and local employees. One survey conducted in the late 1960s indicated that there were 662 associations of municipal public employees, with about 265,000 members in 438 cities. An association of state employee groups, known as the Assembly of Government Employees, claims that its affiliates represent more than half a million employees.

The unusual expansion of public-employee unionism in the 1960s can be partially explained by the same factors discussed above with regard to white-collar unionism. Government employees found a growing disparity between their wages and fringe benefits and those gained by unions in private employment. Generally rising living standards were accompanied by inflationary price movements which made the traditional "security" of government employment seem less attractive. However, a major contributor to the thrust of government unionism occurred in early 1962 with the issuance of President Kennedy's Executive Order 10988. This order sanctioned union organization among federal employees and was followed with parallel legislation in a number of states. Union victories in a number of major cities had a snowballing effect on union growth elsewhere.

President Nixon's Executive Order 11491, which became effective January 1, 1970, updated and expanded the first governmentwide labor-relations code:

> *The order eliminated informal and formal representation rights, permitting an employee organization to acquire recognition only as the exclusive representative of employees in the bargaining unit once a majority has designated it as agent. Exclusive recognition carries the right to negotiate collective bargaining agreements with agency management, although no agreements may contravene applicable laws and regulations, published agency policies and regulations, or controlling collective bargaining agreements at higher agency levels.*
>
> *The order is administered by a Federal Labor Relations Council, which decides major policy questions; a Federal Services Impasses Panel, which has authority to break negotiation deadlocks; and the Assistant Secretary of Labor for Labor–Management Relations, who has authority to determine the appropriate unit for bargaining, supervise representation elections, and decide unfair labor practice charges and alleged violations of standards of conduct for labor organizations.*[2]

With the growth of union membership in government employment, collective bargaining demands have grown in scope and intensity. Work stoppages have also inevitably grown, and these have given rise to extensive discussion of procedures for dispute settlement. These issues arising from collective bargaining are discussed further below.

Associations of teachers and other professionals

Among the most interesting developments in the unionization of white-collar employees has been the growth of collective bargaining among professionals. As noted above, the bargaining agencies are more likely to be called associations than unions, but their procedures in negotiations, and sometimes in strike action, increasingly resemble those of blue-collar unions.

The most notable extension of collective bargaining in professional fields has been among engineers, nurses, teachers, performing artists, and to a lesser extent among journalists and airline pilots. It should be noted, however, that unions affiliated with the AFL–CIO have had only limited success in recruiting professional employees generally. A much more common development is

---

[2]The Bureau of National Affairs, Inc., Washington, D. C. 20037, 1970.

the transition of professional societies and associations into "quasi-unions" which become the collective-bargaining agents on behalf of their employees.

There are several reasons for the recent growth and probable continued growth of these quasi-unions rather than traditional unions among professional workers:

1. Professional associations already have a large and well-established membership.

2. Professionals feel that it is more respectable to belong to an association which places principal stress on professional growth and concerns even if collective bargaining and a quasi-union status are given increasing weight. Unions of the AFL–CIO variety are often viewed by professionals as organizations that would reduce their social and professional status.

3. Professionals often feel that a quasi-union could do a much more effective job than a full fledged union in representing their professional interests, such as the maintenance of standards for entry and continuance in the profession.

Among the most prominent of the unions and quasi-unions for professionals in public service are those for school teachers. In this field there has been intense competition between the American Federation of Teachers, affiliated with the AFL–CIO, and the National Education Association, a quasi-union or professional association that has turned increasingly toward collective bargaining. It is generally felt that the NEA's growing concern with collective negotiations has been primarily prompted by rivalry with the aggressive and bargaining-minded AFT. There is some controversy as to whether total membership of teachers in unions and quasi-unions has been enhanced or limited by the rivalry between the two organizations. There is no doubt, however, that in the past decade membership in both has grown remarkably. The AFT remained relatively small until the 1960s, but a victory in the battle for representation of New York City's teachers in the early '60s gave great impetus to expansion of its membership and by 1970 the AFT had 275,000 members, a fivefold increase over its membership in 1962. Nonetheless, the AFT still represents less than 12 percent of the approximately 2.3 million teachers in public education. The NEA represents almost one half the total. It is estimated that approximately 60 percent of the teachers in the United States belong to an organization that actively engages in collective bargaining negotiations.

The reasons why collective bargaining activity among teachers has so greatly increased are similar to those noted above for white-collar and professional employees as a whole; and the same causal pattern applies to the growth of associational bargaining among nurses, engineers, and other professionals.

The experience abroad

The composition of union membership in a number of European countries has changed in a manner similar to that of the United States in recent years. The same forces have stimulated the growth of unionism and collective bargaining among white-collar and government employees. As in this country, the further extension of organization to white-collar workers and improvements in the legal status of public employee bargaining have become key issues in union circles. Since European trends in industrial relations have often preceded those in the United States, it is constructive to note recent developments abroad.

As in the United States, white-collar and government collective bargaining have reflected the structural patterns found in blue-collar private employment. In the Scandinavian countries, where collective bargaining has been highly centralized for some time among blue-collar workers, similar centralization has developed in the union–management relations in the white-collar field. Indeed, some white-collar unions have gone even further in this direction than their counterparts in manual trades; for example, the Swedish Union of Clerical and Technical Employees negotiates a single contract for all white-collar employees in all manufacturing. In Britain, too, collective bargaining for clerks and draftsmen also results in negotiated national agreements with employers' associations. Industrywide bargaining for white-collar workers also has developed in Germany.

On the other hand, in those countries with a less centralized system of union–management relations, such as the Netherlands and France, white-collar negotiations are also localized, and it is even common to have more than one union represent workers in a given white-collar bargaining unit.

In Western Europe, as in the United States and Canada, public employees have made substantial progress in recent years in their legal rights of unionization and collective bargaining. Workers in publicly owned enterprises, such as gas and electricity suppliers, coal mines, and railroads and other public transportation, generally have the same rights of organization, bargaining, and strike activity as employees in the private sector. However, the status of these workers must be distinguished from that of traditional "civil servants." As in North America, Western European civil servants were traditionally considered to be a privileged group, whose permanency of tenure was to serve as a substitute for the right of unionization and collective bargaining. Strikes were forbidden, and strike action could result in penalties specified by legislative statute.

The traditional status of civil servants has changed in the last decade or two, not only in North America but in almost every Western country. Civil servants in European government units have gained the right to negotiate collective-bargaining agreements. Gradually, with liberalized legal positions and with the ever-pressing model of the private sector, government employees have acquired almost all of the collective-bargaining rights enjoyed by workers in the private economy.

However, the American controversy over the civil servant's right to strike continues to have its counterpart in Western Europe. In Scandinavian countries and in France, strikes are permitted for most civil servants if proper notice and other procedural requirements are met. In a number of other European countries, the rights of negotiations have not been accompanied by the right to strike; and even in Scandinavia some groups are frequently excluded, such as those in the police and military forces.

In almost all Western European countries there are special provisions for the settlement of disputes in public employment. In Sweden, for example, disputes which may endanger national health and safety are handled through a special agreement negotiated between the unions and the government. In Norway and Denmark, disputes which we in this country would term "national emergency disputes" may be settled through special legislation imposing compulsory arbitration. And Britain also has a system of compulsory arbitration to resolve unsettled disputes involving civil servants.

In many European countries, wages and other benefits negotiated through collective bargaining must be ratified by an appropriate legislative body. However, given the number of years of experience with this procedure, the ratification has tended to become a formality, and in several countries is no longer even required.

As collective bargaining by civil servants becomes more commonplace in Western Europe, we find the development of groupings of unions or joint bargaining committees, and in some cases, the desire to influence basic civil service regulations has led to the amalgamation of public-employee unions. This growth, broadening, and amalgamation of public-employee unions in Western Europe make it likely that similar structural changes will occur as public-employee collective bargaining gains greater legal stature in the United States.

Conclusion

The big question about collective bargaining in the United States at the present time, from the standpoint of occupational gains and procedures, is whether the complex pattern of organization, procedures, and techniques developed over the decades in private, blue-collar employment is transferable to white-collar workers and professionals, and especially those in public employment. The tendencies in this direction are obvious. Much of the recent growth of unions in the white-collar and public sectors can be explained by increasingly sympathetic federal, state, and local legislation. These legal aspects of collective bargaining, especially the transition from the private to the public sector, are discussed in more detail in Chapter 9.

Readings

Anderson, Arvid, "Collective Bargaining in Municipal and State Sectors: Some Lessons and Guidelines," in *Good Government, Summer, 1971* (National Civil Service League, 1971).

Chamberlain, Neil W., and James W. Kuhn. *Collective Bargaining.* New York: McGraw-Hill Book Co., 1965.

Davey, Harold W. *Contemporary Collective Bargaining,* 3d ed. Englewood Cliffs, N. J.: Prentice-Hall, 1972.

Dunlop, John T., and Neil W. Chamberlain, eds. *Frontiers of Collective Bargaining.* New York: Harper & Row, 1967.

Goldberg, Joseph, "Changing Policies in Public Employee Labor Relations," *Monthly Labor Review* (July 1970).

Hart, Wilson R. *Collective Bargaining in the Federal Service.* New York: Harper and Row, 1961.

Healy, James J., ed. *Creative Collective Bargaining.* Englewood Cliffs, N. J.: Prentice-Hall, 1965.

Lieberman, Myron, and Michael H. Moskow, *Collective Negotiations for Teachers.* Chicago: Rand McNally and Co., 1966.

Moskow, Michael H., J. J. Loewenberg, and E. C. Koziara. *Collective Bargaining in Public Employment.* New York: Random House, 1970.

"Negotiation Impasse, Grievance, and Arbitration in Federal Agreements," *BLS Bulletin No. 1661.* Washington, D. C.: U. S. Government Printing Office, 1970.

Perry, Charles R., and Wesley A. Wildman. *The Impact of Negotiations in Public Education.* Worthington, Ohio: Charles A. Jones Publishing Company, 1970.

Prasow, Paul, and Edward Peters. *Arbitration and Collective Bargaining.* New York: McGraw-Hill Book Co., 1970.

Roberts, Harold S. *Labor–Management Relations in the Public Service.* Honolulu: University of Hawaii Press, 1970.

Slichter, Sumner H., James J. Healy, and E. Robert Livernash. *The Impact of Collective Bargaining on Management.* Washington, D. C.: Brookings Institution, 1960.

Stern, James L., "Collective Bargaining Trends and Patterns," *Review of Industrial Relations Research, Volume II.* Madison, Wis.: Industrial Relations Research Association, 1971.

Stevens, Carl M., *Strategy and Collective Bargaining Negotiations.* New York: McGraw-Hill Book Co., 1965.

Wellington, Harry H., and Ralph K. Winter, Jr. *Structuring Collective Bargaining in Public Employment.* Washington, D. C.: Brookings Institution, 1970.

Windoes, Frederic, "Effects of Collective Negotiation on School Administration," *Public Personnel Review* (April 1972).

Chapter Nine

Collective-Bargaining Issues: Strikes and Inflation

Introduction

Disadvantages and alternatives

An industrialist was once heard to state:

Collective bargaining is a very bad method for determining wages and conditions of employment. It establishes an adversary relationship, pitting workers against management and stressing conflict rather than cooperation. It frequently results in work stoppages which deprive employees of income, and it reduces production to the detriment of the public interest. In order to avoid strikes or because of collusive agreement between the parties, wages are pushed to excessive levels, causing either unemployment or inflation.

He then concluded, lamely,

The only good thing you can say about collective bargaining is that it is better than any of the alternative methods for determining wages and conditions of employment.

This statement summarizes the quandary posed by collective bargaining. Many questions are raised concerning the tactics employed in collective-bargaining negotiations, especially strike action, and many more questions are raised concerning the consequences of collective bargaining. However, in appraising any of our economic institutions, we must weigh the costs and the benefits of that institution against the costs and benefits of potential alternatives. It is especially important to measure these costs and benefits in social-psychological terms as well as in terms of economics. From such an appraisal one quickly concludes that there are no cost-free alternatives, and it becomes a matter of making a careful comparative analysis.

Little benefit would appear to be derived from strikes per se, and yet strikes are an essential element of the collective-bargaining system in this country. Union leaders are wont to assert that without the threat of a strike —occasionally reinforced by a "live performance"—efforts to obtain their demands from management become mere "sound and fury, signifying nothing."

However essential the freedom to strike is to our collective-bargaining system, it is clear that a prolonged strike may cause considerable hardship for the union members involved and may drive a business establishment over the brink of bankruptcy. Even more serious, some strikes in essential industries may create a national emergency or, even if local in nature, may seriously endanger public health and safety. As noted in the preceding chapter, the right to strike has been generally curtailed in public employment, and its use in such disputes poses especially difficult problems.

However, an analysis of strikes and what to do about them must begin with a study of the causes of strikes, the statistical measurement of the seriousness of strikes, the trends in strike statistics, and a careful examination of the true extent of "national emergency" strikes. Armed with this knowledge, we can then discuss alternatives.

If the alternatives to the strike involve some form of government prohibition or compulsory arbitration, unions may declare that their principal coercive weapon has been removed, that the institution of collective bargaining has become a "paper tiger," and that unionism itself, having lost its principal raison d'être, is on the road to destruction. The destruction of unionism would lead either to a return to the employer's unilateral determination of wages and conditions of employment, or else to government control of a major part of the decision-making processes in private industry.

These propositions must be tested. Even if the dire predictions were true, there are clearly other alternatives which do not go so far as to eliminate completely the right to strike. Such compromise alternatives must also be compared in gains and costs with an unlimited right to strike. This appraisal is made in subsequent sections of this chapter.

Also to be studied is the frequent assertion that collective bargaining is a vehicle of inflationary wage–price pressures. A detailed analysis of such wage determination and the inflationary effects of wage increases is contained in Chapters 14 and 20. But in this chapter the question under study is how the structure of collective bargaining influences the wage demands and wage settlements that might lead to inflation. The key question is whether unions and collective bargaining can be held responsible for a rising wage–price spiral in the present structural context. Here again the advantages and disadvantages of present institutional arrangements must be weighed against alternative possibilities.

Voluntarism and responsibility

A broader question, to which the specific issues raised above are related, is whether an essentially voluntaristic political economy can be preserved if the present collective-bargaining system is eliminated or greatly altered. If collective bargaining can no longer serve as a mechanism for determining wages, and if it is unlikely that the clock will be turned back to the earlier era of unilateral employer determination, the decision-making processes are likely to shift from private to government sectors. Given the political realities, government determination of wages is likely to be followed quickly by government determination of prices—a serious departure from a basically private-enterprise economy. At the same time, equally a key question is whether unions and management can "behave responsibly" from the standpoint of the public interest under the present collective-bargaining system. Can policies responsible to the public interest emerge from a voluntaristic milieu in which private parties have great autonomy? These are not new questions, and they have beset other aspects of our economy. However, they are becoming increasingly crucial in the collective bargaining sphere. This chapter will be concerned with the current aspects of some traditional problems.

Should the power to strike be limited?

Any analysis of the effects and possible alternatives to strikes must begin with their causes. After discussing and classifying the causes and types of strikes, we move in this section to measures of the extent and seriousness of strikes and a review of the arguments for and against the strict limitation of strikes, especially in the public sector, and conclude with a discussion of the alternatives to strike action.

Causes and types of strikes

Bargaining power, withholding power, and work stoppages   If unions come into being in order to enhance the bargaining power of labor, the essence of that power is the possibility of a collective withholding of labor's services. The older conventional notion of bargaining power, as expressed in the writings of John R. Commons and other early scholars in the field, is the relatively simple implicit concept that bargaining power is basically withholding power. The measure of a union's bargaining power was to be found in its ability to "hurt" the employer by bringing his production to a halt by withdrawing the essential labor.

In more recent writings on the theory of bargaining power, the concept has developed a more complex meaning: the ability to influence wage rates, or to cause price inflation, or to hurt the other party, as is seen in the actual results of the marketplace. In this view, bargaining power not only results from the subjective tastes, propensities, and emotional outlooks that make one group of workers more likely to withhold labor than another group, but also results from a wide variety of environmental factors such as market conditions, the state of technology, and the legal framework.

Unfortunately, it is not easy to disentangle the subjective preferences and propensities from the objective limits and constraints that determine the bargaining power of a union or an employer. The discussion in Chapter 13 indicates that the exercise of bargaining power is constrained within limits imposed by market forces of supply and demand for the product and for labor, as well as by factors determining the productivity of labor which limit the range that remains for the exercise of bargaining power. Further precision may be approached through knowledge of the preference functions of unions and management with regard to maximization goals: although we customarily assume that employers attempt to maximize profits, considerable variation in outcome of collective bargaining occurs depending upon whether unions attempt to maximize the increase in wage rates, the increase in membership, the increase in the total wage bill, or some complex function of "political" power and prestige. As noted in Chapter 13, Hicks and a number of others more recently have attempted to give additional precision to the outcome of bargaining by relating union and management policies to willingness and ability to strike or sustain a strike. However, the willingness of a union to strike or of an employer to sustain a strike is related, in turn, to the market and technological conditions in which they find themselves as well as to their subjective propensities and preferences. Thus, we come full circle in our effort to define and measure bargaining power as an influence on wage determination. In spite of recent efforts, a substantial area of indeterminacy remains in the negotiations of unions and management, and the willingness of a union to strike and of an employer to withstand the strike are frequently unknowns that contribute significantly to the area of indeterminacy.

It must be kept in mind, however, that a work stoppage by labor is only one means of withholding services in order to put pressure on management. It is an extreme form of withholding, but absenteeism, tardiness, slowdowns, and voluntary quits are also forms of withholding labor. In one sense, the relationships between labor and management at the workplace can be viewed as an exchange. As in many interpersonal relationships, each party hopes to gain from the other whether the gain be in the form of material advantage or some intangible such as social approval. But in order to gain, the worker and management must also incur costs, for the other party expects to receive gains in return. Just as management hopes to gain an efficient productive contribution from the worker, the worker hopes to gain economic, social, and psychological security and well-being from his relationship with his company. The gains derived by the worker usually involve some cost expenditure by the company, and the gains derived by the company usually involve some cost in productive energy for the worker, the opportunity cost of turning out goods and services for this employer rather than for some other employer or the enjoyment of nonwork activity.

When an employer feels that the gain he derives from a worker's productive contribution is not what it should be, the employer may well withhold expenditures that constitute the worker's gain. That is, the worker may be discharged or he may be penalized through suspension and loss of pay. Similarly, if the worker feels that his gain from the employer is not commensurate with his own productive contribution to the employer's gain, the individual worker may well withhold his labor through actions or inactions that are less dramatic and less obvious than a collective work stoppage. Students of human relations in industry have long been impressed with the prevalence of individual withholding of labor through absenteeism, turnover, slowdown, etc.; such withholding frequently occurs even within nonunion establishments, and through informal agreements among individuals in such establishments; the subtle withholding of labor may be a collective or group phenomenon. A union may simply formalize the process of individual withholding of labor to protest what the workers consider to be an unfair exchange relationship between worker and management, and to increase the worker's gain relative to the company's gain from the exchange relationship.

Workers might restrict their output from the fear that temporary production at peak efficiency may come to be expected by the employer as a permanent norm of production, or from the fear that "there is only so much work to go around" and that the employee may "work himself out of a job." Regardless of the rationality or irrationality of such views, they are known to be widespread, and they result in a withholding of labor even in the absence of unions.

Thus, work stoppage from strikes must be viewed in a broad context of various forms and reasons for the withholding of labor, even in the absence of a union. Although such withholding is frequently adopted as a means of increasing bargaining power and therefore gain from the employer, there are many other causes at work and the withholding may take many forms other than outright work stoppage.

When a union calls a strike it may simply be reflecting the individual discontents that characterize worker attitudes in a particular industry or establishment; it may reflect economic conditions that drive the workers to a strike in desperation or prompt the workers to strike in anticipation of favorable opportunities; or it may reflect the wishes and attitudes of union leaders who hope to consolidate or enhance their own position through the publicity and/or prestige associated with the work stoppage.

Causal types   Strikes may be classified by causes, by characteristics, or by effects. Causes are commonly distinguished as follows:

a. Recognition strikes   A common cause of strikes in the period prior to the passage of the National Labor Relations Act in the United States, and still prevalent in many countries, was the desire to force the employer to recognize the union as the bargaining representative of the workers in his establishment. Although such strikes have declined markedly in recent years, they may still occur when unions feel that they cannot get the majority vote in a representational election or when they are either not covered or do not want to be covered by legislation establishing an election procedure.

b. Economic strikes   The most common cause of strikes is the effort to use a work stoppage to increase bargaining power for higher wages, fringe benefits, and other terms and conditions of employment. Although there may be some underlying factors of a social-psychological nature that are not readily known to an outside viewer, economic gain is most frequently cited as the cause of work stoppages in the United States.

c. Jurisdictional strikes   A relatively small proportion of strikes occurs because one union is competing with another for the membership or the work in a particular industry. Such strikes are most frequently found in the building and construction trades where one group of skilled craftsmen, such as carpenters, may feel that the union representing another skilled craft, such as plumbers or bricklayers, is being given jurisdiction over work considered by the carpenters to be in their domain. The employer in such circumstances may be an innocent victim who cannot favor one union without arousing the enmity of the other.

d. Political strikes   There are two different species of political strike. In the 1930s and 1940s in the United States it was often felt that communist-led unions were striking for ideological reasons rather than for economic gain. Such ideologically motivated strikes are now more common in Europe. This type of political strike may be motivated more by a desire to embarrass the government in power than to advance the economic or social welfare of union members in a particular plant. The publicized objectives of these strikes may be such "legitimate" goals as wage increases or employment security, and in fact, gains in these areas may occur as a by-product of the strike. Union officers or the leaders of ideological factions within a union who wish to bring about political strikes must take care to win and maintain the support of rank and file members who may not share their ideology.

A second type of work stoppage, sometimes called a "political" strike, is related to the "politics" of the union rather than to the larger polity of the nation. As has been noted in the discussion of union wage policy, union leaders, as elected officials, must sometimes take actions that are directed more at the advancement of the union as an institution or of their own personal position within the union than at the immediate economic goals of their members. Just as comparisons with other union gains within an industry or a community may induce a particular union to establish wage goals that may not have a direct economic rationale, the politics of the union may persuade a union leader to call a strike to demonstrate a militancy that at least parallels that of other unions in the "orbit of comparison." Here, too, the announced goals will undoubtedly be economic—wages, hours, and working conditions—but the more basic motive may stem from the restlessness of the rank and file which looks enviously at the militant strike action of rival unions.

e. Sympathy strikes   Union A may strike not in pursuit of its own direct economic advantage but wholly in support of Union B, engaged in a strike for the advantage of B's members. This is especially valuable when the sympathy strikers are in crucial occupations, and can thereby enhance the power of a union whose members are not occupationally placed in a strategic bargaining position. Thus, retail workers who may be readily replaced by supervisory personnel or by newly hired employees are especially anxious to obtain the sympathy and support of the Teamsters Union, for truck deliveries are essential to the continued operation of the retail establishment.

Closely related to the sympathy strike is the *secondary boycott.* In this instance, workers in one union may refuse to handle goods that come from a "struck" plant. It is more common for the Teamsters Union to refuse to handle "hot cargo" than for them to conduct a sympathy strike. The legal status of a secondary boycott has undergone considerable fluctuations over the years, and was discussed in detail in Chapter 7.

Also closely allied to sympathy strikes is the simple refusal of members of one union to cross the picket lines set up by another union. The two unions concerned may be in the same firm or, in the case of the Teamsters, they may have no connection other than the common handling of a product at different stages of its production and distribution.

Although this common classification of strikes by causal factors is of some value in understanding collective bargaining, it is important to remember that in practice one can almost never disentangle the various causal strands. Economic issues are almost always the publicized reason for the strike regardless of the more fundamental motivating variables. Thus, in

1971, by the official figures of the Bureau of Statistics, about 92 percent of the total man-days lost because of strikes that year were over economic issues and working conditions, slightly over 7 percent involved union organization and union security, whereas only .7 percent were caused by interunion or intra-union disputes. It is clear that political factors or sympathetic activities, which may be of crucial importance in explaining a strike, are not readily recorded. Only those intimately acquainted with a particular union–management relationship can be expected to know the true cause of a strike, and government statisticians cannot be blamed for dutifully recording the publicized economic issue.

Another useful approach to a causal classification of strikes might emphasize the reasons for the parties' failure to agree. It is often assumed that all strikes are avoidable, given the overriding commonality of interest between union and management. Under this assumption, strikes occur only because union and/or management are insufficiently informed of their own true best interests, or because the negotiators are inept, or because the bargaining apparatus is insufficiently organized. This type of reasoning is implied in the Hicksian model set forth in the concluding section of Chapter 13. Under this assumption, if the union and management negotiators "only knew the facts and were able men" there would be no strikes.

Even though this is an oversimplified view of strike causation, it is undoubtedly true that many strikes occur simply because one party or the other did not have relevant information, misconstrued the other party's intentions, bluffed or called a bluff when he should not have done so, and tried to reach agreement through a bargaining mechanism that was ill suited to agreement. All those intimately acquainted with labor–management relations have their favorite stories of such strikes that "never should have happened." Human error is at least as widespread in collective bargaining as it is in other fields.

However, it does not further an understanding of union–management relations to accept the simplistic views stated above concerning the avoidability of all strikes. Although unions and managements have overriding common interests, they also have conflicting and competing interests. Note that most strikes are over the issue of wages—which is not surprising when we consider that the wage is a cost of production for the employer, an item he hopes to keep at reasonably low levels for efficient and profitable production, but which, at the same time, is frequently the sole source of livelihood for the union member, an item to be pushed as high as circumstances permit in the interest of rising living standards. Similar conflicts of economic interests occur over fringe benefits and working conditions, which constitute a cost item for the employer and a source of comfort and economic security for the union member.

Even though both parties have an overriding interest in keeping the establishment and the employment relationship in existence, as is noted in Chapter 13 there is frequently a wide area of indeterminacy between the harsh upper and lower limits set by economic factors even if these limits were known to the parties. Given the conflicting positions of union and management on some economic issues, the strike may be needed to help them "see the light." Only as they see their profits shrink or their paychecks dwindle under a work stoppage, can some management and union officials be expected to moderate their bargaining positions in favor of a settlement. Admittedly, a truly clairvoyant union and management negotiator may be able to predict the occurrence of a strike, its duration, and its effect on the positions of the parties. Certainly, "full information" of this type would make most strikes avoidable. But this calls for a foreknowledge of the other party's reactions— reactions not even yet known to that other party himself.

When we move from the strictly economic issues to such questions as union organization, union security, or the political aspects of unions, we gain further insight into the reasons for disagreements leading to a strike. One or both parties may assign value to a strike quite aside from any economic benefit that may result from it. Union leaders may feel that a strike is needed to gain union security, to galvanize the loyalty of the rank and file, to match the militancy of rival unions, to displace or embarrass rival unions, or to embarrass the government in power. An employer may undergo a strike that he knows will bring him no economic benefits in the short run, and perhaps even in the long run. He may hope a strike will undermine the union security or rank and file support; or he may be under pressure from an important supplier, financial agent, or client "to hold the line" even though this is contrary to his own judgment.

Thus, the causes of any particular strike are likely to be complex, and in some cases the complexity will be such as to defy useful analysis. Seldom will a strike fall within any one of the causal classifications described above. Nonetheless, the classifications are useful as tools of analysis in understanding or predicting strike activity.

Classification of strikes by other characteristics   In addition to causal types, there are a number of other ways in which strikes can be classified. Two such classifications discussed here are the tactics of coercion and the locus of the coercive activity.

a. The tactics of coercion   Although strikes usually involve a total stoppage of work by union members, there are partial strikes that may result only in a slowdown of production rather than complete cessation. A major advantage of the slowdown for union members is that it is more difficult to identify, and it may therefore permit union members to continue to receive compensation while putting subtle pressure on the employer to reach agreement on the union's terms. Of course, an employer who observed such a slowdown of activity may discharge particular employees, but such accusations are not readily proved, and the disciplinary process is often circumscribed by contractual rules that prevent quick and decisive employer action. Alternatively, the employer may "lock out" the workers if he suspects that the union is engaging in a coercive slowdown. This employer tactic is further discussed below.

One of the variants of the slowdown is called "work to rule." This device and nomenclature are more common in Great Britain than in the United States, but it has been used in one form or another in many countries. Since production or service in almost all industrial establishments proceeds efficiently only through a cooperative effort of informal agreements, procedures, and activities, workers who insist on producing only in accordance with the strict rules of some written job description or departmental mandate—often very outdated—can usually manage to seriously reduce productive efficiency. When berated by their supervisors, these workers can profess their adherence to some written rules and thereby avoid penalty. However, given the timing of such adherence to rules and the resultant slowdown during a period of negotiating conflict, the employer is usually under no illusion as to the steps he must take to restore the spirit of informal cooperation which will bring about a resumption of productive efficiency.

Somewhat related to the slowdown in production is the "sabotage" of production. In a sense this may be considered a slowdown carried to an extreme conclusion. It may involve isolated or extensive incidents of damage to machinery or destruction of parts or products. Because of its illegality, unions are not likely to admit that they condone such practices, and there is little evidence of the use of sabotage in American industry. When it does occur, it can usually be traced to an individual worker carried away by the passions of the moment. And yet such individual actions can put coercive pressure on an employer.

The sit-down strike, also illegal, places additional pressure on an employer through his fear that striking employees who refuse to leave the plant will cause damage to machinery or product, especially if efforts are made to dislodge them. The sit-down tactic gained fame during the new organizing drive of industrial unions in the rubber and automobile industries in the 1930s, but has seldom been used in recent years. However, isolated sit-down strikes are still occasionally reported, and readers will recognize the affinity of sit-down strikes with sit-ins by students and minority groups in the 1960s and 1970s on behalf of social, political, and educational causes.

Strikers usually take their place outside of the struck establishment and picket. Picketing itself may take a variety of forms and degrees of coercion. Peaceful, nonobstructive picketing is generally protected by constitutional guarantees; however, even here the legality of the picketing depends upon the purpose of the strike that the picketing supports. Mass picketing or militant picketing, which obstruct traffic or intimidate potential workers, have frequently been employed during a strike, and have also frequently been subject to legal counteraction. The legal status of such activity was discussed in Chapter 7.

The timing, duration, and locus of a strike may also be part of the union's general tactical offensive. Sometimes, as in the telephone industry, it is found more effective to call brief sporadic strikes in various locations, hoping to keep management off guard in an industry where if the employer is given sufficient time for planning supervisory employees can frequently keep operations going during a strike. Such strikes appear to be more common in European countries than in the United States. Wildcat, or unauthorized, strikes may sometimes serve the same purpose. These are strikes called by local groups of union members, ostensibly without the authorization of the official union leadership. When they are truly unauthorized, as they frequently are, they may be directed as much against the union leaders as against management. However, such strikes may be only officially "unauthorized" and actually be condoned by the union leadership as a method of pressuring the employer when an authorized strike would not have legal sanction and might result in legal penalties.

Employers, too, possess a variety of tactics to pressure a union before or during a breakdown in negotiations. He may use the "lockout" by refusing to permit strikers or other employees to enter the establishment. This tactic is most frequently used by employers in a multi-unit bargaining relationship when the union has decided to single out a particular employer for strike action, hoping that the continuance of production in competing firms may force the struck employer to reach terms with the union more quickly. To avoid such divisive results, other employers in the industry may lock out their workers in sympathy or in support of the struck employer. As noted below, this employer tactic is now limited by law.

Although in the past—and still on occasion in the present—employers have used strike breakers, detective agencies, and a variety of coercive tactics, at the present time their principal tactic during a strike is recourse to legal action. As is noted in Chapter 7, the circumstances of the strike may well permit the employer to obtain an immediate injunction against a union, thereby bringing the strike to a halt.

b. The locus of the strike   Strikes may also be classified according to the area they cover, which will usually be coextensive with the size of the bargaining unit. Since most bargaining units are confined to a particular establishment, so will most strikes be. However, where regional or industrywide bargaining units and agreements exist, as in trucking or in coal mining, the strikes that result from a breakdown in negotiations are also likely to be regional or industrywide. If one union gives sympathetic support to another the result may be an extensive strike going beyond customary bargaining units. When such sympathy strikes cover a large number of industries in a country, region, or community, they have often been called "general strikes." These have been more common in Great Britain and European countries than in the United States, where few strikes have gone beyond a number of key unions engaged in sympathetic, concerted strike action within a municipality.

Measures of strike activity

Persons absorbed by the newspaper headlines would assume that unions are highly prone to strike activity and that settlements are seldom reached without a prior strike. Actually, the opposite is true. Almost all collective bargaining agreements are reached through peaceful negotiations, and compared to the total number of labor–management agreements reached each year strikes are a rare phenomenon.

There are various measures of the extent and seriousness of strikes. Each has a useful purpose, but some are more sensitive indicators of strike activities than others:

1. *The number of strikes*

2. *The number of workers involved in strikes*

3. *The number of days lost in strikes*

4. *The number of man-days lost*

5. *The percent of union members involved in strikes*

6. *The days lost through strikes per union member*

7. *The percentage of estimated available working time lost in strikes*

Although not all of these measures can be applied to lengthy time periods, the U. S. Bureau of Labor Statistics has gathered data on some of the key statistical measures over an extended period of time. Some of these time trends are indicated in Table 9/1 and in Figures 9/1 and 9/2.

Table 9/1.   United States strike record, 1926–1970.

Year	Number of strikes	Number of workers involved (millions)	Number of man-days lost (millions)	% of estim. available working time lost
1926	1,035	0.33	26.0	0.37
1927	707	0.33	12.6	0.17
1928	604	0.32	5.4	0.07
1929	921	0.29	3.3	0.05
1930	637	0.18	6.9	0.11
1931	810	0.34	10.5	0.23
1932	841	0.32	16.9	0.36
1933	1,695	1.17	19.6	0.38
1934	1,856	1.47	15.5	0.29
1935	2,014	1.12	13.9	0.21
1936	2,172	0.79	28.4	0.43
1937	4,470	1.86	9.2	0.15
1938	2,772	0.69	17.8	0.28
1939	2,613	1.17	6.7	0.10
1940	2,508	0.58	23.0	0.32
1941	4,288	2.36	4.2	0.05
1942	2,968	0.84	13.5	0.15
1943	3,752	1.98	8.7	0.09
1944	4,956	2.12	38.0	0.47
1945	4,750	3.50	38.0	0.47
1946	4,985	4.60	116.0	1.43
1947	3,693	2.20	34.6	0.41
1948	3,419	1.90	34.1	0.37
1949	3,606	3.00	50.5	0.59
1950	4,843	2.40	38.8	0.44
1951	4,737	2.20	22.9	0.23
1952	5,117	3.50	59.1	0.57
1953	5,091	2.40	28.3	0.26
1954	3,468	1.50	22.6	0.21
1955	4,320	2.70	28.2	0.26
1956	3,825	1.90	33.1	0.29
1957	3,673	1.40	16.5	0.14
1958	3,694	2.10	23.9	0.22
1959[*]	3,708	1.88	69.0	0.61
1960	3,333	1.32	19.1	0.17
1961	3,367	1.45	16.3	0.14
1962	3,614	1.23	18.6	0.16
1963	3,455	1.03	17.8	0.15
1964	3,655	1.64	22.9	0.18
1965	3,963	1.55	23.3	0.18
1966	4,405	1.96	25.4	0.19
1967	4,595	2.87	42.1	0.25
1968	5,045	2.65	49.0	0.28
1969	5,700	2.48	42.8	0.24
1970	5,716	3.30	66.4	0.37
1971	5,135	3.26	47.4	.26
1972	5,100	1.70	26.0	.14

[*]Longest steel strike of record during last quarter.
Source of data: Bureau of Labor Statistics, U.S. Department of Labor.

Figure 9/1.   Number of strikes and man-days lost due
to strikes, 1926–70.

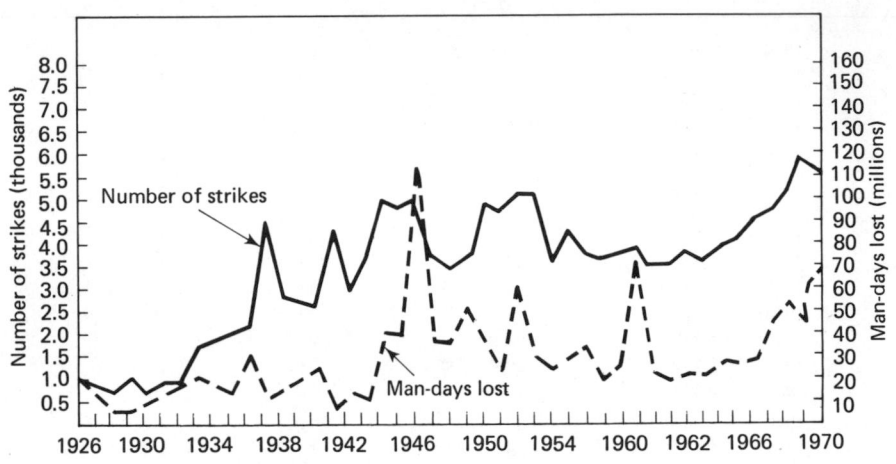

Source of data: Bureau of Labor Statistics, U.S. Department of Labor.

If one examines only the number of strikes, the number of workers involved, or the number of man-days lost through strikes, the figures appear to be large and impressive. Thus, in each of the years 1952, 1953, and 1968–

Figure 9/2.   Strike trends in the United States,
1926–70.

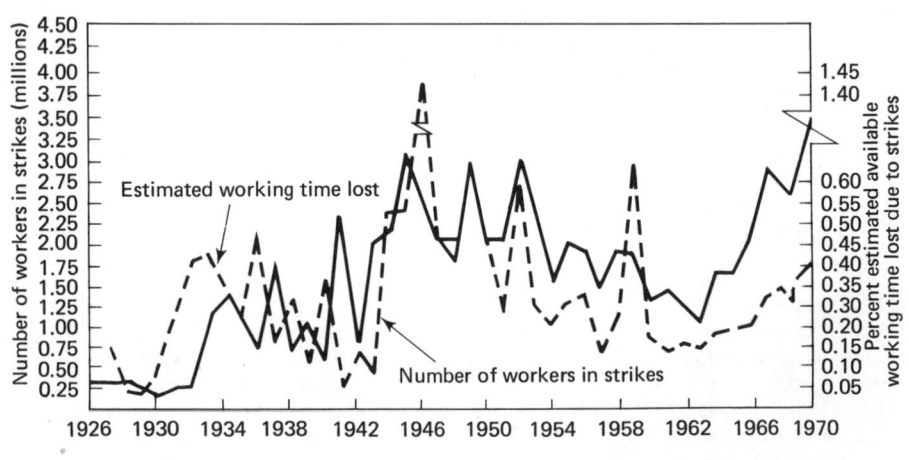

Source of data: Bureau of Labor Statistics, U.S. Department of Labor.

1972 there were over 5,000 strikes; and in 1952, 1970 and 1971 there were over 3 million workers involved in strikes. In 1946, 116 million man-days were lost in work stoppages, and more recently in 1970 there were 66 million man-days lost.

However, when these numbers are related as percentages to the total number of contracts negotiated, the total number of workers employed, or the total estimated work time available, the resultant percentages indicate the relative unimportance of strike activity. In the first quarter of 1970 only 0.15 percent of total working days were lost because of strikes, and as can be seen in Table 9/1, this percentage is not far out of line with the percentages recorded in a number of years of the decade of the 1960s. At the high point in 1970, only 0.37 percent of estimated available working time was lost because of work stoppages. During the past 40 years, only in the hectic strike year of 1946 did the percentage of estimated available working time lost in strikes exceed one percent.

Moreover, as can be seen in Table 9/1 and in Figures 9/1 and 9/2, the trend of strike activity since 1926 is not such as to lead to the conclusion that strikes are becoming a more serious problem in American society. Thus, in 1926 the percentage of estimated available working time lost through work stoppages was considerably higher than in 1972, and no lower than in 1970, the worst year in over a decade. In the turbulent years of the 1930s and the 1940s, strike activity as a percentage of total working time reached heights far beyond those registered in the two succeeding decades with the exception of a few years in which very prolonged strikes in one or two industries greatly affected the total. One is struck by the fluctuations in strike activities during various periods. There appears to be some relationship between the fluctuations in strike activity and the movement of the business cycle. Generally, strikes increase in a period of prosperity and fall in a period of depression, somewhat reflecting the union's expectations of successful strike action. Statistics in a number of other countries also indicate that in recent years the tendency to strike is lower than in earlier decades. Ross and Hartman, who analyzed comparative time trends of strike activity in a number of countries, have drawn some conclusions as to the reasons for the declining use of the strike. They suggest that employers have developed more sophisticated policies and effective organizations for the peaceful settlement of collective-bargaining negotiations. The role of the government as an employer has increased, and with this increase, strikes have declined. In a number of countries unions have concentrated on political activities rather than on strike action.

Although signs indicate that compared to the total number of contracts negotiated peacefully the use of the strike has continued to decline, one hesitates to write its epitaph in view of the flurry of strike activity from time to time in recent years. Clearly, the strike is still a highly prized weapon in the hands of union leaders, and when 3.3 million workers are involved in strikes in recent years, such as in 1970, one can hardly write off this form of union pressure in collective bargaining.

From the standpoint of the public interest, perhaps the most important measure of strikes is the cost of work stoppages to employers, workers, and consumers. Unfortunately, this measure is not readily obtained. If a strike is prolonged, it may involve considerable cost for the employer and the union. However, here, too, the newspaper headlines may be misleading. Undoubtedly, there was substantial loss of production, profits, and wages during the lengthy coal mining, steel, and automobile strikes of the last two or three decades, but analyses have shown that production, profits, and overtime wages were often at unusually high levels when the strike was anticipated, and they were also at unusually high levels while the backlog was being met after the strike. In these and many other industries there are periods of seasonal slack or conditions of chronic underutilization of capacity. A strike merely consolidates a longer period of inactivity into one shorter period of complete work stoppage, and the long-run loss to the employer and the union is often not as great as one would assume.

Strikes cost society even less than they cost the employer and union involved. Very few strikes are industrywide or nationwide; and therefore firms that are not involved in the strike can increase their production to meet the demands that cannot be met by the struck firms. As noted above, even in some strikes which come close to being industrywide, as in coal, steel, or automobiles, overproduction frequently occurs in anticipation of the strike, and this surplus is used to meet orders during the strike.

Even though the foregoing account tends to minimize the overall significance and costs of strikes in general, it should be noted that there are some strikes which can seriously interfere with public health and safety. These are often called "national emergency strikes," but local emergencies can also result from a strike in public utilities or in vital public services. The national emergency provisions of the Taft-Hartley Act, passed in 1947, have been used sparingly since the passage of the Act. Although serious students of labor–management relations cannot always agree that national emergencies actually occurred in each of these instances, the strikes or threats of strike had sufficiently serious implications to induce the President of the United States to invoke the national emergency provisions. The Taft-Hartley Act was used to end strikes or end the threat of strikes in such industries as aerospace, atomic energy, coal mining, the maritime trades, basic steel, shipbuilding, telephones, smelting, meat packing, and stevedoring.

If the railways and airlines were covered by the Taft-Hartley Act, the national emergency provisions would undoubtedly have been used much more frequently. The railways come under the Railway Labor Act, and the dispute-settlement provisions of this Act have been invoked many times since its passage, often with only limited ultimate success. The strike and dispute settlement provisions of the Taft-Hartley and Railway Labor Acts are discussed in further detail in Chapter 7.

Thus, it must be concluded from the record of strike activity that strikes as a whole are not a problem of overriding importance to the public interest. However, strikes in some industries can threaten public welfare, health, and safety; and even when these threaten or occur in private industry no constituted governing authority can sit idly by and permit them to occur or continue.

Strikes in the public sector

Although in the last couple of decades strike activity has not markedly increased in the United States as a whole, work stoppages in the public sector have sharply risen. The increase has parallelled the rise in public employee unionism, and it also reflects a growing militancy among these union members. Since strikes in government employment raise questions going beyond the usual issues raised in strike activity, we must be concerned not only with their growing number and seriousness, but also with the right to strike in public employment as compared with the private sector.

The rising trend of strikes in government   In 1958 there were only 15 recorded stoppages among public employees in the federal, state, and local governments (see Table 9/2). Only 1,720 workers were involved and only 7,510 man-days were lost because of stoppages during the year. Ten years later there were 254 stoppages, and the total number of workers involved had risen to over 200,000 with more than 2½ million man-days lost because of strikes in the public service. A new high of 412 strikes was set in 1970, with over 333,000 workers involved and over 2 million man-days lost in Federal and local units.

As has been noted in earlier discussions of labor-market trends, the greatest expansion of employment in the United States has been in state and local government. Especially at the municipal level, the growth in the number of workers has been accompanied by a growing number of unions and strike activity. Whereas in state government only 60 man-days of strike idleness were recorded in 1958, within a decade the number of man-days lost had grown to almost 43,000, followed by a dramatic rise to 152,000 in 1969. In local government, the number of stoppages in the ten-year period increased from 14 to 235; the number of workers involved in strikes grew from 1,690 to over 190,000; and the number of man-days lost increased from 7,450 to almost 2½ million. Figures for 1969 reflect continued large increases in the total number of strikes, although in all fewer workers were involved than in the record year 1968.

The seriousness of this strike trend is underlined by the fact that more and more strikes are taking place in occupations traditionally considered as prohibited areas for work stoppages. In the last few years, it has not been at

Table 9/2. Work stoppages in government, 1958-68*

Year	Number of stoppages	Total workers involved	Man-days idle during year	State government			Local government		
				Number of stoppages	Workers involved	Man-days idle during year	Number of stoppages	Workers involved	Man-days idle during year
1958	15	1,720	7,510	1	30	60	114	1,690	7,450
1959	25	2,050	10,500	4	410	1,650	21	1,640	8,850
1960	36	28,600	58,400	3	970	1,170	33	27,600	57,200
1961	28	6,610	15,300	–	–		28	6,610	15,300
1962	28**	31,100	79,100	2	1,660	2,260	21	25,300	43,100
1963	29	4,840	15,400	2	280	2,160	27	4,560	13,300
1964	41	22,700	70,800	4	280	3,170	37	22,500	67,700
1965	42	11,900	146,000	–	–	1,280+	42	11,900	145,000
1966	142	105,000	455,000	9	3,090	6,010	133	102,000	449,000
1967	181	132,000	1,250,000	12	4,670	16,300	169	127,000	1,230,000
1968	254++	201,800	2,545,200	16	9,300	42,800	235	190,900	2,492,800
1969	411	190,000	745,700						
1970	412	333,500	2,023,300						
1971	327	151,400	893,000						

*Includes stoppages lasting a full day or shift or longer and involving 6 workers or more.
**Includes five stoppages of federal employees, affecting 4,190 workers, resulting in 33,800 man-days of idleness.
+Idleness in 1965 resulting from a stoppage that began in 1964.
++Includes three stoppages of federal employees, affecting 1,680 workers, resulting in 9,600 man-days of idleness.
++Includes three stoppages of federal employees, affecting 1,680 workers, resulting in 9,600 man-days of idleness.
+++Breakdown for state and local government not available 1969-1971.
Data on stoppages and workers refer to stoppages beginning in the year; man-days idle refer to all stoppages in effect during the year. Because of rounding, sums of individual items may not equal totals given.
Source: U.S. Bureau of Labor Statistics, "Summary Report: Work Stoppages 1970, 1971."

all unusual to find that in a growing number of large and small communities across the nation teachers are on picket lines rather than in classrooms when school is scheduled to begin in September. Whole school systems in such large cities as New York and Detroit have been closed by strikes conducted by the local affiliates of the National Education Association or the American Federation of Teachers.

Even more serious from the standpoint of essential services, there has been a growing number of strikes by policemen and firemen in large and small cities, and garbage collectors and welfare workers have walked off the job in work stoppages in New York and other municipalities feeling the squeeze between the taxpayers' revolt and the municipal workers' demands for equity in compensation as compared with private industry. There has even been a growing number of strikes among doctors and nurses in municipal hospitals, a phenomenon that would have horrified even the participants not many years ago. And subway and bus workers have increasingly threatened to paralyze municipal transport in New York and a number of other large cities, and have occasionally demonstrated that their threat is not an idle one.

The growth of public-employment strikes has only recently spread to those employed by the federal government in spite of the higher concentration of union members on the U. S. payroll. As is noted in Table 9/2, stoppages by federal employees accounted for a small percentage of man-days of idleness in the past decade. However, there has been growing strike activity among the highly organized postal workers, similar to the strikes of postal workers in Great Britain, France, and Canada. With the growth of work stoppages in public employment at the state and local levels, it would appear to be only a matter of time before strike activity also assumes greater significance at the federal level.

However, the increased number of strikes and man-days of idleness in public employment must be seen in perspective. Although, contrary to the strike record in private employment, work stoppages by government workers have shown a markedly increasing trend, in 1968 only about 10 days were lost through strike activity for every 10,000 days worked in the public sector, as compared with a ratio of 20 days lost for 10,000 days worked in private industry. This indicates that public-sector strikes are settled more quickly.

As in the private sector, differences over economic issues are primarily responsible for stoppages in the public sector. Of the 254 strikes in 1968, the reasons given for 196 were disputes over salary and fringe benefits. However, as in the early days of organization in private industry, strikes for union recognition were also prominent, with 60 of the stoppages being placed in this category. As with private industry, work stoppages in the public sector derive from complex causes, and the motivations cannot be pigeonholed. Although the ostensible reason for public employees' strikes is usually economic, such factors as union security and internal politics also play an important complementary role.

The right to strike in the public service   What is amazing about the rapid increase in strikes in public employment is that most of these are considered to be illegal. In the United States today the formal legal doctrine has changed very little from that expressed by Calvin Coolidge, then Governor of Massachusetts (1919), when as a result of a strike of Boston policemen he declared, "There is no right to strike against the public safety by anybody, anywhere, anytime." This view has been reaffirmed by American presidents ever since. Most states and municipalities have similar formal prohibitions against strike activity by their civil servants.

The fact that public employees are striking in growing numbers in the face of legal prohibition adds further to the seriousness of the issues raised by public-employee strikes. The deliberate flouting of the law, often with impunity, jeopardizes the status of rule by law, a cardinal tenet of a democratic society. And yet, the fact that such strikes are increasing, apparently with society's tolerance, makes it necessary to conduct a critical appraisal of the right of public servants to strike. The specific legal enactments and legal status of public employees' strikes are discussed in further detail below.

The major arguments against strikes of public employees are (1) the danger of interference with essential services, and (2) the danger of a strike against the government, the embodiment of all the people of a community or of a nation.

Those who argue in favor of lifting the prohibition against public-employee strikes have less trouble with the issue of interference with essential services than they do with the question of political processes. They contend that the strikes of many public employees, such as teachers or state house clerks, do not involve essential services, the temporary stoppages of which endanger the public health and safety. Such proponents stress that the only legitimate test for the prohibition of strikes is the essentiality of service or product, whether the workers are employed in public or in private activities. For example, strikes by private maritime workers may be much more detrimental to the public interests than strikes by teachers.

However, as has been revealed by analysis of the use of national emergency strike provisions under the Taft-Hartley Act, it is no easy matter to define essentiality of service. Most would agree that policemen, firemen, doctors, and nurses should be placed in this category. But what of sanitation and transit workers? And does not the impact on the public welfare depend upon the length of the work stoppage? Although a one-week strike by teachers may cause no more than annoyance to mothers who find their children at home rather than at school, such a strike continued for many weeks, as have some private industrial stoppages, may be thought to be a serious impairment of the public welfare. A two-day strike by garbagemen can be the source of jokes on television, a one-week strike can be a source of major annoyance, and a two-week strike can be intolerable. Similar time considerations apply to strikes of transit workers and medical personnel.

Even so, as is discussed in the succeeding section, some procedure for determining local, state, as well as national, emergencies can be devised to determine the legality or continuance of some public employee strikes as compared with others.

A more complicated issue for those who would lift the ban on public-employee strikes is the argument that "you can't strike against the government." There are economic limits to the pressures of bargaining power and coercive tactics in the private sector that are absent in public employment. Private employers who must react to a work stoppage are constrained by the product market and their product position, and the public interest is preserved because competing employers are usually available to supply needed products and services. But there are no marketplace and profit-maximization constraints on the public employer who faces a striking union, and the public can seldom turn to an alternative source of the service cut off by a work stoppage.

It is held that the government is the final arbiter in disputes and work stoppages between unions and management. It can play a neutral role in insuring that the public interest is not endangered by a work stoppage. But when the strike is against the government itself, who will serve as the neutral arbiter? Should one segment of the community strike to force the community as a whole to bend to its will?

In spite of these arguments against public-employee strikes in the public service, the *de facto* tolerance of them leads to the conclusion that there will be a progressive modification of the outright prohibition against such strikes in the United States. Steps in this direction have already been taken in a number of other countries.

Regardless of the future course of legal strike prohibitions in public employment, there will be a continuance of current efforts to find alternatives to the strike as a means of settling public-employee disputes. The efforts to find alternative peaceful means of dispute settlement, long prominent in the private sector, assume more crucial importance in public employment.

Alternatives to strikes   The important role that strikes have played in the system of free collective bargaining has led to a search for alternative dispute-settlement procedures stopping short of outright legal prohibition. In public employment, a number of the procedures that have long been used in the private sector to help prevent strikes are being used as an alternative to the right to strike. These procedures are discussed below for both private and public sectors.

Mediation and conciliation   In the United States the Federal Mediation and Conciliation Service maintains a staff of trained mediators and conciliators to help resolve labor–management disputes before strikes occur or to bring the parties together in order to end strikes. Many industrial states also have professional staffs of mediators and conciliators under a variety of agency titles.

The specific job duties of a mediator or conciliator are not easily defined, since mediation is an art rather than a science. In almost all cases it is a voluntary process, with services offered by the appropriate government agencies and only rarely refused by the disputants. Rather than make any formal recommendation for settlement of the dispute, the mediator tries to bring the two parties together, to reduce the area of their differences, and to make informal suggestions that may smooth the path toward a voluntary agreement. He has no formal authority, and his powers rest primarily in his persuasiveness and in the trust that he generates in the two parties.

No two mediators will follow the same tactics or strategies, and the tactics adopted by a mediator will probably differ from case to case as circumstances warrant. For example, even though it is his purpose to bring the parties together, a mediator may find it more expedient at first to keep the parties in separate rooms, shuttling back and forth in his efforts to suggest compromises that will reduce their differences. Only when his unilateral discussions with each party have convinced him that little difference remains will he bring the parties together for a face to face confrontation which may result in the final compromise that eliminates the small remaining area of dispute. At times he will be conciliatory in tone, at times firm, and at times, especially in emergency disputes, he may be insistent and even demanding. The art comes in knowing the appropriate moment and circumstances under which these different tactics should be adopted.

It is not possible to measure the precise impact of voluntary mediation on dispute settlement since it is not always possible to know what would have happened in the absence of the mediator. There seems to be little doubt that mediators at the federal and state government levels have made important contributions to peaceful settlements of labor–management disputes, and that their efforts are generally welcomed by the parties sincerely interested in avoiding a strike.

Even though most of the mediation and conciliation practiced in this country is conducted on a voluntary basis, the procedures have been embodied in the legal process of dispute settlement under the Railway Labor Act covering the railroad and airline industries and under the "emergency dispute" provisions of the Taft-Hartley Act and similar state legislation. Also, under some state statutes dealing with public-employee disputes mediation is required before more advanced steps in the settlement procedures are taken.

Voluntary arbitration   As distinct from mediation and conciliation, in arbitration a third party makes a formal decision that settles the labor–management dispute. If the parties have so agreed prior to the arbitration, the arbitrator's decision is final and binding upon the parties. In spite of this binding feature, almost all the private union–management contracts in the United States have an arbitration provision that may be considered voluntary. It is voluntary in the sense that the parties have voluntarily agreed to insert it into the contract even though the contractual provision asserts that the decision of the arbitrator must be accepted by both parties.

These voluntary arbitration provisions in private industry are almost always included as the final step in the grievance procedure. Thus, the provisions are used for the administration and interpretation of an existing agreement rather than for the settlement of disputes over the terms and conditions of a new contract. Since accumulated grievances can be as much a source of possible strike action as a dispute over new contractual terms can be, voluntary arbitration in grievance settlement is an important step toward peaceful resolution of labor–management differences. Among the most common grievances going to arbitration are discharge and discipline, seniority rights in promotions, job-classification disputes, job evaluation and wage-incentive programs, and such fringe benefit applications as paid vacations, paid holidays, and health and welfare plans. Neutral arbitrators are frequently selected by the parties from lists provided by the Federal Mediation and Conciliation Service, the American Arbitration Association, or state agencies in the labor–management field. Arbitrators are most commonly drawn from the ranks of attorneys, judges, clergymen, and university professors.

Although voluntary arbitration as a final step in the grievance procedure is much less common in public-employee contracts, there has been a notable tendency for its adoption in contracts representing hourly rated employees at the state and local levels. There has also been a notable increase in the use of voluntary arbitration in contracts covering teachers and other professional employees. Because provisions that have long been common in private labor–management relations have been appearing in the collective-bargaining agreements of public employees, it would seem just a matter of time before voluntary arbitration receives widespread acceptance in the public sector.

Compulsory arbitration   When binding arbitration is imposed by statute it is usually called "compulsory arbitration." In such cases the decision of a neutral party or a neutral panel of arbitrators to settle a dispute must be accepted by the parties. Unlike voluntary arbitration, discussed above, compulsory binding arbitration has almost invariably been directed at disputes over new contract terms.

Some of the Australian states have had forms of compulsory arbitration for many years, and it has been sporadically adopted in other countries and occasionally in private sectors in the United States. By and large, however, in the United States compulsory arbitration has been avoided in private industry on grounds of constitutional rights as well as the essentially voluntary nature of collective bargaining in this country. However, binding compulsory arbitration has been adopted by some states for public employees offering essential services. Pennsylvania and Rhode Island provide for compulsory arbitration as a final procedure in the settlement of disputes involving policemen and firemen. Wyoming has applied this procedure only to firemen. Although the statute in Rhode Island provides for compulsory arbitration of disputes involving teachers, the binding aspect of the award is limited to "all matters not involving the expenditure of money." Where adopted, compulsory arbitration provisions have been extensively used: over 60 cases went to arbitration in Pennsylvania in 1968 alone, the statute's first year in effect there. Unlike some of the earlier cases of compulsory arbitration in private industry, the courts in Rhode Island, Pennsylvania, and Wyoming have upheld the constitutionality of the arbitration statutes in public employment.

Although compulsory arbitration, as a substitute for the right to strike, may appear to be a viable solution in disputes that threaten the loss of essential services, the widespread use of compulsory arbitration has serious implications for the continuance of a voluntary collective-bargaining system. There is some evidence that it reduces the willingness of the parties to bargain since the party with less bargaining power can often advance his cause by adhering to an extreme position in hopes that the arbitrator will find it acceptable. One party or the other may well conclude at the outset of negotiations that a decision by the arbitrator would be more in its favor than any settlement they could possibly negotiate.

Fact-finding   Unlike the mediator, the fact-finder establishes the relevant facts in the dispute, analyzes them, and issues a recommendation for settlement of the dispute. Unlike the arbitrator's recommendations, however, those of the fact-finder are seldom binding.

Fact-finding procedures are part of the statutory requirements of the Railway Labor Act (1926) and of the Taft-Hartley Act, also known as the National Labor Relations Act (1947). During the cooling off period in which the parties are enjoined from engaging in a work stoppage, boards or committees are empowered to investigate the facts of the dispute and make a report.

Use of fact-finding has been most widespread in state statutes dealing with public-employee disputes. Here, after a period of required mediation by state officials, parties that have reached an impasse over one or more issues are required to petition a state labor-relations agency for appointment of a fact-finder. The fact-finder hears the arguments of both parties on the issues at impasse and issues his report, including recommendations for a settlement of each of the impasse issues, to the parties and to the state agency. His recommendations may be used to bring pressure on the other side either through newspaper publicity or through legislative action. However, analysis of the disposition of fact-finding awards in New York State and in Wisconsin indicates that there have been notable rejections of the fact-finder's recommendations. But many times disputed issues submitted to fact-finding have been settled through further negotiations after a fact-finder's recommendations, and the recommendations may have contributed to the area of agreement between the parties.[1]

Unions and inflation

Although strikes are to be deplored, some employers contend that strikes are often the only alternative to giving in to a union's inflationary wage demands. The relationship of collective bargaining, full employment, and wage–price movements will be discussed in Chapter 20; in this section, we relate the problem of inflation to the structure and policies of unions and collective bargaining.

Bargaining structure and inflation

With the removal of wage and price controls following World War II, this country experienced one of its most severe periods of wage–price spirals. Unions in such major industries as steel, autos, and coal-mining sought and obtained substantial money wage increases, only to see their gains greatly diminished by even larger increases in the price level. Riding on a wave of pent-up demand, employers seemed to have almost unlimited ability to raise prices in response to a union-demanded wage increase. Unions used the sharp rise in living costs as an excuse for their continuing wage demands, employers used the resultant negotiated increases as an excuse for raising prices, sometimes more than in proportion to the wage rise. If wages and prices rose to levels that appeared to endanger the continuance of product demand, the continuing surge of consumption, private investment, and government spending were sufficient to take the higher priced goods off the market.

There is a story that under these post-World War II circumstances Walter Reuther, the late president of the United Auto Workers Union, decided that the statesmanlike policy would be to forgo the money wage increase in order to stem the tide of rising prices which threatened real wage gains for his members. This policy had been strongly pushed by economists inside and outside of government. If wage demands were moderated, employers would no longer have a need or excuse for raising prices and the inflationary wage–price spiral could be halted. The story goes on, however, that older and wiser union leaders advised Reuther of the foolhardiness of his proposed policy. He was told that his union membership, even though it was among the largest

---

[1]Michael H. Moskow et al., *Collective Bargaining and Public Employment* (New York: Random House, 1970), pp. 279–280.

in the country, was still only a fraction of the nation's work force. Consequently, to forgo a money wage increase for his members would do little to stem the rise of wages in the economy as a whole. Prices would continue to climb, and the only result of a sacrifice of money wage increases for auto workers would be a loss of real wages amidst the continuing inflation. The auto workers then continued to demand and to receive substantial money wage increases throughout the remainder of the 1940s, and the price level continued to rise, thereby reducing the real wage gains of the auto workers and other union members.

This widely held story, true or not, demonstrates the dilemma of unionism and collective bargaining in an inflationary era. Although there are differences among the labor-relations analysts as to whether unions can raise wages excessively and "cause" inflation, much of the public and many government officials continue to condemn unions for doing so. The argument is often related to their strike power, discussed above, and to their so-called monopoly power.

But the Walter Reuther story illustrates the difficulties facing a union even if it were convinced of its contributions to inflation and even if it wanted to reduce its inflationary impact. The structure of collective bargaining in the United States is not such as to bring about "responsible" union policy if responsibility is defined as a concern for broad movements of the national price level. Many thousands of separate collective-bargaining agreements are negotiated each year, each one representing a very small fraction of the total unionized work force. And the unionized work force represents only a fraction of the total labor force in the U. S. economy. Each of these negotiated agreements contributes only an infinitesimal addition to the total wage bill. And yet, added together, they represent a serious cost increase for the employer and a substantial increase in the purchasing power of consumers.

Admittedly, a number of large unions are pattern-setters. Their substantial negotiated wage increases are first paralleled by unions in satellite relationships in the same industry or related industries, and then spread by a demonstration effect to thousands of union and nonunion workers in other sectors of the economy. Should the pattern-setters, such as the auto workers' union, be more restrained than others? Walter Reuther was persuaded to the contrary, and given the political nature of a trade union it is likely that a union leader's position would be in jeopardy if he sacrificed his members' wage increase even were it shown that it would help to establish a pattern to be followed by other unions.

Employer resistance and inflation

The strike issue, discussed in the first part of this chapter, cannot be separated from the inflation issue. As has been noted above, strikes increase in a period of full employment and prosperity, a period likely to be characterized by inflationary price rises. Thus, it cannot be held that employer resistance to union wage demands crumbles in such a period. Apparently, many employers continue to resist union pressures even though their ability to pay higher wages is enhanced by an active demand for their products.

It must be borne in mind, however, that even in a period of inflationary full employment man-days lost through strikes constitute only a very small percentage of total man-days of work available. For every employer who is willing to undergo a strike rather than accede to union wage demands in an inflationary period, there are a hundred who settle without a strike, and this settlement is likely to reflect the buoyant state of union expectations and product demand. Certainly, many employers would consider it contrary to their goals of profit maximization to undergo a strike—and the consequent loss of customers to their competitors—rather than raise wages and prices in an economic environment when such increases are readily accomplished.

Even when a long strike ensues in a period of inflationary wage–price spirals, there are those who feel that the strike is part of the collective-bargaining game. When government officials are closely scrutinizing all price increases for their possible inflationary implications, a prominent pattern-setting industry does well to blame its price increases on a preceding wage increase. And to demonstrate how sincerely the company's management attempted to avoid both the wage and price increases by resisting the union's demands, they may point to the union's work stoppage.

Some suggested remedies

The dilemma of full employment and inflation will be discussed in some detail in Chapter 20. The possible solutions include:

1. *abandonment of the goal of full employment (say to the extent of an unemployment level of 6 percent of the labor force or more);*

2. *some variation of wage and price controls;*

3. *structural changes in collective bargaining and/or industry and employment;*

4. *abandonment of the goal of price stability.*

Abandonment of full employment   Although recent government policies have tried to stem inflationary pressures by reducing total demand and by permitting unemployment rates to rise to relatively high levels, there are clearly limits to such policies in a political democracy. Ever since Herbert Hoover's administration, at least, governments have been wary of high rates of unemployment at election time, and there have been convincing examples of the loss of elections because of an administration's serious departure from the goal of full employment. Recent years have demonstrated how difficult it is to fight inflation by reducing demand and consequently production without having unemployment rise to socially and politically intolerable levels. Aggregate economic policy has not yet reached that scientific state in which just the right balance at just the right time (that is, election time) can be guaranteed.

Thus, quite aside from the loss of economic welfare, and the economic hardship that may well result for unemployed families, political realities place severe limits on the policy of unemployment as the solution to inflationary pressures.

Wage–price controls   As will be noted in Chapter 20, the conventional wisdom was that wage and price controls could not work in any period other than large-scale war. Wage and price controls entail rationing of goods and call for extensive cooperation by producers and consumers. In the absence of a compelling national crisis, it is held that such cooperation will not be forthcoming, and therefore the enforcement of wage and price controls will call for enforcement policies approaching those of a police state.

Until 1971 this reasoning kept government wage and price policies far short of outright controls. The range of policies ran from "jawboning," that is, attempting to persuade unions and management to act responsibly, to wage–price guideposts—that is, unions and managements were urged to permit wage increases that did not exceed the rise in national productivity (approximately 3 percent)—to a hands-off policy in the hopes that the workings of the market would keep labor and management in line.

The major drawback of jawboning and guideposts is that they are contrary to the basic premise of an enterprise system in which the parties, both union and management, are expected to seek maximum gain. When only some unions and management adhere to the guideposts or attempt to act "responsibly," considerable inequities result, and as in the story of Walter Reuther, cooperating parties are likely to be considered by their fellows to be more foolhardy than responsible.

Despite the caveats concerning outright wage and price controls, in late 1971 the administration did impose a wage–price freeze followed by the current system of supervised and regulated adjustments, that has evolved into a system of semi-enforced guideposts. That these controls have been generally well accepted by our society reflects the seriousness of our prevailing economic condition. Unemployment was relatively high, yet inflation showed signs of moderation only after three years of sharply rising prices, and the foreign trade balance and the dollar were in a perilous state.

Chapter 20 deals with the economic implications of controls, but it is appropriate here to note the effect of the recent strong controls on industrial relations. The evolving pattern closely fits the description of government's role in the bargaining process presented at the outset of the previous chapter. There it was stated that the extent of government intervention in union–management relations reflects the government's role relative to that of private enterprise in the economy as a whole.

Now we have modified controls, and we have Wage and Price Boards. Collective bargaining over wages is bound within the framework set by these Boards. These formal limits have been relaxed under Phase III, initiated in early 1973, but the framework for their reimposition remains. The sharp resumption of inflation that immediately followed Phase III serves as a strong reminder that these limits, while not now applied, can be easily reinstituted. What is more, though on an unofficial basis, union wage policy is now set by the AFL–CIO leadership to a greater extent than ever before. Controls and Boards have brought about subtle changes in individual union bargaining power. While we still have our traditional pluralistic bargaining system, wage contracts are more and more influenced by the bargaining power of union representatives on a national board, a process more typical of European than American unionism.

Structural changes   Proposed structural changes range from "break up the big unions and fractionate the collective-bargaining system" to "break up the monopolistic companies and do away with administered prices." As noted above, the highly decentralized collective-bargaining system in the United States (as compared with the more centralized systems in a number of European countries) may further inflationary pressures. It is not likely that any far-reaching steps can be taken to alter the basic structure of American collective bargaining, but even if this were possible there is little reason to think that further fractionation would help. It would be more useful to experiment with greater centralization in the hope that a centralized collective-bargaining agency would at least be in the position to see the effects of its negotiations on the economy and, if it wished to do so, might act more "responsibly."

Another type of structural change that has been vigorously proposed would involve the cooperation of both union and management. This proposal embodies changes in the labor market and the employment relationship through manpower policies, through an improved employment service, skill

training programs, mobility policies, and other measures to improve the efficient functioning of the labor market, whereby it is hoped that inflationary
pressures at high levels of employment could be reduced.[2]

The abandonment of price stability   Although few
knowledgeable government authorities still hold to the notion that prices can
be kept stable, there is still a marked difference of opinion as to how high
prices should be permitted to rise. Until Phase III the United States had been
more concerned about constraining inflation than about maintaining full
employment. A number of European and Asian countries have been much
more tolerant of inflationary price rises, and they have apparently been able
to prosper under conditions of inflation that the United States has felt to be
intolerable.

Those who argue that the best solution to the full-employment–collective-bargaining–inflation dilemma is to simply accept inflation are prone to
stress some of the benefits of inflation. They note that the full employment
that usually accompanies inflation reduces poverty, and that many businessmen profit from a situation in which they can buy at one price and sell at a
higher price. However, inflation poses serious dilemmas for the U. S. balance
of payments and it causes hardship for those on relatively fixed incomes. A
policy of inflation as the most viable solution have to solve these problems.

Conclusion

The major question facing the future of collective bargaining in the
United States is whether it can remain a voluntaristic system and the principal
means by which wages, hours, and working conditions are established in
American industry. Public concern over strikes, especially those affecting an
essential service or product, and over inflationary wage settlements poses a
serious threat to present institutions in the labor–management field. The
preceding discussion has attempted to place both the issues of strikes and of
inflation in perspective. Strikes as a whole should be distinguished from
strikes which endanger the public health and safety; only the latter need to
be a matter of public and legislative concern. A growing number of procedures have been devised and proposed to further the settlement of disputes
without a strike; and many of these procedures stop far short of an outright
prohibition of strikes.

---

[2]For a spirited discussion of this approach, see Charles C. Holt et al., *The Unemployment-Inflation Dilemma: A Manpower Solution* (Washington, D. C.: The Urban Institute, 1971).

Similarly, the advantages and disadvantages of inflation must be viewed against the background of the steps needed to stop inflation. There is no informed agreement concerning the extent to which unions and collective bargaining contribute to inflationary pressures. However, even if their culpability in this regard could be fully established, their inflationary role could be ended only through far-reaching structural change in the American economy. Like strikes, the costs and benefits of inflation must be weighed carefully against the costs and benefits of alternative courses of public action.

Readings

Aaron, Benjamin, "National Emergency Disputes: Is There a 'Final Solution'?," *Wisconsin Law Review,* Vol. 1970.

Ashenfelter, Orley, and George E. Johnson, "Bargaining Power, Trade Unions, and Industrial Strike Activity," *American Economic Review* (March 1969).

Doering, Barbara, "Impasse Issues in Teacher Disputes Submitted to Fact Finding in New York," *Arbitration Journal,* Vol. 27 (1972).

Edelman, Murray, and R. W. Fleming, *The Politics of Wage-Price Decisions.* Urbana: University of Illinois Press, 1966.

Kornhauser, Arthur, Robert Dubin, and Arthur M. Ross, eds. *Industrial Conflict.* New York: McGraw-Hill Book Co., 1954.

Perlman, Richard, ed. *Inflation: Demand-Pull or Cost-Push?* Boston: D. C. Heath, 1965.

Perlman, Richard, ed. *Wage Determination: Market or Power Forces.* Boston: D. C. Heath, 1964.

Ross, Arthur M., and Paul T. Hartman. *Changing Patterns of Industrial Conflict.* New York: John Wiley and Sons, 1960.

Twentieth Century Fund Task Force on Labor Disputes in Public Employment. *Pickets at City Hall.* New York: Twentieth Century Fund, 1970.

Work Stoppages in Government, 1958–1968, BLS Report 348 (Washington, D. C.: United States Department of Labor, 1970).

Part Four   Labor-Market Analysis

Chapter Ten

The Pricing Mechanism and Resource Allocation

The pricing of resources

It is obvious that productive resources have prices, just as consumer goods do: the price of labor is the wage rate; the price of money is interest; the price of land use is rent; and the price of entrepreneurial talent is profit. The production of most goods requires the use of all four resources, and the price of a good is the sum of the dollar contributions made by all the factors. Distribution theory has to do with the basis on which each factor is remunerated; it is analytically a complicated subject. In addition, the size of the share that "ought" to be imputed to the various factors is a source of constant controversy among the recipients.

The derived demand for resources

Final goods and services are demanded because they satisfy certain wants: basic wants, such as those for food, clothing, and shelter, or less fundamental wants, such as the desire for color television or backyard swimming pools. The desires for some goods may have been created by advertisers who are especially gifted in widening, each day, the range of goods consumers feel they cannot do without. In any case the goods are bought for consumption, often within a fairly short period of time.

The demand for resources is of a different origin. Resources are demanded because they can be used to produce goods and services. Accordingly, the demand for a resource is a *derived* demand, dependent on a prior demand for the good it helps to create. Entrepreneurs demand the services of textile workers, for example, because consumers demand textile products. In the aggregate, the demand for textile workers is the sum of the demands of all textile manufacturers, each of whom is weighing the cost of the worker (and other resources) against the price of the product he expects to sell. In market terms, the relevant demand for labor of a particular type is the demand schedule applicable in a given labor market, which may be quite restricted geographically.

Elements of resource demand   The primary determinant of resource demand is the schedule of demand for the commodity it produces. At any time the quantities of the good that buyers will purchase at different prices depend in turn on the tastes, incomes, and alternative goods on the market. These conditioning factors are always changing: tastes shift in accordance with fashion and fad; incomes rise and fall; goods that substitute for or complement the commodity under consideration change in form and price. It follows that industry's demand for the labor used to produce the commodity is also constantly shifting. An increase in demand for airline travel brings with it an increased demand for stewardesses; if railway passenger traffic is declining, so, too, is the employment of railway porters. A demand shift may be quite sharp, as in the sudden demise of a fad and its producers. Or it may be a gradual change taking place over several years, like the shift away from railway travel. The timing of the shift is a critical element in the adjustment of the resource, a gradual change enabling labor to accommodate itself to the necessary job transfers with a minimum of dislocation.

A second condition on the demand for a resource is its productivity. Historically, we have experienced increases in output per man-hour, albeit the rate of increase has differed from one year to the next, and more significantly, from one period to another. Increases in productivity originate either in the resource itself or in the accompanying resources. In the first instance, the quality of the resource may be improved; for example, the more highly educated and trained the labor force, the greater will be its productivity. Improvements in the quality of labor thus tend to increase the quantity that will be demanded at any given wage, since the output per unit of labor is increased. In the second case, the quantity or quality of the accompanying factor may be increased, with the result that each unit of labor has more capital with which to work. Each hour of work is thus more productive because more capital is invested. Technological advances have the effect of increasing output per man-hour through improvements in the techniques of production, in the extent of mechanization, in the utilization of automatic machine controls.

A third influence on the demand for a given resource is the prices of other resources. The price of related commodities affects the demand for a given commodity; the effects differ according to whether the commodities are substitutes or complements. When we turn to the demand for resources, we find that within rather wide limits most resources are substitutes one for the other. For example, a rise in the wage rate of labor may cause a producer to introduce labor-saving machinery; the firm will then use more machinery and fewer men to produce the same final output. In any event, there is normally a substitution effect that tends to shift the demand for a given resource in the same direction as the price of competitive resources. Thus, an increase in the price of machinery will tend to augment the demand for labor, and a decrease in the price of machinery will tend to have the opposite effect.

But there is not only a substitution effect; there is also an output effect. The prices of resources determine the cost of production and, therefore, the supply of a commodity. If the price of a resource to a firm or industry increases, a general increase in cost and a decrease in output may result. Because of the substitution effect, the postulated resource price increase may increase the demand for a competitive resource. At the same time, the output effect of the price rise may offset, or more than offset, the substitution effect. Hence if the price of factor K increases, the demand for factor L may increase because of the substitution effect. Nevertheless, the increase in the price of K may cause such a reduction in total firm or industry output that the output effect entirely cancels the substitution effect. Thus, overall, an increase in the price of factor K may cause a decline in firm or industry demand for factor L, even though K and L are substitutes one for the other.

In summary, when resources are competitive, that is, substitutable, the output and substitution effects tend to shift the demand-for-resource curve in opposite directions. The output effect may indeed be strong enough to overwhelm the substitution effect.

When resources are complementary, the output and substitution effects work in the same direction, thereby reinforcing one another. Assume that factors K and L are production complements in a particular firm or industry. The more K is used, the greater must be the use of L. If the price of K increases, the quantity of K demanded will decline, causing a decline in the demand for L. At the same time, the increased price of K causes an increase in cost and a consequent decrease in output. A decline in output, in turn, will mean that less of both K and L are used. Hence, the increased price of K causes a decline in the demand for L attributable both to the substitution and to the output effects.

When the market for resources as a whole is considered (as opposed to supply and demand within a particular factor market), the resultant direction of substitution and output effects is unclear. A general rise in wages would tend to lead to a substitution of capital for labor, assuming a steady level of total production, and some unemployment of capital. But an output effect would ensue only if general wage increases lead to a decline in aggregate demand or total production. Whether such a decline would result has been a subject of much theoretical analysis and empirical investigation, which is reviewed in Chapter 14 in the study of unemployment theories.

Since the demand for a resource is derived from the demand for goods and services, it follows that some of the market characteristics of the product itself will apply to the demand schedule for the resource. The carryover is particularly important in the case of price elasticity of demand.

Elasticity of resource demand   Price elasticity of demand is a measure of the percentage change in quantity purchased in response to a percentage change in price. In accordance with the "law" of demand, the quantity of a good purchased increases as its price decreases; the concept of elasticity raises the question of *how much* the quantity increases with a given price decrease.

Consumer reaction to a change in price varies from one product to another. What is the reaction to a cut in the price of automobiles? Would the quantity of cigarettes bought change significantly if the price were raised by say, 10 percent? In each case, what would be the effect of a change in the price of only one brand of the product? In an extreme case, a change in price may result in no change in the quantity purchased; this limiting case is one of complete inelasticity. At the other extreme—the case of a purely elastic demand—a very small change in price may occasion an infinitely large change in the quantity bought. A seller considering a change in price clearly must make some guess as to the degree of elasticity of the demand curve he faces, and thus estimate the effect of the price change on his total revenue.

The elasticity of demand for a resource is dependent in part on the elasticity of the underlying commodity demand. If the quantity of a product bought is relatively insensitive to a price cut, there is little incentive for the seller to lower price. If price does fall, moreover, there is no reason for the producer to hire additional workers; the demand for labor, along with that for the commodity, is inelastic. But there are other factors affecting the elasticity of demand for a resource. Just as with the demand for goods, the elasticity of resource demand is influenced by the availability of substitutes. The greater the substitutability of other factors of production—machines for labor, for example—the greater is the elasticity of demand for the resource in question. If the producer can easily shift from one resource to another, he will do so when the price (which is cost to the producer) of a particular factor rises. Hence, a small increase in the wage rate can result in a relatively large reduction in the quantity of labor demanded.

Resource supply: the special case of labor

Limitations on the quantities of resources available place the ultimate constraints on the volume of goods that can be produced. At any time there is limited land, limited capital, and a limited number of workers. Through time, some of these constraints can be eased: more land can be made arable, more capital can be accumulated. In the case of labor, the quantity available for hire may change somewhat within a very short period of time, depending on incentives offered, on types of jobs that become available, and on institutional arrangements governing the amount of labor each worker normally offers.

The supply of a good is normally a positive function, the quantity offered for sale increasing as the price increases. This positive relationship between price and quantity exists because at higher prices it becomes more remunerative to increase output. The commodity's upward-sloping supply, in conjunction with its negatively-sloping demand curve, permits the market for the good to be cleared at the one price which satisfies both buyers and sellers. But the quantity of labor offered does not necessarily rise with increases in the wage offered; under certain circumstances the amount of labor may decline with increases in wage rates.

Consider, for example, the economy's supply of labor during a short period of time. Employers may bid up the wage rate, and to some extent the higher wage is likely to increase the quantity of labor offered, primarily by drawing into the labor force some marginal workers: housewives who formerly found the pay unattractive, possibly retirees and students who will work on a part-time basis. As wages rise further still, there may be an offsetting tendency, however, for the family to feel that it can live on one income. Wives may then prefer to stay at home, and children to stay in school. Associated with higher incomes may also be a tendency for the hours of work per week or per year to decline. Within some range of wages, fewer hours may therefore be offered at higher wages than at low. Thus within the short run, the supply of labor for the economy may bend backward; certainly it is extremely inelastic with respect to wages. Detailed discussion of the aggregate and individual supply of labor will be postponed to Chapters 11 and 12, immediately following.

Wage rates and levels of employment

Given the negatively sloped demand for labor and assuming for the moment a labor supply function that is positively inclined, it is easy to see that the intersection of these aggregate curves determines the wage rate and the quantity of labor employed. Changes in the conditions of demand or supply, moreover, affect the wage and the number of workers employed in the same manner that a shift in the demand for or supply of a commodity would affect commodity price and volume of sales. An increase in the demand for cotton textile workers, for example, occasioned by the imposition of a tariff on the importation of Japanese-made synthetics, may temporarily raise both the wage rate and the number of workers hired. The supply of young workers decreases suddenly each September as students reenter high school and college, thereby lowering the number of persons at work (unless some offsetting rise in workers appears from another source). In long-run terms, offsets have clearly emerged in the changing labor force habits of males and females: young and older men are now less frequently in the labor force than ever before, whereas more women are workers.

The extent to which a shift in the demand for or supply of labor changes the wage rate, and the extent of its effect on employment, depend on the elasticity of the curves themselves. If in a labor-market area only a slight increase in the weekly salary offered could persuade large numbers of married women to take jobs as secretaries, the supply of secretaries is extremely elastic in the relevant price range. Industry could therefore find enough additional personnel of this category by offering a small salary increase. By contrast, the supply of physicians and dentists can be increased only after a lengthy educational period. Generally speaking, the supply of labor is more elastic, the longer the time period under consideration. The elasticity of demand for labor of a particular type varies also for reasons indicated above, and this degree of elasticity dictates the wage effect and the employment effect of a given shift in labor supply.

Through time, the demand for labor of any given classification shifts as commodity demands shift, and as technology improves. The supply of labor in various categories also changes, the aggregate supply for an economy growing with the growth in population. One of the most important questions now being posed for advanced economies is that of the overall balance between the demand for and supply of labor, given two major trends: the rapid pace of mechanization in industry, which eliminates many sources of employment, and the high growth rate in population and labor-force size. The possibility of unemployment inevitably hovers over such an economy. In the United States of the early 1960s the rate of growth was not high enough to

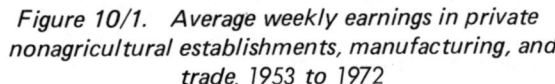

Figure 10/1.   Average weekly earnings in private nonagricultural establishments, manufacturing, and trade, 1953 to 1972

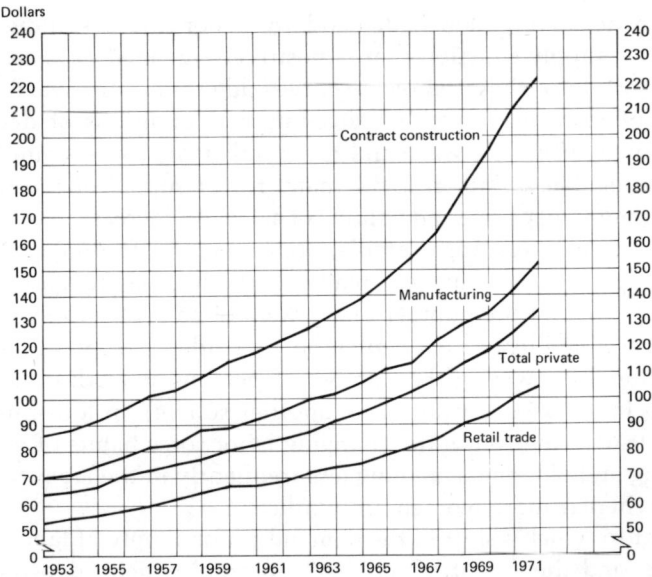

Source: Employment and Earnings, June 1973; Monthly Labor Review, June 1973

generate the necessary number of new jobs—an estimated 3 million per year
—to prevent unemployment. So although total employment increased, year
after year, the problem of unemployment persisted.

An explanation of unemployment, held more in the past than currently,
is the downward rigidity of prices and wage rates. In the classical explanation,
the impact of improved technology and increased output is felt on prices; the
gains from real growth are thus passed on to the consumer in the form of
lower prices and greater volumes of goods. But during the last three decades
neither prices nor wages have fallen. Instead, workers have shared in the
rising output of the economy in accordance with their rise in money wages,
these money wages made possible by an expansion in the supply of money
and credit. As a result, output has expanded, wages have risen, the number
of jobs has grown (although not fast enough to absorb all who wish to work
at going rates of pay), and even in periods of serious unemployment, prices
have continued to rise. Such an upward sweep is not viewed with alarm by
workers whose jobs are secure, nor by entrepreneurs whose profits are rising.
But the unemployed man, the family living on an annuity or other fixed
income, or the worker whose wage lags behind the price change, is likely to
protest that the trend creates certain inequities.

Resource allocation and consumer welfare

Efficient allocation of scarce resources over the wide range of possible
uses is the major function of any economy. Most national goals that are
emphasized from time to time—full employment, a high rate of growth,
industrialization, improved standards of living—are goals whose attainment
depends primarily on the extent to which the economy is able to channel its
factors of production into the areas of greatest demand. For only when resources move freely and quickly from one use to another, in accordance with
the buyers' preferences, are consumers' interests being served.

In the ideal economy there are no restraints on the mobility of productive
resources. Labor and capital then move into the industries and firms that are
bidding for them, as evidenced by the resource prices being offered. Leaving
low-wage jobs, workers quickly shift into employment at higher wage rates,
and this movement continues until the wage differential for a particular job
is eliminated. When the workers quit their low-paying jobs, the effect is to
raise the wage in that area, by cutting back the supply of labor. When they
enter the high-wage jobs, the effect is to lower the wage, by increasing the
supply of labor. As a result, the wage paid by the two employers for a
particular job tends to become equal, and there is therefore no longer a wage
reason for changing jobs.

It is easy to see that such mobility improves the lot of the low-wage
worker. Were he forced to stay in the less productive job, he would continue

to earn the lower wage. But what of the merits of the movement from the public's vantage point? Is the higher wage not reflected in higher costs of production and prices? In fact, the opposite happens. When he moves into the more productive job the worker is able to contribute his services in such a way as to add more to total output. Each hour of labor, producing more goods, can be remunerated at a higher rate of pay. The consumer gains the increase in goods which (assuming no price rigidities) should lower the price, not raise it. It is thus the higher productivity that makes the higher wage rate possible for the worker and the greater volume of goods available to the consumer.

For these gains to accrue to the consumer and the worker, the economic process must be highly responsive to consumer demand. Prices must be flexible, workers and other resources must be mobile. In order for these two conditions to prevail, there must be complete knowledge of market conditions on the part of all the participants. In brief, the economy must be purely competitive. To the extent that such a competitive ideal is not achieved, the consumer's welfare suffers. Restraints on the movement of resources from one employment to another, or any withholding of the supply of labor or goods in order to maintain prices, act to restrict the total output of the economy. The consumer then suffers a loss in the potential supply of goods and services he could enjoy.

Monopoly restraints exist throughout the economy. They pervade the markets for goods, the pricing of labor services, the management of financial institutions. Furthermore, even in the absence of deliberate control, significant impediments to resource mobility exist. The low-wage worker in one state does not always know that the pay is higher in the next state, nor would he always be willing to move his family in order to take advantage of the better wage. Lack of knowledge, family ties, personal preferences, nonwage inducements of all sorts reduce the worker's geographical mobility. In other words, immobility may reflect a rational decision or an irrational decision according to whether or not the economic and noneconomic costs of moving are greater than the economic and noneconomic benefits.

Labor's price and labor's income

The price of a commodity is normally displayed in some conspicuous place—if not on an attached price tag, in some equally convenient manner. A shirt costs ten dollars, and the customer has only to decide whether that expenditure is worth more to him than some alternative use of his ten dollars. The seller is always willing—even eager—to sell at the price he has set, since presumably that price covers costs and a margin of profit.

But the man who sells his labor has to make a far more complicated decision. He must weigh factors in addition to the wage rate offered him: the location of the job, and whether he would be involved in a long commuting trip twice a day, or possibly even have to move his family; the fringe benefits available—vacation time, sickness insurance, retirement annuity, the prospects for promotion. A rational decision as to which job to take necessarily involves some consideration of all such variables, in addition to the primary wage rate. Businessmen must also make decisions based on many variables, when choosing location, expansion, or contraction of operations. But they can all be tied to the profit motive, and be based on dollars and cents considerations. The worker, however, tied to his service, has nonmonetary factors clouding his work decision.

Nonwage considerations in job choice

A number of studies of the job search have concluded that workers usually have very little information on the total spectrum of jobs available, either in their own or in nearby communities, particularly if these workers are among the lower socioeconomic groups, who are less likely to be familiar with the channels of publicity, and who may not read newspapers regularly. Even when employment opportunities are well known, however, the choice is often made on a nonwage basis.

How much advantage does the worker attach to living in the region of the country with which he is familiar? Obviously, it is very difficult for a rural resident of Tennessee to adjust to the demands of living in Chicago, even when the city offers satisfactory job opportunities. The record shows a high propensity for workers to quit and return to their native states after only brief periods in industrial centers, although working conditions at home have seldom improved. Attempts to solve some of the migration problems—housing, social services, etc.—have met with limited success. Cost-of-living differences, real or imagined, frequently impede the movement of labor into areas of job surplus, or at the least make it necessary for the high-cost area to offer substantially higher rates of pay in order to attract workers.

The regional factor is only one of many, however. In recent decades the fringe benefits that go with a job have become increasingly important. In a sense, fringes can be considered as part of the wage: the employee receives part of his remuneration in the form of a deferred annuity for old age, for example, or in the guise of medical insurance for himself and his family. He may view an extra week's vacation as a type of salary offset. The higher the pay, and hence the higher the income tax liability, the greater the appeal of fringe benefits that are not taxable.

In many instances, workers feel that the presence of a labor union is the best assurance of fair treatment on the job; in some cases, workers have been known to oppose the formation of a union, viewing it as a threat to job stability. Personal conflicts between workers and foremen or other officials of the firm create a bad image for a particular company, while good personnel

224 Chapter Ten The Pricing Mechanism and Resource Allocation

relations provide a favorable picture for another. In recent years, different companies have displayed markedly different attitudes toward the hiring of blacks in jobs formerly closed to them. For these and other reasons, workers in a labor-market area may characterize an employer as a good or a bad one to work for, even when the wage differential is in the latter's favor.

From wage rate to spendable income

Nevertheless, among employees who are paid on an hourly basis, the wage rate is the first and most significant variable. Labor has often engaged in long and expensive strikes for an increase of a few cents an hour in the wage rate. In the Broadway hit musical *Pajama Game,* which was based on Richard Bissell's book, *7½ Cents,* the factory workers chant their demands: "Seven and a half cents doesn't mean a helluva lot." But then they go on to point out that seven and a half cents every hour, every day, does in fact mean a great deal.

It is clear that only such a translation of hourly pay into weekly, monthly, and annual income makes the demand a meaningful one. An increase of ten cents an hour raises the fulltime worker's income four dollars a week, about seventeen dollars a month, more than two hundred dollars a year. These are respectable increments, at least in periods of relative price stability, although at first glance the amount seems trifling.

Wage increases are frequently based on a percentage of the hourly rate, rather than being a flat cents-per-hour raise. Since percentage adjustments give larger raises to the higher-paid workers, there is a tendency for the wage dollar differentials under such schemes to widen. As subsequent analysis will show, there are now marked differences in the rates of pay for various jobs. In broad terms, one has only to observe the wide disparities between the average earnings in manufacturing, contract construction, and trade (Figure 10/1). Average earnings in contract construction are twice as high as those in wholesale and retail trade. Even workers in manufacturing earn only two-thirds as much as construction workers. The differentials have widened somewhat since 1960, primarily because of the greater increase in pay for construction workers. In the two and one-half decades between 1947 and 1972, these workers gained over 240 percent in current dollars, or 84 percent in constant spendable dollars.[1]

Practically all workers have gained real income during the past twenty years, albeit not as much as construction workers. To demonstrate that labor is financially better off now than in some earlier period requires more than a comparison of hourly wage rates, obviously; what of the number of hours

[1]Carol M. Utter, "Hours and Earnings Trends in Private Industry," U. S. Department of Labor, Bureau of Labor Statistics, *Employment and Earnings and Monthly Report on the Labor Force,* 14 (December 1967), 12.

Table 10/1.   Average weekly earnings and hours of
production workers on private nonagricultural
payrolls

	Total private			
Year	Average weekly earnings	Current dollars	1967 dollars	Average weekly hours
1947	$ 45.58	42.6	63.7	40.3
1948	49.00	46.0	63.8	40.0
1949	50.24	48.2	67.5	39.4
1950	53.13	50.0	69.3	39.8
1951	57.86	53.7	69.0	39.9
1952	60.65	56.4	70.9	39.9
1953	63.76	59.6	74.4	39.6
1954	64.52	61.7	76.6	39.1
1955	67.72	63.7	79.4	39.6
1956	70.74	67.0	82.3	39.3
1957	73.33	70.3	83.4	38.8
1958	75.08	73.2	84.5	38.5
1959	78.78	75.8	86.8	39.0
1960	80.76	78.4	88.4	38.6
1961	82.60	80.8	90.2	38.6
1962	85.91	83.5	92.2	38.7
1963	88.46	85.9	93.7	38.8
1964	91.33	88.6	95.3	38.7
1965	95.06	91.9	97.2	38.8
1966	98.82	95.6	98.4	38.6
1967	101.84	100.0	100.0	38.0
1968	107.73	106.6	102.3	37.8
1969	114.61	113.6	103.5	37.7
1970	119.46	121.2	104.2	37.1
1971	126.91	129.7	106.9	37.0
1972	135.78	137.9	110.1	37.2

Source: *Employment and Earnings*, March 1973.

worked, the decrease in the value of money, the imposition of higher taxes? Summarizing the changes that have occurred since 1947, a recent Labor Department study noted that the production worker has improved his status, almost doubling during the period, as measured by the rise in spendable earnings. The increase in weekly earnings shown in Table 10/1 was accompanied by a decrease of about 3.5 hours of work per week.

Annual improvements in levels of living are clearly related to the rise in spendable income; in fact, this "average" change in real income is perhaps the

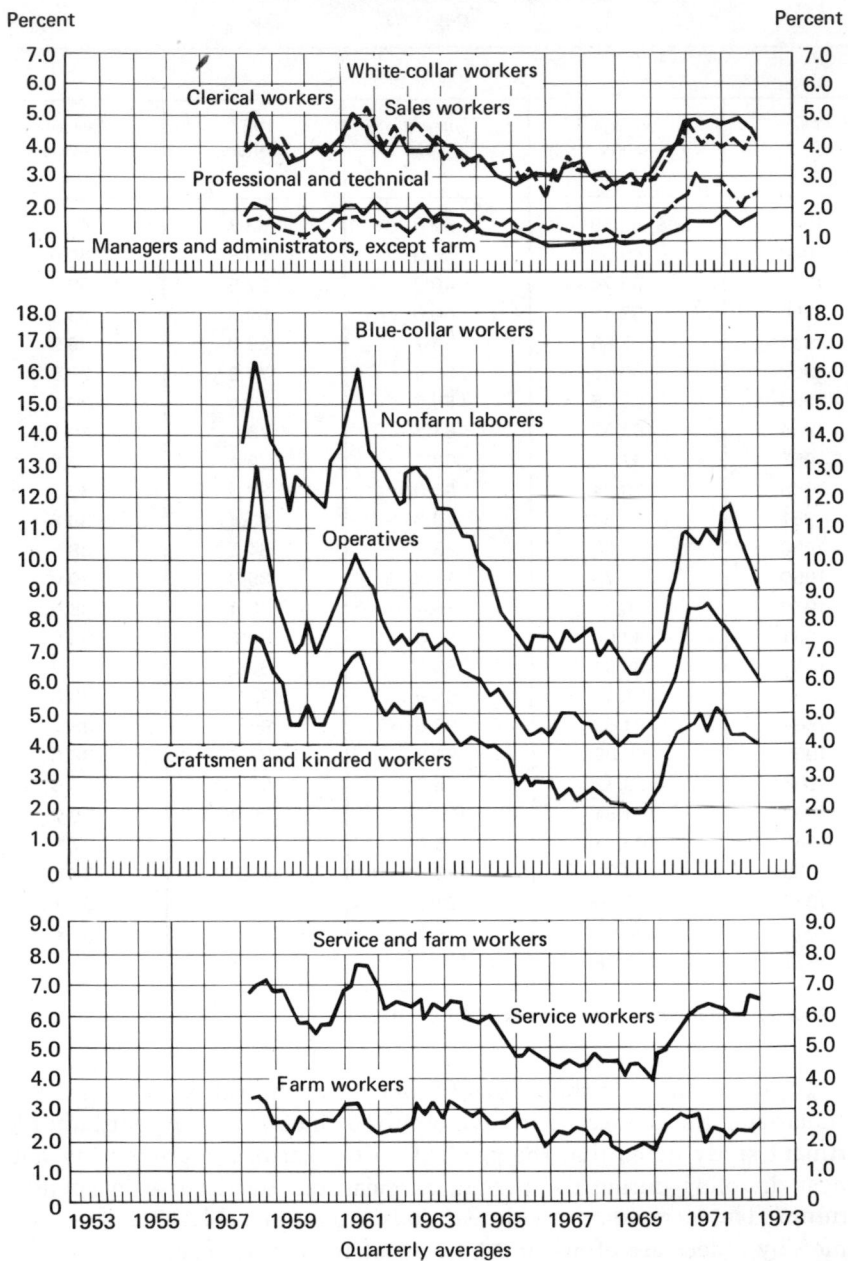

Figure 10/2. Unemployment rates by occupation, 1958 to date (seasonally adjusted)

Source: Employment and Earnings, March 1973.

best single indicator of labor's economic progress, although it must not be supposed that all workers share equally in the advance.

Unemployment and earnings

A gradual decline in the number of hours worked per week or per year has come to be expected. Workers have taken a portion of their economic growth in the form of added free time throughout the twentieth century; average working time has declined from 68 to less than 40 hours per week. Much more difficult to absorb, either by the worker or by the economy, are the sudden cessations of all work for some employees, occasioned by cutbacks in production or by changes in production techniques. Periods of unemployment, albeit often short-term, reduce the worker's income from the going rate of pay usually to the level provided by unemployment compensation, which averages only about one-third of the wage.

The spendable income actually available to a worker employed at any particular wage rate is thus dependent in part on the stability of his job. What are his chances of earning full wages for fifty-two weeks of the year? The probabilities differ, largely in accordance with his occupation group, and with his age and experience in the labor force. Figure 10/2 shows unemployment rates for blue-collar, service, white-collar and farm workers in recent decades. It is evident that one's chances of being out of work are much greater if he is in a blue-collar or service job. Farm workers, less often unemployed, may be underemployed, instead. Only the white-collar employee is relatively safe from job loss.

The hazards of job loss are also greater for certain age groups, notably the very young worker. Teenagers, lacking skill, job experience, or seniority, are usually the first to be laid off in any cutback in a work force. Or they may be unemployed without even getting a first job (Figure 10/3).

Men who have worked for many years have built up seniority rights that protect them to some extent from the threat of job loss. But when older workers—those aged 45 and over—do lose their jobs, the duration of their unemployment is much longer.

The importance of such interruptions in earnings cannot be overlooked, in the total picture of labor's income. The pricing mechanism that serves to allocate goods operates to set wage rates as well, and to divert labor resources into demand areas. In the process of such direction, temporary dislocations occur and labor's earnings are diminished for some part of the workyear. In the final analysis, the price of labor, that is, the wage rate, is of less significance to the worker than his annual spendable income, which reflects not only the rate of pay, but the number of days of work available to him in a year.

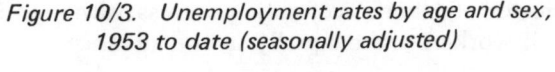

*Figure 10/3.   Unemployment rates by age and sex,
1953 to date (seasonally adjusted)*

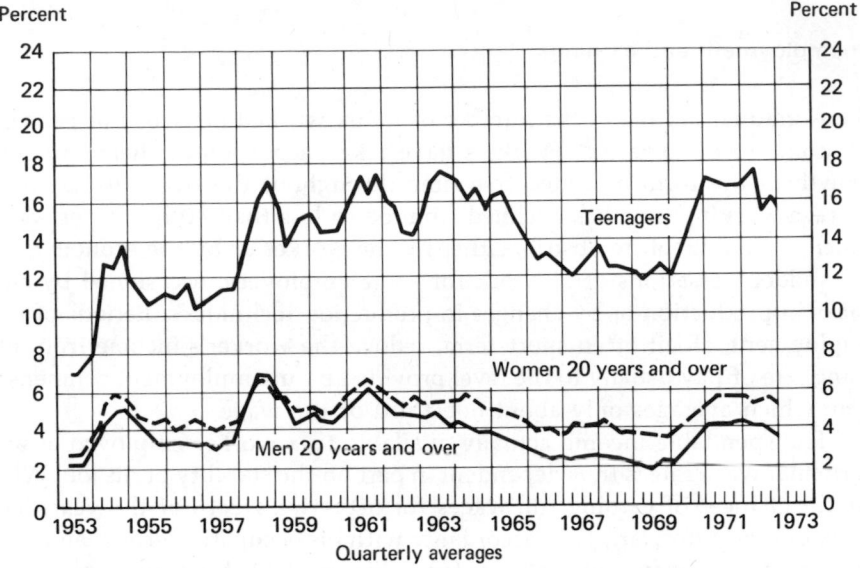

Source: Employment and Earnings, March 1973.

The allocation of labor to
industrial sectors

Expanding sectors of the economy must draw labor from other jobs, or else their expansion is stifled. In order to attract workers, newer industries offer higher wages, better fringe benefits, faster promotions—whatever inducements effectively bid the needed labor from its alternative use. In the complex interchange that has occurred in the American economy during recent years, certain overall industrial trends are discernible.

First, it is obvious that employment is going up in everything except agriculture and mining. Figure 10/4 shows the growth in employment in goods-producing and service-producing industries, respectively. In the former, agricultural jobs have declined by more than a third in the two decades, while mining has dipped by about the same proportion. Although durable and nondurable goods-production jobs and those in construction have increased, the rise has been small in comparison with the gains, of about a third, made by wholesale and retail trade, and the approximate doubling of jobs in services and state and local governments.

In a declining industry such as mining, an impact is usually felt on both the level of employment and the wage rate. In relation to other sectors, both

Figure 10/4.   Nonagricultural payroll employment by
industry, 1953 to date (seasonally adjusted)

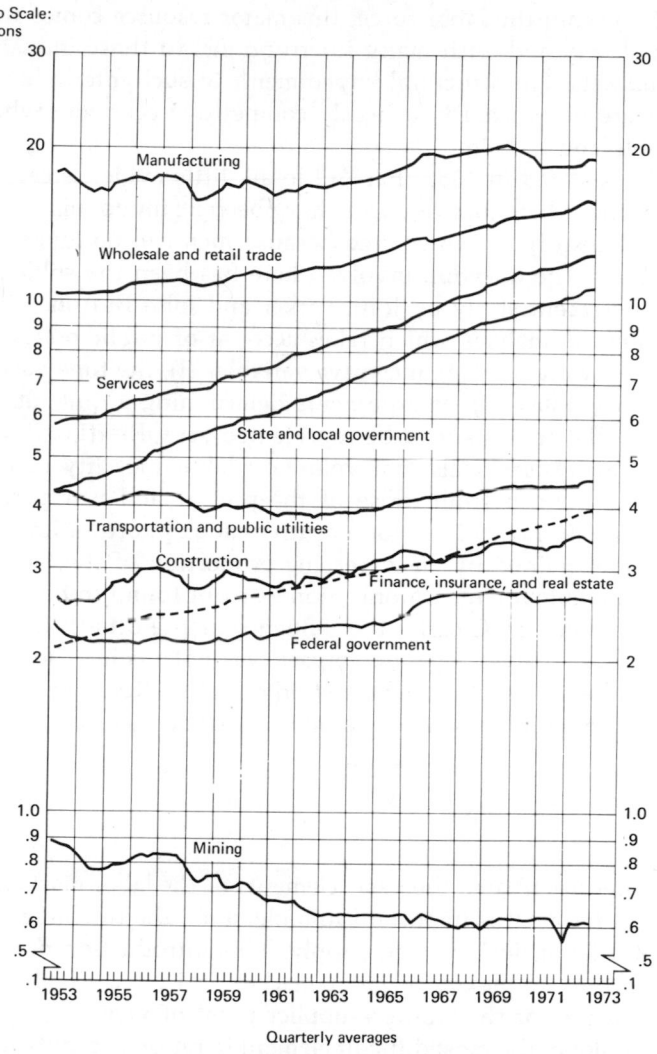

Quarterly averages

Note: Data for 2 most recent months are preliminary.

Source: Employment and Earnings, March 1973.

effects have been pronounced: mining employees gained the smallest increase in hourly earnings of any group of nonagricultural workers during the period —further evidence of the drain away from those areas where demand is declining. A breakdown of employment change by finer industry division would reveal declines in some manufacturing establishments and increases in others, also in accord with changes in consumer demand. Through such sectoral shifts within the labor force, this major resource comes to be allocated, albeit slowly and with many interruptions, to those industries with expanding markets. The structural impediments to such interindustry transfers of labor are minimized in a highly competitive economy whose labor force is flexible and mobile.

Arthur Ross stated in 1958 that "all in all, little evidence can be found for the proposition that labor resources have become immobilized and a new industrial feudalism has been created because men can no longer afford to quit their jobs."[2] The question involved here has been the subject of little analysis until a recent study by John Parker and John Burton. They introduced a theoretical analysis which takes account of public policy variables (P), opportunity variables (O), incentive variables (I), the time variables (T), and all other variables (X), as arguments determining a quit rate, QR. (In equation form, the analysis may be represented as: $QR=f(I,O,P,X,T)$.)

Statistical analysis reveals that voluntary labor mobility in the period 1949–1966 has declined from those of the prewar and war periods. This conclusion holds after correction for incentives and opportunities. Part of the decline can be explained by an increasing proportion of the labor force in nonproduction employment. Unionization was not found to be a significant variable in this analysis. Clearly, the influence of the other variables (X) is significant and an analysis of their impact was not made. The subsequent conclusion, at the least, is that the question raised by Ross needs total reexamination; at this point, his view would seem to be incorrect.

Summary

This chapter has treated the basic elements of the labor market, but only in the broadest terms. It is important to understand the fundamental factors that lie behind labor demand and supply. This introduction does no more than point up the complexity of labor-market decisions, whether from the employer-demander or the worker-supplier point of view.

For the employer the most difficult element in rational, profit-maximizing decision-making is the fact that the demand for labor is derived from product-market conditions. For the worker, his inextricable tie to the service he renders—a service that costs him time and effort—makes utility-maximizing difficult.

The chapter that follows analyzes labor markets and labor supply and demand in more detail. Interrelationships among individual decisions and the economy as a whole are also studied.

---

[2]J. Burton et al., eds. *Readings in Labor Market Analysis.* New York. Holt, Rinehart and Winston, 1971, p. 266.

Readings

Ferguson, C. E. *Microeconomic Theory*, Rev. Ed. Homewood, Ill.: Richard D. Irwin, Inc., 1969.

Hicks, J. R. *The Theory of Wages.* New York: The Macmillan Co., 1932.

Rothschild, K. W. *The Theory of Wages.* Oxford: Basil Blackwell, 1954.

Stigler, George. *Production and Distribution Theories.* New York: The Macmillan Co., 1941.

_____. *The Theory of Price,* 3d ed. New York: The Macmillan Co., 1966.

Chapter Eleven

Wages and Employment in the Firm

Introduction

The behavior of the individual firm operating within the market system is now to be considered. Here the questions have to do primarily with the firm's decisions as to how many workers of a particular type to hire at the going wage rate, or with the appropriate combination of labor and capital. As we shall see, the firm's ability to set the wage rate unilaterally is limited to certain types of market structures. Since the firm's decisions on the quantity of labor it will hire depend on its particular input–output relations, we must first review the theory of production as it affects the demand for labor under different sets of market conditions. Throughout the analysis of firm behavior, it is assumed that profit-maximization is the firm's major goal. Other models could be drawn; we could show the firm that attempts to maximize sales, for example, subject to some minimum profit constraint. Microeconomic theory texts provide the interested student with further models of this type.

The theory of production with one variable input

A brief review of the theory of production requires a number of simplifying assumptions. In particular, assume that production takes place in the short run, with a given state of technology, the short run being defined as a period too short for the quantity of the fixed factor of production to be changed. Suppose further that there are only two factors of production: labor and capital. In the short run, capital is the fixed factor and labor the variable factor. Finally, we will assume that production takes place under conditions of variable proportions, meaning that labor and capital can be used in different proportions in the production process, to produce the same output. The physical relation between a firm's inputs of capital and labor and its output of goods is called a production function. A production function for a firm operating under our assumptions is presented in Table 11/1. Note that as

Table 11/1. A production function with one variable input

Units of capital	Units of labor	Total physical product
10	0	0
10	1	13
10	2	44
10	3	81
10	4.	112
10	5	125
10	6	108

additional units of labor are added to the fixed amount of capital, total output increases, at first, by greater and greater amounts. This initial condition arises from the fact that a given plant or piece of capital equipment is designed to operate most efficiently with some specific amount of labor. Once this most efficient level of employment is reached, output continues to increase, but by smaller and smaller increments, as more workers are added. Finally, a point is reached beyond which further employment would cause a decrease in output.

The production function in Table 11/1 is presented graphically in Figure 11/1 by a curve measuring total output or total physical product, which increases first at an increasing rate, then at a decreasing rate, eventually reaches a maximum, and finally declines.

Figure 11/1. Production function demonstrating the relationship between output and the variable input—labor.

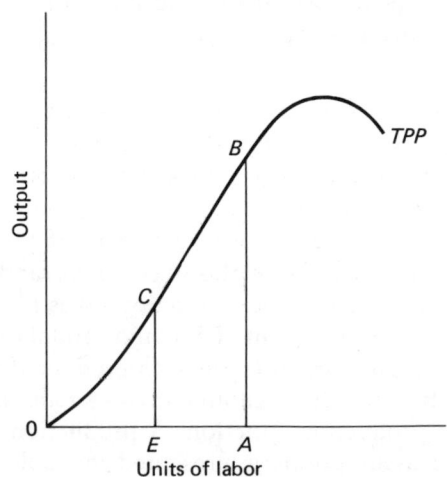

Table 11/2. Total, average, and marginal physical
product

Unit of labor	Total physical product	Average physical product	Marginal physical product
0	0	0	—
1	13	13	13
2	44	22	31
3	81	27	37
4	112	28	31
5	125	25	23
6	108	18	−17

The shape of the production function in Figure 11/1 reflects the law of diminishing returns. The law of diminishing returns holds that the addition of successive units of a variable factor to a given amount of the fixed factors leads at first to increasing increments to total output; but at some point the additions to total output will start to decline. The bell-shaped production function presented in Figure 11/1 depicts the situation of a firm as it successively adds one additional variable factor to the fixed factor in the short run.

In Table 11/2 the average physical product and marginal physical product curves are derived from the production function presented in Table 11/1 and Figure 11/1.[1] In review, the average physical product is defined as the total output (total physical product) divided by the number of units of the variable input employed; the marginal physical product is defined as the change in total physical product resulting from a change of one unit in the use of the variable input.

These average physical product and marginal physical product curves are shown in Figure 11/2. Note that both the average physical product and the marginal physical product curves first rise, then reach a maximum, and finally decline, with the marginal product becoming negative after some point. In addition to the definitions of total, average, and marginal products, we should note their relationships. Geometrically, the average physical product at any given point on the total physical product curve is the slope of a ray from the origin to the total physical product curve at that point. Similarly, the marginal physical product at any point is the slope of the tangent to the total physical product curve.

When the total physical product curve reaches a maximum, its slope is zero. Therefore, by our definition, marginal physical product is zero when total physical product is maximized. Marginal physical product will be a maximum where the slope of the total physical product curve is a maximum. This is the point of inflection of the total physical product curve or, more

---

[1]Note that the total, average, and marginal physical product are graphed as continuous functions and do not specifically represent the data presented in Table 11/1.

Figure 11/2. *APP* and *MPP* curves

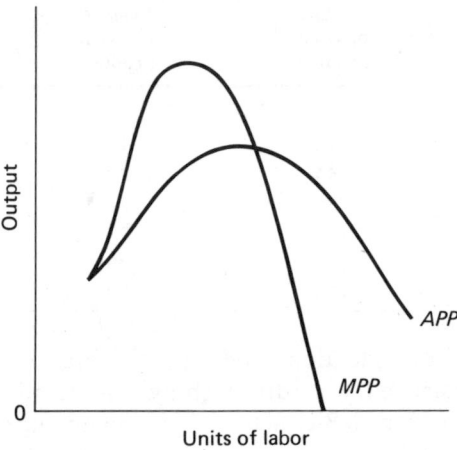

simply, the point at which total output ceases to increase at an increasing rate and begins to increase at a decreasing rate. Average physical product will be maximized when the slope of a ray drawn from the origin to the total physical product curve is a maximum. This will occur at the point where the ray from the origin is just tangent to the total physical product curve.

An example of average product and the maximum level of marginal product is drawn in Figure 11/1. *OA* units of labor would, with supporting fixed capital, produce *AB* units of output. Hence, from the definition of average product, $AP = \frac{TPP}{L}$, where L is the number of units of labor employed, average product in this case equals $\frac{AB}{OA}$.

Marginal product equals the rate of change of total product with respect to a small change in the amount of labor employed, that is, $MPP = \frac{\Delta TPP}{\Delta L}$. Thus marginal product is the slope of the tangent drawn to the total product curve. The slope is a maximum at *C*, the point beyond which the tangent would touch the curve from above, rather than from below. That is, tangent lines would become successively flatter beyond *C*, whereas they were becoming steeper moving up to *C*. Translating the geometry into economics, marginal product rises at employment below *OE*, the amount of labor producing *EC* output, and falls when more than *OE* units are employed. *C* is the point of diminishing returns.

The marginal physical product curve shows the addition to total product attributable to the addition of one unit of the variable factor. If marginal physical product exceeds average physical product, this means that a number greater than the average is being added into the old total. When the new average is computed, it must be greater. Therefore, when the marginal physical product curve lies above the average physical product curve, the average physical product must be rising. The same analysis can be used to show that when the marginal physical product lies below the average physical product, the average physical product must be declining. If the marginal physical product lies above the average physical product when the average physical product is rising and below it when the average physical product is falling, it follows that the marginal physical product must equal the average physical product when the average physical product is at its maximum.

These relationships are illustrated in Figure 11/3, where total physical product is maximized (and marginal physical product is zero) at point C. At the point of inflection of the total physical product curve (A), marginal physical product is at its highest. Average physical product is greatest at the point at which a ray drawn from the origin is just tangent to the total physical product curve (B). Finally, the marginal physical product and average physical product are equal where average physical product is maximized.

The behavior of the total, average, and marginal physical products, as illustrated in Figure 11/3, delineate three stages of production for the firm. Stage I is defined as the range of variable input (labor) usage over which the average physical product is rising. In this stage the fixed input, capital, is being used in uneconomically large proportions relative to labor. Each additional unit of labor increases the average output of labor; for this reason, the rational producer would not operate in this range. Stage III is defined as the

Figure 11/3. Relationship between TPP, APP, and MPP.

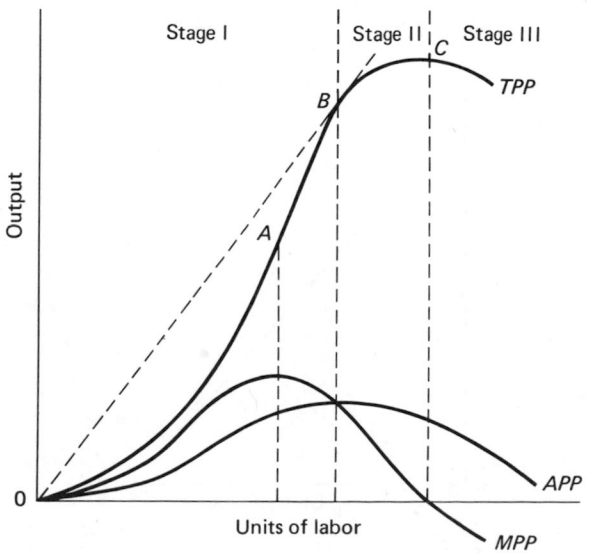

range of variable input (labor) usage over which total physical product is declining. In this stage, labor is being used in uneconomically large proportions relative to the fixed stock of capital. Each additional unit of labor causes total output to decline, and again, the rational producer would not operate in this range. Accordingly, production must occur in Stage II. The only relevant portions of the average and marginal product curves are, therefore, the declining segments in the second stage of production.

The firm's demand for labor

The profit-maximizing entrepreneur will hire labor (or any resource) up to the point at which the addition to total output attributable to the last unit of labor is just equal to its cost. In symbols, equilibrium employment of labor occurs where $MR = MC$. Under perfect competition in both product and resource markets, this equation becomes $MPP \times P = W$, where P is the product price and W the wage rate. By definition of a perfectly competitive product market, P is a constant; thus, employment of labor is determined by the relationship between labor's marginal physical product schedule and the wage rate.

Since the only relevant range of production for a rational entrepreneur is the range of decreasing marginal physical product, it follows that the demand curve for labor must be negatively sloped, with more labor hired, and MPP falling, as the curve falls (Figure 11/4). The slope of the demand curve for labor depends upon the character of the production process. For example,

Figure 11/4.   Demand curve for labor

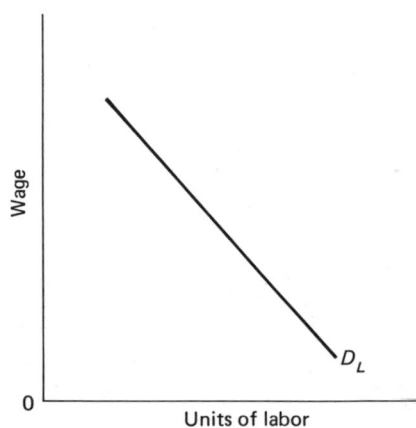

if the process is characterized by a large amount of capital combined with relatively few workers, the marginal physical product of labor curve falls very quickly and, hence, the demand curve for labor is relatively inelastic. Carrying this case to the extreme, if there is only one technical combination of labor and capital at which the firm can feasibly operate, the demand curve for labor is perfectly inelastic (a vertical line) at the desired level of employment. On the other hand, if the production process is characterized by a small stock of capital and a very large number of laborers, the marginal physical product curve and, hence, the demand curve for labor tends to be relatively elastic.

Demand–supply conditions in different markets

It is necessary to draw distinctions among the several types of markets in which the products sell, and among the types of markets in which the prices of the resources are determined. Depending on the market conditions, the price behavior varies for both the product and the resource used to produce it. It follows, therefore, that the quantities of the resource demanded by the firm can be explained only within the frameworks of the product and resource markets. We have just touched on this issue in the presentation of a labor-demand schedule with perfect competition in both markets; in this section we detail equilibrium wage-employment positions under all four types of market conditions: perfect competition in both factor and resource markets, imperfect markets for both, and both cases in which one operates in a perfectly competitive market and the other does not.

Demand for labor: pure competition in the product market

Pure competition in the product market is characterized by a large number of small firms producing a homogeneous product under conditions of perfect knowledge and perfect resource mobility. Each firm is so small that its actions have no effect on the market price of the product. The purely competitive firm can sell all it can produce at the going market price. The equilibrium price of the product is determined by the equality of the market demand for and the supply of the commodity.

The value of an additional employee to the firm can be measured in money terms. His marginal output (MPP_L) is sold in the market at some predetermined price, yielding revenue to the firm. The value of an additional employee in money terms is the change in total revenue (marginal revenue) derived from selling the laborer's addition to output. This concept, called the marginal revenue product of labor (MRP_L), is defined as the addition to total revenue attributable to the employment of one more unit of labor. The marginal revenue product of labor equals the marginal physical product of labor times the marginal revenue of the output, or $MRP_L = (MPP_L)(MR)$.

Under conditions of pure competition, the demand for the product is perfectly elastic, and the price of the product equals its marginal revenue. Therefore, the marginal revenue product of labor will also equal the marginal physical product of labor times the market price of the output, or $MRP_L = (MPP_L)(P)$. The derivation of the marginal revenue product of labor for a firm operating under conditions of pure competition in the product market is presented in Table 11/3.

Table 11/3.   Marginal revenue product of labor under pure competition

Units of labor	Total physical product	Marginal physical product	Marginal revenue or product price	Marginal revenue product
0	0	—	$2	—
1	13	13	2	$26
2	44	31	2	62
3	81	37	2	74
4	112	31	2	62
5	125	23	2	46
6	108	−17	2	−34

According to the rules for profit maximization, the firm will continue to add labor units to the production process until the MRP_L=wage. As a result, the demand for labor, under perfect competition, can be represented by the MRP_L curve with slight qualification. As with all marginal-average revenue curve relationships, the VMP_L curves crosses the VAP_L curve at the latter's maximum point. As a result, all wage-labor input quantity combinations on the VMP_L curve to the right of the VMP_L–VAP_L intersection represent conditions where total revenue (TR) is greater than total variable costs (TVC). It could alternatively be stated that the firm will remain in operation as long as the wage rate is less than the VAP_L. Consequently, the short-run demand curve for labor is represented by the VMP_L curve when it is below the maximum VAP_L. Under pure competition, $VAP_L = MRP_L$, since the product price does not change (decline) the employed, and output, increase. Graphically, the short-run demand for labor is represented by the solid segment in Figure 11/5, on the MRP_L, or VMP_L curve.

Graphically, since the MRP_L is simply a scalar (P) multiple of the MPP_L, it is identical in slope to the MPP at all points. The same is true of the VAP_L and the AP_L curves. Figure 11/5 is merely a dollar valuation of Figure 11/2.

Figure 11/5. The short-run demand curve for labor for a perfectly competitive firm

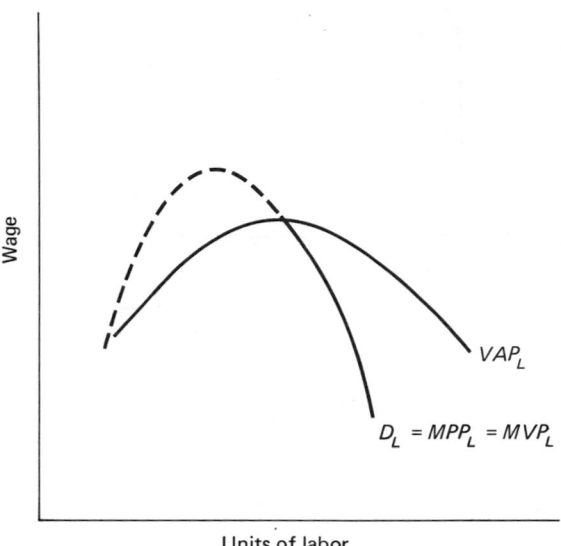

Supply of labor: pure competition in the resource market

Pure competition in the resource market is analagous to pure competition in the product market. Each firm is too small to have any influence on the existing wage rate; therefore, each firm can hire all the labor it needs at the existing market wage. The market wage is determined by the intersection of the market demand for and supply of labor; the firm cannot hire labor at a lower rate and it has no incentive to pay a higher one, since it can hire all the labor it needs at the going rate. This situation may be the same for a small employer in a large labor market.

The supply of labor to a competitive firm is viewed as a horizontal line at the level of the market wage; in other words, the supply of labor is perfectly elastic. The perfectly elastic supply of labor curve for the purely competitive firm is illustrated in Figure 11/6 where OW is the existing market wage. If the firm can hire all the additional laborers it needs at the existing market wage, the change in total cost from hiring one more unit of labor will, of course, be equal to the market wage. That is, the supply curve of labor, which equals the wage at any level of employment, is also the firm's marginal labor cost curve.

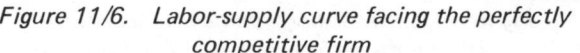

Figure 11/6. Labor-supply curve facing the perfectly competitive firm

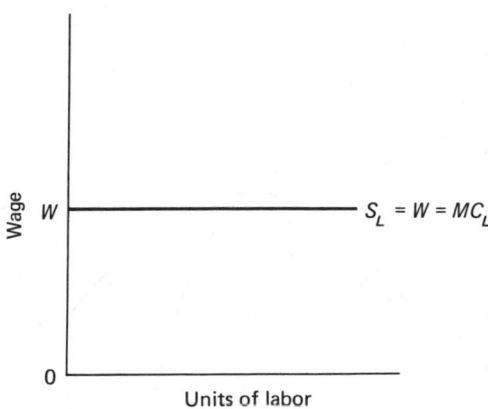

Wage

W ———————————————————— $S_L = W = MC_L$

0

Units of labor

Equilibrium level of employment: pure competition in the product and the resource markets

We have noted that the profit-maximizing entrepreneur will hire labor up to the point where the addition to total revenue attributable to the last unit of labor employed just equals the addition to total cost from employing that unit of labor, or where $MRP_L = MC_L$. For the purely competitive firm, this is the same as stating that he will hire labor up to the point of the intersection of the demand and supply curves for labor. This equilibrium level of employment is illustrated in Figure 11/7.

The equilibrium level of employment is ON and the wage paid by the firm equals OW, the market wage. This equilibrium level of employment of the firm will be changed by any changes in its demand for or supply of labor. A change in the firm's demand curve for labor could result from changes in the productivity of labor and/or the price (or marginal revenue) of the product. A change in the supply of labor to the firm would result from any change in the market wage, or in other words, from any changes in the market demand for or supply of labor.

In the preceding analysis determination of the firm's demand for labor assumed that labor was the only variable input. When we remove this assumption, making labor one of several variable inputs, the demand curve for labor is no longer the marginal revenue product of labor. The variable inputs are now interdependent in the productive process; that is, the productivity

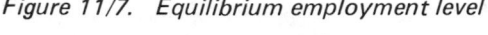

Figure 11/7. Equilibrium employment level

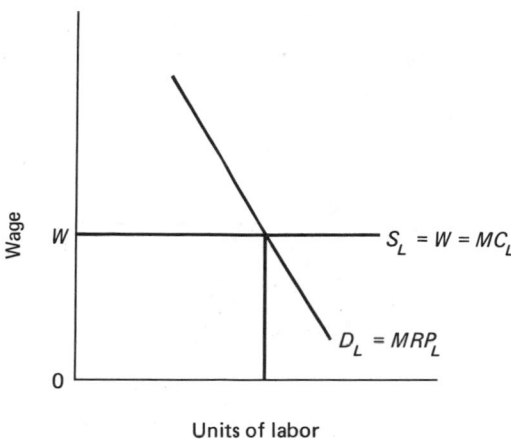

Units of labor

of one resource depends on the quantities of the others used. A change in the price of labor therefore changes the quantity of the other variable resources utilized. This changes the productivity of labor and shifts labor's marginal revenue product curve.

Such a change is illustrated in Figure 11/8. Assume that there are now two variable inputs: capital and labor. Equilibrium initially exists at point E, the intersection of MRP_L , and the market wage OW. If the market wage falls to OW_1, the new supply of labor curve for the firm is S_{L1}. The fall in the price of labor causes the marginal revenue product of labor curve to shift over to MRP_{L1} and new equilibrium will be achieved at point F, where MRP_{L1} equals the market wage OW_1. Other points similar to point F can be derived. The demand curve for labor is represented by these successive equilibrium points, or line EF.

Why does labor's marginal revenue product curve shift to the right when the price of labor falls? This movement is explained by the impact of the lower price of labor on the level of output and the quantity of capital used. A lower price of labor causes the firm to substitute labor for capital. This effect alone would cause the marginal product of labor curve to shift to the left, because each unit of labor has less of the other resources, both fixed and variable (capital), to work with. However, the lower price of labor and the larger quantity of labor used tends to increase output for any given cost outlay. This effect taken separately usually results in an increased use of both labor and capital and a shift in the marginal physical product of labor curve to the right. The lower price of labor lowers the firm's marginal cost of production for a given level of output, and then increases its equilibrium level

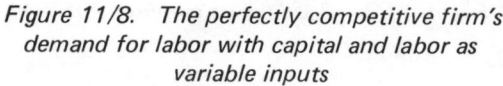

Figure 11/8.   The perfectly competitive firm's
demand for labor with capital and labor as
variable inputs

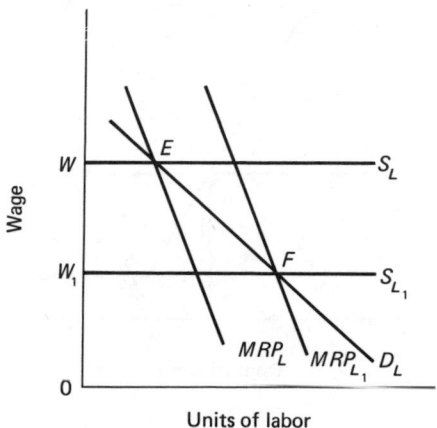

of output, product price remaining unchanged. This increase in output similarly moves the marginal physical product of labor curve to the right. The
aggregate effect of these three component moves is to shift the marginal
physical product of labor curve to the right. If the price of the product remains
constant, the marginal revenue product of labor curve must also shift to the
right.[2]

In summary, the demand curve for labor will tend to be more elastic when
labor is one of several variable inputs. Moreover, the better the substitutes
available for labor, the more elastic its demand curve will be. The firm's
equilibrium level of employment will still be determined by the intersection
of the demand and supply of labor of the firm. However, under the assumption of more than one variable input, the firm's demand curve for labor is no
longer the marginal revenue product.

Demand for labor: imperfect competition in the product market

All the previous analysis has assumed that firms operate in a purely
competitive environment. In reality, the economy is characterized by many
imperfectly competitive markets; pure competition is the exception rather
than the rule.

[2]For an excellent analysis of this topic using indifference curves, see C. E. Ferguson. *Microeconomic Theory*,
Rev. Ed. (Homewood, Ill.: Richard D. Irwin, Inc., 1969), pp. 365–368.

The distinguishing feature of all imperfectly competitive market structures—monopoly, oligopoly, and monopolistic competition—is this: they are
faced with a downward sloping demand curve for their product. Such a
demand curve implies that the imperfectly competitive firm's production
decisions have some effect on the market price of the product. In particular,
the imperfectly competitive firm must lower its price to sell additional units
of its output.

Under conditions of a downward sloping demand curve for the product,
the marginal revenue of the firm will also be decreasing, and will lie below
the demand curve for the product. The marginal revenue (the revenue from
the sale of an additional unit of output) is less than its market price, a
relationship illustrated in Table 11/4. A graph of the data in Table 11/4
would reveal that the marginal revenue curve lies below the demand curve
for the product. Specifically, it would bisect lines drawn from the demand
curve to the price axis. The general shape of the demand curve for the product
and, hence, the marginal revenue curve is determined by the specific market
structure, that is, monopoly, oligopoly, or monopolistic competition.

Table 11/4.   Demand and marginal revenue under
imperfect competition

Units of output	Product price	Total revenue	Marginal revenue
5	$10	$50	—
10	9	90	40
15	8	120	30
20	7	140	20
25	6	150	10
30	5	150	0
35	4	140	−10

If we assume once again that labor is the only variable input, the general
rule that the firm's demand curve for labor is the marginal revenue product
curve of labor is a rule that holds also for conditions of imperfect competition
in the product market.

But in the case of imperfect competition, the marginal revenue product
no longer simply equals $MPP \times P$. This term is designated the *value of
marginal product,* or *VMP.* Under perfect competition in the product market,
then, $MRP = VMP$.

Under imperfect competition in the product market, however, points on
the labor demand schedule are at the equality between the wage and the
addition to revenues of the marginal worker, or wage equals $MPP_L \times MR$.
This addition differs from *VMP* because the product price is no longer constant, but falls as more output is produced when more labor is hired, making
MRP lower under imperfect competition for a given level of employment.

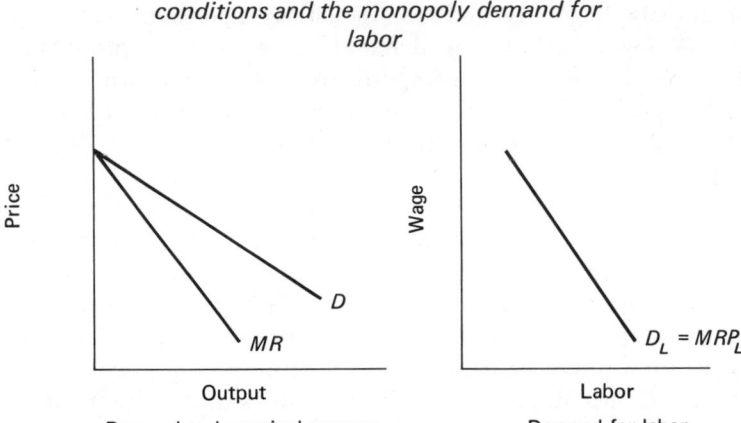

Figure 11/9. Monopoly demand and revenue
conditions and the monopoly demand for
labor

The imperfectly competitive firm's demand curve for labor will be shaped according to the demand and marginal revenue conditions in the product market, that is, the market structure. The remaining portion of this section will consider the firm's demand for labor under the different imperfectly competitive market structures.

Monopoly   Pure monopoly is characterized by a single producer of a product, barriers to entry into the industry, and no close substitutes for the product. Since the monopolist is its only producer, the demand curve for his product is the market demand curve for the product; and it is therefore downward sloping.

The downward sloping demand curve for the product yields a marginal revenue curve that slopes down and lies below the demand curve at all points. If the marginal revenue curve slopes down, the monopolist's demand curve for labor (the marginal revenue product curve) must also slope down. Figure 11/9 presents a graphical illustration of monopoly demand and revenue conditions and the resulting monopolistic demand for labor. The monopolist's demand for labor, *ceteris paribus,* tends to be less elastic than the purely competitive firm's demand for labor, since both the marginal physical product and the marginal revenue are decreasing in the relevant range of production.

Monopolistic competition   Monopolistic competition is defined as a large number of firms producing a slightly differentiated product, with no significant barriers to entry or exit from the industry. Under these conditions the demand curve for the firm's product will be highly but not perfectly elastic. The exact slope will depend on the amount of product differentiation and the number of producers in the market.

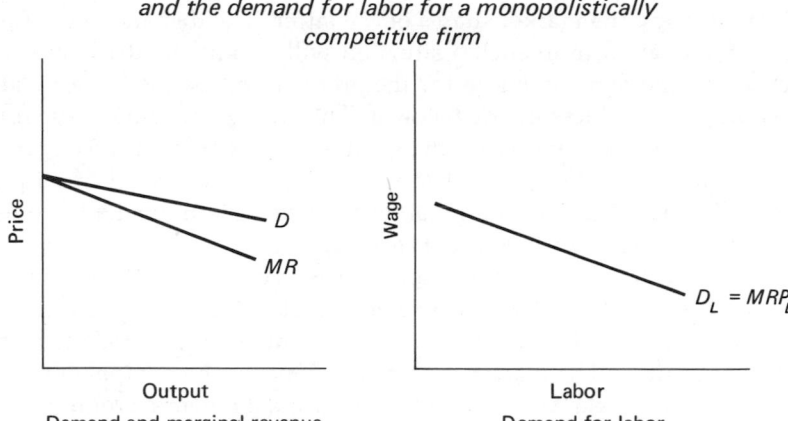

Figure 11/10. Demand for revenue conditions (left)
and the demand for labor for a monopolistically
competitive firm

Output
Demand and marginal revenue

Labor
Demand for labor

As in the analysis of monopoly presented above, the downward sloping demand for the product results in a downward sloping marginal revenue curve and hence a downward sloping demand curve for labor. Figure 11/10 presents the monopolistically competitive firm's demand curve for labor, which will tend to be more elastic, *ceteris paribus,* than the monopolist's demand for labor but not as elastic as that of the purely competitive firm.

Oligopoly   Oligopoly is characterized by a few large producers who are mutually interdependent; the actions of one firm affect the other firms. Oligopolists may produce homogeneous products (in a pure oligopoly) or differentiated products (in a differentiated oligopoly). The mutual interdependence of oligopoly invites collusion among the firms in order to increase profits. Therefore, oligopolies may be characterized by independent action, formal collusion such as centralized cartels, or informal collusion, that is, informal price-setting agreements or price leadership by either the low-cost or the dominant firm in the industry.

This range of possibilities allows the oligopolistic market structure to take any one of a number of forms. Each different market condition will tend to yield a different demand curve for the oligopolist's product. A comprehensive analysis of oligopoly would need to consider a number of different possible market conditions: homogeneous or differentiated products, independent action or collusion, etc. In this analysis we will consider only one specific type of oligopoly.

Assume that the structure is that of the pure, independent-action oligopoly. The firms act so as to ignore price increases of rival firms, but they follow price decreases. The rationale for this assumption lies in the fact that if one firm lowers price other firms follow, so as to retain their market shares; if one firm raises prices, however, the other firms will not follow, because the customers of the new higher-priced firm will shift to the lower-priced firms, thereby increasing the market shares of the latter. The demand curve for the product of a single firm in such a situation will be kinked at the prevailing market price. The demand curve for the product will be more elastic above the existing price and less elastic below it. This kinked demand curve for the product will yield a discontinuous marginal revenue curve for the oligopolist. The marginal revenue curve will be discontinuous at the level of output of the kink. The discontinuous marginal revenue curve will yield a discontinuous demand for labor, as illustrated in Figure 11/11.

In summary, the demand curve for labor is a function of the productivity of labor and the market structure. The market structure affects the elasticity of demand for the product, which in turn determines the shape of the marginal revenue curve. The marginal revenue is one of the components of the marginal revenue product of labor, and the marginal revenue product of labor curve is the firm's demand curve for labor.

Equilibrium level of employment: imperfect competition in the product market

Let us assume that the firm hires labor competitively. This assumption of pure competition in the resource market allows us to retain the perfectly elastic supply curve of labor for the firm. Therefore, the supply of labor curve for the firm will be a horizontal line at the market wage. The equilibrium level of employment will be that level at which the imperfectly competitive firm's demand for and supply of labor are equal. The firm's equilibrium position in the three different market structures of imperfect competition is presented in Figure 11/12, where ON is the equilibrium level of employment and OW the market wage. Several summary points regarding these three equilibria can be made.

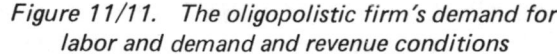

Figure 11/11. The oligopolistic firm's demand for labor and demand and revenue conditions

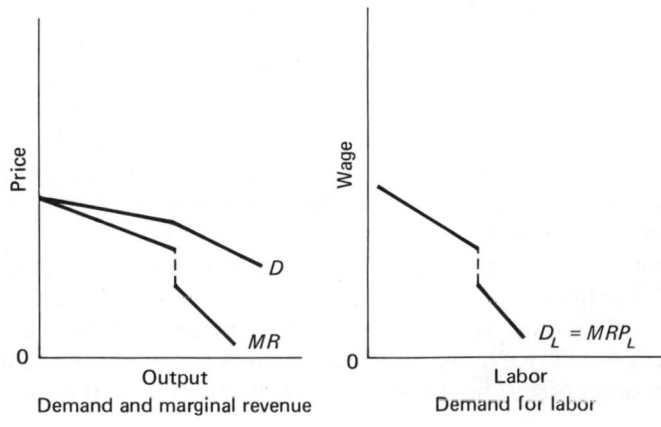

1.   The equilibrium position of the oligopolistic firm in Figure 11/12 merits special reference. If the market wage either increases or decreases but still intersects the demand curve for labor in the discontinuous section, the employment level of the firm will not change. If the market wage decreases enough so that it no longer intersects the firm's demand for labor curve in the discontinuous section, the level of employment will be expanded by the firm. Similarly, if the market wage rises so that it no longer intersects the demand for labor curve in the discontinuous section, the firm will be moved to reduce employment. Hence, in the case of oligopoly, considerable variation in the market wage may occur with no corresponding change in employment.

Figure 11/12.   Equilibrium positions for the firm in imperfectly competitive product markets

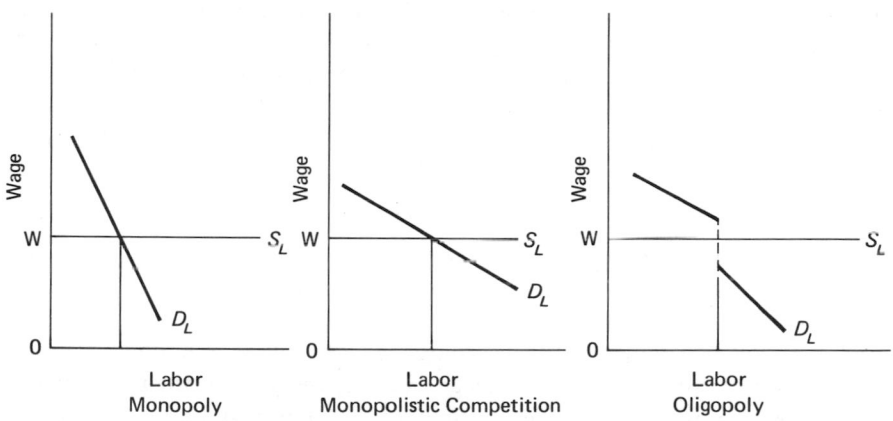

	Labor	Labor	Labor
	Monopoly	Monopolistic Competition	Oligopoly

2.   It is possible to determine the equilibrium level of employment for the imperfectly competitive firm when labor is not the only variable input. The demand curve for labor is derived, using the same procedure as for the purely competitive firm. The analysis of the demand for labor when there is more than one variable input presented in the section under pure competition applies to monopoly, oligopoly, and monopolistic competition as well: the equilibrium level of employment will occur at the intersection of this derived demand curve for labor and the supply curve of labor for the firm.

3.   The notion of exploitation can now be analyzed. The concept of "monopolistic exploitation" has been defined as a condition in which a resource, such as labor, receives as a return something less than the value of its marginal product.[3] The value of the marginal product of labor is the market value of the laborer's marginal output, or the marginal physical product of labor times the market price of the output. We have shown that as long as pure competition exists in the resource market, the wage for workers will tend

---

[3]See Joan Robinson, *The Economics of Imperfect Competition* (London: The Macmillan Co., 1933), p. 281.

toward the value of the marginal product, which in the special case of this market is the same as the marginal revenue product of labor. When conditions of pure competition prevail in the product market, with the price of the product equal to its marginal revenue, the marginal revenue product of labor equals the value of the marginal product of labor, and exploitation will not exist. But the imperfectly competitive firm is faced with a downward sloping demand curve for its product. Marginal revenue to the firm will be less than the price of the product at all levels of output. If marginal revenue is less than the price of the output, the marginal revenue product of labor must be less than the value of the marginal product of labor, and monopolistic exploitation will occur.

In summary, as long as there is any type of imperfect competition, which in graphical analysis is indicated as a downward sloping demand curve for the product, monopolistic exploitation of resources occurs. The use of the term "exploitation" may seem inappropriate if some types of imperfect competition, such as product differentiation in monopolistic competition, are deemed desirable by the consumers of the economy.[4] Moreover, it is clear that the concept of monopolistic exploitation applies to all factors of production, not just to labor.

Supply of labor: imperfect competition in the resource market

Imperfect competition in the resource market occurs whenever a firm is large enough to affect the market wage by its employment practices, such as when there are one or a few large purchasers of labor in a given market, or when the labor itself is very specialized, so that even a small firm prices a significant share of the total labor available. These conditions are called monopsony and oligopsony, respectively.

The imperfectly competitive hirer of labor must raise wages to hire more workers, and he is therefore faced with an upward sloping supply curve of labor. In the case of monopsony, the firm's supply of labor curve is identical to the market supply of labor. In determining the profit-maximizing level of employment, the imperfectly competitive hirer must consider the marginal expense of hiring an additional unit of labor, or the marginal resource cost of labor (MRC_L), which is defined as the change in total cost arising from the hiring of one more unit of labor. The derivation of the marginal resource cost of labor for an imperfectly competitive firm is presented in Table 11/5. The upward sloping supply of labor and the resulting marginal resource cost of labor presented in Table 11/5 are graphed in Figure 11/13.

---

[4]See E. H. Chamberlin, *The Theory of Monopolistic Competition* (Cambridge, Mass.: Harvard University Press, 1933).

Table 11/5. Monopsony and the marginal resource cost of labor

Units of labor	Wage	Total cost of labor	Marginal resource cost of labor
1	$1.50	$ 1.50	—
2	2.00	4.00	$2.50
3	2.50	7.50	3.50
4	3.00	12.00	4.50
5	3.50	17.50	5.50
6	4.00	24.00	6.50

It is important to note that for any imperfectly competitive hirer of labor, the marginal resource cost of labor curve will lie above the supply curve of labor. Since the average resource cost, or wage, is measured along the supply curve of labor, it follows that at any given level of employment the marginal resource cost will exceed the wage paid.

Equilibrium wage and level of employment: imperfect competition in the resource market

As noted earlier, a firm that maximizes profits hires labor up to the point where the marginal cost of hiring the last unit of labor just equals the marginal revenue derived from its use. For conditions of imperfect competition in the labor market, this means hiring labor up to the point where the marginal revenue product of labor equals the marginal resource cost of labor.

Figure 11/13. Supply of labor and the marginal resource cost of labor in imperfectly competitive resource markets

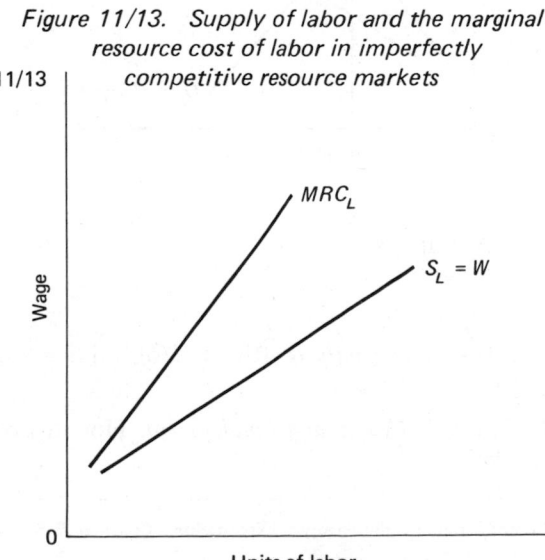

The equilibrium wage and level of employment for a firm operating under conditions of imperfect competition in the resource market is presented in Figure 11/14. The equilibrium level of employment, *ON*, occurs at the intersection of the marginal revenue product curve and marginal resource cost curve. To determine the equilibrium wage we must refer to the supply curve of labor. *ON* units of labor can be hired at a wage of *OW*. Therefore, the profit maximizing firm will hire *ON* units of labor at a wage of *OW*. Note that the monopsonist pays labor a wage, *OW*, which is less than labor's contribution to total revenue, *EN*. When labor is paid a wage less than its marginal revenue product "monopsonistic exploitation" is said to occur.[5] Further consideration of this concept will follow in the next chapter's discussion of the market wage.

Figure 11/14. Equilibrium wage and employment levels for the firm in imperfectly competitive resource markets

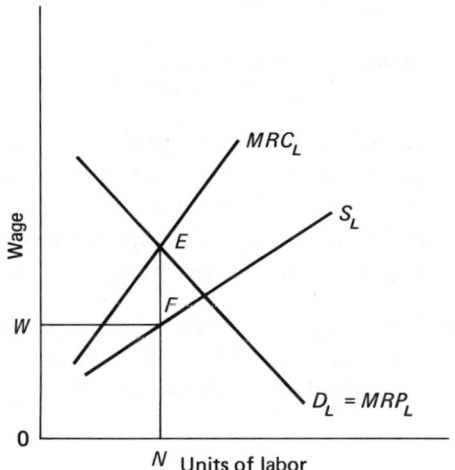

Readings

Boulding, Kenneth. *Economics Analysis,* 4th ed., Vol. 1. New York: Harper and Row, 1966.

Cartter, Alan M. *Theory of Wages and Employment.* Homewood, Ill.: Richard D. Irwin, Inc., 1959.

[5]See G. Bloom, "A Reconsideration of the Theory of Exploitation," *Quarterly Journal of Economics,* 55 (May 1941), 413-43.

Cassels, John M., "On the Law of Variable Proportions," in *Explorations in Economics*. New York: McGraw-Hill Book Co., 1936.

Chamberlin, E. H. *The Theory of Monopolistic Competition.* Cambridge, Mass.: Harvard University Press, 1933.

Clark, J. B. *The Distribution of Wealth.* New York: The Macmillan Co., 1902.

Ferguson, C. E. *Microeconomic Theory*, Revised Edition. Homewood, Ill.: Richard D. Irwin, Inc., 1969.

Hicks, J. R. *The Theory of Wages.* London: The Macmillan Co., 1932.

Perlman, Richard. *Labor Theory.* New York: John Wiley and Sons, 1969.

Robinson, Joan. *The Economics of Imperfect Competition.* London: The Macmillan Co., 1933.

Stigler, George J. *Production and Distribution Theories.* New York: The Macmillan Co., 1941.

Chapter Twelve

Wages and Employment in the Labor Market

Introduction

In the last chapter, we discussed the behavior of the individual firm within the free-price system. There we raised the particular question of how many workers the firm would hire in order to maximize profits, given the overall conditions set by aggregate demand for goods and for labor's services, and given the market structure of which the firm was a part.

It is now time to deal in somewhat more detail with the market structure. Specifically, we shall analyze the market demand for labor under conditions of both pure and imperfect competition, and then derive a market supply schedule for labor, using the indifference-curve approach. With the market demand and supply tools, it is then possible to comment on the nature of monopolistic and monopsonistic exploitation of labor, which occurs when the wage paid to labor is less than the value of its marginal product.

The market demand for labor

In analyzing the market demand for labor, we must consider how a change in the wage affects the level of employment and the output of all the firms in the market. When all firms expand or contract output, the market price of the commodity changes. A change in the market price of the commodity and in the marginal revenue shifts the demand schedule for labor.

Pure competition in the product market

The derivation of the market demand for labor under conditions of pure competition is illustrated in Figure 12/1. We assume for simplicity that labor is the only variable input. The left panel, representing the typical firm in a purely competitive market, is initially in equilibrium at a market wage of OW, with the firm's demand curve for labor MRP. Each firm hires On units of labor at the market wage OW. The total amount of labor employed in the market will be the summation of the individual firm's employment, or ON in the right panel. Therefore, A is one point on the market demand curve for labor.

Let the market wage fall to OW_1. The lower price of labor will induce firms to expand their employment. When all firms expand the quantities of labor used, in response to the lower wage, total output expands. If the output of all firms increases, the market supply of the commodity increases, or shifts to the right. The increase in the market supply of the product will cause its price to fall.

For a purely competitive firm, the market price of a product equals its marginal revenue. Thus, each firm will be faced with a lower marginal revenue for its output. The lower marginal revenue will shift the marginal revenue product of labor curve to the left. In the left-hand panel of Figure 12/1 this shift is indicated by moving from MRP to MRP_1. To maximize profits, each firm will equate the new market wage with the new marginal revenue product of labor. The new equilibrium position will be at point B with each firm now hiring On_1 units of labor at the market wage OW_1. The market level of employment at the new wage, OW_1, will be ON_1. Therefore, B is a second point on the market demand curve for labor. It should be noted that the effect of the shift from MRP to MRP_1 is to cause the industry's product demand curve to decline, and that the consequent market demand curve is less elastic than the summation of the individual firms' demand curves. Other points similarly determined constitute the market demand curve for labor.

The competitive market demand for labor represents the summation of the individual firms' demands for labor or marginal revenue product curves. However, as explained in the above paragraph, the market demand is not the direct or horizontal summation, but the summation of the marginal revenue products consistent with a given level of employment and output. For any level of employment and output, the relevant point of the market demand

Figure 12/1.   Market demand for labor derivation
under perfect competition

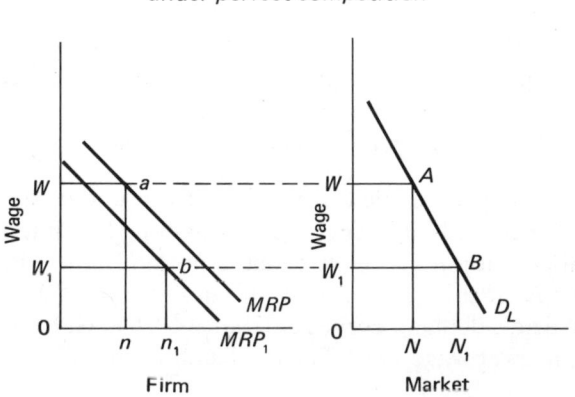

curve for labor represents the summation of the marginal products of labor multiplied by the marginal revenue associated with that level of output. Therefore, the market demand curve for labor is the marginal revenue product curve for the market as a whole.

As noted before, under conditions of pure competition in product market, marginal revenue will equal the market price of the product; hence, the marginal revenue product will equal the value of the marginal product, or $MRP_L = (MR)(MPP_L) = VMP_L = (P)(MPP_L)$. Thus, the competitive market demand curve for labor is also the value of the marginal product of labor curve for the market as a whole.

Imperfect competition in the product market

If the product market were monopolistic, the market demand curve for labor would surely be the demand curve of the monopolist. Since each monopolist is the sole supplier of his product in the market, the effect of a change in the wage on the quantity of output produced, and thus on the market price and marginal revenue of the product, is accounted for in the marginal revenue product curves. In other words, since an individual monopolist's demand curve for labor is downward sloping, it can be used to show the effect of a change in the wage on employment, output, market price of the product, and the marginal revenue product of labor.

If the employers of labor in the market are oligopolists or monopolistic competitors, the market demand curve for labor is not simply the horizontal summation of the individual firms' demands for labor. When the wage falls, all firms in the market will expand output and the market price of the product falls, just as in a purely competitive market. A change in the product price changes marginal revenue and, consequently, the firm's demand curve for labor. The graphical derivation of the market demand curve for labor for an oligopolistic or monopolistically competitive market is similar to that in Figure 12/1 depicting a purely competitive market.

The imperfectly competitive market demand curve for labor represents the summation of the individual firms' demands for labor or marginal revenue product curves. Under conditions of monopoly, firm and market curves are one and the same; under conditions of oligopoly or monopolistic competition, the demand curve is the summation of the marginal revenue products consistent with a given level of employment and output. Therefore, the imperfectly competitive market demand curve for labor (as in the purely competitive case) is the marginal revenue product curve of labor for the market as a whole. However, under conditions of imperfect competition in the product market, marginal revenue will be less than the market price of the product; hence, marginal revenue product is less than the value of the marginal product, or $MRP_L = (MR)(MPP_L) < VMP_L = (P)(MPP_L)$. Thus, the imperfectly competitive market demand curve for labor, *ceteris paribus,* will lie to the left and below the competitive market demand for labor curve.

The market supply of labor

The market supply curve for labor shows the different quantities of a particular kind of labor that will be placed on the market at all possible wage rates. The precise shape of the market supply curve is difficult to determine, but we can gain insight into this problem by analyzing the supply of labor offered by an individual.

The supply of labor from an individual

In analyzing an individual's supply of labor we use indifference curves, which depict an individual's tastes and preferences for work, leisure, and income, among other arguments. Specifically, an indifference curve shows the different combinations of two commodities that yield equal satisfaction to the individual.

In Figure 12/2 the quantity of good X is measured along the horizontal axis and that of good Y along the vertical axis. We can derive a set of indifference curves, I_1, I_2, I_3, etc., which describe the consumer's preferences between goods X and Y. The characteristics of these indifference curves are: (1) they slope downward to the right; (2) they are convex to the origin; and (3) they do not intersect. Higher levels of satisfaction are shown by higher

Figure 12/2.   Indifference curve map for the
individual

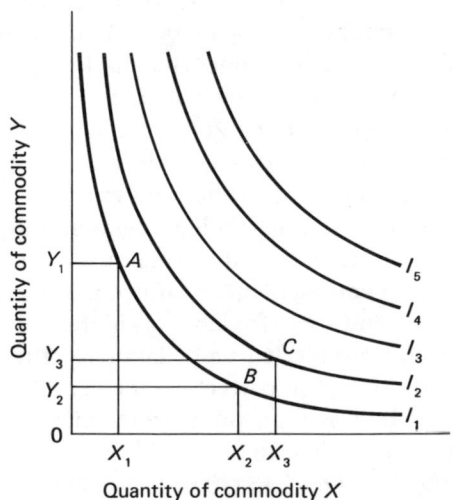

Quantity of commodity X

(farther to the right) indifference curves. Any one indifference curve, such as I_1, indicates all the combinations of goods X and Y that yield equal satisfaction to the individual.[1]

In Figure 12/2, two combinations of goods X and Y, represented by points A and B, yield the same satisfaction to the individual. He would therefore be indifferent with respect to a choice between these two combinations of X and Y. Point C on indifference curve I_2 represents a higher level of satisfaction and therefore would be preferred to either A or B.

Suppose that an individual has the opportunity to work for as many hours as he pleases at a fixed hourly wage. We can postulate a set of indifference curves that describe his preferences between work and income (or leisure and income). In Figure 12/3 income is measured on the vertical axis; leisure, measured from left to right, and work, measured from right to left, appear on the horizontal axis. The individual's satisfaction is regarded as a function of income and leisure. Movement along a given income–leisure indifference curve leaves the individual's level of satisfaction unchanged, and movement to a higher indifference curve increases the level of satisfaction.

The shape of the income–leisure indifference curve indicates that an individual desiring to maintain a certain level of satisfaction would be willing to accept a decrease in income only if it were accompanied by an increase in leisure, and vice versa. Furthermore, the more income and the less leisure the

Figure 12/3. The work-leisure-income indifference map for an individual

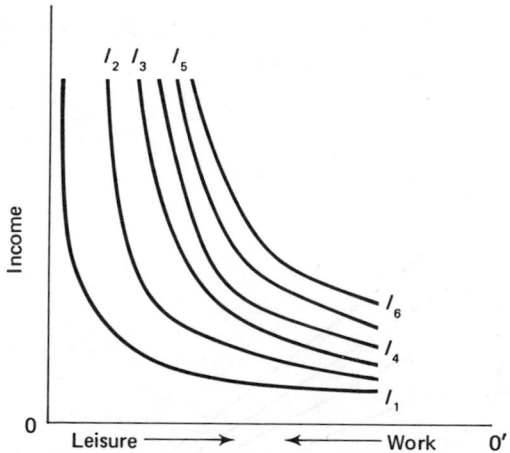

---

[1]For a more detailed discussion of the characteristics of indifference curves and their derivation from the three-dimensional utility surface, see C. E. Ferguson. *Microeconomic Theory*, Rev. Ed. (Homewood, Ill.: Richard D. Irwin, Inc., 1969), pp. 14–25.

individual has, the more important leisure is to him as compared to income, and vice versa. In other words, if the individual has a very high income and little leisure, he would be willing to give up a considerable amount of income to get additional leisure. Similarly, if he has a very low income and a large amount of leisure, he would be willing to forgo a considerable amount of leisure to secure a small increase in income. If the individual's income increases (decreases) while the amount of leisure remains the same, the individual's level of satisfaction increases (decreases); on the indifference map in Figure 12/3, this entails a movement to an indifference curve farther to the right (left).

Income–leisure indifference curves differ from those of two commodities in one important respect: they cannot cross either axis. In the absence of outside funds, some income must be earned if for no other reason than to avoid starvation. An indifference curve cannot cross the Y-axis because no one can work all the time; some nonworking time is necessary.

The necessity for leisure relates to the fundamental characteristic of work: labor services are tied to the worker and require time and effort. This explains the necessary trade-off between income and leisure. Unlike the firm, which can act as a profit maximizer, the worker cannot maximize his monetary returns, his income from work. He does try to maximize his satisfaction or utility from an optimum combination of income and leisure, but this is a much more subjective decision than faces the firm, and leads to individual differences in the labor supply in response to the same wage rate.

The relation between the wage rate, leisure, and income can be illustrated by a simple example. Let us assume that an individual's income is made up

Figure 12/4.   Income line series for different wage rates

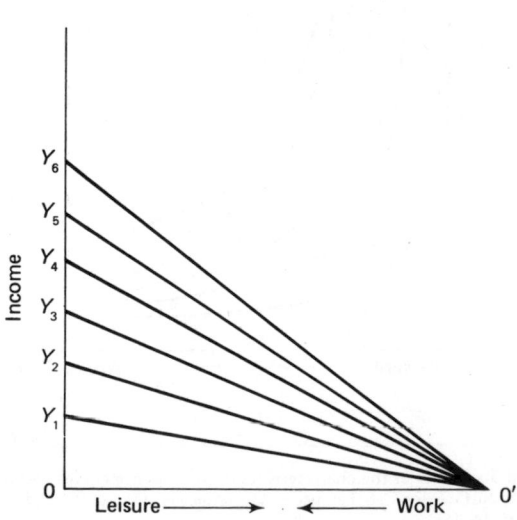

entirely of the earnings from his labor services. When he is working, his income will be the constant wage times the number of hours worked, or $Y = (W)(L)$. This income equation can be graphed as a straight line with a Y-intercept of $Y = (W)(L)$ and an X-intercept of zero work, or maximum leisure. The slope of the income line will be the wage rate, W. Figure 12/4 shows a series of income lines representing different possible wage rates. Income lines with steeper slopes represent higher wage rates.

To determine the worker's preference between leisure (or work) and income at each wage level, we combine the indifference curves and the income lines into a single diagram. The point of tangency between the income line and an income–leisure indifference curve will define the equilibrium position for a worker. Figure 12/5 shows his income line for a constant wage, W, and three of the indifference curves that make up his income–leisure indifference map.

Note that the wage of $W\left(\frac{oy}{oo'}\right)$ permits the worker to achieve different combinations of income and leisure: points A, B, and C, for example. He is indifferent as to the choice between combinations A and C; they lie on the same indifference curve. He would prefer combination B to either A or C, since B lies on a higher indifference curve, meaning that combination B permits a greater amount of satisfaction. Given the fixed wage, he would not be able to achieve any combination of income and leisure, such as point D, which yields a still higher level of satisfaction. The point of tangency between the income line and highest indifference curve represents that combination of income and leisure which gives the individual the greatest total satisfaction consistent with a given wage.

Figure 12/5.   The worker's equilibrium work–income position

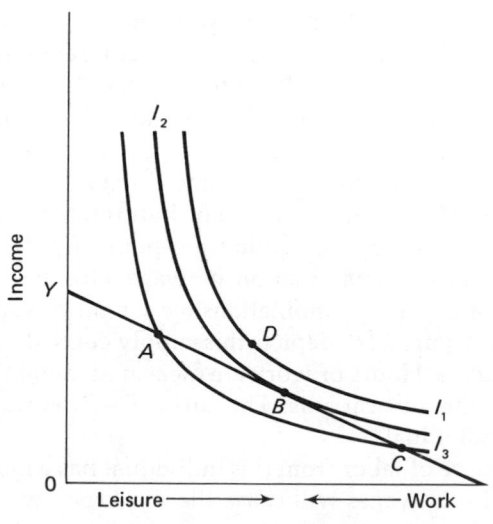

Figure 12/6.   Different equilibrium income–leisure
positions for an individual at different wage rates

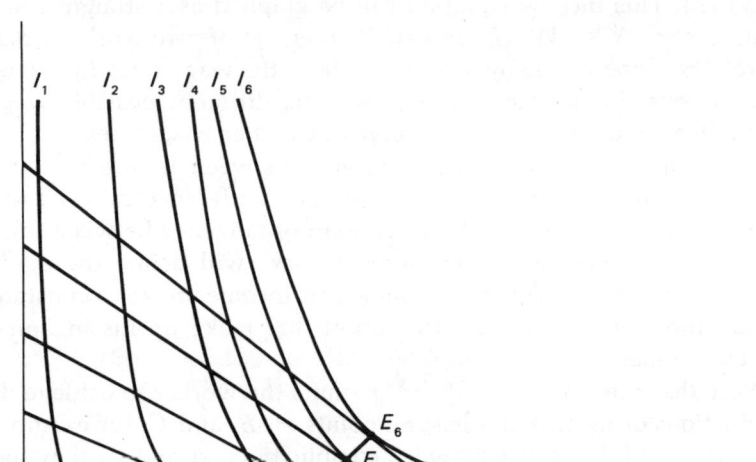

The choice between income and leisure that the individual will make, as
the wage changes, can be illustrated by including income lines for many
different wage rates. Figure 12/6 illustrates the different income–leisure equilibrium positions for an individual at different possible wage rates. Note that
the higher the rate, the greater the income that accompanies any given volume of leisure. Stated differently, the higher the wage, the higher the cost of
any hour of free time, measured as income foregone.

It is a short step from such a system of indifference curves to the supply
curve for labor. Each successive equilibrium point, E_1, E_2, E_3, etc., in Figure
12/6 indicates a specific combination of wage rate and quantity of labor
supplied. From this series of combinations we can plot a supply curve of labor
for the individual. Figure 12/7 depicts this supply curve drawn from the series
of indifference curves. Hours of work are measured along the horizontal axis,
the wage rate on the vertical axis. The curve E_1–E_6 is the supply curve for
labor from the individual.

The supply curve of labor from this individual has a negative slope at low
wages, where a rise in wages will cause the worker to work less. But in this

Figure 12/7. The individual's supply of labor

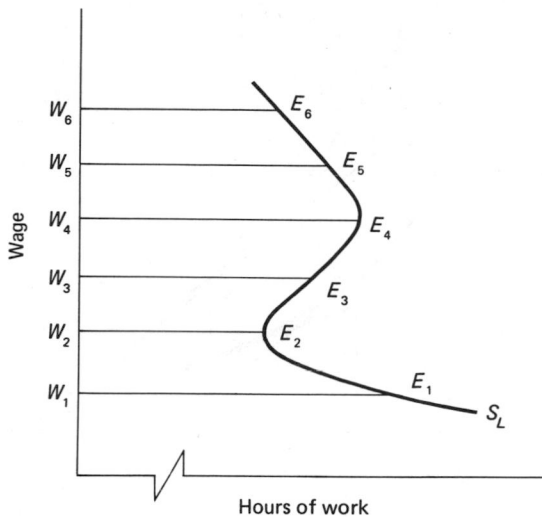

case there is a turning point, after which a rise in the wage elicits more labor services from the individual. Finally, there is another turning point beyond which further wage raises reduce the quantity of labor the individual offers.

The exact shape of a particular worker's supply curve of labor is determined by the nature of his income–leisure indifference map. The shape of the indifference curves in our example is predicated on certain assumptions concerning the utility of leisure and income to the worker, and a concept of some minimum subsistence standard of wages.[2] Individual preferences for income over leisure, and vice versa, are reflected in the worker's indifference curves, and the indifference curves in turn indicate the shape of his supply curve of labor. Income–leisure indifference maps can indicate supply curves of labor that are positively sloped, negatively sloped, backward bending, or winding in and out. Therefore, we come to the conclusion that it is possible for individual labor supply curves to take on a variety of shapes.

Uncertainty over the shape of the individual labor supply schedule arises because the worker is subject to two conflicting influences in his income–leisure decision. The *substitution effect* of a wage increase induces the worker to supply more hours of work and take less leisure, since leisure has now become more expensive to him. The *income effect,* on the other hand, increases his demand for leisure. With a higher income level from the same work effort, he tends to buy more of almost everything, including leisure.

---

[2]For two slightly different sets of assumptions yielding similarly shaped curves, see Kenneth E. Boulding. *Economic Analysis,* 4th Ed., Vol. 1 (New York: Harper and Row, 1966), pp. 613–616, and Richard Perlman. *Labor Theory* (New York: John Wiley and Sons, 1969), pp. 4–13.

Figure 12/8.   Income and substitution effects

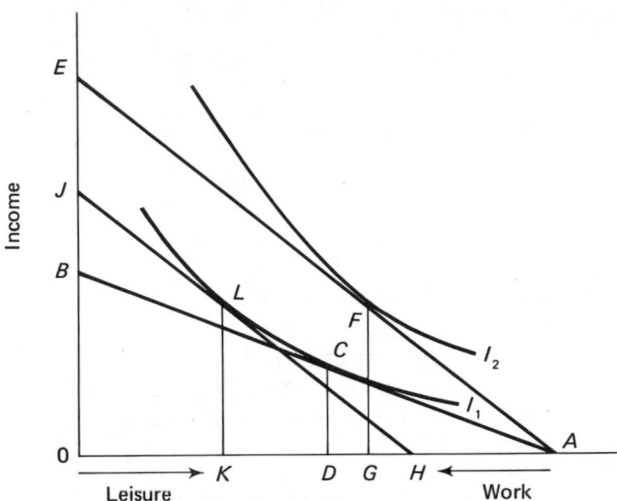

We isolate these two effects in Figure 12/8 by dividing a wage increase from *AB* to *AE* into two components.

An intermediate wage line to *AE* is drawn as *HJ*, to measure the substitution effect. Leisure has become more expensive with the rise in the wage rate, and like the substitution effect for all "goods" when they become more expensive, we tend to buy less leisure as its price rises. From the substitution effect alone, the amount of leisure "purchased" would fall from *OD* to *OK* with our purchase of all other goods rising from *DC* to *KL*.

But the income effect from the wage increase, or rise in the price of leisure, provides the big difference in demand for leisure compared to that for other goods. For all other commodities a rise in its price would have a negative income effect. Note, however, that in the case of leisure, a rise in its price represents an increase in wages, the source of income for the worker. Hence, the income effect is positive, contrary to the direction of the substitution effect and not consistent with it as in the case of price changes of other consumption goods.

Whether or not the worker will demand more or less leisure (supply less or more labor) as a result of wage increases depends on the relative strength of the two effects. Our example, Figure 12/8, is drawn to show a case in which the income effect, the movement from *L* to *F*, outweighs the substitution effect and this wage increase leads to an increase in the quantity of leisure demanded (decrease in the supply of labor offered). But there is nothing necessary about this conclusion. It would be just as possible for the income effect to be weaker than the substitution effect; in this case, labor supply would increase as the wage rose.

The conflict between substitution and income effect from a wage increase makes two definite patterns that apply to the consumption change following price movement of other goods no longer applicable to the leisure–income relationship.

First, the direction of the labor supply curve becomes uncertain. When the substitution effect outweighs the income effect, the supply schedule becomes positively sloped, and it is negatively sloped when the income effect dominates. This is the same thing as saying that if the wage increases and the substitution effect rules, the quantity of leisure demanded will fall, with opposite changes for a wage decline.

Second, the Giffen paradox, relating to demand increases with rising price, loses its peculiarity for leisure. When its price rises, it would not be odd for more of it to be demanded, for the income effect, which now operates positively to demand more leisure, may overturn the substitution effect; that is, there is nothing odd that an individual's offer of market labor falls with a higher wage.

If we assume, or rather acknowledge, that "income," standing for all other goods, is a "normal" good, there is one important limitation to the shape of the supply schedule. It cannot have an elasticity greater, negatively, than –1.

To show this, note that earnings equal the wage rate multiplied by the number of hours worked. Then if "income" is a normal good, when the wage rate rises, total income must also increase. This means that the product of wage rate and hours must exceed this product at the lower wage. Now, elasticity is –1 if the products remain the same, if the percentage fall in hours just equals the percentage increase in the wage rate. Thus, to meet the condition that income be a normal good, if the supply schedule is negatively sloped, its curvature at any point has an elasticity of –1 at its outer limit.

Household labor supply—working wives

To consider the household supply of labor further complicates the explanation of the individual labor supply schedules because leisure cannot be shared. If it could be, and assuming potential labor supply from husband and wife alone (neglecting possible earnings of older children and other household members), the previous analysis would have to be modified. For if the husband could earn more than the wife, he could keep increasing his labor supply and she could give him some of her "cheaper" leisure.

If this seems fanciful, it nevertheless explains in part why a rational family decides the wife should work, even though she earns less per hour than her husband earns from working an additional hour. Suppose he could earn $4.00 for an additional hour's work and she $2.00. She would then offer an hour of household market labor if his valuation of leisure is $4.00 at the margin (putting him at his equilibrium earnings–leisure position), as long as her value of leisure is less than $2.00 per hour.

The labor supply of the wife depends on two somewhat unrelated elements, her husband's earnings and her own potential earnings, both related to household income needs and goals. The husband's income acts as a deterrent to the labor supply of the wife. The effect of his earnings is to provide a pure negative income effect on the wife's labor supply. The higher her husband's income, the less market effort the wife would supply. In fact, if his income rises high enough, she would choose not to work at all. Figure 12/9 presents this situation graphically.

Let I_1, I_2, and I_3 represent three indifference curves in the wife's income–leisure preference map. AB is her wage-rate ray, the slope of which we will assume is unaffected by her husband's earnings. If he did not work at all, she would work AC hours, earn CP dollars, and enjoy OC hours of leisure.

If the husband earned AE dollars (per week), the effect would be to lift the wife's wage ray upwards, beginning at E to form the new ray EF parallel to AB. With leisure a normal good making higher indifference curves steeper, her new equilibrium point would lie on I_2 to the right of P at P_1.

If the husband's income rose to AG, she wouldn't work at all. At zero hours of work, at point G directly above A, the market value of her labor, represented by the slope of GH, would be less than her valuation of her last,

Figure 12/9.　The effect of the husband's income
on the labor supplied by the wife

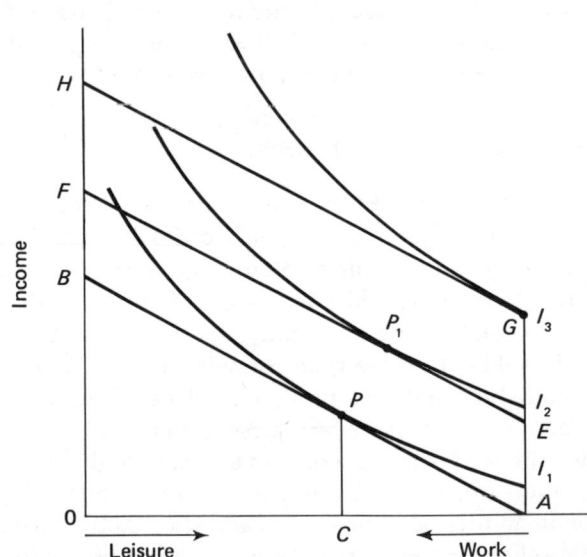

or 168th hour of leisure, represented by the slope of the indifference curve, I_3, touching G.

This analysis of the effect of the husband's earnings on the wife's labor supply does not take into account factors other than household earnings. It assumes that the wife's work decision is made dependent on, and after her husband's earnings are included in, household income. It does not take into account the fact that increasingly, women's work decisions are made interdependently and simultaneously. But this analysis does fit the traditional facts of economic life. While more and more married women have been entering the labor force, it is still true that among young marrieds only about 40 percent of the wives work. The world of market work is still pretty much a man's world. If the trend toward increasing work by wives continues, however, the effect of husbands' earnings on wives' participation will be reduced. Work decisions will be made simultaneously and the simplicity of our analysis will yield to sexual equality.

Despite the rise in husbands' income over time, with its negative effect on wives' labor effort, we know that married women have been increasing their labor-force participation rate. To explain this seemingly contradictory pattern, we need only look at the concomitant positive influence on their labor supply—increases in their potential earnings. That wives have increased their participation so strongly and steadily over the past generation in the face of higher income from husbands, indicates a strong positive relationship between their earnings and work effort, or positively sloped labor supply schedule, at least with respect to the decision of whether not to work at all in the market.

To explain the wives' positive labor supply schedule we must drop the unrealistic classification of time into only two categories—work and leisure. Market work represents unpleasant or nonconsumption use of time, but so do lots of other things we do that take time to perform. For example, commuting can be considered *nonmarket work time.* "Nonmarket" means that there is no monetary compensation for the effort, and "work" designates this time as not giving any consumption utility. Men commute and they also do odd jobs around the house, but by far the bulk of nonmarket work time is contributed by the wife in the performance of housework duties.

With three classifications of time, we can see that it is theoretically possible for a wife to increase both her market effort and her leisure time by reducing her housework. But to get the same housework done with less expenditures of time and effort requires the use of substitutes for the wife's effort. These substitutes—domestic service, appliances, prepared foods, etc. —are available, but at a cost.

Accordingly, the higher the wage the wife receives, the more easily can the household afford to buy substitutes for her housework time. There are few reliable studies of housework hours, but it is likely that with rising wages for women, improving educational levels that equip women for higher paying jobs, and better household technology, the labor supply of wives has increased without a substantial decrease in their leisure. In fact, as was noted previously, it is possible that wives today are enjoying more leisure than their mothers did, even though they work much more in the market.

Determinants of the market supply of labor

When we speak of the market supply of labor, we are discussing not the supply of labor to the economy as a whole, but the supply of labor of a particular kind to a certain well-defined group of employers, such as the firms in a specific industry. The total supply of labor offered to employers depends on two factors: the number of hours each worker is willing to work, and the number of workers.

If we suppose that the number of workers available to a specific market is fixed, the market supply of labor will be determined by the number of hours each worker is willing to work. As we have noted above, the supply curve of labor for an individual can take a variety of shapes. The market supply curve of labor of a particular kind, being the summation of the supplies of labor from the individuals in that market, can also take any one of several shapes; the summation of these curves is indeterminate. An exception to this generalization occurs if all workers have identical income–leisure preferences; but such an identity is unlikely. If the number of hours that an individual worker can work is fixed, the market supply of labor will, of course, vary by the number of workers available to a specific market. In this case there is a direct relation between the wage and quantity of labor offered. As the wage in a specific occupation, industry, or market rises, workers will be drawn from other occupations, industries, or markets. Under these assumptions, the market supply of labor to the industry raising its wage will be positively sloped; higher wages will increase the quantity of labor offered.

The behavior of the actual market supply of labor will be some combination of these two partial solutions. If the number of laborers in a specific industry or occupation cannot easily change, the market supply of labor curve may slope up, it may slope down, it may be backward bending, or it may wind in and out. This situation is likely to occur in the short run, when an industry or occupation is characterized by highly specialized labor, since this type of labor generally requires time-consuming human capital investment. On the other hand, if the number of laborers in an industry or occupation can vary easily, the market supply curve of labor will slope upward. This situation typifies the behavior of nonspecialized labor in both the short-run and long-run and in many instances, that of specialized labor in the long-run. In summary, the market supply of labor tends to slope upward in both the short run and the long run, except in the short run for specialized labor.

Figure 12/10. Labor-market equilibrium

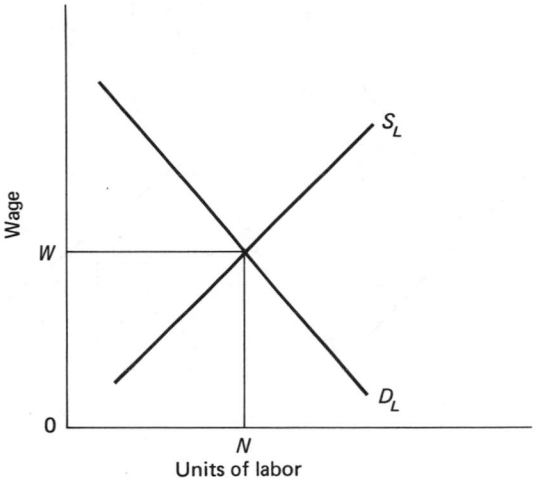

Labor-market equilibrium

Any labor market characterized by competitive hirers of labor is in equilibrium when the market demand for labor and the supply of labor are equal; this equality sets the equilibrium market wage and level of employment. In Figure 12/10, illustrating such an equilibrium in a labor market, the market wage is OW and market level of employment is ON.[3]

At a given market wage, the supply curve of labor to the typical firm under conditions of pure competition in the resource market is a horizontal line. The individual firm may hire any quantity of labor at the going wage. In Figure 12/11, the left panel illustrates this labor-market equilibrium, where D_L is the market demand for labor and S_L the market supply. The demand curve for labor (or marginal revenue product of labor) of the typical firm is shown in the right panel.[4] The market wage, OW, and the market level of

---

[3]It should be noted that the analysis presented in Figure 12/8 applies to either pure competition or imperfect competition in the product market as long as pure competition exists in the resource market. Under conditions of pure competition in the product market, D_L represents the competitive market demand for labor and is also the marginal revenue product and value of the marginal product curve for the market as a whole. Under conditions of imperfect competition in the product market, D_L represents the imperfectly competitive market demand for labor and is also the marginal revenue product curve for the market, but lies to the left of the value of the marginal product curve for the market.

[4]Figure 12/11, like Figure 12/10, represents either pure competition or imperfect competition in the product market with pure competition in the resource market. If D_L in the left hand panel is the competitive market demand for labor, MRP_L in the right hand panel represents the marginal revenue product of labor curve for the typical competitive firm. On the other hand, if D_L is viewed as the imperfectly competitive market demand for labor, MRP_L represents the marginal revenue product of labor curve for the typical imperfectly competitive firm.

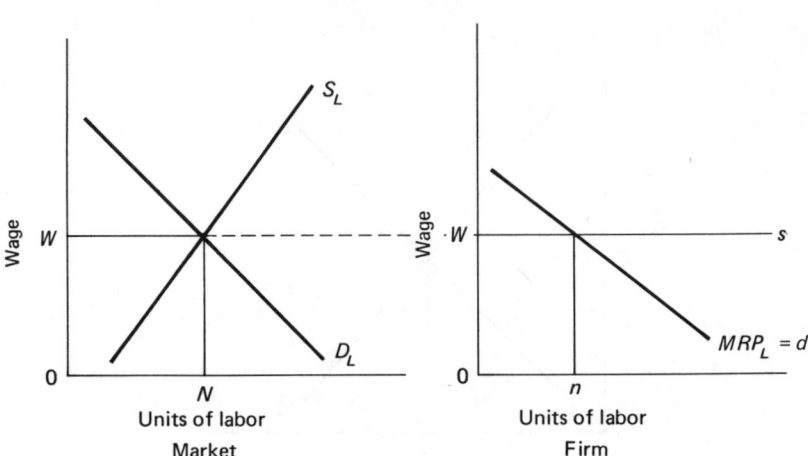

Figure 12/11.   Equilibrium in the market and for the
individual firm

Market	Firm
Units of labor	Units of labor

employment, *ON*, are reflected as an infinite supply of labor at a constant price to the competitive hirer of labor. The number of workers hired by the firm at the going wage is determined by the intersection of this wage (or cost) and the firm's demand curve for labor. Thus, the equilibrium level of employment for the firm is *On*. The market level of employment, *ON*, will equal the summation of each firm's quantity of labor employed.

Monopolistic and monopsonistic exploitation

Suppose that we are considering a case in which both the product and resource markets are competitive. In Figure 12/12 the competitive market demand for labor is D_L and the market supply of labor is S_L. Equilibrium is attained at point *E*. The market wage is *OW* and the level of employment is *ON*. Since the competitive market demand curve for labor is also the marginal revenue product and the value of the marginal product curves for the market as a whole, labor is paid a wage, *OW*, equal to its marginal revenue product and to the market value of its marginal product.

Let us now assume that there is monopoly in the product market and pure competition in the resource market. In Figure 12/12 the monopoly market demand for labor is D_{L1}. Note that the monopoly market demand lies to the left and below the competitive market demand for labor, D_L. Equilibrium is attained at point E_1. The market wage is OW_1 and the level of employment is ON_1. The effect of monopoly in the product market is to set a market wage and a level of employment that are lower than those set in the competitive situation. The difference between the competitive market wage and the mo-

Figure 12/12. *Monopolistic and monopsonistic equilibrium positions*

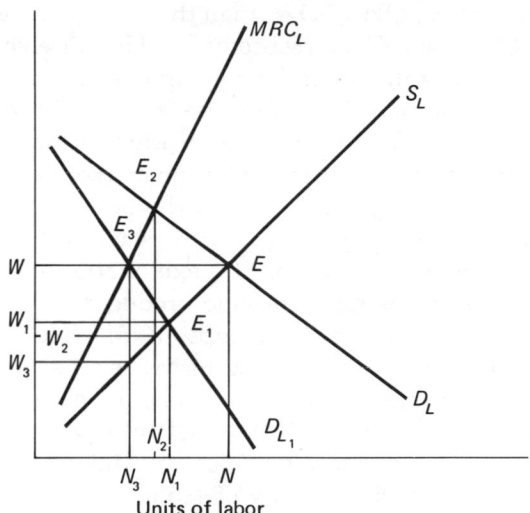

Units of labor

nopolistic market wage is the amount of monopolistic exploitation, or OW $-OW_1 = WW_1$. Since the monopolistic market demand curve for labor is also the marginal revenue product of labor curve for the market, and lies below the value of the marginal product curve for the market, labor is paid a wage, OW_1, equal to its marginal revenue product and less than the market value of its marginal product. Thus, monopolistic exploitation is characterized by a market wage that is less than the value of the marginal product of labor.

Alternatively, assume that there is monopsony in the resource market and competition in the product market. Since the monopsonist is the only firm hiring labor in the market, his supply of labor must be the market supply of labor. Similarly, the competitive market demand, D_L, is the monopsonist's demand for labor. Market equilibrium, however, is not attained at point E, because in order to maximize profits, the monopsonist will equate the marginal resource cost of labor and the marginal revenue product of labor (D_L). Equilibrium is therefore at point E_2. The market wage is OW_2 and the level of employment is ON_2. The effect of monopsony in the resource market is to reduce the market wage and restrict the level of employment below the competitive levels. The difference between the competitive market wage and the monopsonistic market wage is the amount of monopsonistic exploitation, or $OW - OW_2 = WW_2$. At a level of employment of ON_2, the marginal revenue product and the value of the marginal product of labor is equal to N_2E_2, and, hence, labor is paid a wage, OW_2, that is less than both its marginal revenue product and the value of its marginal product.

Finally, assume that there is monopoly in the product market and monopsony in the resource market. The relevant market demand for labor under these conditions is D_{L1}. Equilibrium is attained at point E_3. The market wage is OW_3 and the level of employment is ON_3. Note that the monopoly–monopsony market wage, OW_3, is less than the wage under either monopoly or monopsony, OW_1 and OW_2 respectively. The difference between the competitive market wage and the monopoly–monopsony market wage is the amount of exploitation, or $OW - OW_3 = WW_3$. The portion WW_1 is attributable to monopoly in the product market and is the result of the monopolist's paying labor a wage less than the market value of its marginal product. The portion W_1W_3 is uniquely attributable to monopsony and is caused by the monopsonist's paying labor a wage less than its marginal revenue product. Thus the monopsonistic exploitation means that labor is paid a wage less than its marginal revenue product.[5]

Monopsony power and, hence, monopsonistic exploitation arise when labor is specialized to only one or a few firms, or when labor is relatively immobile between firms and markets. A number of measures to counteract monopsony have been suggested. These fall into two general categories: minimum resource prices or, more specifically, minimum wages; and measures designed to increase the mobility of labor.

Minimum wages may be set by the government or by organized groups of laborers such as unions. Ideally, the minimum wage is set so as to increase both the wage and the level of employment and to eliminate the monopsonistic exploitation of labor. Analysis of the actual effect of minimum-wage laws on the level of employment and the amount of monopsonistic exploitation runs in much the same terms as the analysis of the effect of administered union wages. Consequently, a more thorough analysis is deferred to the next chapter, which is devoted to a discussion of the economic effects of unions. It should be noted that minimum-wage laws do not attack the causes of monopsony, but only attempt to remedy its effects. Finally, attempting to set a specific wage that eliminates monopsonistic exploitation yet does not cause unemployment is a difficult if not impossible task.

Measures to increase the mobility of labor attack the causes of monopsony more directly. If labor is highly mobile between geographical regions, industries, firms, specific employment classes, etc., the monopsonistic power of any employer is significantly reduced. In fact, if labor is perfectly mobile and has perfect knowledge of other employment opportunities, monopsonistic exploitation will occur only if a kind of labor is specialized to a particular employer. Measures frequently suggested as means of increasing the physical mobility of labor and/or the extent of labor's knowledge of other employment opportunities are: comprehensive increases in the educational level of the population; increasing emphasis on vocational training and retraining programs; establishment of federal employment exchanges; and subsidization of worker migration.

---

[5]See C. E. Ferguson, *op. cit.*, pp. 408–410.

Readings

Bloom, G., "A Reconsideration of the Theory of Exploitation," *Quarterly Journal of Economics,* Vol. 55 (May 1941), 413–443.

Boulding, Kenneth. *Economic Analysis,* 4th Ed., Vol. 1. New York: Harper and Row, 1966.

Cartter, Allan M. *Theory of Wages and Employment.* Homewood, Ill.: Richard D. Irwin, Inc., 1959.

Chamberlin, E. H. *The Theory of Monopolistic Competition.* Cambridge, Mass.: Harvard University Press, 1933.

Clark, J. B. *The Distribution of Wealth.* New York: The Macmillan Co., 1902.

Hicks. J. R. *The Theory of Wages.* London: The Macmillan Co., 1932.

Mosak, Jacob, "Interrelations of Production, Price, and Derived Demand," *Journal of Political Economy,* 46 (1938), 761–787.

Perlman, Richard. *Labor Theory.* New York: John Wiley and Sons, 1969.

Robinson, Joan. *The Economics of Imperfect Competition.* London: The Macmillan Co., 1933.

Stigler, George J. *Production and Distribution Theories.* New York: The Macmillan Co., 1941.

Chapter Thirteen   Unions, Wages, and Employment

Introduction

"It is a perennial question," wrote Clark Kerr,

whether trade unionism plays the role of Robin Hood or Jesse James. Robin Hood was the legendary hero of the people, albeit he is now considered a subversive character in some quarters, who robbed the rich to aid the poor and did so in a most sportsmanlike manner. Jesse James was the bad man who robbed the rich and the poor alike with nothing but loss to society. [1]

Interesting as the question is, there is little chance of finding an answer satisfactory to all interested parties and certainly not to the contending parties, labor and management. Nor would the labels good men and bad men change the complex nature of labor–management negotiations, regardless of how the two groups are identified. It is important, however, to analyze the effects of trade-union action on the wage rate, the numbers of workers employed, and the possible impact of union activity on the overall movement of incomes and prices. In the discussion at hand we shall be concerned with the economic effects of unions in different market conditions, and with the range of possible goals that unions may seek to achieve. Following this chapter, we discuss wage and employment goals of employers, and the resulting indeterminacy of contract terms on these crucial economic factors.

Economic effect of unions

Using the labor-market equilibrium models developed in the preceding chapter we can indicate in general the effects of a bargained union wage upon the market, the firm, and the workers. For illustrative purposes, consider the

---

[1] Clark Kerr, "Trade-Unionism and Distributive Shares," *Papers and Proceedings of the Sixty-Sixth Annual Meeting of the American Economic Association,* Vol. 44: No. 2 (May 1954), p. 279.

case of a positively sloped market supply of labor, and a union that is capable of organizing all the laborers in the market.

Pure competition in the labor market

Suppose at first that the labor market is purely competitive and that there is no union. The equilibrium market wage and level of employment are determined by the intersection of the market demand and supply curves of labor. The equilibrium level of employment for the typical firm in the market is set at the point where the market wage equals the marginal revenue product of labor. This situation is illustrated in Figure 13/1, where the equilibrium market wage is OW and the level of employment is ON. The typical firm will hire On units of labor.

Let us now introduce a union that organizes all the laborers in the market. The effect of such a union is to make the market supply of labor perfectly elastic at the bargained union wage; in brief, the union bargaining agency sets a certain wage rate, which purchasers of labor in the market must pay to all the laborers they employ. The market supply curve of labor will therefore be a horizontal line up to the point where it intersects the existing market supply curve of labor. In Figure 13/1, suppose the union sets the wage at OW, the competitive equilibrium wage. The relevant supply of labor curve is then WaS_L. The equilibrium market level of employment is ON and each firm employs On. In other words, if the union does not attempt to raise the wage above the equilibrium level, employment does not change.

Suppose, however, that the union does attempt to raise the wage of its members above the competitive level. In Figure 13/1 let the bargained wage be OW_1. The relevant market supply of labor curve is then $W_1 bS_L$. The level of employment in each firm will be On_1. The effect of the union action in this competitive labor market is to raise the wage and reduce employment. Take a closer look at the effect of the higher union wage on the laborers in the market. In Figure 13/1, ON_2 laborers are willing to work at the union wage, OW_1. However, the firms in the market are willing to employ only ON_1 workers. Therefore, we have $N_1 N_2$ workers who are unemployed at the going wage. Although the workers who are employed (ON_1) clearly benefit from the higher wage, $N_1 N$ workers who were employed at the competitive wage are now unemployed at the higher union wage.

If the demand for labor is inelastic, the rise in the wage rate increases the total wage bill, even though employment falls. Therefore, the union could theoretically divide the total wage bill among the workers who were formerly employed, thereby allowing these workers to benefit. One way of achieving this division would be to keep employment at the nonunion level (ON), meanwhile lowering the workweek for all employees. However, even when this is possible, there are still workers in the market (NN_2) who are unemployed. If the demand for labor is elastic, a rise in the wage will decrease the

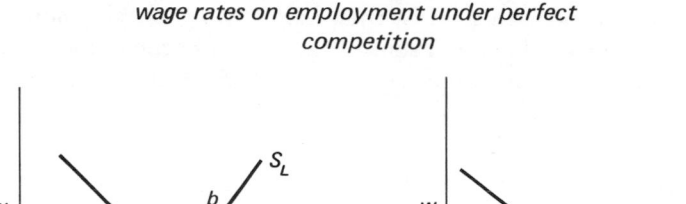

Figure 13/1.   The effect of union efforts to alter
wage rates on employment under perfect
competition

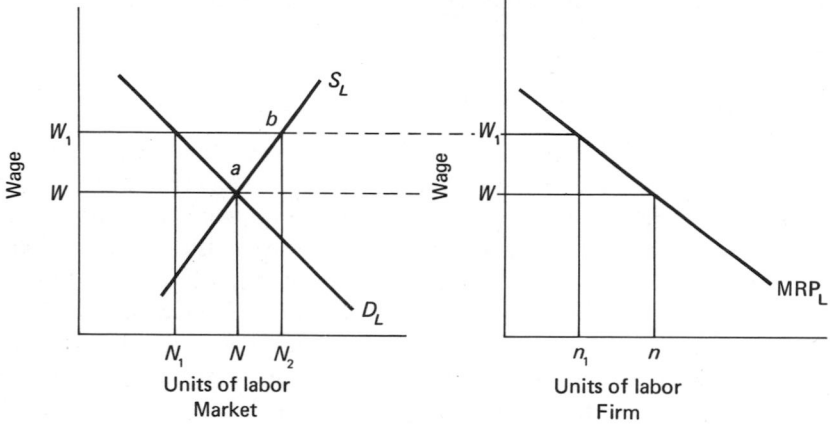

total wage bill. In this case, the employed workers still benefit, but it is not possible for the union to compensate the workers who are now unemployed because of the higher wage. Also, there is an additional group of workers not available previously who are now willing to work at the higher wage but are unable to find employment.

In summary, in a purely competitive labor market a union that succeeds in raising the wage above the competitive level will invariably create some unemployment. All the workers employed at the competitive equilibrium position will benefit only if the demand for labor is inelastic and the union is successful in maintaining the level of employment while reducing the workweek. If the demand for labor is elastic, or if the union is unable to maintain the level of employment while reducing the workweek, only those laborers who remain employed will benefit from the higher union wage. Thus, the wage action of a union in a purely competitive market does not necessarily benefit all the union members.

Furthermore, even the situation in which an overall gain could be realized depends on two important conditions. First, the union must organize the whole labor market. Otherwise, union workers would be replaced by nonunion workers who were willing to accept the lower, competitive wage. In fact, if the labor market were truly competitive beforehand, that is, with so many workers that none could hold out for the higher wage, and the union only managed to organize a small part of the market, all union members would be replaced.

Second, even if the union organized the work force and labor demand were inelastic, the gain in dollars for each union worker from the higher wage might actually be offset by the dissatisfaction at having the workweek cut.

Although the workers would now have higher income from less effort, which seems like the best of both worlds, they might want to offer more hours at the now higher wage. Thus, in a sense they would become underemployed. To succeed, work sharing requires a great deal of union discipline and solidarity.

Imperfect competition in the labor market

If the labor market is characterized by imperfect competition, the effect of a union upon the level of employment will be considerably different from that described above. The typical situation for monopsonistic competition, a term used to express any degree of imperfection in the labor market, is pictured in Figure 13/2. In the absence of a union, equilibrium is attained at point a. The level of employment is ON and the market wage is OW.

Suppose now that the workers organize themselves into a union, which bargains for and gets a wage of OW_1. The firm must pay at least OW_1 for each unit of labor used, and the supply curve of labor now faced by the monopsonist is W_1bS_L. The change in the supply curve of labor changes the marginal resource cost of labor. For any units of labor up to N_1 the monopsonist must pay a wage of OW_1; hence each additional unit of labor from zero to N_1 adds OW_1 to the total cost of labor. The marginal resource cost of labor for each unit of labor from zero to N_1 is OW_1, the new marginal resource cost of labor coinciding with the W_1b segment of the supply of labor curve out to N_1 units. But for any units of labor past N_1 the monopsonist is faced with the upward sloping section, bS_L, of the supply curve, and the corresponding section of the marginal resource cost of labor is $dMRC_L$. Thus, the marginal resource cost curve that corresponds to the supply curve W_1bS_L is W_1bdMRC_L. This marginal resource cost curve of labor is discontinuous at a level of employment of ON_1 units of labor.

The monopsonist will hire labor up to the point where the marginal revenue product of labor is equal to the marginal resource cost of labor. In Figure 15/2, when the union wage is OW_1 the monopsonist's marginal revenue product curve intersects the marginal resource cost curve in its discontinuous section, at point c. The monopsonist will hire ON_1 units of labor at the union wage of OW_1. The effect of the union is therefore to raise both the wage and the level of employment in the market.

Referring again to Figure 13/2, in the absence of a union ON units of labor were employed and paid a wage of OW. The difference between the purely competitive wage and the monopsonistic wage, or $OW_2 - OW = WW_2$, is the amount of exploitation due to monopsony in the labor market. At the union wage of OW_1, ON_1 units of labor are employed. The amount of exploitation in this case is the difference between the competitive wage, OW_2, and the union wage, OW_1, or the amount WW_1. The amount of exploitation has fallen ($WW_1 < WW_2$) with the presence of the union.

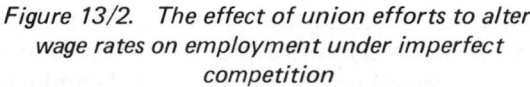

Figure 13/2. The effect of union efforts to alter
wage rates on employment under imperfect
competition

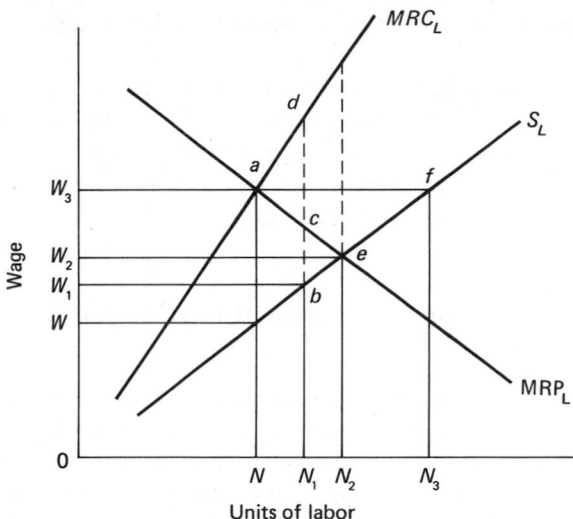

Close inspection of Figure 13/2 reveals that any union wage between OW
and OW_2 partially counteracts the monopsonistic exploitation of labor. If the
union can set the wage at OW_2, the marginal revenue product of labor will
equal the wage, and monopsonistic exploitation will be eliminated. A wage
of OW_2 results in a level of employment of ON_2, which corresponds to the
competitive equilibrium position. This is the maximum amount of employment that can be achieved in this market. Any union wage between OW_2 and
OW_3 will also eliminate monopsonistic exploitation, but at the expense of
some unemployment. For example, if the union sets the wage at OW_3, the
monopsonist will hire ON units of labor. At this level of employment the
marginal revenue product of labor, Na, will equal the wage. However, at this
wage ON_3 units of labor will seek employment, and there will be unemployment equal to NN_3. The wage OW_3 is the highest that the union can achieve
while maintaining a level of employment at least equal to that which would
occur if there were no union; any wage above OW_3 reduces employment
below ON, the level existing in the absence of the union.

In summary, a union that succeeds in raising the wage above the monopsonistic equilibrium level may increase or decrease employment, depending
on how much of a wage increase is achieved. Any wage above the monopsonistic level will either partially or completely eliminate monopsonistic exploitation of labor. However, this counteraction of monopsony may be achieved
at the cost of creating some unemployment.

Again, how well the union members do depends on the degree of organization in the labor market. If the whole market is organized, union employ-

ment is maintained at ON and wage OW_3. But if many workers are unorganized, and the union cannot control hiring through an informal (illegal) closed shop or a union-shop arrangement, total employment would stay at ON but many of the original unionized work force might be replaced by nonunion workers.

The previous discussion has been an *ex post* explanation of the economic effect of a given union wage. Nothing has been said about the objectives of union wage policy, nor have we attempted to explain *ex ante* the determination of the union wage. The next section will consider a number of hypotheses regarding the goals of union wage policy.

Theory of union and firm bargaining

Although many models of union wage policy have been developed, no single explanation commands agreement. The primary problem in developing a union wage model arises from ambiguity as to the goals of unions; no conventional maximizing goal has found general acceptance. Some of the hypotheses advanced to explain union objectives are examined in the discussion that follows.

Maximization of the wage rate or the level of employment

As the goal of union behavior, maximization of the wage rate alone would seem indefensible, for to the extent that the union could unilaterally set the wage and follow a policy of wage maximization, the ultimate result would be one worker at an extremely high wage. Such a goal would never be espoused, of course. Even if the union tries to achieve a maximum wage consistent with reality, this maximum wage can often be reached only at the cost of creating some unemployment. Reduced employment may lead to reduced membership for the union as well as a lowering of the total amount of wages received by those who continue to work.

Alternatively, if the union wishes only to maximize employment, it could theoretically expand employment out to the level of zero wages. In actuality, the supply of labor would put some limit on the level of employment. A union that pursues a goal of employment maximization forces the wage down to the intersection of the demand for and supply of labor, or to the competitive wage. This wage would result in the maximum amount of employment consistent with the given supply of labor. If unions view wages and employment, in part, as substitutes for one another, it seems highly unlikely that the organizations do try to maximize one without regard to the other. Neither wage maximization nor employment maximization seems alone to be a reasonable union goal.

Maximization of the net return

The analogy has often been drawn between a labor union and a business monopoly. The labor union, it is argued, acts as a monopolistic seller of labor. We know that the business monopolist ideally produces that volume of output at which marginal cost equals marginal revenue, since equating marginal cost and marginal revenue maximizes net returns, or profit. Similarly, if a union, realizing it is a monopolistic seller of labor, acts in the same fashion, it will equate the supply price of labor and its marginal revenue.

The concept of marginal revenue, as viewed by the union, merits further consideration. If we view the union as a monopolistic seller of labor, the market demand for labor is the union's demand curve for its product, its labor services. The union's demand curve for its product is also its average revenue curve. Thus, the union's marginal revenue curve is a curve marginal to the market demand for labor. The marginal revenue curve corresponding to a linear downward-sloping demand for labor would be a linear downward-sloping curve that lies below the demand curve at all points. More specifically, the marginal revenue curve will bisect horizontal lines drawn from the price or wage axis to the demand curve for labor.

Figure 13/3 illustrates the case of a union acting as a monopolistic seller of labor. The union equates the marginal revenue (or marginal demand for labor) and its supply price at employment *ON*, and demands a wage of *OW*. Acting in this fashion, the union gains a higher wage and a lower level of employment than occurs in the competitive case.

An interesting variant of the above example occurs when the labor union acting as a monopolistic seller of labor is confronted by a monopsonistic

Figure 13/3.   The union as a monopolistic seller of labor

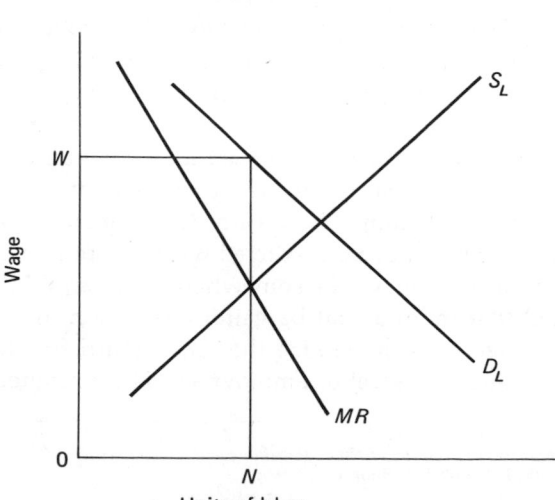

Units of labor

Figure 13/4.   The bilateral monopoly case

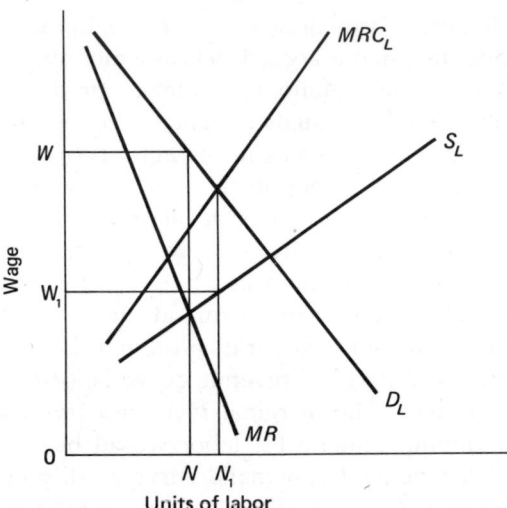

Units of labor

employer of labor. This is the traditional *bilateral monopoly* case. The union as a monopolistic seller of labor will maximize its net return by equating the marginal revenue and the supply price of labor. The monopsonistic hirer of labor will maximize his return by equating the marginal resource cost of labor and the marginal revenue product.

From Figure 13/4 illustrating the bilateral monopoly case, it will be noted that if the union has the power to force the monopsonist to act as a purely competitive hirer of labor, the wage will be OW and the level of employment ON. This combination of wage and employment level will maximize the return for the union. If the monopsonistic employer has the power to force the union to act as a purely competitive seller of labor, the wage will be set at OW_1 and the level of employment at ON_1. This combination of wage and employment will maximize the net return to the monopsonist.

But in bilateral monopoly neither party has all the power. The union can no more induce the monopsonist to act as a competitive hirer than the monopsonist can induce the union to act as a competitive seller. Both the union and the monopsonist are aware of the market conditions that exist; each will attempt to maximize its return. Consequently, the wage and the level of employment cannot be predicted with any precision; we know only that the compromise wage will lie somewhere between OW and OW_1. It has been suggested that in an actual bargaining situation, the level of employment will be set so as to maximize the joint return for the union and the monopsonist.[1] Once the level of employment is determined, the wage is set

---

[1]See Sidney Siegel and Lawrence Fouraker, *Bargaining and Group Decision Making: Experiments in Bilateral Monopoly* (New York: McGraw-Hill Book Co., 1960).

at a point that allows the union and the monopsonist to split the maximum joint return. This tendency to split the joint return is said to become stronger when each party has full knowledge of the other's plans.

The bilateral monopoly model indicates: first, that in a realistic bargaining situation both parties are aware of the existing market demand and supply of labor; second, that the specific demands and their limits will be determined by the shape and position of the demand and supply curves for labor; and third, that there is a range of wage and employment positions within which some compromise between the parties is possible. These concepts are used later in the development of a more sophisticated bargaining model.

Maximization of the wage bill

A trade union has no significant costs of production; accordingly, it has been hypothesized that the labor organization attempts to maximize the total income of its members. Since a seller faced with a downward sloping demand curve for his product maximizes total receipts at the point where the elasticity of demand for the product is unitary, and the point of unitary elasticity of demand corresponds to a level of sales where marginal revenue is zero, a union attempting to maximize total income, or the wage bill, would strive for a wage and employment position at which the marginal revenue is zero. In Figure 13/5, this occurs at a wage of OW and employment of ON.

Whether the union achieves this absolute maximum wage bill will be determined by the supply curve of labor. If the supply curve of labor intersects the demand curve for labor at a level of employment greater than ON,

Figure 13/5. Maximization of the wage bill

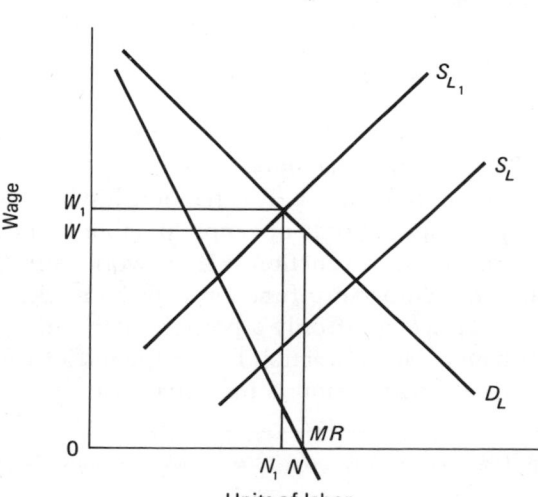

Units of labor

the maximum possible wage bill can be achieved. This situation is illustrated by the intersection of the S_L and D_L curves in Figure 13/5. However, if the supply of labor curve intersects the demand for labor curve at a level of employment less than ON, the union is not able to achieve the maximum wage bill. This possibility is illustrated in Figure 13/5 where the supply of labor curve, S_{L1}, intersects the demand for labor curve at a level of employment of ON_1. This is the maximum volume of employment that can be achieved when the supply of labor curve is S_{L1}. Under these circumstances the wage bill will be maximized at this position, that is, at a wage of OW_1 and a level of employment of ON_1. Any wage above OW_1 will reduce the wage bill, and a wage below OW_1 is not possible.

Maximizing the aggregate payroll of its members appears at first glance to be a logical goal for a union. However, closer inspection reveals a number of difficulties. First, if the demand for labor is generally inelastic, the union strives for a high wage to increase the total income of its members. This leaves unresolved the questions of how many members the union seeks to retain and how much unemployment it is willing to accept. Higher wages and correspondingly lower levels of employment may significantly lower union membership. Persistent unemployment in a given market encourages the emigration of workers to other markets. Second, in order to follow a policy of wage-bill maximization, the union needs a rather sophisticated knowledge of the elasticity of demand for labor; typically, such complete knowledge does not exist. Finally, if the union members were employed by a number of different firms, wage-bill maximization would require that the union make different wage demands on different employers, each demand related to the firm's elasticity of demand for labor. Observation of union wage and employment policies belies such behavior. Once again we must conclude that the goal of maximizing the wage bill has little general applicability in explaining union wage and employment strategy.

Maximization of union membership

Another pattern of behavior emerges when the union tries to maximize its membership. Let us assume the union can identify the number of members that it can expect at different wages. This relationship between the wage and union membership is a special type of supply of labor function and has been called the union-membership function.[2] If all workers in the market were organized, the union-membership function and the market supply of labor would be identical. However, if only a portion of the labor market is organized, the union membership function lies to the left of the market supply curve of labor. Partial organization is the usual case.

---

[2]See J. T. Dunlop. *Wage Determination under Trade Unions* (New York: The Macmillan Co., 1940), Chapters 3 and 4.

Figure 13/6.   Maximization of union membership

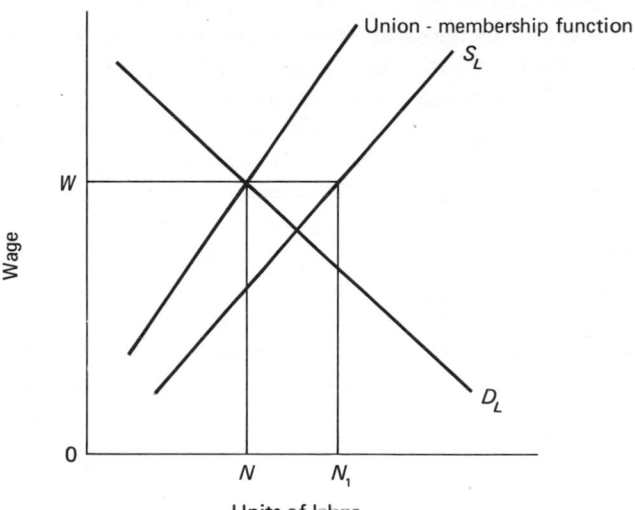

When the union goal is the maximum number of members, the appropriate wage and employment combination is that which brings the demand for labor into equality with the supply of union members. In Figure 13/6 the demand for and supply of labor and the union membership function are illustrated. The maximum union membership is determined by the point of intersection of the demand for labor and the union membership function. Therefore, the union would demand a wage of OW. Employment at this wage is ON.

In this case, the intersection of the demand curve for labor and the union membership function determine a wage above the competitive wage and a level of employment below the competitive level. At the membership-maximizing wage of OW there would be NN_1 unemployment of nonunion laborers. Only if the union membership function is identical to the supply of labor curve would the union wish to set the wage and employment at the competitive level. In summary, if only a portion of the labor market is organized, a union attempting to maximize its membership would seek a wage above the competitive level and a level of employment below the competitive level. Such a position results in the unemployment of nonunion workers. If the entire labor market is organized, the union maximizes its membership at the competitive wage and there is no reason for unemployment in the market.

A number of objections have been raised regarding the concept and use of the membership function.[3] Consider one objection—that concerning the

[3]See Allan M. Cartter. *Theory of Wages and Employment* (Homewood, Ill.: Richard D. Irwin, Inc., 1959), pp. 84–86.

predicted union reaction to a change in the demand for labor. The membership function presented in Figure 13/6 predicts symmetrical union reaction to both increases and decreases in the demand for labor. In other words, if the demand for labor increases, the union demands a higher wage and employment; and if the demand for labor decreases, the union seeks a lower wage and lower level of employment. Given an equal increase or decrease in the demand for labor, the union's desired wage would increase or decrease by the same amount. The same analysis applies to the union's employment demands. This type of action presumes that the relative values of wages and employment to the union are the same, above or below the current position. But union reaction to changes in the demand for labor does not seem to support this supposition. The commonly observed union reaction to an increase in the demand for labor is to seek wage increases primarily, these raises accompanied by only small increases in employment. On the other hand, the usual union reaction to a decline in the demand for labor is to resist wage decreases even at the cost of a considerable reduction in employment.

Optimum combination of wages and employment

None of the single-value maximizing goals discussed above satisfactorily explains union behavior. Each goal—maximizing the wage, maximizing employment, maximizing net returns, maximizing the wage bill, maximizing union membership—is too restrictive to be generally applicable in explaining union action. Alternatively, one may look for the explanation by asking whether the union seeks some optimum combination of wages and employment. In other words, we must ask what priorities or preferences the union sets in considering the various alternative goals.[4]

Union wage and employment preferences   A theory of optimum choice requires two sets of relationships: one describes all the different combinations of the wage and employment that the union can possibly achieve, and the other describes the union's system of preferences between the wage and employment combinations. We have seen that the demand and supply functions of labor will act to limit the different wage and employment combinations that are attainable. The union's preferences with respect to the different combinations of wages and employment can be illustrated by a system of indifference curves.

We can postulate a set of indifference curves that describe the preferences of the union as to wages and employment. Such indifference curves are

---

[4]See William Fellner. *Competition Among the Few* (New York: Alfred Knopf, 1951).

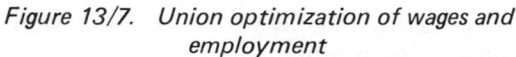

Figure 13/7. Union optimization of wages and employment

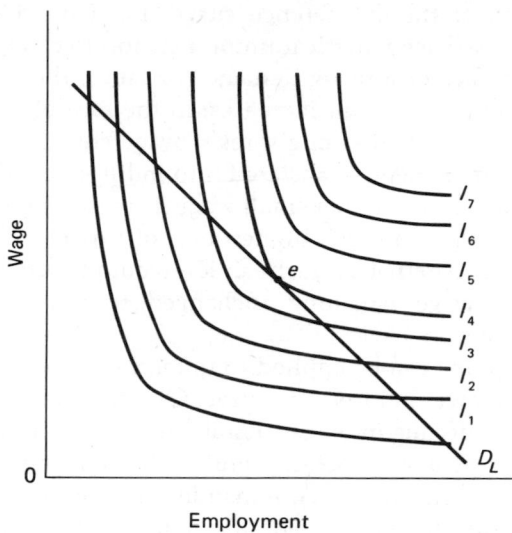

Employment

illustrated in Figure 13/7. Any single curve represents the combinations of wages and employment that yield equal satisfaction to the union, indifference curves farther to the right indicating higher levels of satisfaction for the union. Point *e* is assumed to be the current wage and employment combination.

The shape and position of the indifference curves in Figure 13/7 are dictated by the relative values the union puts on wages and employment; the shape of a single indifference curve reflects the union's view as to the substitutability of wages and employment. If wages and employment were perfect substitutes in the eyes of the union, that is, a given relative increase in the wage and an equal relative decline in employment would leave union satisfaction unchanged; the indifference curve between the wage and employment would then be a straight line. If wages and employment were viewed as not substitutable at all by the union—the union considers itself no better off in having a higher or lower wage for a given level of employment, and vice versa—the indifference curve would be a right angle at the present wage and employment combination.

Neither of these two extremes realistically describes the union attitude toward changes in wages and employment. Instead, unions view wages and employment as imperfect substitutes for each other. In order to leave union satisfaction unchanged, a large increase in employment would be needed to compensate for a small wage decline; and vice versa. Union preference of this type creates indifference curves that are sharply angled at the present wage and employment position. The indifference curves in Figure 13/7 have been drawn on the assumption that unions view wages and employment as highly imperfect substitutes for each other.

The position of the indifference curves in Figure 13/7 represents the previously discussed asymmetrical union reaction to changes in the demand for labor. In the face of a rising demand for labor, the union would prefer wage increases to employment increases; in the face of a declining demand for labor, the union would strongly resist wage cuts even if the alternative is a decline in employment. Translated into indifference-curve terminology, the union would require a rather small wage increase, employment remaining unchanged, to move to a much higher level of satisfaction, or much higher indifference curve. Alternatively, the union would require a large increase in employment, the wage remaining unchanged, to move to a slightly higher level of satisfaction.

Similar reasoning can be applied to union movement to a lower level of satisfaction, or a lower indifference curve. Observation of union action indicates that a small decline in wages, employment remaining unchanged, will cause union satisfaction to decline significantly. On the other hand, a large decline in employment, the wage remaining unchanged, would be required to lower union satisfaction to an equal extent. Inspection of Figure 13/7 will indicate that the position of the indifference curves reflects this asymmetrical union behavior.

To find the best combination of wages and employment for any given demand for labor, we find the point where the demand for labor is just tangent to a wage–employment indifference curve. This point represents that combination of wages and employment that gives the union the greatest satisfaction consistent with a given demand for labor. Any change in the demand for labor would change the union's maximum satisfaction position. In Figure 13/8, different demands for labor are combined with the union's wage–employment indifference map as presented in Figure 13/7. The desired union wage and employment positions for differing demands for labor are indicated by e_1, e_2, e_3, etc.

Connecting points e_1, e_2, e_3, etc., in Figure 13/8, we have a locus of points that defines the union's wage and employment preferences as the demand for labor changes. This curve has been called the *union wage-preference path* (WPP_u). The typical union wage-preference path is sharply kinked at the existing wage. As we have noted, the shape of the union wage-preference path reflects the fact that unions view wages and employment as imperfect substitutes. A union's response to an increase in the demand for labor will differ from its response to a decrease.

A typical union wage-preference path is depicted in Figure 13/8. The existing wage and employment are OW and ON respectively. If the demand for labor increases from D_L to D_{L1}, the union seeks a wage of OW_1 and employment of ON_1. Alternatively, if the demand for labor declines from D_L to D_{L2}, the union demands a wage and employment combination of OW_2 and ON_2.

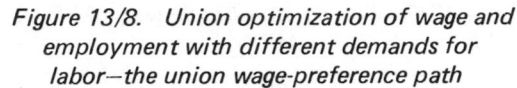

Figure 13/8. Union optimization of wage and employment with different demands for labor—the union wage-preference path

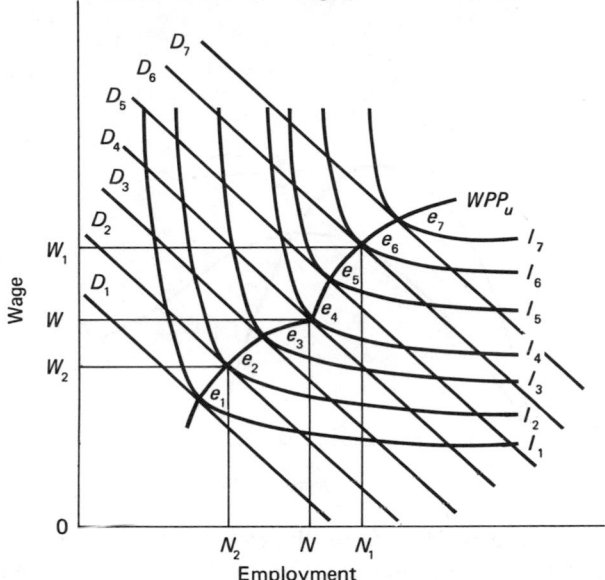

If the union could unilaterally set the wage, the resulting wage and employment position would lie on the union wage-preference path. However, our earlier discussion of bilateral monopoly indicated that the employer also has certain preferences with respect to wages and employment and that it is unlikely that either party will have all the power. Therefore, the union wage-preference path is an incomplete picture of a realistic bargaining situation. We must also inquire into the nature of the employer's preference with respect to wages and employment.

                      Employer wage and employment preferences   In the following discussion we will assume that the rational employer will attempt to maximize profits; the desired wage and employment combinations will be those that maximize profits for the employer. We therefore must analyze the relationship between the demand curve for labor and the employer's level of profits.

The employer does not have the problem that faces the union of weighing the employment effects of his wage policy. If he could maximize his profits by cutting his work force down towards zero he would do so. If he could pay zero wages he would be happy to do so. But he is constrained by labor-supply conditions. He is dealing with a union which resists wage declines except in the case in which there is a shift in the labor demand schedule.

Let us assume that the employer uses only one variable factor of production, labor. In Figure 13/9, typical average and marginal revenue product of

*Figure 13/9.   The relationship between ARP$_L$ and
                              MRP$_L$*

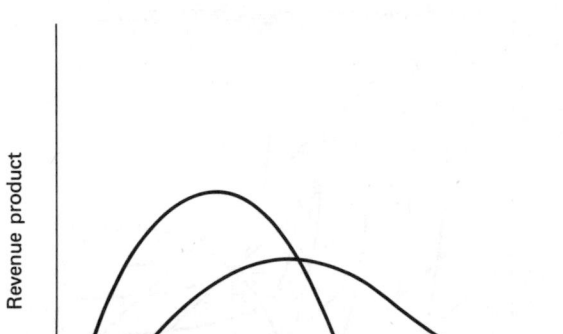

Units of labor

labor curves for such a producer are illustrated. These curves can easily be
derived from the average and marginal product curves presented in Chapter
11, by multiplying the marginal and average product of labor times the price
of the product that labor produces. From the geometric relationship of the
average to the marginal, we know that the marginal revenue product curve
will intersect the average revenue product at its highest point.

If labor were paid its average revenue product, the entire value of the
output would go to labor. In other words, by paying labor its average revenue
product the employer would incur a loss equal to the cost of the fixed factors
of production. The theory of the firm tells us that this is the shutdown point
for the rational employer. For a given level of employment, a wage greater
than the average revenue product of labor will cause the firm to shut down
completely. Therefore, the average revenue product curve can be interpreted
as a wage–employment frontier above which the firm will cease to operate.
Given any combination of wages and employment lying inside the average
revenue product curve, the firm will continue to operate in the short run.

A "zero profits" curve can be directly derived from the average revenue
product or "shutdown" curve. Zero profits occur when the total revenue
product of labor (total revenue) just equals the sum of the total payments to
labor and to the fixed factor or factors of production (total cost). In average
terms, zero profits occur when the average revenue product of labor just
equals the sum of the average payments to labor (the wage) and the average
fixed cost per worker. Thus, if we subtract the average fixed cost per worker
from the average revenue product of labor, we have the wage rate which
yields a zero level of profits to the employer. The difference between the

Figure 13/10. ARP_L, MRP_L, and $ANRP_L$ curves

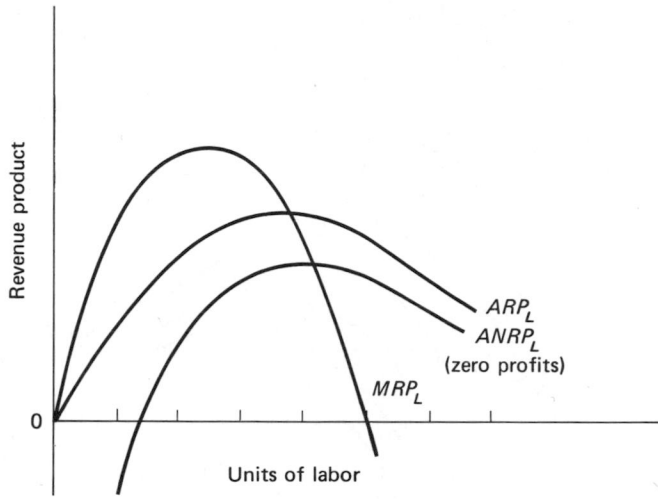

average revenue product of labor and the fixed cost per unit of labor is called the average net revenue product of labor.[5] A typical average net revenue product of labor curve is illustrated in Figure 13/10.

The average net revenue product curve in Figure 13/10 represents all the wage and employment combinations that yield a zero level of profits to the employer. Since the wage and employment preferences of the employer are dependent upon the profitability of the different wage and employment combinations, the employer is indifferent with respect to the different wage–employment combinations lying on the average net revenue product curve. Thus, the average net revenue product curve is a special type of employer wage–employment "indifference" curve, measuring satisfaction in terms of profits. It should be noted that marginal revenue product, or demand curve for labor, will intersect the average net revenue product curve where the latter is at its maximum.

We can now construct curves analogous to the average net revenue product curve for varying profit levels. A positive level of profits for the employer can be interpreted as an increase in the fixed costs. For example, the wage and employment combinations that yield a given level of profits to the firm can be found by averaging the sum of the fixed costs and profits and subtracting this figure from the average revenue product of labor. This calculation will produce a curve representing the wage–employment combinations that yield a constant level of profits to the employer. Such a curve will lie below the average net revenue product of labor. Similar curves for varying levels of

[5]Allan M. Cartter. *Theory of Wages and Employment* (Homewood, Illinois: Richard D. Irwin, Inc., 1959), pp. 49, 95–97.

*Figure 13/11.   ARP$_L$, MRP$_L$, and the employer's
wage employment indifference map*

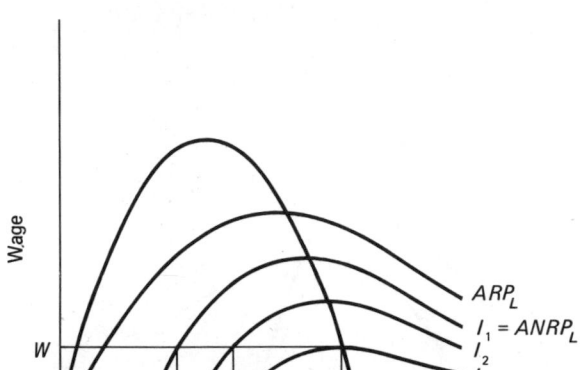

Units of labor

profit can be constructed. A system of employer wage–employment "indifference" curves, I_1, I_2, I_3, etc., is illustrated in Figure 13/11. Any single curve
represents the combinations of wages and employment that yield equal levels
of profits for the employer. Curves farther down to the right indicate higher
levels of profits for the employer.

If the wage is *OW*, the maximum profit level of employment for the firm
is *ON*. ON_1 and ON_2 are also possible employment positions for the firm,
but each of these lies on a higher curve indicating lower levels of profit. It
can be seen that the demand curve for labor (marginal revenue product curve)
indicates the profit-maximizing level of employment for any given wage.
Thus we come to an important conclusion concerning the employer's wage
and employment preferences: for any given wage, the employer would prefer
to expand employment out to a point lying on his demand curve for labor.
Such a position will yield maximum profits consistent with the given wage.

We can also indicate the employer's reaction to change in the demand for
labor through the use of the equal-profits curves developed above. Employer
reaction to changes in the demand for labor is illustrated in Figure 13/12. If
the current wage is *OW*, the employer will maximize profit at point *e* on
demand curve D_L. The profit maximizing level of employment is *ON*. The
level of profits at this position is represented by the equal profit curve *I*.

If the demand for labor increases to D_{L1}, the entire system of equal-profit
curves will shift up. This is indicated by moving the equal-profit curve from
I to *I'*. If the employer moved to point *a* on demand curve D_{L1}, the level of
profits would remain unchanged. In this case all the gains resulting from the

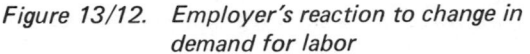

Figure 13/12. Employer's reaction to change in
demand for labor

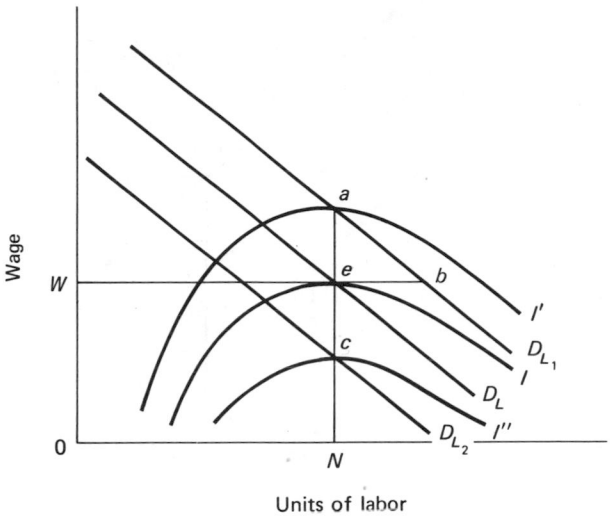

Units of labor

increase in the demand for labor would go to labor in the form of higher
wages. Employment remains unchanged. However, if the employer can move
to point b on curve D_{L1}, he will realize an increase in profits. It is obvious
that the demand curve for labor will intersect an equal profit curve lower than
I' at point b. Lower curves indicate higher levels of profits for the employer.
Point b on demand curve D_{L1} is the most profitable point the employer can
hope to achieve without reducing the wage. Thus, if the demand for labor
increases the employer would prefer to keep the wage at the current level and
expand employment out to a point on the new demand curve for labor.

In Figure 13/12, a decrease in the demand for labor from D_L to D_{LZ} will
shift the entire system of equal profit curves downwards. Movement from
point e on curve D_L to point c on curve D_{LZ} will maintain the existing level
of profits for the employer. Point c on curve D_{LZ} is the most profitable
position the employer can hope to achieve. Any point above c on curve D_{LZ}
will lie on a higher equal-profit curve, indicating a lower level of profit for
the employer. Thus, if the demand for labor decreases, the employer would
prefer to keep employment at the current level and decrease wages to a point
on the new demand curve for labor.

The curve ceb in Figure 13/12 defines the employer's wage and employment preferences as the demand for labor changes. This curve has been called
the employer wage-preference path (WPP_E), the typical employer wage-
preference path is a right angle at the existing wage. The shape of the employer wage-preference path reflects the employer's profit-maximizing
behavior, as he responds to increases or decreases in the demand for labor.

Figure 13/13.   The employer wage preference path

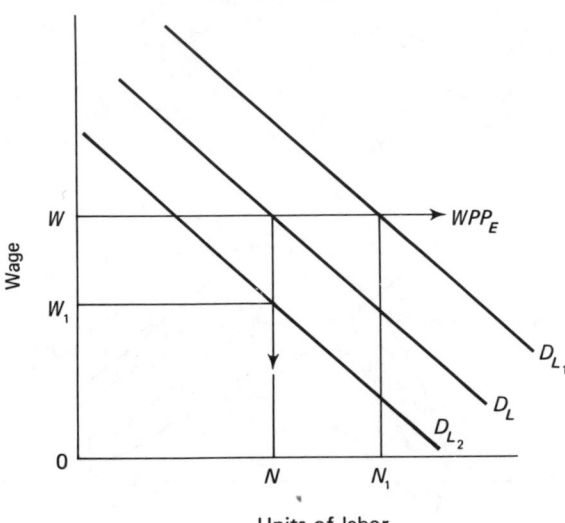

Units of labor

A typical employer wage-preference path is depicted in Figure 13/13. The existing wage and employment are OW and ON respectively. If the demand for labor increases from D_L to D_{L1}, the employer seeks a wage of OW and employment of ON_1. Alternatively, if the demand for labor declines from D_L to D_{L2}, the employer would prefer a wage and employment combination of OW_1 and ON.

If the employer could unilaterally set the wage, the resulting wage and employment position would lie on its wage-preference path. Once again, this is an incomplete picture of actual wage determination because it considers only one of the two interested parties. A comprehensive picture of the bargaining situation can be portrayed only by combining the wage-preference paths of the union and the employer.

Bargaining range   By analysis of such combinations, the range of possible wage settlements can be illustrated in Figure 13/14. Assume the current wage and employment position is at point e on the demand curve for labor D_L. Assume that the demand for labor increases from D_L to D_{L1}, labor's maximizing position. The union would prefer to move along its wage-preference path to point a; the employer would prefer to move along his wage-preference path to point b. Ideally, the bargained wage will lie between points a and b on demand curve D_{L1}. Similarly, if the demand for labor declines to D_{L2}, the union would prefer to move to point c and the employer would prefer to move to point d. The wage settlement will likely lie between points c and d on demand curve D_{L2}.

Figure 13/14.   The bargaining range

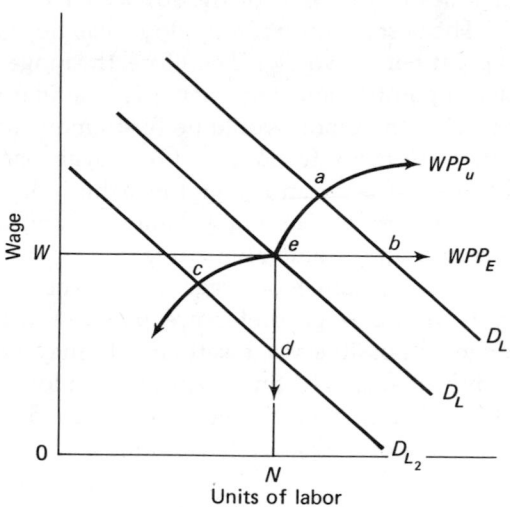

The supply curve of labor represents the maximum amount of employment that can be achieved at any wage. Depending on its position, the supply
curve may limit the range of possible wage settlements indicated in Figure
13/14. Assume that the market supply of labor curve is S_L in Figure 13/15.
The current wage and employment is indicated by point e on the demand
curve for labor D_L. If the demand for labor increases to D_{L1}, the union would

Figure 13/15.   The effect of the supply of labor on
the bargaining range

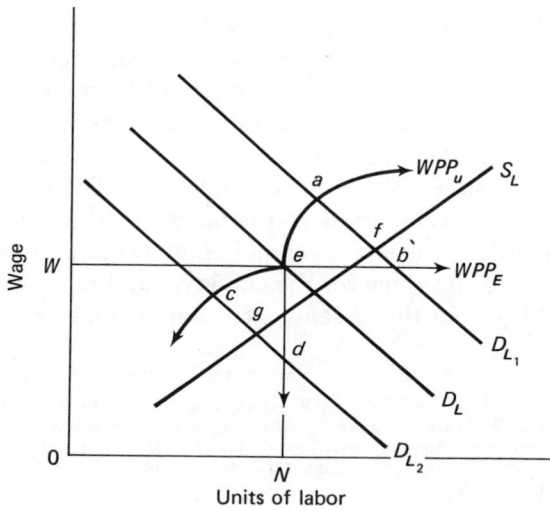

prefer to move to point a and the employer would prefer to move to point b. However, point b lies to the right of the supply curve of labor and thus cannot be achieved. The best position the employer can hope to achieve under these conditions is point f on curve D_{L1}. Therefore, the range of possible wage settlements is between points a and f on curve D_{L1}. Similarly, if the demand for labor declines to D_{L2}, the union would prefer to move to point c and the employer would prefer to move to point d. Once again, point d lies to the right of the supply curve of labor and cannot be achieved. The best position the employer can hope to achieve is point g. Thus, the range of possible wage settlements is between points c and g on curve D_{L2}.

In summary, the likely range of wage settlements can be explained through the analysis of the wage-preference paths of the union and the employer. This range of possible wage settlements may be limited by the existing market supply of labor. The final wage and employment position will ideally lie along this range of possible settlements, the final position being determined in the process of collective bargaining.

A theory of the wage rate under collective bargaining

Traditional theory has held that the wage under collective bargaining is indeterminate within the prescribed bargaining range. However, a number of recent theories have been developed that attempt to define the equilibrium wage rate.[6] In this section we will consider one such model, that presented by Professor Hicks in his *Theory of Wages*.

In his model, Hicks introduces the concept of the *employer's concessions curve* and the *union's resistance curve*. The employer's concessions curve describes the highest wage the employer will be willing to pay, rather than undergo a strike of a certain length. The union's resistance curve describes the lowest wage the union will be willing to accept before calling a strike of a specified length. The concessions and resistance curves are illustrated in Figure 13/16. The wage rate is measured along the vertical axis, and time (length of the strike) is measured along the horizontal axis. The wage rates OW and OW_1 can be viewed as the limits to the range of wage settlements derived through the analysis of the employer and union wage-preference paths. OW is the profit-maximizing wage for the employer and represents the wage the employer would pay in the absence of a union. OW_1 is the satisfaction-

[6]See Carl M. Stevens. *Strategy and Collective Bargaining Negotiation* (New York: McGraw-Hill Book Co., 1963), pp. 15–25; J. Pen. *The Wage Rate under Collective Bargaining,* translated by T. S. Preston (Cambridge: Harvard University Press, 1959); Alan M. Cartter, *op. cit.,* pp. 116–126; T. C. Schelling, "An Essay on Bargaining," *American Economic Review,* 46 (June 1956), 281–306; J. R. Hicks, *Theory of Wages* (New York: The Macmillan Co., 1932).

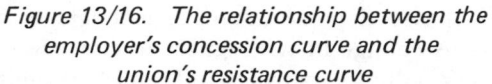

Figure 13/16. The relationship between the
employer's concession curve and the
union's resistance curve

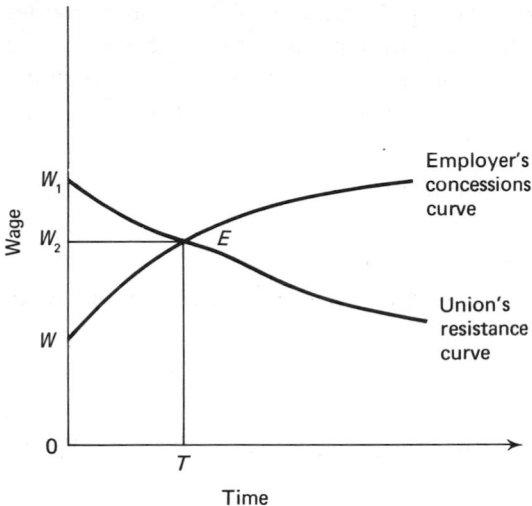

maximizing wage for the union and represents the wage the union would set
if it had all the power.

The employer's concessions curve starts at a wage of OW and rises as the
estimated length of the strike increases; the longer the strike is expected to
last, the higher the wage the employer will pay in order to avoid the work
stoppage. However, the employer's concessions curve cannot rise above the
wage that would cause him to shut down completely. As noted previously,
if labor were the only variable input, this would be a wage equal to the
average revenue product of labor. The union's resistance curve starts at a
wage of OW_1 and declines as the estimated length of the strike increases. The
longer the strike, the more the union is willing to give ground.

The employer's concessions curve and the union's resistance curve intersect at point E corresponding to a wage of OW_2. Thus, if both parties estimate
the length of a strike to be OT, a determinate equilibrium wage is established
at a wage rate of OW_2. At a wage above OW_2 the employer would prefer
a strike, and at a wage below OW_2 the union would prefer a strike.

The Hicks model is one of the earliest analyses of the wage rate under
collective bargaining. Its usefulness is limited by the nature of the assumptions involved. The equilibrium wage is predicated under the assumption that
both the employer and the union estimate the length of the strike to be OT;
yet this assumption is difficult to justify. Another limitation of the model lies
in the static, two-dimensional nature of the concessions and resistance curves.
The model assumes that each party's willingness to concede or resist depends
solely upon the estimated length of a strike. In fact, the willingness of one

party to concede will also depend upon his estimate of the other party's willingness to resist. A change in willingness to concede by one party may affect the other party's willingness to resist. Despite its limitations, however, Hicks's presentation does point up one of the major variables involved in the determination of the wage under collective bargaining. As a pioneering work in this area, it laid the groundwork for recent and much more sophisticated bargaining models that appeared in the literature.

Readings

Cartter, A. M. *Theory of Wages and Employment.* Homewood, Ill.: Richard D. Irwin, Inc., 1959.

Dunlop, J. T. *Wage Determination under Trade Unions.* New York: The Macmillan Co., 1944.

_____, ed. *Theory of Wage Determination.* New York: The Macmillan Co., 1957.

Fellner, W. J. *Competition among the Few.* New York: Alfred A. Knopf, 1951.

Ferguson, C. E. *Microeconomic Theory,* Rev. Ed. Homewood, Ill.: Richard D. Irwin, Inc., 1969.

Hicks, J. R. *The Theory of Wages.* London: The Macmillan Co., 1932.

Reder, M., "The Theory of Union Wage Policy," *Review of Economics and Statistics,* 34 (February 1952), 34–55.

Robinson, Joan. *The Economics of Imperfect Competition.* London: The Macmillan Co., 1933.

Ross, A. *Trade Union Wage Policy.* Berkeley: University of California Press, 1953.

Taylor, G. W., and F. C. Pierson, eds. *New Concepts in Wage Determination.* New York: McGraw-Hill Book Co., 1957.

Chapter Fourteen   Wages and Employment in the Economy

Introduction

The central role that price plays in allocating resources to alternative uses in the productive process has been emphasized in the preceding discussion. Labor economics must concern itself with questions of price under various market structures because in the determinants of price lie also the determinants of the real wages of workers, their distribution among different industries and occupations, and their relative share of the total output.

Just as the price of products requires macro- and micro-analysis, pricing of labor services must be analyzed both in aggregate terms and from the perspective of the single firm. Accordingly, having treated micro-issues in the previous chapter of this section, we shall deal in this chapter with the factors that determine the economywide demand for labor, and the aggregate supply of labor, or the labor force.

In the immediate analysis we shall sketch out a highly generalized body of theory pertaining to wages and employment in the economy as a whole. To do so, certain simplifying assumptions are made. We shall suppose that the units of labor in any particular model are homogeneous—that is, of the same type or occupation, and the same efficiency. Labor of a different type therefore requires a separate analysis. The wage rate, as used here, is assumed to be a proxy for all forms of remuneration to the employee. It thus includes all employee benefits, such as pensions. With these and other assumptions that will be noted in the course of the analysis, we may now turn to questions of the demand for and the supply of labor to the economy.

The economy's supply of labor

The supply of labor is defined as the quantities of labor that would be offered on the market at different wage levels. Since the concept of labor supply is central to the ensuing discussion, two points merit elaboration.

First, the "supply of labor" refers to a schedule of the various combinations of wage rates and quantities of labor offered by persons in the economy: 100 man-hours would be offered at an hourly rate of $2.00, 125 hours at a rate of $2.10, 150 hours at a rate of $2.20, etc. It follows from this definition that a change in the supply of labor is a shift of the entire schedule or curve; a decrease in the supply of labor means that there is less labor offered at all possible wage rates. By contrast, a change in the "quantity of labor supplied" indicates merely a movement within a given schedule or along a supply curve. Such changes in the quantity of labor supplied occur when the wage rate itself goes up or down. To elaborate further: if because of a rise in the wage rate, additional workers enter the labor force or existing workers now desire to work more, there has been an increase in the quantity of labor supplied. If on the other hand, population grows and thereby increases the size of the available labor force at any wage, the supply of labor has increased.

Second, "labor" is broadly defined to take account of both the numbers of workers and the number of hours worked. Changes in the supply of labor and/or the quantity of labor supplied can therefore result from changes in the number of workers or the number of annual hours per worker.

Since the most important determinant of the quantity of labor supplied is the going wage rate, the discussion that follows will be concerned primarily with this variable.

The short-run supply of labor

The supply curve of labor may be analyzed in either the short run or the long run. The short-run supply of labor for the economy is defined as a period so short that changes in the wage rate cannot affect the size of the population. The long run is a period in which changes in the wage rate do influence population size. In accordance with these delineations, it is evident that the short-run supply of labor for the economy is constrained by the total population; a rise in the wage rate will not substantially increase the number of workers available. This constraint tends to make the short-run supply of labor for the economy relatively inelastic. If the quantity of labor supplied did not respond at all to changes in the wage rate, the supply of labor curve would of course be perfectly inelastic.

Although by definition population size does not change in the short run, the quantity of labor supplied nevertheless responds to changes in the wage rate. This response has two opposing effects. An increase in the wage rate may encourage some of the existing labor force to work more hours, and will encourage some marginal workers—married women, youths, retired workers —to enter the labor force. On the other hand, an increase in the wage rate may encourage some in the existing labor force to work less (depending on the relative values they place on income and leisure). But in general by responding to higher wages and widened employment opportunities, the "hidden unemployed," the secondary workers in the labor reserve, tip the balance in favor of an expansion in quantity supplied. In summary, the short-run supply of labor for the economy is an upward sloping, relatively inelastic curve.

Not only must this general rule applying to the short-run supply of labor be noted, it is also important to observe that the supply of labor for a specific segment of the economy tends to be more elastic than the supply of labor for the whole economy. This higher elasticity results from the mobility of labor between sectors, regions, markets, etc. Higher wage rates in one sector are likely to draw laborers away from another sector. The physical quantity of workers available to any given part of the total economy in the short run is thus not as fixed as the quantity of labor available to the total economy in the short run.

The long-run supply of labor

The long-run supply of labor is influenced by the factors that determine the short-run supply of labor; in addition, it takes account of population growth. Population increases may occur in response to changes in real wages, or in response to changes in nonwage factors of social and cultural origin— for example, attitudes toward family size and birth control measures, the levels of aspiration for the education of children, etc., affect family size. Changes in these attitudes are not predictable and in many cases are very difficult to quantify; it is nevertheless important to keep them in mind throughout any discussion of the long-run supply of labor. These factors are interrelated with wages. Nineteenth-century economists held that wage increases led to population growth. Indeed, population did tend to grow with income. But in recent years, especially in the United States, rising wages and incomes have been associated with birthrate declines. Thus, the effect of wages and income on population is too uncertain to predict the shape and slope of the long-run supply curve for labor.

The economy's demand for labor

Marginal productivity theory affords a framework for analyzing the demand for labor. In origin, the concept of marginal productivity was hinted at in the writings of a number of economists during the nineteenth century.[1] However, it was not until the 1880s and 1890s that the work of economists

---

[1]T. H. von Thunen. *Der Isolierte Staat* (1826); Mountifort Longfield. *Lectures on Political Economy (1834)*; Henry George. *Progress and Poverty* (1879).

in America and Europe formalized the marginal productivity theory of wages, the name most commonly associated with the development of the concept being that of the American economist, John Bates Clark.[2] This theory, which was applied to the analysis of labor demand in the previous chapter, also serves as the explanation of the economy's labor-demand schedule.

If labor continues to be hired up to the point at which the wage equals its marginal value productivity, marginal value product is therefore the demand curve for labor. The demand curve for labor in a simple two-factor economy can be represented, therefore, by the downward sloping marginal value product curve illustrated in Figure 14/1. Shifts in the quantity of labor demanded may be distinguished from shifts in the demand for labor. If the wage is OW, OL units of labor are demanded. If the wage rate falls to OW_1, OL_1 units of labor are then demanded. This is a change in the quantity of labor demanded. By contrast, a change in the demand for labor occurs when prices or the marginal productivity of labor curve shifts. In our two-factor economy, the amount of the capital input determines the height of the product curves. A change in the stock of capital causes the product curves to shift; the greater the amount of capital available the greater the total, average, and marginal products. Since an increase in the stock of capital increases the capital per unit of labor, the marginal physical product of labor and hence the demand for labor rises with expansions in the stock of capital.

Figure 14/1.   The demand for labor curve

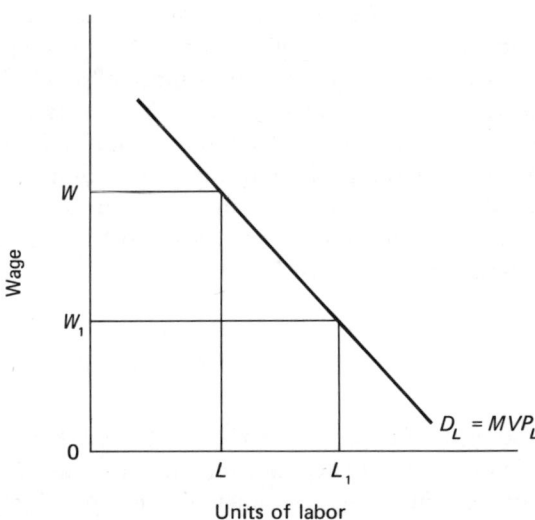

[2]John Bates Clark. *The Distribution of Wealth* (New York: The Macmillan Co., 1902). The analysis of the demand for labor and the distribution of output presented here is a summary of Clark's distribution theory. One important difference should be noted: Clark stated that the marginal productivity principle determines wages, however, most modern theorists consider the principle to determine only the demand for labor. The supply of labor must also be considered in the development of a theory of wages. This latter view is adopted here.

Similarly, if the quantity of labor is assumed to be constant and the quantity of capital to be varied, capital is subject to diminishing marginal returns. The downward sloping marginal product of capital is then the basis of demand curve for capital.

In summary, the demand curve for labor is represented by the downward sloping curve of the marginal value product of labor. The quantity of other inputs used in combination with labor combines with the state of technology to determine the position of the curve. An increase (decrease) in the quantity of other inputs available will increase (decrease) the demand for labor. In our two-factor economy an advance in technology will have the same effect as an increase in the stock of capital: both will increase the marginal physical product of labor and hence the demand for labor.

The distribution of output

The marginal productivity concept helps to explain labor's return, and the return to capital. In the left panel of Figure 14/2, MPP_L indicates the demand curve for labor when labor is assumed to be the variable input, with capital fixed in quantity, and the price level assumed to be constant. If OL units of labor are employed, the equilibrium wage will be OW. Since the marginal physical product of labor measures the addition to output from increments of labor, the area under the marginal physical product curve measures total output. When OL units of labor are employed, total product is the area $OAEL$. Labor's share of this total output, the wage times the number of laborers employed, is therefore the area $OWEL$. Capital's share is the residual amount, or the area of triangle WAE.

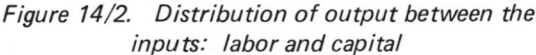

Figure 14/2. Distribution of output between the inputs: labor and capital

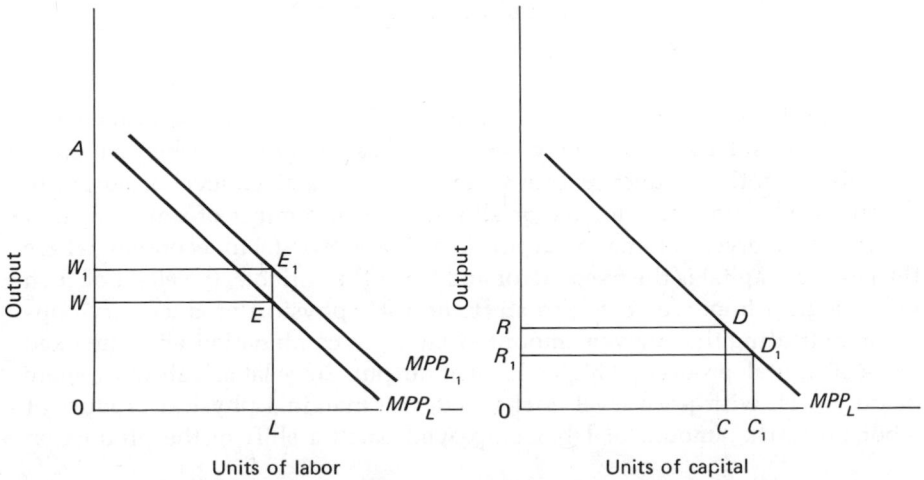

In the right panel of Figure 14/2, capital is assumed to be the variable input and labor the fixed input. If OC units of capital are employed, the return per unit of capital is OR. Total output is the area $OBDC$; capital's share of this output will be $ORDC$, and labor's share will be RBD. As Clark pointed out, the returns to labor and to capital are the same, regardless of which is treated as the variable factor. Hence, in Figure 14/2 the area of $OWEL$ (labor's share) in the left panel is equal to the area of RBD in the right panel, and area $ORDC$ in the right panel (capital's share) is equal to area WAE in the left panel.

To illustrate changes in the returns to the two factors, refer again to Figure 14/2. Assume an increase in the supply of capital to OC_1, in Figure 14/2. Referring to the right-hand diagram, the return to capital falls to OR_1, and labor's residual total return increases to the area of R_1BD. Capital's return, $OR_1D_1C_1$, will be higher or lower than $ORDC$, depending upon the elasticity of the marginal physical product of capital. If the marginal physical product curve of capital is elastic in the relevant range, capital's total return will increase ($OR_1D_1C_1 > ORDC$). If the marginal physical product curve of capital is inelastic in the relevant range, capital's return will decline ($OR_1D_1C_1 < ORDC$).

Regardless of the direction of change in capital's return, labor's return will increase if more capital is used. An increase in the stock of capital shifts the entire marginal physical product of labor curve from MPP_L to MPP_{L1}. If the quantity of labor available is OL, the new equilibrium wage will be OW_1. Labor's return of output thus rises from $OWEL$ to OW_1E_1L. Total return for capital will fall and for labor will rise, indicating an increase in labor's share if the marginal physical product curve of capital is inelastic. Only in the case of a very elastic marginal physical product curve of capital could capital's share increase.

Technological progress and factor shares

Up to this point in the discussion the possibility of technological change has been considered only briefly. Technological progress can be defined as any change in the production function that allows a given level of output to be produced with fewer inputs, or allows a given number of units of input to produce a larger volume of output. In a simple two-factor economy where the stock of capital is the fixed factor and labor the variable, the effect of such technological improvement is to shift the total physical product curve upward, indicating that a given amount of labor, in combination with the fixed stock of capital, produces a higher level of output. Since labor's absolute share of output is, with price level unchanged, the marginal physical product of labor times the amount of labor employed, such a shift in the production function raises the marginal productivity of labor and thus increases its absolute share.

Let us no longer consider the stock of capital fixed, and examine the effect of technological progress in an economy in which both labor and capital are variable inputs. Conceptually, labor and capital could be combined with some fixed factor such as land, or in the long run they could be the only factors of production.

When labor and capital are both treated as variable factors in the production process, input substitution becomes possible, when a given level of output may be produced by more than one combination of labor and capital. For example, a certain quantity of output may be produced with six units of labor and four units of capital or four units of labor and six units of capital; in short, we may substitute labor for capital while leaving the level of output unchanged. The ratio of the amount of capital to the amount of labor used is called the capital–labor ratio.

In equilibrium, when both labor and capital are variable inputs, their real rates of return are their respective marginal productivities: labor is paid its marginal physical product, as is capital.[3] The absolute amount going to labor is the marginal physical product of labor times the number of units of labor used, and the amount going to capital is, similarly, the marginal physical product of capital times the quantity of capital used.

The nature of technological change clearly affects the relative shares of output going to labor and capital. Classifying technological progress as labor-using, neutral, or capital-using, we can define labor-using technology as the type that increases the marginal physical product of labor relative to the marginal physical product of capital at the existing capital–labor ratio; there is therefore an incentive to use more labor relative to capital. Neutral technological progress leaves the relative productivities of labor and capital unchanged, while capital-using technology increases the productivity of capital relative to that of labor at the existing capital-labor ratio. In the latter case, more capital is used.[4]

Over time, changes in the relative shares going to capital and labor are affected by the nature of technological progress. Labor-using technology raises the rate of return to labor (MPP_L) relative to that of capital (MPP_C) and decreases the capital-labor ratio ($\frac{C}{L}$); thus labor's relative share of output must rise and capital's relative share of output must decline. By the same line of reasoning, neutral technological change leaves the relative shares of capital and labor unchanged, and capital-using technology increases the relative share of capital and decreases the relative share of labor.

---

[3]In symbols, under equilibrium conditions, $W = MPP_L \times P$, so that, $W/P = MPP_L$ and $W/P = W_R$, the real wage of labor. The same relationships hold for capital.

[4]This definition of technological progress was first posed in John R. Hicks, *The Theory of Wages* (London: The Macmillan Co., 1932).

In summary, if labor is the only variable input in the economy, technological advance will invariably increase its absolute return. If both labor and capital are variable inputs in the economy, the relative share of labor increases, decreases, or remains the same depending on whether technological advance is labor-using, capital-using, or neutral. Absolute return to labor may decline when technological advance is capital-using.

Employment and unemployment

Classical theory

In classical theory the equilibrium wage and the level of employment are determined by the intersection of the aggregate demand for and supply of labor. The demand for labor is labor's marginal value product curve and the supply of labor is assumed to be directly related to the wage. In an analysis based on output, the real wage equals the marginal physical product of labor. But laborers in the economy are paid in money, not real wages.

Equilibrium is assumed to be at full employment in the classical analysis; there is no involuntary unemployment. Given the economy's production function (TPP), the full employment level of output is determined, as illustrated in Figure 14/3. Here it can be seen that any real wage above the equilibrium wage ($\frac{W}{P}$), say at $\frac{W_1}{P}$, generates some amount of involuntary unemployment, $N^1 N$. But as workers compete for jobs they bid down the money wage. With a constant price level, falling money wages result in falling real wages. As wages decline, the number of workers hired increases toward ON. This process of adjustment continues until all the workers who want jobs at the going wage are hired. Thus, classical employment theory relied on adjustments in the real wage, through flexible money wages, to bring about full employment.

The possibility that the full employment level of output, once produced, would not find a market was not considered; Say's Law—that "supply creates its own demand"—was assumed to operate. More precisely, for any level of output, the income created producing the output was assumed to result in a level of spending sufficient to purchase all the goods produced. The possibility of a deficiency in the aggregate demand for output was therefore not entertained in the classical theory. Through the quantity theory of money, the money supply was assumed to determine the price level and money wage. The effect of the money supply on the real wage and on employment was assumed to be neutral.

The classical theory of employment, in summary, held that at the equilibrium real wage there could be no involuntary unemployment. Under the assumptions that both the demand for and supply of labor are functions of the real wage, and that money wages are flexible, downward wage adjust-

Figure 14/3. *Classical employment theory*

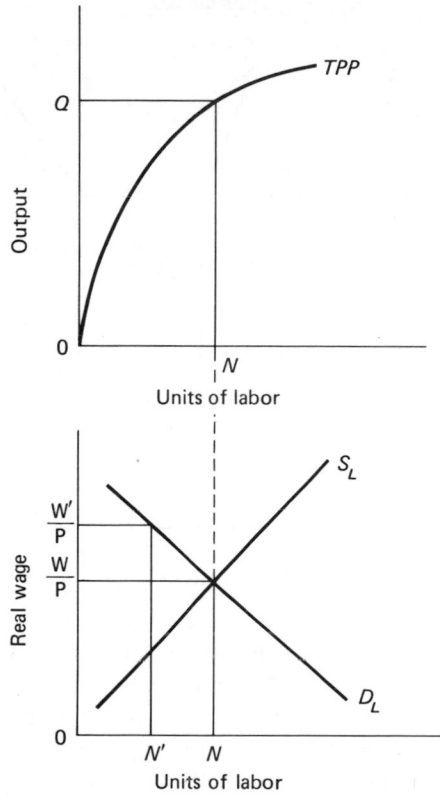

ments act to eliminate any temporary imbalances in demand–supply conditions of labor. Changes in the money supply, being neutral, do not affect the level of real wages.

Keynesian theory

John Maynard Keynes attacked the classical theory of wage and employment on a number of grounds.[5] He reasoned that workers operate under a "money illusion"; they measure their well-being in terms of money, not real wages, and they therefore bargain for and react to changes in money wages. This money illusion also encourages laborers to resist falling money wages, even when accompanied by falling prices, thus tending to make money wages rigid in a downward direction. The growth of strong unions, which invariably resist money wage cuts for their members, adds to this downward rigidity.

---

[5]John Maynard Keynes, *The General Theory of Employment, Interest, and Money* (New York: Harcourt Brace Jovanovich, 1936).

Figure 14/4.   The classical demand and supply of
labor curves

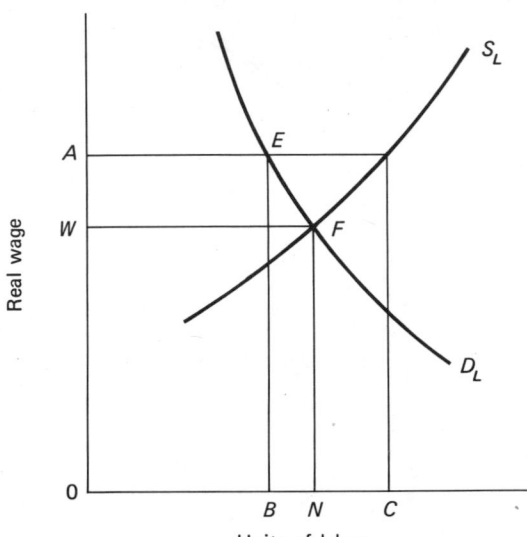

But Keynesian unemployment theory does not rely on downward wage rigidity. In its simplest form Keynes denies the universality of Say's law that supply creates its own demand. Wages are not only a cost of production but also a source of income. Accordingly, the level of employment, and the real wage are both determined by the level of aggregate demand. Then—again, emphasizing that Keynes and his modifiers allow for varied adjustments to this simplified description of the theory—even if wage earners accepted lower money wages, they would be powerless to reduce their real wage to the level required to establish full employment.

Keynesian analysis can use the classical labor demand and supply curves to show the persistence of underemployment equilibrium, a state of substantial unemployment that will remain unchanged until a rise in aggregate demand increases employment and lowers the real wage.

In Figure 14/4, we repeat the labor supply and demand curves of the classical theory. We have ignored the Keynesian postulate of money illusion. The level of aggregate demand determines a real wage of OA, with employment of OB and unemployment at BC. Although there is excess supply of labor, E is an equilibrium point, because even if workers must lower money wages, this practice will only drive prices down, keep real wages steady and do nothing to reduce unemployment, which will be eliminated only when aggregate demand rises, pushing real wages down and establishing a full employment equilibrium at F of ON units of labor.

In other words, to secure full employment, the Keynesian answer is to increase aggregate demand through monetary and fiscal policy. Undoubtedly, recovery from a deep depression, such as that underway when Keynes wrote, requires an expansion in total demand. But in recent times a new theory of unemployment has arisen to explain the unemployment that characterizes relatively prosperous periods. This theory, called the structural hypothesis, received wide recognition and consideration during the late 1950s and early '60s, but is still of interest today, because it relates to the inflationary pressures associated with moving the economy towards full employment.

The structural hypothesis

The structural hypothesis holds that when total unemployment is relatively low, at least compared with depression levels, say at about 5 percent, at least some of the unemployment is structural in nature. That is, while total demand might be sufficient, or nearly so, to provide full employment, unemployment results because many of those out of work do not have the ability or skills to fit job openings. Thus the structural argument is related to recent sharp changes in technology and consequent shifts in labor demand. We have previously discussed these shifts, away from the unskilled and uneducated towards those with training and education.

Significant differential unemployment rates among labor-force groups seem to support the structural argument. Unemployment rates for the skilled and college graduates are much lower than those for the unskilled and high school graduates, but differential rates in themselves are not enough to validate the structural hypothesis. Structural unemployment can only be a product of good times. Even if the unemployment rate for one group is much higher than for another, indicating *structural imbalance,* structural unemployment can occur only if there is an actual labor deficit in the latter group, that is, an excess of vacancies over job seekers. In bad times there is little likelihood of excess vacancies in any significant sector of the labor force.

In the absence of good vacancy data, it is impossible to measure the magnitude of structural unemployment if it is indeed present, even in prosperous periods. But if structural elements are present, serious labor bottlenecks would tend to occur as the economy approached full employment, and the problem of inflation would be magnified. Policy makers would face a more pronounced trade-off between rising prices and reduced unemployment in reaction to measures designed to restore full employment to a recession economy. (Analysis of this trade-off receives fuller treatment in Chapter 20.)

Interest in structural unemployment waned in the mid-'60s when full employment was approached with relatively stable prices, indicating that the previous long recession was attributable to inadequate aggregate demand and not to structural elements. But the upward sweep of prices beginning in 1966 rekindled interest in the structural hypothesis.

Readings

Cartter, A. M. *Theory of Wages and Employment.* Homewood, Ill.: Richard D. Irwin, Inc., 1959.

Edwards, Edgar A., "Classical and Keynesian Employment Theories: A Reconciliation," *Quarterly Journal of Economics,* 73 (August 1959), 407–428.

Ferguson, C. E. *Microeconomic Theory.* Rev. Ed. Homewood, Ill.: Richard D. Irwin, Inc., 1969.

Keynes, J. M. *The General Theory of Employment, Interest, and Money.* New York: Harcourt Brace Jovanovich, 1936.

Long, Clarence D., "The Illusion of Wage Rigidity: Long and Short Cycles in Wages and Labor," *Review of Economics and Statistics,* 42 (May 1960), 140–151

Mishan, E. J., "The Demand for Labor in a Classical and Keynesian Framework," *Journal of Political Economy,* 72 (December 1964), 610–616.

Patinkin, D. *Money, Interest, and Prices.* New York: Harper and Row, 1965.

Perry, G. L. *Unemployment, Money Wage Rates, and Inflation.* Cambridge, Mass.: M.I.T. Press, 1966.

Pigou, A. C., "The Classical Stationary State," *Economic Journal,* 8 (December 1943), 343–351.

Stigler, George. *Production and Distribution Theories.* New York: The Macmillan Co., 1941.

Part Five

Poverty, Income Security, and Public Policy

Chapter Fifteen

Income for Workers and Nonworkers: The Problem of Poverty

Introduction

Poverty in America has been the focus of much public attention during the past two decades. Indeed, a quick review of the literature reveals a recurrent theme that poverty is a new problem, peculiar to this day and age. Yet, as Chapter One indicated, there are many similarities between nineteenth and twentieth century appraisals of poverty; both accounts stress the size of the income gap between rich and poor. Relative deprivation, readily apparent in any society characterized by extremes in income distribution, is of concern to students of labor economics, who look for alleviation of the problem mainly in the form of improved earnings for the poor. It is important to consider also the alternatives to earnings—particularly public transfers of income—since many adults suffer interruptions in work through unemployment and disability. Moreover, some groups, such as the young and the old, are without earnings for longer and longer periods as the age of entry to the work force rises and the period of retirement lengthens.

After a review of the data on the current distribution of income, our attention is directed to the poor, those who work and those who do not work. Identifying the groups most susceptible to poverty helps to explain its causes, and to suggest possible policy alternatives. The latter sections of this chapter describe the growth of income transfers in this country and the reasons for this growth.

Subsequent chapters of this section discuss the programs now underway for providing income for the unemployed and the disabled, and for the retired. Finally, the question of a guaranteed income for all—an issue that is under constant debate—is considered.

The current concern with poverty

A poll of undergraduates reveals that most consider their families to be middle class. This belief persists, even when "middle" is specified as middle-income, and refers to the middle third of the income distribution. Students from families with very high incomes—one notable case was a student whose father earned $60,000 per year—are likely to compare their incomes with those that are higher, and conclude that they are therefore middle-income.

Distribution of money income

A more realistic appraisal of one's relative income status can be drawn by considering the income distribution pattern for the nation. As Table 15/1 shows, the median for all families in 1970 was $9,867; for individuals, the median was $6,868.

International comparisons   To characterize the material conditions of life in American society as affluent or poor is to compare them to conditions prevailing in other times and places. Relative to other countries, we have the highest per-capita income in the world, as Table 15/2 shows. In fact, our dollar income averages over $1,200 more per year than that in the next highest-income country. But however affluent the nation may be in comparison with other countries, as families we are far from our dreams of well-being.

Changes in the nation's income   Indicators of aggregate wealth and high income are easy to cite. Gross national product—the money value of goods and services produced in a year—almost doubled during the past decade, and more than tripled in less than twenty years. The 1970 GNP was $975 billion, or almost twice its 1960 level of $504 billion and nearly three and one-half times its 1950 magnitude of $285 billion. Even with a substantial growth in population (a rise of one-third, from 150 million in 1950 to over 200 million in 1970, with half of this increase occurring during the past decade), per-capita income tripled during the two decades following World War II and rose by over a third in the most recent decade.

The range of family incomes   As per-capita income has increased, the range of dispersion of actual incomes around average income has narrowed. Increasing productivity and the maintenance of near-full employment of the labor force have pushed up the bottom of the income distribution, while steeply progressive income taxes have significantly limited its rise at the top. Thus, income is higher in total than ever before, and it is somewhat more evenly distributed over a large proportion of the population. As Table 15/1 shows, family and individual incomes are now heavily concen-

Table 15/1 Family income, 1947, 1950, and 1958 to 1970—families by total money income

(Families as of March of the following year. This report excludes inmates of institutions. It includes members of the Armed Forces in the United States living off post or with their families on post but excludes all other members of the Armed Forces; the survey included about 1,164,000 members.)

Total money income	1970	1969	1968	1967	1966	1965	1964	1963	1962	1961	1960	1959	1958	1950	1947
Number thousands	51 948	51 237	50 510	49 834	49 065	48 279	47 835	47 436	46 998	46 341	45 456	45 111	44 232	39 929	37 237
Percent	100.0	100.0	100.0	100.0	100.0	100.0	100.0	100.0	100.0	100.0	100.0	100.0	100.0	100.0	100.0
Under $1,000	1.6	1.6	1.8	2.1	2.2	2.9	3.2	3.8	4.2	5.0	5.0	5.1	5.6	11.5	10.8
$1,000 to $1,999	3.0	3.1	3.4	4.4	5.2	6.0	6.3	6.8	7.4	7.7	8.0	8.3	8.7	13.2	16.6
$2,000 to $2,999	4.3	4.6	5.1	6.0	6.6	7.2	8.1	7.9	8.3	8.7	8.7	9.3	9.8	17.8	22.0
$3,000 to $3,999	5.1	5.3	6.1	6.3	6.7	7.7	8.4	8.7	9.2	9.4	9.8	10.1	11.2	20.7	19.7
$4,000 to $4,999	5.3	5.4	6.0	6.5	7.0	7.9	8.6	9.0	9.9	10.5	10.5	11.7	13.4	13.6	11.6
$5,000 to $5,999	5.8	5.9	6.9	7.8	8.4	9.3	9.9	11.1	11.5	11.7	12.9	13.2	13.7	9.0	7.7
$6,000 to $6,999	6.0	6.4	7.6	8.3	9.3	9.5	9.9	10.2	10.9	10.2	10.3	11.0	10.7	{ 5.2	
$7,000 to $7,999	6.3	7.3	8.2	8.9	9.3	9.7	9.3	9.1	8.6	9.1	8.7	8.4	{ 16.8		{ 8.9
$8,000 to $9,999	13.6	14.4	15.2	15.4	15.3	14.5	13.9	13.4	12.3	11.6	11.3	10.6		5.8	
$10,000 to $14,999	26.8	26.7	25.0	22.4	20.8	17.7	16.2	14.5	12.8	11.3	10.6	9.1	7.6	{ 3.3	{ 2.7
$15,000 to $24,999	17.7	15.6	12.1	9.6	7.5	6.2	5.2	4.4	4.0	3.6	2.8	2.4	1.9		
$25,000 and over	4.6	3.6	2.6	2.4	1.6	1.4	1.1	1.0	0.9	1.1	0.9	0.7	0.5		
Median income dollars	9 867	9 433	8 632	7 974	7 500	6 957	6 509	6 248	5 956	5 737	5 620	5 417	5 087	3 319	3 031

Source: Bureau of the Census, Current Population Reports, Consumer Income, Series P-60, No. 78 (May 20, 1971).

trated in the $4,000–$15,000 range; about two-thirds of the families and individuals have incomes within this bracket. Only a very small percentage of income recipients has $25,000 a year or more.

The equality of income distribution   If income-distribution equality is taken to mean that each quintile of the total number of income recipients receives exactly 20 percent of distributed income, then it can be seen from Table 15/3 that income has been unevenly distributed in the United States, for both families and unrelated individuals, for the years 1947 through 1969. In the lowest quintile, families and unrelated individuals received far less than their equal share over this period, despite some move-

Table 15/2   Per-capita national income in
selected countries, 1965, 1969
(In U.S. dollars)

Country	Per-capita national income	
	1965	1969
United States	$2,893	4151
Argentina	740	—
Australia	1,620	2434
Brazil	217	318
Canada	1,825	3068
Chile	515	557
France	1,436	2485
West Germany	1,447	2246
Israel	1,067	1450
Italy	833	1420
Japan	696	1396
Korea	88	213
Mexico	412	511[a]
Netherlands	1,265	1976
Nigeria	63	—
South Africa	509	682
Switzerland	1,928	2642
United Kingdom	1,451	1817
Venezuela	745	860
Viet Nam	113	171[a]

Source: United Nations, Yearbook of National Accounts Statistics, 1969, Vol. II. International Tables; Table 1A: Estimates of Total and Per Capita National Income Expressed in United States Dollars.

[a] 1968 data.

ment toward equality. The improvement for unrelated individuals was relatively greater than for families. This sequence also is true, to a lesser extent, for the second and third quintiles. The fourth quintile received an overlarge share over this period, with the share going to unrelated individuals growing faster than that of families. The highest quintile experienced a decline in the share received with unrelated individuals losing relatively more. Despite these changes in distribution, a great deal of inequality in distribution remains.

Inequality of income distribution is measured by a Lorenz curve, which plots the percentage of income earned against the percentile of the population by income. Figure 15/1 shows a typical Lorenz curve. The straight line depicts a situation of equal income distribution, with the lowest 10 percent, highest 10 percent, and intermediate 10 percentiles of the population each receiving exactly 10 percent of total income. The curve shows the actual distribution, with higher percentiles earning an increasing share of total income.

The size of the bow—the distance of the curve from the line—measures the degree of inequality. The statistic used to measure inequality is the Gini coefficient, the ratio of the area between the curve and the line (*OA* in Figure

Table 15/3   Income distribution

Percent of aggregate income received by each fifth and top 5 percent of families and unrelated individuals: 1947 to 1969

Item and income rank	1947	1950	1955	1960	1965	1967	1968	1969
Families	100.0	100.0	100.0	100.0	100.0	100.0	100.0	100.0
Lowest fifth	5.0	4.5	4.8	4.9	5.3	5.4	5.7	5.6
Second fifth	11.8	12.0	12.2	12.0	12.2	12.2	12.4	12.3
Middle fifth	17.0	17.4	17.7	17.6	17.6	17.5	17.7	17.6
Fourth fifth	23.1	23.5	23.7	23.6	23.7	23.7	23.7	23.4
Highest fifth	43.0	42.6	41.6	42.0	41.3	41.2	40.6	41.0
Top 5 percent	17.2	17.0	16.8	16.8	15.8	15.3	14.0	14.7
Unrelated individuals	100.0	100.0	100.0	100.0	100.0	100.0	100.0	100.0
Lowest fifth	1.9	2.3	2.5	2.6	2.6	3.0	3.2	3.4
Second fifth	5.8	7.0	7.3	7.1	7.6	7.5	7.8	7.7
Middle fifth	11.9	13.8	13.4	13.6	13.5	13.3	13.8	13.7
Fourth fifth	21.4	26.5	25.0	25.7	25.1	24.4	24.4	24.3
Highest fifth	59.1	50.4	51.9	50.9	51.2	51.8	50.8	50.9
Top 5 percent	33.3	19.3	21.7	20.0	20.2	22.0	20.4	21.0

Source: Dept. of Commerce, Bureau of the Census; *Current Population Reports,* Series P-60, No. 75, and unpublished data.

Figure 15/1.   Lorenz curve of income distribution

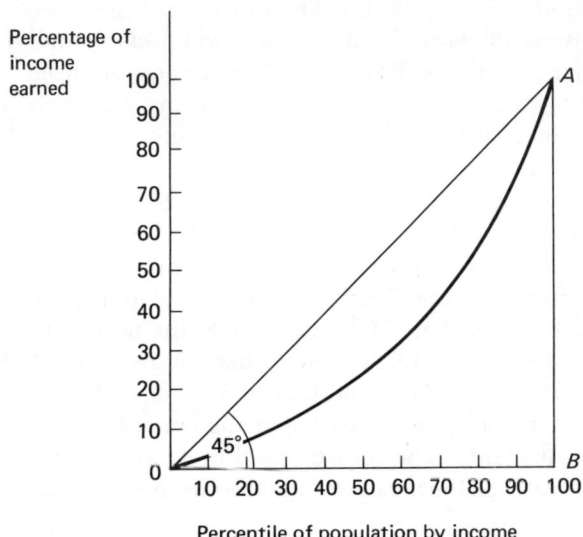

Percentile of population by income

15/1) to the area under the line (*OAB*). Thus, a Gini coefficient of zero represents perfect equality of income, while a value of 1 represents perfect inequality, the theoretical result with one person receiving all the income. The current Gini coefficient for the United States is approximately .40. The trend over the last two decades has moved very slightly toward greater inequality, that is, toward a higher Gini coefficient.

How much is enough?

We might quickly agree that the 4.6 percent (in 1970) of the families with incomes of more than $25,000 are well off (at least as long as we don't poll those high-income families, who would surely protest). But how close to adequacy are those incomes that are significantly lower? How high a level of living can actually be attained by the family with an income near the median, for example? Remember, the median is about two and one-half times the income used as the poverty threshold.

The costs of maintaining three different levels of living have been estimated by the Bureau of Labor Statistics. For the lowest of these budgets a family of four persons needed $6,960 in 1970; the moderate level cost $10,664; and the higher $15,511. The family used for these estimates included a husband employed full time, a wife who did not work, a girl of 8 and a boy of

13 years. Costs of achieving the three levels vary with family size and the age of its members.

The living standards that could be assured by these incomes were far from lavish. Food costs in the lower level were based on the Department of Agriculture's low-cost food plan used for public assistance allowances. Housing costs covered rental quarters of a five-room, one-bath unit. Public transportation is to be used where available, with a used car, eight years old, allowed in other cases. The clothing allowance totaled $807 a year for all family members. For the moderate budget, food costs were based on USDA's moderate-cost food budget totaling $2,452; a total housing allowance of $2,501, or about $225 per month was made; a two-year-old used car, to be traded in after 4 years, was included for some of the families. Even on the higher budget, the allowances for housing, clothing, transportation, and medical care were modest.

Even so, how many families could afford to live at these levels? More than a third of the families had incomes below the $6,960 required for the lowest budget standard. Another fifth of the families could afford the lowest, but not the moderate level which cost $10,664 per year. Still another 25 to 30 percent are above the moderate standard, but have less than the $15,511 required for the third level of living. About five out of six families have less than enough income to meet the cost of the top budget. Or in brief, one out of three families cannot meet the low-budget standard, and one out of two families cannot afford the moderate standard.

The working and nonworking poor

The preceding summary of the incomes of most American families, and the consumption levels these incomes afford, points up the painful conclusion that the poor are only one of the groups who worry about money. The line between the poor and the near-poor is a fine and arbitrary one; the new designation, low-income, is an improvement because it suggests a relative rather than an absolute standard. Any interruption of employment, or unusual expense, or failure to control expenditures rigidly, immediately catapults the marginal family into poverty.

Susceptibility to poverty

Attention might therefore well be focused, not exclusively on the group that at the moment falls at the very bottom of the scale, but instead on those characteristics that render a large proportion of all families in the economy quite vulnerable to the virus of poverty.

Age and poverty   About one-fourth of all persons
aged 65 or over were below the poverty line in 1970. In total, the aged
constituted 18.5 percent of the poor people of the nation, and only 8 percent
of the nonpoor. Figure 15/2 shows the extent of poverty by age and sex.

Since the aged couple is not likely to have a wage earner, the income
received is usually made up of Social Security benefits, frequently a welfare
payment, possibly a private pension claim, sometimes parttime earnings. But
none of these sources except earnings keep pace with rises in the price level,
nor do they reflect the increase in incomes that are generated by economic
growth. As a result, the difference between the incomes of the wage earners
and those of the retired members of the population grows wider, the higher
the rate of economic growth.

The median income of aged couples is less than half that of younger
couples. Similarly, the older person who lives alone also lives at a much lower
level than his younger counterpart. The significance of earnings in explaining
these differences should be emphasized. When work experience is the same
for young and old families with male heads, the older families fare almost as
well. The poorest of the poor—aged women living alone—are frequently
women who are too old to work, many of them widows who have never
worked outside the home and who therefore have no earning capacity.

Children of the poor   In her earlier work, Orshansky
illustrated dramatically the plight of the dependent child in a poor family. In
the mid-'60s, she estimated, 3 out of 5 children in families headed by women
were being brought up in poverty. By 1970, income levels had risen substantially, but children under 14 years of age still constituted one-third of all the

Figure 15/2.   The poor by age and sex, 1969

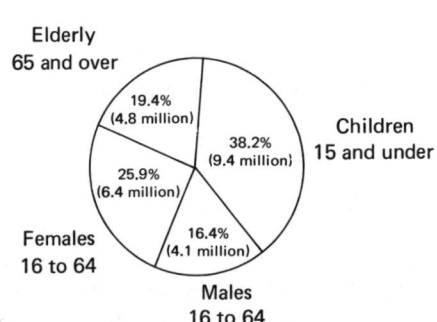

Source: Office of Economic Opportunity, 1971.

poor, numbering more than eight and one-half million. Children in large families were especially vulnerable; about half of all poor children are in families with at least five children.

Many families with four or five youngsters had insufficient income to support even two or three . . . For example, of the families poor in 1966 with a woman head and four children, one-half had less than $2,300 income for the year . . . This median was 40 percent less than the minimum of $3,900 required to enable a nonfarm family of this size to stay above the poverty line and was not even enough for a mother and two children.[1]

Women in poverty   Children who are in households headed by women are almost inevitably poor, as the preceding discussion noted. It follows that the mothers of these children are similarly poor, and that their chances of holding jobs while caring for their children are scant. But even when they work, women earn less than men. During the main portion of the worklife—up to age 55—a woman's family is nearly six times as likely to be poor as a man's. The gap narrows in later years, since neither the man nor the woman is likely to be working, and since social security and other public benefits are not dependent on sex.

Of all the poor, women outnumber men 8 to 5. Partly because women live longer than men, there are many more aged women living in poverty; here the ratio is 2 to 1. From these figures, it is easy to understand Orshansky's comment: "A woman has two chances to get into poverty. She can marry into it, or she can make it on her own."

The Southern poor   People who live in the South have traditionally had lower incomes, on the average, than those in other sections of the country. In 1970, the picture was no different. Almost 15 percent of families in the South fell in the low-income category, as compared with 8 percent of those in the North and West. Of the unrelated individuals living in the South, 40 percent were low-income; the proportion of the North and West was 30 percent.

Incomes at the higher levels are rare in the South. In the late '60s only one family in five had an income of $10,000 or more, in contrast to the one-in-three proportion prevailing elsewhere in the nation. Among the non-whites of the South, only one family in 20 had a $10,000 or higher income;

---

[1]Mollie Orshansky, "The Shape of Poverty in 1966," *Social Security Bulletin* (March 1968), p. 18.

nonwhites elsewhere had almost a one-in-five proportion in that higher range. The median family income differs markedly: about $6,500 for those in the South, compared with over $8,000 in other areas, with the non-white figures being about $3,800 in the South and $6,500 elsewhere.

The South's lower incomes reflect several factors: the high proportion of blacks, whose earnings are lower than those of whites, even in the same jobs; the lower levels of industrialization and hence the lower productivity of the Southern worker; the dominance of agriculture, textiles, and other low-wage employment. Because of their low productivity, a large proportion of those employed in the South remain poor despite their full-time jobs. For nonwhite men, the figure is particularly startling: even in the mid-'60s one-third of these men, fully employed throughout the year, remained below the poverty line. In the rest of the country, the rate was 10 percent.

Poverty and race   As Figure 15/3 illustrates, a black is three and one-half times as likely to be poor as a white person. Although the plight of the blacks who live and work in the South is particularly severe, they suffer employment and wage discrimination in other regions of the nation as well. The slow process of increasing their education and skills and hence their productivity has had only marginal effect up to now; discrimination, albeit illegal, continues to influence market decisions.

The fact that one in three blacks is poor (as compared with one in ten whites) does not mean that most poor people are black. Because of their larger numbers, whites make up the major proportion of the poor—more than

Figure 15/3.   The incidence of poverty by race, 1969

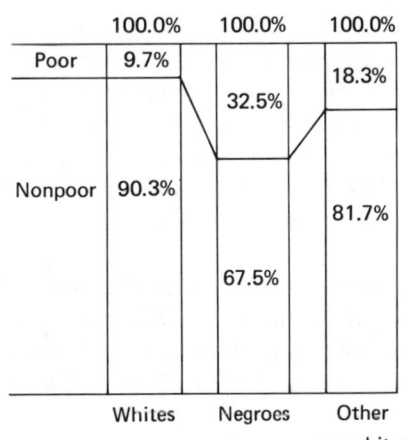

Source: Office of Economic Opportunity, 1971.

two-thirds of the total. The employment problems of low-income persons are much the same, however, regardless of race: they lack stable and productive jobs.

The working poor

The numbers of blacks in the South who earn less than enough to graduate out of poverty, even when they work full-time, refutes the proposition that a full-employment economy will eliminate the problem. While it is certainly true that the economic position of the low-income group gains in periods of prosperity and high growth, it is also true that many in that group are not able to earn, when fully employed, the $3,000 to $4,000 necessary to meet the minimum living standard. Nor is the problem of low earnings peculiar to blacks. In the South, 7 percent (and in the rest of the country, 4 percent) of the fully employed white men had earnings below the poverty threshold at the midpoint of the prosperous 1960s.

The attachment of the poor to the labor force is illustrated in Figure 15/4. Note that 58 percent of the poor are not expected to work because they are in school or are old, ill, or disabled. Another 6.5 percent are aged 14 or over but still in school, while the 11.6 percent aged 14–64 are neither working nor out of work because of school, illness, or disability. The remaining one-fourth of the poor were working, most of them part-time. Finally, we see that only 8 percent of the poor were full-time year-round workers. It is easy to generalize that poverty results mainly from lack of work.

Being without a job for any length of time almost certainly guarantees poverty. But unfortunately, having a steady job does not guarantee that the worker will not be poor. Certain types of jobs carry low rates of pay, regardless of where they are performed, although the hourly rate may be significantly lower in the South than elsewhere. Farming is an obvious case in point. Even when allowance is made for the value of homegrown food, lower housing costs, etc., farm incomes lag behind those of any other occupational group. Unskilled workers receive the lowest wages in industry, and domestic servants, largely women, can seldom earn more than the minimum wage. Three out of 5 female domestic workers continue to have incomes below the poverty scale. At a minimum of $1.80 per hour, for example, earnings for a 40-hour week, 52 weeks of the year, total less than the $3,944 cutoff established in 1970 for the 4-person family. Assuming no interruption of employment, the worker earning that rate would fall short of the amount necessary to pull his family out of poverty, even before taxes, payroll deductions, etc., were taken into account.

Threats to job stability are numerous for those workers at the bottom of the occupational ladder. Since the jobs require very little skill or experience, the supply of workers is normally quite plentiful, partly because new entrants to the labor force begin their work at this level. Employers are thus able to

Figure 15/4. The poor: their attachment to the labor force, 1969

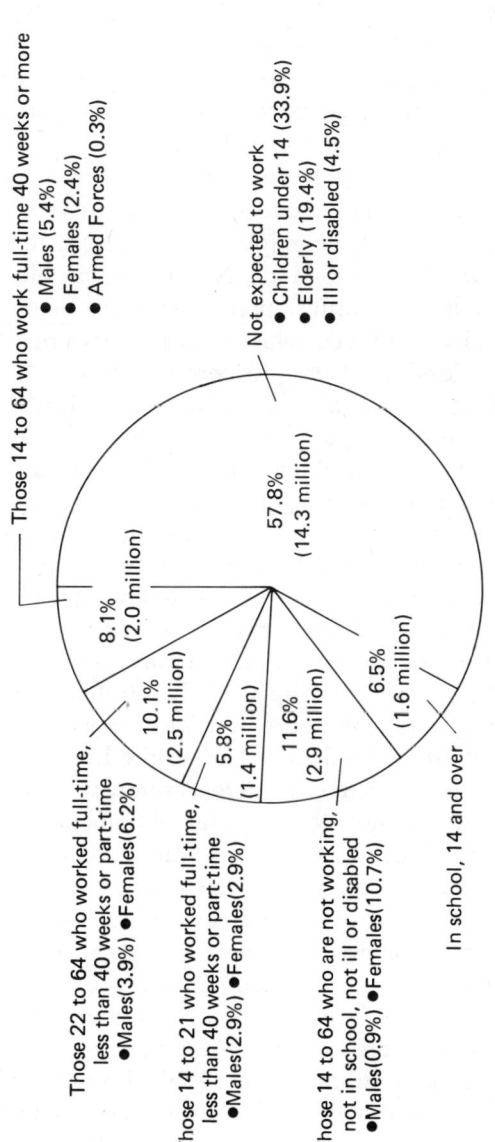

Those 14 to 64 who work full-time 40 weeks or more
● Males (5.4%)
● Females (2.4%)
● Armed Forces (0.3%)

Not expected to work
● Children under 14 (33.9%)
● Elderly (19.4%)
● Ill or disabled (4.5%)

57.8%
(14.3 million)

8.1%
(2.0 million)

Those 22 to 64 who worked full-time,
less than 40 weeks or part-time
●Males(3.9%) ●Females(6.2%)

10.1%
(2.5 million)

Those 14 to 21 who worked full-time,
less than 40 weeks or part-time
●Males(2.9%) ●Females(2.9%)

5.8%
(1.4 million)

11.6%
(2.9 million)

Those 14 to 64 who are not working,
not in school, not ill or disabled
●Males(0.9%) ●Females(10.7%)

6.5%
(1.6 million)

In school, 14 and over

Source: Office of Economic Opportunity, 1971.

draw on a large pool of young workers, whose educational qualifications are better than those of older workers. A highschool diploma has come to be a requisite for most jobs, even when the job content clearly requires little formal education. As a result, older men whose education terminated in an earlier era and short of a highschool diploma, once unemployed, are often replaced by younger men or women. The highschool dropout suffers a similar disadvantage in the labor market.

The unemployed worker does not usually stay unemployed throughout the year, except in periods of recession and cutbacks in the entire economy. When unemployment is temporary, the effect is to reduce annual income, frequently below the poverty line, but not to place the family on welfare. Unemployment insurance is a short-term source of income at best, and frequently not available at all. Partial unemployment accounted for a significant portion of the poverty in 1966: one poor family out of five was headed by a man who had been out of work for a part of the year. For families headed by women, unemployment was twice as high among the poor as among the unpoor families.

Earnings and productivity

The income problems of the working poor are complex, involving at the outset at least two variables: the amount of time worked, and the rate of pay per hour or week. If the problem turns primarily on the shortage of jobs, resulting in frequent layoffs and interruptions in income, policy makers must direct their attention to stimulating the rate of growth and job creation. If, instead, the worker's hourly pay persists in remaining so low that he cannot hope to achieve an adequate level of living, the course of action lies in another direction. Specifically, he must improve his productivity on the job and the results of that improvement must be reflected in his paycheck.

The relationship between any one worker's output and his earnings appears at first glance to be a remote one. If he is a part of a large plant, where thousands of workers combine their efforts to produce a good, or a series of goods, which then sell at the market price, it is difficult to trace the influence of his individual efforts on total output. To argue that his wage is determined by the value of the marginal product—as was discussed in Part Four—is to invite the counterargument that there is no way of knowing whether such is the case, since we cannot measure any one man's productivity.

Without repeating the analysis of wage theory at this point, it is well to remember that the concept of marginal value product includes two components: the *amount* produced, and the *price* at which it sells in the market. The first is a physical measure: a bolt of cloth, 10 bushels of wheat, 2,000 bricks. The second reflects the worth of the product to the buyer. Depending on how buyers value the good produced, the value of the work itself is high or low.

We tend to place a high value on a visit to a physician, for example, even if we get only five minutes of his advice, but an hour's work by a garbage collector is thought to be worth much less pay.

The only way the garbage collector can increase his hourly rate is to perform more work in an hour, possibly with better equipment or improved knowledge, or to withdraw his service until the buyer raises the amount he is willing to pay for the service. But his ability to do the latter is limited, since the service is one that can be performed with a minimum of training, and other men may be willing to do the job for the going rate. If the latter is not the case, a significant rise in the pay demands of the garbage collector is likely to lead to reduction in the number of men used and increased mechanization of the service. In either case, the relatively unskilled worker is likely in the short run to have a fairly narrow range within which he can raise his hourly rate; in the long run, the increase depends largely on the susceptibility of the job to machine replacement.

Certain services, notably those of physicians, lawyers, professors, etc., command relatively high rates of pay because they are in short supply and they cannot easily be performed by machines. The number of persons who can perform these services remains scarce because of the time and expense in preparing for the professions; this scarcity is reflected in the price the public is willing to pay for these particular services. In other professions, partly because the length of the training is shorter, earnings are significantly lower; secondary school teachers and nurses, for example, tend to be fairly low-paid professions, although a shortage of teachers persisted for many years and nurses continued to be in short supply at going rates of pay. Failure of these two services to command higher salaries is undoubtedly due in part to the fact that they are performed mainly by women, who have fewer alternative job choices, and due also in part to the low priority we give to these services, as compared with other goods and services we would like to purchase.

Earnings vary also in other jobs and industries, with the highest pay going to employees in contract construction, the lowest to those in wholesale and retail trade. In 1970, gross hourly and weekly earnings of production workers in private nonagricultural establishments were as follows:

Industry	Hourly	Weekly
All private industries	$3.22	$119.46
Manufacturing	3.36	133.73
Durable goods	3.56	143.47
Nondurable goods	3.08	120.43
Mining	3.84	163.97
Contract construction	5.25	196.35
Wholesale and retail trade	2.71	95.66
Finance, insurance, and real estate	3.08	113.34

On a weekly basis, earnings going to production workers were twice as high in construction as in trade. One explanation for the construction workers' advantage is their ability to restrict the number of workers joining their ranks, and the effective bargaining positions of the craft unions in construction.

The pricing of factors of production

A laissez-faire economy depends on the price mechanism not only to allocate consumer goods but also to apportion resources—men, machines, natural resources—among their potential uses. In relying on price to allocate the total output of goods and services among consumers, we recognize that if the price mechanism were withdrawn, we would have to substitute some alternative scheme for distributing goods. Scarcity of goods, and ultimately scarcity of resources used to produce goods, makes it necessary to have an allocative device that will ration the supply.

If every family in the nation wants a new television set, not every family can in fact have one. What appears to keep everybody from having a television set is a price that to a larger number of people is prohibitive; in reality, there are fewer sets available than there are people who would like to have one, and price merely rations the existing supply. If more people are willing to pay the going price for sets than can be accommodated with that supply, the price will tend to rise and thereby make it profitable for industry to build more sets. Every time the price rises, it induces business to produce more sets; simultaneously, it shuts people out of the market who will not pay the higher price.

The same pricing principles apply to resources—labor, for example. We rely on the wage or salary offered for a service to ration the supply of that service to the potential buyers; moreover, a shortage of any particular talent relative to its demand at the going price results in a bidding for the scarce resource, and consequently a rise in its price. This rise in price should then attract more people into the desired area. If plumbers' wages rise, more men are attracted into plumbing; if dentists' incomes rise, more students go into dentistry. Upward price movements ought to draw labor into the fields that are most in demand and conversely, a fall in the wage offered drives workers out of a declining trade. There is scarcely any demand for a village blacksmith in 1973, for example.

The pricing mechanism has obviously been an imperfect allocator of labor; the mobility of manpower resources is not sufficient to insure smooth transitions from job to job, industry to industry, location to location, in accordance with shifts in demand for products (and hence the labor producing them), or for services. In some cases, the device seems hardly to work at all. The example often cited is that of public school teachers. The price for this profession seems to move up only very slowly, despite public clamor and supposedly a great demand for teachers. But closer inspection reveals a difference between the public's need and its actual demand (as indicated by price and quantity). The only way the need can be translated into effective demand is for people to tax themselves and pay a higher price for the service. When people don't tax themselves, teachers' salaries don't go up and students are not drawn into teaching, or at least not by the appeal of salary.

In an economy in which one's income is dependent on the work he does, or upon his ownership of property—an economy in which a man must own something, if only a marketable skill, in order to draw an income—it is nevertheless true that certain persons throughout their lives, and all persons at some times during their lives, do not earn incomes. Different societies meet the needs of the dependent groups in different ways. In our own economy, the methods of spreading income to these groups have changed significantly in recent decades, through the adoption of broad social policies calling for a nationwide network of public expenditures.

We have always recognized the needs of persons who without work are also without income. But in earlier times there was far greater reliance on families as the source of support; most of the nonworkers were attached to families in which there was a wage earner or a property owner. In an advanced industrial society, as support patterns have become far more complicated, the uncertainty of income is commonplace. Whether any individual will be able to earn his living by work throughout his adult life cannot be predicted. There are hazards that plague the hard-working, the intelligent, even the well-educated person. There is always a chance of accident; there is always the chance of early death of the breadwinner; there is always the threat of unemployment.

Analysis of the incomes derived from labor or the ownership of capital (rent, interest) or for running a business (profit), often referred to as factor payments, comprise the study of distribution, to which economists have devoted a great deal of attention. Our earlier discussion of wage theory summarized the principles of distribution as they apply to the factor that receives the largest share of aggregate income in this country. But questions about economic security lead us into areas in which nonfactor, or transfer, payments provide the bulk of the support. Unemployment insurance, for example, is the major source of income for certain groups of people for short periods of time, and Social Security benefits provide most of the support for large numbers of retirees for quite long periods of time.

The growth of income transfers

Growth in the volume of transfer payments invites analysis of somewhat broader issues related to the changing patterns of income distribution. Two questions are posed at the outset: (1) What are the social forces that have brought about the trend toward greater transfers of income to nonworking groups? (2) To what extent and in what form will these transfers continue to grow? Current attempts to improve educational and training levels, for example, which increase the number of years before earnings begin, suggest the probability of increased expenditures for young adults.

Reasons for the growth

Of the many factors involved in the growth of income maintenance for persons not at work, one broad development—the rise in productivity per man-hour—is of particular significance. In fact, it might be said that in large measure increases in productivity both originated the need for income transfers (by requiring a more highly educated labor force, by increasing the pressure for retirement as less labor per unit of output is required, by increasing unemployment, at least in the short run, and so forth) and provides the means of meeting this need, that is, an increased total product. Needless to say, an increased capacity to support nonworking groups does not mean that society chooses to allocate its output in such a manner. Conceivably, larger volumes of goods could continue to be distributed functionally, leaving nonworking persons and their families dependent upon private charity, savings, support by relatives, and the like. In the United States, the initial decision to allocate a portion of the nation's output to persons not currently at work was actually made at a point in the nation's history when the total output was extremely low, and when the major economic problem—unemployment—sprang not from any sudden or sharp rises in productivity, but from financial collapse and the ensuing decline in aggregate demand for goods. Thus, significant transfers of income originated in a situation in which rising productivity played no immediate role.

Since the end of World War II, increases in productivity have been a major concern throughout the world. In the United States the desire for a higher rate of economic growth (and a faster rise in productivity) has been fed by the knowledge that many other nations were enjoying growth rates considerably in excess of ours. Yet productivity growth in this country has been impressive. This increase in output per man-hour, enabling the economy to produce larger and larger volumes of goods with little or no expansion in the number of man-hours required, is precisely what gives rise to the argument that increases in productivity in fact create the need for transfers of income. Inevitably, the short-run problem of technological unemployment arises, making it necessary to provide temporary income for disemployed workers and their families. But longer-run considerations are involved in financing intergenerational shifts in income. To provide retirement income or income-maintenance during a lengthened period of education, several years' income is required. Moreover, the particular employment problems of the very young worker in recent years have made it quite clear that the alternative to increased expenditures for education is increased expenditures for unemployment compensation.

Given present trends toward longer periods of education and reduced work activity for older men, it is not unlikely that the number of years a man spends outside the labor force could increase significantly during the coming decades. For example, it is not unrealistic to suppose that the average age of full-time entry to the labor force will rise by two years while the retirement age drops by the same amount within a decade or two. A man would then have an additional four years in which he would be supported by nonwage income. In addition, it seems likely that most new increases in life expectancy will be added to the number of years spent outside the labor force. The former division of any extra years of life between working and not working will change as job opportunities, particularly for older men, diminish.

Sources of income for the nonworker

Since output is increasing without any substantial increase in man-hours worked, it is clear that a man can expect his lifetime output to remain at least at its present level, even if his worklife declines, or his total man-hours of work decline through a shortened workweek. In essence, the man who in the future will work from age 20 to age 60 will produce at least as much as the man who in an earlier period worked from age 18 to age 65; and very likely, the output of the man with the shorter worklife will be greater, particularly if it can be supposed that his health is better than that of the worker of earlier generations, and if the number of years he is forced to spend in involuntary unemployment is at least not increased.

If a man's total output is in fact rising even though he is spending an increasing number of adult years outside the labor force, the problem of supporting him and his family through a lengthened educational period and a lengthened retirement period can be viewed in part as a problem of spreading total earnings through the lifespan, rather than concentrating them during the working years. A partial leveling of the income stream need not, of course, provide the same income for each year of adult life. In fact, given the changing pattern of financial needs and expenditures through the family cycle—education, marriage, birth of first child, support of older children, the husband-and-wife family in which at least the head is still at work, and finally, the retirement period for two, and then one person—the annual income ideally would vary in accordance with changing needs. Nevertheless, it becomes increasingly important that the life earnings of husband and wife be viewed in the perspective of their lifetime needs, and that these earnings be spread somewhat more evenly through adult life, rather than being concentrated within the years of actual labor-force activity.

For the individual family, savings, the acquisition of a private pension claim, and the building up of equity in a home are the most frequent examples of deferred consumption during relatively high-income years in return for money or real income during retirement. The family that envisions its long-range as well as its short-run financial needs, and budgets its expenditures and savings accordingly is thus evening out its expenditures. In so doing, the family is merely extending a budgeting principle applied monthly by many families whose income is not received in twelve equal installments, but who divide their annual total income by twelve and then regulate their expenditures in accordance with this average.

In the aggregate, a society's capacity to support adults for longer periods of education and in retirement depends upon that society's capacity to produce, and its willingness to redistribute income. The productive potential of the American economy, which is expected to make ever greater strides under the continued technological thrust of the era, is clearly capable of rendering an output sufficiently large to provide for its members both an adequate supply of goods and an increased number of years free of work. Shifts in the pattern of distribution that enable nonworking adults and their families to share in the national product, principally typified up to now by the OASDI (Social Security) program, may gradually be extended on a much broader scale to young nonworking adults and their families.

A rationale for transfers?

In classical wage theory, earnings are derived from the worker's productivity; under competitive conditions, the wage rate tends to approach the value of the marginal product. Payment of wages below the marginal product cannot persist, since competition for workers will drive up the wage and conversely, attempts to hold wages above the value of the marginal product result in unemployment rather than higher real wages.

Despite widespread criticism, the notion that real wages are a function of productivity continues to hold sway. Union negotiators base their claims for wage increases on the fact that their productivity is rising, and public officials argue that inflationary pressures can be contained only if the rise in wage rates is limited to the rise in productivity. Although the question of whose productivity is to serve as the basis for wage increases is often vague, there is a clear implication that real wages are dependent on current productivity.

Such a rationale for transfers of income is of course lacking, since no service is rendered during the period of the transfer, if at all. Income claims originate from a variety of circumstances: childhood and the human investment period before earnings begin; unemployment, after previous work has provided entitlement; retirement, again after service in covered employment; disability; inability to earn because of old age or youth, etc. There is a common element in all instances, however: each recipient, for one reason or another, is either unable or is severely restricted in his ability to work for pay. The proposed Family Assistance Act of 1970, which would have required that parents (with the exception of mothers with preschool age children) register for work, is further evidence of our belief that income claims should accrue only to persons who cannot acquire earnings.

The growing importance of transfers, particularly during youth and old age, calls for a reexamination of this rationale. The reasons people do not work for pay have become an extremely complex matter, involving institutional barriers to employment, as in child labor laws and compulsory retirements; levels of aspiration and estimates of the costs and returns from higher education; rates of time preference for goods; leisure-versus-goods preferences, etc.

Even more significant are the lengthening periods of man's life in which his income is determined by the level of transfers. As long as the basis for a transfer is the need to provide short-run financial support until work can be resumed, the tendency is to make the payment minimal; it is, after all, a temporary expedient. But when the period stretches to two decades at the end of life, and in many instances to as much as two and one-half decades prior to labor force entry, the nonearning years assume a different dimension. The question then emerges: on what basis is the income level during the nonworking years to be determined? Labor productivity, albeit an imperfect basis for determining earnings even during worklife, ceases to be an index of a man's "worth" when he ceases to work. Nor is the amount of financial support given a student necessarily related to his anticipated worklife productivity.

The theory of income distribution that is couched in marginal productivity terms has never been altogether satisfactory. It is less so when a large portion of one's lifetime income takes the form of an income claim against a current output that he did not help to produce; or conversely, when the workers' output is shared with the nonworking members of society. In a public transfer, the income spreading is horizontal in nature; taxes reduce net incomes of workers, transferring income claims against the current output to nonworkers. A private transfer, too, reapportions the annual product between wages and transfers. But the receipt of a private pension has a vertical dimension as well: the recipient has acquired the claim because in some previous period he has presumably foregone a portion of his earnings (in addition to that taxed away for public pensions), with the understanding that he would later be reimbursed, with interest. The public retirement transfer is essentially one from a generation of workers to a generation of retirees, whereas the private pension is a transfer from a generation of workers to a particular group of retirees. The total product may of course be larger because of the previous saving of the private pensioner, who used his current earnings to further capital accumulation, rather than to finance his current consumption.

In summary, income-distribution analysis in its modern context is complicated by the time dimension—the fact that much lifetime income is not received in the period when the work is actually performed—and by the issue of public-versus-private transfers, which influence the size of the income claims of certain groups via-à-vis all other consumers. For policy considerations, some rationale for the size and source of income transfers would be of immense value in delineating certain questions: To what extent does the present temporal distribution of income approach the desired distribution? If reallocation is indicated, what is the role of public, and that of private, transfers? Can we identify certain groups—educational, occupational, geographic—who are poor at certain ages but not at others? The more pressing questions of income allocation seem today to be found in the contrasts between the status of the working and that of the nonworking male (whose labor-force status is to some extent a function of age), rather than in the traditional study of functional shares.

Readings

Batchelder, Alan B. *The Economics of Poverty,* 2d Ed. New York: John Wiley and Sons, 1971.

Bowen, William G.; Frederick H. Haibison; Richard A. Lester; and Herman M. Sumers, eds. *The Princeton Symposium on the American System of Social Insurance.* New York: McGraw-Hill Book Co., 1968.

Budd, Edward C., ed. *Inequality and Poverty.* Englewood Cliffs, N. J.: Prentice-Hall, 1965.

Gallaway, Lowell E., "The Foundations of the War on Poverty," *American Economic Review,* 55 (March 1965), 122–131.

Kreps, Juanita M. *Lifetime Allocation of Work and Income.* Durham, N. C.: Duke University Press, 1971.

Lampman, Robert J., "Approaches to the Reduction of Poverty," *American Economic Review,* 55 (May 1965), 521–529.

Levitan, Sar; Wilber Cohen; and Robert Lampman, eds. *Towards Freedom from Want.* Industrial Relations Research Association, 1968.

Myers, Robert J. *Social Insurance and Allied Government Programs.* Homewood, Ill.: Richard D. Irwin, Inc., 1965.

Thurow, Lester, "The Causes of Poverty," *Quarterly Journal of Economics,* 81, (February 1967), 39–57.

Weisbrod, Burton A., ed. *The Economics of Poverty.* Englewood Cliffs, N. J.: Prentice-Hall, 1965.

Chapter Sixteen Economic Assurance: Income for the Unemployed and the Disabled

Introduction

Achieving full employment in the American economy is difficult; maintaining such a state for any length of time is almost impossible. Even during the highly prosperous second half of the 1960s, significant levels of unemployment persisted: by the early 1970s, the unemployment rate climbed toward 6 percent, or close to 5 million workers out of a labor force of 85 million. In facing a problem of this magnitude, we have found it necessary to adopt a series of policies and programs, some short-run and some much longer-range.

Long-run solutions to job scarcity lie primarily in the area of fiscal and monetary policy. Along with measures designed to stimulate economic activity and job creation, however, public programs that insure qualitative improvement in the labor force are also required; hence the emphasis on education and manpower training. While these two sets of policies are at work to restore jobs to the jobless, the jobless must have some means of supporting themselves and their families. For most workers, savings are scant and idleness means deprivation. A temporary source of income to replace earnings is therefore essential if the family is to avoid the relief rolls. For the economy, too, the generation of income and expenditures may be critical in preventing further declines in economic activity; unemployment insurance is commonly regarded as an important "built-in stabilizer."

Unemployment insurance

Prior to the passage of the Social Security Act, only Wisconsin had a state law providing benefits to workers out of jobs. Under the federal act the other states were induced to pass such laws; a uniform tax was levied on the payrolls of industrial and commercial employers of eight (later reduced to four) or more employees during at least 20 weeks of the year. Employers in a state whose unemployment insurance law met the federal guidelines could offset the state tax against the national tax up to 90 percent of the latter. By mid-1937 all states had enacted laws satisfactory to the federal government, although the provisions of the state laws varied a great deal.

Coverage under the state laws

Employees covered for unemployment insurance are usually those specified in the Federal Unemployment Tax Act: industrial and commercial workers in private industry. Often exempted, therefore, are several large groups: agricultural workers, domestic servants, state and local government employees, most employees of nonprofit organizations, self-employed workers, plus employees of private firms having fewer than four workers in 20 weeks a year.[1]

Several states extend coverage to some of these groups, however. About half the states cover firms with fewer than four employees, and over half the states include state and local government workers. Four states have laws covering nonprofit organizations. Agricultural workers are covered in Hawaii and Puerto Rico, and domestic workers in Hawaii and New York. Special federal legislation extended coverage to federal civilian employees and ex-servicemen. Railroad workers also have a separate federal law. All told, about 50 million workers, or three-fourths of all wage and salary workers were in covered employment in the mid-1960s.

Eligibility for benefits

To qualify for unemployment benefits, a worker must be "ready, able, and willing to work, must be unemployed and not disqualified, and must be registered for work at a public employment office." In determining his eligibility, the state examines a worker's employment in the base period—usually four quarters preceding the claim for compensation. Minimum earnings during this period range from $300 to $800, with additional requisites as to the timing of these earnings. Twenty-one states prohibit the payment of benefits in a second year, without an intervening period of employment.

Further tests of qualification include the worker's availability for work, as evidenced by his filing a claim and registering for work at a public employment office. He may be disqualified for benefits if he left his previous job without good cause; if he was discharged for misconduct on the job; if he refuses, again without good cause, to accept suitable work; if he is unemployed due to a labor dispute. Disqualification may postpone benefits, reduce

[1] *Social Security Programs in the United States* (Washington, D. C.: U. S. Department of Health, Education, and Welfare, Social Security Administration, 1966), pp. 47–62.

the amount, or cancel them altogether until he has returned to work and established additional wage credits. In most states, certain types of remuneration—workmen's compensation, retirement benefits under the Social Security Act, employer pension, or wages in lieu of notice or dismissal payments—reduce the unemployment benefit by the amount of the other remuneration.

The range of benefits

Average benefits for all states combined are about one-third of average wages in covered employment. The minimum is usually $10 a week, and the maxima range from $40 to $90. Benefits are related to the worker's past earnings—a fraction, say 1/26, of the wage in the base period; all benefits are subject to some dollar maximum (Table 16/1).

Benefits are also available for partial unemployment, as are additional allowances for dependents. For the latter, the amounts are small: $1 to $6 per week. All but three states require a waiting period after the worker becomes unemployed (usually a week) before compensation begins. Eight states and Puerto Rico allow extensions of benefits (usually 50 percent) after the regular claims have been exhausted, if the state's level of unemployment reaches a preset level.

In addition, training allowances under the Manpower Development and Training Act of 1962 are payable to adults who are undergoing job training, the amount of these allowances being based on the state's average weekly unemployment benefit. These allowances may be increased for dependents, and may include costs of transportation or daily commuting for the training. State unemployment insurance systems administer the system of training allowances, but the cost is paid by the federal government out of general revenues.

Financing and experience rating

The Federal Unemployment Tax Act levied on employers a permanent tax of 3.1 percent of the first $3,000 of the worker's earnings in covered jobs. Any contributions to an approved state system may be credited against this federal tax, up to 2.7 percent of taxable earnings. There is no Federal tax on employees, but three states (Alabama, Alaska, and New Jersey) do tax employees. While 34 states charge contributions on the first $3,000 of earnings as in the federal law, the others tax $3,600 to $7,200 in wages.

Experience rating is allowed in all state laws except that of Puerto Rico. Under this rule, employers with favorable unemployment records are taxed less than 2.7 percent of their payrolls. The range of actual tax liability runs from zero to 5.1 percent, with the average being 2.2 percent of taxable pay-

Table 16/1. *Selected benefit provisions under State unemployment insurance laws, January 1, 1971*

State	Weekly benefit amount for total unemployment			Duration of benefits (weeks)[3]	
	Computation (fraction of high-quarter wages unless otherwise indicated)[1]	Minimum[2]	Maximum[2]	Minimum[4]	Maximum
Alabama	1/26	$12	$50	13	26
Alaska	2.3–1.1 percent of annual wages, plus dependents' allowance.	[2]18–23	[2]60–35	14	23
Arizona	1/25	10	50	12+	26
Arkansas	1/26 up to 1/2 of State average weekly wage.	15	50	10	26
California	1/24–1/27	25	65	[3]12–14+	[3]26
Colorado	60 percent of 1/13 of claimant's high-quarter wages up to 60 percent of State average weekly wage.	14	77	10	26
Connecticut	1/26 up to 60 percent of State average weekly wage, plus dependents' allowance.	15–20	82–123	[3]22+	[3]26
Delaware	1/25	10	65	16+	26
District of Columbia	1/23 up to 1/2 of State average weekly wage, plus dependents' allowance.	8–9	[2]73	17+	34
Florida	1/2 of claimant's average weekly wage.	10	47	10	26
Georgia	1/25	12	50	9	26
Hawaii	1/25 up to 66-2/3 percent of State average weekly wage.	5	86	[3]26	[3]26
Idaho	1/26 up to greater of 52-1/2 percent of State average weekly wage or $40.	17	59	[3]10	[3]26
Illinois	1/20–1/25 plus dependents' allowance.[1]	10	45–88	[3][4]10–26	[3]26
Indiana	1/25 plus dependents' allowance.[1]	10	40–52	12+	26
Iowa	1/22 up to 1/2 of State average weekly wage.	9	61	11+	26
Kansas	1/25 up to 1/2 of State average weekly wage.	15	60	10	26
Kentucky	1/25 up to 55 percent of 85 percent of State average weekly wage.	12	56	15	26

Table 16/1. (continued)

State	Weekly benefit amount for total unemployment — Computation (fraction of high-quarter wages unless otherwise indicated)[1]	Minimum[2]	Maximum[2]	Duration of benefits (weeks)[3] Minimum[4]	Maximum
Louisiana	1/20–1/25	10	[5]55	12	28
Maine	1/22 up to 52 percent of State average weekly wage.	10	57	[4]11+–30	[4]26
Maryland	1/24 plus dependents' allowance.	10–13	[2]65	26	26
Massachusetts	1/2 of average weekly wage up to 52-1/2 percent of State average weekly wage, plus dependents' allowance.[1]	12–18	69–104	[4]5+–30	30
Michigan	63–55 percent of average weekly wage, plus dependents' allowance.[1]	[2]16–18	53–87	11	26
Minnesota	50 percent of claimant's average weekly wage.	15	57	13	26
Mississippi	1/26 up to lesser of 1/2 of State average weekly wage or $40.	10	40	12	26
Missouri	1/25	3	57	[4]10+–26	26
Montana	1/23–1/28	13	42	13	26
Nebraska	1/19–1/23	12	48	17	26
Nevada	1/25, plus dependents' allowance up to lesser of $20 or 6 percent of high-quarter wages.	16–24	47–67	11	26
New Hampshire	1.7–1.0 percent of annual wages.	13	60	26	26
New Jersey	66-2/3 percent of claimant's average weekly wage up to 1/2 of State average weekly wage.	10	72	12+	26
New Mexico	1/26; not less than 10 percent nor more than 1/2 of State average weekly wage.	12	58	18	30
New York	67–50 percent of claimant's average weekly wage.	20	75	26	26
North Carolina	2.0–1.0 percent of annual wages up to 1/2 of State average weekly wage.	12	54	[3]26	[3]26
North Dakota	1/26 up to 1/2 of State average weekly wage.	15	54	18	26
Ohio	1/2 of claimant's average weekly wage, plus dependents' allowance.[1]	10–16	47–66	20	26

See footnotes at end of table

Table 16/1. (continued)

State	Weekly benefit amount for total unemployment Computation (fraction of high-quarter wages unless otherwise indicated)[1]	Minimum[2]	Maximum[2]	Duration of benefits (weeks)[3] Minimum[4]	Maximum
Oklahoma	1/26	16	49	10+	26
Oregon	1.25 percent of base-period wages.	20	55	11+	26
Pennsylvania	1/23–1/25 or 1/2 of full-time weekly wage, if greater.	11	60	[3]18	[3]30
Puerto Rico	1/15–1/26, up to 60 percent of State average weekly wage.	7	46	[3]20	[3]20
Rhode Island	55 percent of claimant's average weekly wage up to 60 percent of State average weekly wage, plus dependents' allowance.	12–17	71–91	12	26
South Carolina	1/26 up to 1/2 of State average weekly wage.	10	53	10	26
South Dakota	1/22–1/24	12	47	[4]10+–16	26
Tennessee	1/26	14	50	12	26
Texas	1/25	15	45	9	26
Utah	1/26 up to 1/2 of State average weekly wage.	10	56	[4]10–22	36
Vermont	1/2 of claimant's average weekly wage for highest 20 weeks up to 1/2 of State average weekly wage.	15	61	[3]26	[3]26
Virginia	1/25	18	59	12	26
Washington	1/25 of high-quarter wage up to 1/2 of State average weekly wage.	17	72	[3][4]8+–21+	[3]30
West Virginia	1.6–0.9 percent of annual wages up to 45 percent of State average weekly wage.	12	58	26	26
Wisconsin	63–50 percent of claimant's average weekly wage up to 52-1/2 percent of State average weekly wage.	11	72	14+	34
Wyoming	1/25 up to 1/2 of State average weekly wage.	10	[2]56	[4]11–24	26

See footnotes following page

Table 16/1. (continued)

[1]When States use a weighted high-quarter formula, annual-wage formula, or average-weekly-wage formula, approximate fractions or percentages are figured at midpoint of lowest and highest normal wage brackets. In Massachusetts for claimants with average weekly wage of $66 or less, computation based on weighted schedule (approximately 1/21-1/26 of high-quarter wage). When dependents' allowances are provided, the fraction applies to the basic benefit amount. In Illinois and Indiana no dependents' allowance paid to claimants qualified only for basic maximum benefit or less. In Michigan and Ohio claimants may be eligible for augmented amount at all benefit levels but benefit amounts above basic maximum available only to claimants in family or dependency classes whose average weekly wages are higher than those required for maximum basic benefit amount.

[2]When two amounts are given, higher includes dependents' allowances. Higher for minimum weekly benefit amount includes maximum allowance for one dependent; Michigan—for one dependent child or two dependents other than a child. In the District of Columbia and Maryland, same maximum with or without dependents. In Alaska, maximum for interstate claimants is $20 and no dependents' allowances are paid to interstate claimants not enrolled in an approved training course; in Wyoming, maximum amount for interstate claimants may be less than that shown.

[3]Benefits are extended under State program by 50 percent when unemployment in States noted reaches specified levels; in Connecticut by 13 weeks and in North Carolina, by 8 weeks. In Puerto Rico, benefits are extended by 32 weeks in certain industries, occupations, or establishments when a special unemployment situation exists.

[4]For claimants with minimum qualifying wages and minimum weekly benefit amount. In States noted, range of duration applies to claimants with minimum qualifying wages in base period; longer duration applies with the minimum weekly benefit amount; the shorter duration applies with maximum possible concentration of wages in the high quarter, and therefore the highest weekly benefit amount possible for such base-period earnings. In Maine, benefits are not exhausted until claimant receives $300; thus duration may be as long as 30 weeks for some claimants.

[5]$60, effective Aug. 1, 1971.

Source: Social Security Administration, *Social Security Programs in the United States,* 1971, pp. 60-62.

rolls. This provision was intended to help stabilize employment. However, since an individual employer's control over the demand for his product—and hence his need for employees—is usually very limited, tax rates are more likely to be lowered by the state of the economy than by any intracompany attempts to keep its unemployment low.

Economics of unemployment compensation

The many causes of unemployment are usually grouped under two over-all headings: demand inadequacy and structural impediments. Since unemployment occurs for different reasons, solutions to the problem and the treatment accorded the unemployed must differ also. In outlining programs to aid the unemployed, Joseph Becker and his associates[2] distinguish between those who need only income maintenance and those who need something more. The first group need *alleviative* action: temporary, even partial, replacement of earnings to tide them over a short interruption in their working arrangements. The second category of unemployed need an improvement in their education, work skills, or location, in order to find satisfactory jobs. These *curative* programs are more expensive per worker, they take longer to complete, and they should have a more profound effect on the subsequent earnings pattern of the worker. Unemployment insurance is primarily alleviative in function, as are programs providing for severance pay, early pensions, and welfare allowances. In contrast, area redevelopment, public works, job-training programs, and public employment services are curative for the most part.

The authors in Becker's book make a second distinction between *economic* and *welfare* programs. *Economic* programs attend to the needs of those unemployed persons who normally have jobs; they make previous employment a condition of eligibility, or they tie benefits to the value of work performed by the person hired. Again, unemployment insurance is an example of an economic program, as are arrangements for early pensions, public works, job retraining, area redevelopment. *Welfare* programs for the unemployed usually rely on a means test, rather than previous job experience, to determine eligibility; benefits are based, too, on need rather than prior earnings, so that unemployment assistance becomes very similar to general welfare assistance which applies to all in need, not just the unemployed. As the authors note, there is a strong preference in this country for economic programs, and a willingness to resort to welfare or relief measures only when such devices as unemployment insurance fail to reach all the unemployed.

---

[2]Joseph M. Becker, S. J., ed. *In Aid of the Unemployed* (Baltimore: The Johns Hopkins Press, 1965).

Shortcomings of the program

Many of the deficiencies of the present unemployment insurance scheme are evident from the foregoing description. Consider the limitations on coverage, for example. About one-fourth of the nation's wage and salary workers remain outside the system for one or more of the following reasons: employment in a firm of fewer than four workers; employment in a nonprofit institution; or working for a state or local government. Some states have extended coverage to some of these groups, but the workers who have no protection can be brought under the laws only by federal action or by a series of liberalizing state amendments.

Along with coverage, the issue of adequacy of the benefit is a critical question. Despite general agreement that the benefit ought to match at least half of the weekly wage lost during unemployment, the average is closer to one-third. There are other related questions: what allowances should the worker with dependents receive? Twelve states now have systems for such supplements to the worker's benefit. Should dependents be taken care of through an allowance for higher maximum benefits?

The length of time a worker may draw unemployment insurance is another perennial question. Duration of benefits has been increased during the last three decades, so that the covered worker who loses his job now normally has access to about 24 weeks of benefits. But it is evident that this is often not long enough, particularly during periods of recession. In some states attempts have been made to establish extended benefits to certain groups of workers. Alternatively, it has been recommended that the federal government underwrite benefits beyond 26 weeks.

None of these shortcomings are insurmountable, if it were not for the expenses involved. Financing an improvement in benefit levels, or an extension of coverage, or a lengthened duration period, remains an issue that the various states have found extremely difficult. Unemployment insurance reserves have dipped very low during the brief recessions of the post World War II era, and continuation of the programs at their present levels has been sometimes in question. Improvements can be made, therefore, only if additional funds are made available by the federal government, or if states raise their tax rate or enlarge the tax base. Increases in payroll taxes are generally opposed, since they tend to be regressive, or at least the incidence is uncertain. For the most part, financial relief could more reasonably come from federal sources, either as training and relocation allowances for special programs, or as general revenues to support supplementary programs of insurance.

Supplementary unemployment benefits

The limitations of public systems of unemployment compensation have led to long and serious consideration of the action industry might take in absorbing an additional share of unemployment costs. The rationale for privately financed supplementary unemployment benefits, the cost of which is borne by the employer, is much the same as that for merit rating under the system of public benefits: the firm is encouraged to stabilize its employment in order to avoid the cost of supporting any of its workers who are thrown out of jobs.

The first supplementary unemployment benefits plan was developed by the United Automobile Workers and the Ford Motor Company, and signed in 1955. Subsequently, other automobile companies agreed to the same contracts, and the United Steelworkers negotiated somewhat similar plans in the steel and can industries. In the mid-'60s, about two and a half million workers had supplementary unemployment coverage; more than two-thirds of the workers in the automobile, rubber, aluminum, agricultural-implement, and can and steel industries were included in these plans.

In the initial agreement, the automobile companies agreed to pay 5 cents per hour for each hour worked by the covered workers, the proceeds of these contributions being used to provide supplements to the compensation afforded by the state. The maximum amount available to any unemployed worker was 65 percent of his wages for as much as 52 weeks. At present the General Motors plan allows 62 percent of gross earnings, and a weekly $1.50 each for as many as 4 dependents. The United States Steel Company sets the total benefit at 60 percent of earnings, up to $37.50, plus dependents' allowances. Since the benefit is a sum of the state's payment and that of the supplementary unemployment benefit, it is not possible for the worker to receive more than the 60 to 65 percent of wages specified; there is great advantage to the unemployed, however, in the fact that duration is extended to 52 weeks of the year.

Supplementary unemployment benefit contracts were not significantly expanded during the 1960s, although the issue of guaranteed annual wage, or minimum income, or negative income tax, is ever present. Current attention to matters of minimum income guarantees for all persons, at public expense, has tended to overshadow all other developments in this area.

Short-run and long-run unemployment

Maintaining incomes during unemployment is a complex problem, involving questions of the level of income to be maintained, the relationship of the benefit to previous earnings, issues of work incentives, and the duration of compensation. Many of these same questions haunt the policy makers who are now trying to devise rules for a guaranteed minimum income for all.

But even if the issue is narrowed somewhat by a fairly arbitrary set of goals, the essence of the problem remains. Suppose it was agreed that the goal would be an average wage replacement of 50 percent; a coverage extended to all wage and salary workers; duration of 26 weeks, or half of the year, after which the worker would have to resume covered employment to qualify for further compensation. Since the availability of jobs is not necessarily improved just because unemployment insurance benefits have expired, the need for income maintenance may continue long beyond its guarantee of 26 weeks. Or conversely, the need may have disappeared long before benefits expired, because the unemployed worker quickly found a new job.

Unemployment compensation, even under the best arrangements, remains a temporary expedient for what is expected to be a temporary problem. It was not designed to deal with the long-term unemployment that is characteristic of certain areas of the country or certain groups of workers; nor is it equipped to maintain even partially the incomes of such masses of families as fell jobless in the early 1930s. Any attempt to accommodate the various state unemployment-insurance programs to massive or prolonged unemployment is futile. Given the tax arrangements for funding the systems, all else follows: limited coverage, short duration, low levels of benefits.

It is clear that the needs of certain groups cannot be met by unemployment compensation, unless the states drastically change their tax rates or base, or alter their thinking that a worker must earn his right to benefits. Under present arrangements, to be eligible for compensation the worker must have acquired claims by his having worked in a covered job. Clearly, many of the unemployed do not qualify, at any time: they have no record of earnings in a covered occupation, or they have exhausted such benefits. Teenagers, for example, who have the highest unemployment rates of any group of workers, have no credits from earlier employment and hence no eligibility for benefits. Older workers, on the other hand, who have the highest incidence of long-term unemployment, have previous earnings records but have frequently exhausted their benefits.

The worker who is only marginally attached to the labor force—because he is unskilled or inexperienced, or older and displaced from the job to which seniority rules apply, or because he is a part-time worker—has little, if any, income support from the unemployment-insurance schemes. Many of these workers need the support even more than the worker whose loss of a job is temporary but who is nevertheless fully covered. This suggests that the unemployed are a heterogeneous group, in need of a series of income supplements. Compensation for being out of a job for a brief period is a much less severe problem, which can be dealt with through unemployment insurance, with some improvement in compensation levels, coverage, and duration of benefits. Maintaining the income of the marginal or uncovered worker is far more challenging.

Income for the disabled

Inability to earn income may be due to physical or mental disability, as well as to lack of jobs; to sickness, as well as to old age. To the individual worker and his family, the reason for the disappearance of earnings is not important; but the necessity for some form of replacement is critical to the family's welfare. Similarly, premature death of the breadwinner must somehow be compensated for, lest the family soon be added to the welfare rolls.

In the United States there are no family allowances, and insurance against illness and disability are usually related to the worker's labor-force attachment. This means that support for the sick or disabled man or woman generally derives from the work situation, rather than from a social guarantee of income at some minimum level. And since the benefit is work-related, it is available only to those persons who have been at work in a covered job during some previous period. These qualifying conditions limit disability payments to certain workers under certain conditions. Additional limitations to eligibility have to do with the degree of injury (i.e., whether it is total or partial); the length of time the impairment will last (permanent or temporary); whether the injury was suffered on the job; and in the case of partial disability, the state in which the injury or illness occurred.

Workmen's compensation benefits

The cost of compensating a worker for injury suffered on the job is now generally viewed as a cost of doing business, in the same way that business is expected to carry insurance on plant and equipment. Workmen's compensation is therefore not optional with the business firm; in all states there are now laws setting forth the conditions for compensating workers who were injured at work or contracted illnesses associated with the job.

Such guarantees were not always made to workers.[3] Early in the century the federal government enacted legislation covering its civilian employees. But attempts to gain state-by-state passage of accident-insurance laws were frustrated by the employers' counterclaims of employee responsibility. The common law defenses used by the employer were three. The worker, he argued, assumed certain risks when he came on the job; this *assumption of risk* relieved the employer of liability for damages in any accident that occurred. Or alternatively, the employer held that the worker was at fault in the accident, and this amounted to *contributory negligence.* Finally, employers could enter a *fellow-servant plea:* the accident resulted from negligence on the part of a co-worker who was thus responsible, if anyone was. With the aid of these protective doctrines, employers were able to avoid financial responsibility for injuries on the job during the early 1900s.

But by 1920 all but six states had passed laws providing, in varying degrees, for cash benefits and medical care for accidents suffered on the job, and for survivors' benefits, at employer expense. At present, all states have

---

[3]For a discussion of the details of these laws, see Herman M. Somers and Anne R. Somers. *Workmen's Compensation* (New York: John Wiley and Sons, 1954).

laws providing for compensation to the worker without regard to who is at fault in the accident. The terms of coverage and eligibility vary from state to state, however, as do the sizes of benefits.[4]

Coverage   In total, state and federal laws extended workmen's compensation to about 50 million employees, or about three-fourths of all wage and salary workers, in the mid-sixties. Exemptions of coverage are often made for domestic servants, farm and casual labor, employees of nonprofit organizations, and workers in firms of three or fewer employees. More than half of the state laws are compulsory; the employer is required to pay certain levels of compensation for various injuries. The other states—23 in all—allow the employer to act on his own, with the provision that in the event of injury or illness from the job, he may not rely on the common law defenses. Depending on the state's law, employers may carry insurance against accidents or simply prove their own capacity to absorb the possible cost. In some states insurance must be carried with a special state insurance fund.

Eligibility   Workers are usually eligible for benefits for any injury (or to the heirs, for death) "arising out of and in the course of employment." Exceptions are noted in cases of misconduct or negligence. Such occupational illnesses as silicosis, caused by breathing dust, are compensated for in much the same way as industrial accidents.

The amount of compensation varies from state to state, as Table 16/2 shows. Benefits usually range from 60 percent to two-thirds of the weekly wage when the accident occurs, with some states varying the amount to account for dependents. But since most states set a dollar maximum on the weekly benefit, the higher-paid worker is not likely to receive the specified percentage.

Temporary and permanent total disability   In most cases, compensation payments are made to persons who are totally disabled, but not permanently. Under most state laws, weekly maximum payments of at least $40 (including allowances for dependents), and more than half the states allow a high of $50 or more. The duration of benefits for temporary total disability ranges from 208 to 500 weeks. Some states have no limits on the length of time benefits may be drawn, whereas some laws limit the total amount that can be paid, the range being from $10,750 to $35,000.

---

[4]For details of these programs, see *Social Security Programs in the United States, op. cit.,* pp. 62–76.

Table 16/2. Minimum and maximum benefits for temporary total disability under workmen's compensation laws, January 1, 1971

State	Maximum percentage of wages	Maximum period	Payments per week		Total maximum stated in law
			Minimum	Maximum	
Alabama	[1]55–65	400 weeks	$15, or average wage if less.	$50	$20,000.
Alaska	65	Duration of disability.	$25, or average wage if less.	$127	$20,000.
Arizona	65	433 weeks	$30, if worker is 21 years of age, or over, plus $2.30 for total dependents.	$150, plus $2.30 for total dependents.	
Arkansas	65	450 weeks	$10	$49.00	$19,500.
California	[2]61 3/4	240 weeks	$25	$87.50	$15,200.64.
Colorado	66 2/3	Duration of disability.	$13	$59.50[3]	([3]).
Connecticut	66 2/3	Duration of disability	$20	60% of State's "average production wage" ($84–$126).[1]	
Delaware	66 2/3	Duration of disability.	$25, or actual wage if less.	$75.	
District of Columbia	66 2/3	Duration of disability.	$18, or average wage if less.	$70	$24,000.
Florida	60	350 weeks	$12, or actual wage if less.	$56.	
Georgia	60	400 weeks	$15, or actual wage if less.	$50	$18,000.
Hawaii	66 2/3	Duration of disability.	$18, or average wage if less.	$112.50	$35,100.
Idaho	[1]60	400 weeks;[4] thereafter $26 per week ($33 if dependent wife), plus $8 to $48 for children, for duration of disability.	$26 ($33 if dependent wife) to $81[1]	$43 to $99.00[1] (see col. 3).	

Table 16/2. (continued)

State	Maximum percentage of wages	Maximum period	Payments per week		Total maximum stated in law
			Minimum	Maximum	
Illinois	[1]65–80	Duration of disability until equivalent of death benefit is paid, except in specific injury cases limited to 64 weeks.	$31.50 to $49[1]	$74 to $91[1]. After first 64 weeks reduced to $59 to $71.	$18,000– $25,200.
Indiana	60	500 weeks		$57	$25,000.
Iowa	66 2/3	300 weeks	$21 $18, or actual wage if less.	50% of State's average weekly wage, ($61).	
Kansas	60	415 weeks	$7	$56	$23,240.
Kentucky	66 2/3	425 weeks[4]	25% of 85% of the State's average weekly wage ($24).	55% of 85% of the State's average weekly wage ($52).	
Louisiana	65	300 weeks	$12.50, or actual wage if less.	$49.	
Maine	66 2/3	Duration of disability.	$18	2/3 of State's average weekly wage ($72.92).	
Maryland	66 2/3	208 weeks	$25, or actual wage if less.	$55[5].	
Massachusetts	66 2/3	Duration of disability.	$20, or average wage if less, but not less than $10 if normal working hours are 15 or more.	$70, plus $6 for each total dependent; aggregate not to exceed workers' average weekly wage.	$18,000. plus dependents' allow- ances.[6]
Michigan	66 2/3	Duration of disability.	$27 to $42	$79 to $108[1] [7].	
Minnesota	66 2/3	350 weeks	$17.50	$70.	
Mississippi	66 2/3	450 weeks	$10	$40	$15,000.
Missouri	66 2/3	400 weeks	$16, or actual wage if less.	$63.50.	

(See footnotes at end of table.)

State	Maximum percentage of wages	Maximum period	Payments per week Minimum	Payments per week Maximum	Total maximum stated in law
Montana	[1]50–66 2/3	300 weeks	$39.50 (reduced by $5 after 26 weeks).	$42 to $65[1] (reduced by $5 after 26 weeks).	
Nebraska	66 2/3	300 weeks[4]; thereafter 45% of wages, maximum $41.00.	$35 or actual wage if less, first 300 weeks; thereafter $31, or actual wage if less.	$55 (see col. 3).	
Nevada	[1]65–90	433 weeks	No statutory minimum	$57.75 to $79.96.[1]	
New Hampshire	66 2/3	312 weeks; thereafter annual extensions in the discretion of the labor commissioner.	$20, or average wage if less.	$69.	
New Jersey	66 2/3	300 weeks	$15	2/3 of State's average weekly wage ($95).	
New Mexico	60	500 weeks	$24, or actual wage if less.	$48	$24,000.
New York	66 2/3	Duration of disability.	$30, or actual wage if less.	$95.	
North Carolina	60	400 weeks[8]	$10	$50	$18,000.[8]
North Dakota	80	Duration of disability.	Same as maximum	55% of State's average weekly wage, plus $5 for each dependent child ($59), but not to exceed worker's net wage after taxes.	
Ohio	66 2/3	Duration of disability.	$25, or actual wage if less.	$63 for the first 12 weeks; thereafter $56.	$10,750.
Oklahoma	66 2/3	300 weeks; may be extended to 500 weeks.	$15, or actual wage if less.	$49	

Table 16/2. (continued)

State	Maximum percentage of wages	Maximum period	Payments per week		Total maximum stated in law
			Minimum	Maximum	
Oregon	66 2/3	Duration of disability.	$30, or 90% of actual wage if less.	$60 to $80.[1]	
Pennsylvania	66 2/3	Duration of disability.	$35, or 90% of actual wage if less, but in no event less than $22.	$60.	
Puerto Rico	66 2/3	312 weeks	$10	$45.	(⁹).
Rhode Island	66 2/3	Duration of disability.[9]	$30	60% of State's average weekly wage ($70.33), plus $6 for each dependent; aggregate not to exceed worker's average weekly wage.	
South Carolina	60	500 weeks	$5	$50	$12,500.
South Dakota	55	312 weeks	$27, or average wage if less.	$50	$18,800.
Tennessee	65	Duration of disability.	$15, or average wage if less, but in no event less than $12.	$47.	
Texas	60	401 weeks	$12	$49.	
Utah	60	312 weeks	$27 to $45,[1] or actual wage if less.	$47 to $65.[1]	$14,664–20,280.[1]
Vermont	66 2/3	330 weeks[4]	1/4 of State's "average weekly wage" ($31), plus $3.50 for each dependent child under 21, or average wage if less.	1/2 of State's "average weekly wage" ($61), plus $3.50 for each dependent child under 21.	
Virginia	60	500 weeks	$14	$62	$24,800.

(See footnotes at end of table.)

State	Maximum percentage of wages	Maximum period	Payments per week		Total maximum stated in law
			Minimum	Maximum	
Washington	66 2/3	Duration of disability.	Same as maximum	$42.69 to $81.23.[1]	
West Virginia		208 weeks	$26	50 % of State's average weekly wage ($65.50)	
Wisconsin	70	Duration of disability.	$8.75	$79.	
Wyoming	66 2/3	Duration of disability.	$33.46 to $49.62[1]	$43.85 to $63.46.[1]	
United States: Federal employees	[1]66 2/3–75	Duration of disability.	$66.65[10] or actual wage if less.	$429.12.[10]	
Longshoremen	66 2/3	Duration of disability.	$18, or average wage if less.	$70	$24,000.

[1] According to number of dependents. In Idaho, Oregon, Washington, and Wyoming, according to marital status and number of dependents. In Illinois, according to number of dependent children under 16, or under 18 when not emancipated. In Connecticut, $5 for each dependent child under 18, up to 50 percent of the basic weekly benefit.

[2] The California law provides for 65 percent of 95 percent of actual earnings, or 61-3/4 percent.

[3] Colorado: If periodic disability benefits are payable to the worker under the Federal OASDHI, the workmen's compensation weekly benefits shall be reduced (but not below zero) by an amount approximating one-half such Federal benefits for such week. If disability benefits are payable under an employer pension plan, the workmen's compensation benefits shall be reduced in an amount proportional to the employer's percentage of total contributions to the plan. Colorado does not limit total maximum for disability from accidental injury, except that if payable in lump sum, maximum is $18,623.50.

[4] If total disability begins after a period of partial disability, the period of partial disability is deducted from the specified period for temporary total.

[5] Maryland: Two-thirds of wage not to exceed $55 per week for first 42 days of temporary disability. After 42 days 2/3 of wage not to exceed 2/3 of State's average weekly wage ($85.68 as of 1/1/71). Maximum limit for 208 weeks.

[6] Massachusetts: Total maximum $18,000 for temporary total and permanent partial disability.

[7] Michigan: The maximum benefit rate is adjusted annually on the basis of a $1.00 increase or decrease for each $1.50 increase or decrease in the State's average weekly wage.

Table 16/2. (continued)

[8]North Carolina: The 400 weeks and **$18,000** do not apply in cases of permanent total disability resulting from an injury to the brain or spinal cord or from loss of mental capacity caused by an injury to the brain.
[9]Rhode Island: After 500 weeks, or after $32,500 has been paid, payments to be made from second-injury fund for period of disability.
[10]Federal employees: Based on 75 percent of the pay of specified grade levels in the Federal civil service.
Source: Social Security Administration, *Social Security Programs in the United States, 1971.* p. 76–80.

Permanent partial disability   Partial disability may result from the loss of an eye or a limb, for example, or from back or head injuries. The former group, termed specific or schedule injuries, are compensated for in the same manner as total disability, but for a stipulated length of time. General injuries of the second type usually result in the payment of some percentage of the wages lost from the injury.

Death and medical benefits   Survivors of workers who are fatally injured on the job receive compensation, usually in the form of weekly or monthly benefits, either up to some total amount, or until the widow dies or remarries and the children reach age 16 or 18. In most states the amount of the benefit is related to earnings, with allowance for dependents. Medical care following accident or illness from the job is provided; in most states there is no limit on the time or amount of aid furnished.

Financing   The employer pays the cost of accident and illness compensation, with a few states allowing for small employee contributions for health benefits. The costs to the employer vary, depending on the hazardousness of the work, the level of benefits guaranteed, and the type of insurance carrier used. An employer's cost, on the average, amounts to about 1 percent of his payroll. But the range is wide, from 0.1 percent for clerical jobs to 20 percent in some hazardous areas. Although insurance costs are met by the employer, the employee who has a disabling accident suffers a far greater financial cost in the form of wages foregone, perhaps for the rest of his life.

Temporary disability insurance

Only four states—California, New Jersey, New York, and Rhode Island —have laws providing for wage-loss compensation in cases of temporary nonoccupational illness or disability. In these states, most industrial and commercial wage and salary workers in private industry are covered. Employers are required to provide protection through insurance with a commercial carrier, with the state-operated fund, or by "contracting-out" of the state fund. More than 12 million workers, or about one-fourth of the employed wage and salary workers in private industry now have some temporary disability insurance coverage.

Disability is usually defined as the inability, "by reason of a physical or mental condition, to perform regular or customary work."[5] Pregnancy quali-

---

[5] *Ibid.*, p. 77.

fies as such a condition in certain instances. When workmen's compensation is being received, payments of disability insurance are either not allowed or are a limited addition to the compensation. Receipt of unemployment insurance payments also disqualifies a claim for disability benefits. Eligibility is established only by persons with a substantial attachment to the labor force, as demonstrated by past employment or earnings. In New York, workers qualify after 4 consecutive weeks of covered work, in New Jersey, after 17 weeks of employment during the previous year, and in Rhode Island, after 20 weeks. California required earnings of $300 in the base period.

The benefit amount is related to the worker's previous wage, but in all four states there are dollar limits on the benefit. As Table 16/3 indicates, computation of the weekly benefit involves a percentage of the wage—about 50 percent—subject to the stated maximum. These benefits may be drawn for as many as 26 weeks. In California, hospital costs are partially met: $12 a day for 20 days on any one disability is available to the beneficiary.

In contrast to the financial arrangements for workmen's compensation, the cost of temporary disability insurance is borne largely by the employee. Employee payroll taxes are collected to meet the costs in California and Rhode Island; in New Jersey and New York, payroll taxes are levied on both employer and employee. No government contribution is made in any of the states.

These few state programs, although minimal in coverage and amount of benefit, are a step in the direction of meeting a major problem: no replacement of income for workers who are temporarily sick or disabled from causes not related to work. Unless the disability occurs on the job, workmen's compensation is not available; unless it is total and permanent, the OASDHI (Old Age, Survivors, Disability, and Health Insurance) cash benefit (described below) cannot be claimed. At present, private insurance coverage is the only source of protection for most employees, and the costs of such insurance are prohibitive to the low-income workers.

OASDHI cash disability benefits

Monthly benefits are now available to workers under age 65 who are permanently and totally disabled. Entitlement is based on a very strict definition of disability, however; the worker must be unable "to engage in any substantial gainful activity by reason of any medically determinable physical or mental impairment which can be expected to result in death or which has lasted or can be expected to last for a continuous period of not less than 12 months." Thus, the disability must be judged a permanent one, and it must be so severe that the worker cannot engage in any gainful activity—to be rendered unable to merely do the work he had been doing is not a sufficient basis for entitlement.

These benefits are payable after a 6-month waiting period, and continue until the worker reaches age 65 (when he goes on the retirement rolls), unless

Table 16/3. Selected benefit provisions under State temporary disability insurance laws, January 1, 1971

State	Weekly benefit amount for disability			Duration of benefits (weeks)
	Computation	Minimum	Maximum	
California	1/21–1/23 of high-quarter wages	$25	$87	6–26
Hawaii	55% of average weekly wage	[1]14	66 2/3% of State average weekly wage ($85)	26
New Jersey	66 2/3% of average weekly wage	10	50% of State average weekly wage ($72)	8+–26
New York	50% of average weekly wage	[2]20	75	26
Puerto Rico	1/15–1/26 of high-quarter wages up to weekly benefit amount of $31. One percent of annual wages above $31.	7	[3]78	10+–26
Rhode Island	55% of average weekly wage, plus $3 for each dependent up to $12	[4]12	50% of State average weekly wage ($59)[4]	[5]12–26

[1] Average weekly wage if less than $14.
[2] Average weekly wage if less than $20.
[3] Lower maximum for agricultural workers ($26).
[4] Exclusive of dependents' allowances.
[5] Minimum may be less than 12 weeks for claimants who qualify with only $1,200 of earnings in base period.
Source: Social Security Administration, Social Security Programs in the United States, 1971.

he recovers his ability to work. Coverage is the same for disability purposes as for retirement benefits, and financing the two programs is handled in the same way: from payroll taxes on employer and employee. Determinations of disability are usually made by the state vocational rehabilitation agencies, which attempt also to prepare the injured or ill beneficiary for returning to work. In the mid-'60s the average monthly benefit for a disabled worker without dependents was under $95, with a dependent wife and one or more children, about $200.

With the 1965 Amendments to the Social Security Act, a health insurance program was formulated covering persons aged 65 and over. This medical-expense insurance was not extended to the disabled, however, on the basis that medical care for the disabled would be very expensive. Another way of stating the problem is to say that their need for medical care was great. In any case, disabled persons did not receive medical care coverage in the 1965 legislation. Nor has legislation corrected this omission, despite the recommendations of an advisory council appointed to study the health insurance needs of the disabled.[6]

Financing the costs of not working

Since workmen's compensation and unemployment insurance are provided by state laws, there is wide variation in all aspects of these programs: amounts and duration of benefits, dependents' allowances, coverage, etc. Financial arrangements vary, too, although for the most part payroll taxes, when used, are levied on the employer and not on the employee. In financing these programs, the important question arises: where does responsibility lie for carrying the costs of the nonworking periods? Is it industry's obligation to support the worker who is disabled or unemployed?

John L. Lewis, the late President of the United Mine Workers, argued that industry does in fact have such responsibility; their "cost of caring for the human equity in the coal industry is inherently as valid as the cost of replacement of mining machinery." Similarly, the obligation of the steel industry for its employees was affirmed by a fact-finding board two decades ago.

The machines and plant on which the industry has prospered . . . are not all made of metal or brick and mortar. They are also made of flesh and blood. And the human machines, like the inanimate machines, have a definite rate of depreciation.[7]

---

[6] *Health Insurance for the Disabled under Social Security,* Report of the Advisory Council on Health Insurance for the Disabled (Washington: Government Printing Office, 1969).

[7] Steel Industry Board, *Report to the President on the Labor Dispute in the Basic Steel Industry,* quoted in Charles L. Dearing; *Industrial Pensions* (Washington, D. C.: The Brookings Institution, 1954), p. 61.

Money versus real costs

To some extent government action would seem to support the notion of industry responsibility. Both federal and state legislation now demand that employers make financial provisions for possible periods of unemployment and disability, and that as employers they accept the obligation.

In a deeper sense, however, legislation requiring employer contributions has the effect of shifting some of the costs of unemployment and disability from the worker to society as a whole, or at least to the consumers of products made by the employers. The initial cost of the insurance is borne by the employer in most cases. But rarely does the firm bear the final incidence of the tax, since it, too, is a cost of doing business and is charged off in the price of the product along with the wage cost. The firm has to absorb the cost only when it cannot raise the product price, or lower the remuneration paid to labor and other factors of production—or, in short, when it faces an extremely elastic demand for its commodity and an elastic supply of the factors of production. Unless both of these circumstances exist, commodity price or factor price changes and some part of the tax burden is shifted forward to consumers or backward to labor.

When the consumer suffers a price increase, he may choose not to buy the product. But the more widespread the practice of charging the unemployment and disability cost to the industry, the more general the price rise and the smaller the consumer's chance of avoiding the incidence of the tax. Alternatively, the cost could be borne out of general tax revenues; this is frequently suggested on the basis that the payroll tax, when the employee shares it, is regressive. Federal tax receipts are collected on a progressive basis, the personal income tax being the major source of revenue. State taxes are less so, however, since they include excise and sales taxes that are regressive, and that are much less progressive than federal income taxes. It should be noted that these state taxes tend to maintain the given income distribution, and therefore the structural problem remains unchanged.

If the costs of not working were met from general revenues, the burden would be spread over all taxpayers, rather than being paid by consumers who buy the products of the covered industries and the workers in those industries. Assuming coverage were extended to all workers, the shift would be from consumers and workers to taxpayers; this shift would share the cost somewhat more progressively. But the cost is shared by a very large proportion of the public even now, rather than being paid by industry alone.

The larger costs of not working—measured as product forgone—is also borne by the whole society. It is true that at first glance the family of the unemployed worker absorbs most of the burden, for that family must cut its annual expenditure from, say, $8,000 a year to less than half that amount even under the best unemployment insurance law. What society loses is the full $8,000 worth of goods that the worker would produce if he had not lost his job; the transfer payment he receives does not represent any actual output during that year. The real cost of unemployment and disability can be aggregated to show the dollar value of goods and services forgone. Herein lies the national burden of not working, the burden on all the people in the economy.

Allocating or reducing the costs

Financing unemployment and disability benefits raises questions about allocating the costs of some minimum level of support approved for the worker who is not able to earn an income. Society has progressed in its thinking on allocation, from earlier views that by taking a job the worker assumed the risk of physical injury, and that unemployment was the fault of the unemployed, to its present position that the costs of these two hazards are properly charged to the operation of the business.

The next stage of thought would seem to concern itself not so much with allocating as with reducing the costs of involuntary displacement from work. Such costs could be drastically reduced through measures aimed at keeping people at work. Such measures are not costless, but their returns in the form of increased output have been well documented.

Investments in job training (including basic education) for the unemployed, in relocation of workers and plants, and in job redesign for the disabled and handicapped are investments designed to reduce the longrun costs of unemployment and disability. Yet our expenditures on these programs have been meagre, either in terms of the potential return or in comparison with the resources other economies devote to the problem. It is no accident that unemployment rates are low among highly skilled and well-educated persons, or that nations that emphasize job retraining have practically no idle workers. Until the United States develops similar methods of eliminating some of the structural barriers to employment, the loss in output, which is the real cost of not working, will remain high.

Readings

Becker, Joseph M., ed. *In Aid of the Unemployed.* Baltimore: Johns Hopkins Press, 1965.

Bowen, William G.; Frederick H. Harbison; Richard A. Lester; and Herman M. Somers, eds. *The Princeton Symposium on the American System of Social Insurance.* New York: McGraw-Hill Book Co., 1968.

Health Insurance for the Disabled under Social Security. Report of the Advisory Council on Health Insurance for the Disabled. Washington, D. C.: U. S. Government Printing Office, 1969.

Lester, R. A. *The Economics of Unemployment Compensation.* Princeton, N. J.: Industrial Relations Section, Princeton University, 1962.

Myers, Robert J. *Social Insurance and Allied Government Programs.* Homewood, Ill.: Richard D. Irwin, Inc., 1965.

Somers, Herman M., and Anne R. Somers. *Workmen's Compensation.* New York: John Wiley and Sons, 1959.

Turnbull, J. G.; C. A. Williams, Jr.; and Earl F. Cheit. *Economic and Social Security,* 3d Ed. New York: Ronald Press, 1967.

U. S. Department of Health, Education, and Welfare. *Social Security Programs in the United States.* Washington, D. C.: Social Security Administration, 1966.

Chapter Economic Assurance:
Seventeen Income for the Retired

Introduction

Retirement is a luxury available to only a small proportion of the world's older people. In the United States only about one-fourth of the men aged 65 and over are now in the labor force, and many of these men work only part-time. Time free of work in old age, along with the shortened workweek and later entrance into the labor force, is possible because man can now produce enough goods and services to meet his family's needs in much less than the 12 hours a day customary in the last century. Worklife, too, although longer because of the longer lifespan, comprises a smaller proportion of man's total life. In the late nineteenth century, work commenced in the early teens and ended with death; now males are nearly twenty when they go to work, and they tend to retire at age 65, or earlier. In less productive economies, it is not possible to subsist on the product earned in a short workweek or to keep children in school through their teens. Output per man-hour is so low that all persons have to work for practically all of their lives. Leisure in any form invites starvation.

Worklife changes in the twentieth century

Growth in time free of work has in the longrun been an obvious corollary of growth in output per worker. Establishment of the eight-hour day gave the most dramatic evidence of increasing leisure, but an equally significant change has occurred in the number of nonworking years. A male born in 1960 can expect to spend half again as many years free of work as the male born in 1900. Instead of 16 nonworking years he will have 25; his added life expectancy of 18½ years is divided almost evenly between time in and time outside the labor force. Of the additional nine years spent outside of the labor force, about four are being added to the educational and five to the retirement period of man's life.[1]

---

[1]Seymour Wolfbein, *Changing Patterns of Worklife* (Washington, D. C.: U. S. Department of Labor, 1963).

Decline in labor-force activity of males

The distribution of man's lifetime between working years and leisure years depends primarily on the nation's stage of economic development or, more precisely, on the productivity of labor and hence the extent to which nonworking time can be supported. Male labor-force activity rates at mid-century were highest in agricultural countries and lowest in industrialized countries (Table 17/1). The lower average rates in developed economies are a result of the drop in activity at each end of the worklife; age-specific rates by stage of industrialization reveal sharp differences in the work patterns of young and old men. In agricultural countries the proportion in the 10–14 age group who are active is about six times (and the proportion of 65-and-over males about twice) the proportion at work in the industrialized countries (Table 17/2). It is interesting to note that the current average participation rate for men in the agricultural countries is approximately the same as that for the United States at the end of the last century.

The downward trend among industrially advanced nations continues, with the major declines appearing at the beginning and the end of the work-life span. During the last two decades, the rates of decline in the work activity of young men have differed among the developed economies, as have the rates for men aged 65 and over; yet the overall effect in most countries has been to increase the number of nonworking years for men. Since the scientific and technological progress that increased productivity per man-hour also

Table 17/1. Average activity rates for males for countries classified according to degree of industrialization, population censuses

Degree of industrialization	Standardized for age structure[a]
Industrialized countries[b]	60.5
Semi-industrialized countries[c]	62.8
Agricultural countries[d]	65.1

[a]The age distribution of men in the Netherlands at the 1947 census was taken as the standard.
[b]Twenty-one countries having less than 35 percent of active males engaged in agriculture and related activities.
[c]Thirty countries having 35 to 59 percent of the active males engaged in agriculture and related activities.
[d]Twenty-one countries having 60 percent or more of the active males engaged in agriculture and related activities.
Source: United Nations, Sex and Age Patterns of Particip-ation in Economic Activities, Report 1 of Demographic Aspects of Manpower, Table 3.4, 1962. Figures are unweighted means.

*Table 17/2.   Average age-specific activity rates for
males in countries classified according to degree
of industrialization, population censuses, 1960*

Degree of industrialization	Age in years						
	10–14	15–19	20–24	25–34	45–54	55–64	65 and over
Industrialized countries[a]	4.1[b]	72.4	91.5	96.7	97.6	95.9	37.7
Semi-industrialized countries	13.2[b]	70.3	91.8	96.2	97.1	95.9	61.0
Agricultural countries	23.9[b]	78.4	91.2	96.3	97.5	96.3	70.0

[a]For basis of classification, see Table 17/1.
[b]Excluding countries where a minimum age limit of 15 years was adopted for enumeration of the economically active population. There were three such cases among the industrialized countries, two among the semi-industrialized, and three among the agricultural.
Source: United Nations, *Sex and Age Patterns of Participation in Economic Activities,*
Report 1 of *Demographic Aspects of Manpower*, Table 3.2, 1962.

increased life expectancy, however, the male's average number of working years has also increased. Male worklife expectancy in the United States saw its first downturn in the 1950s, but the number of years spent outside the labor force has grown throughout the century, and it seems likely that additional years of life will henceforth be allocated to education, training, and retirement rather than to work.

The offset: women in the work force

While the participation rate for males in the United States has been steadily declining, the proportion of women employed outside the home has grown. The net result is an overall rate in the 1960s that is not significantly different from that at the beginning of the century. (Shorter-run shifts in sex distribution of the work force are detailed in Chapter 3.) The combined proportion in 1900 was 53.7; in 1965, it was 56.7.

The combined rate conceals marked changes in the labor-force activity of young and old men. Among men aged 65 and over, the decline has been roughly from two out of three men at work to one in three men at work. Specifically, the rate dropped from 63.1 in 1900 to 26.9 in 1965, and is expected to fall to 21.8 by 1980. Men in their early sixties have experienced some decrease in work activity as well; their 1965 rate of 76.5 (in contrast to 94.3 for men aged 45–54) reflected the downturn in work of men in their later years.

But even more striking changes have occurred in the job orientation of women. In the decade and a half, 1950 to 1965, the number of women in the work force increased from 19 to 27 million, with most of the increase coming from married women. In addition, women's worklife expectancy is changing too, largely as a result of changing patterns of childbearing. As Stuart Garfinkle has pointed out, the more children a woman has and the later in life she has her last child, the shorter will be her worklife. Professional women usually have fewer children, and hence longer worklives. Most 18-year-old women will marry, have children, and leave the labor force. But by age 35, most mothers have had their last child and are free to reenter their old job or find new ones. As Table 17/3 shows, a woman of 35 has a worklife expectancy of 24 years. Women who never marry, or who are widowed or divorced, work longer than married women, the never-married having the longest and most continuous work patterns.

Table 17/3.   Average number of years of labor-force activity remaining for selected groups of women in the labor force, 1960

Age	Single women	Married, husband present, no children	Married, husband present, in labor force after birth of last child	Widowed	Divorced
20	45.3	34.9	(1)	41.8	43.3
25	40.5	30.1	(1)	37.0	38.5
30	35.7	26.6	(1)	32.1	33.6
35	31.2	24.4	23.8	27.3	28.8
40	26.3	20.8	19.1	22.5	24.1
45	21.6	16.7	14.5	17.8	19.7
50	17.1	13.7	11.9	13.4	15.5
55	13.1	10.9	9.4	9.8	11.6
60	10.0	8.7	6.9	7.1	8.4
65	7.8	6.5	5.9	6.0	6.7

[1]Amounts not significant.
Source: Stuart Garfinkle, "Work Life Expectancy and Training Needs of Women," U. S. Department of Labor, *Manpower Report*, No. 12, 1967.

The net effect of the greater labor-force participation of the different groups of women, including those who bear children, is to offset the decline in work activity of younger and older men. Age of entry to the labor force for both men and women has been pushed up, giving young people ever-lengthening periods of education and training. Both sexes, too, withdraw from the work force long before old age actually demands that they do so. Retirement is now a lifestage that absorbs a significant proportion of the total lifespan, and together with the education period, these two stages comprise a large portion of adulthood.

Worklife changes and income distribution

The economic implications of these trends in labor-force participation, particularly their import for income allocation, are quickly evident. The study of income distribution has always been a subject of economic analysis, true; but as earlier discussion indicated, such study has been concerned primarily with determining functional shares: wages, rent, interest, and profits. Although these traditional allocation issues have not disappeared from the literature, some of today's urgent questions turn on the division of the national product between persons who are at work and persons who are not—the latter including not only the sick and disabled, but also the young and the old.

Incomes of the aged

Income levels of persons in retirement illustrate the financial position of a group that is largely outside the labor force. In general terms, the low labor-force activity of men aged 65 or over—about one in four men, including the part-time workers—causes most incomes to drop significantly at or near age 65, despite the offset provided by retirement benefits. Nine out of ten of the nation's 20 million older people have retirement income protection of some sort—85 percent are eligible for Social Security and another 5 percent for civil service or railroad retirement benefits. About 15 percent of the aged draw private pensions. Of those persons now reaching age 65, less than 3 percent remain uncovered by a public program.

The amount of the benefit, however, is frequently far too low to provide even a poverty-level income; as a result, about 30 percent of the present aged are classified poor. As our earlier analysis of poverty revealed, an additional 10 percent of the elderly are on the poverty borderline. The aged are therefore more frequently poor than any other group; in the case of the very old, moreover, the chances of bolstering their incomes by working are quite remote.

In 1970 the median income for families headed by persons aged 65 and over was $5,053, as compared with a median of $10,156 for younger families (Table 17/4); for aged individuals the median was $1,951, for younger single persons, $5,021. The median for the aged family was thus 49.7 percent, and that of the older individual 38.8 percent of the incomes of their younger counterparts. In both cases, the aged's proportion has dropped since 1962. A drop in this percentage—for families from 50.6 to 49.7 percent and for individuals from 47.2 to 38.8 percent—means that the wide gap between the incomes of the young and those of the old is growing wider.

As the median indicates, about half the elderly families had less than $5,053 money income in 1970. One-fifth had incomes below $2,000. The plight of the older single person (most often, an aged widow) was even worse. Half of these persons had less than $1,951 and a fourth had less than $1,000. Three out of five aged women living alone are below the poverty line drawn by the Social Security Administration.

Financing retirement under Social Security

The sources of income for the elderly have shifted markedly during the past twenty years, with earnings coming to be a smaller, and income-mainte-nance programs a much larger, proportion of the total. In the late 1960s slightly more than 50 percent of their aggregate income came from social insurance, veterans' and public assistance programs. Earnings accounted for less than 30 percent (about half of the aggregate earnings going to the "younger aged"—those aged 65 to 71—who did not receive OASDI benefits, in most cases because of their earnings), and income from assets another 15 percent of the total. Cash contributions by friends or relatives not living in the same household amounted to one percent of the total income.

The Social Security Act of 1935   The Social Security Act fills in certain income gaps—gaps created by retirement from work,

Table 17/4.   Trend in median money income of families and unrelated individuals, 1960–70

	Families			Unrelated individuals		
		Heads 65-plus			65-plus	
Period	Heads 14 to 64 (amount)	Amount	Percent of 14 to 64	14 to 64 (amount)	Amount	Percent of 14 to 64
1960	$5,905	$2,897	49.1	$2,571	$1,053	41.0
1961	6,099	3,026	49.6	2,589	1,106	42.7
1962	6,336	3,204	50.6	2,644	1,248	47.2
1963	6,644	3,352	50.4	2,881	1,277	44.3
1964	6,981	3,376	48.4	3,094	1,297	41.9
1965	7,413	3,514	47.4	3,344	1,378	41.2
1966	7,922	3,645	46.0	3,443	1,443	41.9
1967	8,504	3,928	46.2	3,655	1,480	40.5
1970	$10,152	$5,053	49.7	$5,021	$1,951	38.8

Source: Bureau of the Census, as supplied by the Administration on Aging, Social and Rehabilitation Service, Department of Health, Education, and Welfare, January 1969; Bureau of the Census, Current Population Report, Consumer Income, Series P-60, No. 78, 1970.

temporary loss of job, physical disability, or lack of earnings by a family head. The overall purpose of the legislation was to prevent financial deprivation for individuals and families for whom earnings are nonexistent or inadequate.

The unemployment insurance program, described elsewhere, is a state-administered program with federal participation. By the Federal Unemployment Tax Act all employers in commerce and industry who employ four or more workers during 20 or more weeks of the year are taxed at a rate of 3.1 percent on the first $3,000 of annual wages paid to each employee; the rate may be lowered for an employer with a stable employment record. In states having unemployment insurance laws that meet federal standards, roughly 90 percent of the payroll taxes go to provide state-administered systems of unemployment insurance benefits. Although the guidelines provided to the states establish minimum criteria, there is nevertheless wide variation in the provisions of the various state laws, particularly in the amounts and duration of benefits.

Federal–state public assistance programs provide cash incomes and services to needy families. The groups included are: old people without adequate means of support, needy families with dependent children, blind persons, the permanently and totally disabled; medical assistance payments are also available to most of these groups. Financed by matching state–federal funds, these programs require a demonstration of need, defined as the family's inability to meet some minimum standard set by the state. Some states place liens on property (such as a home) owned by the recipient, in order to recover the cost of assistance payments. Residence within the state is usually required in order to qualify for assistance. Wide divergences in the amounts different states are willing to make available to the needy have led to repeated demands for a federal program of assistance grants.

The federal–state medical-assistance programs are relatively new. Established prior to the passage of Medicare, the programs provide for the payment of certain medical expenses for persons who are receiving cash welfare payments, or who are in similarly poor financial circumstances.

Retirement benefits under the Social Security Act

Monthly cash benefits are available at age 65 (or at age 62 for women and at a reduced level at 62 for men) to persons who have worked in covered occupations and who, with their employers, have contributed to the Old Age and Survivors Insurance trust fund during worklife. The federal trust fund, established in 1940 as a separate account in the U. S. Treasury, holds the funds collected in payroll taxes and handles the financial operations involved in the payment of benefits. Contribution rate schedules are shown in Table 17/5.

The maximum amount of yearly earnings subject to these rates is currently (in 1973) $10,800; however, this taxable base will rise. From the $3,000 figure established in 1937, the taxable base has been raised several times

Table 17/5. *Social Security (OASDHI) effective and scheduled contribution rates: 1950–1987*

[Rates in percent. OASDHI: Old-age, survivors, disability, and health insurance.]

Period or year	Annual maximum taxable earnings[1]	Employers and employees (each)			Self-employed[4]			Monthly premium for supplementary medical insurance[5]
		Total	OASDI[2]	HI[3]	Total	OASDI[2]	HI[3]	
In effect:								
1950	$ 3,000	1.50	1.50	(x)	[6]$2.25	[6]$2.25	(x)	(x)
1955	4,200	2.0	2.0	(x)	3.0	3.0	(x)	(x)
1960	4,800	3.0	3.0	(x)	4.50	4.50	(x)	(x)
1965	4,800	3.625	3.625	(x)	5.4	5.4	(x)	(x)
1967	6,600	4.40	3.90	.50	6.40	5.9	.50	$3.00
1968	7,800	4.40	3.80	.60	6.40	5.80	.60	4.00
1969	7,800	4.80	4.20	.60	6.90	6.30	.60	[7]4.00
1970	7,800	4.80	4.20	.60	6.90	6.30	.60	[8]5.30
1971	7,800	5.20	4.60	.60	7.50	6.90	.60	[8]5.60
1972	9,000	5.20	4.60	.60	7.50	6.90	.60	
Future schedule:								
1973	$10,800	5.85	4.85	1.00	8.00	7.00	1.00	(NA)
1974	$12,000	5.85	4.85	1.00	8.00	7.00	1.00	(NA)
1975–77	*	5.85	4.85	1.00	8.00	7.00	1.00	(NA)
1978–80	*	6.05	4.80	1.25	8.25	7.00	1.25	(NA)
1981–85	*	6.15	4.80	1.35	8.35	7.00	1.35	(NA)
1986–92	*	6.25	4.80	1.45	8.45	7.00	1.45	(NA)
1993–97	*	6.25	4.80	1.45	8.45	7.00	1.45	(NA)
1998–2010	*	(6.25)	4.80	(1.45)	(8.45)	7.00	(1.45)	(NA)
2011 and thereafter	*	(7.30)	5.85	(1.45)	(8.45)	7.00	(1.45)	(NA)

Table 17/5. (continued)

NA Not available.

X Not applicable.

[1] For self-employed taxable base is total earnings.

[2] Cash benefits for old-age, survivors, and disability insurance.

[3] Hospital insurance for the aged, first effective in 1966.

[4] Self-employed persons brought under program for first time in 1951.

[5] Program began July 1966. Voluntary program financed by equal contributions from participants 65 and older, and the Federal Government. Premium is subject to revision periodically.

[6] 1951 data.

[7] Effective April 1.

[8] Effective July 1.

* Financing: A revised contribution rate schedule was enacted (and later superseded by the schedule in the October amendments), with rates as shown in the table on page 23 under the heading "old law." The earnings base for contribution and benefit purposes was also revised—from $9,000 in 1972 to $10,800 in 1973 and to $12,000 in 1974. The base is to be raised automatically in the future as wages rise, under the following procedure:

Whenever an automatic adjustment in monthly cash benefits is made, a determination will also be made as to whether an adjustment in the maximum amount of annual earnings that will be taxed and credited toward benefits is required. The determination is made by multiplying the contribution and benefit base in effect in the year of determination by the ratio of the average taxable wages (under the social security program) of all employees, as reported in the first calendar quarter of the year of determination, to the average taxable wages of all employees as reported for the latest of (a) the first calendar quarter of 1973 or (b) the first calendar quarter of the year in which the last automatic determination resulted in a base increase or of the year in which a legislative increase in the base was enacted. The product, rounded to the nearest multiple of $300, will be the amount of the contribution and benefit base, effective with respect to remuneration paid after the year of determination. In no case, however, will the base be reduced to an amount lower than the base in the year of determination.

Source: Social Security Bulletin, March 1973, p. 15.

during the past three decades, as earnings have increased, in order to allow for the necessary improvement in benefit levels. Any person who has worked a minimum of ten years in a covered job—the coverage is virtually complete now, having been extended to domestic servants, farmers, and other groups initially exempt—is fully covered for life.

The amount of the retirement benefit is somewhat related to the worker's earnings, but there is a substantial leveling-out of benefits in favor of the lower-income worker. As earnings rise, the wage earner's chances of having the maximum benefit improve. Moreover, a wife's supplement to her husband's primary benefit increases the monthly income by half, and additional payments are made for dependent children. The latter is particularly important to disabled workers. The average benefits in 1970, shown in Table 17/6, are obviously very low; maximum benefits based on the rising earnings base will gradually rise, although not as fast as wages.

Table 17/6.　Average OASDHI monthly benefits in current-payment status, August 1971

Beneficiary	Monthly benefit
Retired workers	$131.50
Disabled workers	145.73
Aged widows and widowers	112.83
Children of deceased workers	90.74

Source: Social Security Administration, *Social Security Bulletin*, Vol. 34.

Work-disincentive effects of Social Security benefits

Benefits not only provide income maintenance during the retirement period; they also encourage retirement. The program contains a retirement test for the receipt of benefits, by limiting the amount of earnings that can be received before benefits begin to be reduced. When earnings exceed a certain level—currently $1,680 per year—benefits are reduced.

This system has the effect of reducing work-incentives of older workers, and partially explains the pronounced steady decline in their labor-force participation. In fact, it is generally believed that one of the indirect goals of the program, established as it was during the deep depression of the 1930s, was to reduce the labor force by encouraging retirement of older workers, and therby lessen the frantic competition for scarce jobs. While in recent years unemployment has not been the burning economic problem it was in the 1930s, the retirement test still deters labor-force participation of older persons.

Indifference curve analysis can explain the negative effects on work incentives of the benefit system. Figure 17/1 presents an equilibrium work–income position for an older worker, with potential earnings described by wage ray *OA*, at *OB*, with income of *BC*.

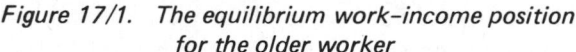

Figure 17/1. The equilibrium work–income position for the older worker

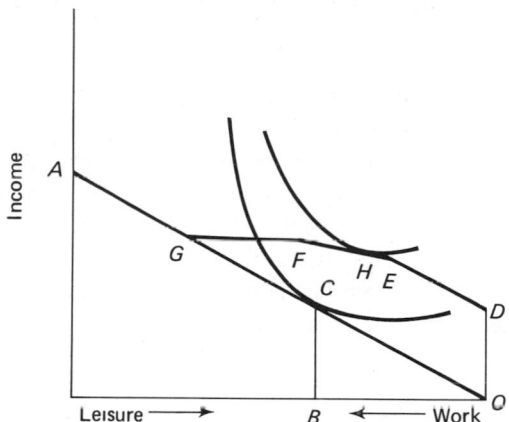

Benefits with no earnings are *OD*. At the same wage rate, the worker received total income along the path *DE*, which is parallel to wage rate *OA*, since the worker's earnings are so low he still "passes" the retirement test and maintains his full benefits.

Beyond *E* up to *F* his total income rate falls by half, as he loses $ .50 of each additional dollar earned in reduced benefits. His income path becomes horizontal up to the point it reaches the wage ray, at *G;* the effective marginal tax on earnings becomes 100 percent, since he loses $1 in benefits for each dollar earned. At *G* his benefits fall to zero and his total income path then follows his wage only.

His new equilibrium point, as a result of benefits, will be at a higher indifference curve (level of satisfaction) but at less work effort. We have drawn the higher equilibrium point along the segment *HF* of the total income path, but it can lie anywhere to the right of *C*. It might even be at zero work effort.

Work incentive is reduced because of the pure income effect of the benefit payment, which raises the income path above the wage ray. Since the marginal income increase is less than the wage at every income segment except *DE,* the negative income effect on work effort is never offset and, on the contrary, is typically reinforced by the substitution effect.

Of course if the initial equilibrium point is well above *G,* the worker would be unaffected by the benefit system and would continue working. Similarly, if the wage ray were much steeper, the negative benefit effects on work effort would arise only at low levels of work, probably at much fewer hours than the equilibrium contribution of the worker to the labor market. Behavior fits theory. Low-wage workers tend to retire; those who enjoy higher pay rates are more likely to keep working after 65.

Economics of aging

The aged person on a fixed income who lives alongside the wage earner whose pay reflects his rising productivity faces a dilemma that results from both the drop in his income once he has retired from work and the relative deterioration in his income position during retirement. As Ida Merriam has pointed out, the latter problem has come to the forefront during the nation's period of sustained economic growth.

> *For the income-maintenance programs . . . the difficult question posed by technologi-cal change and rising national income is not that of determining the benefit amounts of different individuals at the time they retire, but rather that of reaching a consensus as to what happens to their benefits over the subsequent 10, 15, or 20 years.*[2]

If the incomes of retired persons are to be maintained at levels closer to those of economically active persons, whose earnings are always rising, how are such income supplements to be provided? There are few alternatives: one, private savings; two, private pension arrangements; and three, transfers by some taxation-benefit scheme. If retirement income is to be provided by public transfers, a major question remains: how is the transfer to be financed —by payroll taxes or from general revenues?

Private transfers

Most people agree that they should save substantial proportions of their incomes for retirement; most people fail to do so. The private method thus has the advantage of allowing a family to do its own lifetime budgeting and

---

[2]Ida C. Merriam, "Implications of Technological Change for Income," in Juanita M. Kreps, ed. *Technology, Manpower, and Retirement Policy* (Cleveland: World Publishing Co., 1966), p. 171.

saving for old age; it has also the disadvantage of allowing it to do neither. Indeed, the widespread reliance on public and private pensions rests on the premise that many people make no voluntary systematic provisions for retirement income. Since people do not save enough to insure retirement incomes comparable to their current earnings, it is unrealistic to expect them to acquire savings adequate to match the even higher incomes of the future.

Private pension arrangements face much the same difficulty, since they also require more saving now for more consumption during retirement. In order to provide future benefits commensurate with future incomes, and further, provide benefits that would rise through the retirement period, private pension schemes would have to exact much heavier contributions from employers and employees than they now require. Unless these larger contributions are made, employers will find it difficult to unilaterally raise pension benefits above the levels financed by past contributions.

Historically, private pensions were normally unfunded, noncontributory and discretionary on the part of the employer and without rights for employees until the 1940s. Between 1940 and 1968, the number of covered workers rose from 4 million to about 26 million. This growth resulted primarily from Supreme Court support for the NLRB decision that pensions were a legitimate part of collective bargaining, and also from Korean War stabilization policies.

There are several major theories that explain the growth of private pension plans.

Early industrial pension plans were viewed as gratuities or rewards to employees for long and loyal service to the employer. Closely related to this view is the concept that private pensions constitute a systematic and socially desirable method of releasing employees who are no longer productive members of the employer's labor force. As the economy became more and more industrialized and pension plans became more prevalent, there was increasing interest in the view that employers had a moral obligation to provide for the economic security of retired workers.[3]

This represents the human-depreciation argument for private pensions. An alternative argument points to improved total productivity since older workers experiencing declining productivity can be retired, thereby making promotion opportunities available for younger workers from whom this fact and the security pensions provided induce increased productivity. The deferred wage concept is the final argument for pensions. Wages are viewed as the summation of fringe benefits (pensions, etc.) and cash income. Consequently, pension increases generally come at the expense of reduced cash income. This theory is the most widely accepted of those presented above.

---

[3]James H. Schulz, "Economics of Aging: Toward A Full Share in Abundance," Hearings before the Special Committee on Aging, United States Senate, 91st Congress, Part. 10A, pp. 1513–1514.

Table 17/7. Estimated coverage under OASDHI and private retirement plans, December of selected years, 1940–80 (numbers in millions)

Year	Paid employment (including self-employment and Armed Forces)	Covered under OASDHI[1]					Covered under private retirement plans	
		Total						
		Private wage and salary workers[2]	Number	As percent of paid employment	Wage and salary	Self-employment	Number	As percent of private wage and salary workers
1940	47.1	33.5	30.4	64.5	30.4	....	4.1	12.2
1945	57.3	38.1	38.9	67.9	38.9	....	6.4	16.8
1950	61.3	43.5	40.4	65.9	40.4	....	9.8	22.5
1955	65.7	47.8	56.2	85.5	49.5	6.7	15.4	32.2
1960	67.1	50.1	59.0	87.9	51.8	7.3	21.2	42.4
1965	74.5	54.8	66.4	89.1	60.1	6.3	25.4	46.4
1966	77.0	57.3	69.0	89.6	62.8	6.2	26.4	46.1
1967	77.9	58.2	69.9	89.7	64.1	5.8	27.6	47.4
1968	79.4	59.8	71.3	89.8	65.4	5.9	[3]28.6	47.8
Projections:[4]								
1980	94.6	72.9	85.9	90.8			42.3	58.0

[1]Coverage in effect, including State and local employees for whom coverage has been arranged, railroad employees, and all members of Armed Forces.
[2]Full-time and part-time workers, annual average.
[3]Preliminary.
[4]President's Committee on Corporate Pension Funds and Other Private Retirement and Welfare Programs, "Public Policy and Private Pension Programs," January 1965, app. A, table 2.
Source: Social Security Administration.

As of 1968, almost 29 million persons were covered by some private retirement plan. As can be seen in Table 17/7, most of these individuals accumulated OASDHI benefit credits as well.

There are two basic types of private retirement plans: deferred profit-sharing, and pension plans. Only a few million workers are covered by deferred profit-sharing plans. Private pension plans are generally financed by employer contributions, although there are some cases where employees also contribute. About 14 million of those covered participate in plans created by collective bargaining. Half of those covered by collectively bargained plans participate in multiemployer or industry based schemes in which there is a central pool of pension funds from which payments are made.

As can be seen in Table 17/8, the number of beneficiaries has greatly increased since 1940 and is expected to reach 6.6 million by 1980.

One aspect of private pension plans which currently is the subject of much discussion concerns the transferability of pension rights in the event the employee changes jobs prior to retirement or is fired, or more simply, vesting. There is a common hypothesis that the large number of covered

Table 17/8. Beneficiaries under OASDHI and private retirement plans, December of selected years, 1940–80 (in thousands)

Year	Retired workers aged 62 and over receiving old-age (primary) benefits under OASDHI[1]	Beneficiaries under private retirement plans[2]
1940	112	160
1945	518	310
1950	1,771	450
1955	4,474	980
1960	8,061	1,780
1965	11,100	2,750
1966	12,293	3,110
1967	12,768	3,420
1968	13,097	[3]3,760
Projections:[4] 1980	18,261	6,600

[1]For 1966, 1967, and 1968, includes persons with special age 72 benefits. Excludes disabled beneficiaries under age 65.
[2]Includes an undetermined number of retired and disabled workers under age 62 and widows.
[3]Preliminary.
[4]President's Committee on Corporate Pension Funds and Other Private Retirement and Welfare Funds, "Public Policy and Private Pension Programs," January 1965, appendix A, table 3.
Source: Social Security Administration.

workers today and improved vesting protection will have a large beneficial effect on future retirees. Table 17/9 presents projections of private pension income in 1980 based on 1964 benefit levels and alternatively, on an annual 3 percent increase in the benefit level. The results are that benefits will not be of great help under either benefit schedule. Under the 1964 benefit schedule, 60 percent of the beneficiaries will receive $1,000 or less per year while under the second plan 75 percent of the beneficiaries will receive $2,000 or less per year.

To the extent that financial support for retirement is not provided through the private sector, it must of course come from public income-maintenance schemes; controversy continues over the proper division of responsibility between the two sources. Yet dichotomizing man's individual productivity and that of society as alternative sources of support is misleading, since it suggests that the worker can evade responsibility for his retirement income and leave the matter to the government. Such a shift is not possible. The worker pays a tax throughout worklife, as does his employer (this portion of the tax being borne ultimately by the consumer in the form of a higher price, or by the worker in the form of reduced money wage), and these revenues support persons then in retirement. When the worker retires, the generation at work is paying the tax, true, and the retiree receives benefits.

Table 17/9.   Projected private pension income
distribution for retired couples and
unmarried individuals, 1980
(percentage distribution)

Private pension income	Couples[1]		Unmarried individuals[1]	
	1964 level	3 percent trend	1964 level	3 percent trend
Total percent	100	100	100	100
Under $1,000	60	35	72	49
$1,000 to $1,999	33	39	23	34
$2,000 to $2,999	6	17	4	11
$3,000 to $3,999	1	6	1	3
$4,000 to $4,999	(2)	2	(2)	1
$5,000 and over	(2)	(2)	(2)	(2)

[1]Recipients only. Trend refers to annual increase in level of benefits. Same recipient rate is assumed for each run.
[2]Less than 0.5 percent.
Source: Adapted from James H. Schulz, "The Economic Status of the Retired Aged in 1980: Simulation Projections," Social Security Administration, Research report No. 24 (Washington, D.C., Government Printing Office, 1968), table 20, p. 69.

But while the timing may make it appear that he is being supported by society —strictly speaking, all persons not at work or owning capital are being supported by society, since at the moment they are not contributing to output —this interpretation is not valid when considered within the context of man's lifetime.

The issue of public-versus-private financing of retirement is confused by questions of *who* provides the support and *when* he provides it. Increasingly, both young adults and aged persons acquire claims against the national product of any given year without contributing to that year's output by being current members of the labor force. In a broad sense, the young and old may be considered the children and parents of the middle age group, who are the active participants in the production process and who are the current producers of the national output. Since current consumption must come from either current output or capital stock, it can be argued that parents in the middle age group are supporting both their offspring and their aged parents.

Intergenerational support thus conceived, however, is quite different from the traditional pattern in which the children and grandparents in each family were supported by the parents *of that family*. Support of one generation by another is increasingly provided, not within families, but between one whole generation and another. Thus the employed person in the middle age group contributes to the support of young adults through tax payments for financing education, and to the support of retired persons through the OASDHI tax, whether or not he has children or retired parents.[4]

The middle-aged family head still has the option of saving for his own future retirement, in addition to the taxes he pays to support the young and the old generations. Whether he has the income to save is another question. Why has this option not been exercised more rigorously in the past? Has it been due to an inability to predict the future, or to the low levels of income, or to the fact that the wage earner's aspirations have outpaced his real income? These and other explanations abound. But little research has been devoted to the question of why the present generation of retirees accumulated so little in savings. Even more important, study of the savings behavior of today's worker, which might reveal the extent to which future retirees will be able to rely on privately acquired income claims, is equally sparse.

Financing public benefits

Since in the pattern of intergenerational support that is emerging the generation rather than the individual family is the focal unit, the financial arrangements for the necessary transfers of income are increasingly impor-

[4]See Juanita M. Kreps, "The Economics of Intergenerational Relationships," in Ethel Shanas and Gordon F. Streib, eds. *Social Structure and the Family* (Englewood Cliffs, N. J.: Prentice-Hall, 1965), pp. 267–288.

tant. In particular, there is the question of whether payroll taxes on employers and employees should continue to provide the funds for benefits, or whether benefits should be financed in part, at least, from general revenues.

The primary argument against the payroll tax is based on its regressivity, for it places a burden on the low-income worker.[5] Since the tax in the late 1960s applied to only the first $7,800 of earnings, the counterproposal of an increase in the taxable base (as opposed to further increase in the tax rate) was frequently made, until in the early 1970s the tax base was raised to $9,000. Moreover, since the benefit is weighted in favor of the worker who has had low earnings, the regressive effect of the tax is somewhat mitigated. Arguing for the payroll tax is the advantage of having each worker feel that he is paying for his retirement benefit, which then comes to him as a right.

Revenues from the present payroll tax are insufficient to provide benefit increases of the magnitude necessary to significantly improve the economic position of the aged. If benefits are to be raised, it is necessary either to increase taxes (by raising the rate or the taxable base) or to draw from general revenues. Yet further increases in the tax liability of the low-income worker are very hard to justify. If his income is at or below the poverty level he now pays a tax on his earnings, although he is exempt from income tax payments precisely because we reason that his income is too low. When his employer's contribution is also considered—as a reduction in his wages or an increase in the prices he pays—the combined tax will ultimately reduce his income by 10 percent, under the 1967 Amendments to the Social Security Act.[6] Such deductions thus quite heavily tax the earnings of the working poor, and the argument that the funds are used to finance benefits for the nonworking poor is not persuasive.

Alternatively, financing higher benefits from general revenues achieves some income redistribution from high to low incomes, since the primary sources of federal revenues are the progressive personal and corporate income taxes. The greater the reliance on general revenues, therefore, the greater the redistributive effect; proposals that all benefits be financed in this manner have been offered. A more frequent recommendation has been to finance only a portion of the costs—one-third, for example—from general revenues.

In the Congressional hearings on the 1967 revisions of the Social Security system,[7] Colin D. Campbell proposed that the payroll tax be fixed at a rate

---

[5]The degree of regressiveness, however, is subject to debate. See Robert J. Myers, "Employee Social Insurance Contributions and Regressive Taxation," *Journal of Risk and Insurance*, XXXIV (December 1967), 611–615.

[6]There is some disagreement as to the incidence of the employer's portion of the payroll tax. See the Social Security Administration's statement on this point in *Hearings* before the House Committee on Ways and Means, Part 1, 90th Congress, March 1967, pp. 330–331; and the criticism of this position by John A. Brittain, "The Real Rate of Interest on Lifetime Contributions Toward Retirement under Social Security," *Old Age Income Assurance*, Part III, Joint Economic Committee, 90th Congress, 1st Session, 1968, pp. 109–132.

[7]*Hearings, op. cit.*, Parts 1, 2, 3, and 4. See also a summary and analysis of the financing issues by Dorothy S. Projector, "Should the Payroll Tax Finance Higher Benefits under OASDI?" *Journal of Human Resources*, IV (1969), pp. 60–75.

that would allow new persons coming under coverage to receive in benefits during their retirement the amount of their own contributions and those made by their employers. The tax rate required to finance the new entrant's benefit would be lower than the present combined contribution; Campbell estimates 5.4 percent, or 2.7 percent each on employer and employee, which is almost two-thirds of the level-cost rate. The remaining costs—all benefits, that is, that are paid to present retirees in excess of what they paid for— should come from general revenues. Measures to improve income levels of retirees, such as increases in minimum benefits, or benefit increases commensurate with the rise in median family income, would also be financed from general revenues ". . . whenever they increase the benefits of persons without at the same time increasing their tax contribution."[8]

Estimates of the tax rate necessary to pay for any specified level of benefits must take into account the probable rise in earnings during the lifetime of the worker. As taxable earnings increase, the level of benefits that can be supported also increases. John A. Brittain[9] has demonstrated that the rise in real incomes makes it possible for retirees to receive more in benefits than they and their employers paid in taxes; a real rate of interest of about 4 percent can be earned by the average participant, under the growth conditions prevailing in recent years. This real rate of interest is the sum of the rates of growth of per capita wages and population, as Henry Aaron[10] showed in an extension of the earlier "social insurance paradox" set forth by Paul A. Samuelson.[11] The "average" return of 4 percent that Mr. Brittain derives is not applicable to the contributions of wage earners at all levels. Because of the progressiveness of the benefit, the return to contributors with low earnings is higher than that made to high-wage earners.[12]

But even the somewhat higher return to low-income workers is not a valid basis for exacting a portion of that income in taxes, Mr. Brittain argues. The poor must borrow at very high interest rates (36 percent or more), meanwhile being forced to save for a return of 6 or 7 percent.

A 6 or 7 percent ultimate real yield on the 10 percent contribution paid by the young $2,500 earner may sound attractive to some policymakers, but who would presume to call this worker a profligate glutton if he would rather have the 10 per cent now?[13]

---

[8]*Hearings, op. cit.,* Part 3, p. 1390.

[9]John A. Brittain, "The Real Rate of Interest on Lifetime Contributions Toward Retirement under Social Security," pp. 109–132.

[10]Henry Aaron, "The Social Insurance Paradox," *Old Age Income Assurance,* Part V, pp. 15–18.

[11]"An Exact Consumption-Loan Model of Interest with or without the Social Contrivance of Money," *Journal of Political Economy,* LXVI (1958), 467–482.

[12]John A. Brittain, "The Real Rate of Interest on Lifetime Contributions Toward Retirement under Social Security," pp. 124–125.

[13]*Ibid.,* p. 130.

In a summary of the issues involved in the tax-benefit ratio, Dorothy Projector emphasizes the major dilemma: for many families, adequate income in old age can be afforded only at the expense of adequate income during youth.[14]

What are the functions of OASDHI?

Measures to improve the income levels of the aged are defended on different bases: their present incomes are below some index of minimum adequacy—the Orshansky poor or near-poor level, for example; or the aged's incomes are below their own preretirement incomes; or they are below the incomes of younger persons and families who are still at work. In any program designed to raise incomes in old age, the role of federal old-age insurance is clearly central. Yet it is important to ask whether we should rely altogether on Social Security benefits as a means of establishing an adequate minimum income for each retiree, regardless of his past contributions, or whether some minimum income should be provided to all families through a program financed from general revenues. In the latter case, wage-related benefits could then be paid to retirees as an addition to the guaranteed income, from the funds collected in payroll taxes.

Criticism of the OASDHI system is frequently voiced on the grounds that it is an inefficient way to reduce poverty. The President's National Advisory Commission on Rural Poverty commented that little of any increased OASDHI benefit would go to the poor—less than one-fifth, if benefits were raised by 20 percent. Moreover, the Commission indicated that

Under the benefit formulas used, if OASDI payments were increased by 50 percent rather than 20 percent, the poor would get an even smaller percentage of the benefits. This is so because benefits are paid to those who are not poor as well as to those who are poor, and each increase in incomes means that a larger percentage of the benefits goes to those who are not poor.[15]

In a similar vein, Dorothy Projector points out that an expenditure in the form of welfare payments or negative tax supplements would remove more families from poverty than the same expenditure in OASDHI benefits. She suggests that we "recognize that OASDHI cannot solve all problems of income maintenance and . . . move in the direction of creating additional mechanisms for meeting the need for further redistribution of income."[16]

---

[14]Dorothy Projector, "Should the Payroll Tax Finance Higher Benefits under OASDI?," p. 73.

[15] *The People Left Behind.* Washington: The President's National Advisory Commission on Rural Poverty, 1967, p. 87.

[16]Dorothy Projector, "Should the Payroll Tax Finance Higher Benefits under OASDI?," p. 74.

Proposals for providing a universal pension to all elderly persons have been made repeatedly. Eveline Burns has long advocated a doubledecker system of payments, in which a demogrant (a uniform payment to all persons at some specified age) would be supplemented by a wage-related benefit.[17] The former would be financed from general revenues, the latter from payroll taxes. Margaret Gordon has also proposed a flat pension for persons aged 65 and over (or failing this, for all those aged 70 or more), and income-conditioned benefits in addition.[18] The widespread use of such schemes in European countries is cited by both authors.

Poverty in old age is perhaps best alleviated through a universal pension, leaving to social insurance the function generally assigned to it, that is, the replacement during retirement of some portion of previous earnings. Separation of the two components of income of the aged would permit the establishment of some minimum income for all aged persons, regardless of their previous earnings records, while also preserving the present structure of OASDHI benefits and contributions. In her argument for such a scheme, Margaret Gordon points out that a pension of $50 for individuals and $75 for couples aged 65 or over would mean that those now receiving minimum benefits would receive approximately $100 a month (individuals) and $150 a month (couples), or $1200 and $1800 annually. These minima would bring couples almost up to Orshansky's nonfarm poverty line of $1850, and would move the individuals much closer to their poverty level of $1435. Aged individuals and couples now receiving average OASDHI benefits, moreover, would have their incomes raised almost to Orshansky's nonfarm low-income levels for the elderly. The net costs of a universal pension of this amount are difficult to estimate, because of offsetting savings; the annual costs before such savings are deducted would be about $9.9 billion.[19]

If the problem of extreme poverty in old age were to be met by a guarantee of income, either to the elderly or to all persons, it would then be possible to concentrate attention on improving the ratio of pension income to earnings. This ratio is extremely low, and projections indicate that

U. S. pension systems, as they are presently developing, are failing to generate for large numbers of aged persons retirement income sufficient to meet generally accepted international and national standards of pension-earnings ratio adequacy.[20]

---

[17]See her "Social Security in Evolution," *Social Service Review*, XXXIX (1965), 129–140; also, "Income-Maintenance Policies and Early Retirement," in Kreps, ed., *Technology, Manpower, and Retirement Policy*, pp. 125–140.

[18]Margaret S. Gordon, "The Case for Earnings-Related Social Security Benefits Restated," *Old Age Income Assurance*, II, 312–339.

[19]*Ibid.*, p. 336.

[20]James H. Schulz, "Aged Retirement Income Adequacy—Simulation Projections of Pension-Earnings Ratios," *Old Age Income Assurance*, II, 259.

The earnings-replacement function of OASDHI has sometimes been over-looked in the rash of proposals for alleviating poverty.

Financial and real support of nonworkers

Many differences of view as to the financing of OASDHI benefits arise from difficulties inherent in imputing to the system the responsibility for achieving both individual equity and socially defined adequacy.

Individual equity means that the contributor receives benefit protection directly related to the amount of his contributions—or, in other words, actuarially equivalent thereto. Social adequacy means that the benefits paid will provide for all contributors a certain standard of living.[21]

A social insurance scheme which provides only individual equity, by Myers' definition, achieves a temporal reapportionment of a family's income. But redistribution of income between income classes occurs only to the extent that some goal of social equity is sought—a goal that specifies certain minimum incomes, for example, regardless of previous earnings records. Under OASDHI provisions, retirement benefits are only remotely related to previous earnings; still, the rationale that benefits accrue because one pays into the system is apparently important to both workers and retirees.

The strong redistributive effect of old-age insurance programs, examined in a recent study by Benjamin Bridges,[22] will continue to be both applauded and viewed with alarm. But the impact of recent demographic and technological changes on patterns of income distribution apply to the young as well as the old; for both groups the trends would seem to indicate greater support from transfers and less from earnings.

Readings

Bowen, William G.; Frederick H. Harbison; Richard A. Lester; and Herman M. Somers, eds. *The Princeton Symposium on the American System of Social Insurance.* New York: McGraw-Hill Book Co., 1968.

Burns, Evelyn, "Social Security in Evolution," *Social Service Review,* 1965, pp. 129–140.

---

[21]Robert J. Myers, *Social Insurance and Allied Government Programs* (Homewood, Illinois: Richard D. Irwin, Inc., 1965), p. 6.

[22]"Current Redistributional Effects of Old-Age Income Assurance Programs," *Old Age Income Assurance,* II, 95–176.

Carroll, J. J. *Alternative Methods of Financing Old Age, Survivors, and Disability Insurance.* Ann Arbor: Institute of Public Administration, University of Michigan, 1960.

Economics of Aging: Toward a Full Share in Abundance. Hearings before the Special Committee on Aging, United States Senate, 91st Congress, Part 10A.

Epstein, Lenore, "Income of the Aged in 1962: First Findings of the 1963 Survey of the Aged," *Social Security Bulletin,* March 1964, pp. 3–24.

Friedman, Milton, "Old Age Survivors Insurance" in *Capitalism and Freedom,* Chapter 11. Chicago: University of Chicago Press, 1962.

Gordon, Margaret S. *The Economics of Welfare Policies.* New York: Columbia University Press, 1963.

Joint Economic Committee, 90th Congress. *Old Age Income Assurance.* Washington, D. C.: U. S. Government Printing Office, Part III, 1st Session, 1968.

Kreps, Juanita M., "The Economics of Intergenerational Relationships," in Ethel Shanas and Gordon F. Streib, eds. *Social Structure and the Family,* Englewood Cliffs, N. J.: Prentice-Hall, 1965.

Myers, Robert J. *Social Insurance and Allied Government Programs.* Homewood, Ill.: Richard D. Irwin, Inc., 1965.

Turnbull, J. G.; C. A. Williams, Jr.; and Earl F. Cheit. *Economic and Social Security,* 3d ed. New York: Ronald Press, 1967.

U. S. Department of Health, Education, and Welfare. *Social Security Programs in the United States.* Washington, D. C.: Social Security Administration, 1966.

Chapter Eighteen

Economic Assurance: Guaranteed Income

Introduction

The transfer of income between generations, now made primarily through governmental agencies rather than through family units, has come to be accepted as a concomitant of the lengthened lifespan prevailing in advanced countries throughout the world. A rationale for such intergenerational support can easily be deduced, as the discussion in the preceding chapter demonstrates.

Public transfers of income to persons of working age have been provided only under certain circumstances, however. Unemployment insurance and cash benefits to the disabled worker have been the only major sources of public support for males of working age, with aid to dependent children being restricted to families without male heads, until very recently. Unemployment and disability payments, financed by payroll taxes, are viewed as forms of insurance and thus available only to workers who have made contributions, or have had employers who contributed. The male of working age has been eligible for a public transfer, therefore, only by reason of his attachment to the labor force.

Income without work: the rationale

How, then, have we come to the present stage of discussion of a guaranteed income for all? Is the emergence of new approaches to income maintenance due to a recognition of gaps in the existing system? Or is the output of the economy now so large that the nation can "afford" to offer some minimum family income? To what extent does the widespread endorsement of such schemes as the negative income tax, which would be available without references to employment, reflect a belief that work is no longer necessary?

Technology and income guarantees

The workless society has been promised from time to time, usually on the expectation that automation will soon eliminate the need for human labor. Robert Theobald, the widely quoted author of *Free Men and Free Markets,* maintains that "the guaranteed income is a philosophical principle which argues that every man is entitled to a minimum income at a time when machines can produce enough for all." Moreover,

Provision of income as a right will bring us to understand that money itself is an anachronism in a cybernated era. Money was needed to ration scarce goods and industrial services in the past, but it is a highly unsatisfactory means of determining priorities in a cybernated era. Society will find it more satisfactory, in terms of scarce resources, to distribute many types of goods and services without money payments. [1]

A constitutionally guaranteed income, he argues, is essential in an era when human labor is no longer necessary to the production of goods. But the fact that "man has a pathological desire to toil" means that he will not remain idle, but will turn his attention to those pursuits that interest him, once his basic needs are assured. By eliminating money as a means of motivation, he concludes, people will do those things that make the best use of their talents.

Although few economists have agreed with Theobald that work was on its way out, technology's role in the development and persistence of high levels of unemployment during the 1950s and early '60s has been the subject of some concern. Statistics showing that the number of jobs grows each year, despite the inroads of automation, are not completely reassuring; the question is not whether employment increases, but whether unemployment increases, as the labor force expands. And during most of the period following the Second World War, the level of unemployment has been high, ranging from 7 percent to 5 percent of the work force. The rate has fallen below 4 percent only during the Korean War and for a short period during the Vietnam War.

Unemployment of such magnitudes in an era of prosperity and rising incomes and prices inevitably lends support to arguments for guaranteed family incomes. Whether the unemployment is an outgrowth of technological change, or a result of lagging economic growth, the problem of providing income to the unemployed remains much the same. The National Commission on Technology concluded in 1966 that income-maintenance arrangements needed to be reexamined, not because automation made human labor obsolete, but because we could afford to guarantee incomes to all persons.

---

[1]Robert Theobald "The Guaranteed Income in Perspective," in Thomas A. Naylor, ed. *The Impact of the Computer on Society* (Atlanta· Southern Regional Education Board), pp. 64, 71.

"We are convinced that rising productivity has brought this country to the point at last when all citizens may have a decent standard of living at a cost in resources the economy can easily bear."[2]

Thus, not out of fear of technology but because, as a gift of technology, the economy could afford to do so, the Commission proposed minimum guaranteed incomes; "to say don't worry about automation and computers as a cause of unemployment is not to say don't worry."[3] Moreover, as was noted in Chapter 15, the problem of low incomes extends to families whose heads are employed. Mollie Orshansky estimated that in 1966 one-fourth of all poor families were headed by men who had worked throughout the year; among poor families headed by men under age 65, five out of six of the heads worked some time during the year.[4] Supplements to the earnings of these workers are clearly a necessary part of any scheme designed to alleviate poverty.

Insecurity of jobs and earnings

Proponents of a guaranteed income point to the frequency of unemployment and its concomitant interruption of earnings. No family has the assurance that the family head will retain his job month after month, and even short-term unemployment is catastrophic for low-income workers. Savings are low, and asset ownership infrequent; meanwhile, expenditures for basic necessities must continue despite job loss. In periods of rising unemployment, cuts in spending accelerate the downswing, which means that businesses are faced with losses, making further cutbacks necessary and a second wave of job loss very likely. Were minimum incomes provided irrespective of job status, spending would be curtailed less sharply when jobs were lost, and the cumulative effect of job displacement would be minimized. In line with this reasoning, unemployment insurance has been repeatedly cited as a prime example of a "built-in stabilizer."

The need for such a stabilizer grows with any growth in unemployment. During the two and one-half decades immediately following the Second World War the proportion of the labor force that was idle increased in something of a "stairstep" effect: the unemployment level of a recession was reduced during the subsequent recovery, but not to the level of the preceding prosperity. In the years immediately following the hostilities, 1946–48, the economy had little unemployment—an average of 3.6 percent for the three

---

[2] *Technology and the American Economy*, Report of the National Commission on Technology, Automation, and Economic Progress, Washington, D. C., 1966, p. 38. The "cost" here is not reduced total production but rather a transfer by the more affluent of some of their "resources" (earnings) to the poor. Thus, the economy refers to those making the transfers.

[3] Garth L. Mangum, "The Computer in the American Economy," in Naylor, ed., *The Impact of the Computer on Society*, p. 98.

[4] Mollie Orshansky, "The Shape of Poverty in 1966," *Social Security Bulletin*, March 1968, pp. 14–15.

years. This "three percent frictional unemployment," regarded as tantamount to full employment, shot up sharply in 1949–50 to a rate of 5.3 percent.

The Korean War temporarily lowered the level of idleness, but afterwards, in 1954, unemployment rose again to 5.6 percent. In 1955–57, full prosperity returned but this time unemployment dropped only to 4.3 percent. The 1958 recession brought us the highest level of unemployment of the era: 6.8 percent. Again, recovery restored jobs to many but the rate remained around 5 percent during the early 1960s. Not until we had heavy wartime expenditures, and eventually entered the Vietnam War on a full scale did the unemployment rate go below 4 percent. In review, each recession has left its mark; unemployment rises, and some of this rise remains through the succeeding period of prosperity.

In climbing to progressively higher levels of joblessness, the economy left certain groups farther and farther behind. Unemployment is highest among young, untrained workers, blacks, older workers with low levels of education or skill, workers in declining industries. In contrast to an overall unemployment rate of 5 percent, the rate for these groups is often twice as high; in the case of black teenage boys, as many as one in five is frequently idle. Data on the differential incidence of unemployment among particular age, sex, and racial groups were reviewed in Chapter 2. The burden of unemployment thus falls heavily on those workers whose earnings are minimal when they are employed, and who cannot hope to sustain any interruption of earnings by borrowing against the future.

Income maintenance is much easier to justify in an era of persistent unemployment than in a period of job stability. The rationale for a guaranteed income is further strengthened by the recognition that significant proportions of the work force were rendered jobless, despite rising incomes for most of the population and the rising expectations of all persons.

Inequality: earnings of minority groups

These expectations are being fed by the improved techniques of communication and by the pace of the Civil Rights movement. After watching the typical TV family for a while, most people begin to want a similar set of living arrangements. In reality, only a small proportion of all families can afford such a standard, and a far smaller percentage of certain minority groups can do so.

The earnings of black workers are consistently lower than those of white persons in this country, even when job classification is held constant; similarly, when compared by numbers of years of school completed, the black earns less. But the big differences in average earnings arise from the inability of most blacks to gain entry to the higher-level jobs. Throughout history, their educational attainment has been inferior because their access to education has been narrowly limited. Facilities and teachers have been of such poor quality that advancement through the public schools has meant little. Moreover, staying in school through adolescence has been rare, since low family incomes made early job entry a necessity.

The nation's past discrimination in education has helped to rear a black population whose earning capacities are low or nonexistent. For blacks who have reached middle age or beyond, improvements in job productivity through job training are likely to be scant, particularly for those who are functionally illiterate. Unfortunately, the educational opportunities of children in these families are also poor, despite the progress of desegregation, since the children frequently lack adequate diet and health care.

In such cases, the guarantee of some minimum family income would enable the educational process to take hold. Welfare payments, particularly through aid to dependent children, meet some of the need. But income as a matter of right, it is argued, would remove the stigma that follows the welfare check. And until this right is recognized, no true freedom of opportunity exists.

Income without work: the schemes

Reforms of the present system of welfare payments are currently under discussion, in part because of obvious defects, and in part because of the appearance of alternative proposals for guaranteeing minimum incomes. It is generally recognized that the public assistance programs as now run by the various states fail to meet the needs of the poor. Coverage is restricted, earnings are discouraged, desertion of families is encouraged; average benefits vary widely among the states—from a monthly $8.45 per person in Mississippi to $68.55 in New York.

Negative income tax proposals: supplements to earnings

One of the earliest proponents of an alternative plan was Milton Friedman, who in his *Capitalism and Freedom* proposed a simple negative income tax arrangement to replace the present proliferation of public assistance and government welfare programs. Friedman's plan would apply a tax rate of, say, 50 percent to a family's unused exemptions and minimum standard deductions. If the minimum standard deductions for a family of five were $3,700, and their income $2,000, unused exemptions and deductions would be $1,-700. Fifty percent of this amount, or $850, would raise the family income to

$2850. The effective minimum income in this case would be $1850, which would be the maximum payment going to a family with no other income.

Numerous variations on this theme have been composed. They involve a symmetrizing of the present income tax structure, with payments being made by the Internal Revenue Service, upon the receipt of a statement of income similar to an ordinary tax form. They are noncategorical in coverage. Eligibility (in most proposals, based on the family as a unit) would be determined solely by income and family size; consequently, the problems of determining eligibility in exclusionary categories would be eliminated.

Although many variations have been suggested, they all require decisions on the base to which the rate is to be applied, the tax rate, the effective minimum, and a break-even point. Two possible *bases* have been under consideration: (1) the unused exemptions and minimum standard deductions of a family with no taxable income and (2) the poverty–income gap, which is the difference between an officially established poverty line for a family of a particular size and that family's money income. Although the two bases differ substantially only for very small or very large families, the poverty–income gap is generally considered a better indicator of need.

As to tax *rate,* it should be noted that the present public-assistance system operates under what amounts to a 100 percent tax—for every dollar earned, the public assistance allotment is reduced by $1.00. This provides a strong disincentive to work. The negative income tax attempts to provide some work incentive by allowing the poor to keep a percentage of their earnings in addition to the payment. This means a tax rate considerably lower than 100 percent. Not only does a 100 percent rate eliminate the monetary incentive to work; it could result in a much greater cost to the economy.

The effective *minimum income* can be either a stated floor or simply the amount paid on a particular scale to a family with zero income. The *break-even point* is that point at which a family's tax liability equals its guaranteed income, and thus the payment becomes zero.

While endorsing the principle of negative income taxation, Robert Lampman views the scheme as a supplement to other welfare programs. Public-assistance payments should be greatly reduced by negative taxes under his proposals, but he would not eliminate OASDHI benefits, for example.[5] In one of his plans he suggests a $750 allowance for families with incomes up to $1,500, with a reduction of 50 percent in the allowance for any income over $1,500. In this manner, he would provide some work incentive for low-income workers. But since the benefits are clearly inadequate for families with the lowest incomes, the scheme relies on public assistance to supplement

[5]Robert Lampman, "Approaches to the Reduction of Poverty," *American Economic Review, Papers and Proceedings,* 55 (May 1965), 521–529. Also, see his "Programs for Poverty," *Proceedings of the 57th Annual Conference of the National Tax Association* (Pittsburgh: September 1964), pp. 71–81.

the allowance. Another of his plans calls for an effective minimum of $1,500, with the poverty-income level of $3,000 for a family of four, and negative tax rates that vary inversely with the income. If the family's income is $500, their poverty–income gap is $2,500, and payment at 45 percent of the gap would add $1,125, for a total income of $1,625. For a family with a $2,000 income, payment at 25 percent of the gap would add $250 to the income. This plan concentrates its benefits on the poorest of the poor, but like all negative income tax plans, would reach many people who are working and not on relief, yet whose incomes are considered inadequate by today's standard.

James Tobin would have an income guarantee high enough to raise those families with no other income out of poverty, and a tax rate low enough to provide incentives for those who can work. For example, if the guarantee were to equal the $3,000 poverty line for a family of four, and the tax rate were set at 50 percent, a family with an income of $2,000 would receive $2,000 ($3,000 less 50 percent of their previous income), making their total income $4,000. He points out that if the income guarantee is to be sufficient to support a family, and yet provide an incentive to work, it is impossible to avoid making payments to families who are above the poverty line. (In the example given above, the break-even point would be an income of $6,000.)[6]

Any plan that provides a reasonable income (poverty level) floor and less than a 100-percent rate produces what has been called the "notch" effect. If, for instance, a minimum of $3,000 is specified, with a tax rate of 50 percent, and families with incomes over $3,000 are excluded, a family with a $2,000 income would receive $2,000 ($3,000 less 50 percent of $2,000), making their total income $4,000. This would be more than that of a family whose own earnings of $3,500 prohibited them from receiving any assistance. The logical thing for the second family to do would be to curtail its earnings until they dropped below the $3,000 level.

In his review of these and other negative income tax plans, Christopher Green points out that the schemes represent an attack on poverty with a minimum of income redistribution; further, that the plans allow the poor to benefit from tax cuts, where the cuts include an increase in the negative rate. Tax reductions at present do not benefit the poor directly, whether the tax rate is being reduced or the level of personal exemptions and deductions is being raised.[7] With Lampman, he emphasizes the fact that guaranteed incomes are not a substitute for long-range programs designed to increase labor productivity: "It is not inconsistent to provide money income for the poor and at the same time make government expenditures for raising the productivity of the poor."[8]

---

[6]James Tobin, "Improving the Economic Status of the Negro," *Daedalus,* 94 (Fall 1965), 889–895.

[7]Christopher Green. *Negative Taxes and the Poverty Problem* (Washington, D. C.: The Brookings Institution, 1967), p. 61.

[8]*Ibid.,* pp. 8–9.

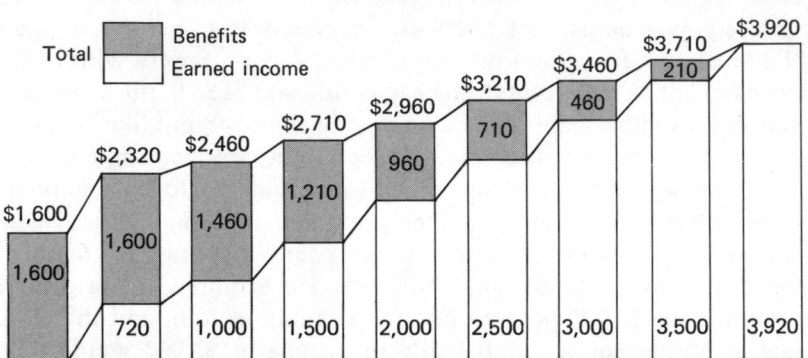

Figure 18/1.   Family assistance benefit schedule
(family of four)

The income earned will enable the Family Assistance recipient to become more self-supporting through the 50 percent retention provision and thus reduce federal payments

Source: Hearings before the Committee on Finance, United States Senate, 91st Congress, Second Session on H.R. 16311, Part 1, p. 182.

The proposed family assistance plan of 1970

The FAP applies the basic principle of the negative income tax to a specific segment of the population. Designed to replace the much-criticized AFDC program, the FAP covers all families with children. Implementation of the program would nationally standardize the eligibility requirements. There are three basic eligibility requirements: that all able-bodied adults, with the exception of mothers with preschool-age children, register for work; that asset holdings total less than $1,500, excluding domestic property and private property needed for work; and that the earnings of a family of four not exceed $3,920.

In the absence of earnings, FAP benefits would be $500 for each of the first two family members and $300 for each of the remaining family members. This would total $1,600 for a family of four. The first $720 of earnings do not alter the benefit schedule. Earnings in excess of this amount have an effective marginal tax rate of .5, since each dollar earned above $720 causes benefit payments to be reduced 50¢. The benefit schedule is pictured in Figure 18/1. Additionally, the states must supplement the FAP benefits up to the January 1, 1970, AFDC payment level or to the poverty level, whichever is smaller.

Currently, there seems little likelihood that an FAP will be implemented. President Nixon supported the plan in 1971 and 1972, but despite passage in the House, it was twice rejected by the Senate. Now the administration has withdrawn its support, and while the program is still debated outside of Congress, it will be at least several years before FAP is reintroduced and passed.

Problems and alternatives

The negative income tax shares with other guaranteed-income plans an essential component: it involves a direct transfer of money to the poor. Consequently, the tax schemes face the same initial problem as other plans offering this guarantee, namely that of minimizing payments to the nonpoor, while at the same time making the guarantee adequate, and avoiding the disincentive characteristic of public-assistance programs. Moreover, any of the plans would be very costly, even if restricted to those below the poverty line.[9] Although calculations of cost must take into account the amount of reduction in public assistance expenditures, it is difficult to see how public assistance can be eliminated entirely, without leaving some families worse off than they are at present.

There would also be difficulties in the administration of such a program. If payment were made at the end of a year on the basis of a statement of that year's income, the money would not be available when it was needed. Payment on the basis of estimated income would likely require adjustment at the end of the year, and it might be almost impossible for a poor family to return overpayments. This difficulty could be eased somewhat by quarterly or monthly statements.

Objections have been raised to having such a program administered entirely by the federal government, not only by opponents of "big government," but by those who feel that local workers can do a better job. It is argued that the need is to individualize benefits, not nationalize them, and that the Internal Revenue Service cannot be expected to be more sympathetic to the problems of the poor than are present welfare officials.

Finally, criticisms of guaranteed-income plans in general are relevant to the negative income tax. There are questions of whether a guaranteed income might lower the already low mobility of the poor, making it even less likely that they will move to sections of the country where jobs are more readily available. Former Congressman Thomas B. Curtis has suggested that any guaranteed income will lower the incentive to save, raise the propensity to consume, and thus threaten investment.[10]

Several alternatives to the negative income tax have been proposed; revision of the public-assistance system is one. Benefits and coverage should be

---

[9]For cost estimates, see *ibid.*, Appendix D, pp. 188–194.
[10]"Income Guarantees: A Spectrum of Opinion," *Monthly Labor Review*, 90 (February 1967), III–IV.

expanded, additional public services provided, and the means test simplified. The poor are not a homogeneous group, the argument runs, and a single program cannot be expected to meet the needs of all. Interestingly enough, the Advisory Council on Public Welfare has suggested a revision of the public-assistance system that would turn it into a form of guaranteed-income plan. The federal government would establish an income floor and provide the states with all the necessary funds. Eligibility would be determined entirely by need. This plan carries the same disadvantage as the present public-assistance system or a negative income tax with a 100 percent rate: it eliminates the monetary incentive to work. Lowering the rate would lead to payments to families above the floor; excluding these families would result in the notch effect.

Daniel Moynihan has suggested a monthly family allotment of $10 per child, regardless of income; 60 percent of all poor families, he points out, have children. However, the objections are raised that this amount is not adequate for the poor, and it also helps families who are not poor and who have 75 percent of the children.

Some economists, Leon Keyserling in particular, feel that while some forms of assistance are necessary and should be expanded for those who cannot or should not work, the emphasis on a guaranteed income is in itself defeatist. They would recommend instead guaranteed full employment, with the government as the "employer of last resort." Keyserling points out that there are more than enough unmet needs in the public sector to avoid the inference of "make work."[11]

The notion of having the government act as employer of last resort was advanced by many writers during the late 1960s; initially it was proposed by the National Commission on Technology, Automation, and Economic Progress. Support for such a program was evidenced by recent sponsorship of bills in Senate and House Committees. But as Garth Mangum has emphasized, public employment to combat joblessness is not a new idea. Unfortunately, the leaf-raking image of the New Deal era continues to mark such attempts to create jobs, though "it is difficult to find fault with leaf raking if there are leaves to be raked."[12]

In rebuttal, proponents of the negative income tax argue that it would be an effective way of filling the poverty–income gap without completely nullifying the incentive to work. It would help the *working* poor—a group largely neglected by present assistance systems. It would eliminate the need for a huge welfare apparatus; it would provide a national assistance minimum, and would eliminate the present wide state variations in welfare payments; and

---

[11]Leon H. Keyserling, "Guaranteed Annual Incomes," *The New Republic,* 156 (18 March 1967), 20–23.

[12]Garth L. Mangum, "Government as Employer of Last Resort," in Sar A. Levitan et al., *Towards Freedom from Want* (Madison: Industrial Relations Research Association, 1968), p. 140.

finally, it would be impersonally and impartially administered, with income and family size being the only criteria.

What we have: a patchwork of uncertainty

In a recent discussion of income transfer programs, Henry J. Aaron identifies three groups of poor: one, the employed and employable (working-age males and childless working-age females); two, those for whom employment is not feasible (the aged, the disabled, and the blind); and three, mothers of working age, for whom jobs may or may not be available and appropriate. Income-maintenance programs aim to replace income losses incurred primarily by the second group, who have suffered either the death of the breadwinner, retirement from work, disability, or some other termination or interruption of earnings. Income supplements, on the other hand, are provided because incomes are recognized as inadequate, and are made without reference to any previous earnings records.[13]

The Social Security Act of 1935 established the major programs of both income maintenance and income supplements. In meeting the income needs of the aged and the disabled, OASDHI cash payments (discussed in detail in the preceding chapter) were made to 13 million households in 1965—about 70 percent to the aged and 30 percent to beneficiaries under age 65. Included in the payroll-financed benefits under the OASDHI system are payments to retirees and their families, to the totally and permanently disabled and their dependents, and to survivors of workers covered by the program; partial support for medical care for persons aged 65 and over is also provided.

In this federal program benefits are related to previous earnings records, but do not vary in amount from state to state. In contrast, unemployment-insurance payments and welfare allowances are in the hands of the states. Unemployment compensation schemes that meet the federal guidelines on coverage, payroll taxes, and general administration, can nevertheless differ substantially in the amount and duration of benefits paid, eligibility for receiving benefits, possibilities for extension, etc., as was noted in Chapter 16.

Families receiving public assistance are subject to even wider variation in minimum allowance; the extremes, referred to earlier, are Mississippi's average monthly payment of less than $9.00 per dependent child, and New York's allowance of almost $70.00. These allowance differentials frequently induce poor families to migrate to those areas offering the most liberal benefit levels. In addition to setting the amount, the state determines eligibility—whether property owned by the recipient is subject to lien, what the residence requirements are, the nature of the means test. Since states are under pressure to keep

---

[13]Henry J. Aaron, "Income Transfer Programs," *Monthly Labor Review*, 92 (February 1969), 50–54.

the assistance rolls low in order to minimize costs, there is little chance that cash payments will be made to all the needy. Orshansky estimates that 5 out of 6 of the households receiving public assistance remain poor, even with the welfare allowance.

Despite the low levels of income provided, public assistance remains the major source of support for millions of families. Old-age assistance went to more than 2 million in 1966, General Assistance and Aid to the Blind about 400,000, and Aid to the Permanently and Totally Disabled 600,000. By far the largest program is that of Aid to Families with Dependent Children, whose recipients totaled 4.7 million at the end of 1966. One author has stressed the fact that, notwithstanding our earlier hopes that the number of public-assistance recipients would dwindle, these large numbers on the relief rolls suggest a need for continued large-scale aid. We must therefore ask ourselves, he concludes, whether these programs are doing the job, and specifically whether the methods used are suitable for the massive scale now necessary in dealing with the poor. In his view, the "limited impact and erratic performance" of present welfare arrangements confirm the view of the 1966 Report of the Advisory Council on Public Welfare: "Only a relatively small segment of the needy are now helped by public assistance programs—about one-fifth of those in families having an annual income of less than $3,000."[14]

Income without work: the issues

Negative income taxation has been classified as a watered down version of social dividend taxation, which in turn is defined as a

> tax-transfer system in which every family begins the year with an income guarantee. . . . The essence of social dividend taxation is that it combines negative and positive taxes in such a way as to build a floor under the income of every family. It requires the tax system to raise revenues to finance the guaranteed minimum income to everybody as well as to finance other public services.[15]

The immediate objection raised to any scheme of guaranteed income is that of the costs involved. Cost estimates vary, depending largely on the size of the individual or family allowance. James Tobin's plan for a basic annual

---

[14]George F. Rohrlich, "Social Assistance, Social Subsidies, and Social Services to Underwrite the Essentials," in Sar A. Levitan et al., *Towards Freedom from Want,* pp. 38–39.

[13]Green, *Negative Taxes and the Poverty Problem,* p. 54.

allowance of $400 per person, with an upper limit of $2,700 per family, was estimated to cost about $14 billion, based on 1962 income data.[16] In the early days of the antipoverty program, the Council of Economic Advisers' figure of $11 billion was widely cited as the cost of raising families to a $3,000 and individuals to a $1,500 minimum. Translated into alternative uses, $11 billion amounted to about one-fifth of the annual defense budget and less than 2 percent of the Gross National Product.

When the economy's output is growing and tax revenues are rising (even without increases in tax rates), aggregate costs of these magnitudes do not appear prohibitive. But an expenditure on any program can be judged as appropriate only when its advantages outweigh those accruing from a similar expenditure on some alternative program. A majority view would probably hold in favor of income supplements over military spending, space explora- tion, and, very likely, over foreign aid. But these budget items do not exhaust the list of possible priorities. What of an alternative expenditure to provide medical and dental care to low-income families? Would improved educa- tional facilities make a more significant long-run contribution to the elimina- tion of poverty? Rather than offer the income directly, would the provision for certain basic needs (housing, food, health care) at public expense be a better use of the funds?

The question of costs is further complicated by the role of work incen- tives. Will the guarantee of some minimum income reduce the amount of effort devoted to work, thereby reducing total output? To the extent that this reduction occurs, the cost of the income-supplement program is higher than the dollar cost of providing the allowance; it must include also the cost of the forgone output. Clearly, one's appraisal of how extensively income is a moti- vating force in getting work done conditions his estimate of the true costs of income guarantees. Moreover, since income supplements must be paid for with tax revenues, one must reckon with a potential reduction in work effort on the part of the group whose incomes are being taxed to finance the allowances.

The disincentive effect of income taxes has been exaggerated, according to George F. Break's English study. In interviews with accountants and solici- tors who were subject to high marginal and average tax rates, and who could control their work hours, he found the following attitude:

When you get right down to it, I am working as hard as I ever worked. I complain bitterly about how little I am allowed to keep of every pound I earn, but I go on working just the same.[17]

---

[16]Tobin, "Improving the Economic Status of the Negro."

[17]George F. Break, "Income Taxes and Incentives to Work: An Empirical Study," *American Economic Review*, 47 (September 1957), 548.

Figure 18/2.   Effects of positive and negative taxes
on work effort

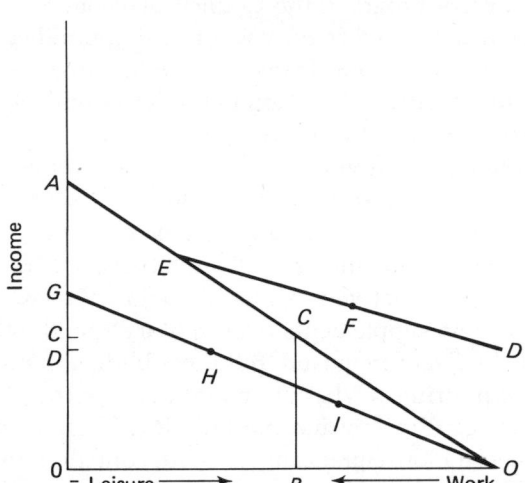

The author notes that several factors will tend to cause workers to offer the same amount of labor, despite the imposition of income taxes: the tendency toward larger families, which increases commitments; higher divorce rates; increasing demand for consumer durables; the entrance of wives to the labor force, notwithstanding higher marginal tax rates; greater domestic and foreign travel which stimulates demand; greater urbanization, with its "bandwagon" effect on consumption patterns; decreasing flexibility of the individual's working habits, which reduces the individual's propensity to change his working hours in response to a tax increase.

The question of whether the members of low-income families would work less if the basic necessities were assured, without reference to work effort, is difficult to subject to empirical test.[18] The threat that certain jobs—the less pleasant, and generally lowest-paying ones—would not get done continues in many quarters to be an argument against income guarantees for the "able-bodied male." Even though such jobs would presumably enable the family to achieve a living standard above the minimum, there persists some skepticism that more income would provide sufficient incentive once a subsistence level of living was assured.

Much of the analysis in the last chapter on the work disincentive effects of Social Security benefits can be applied to negative income tax subsidies. The uncertainty that Break found on how positive taxes affect work effort does not carry over, at least in theory, to the negative tax. Furthermore, the

---

[18]See Martin David and Roger F. Miller, "The Work Leisure Choice Under a Tax and Transfer Regime" (Madison: University of Wisconsin, Social Systems Research Institute, 1968), mimeographed.

work disincentive effect on those above the poverty level leads to understatement of the costs of eliminating poverty through income guarantees, by estimates that ignore this effect.

These pessimistic conclusions can be explained with reference to Figure 18/2, which shows the effect of taxes, negative and positive, on work effort. In the absence of a subsidy program, the worker would be at work-income–leisure equilibrium at OB hours of work and income BC. In this example, the worker is above the poverty level, which we assume equal to the basic zero-earning subsidy, OD.

At some positive tax rate below 100 percent, the subsidy would disappear at total income OE and the income path above that level would follow along the wage ray OA. For the same reasons given to explain the work disincentive effect of Social Security benefits, the worker would reduce his work effort because of the subsidy program; the income path would put him at a higher income, with a negative income effect, with a lower marginal earnings rate, negative substitution effect, than before at the same work effort.

We show his new equilibrium position at F. The actual position depends on his income–leisure indifference map; but it will be at some point to the right of C. Contrast this conclusion with the uncertainty regarding work effort effects of a positive income tax.

A positive tax is depicted by a lower net wage ray OG. (We have assumed a constant income tax rate but this simplification does not mar the analysis.) The new equilibrium point would be either to the left or right of C, say at H or I, indicating more or less work effort as a result of the tax. In this case the income effect of the tax tends to increase work effort while the substitution effect has a negative effect. In short, the overall effect is uncertain, depending on the slope of the labor-supply curve over the wage range. The tax simply lowers the net wage, and the worker would offer more hours of work if his income effect outweighed his substitution effect, that is, if he had a negatively sloped labor supply curve.

Recall that the worker was originally above the poverty level. But as a result of the guaranteed-income program he will take advantage of the subsidy. Thus, to the extent that workers who are not in need decide to receive subsidies, the cost of the program exceeds the amount required to bring every household up to the poverty floor, the so-called total poverty gap. Furthermore, those at equilibrium earnings slightly above E who were not originally eligible for the subsidy might increase their income–leisure satisfaction by working less and receiving a subsidy.

To introduce an optimistic note, this whole analysis rests on a static income–leisure preference map. The poor may have their tastes for consumption altered by rising total income. The question warrants extensive empirical testing.

Programs that might discourage work are thus seen as deterrents to a high growth rate of output. Threats to the *size* of the nation's output are only one part of the objection, however; even stronger protests are heard because of the possible impact on the *distribution* of that output. In general, the distribution scheme espoused for our economy confers income in accordance with productivity. Such a reward system is found acceptable because it is thought to be fair—"a man gets what he is worth and he is worth what he gets." Leaving aside the difficulties of measurement, which might provide evidence as to whether productivity does in fact determine wages, equity under this distributive scheme is frequently challenged on the basis that inadequate educational opportunities limit the productivity, and hence the earnings, of certain groups, for example, blacks, females, and the impoverished. Opportunities available to these groups are also limited by discrimination. Expenditures made for the purpose of improving educational opportunities are thus generally acceptable, since they enable the citizenry to be self-supporting.

The idea of using public funds to provide income, rather than the means of learning to earn income, is in many circles vehemently opposed, as long as there is any work alternative. Even when unemployment is involuntary and unemployment insurance not available, there often lurks the suspicion that laziness is a part of the explanation. The work ethic lends strong endorsement to present wage-employment arrangements, and persons who receive income from public transfers are, by contrast, expected to be old or disabled. How much of our reluctance to underwrite income supplements to men of working age hinges on the religiously based belief that work is good and idleness (except when earned) wicked, and how much on a perceived need to produce an ever-growing output, is difficult to unravel. But taken together within today's social structure, the two notions brake the speed with which income can be separated from work. Elizabeth Wickenden notes the stubborn resistance to change in attitudes:

Many of the old values in which people find comfort have little relevance to the present. Self-reliance has little meaning where ability to earn depends on the availability of a job. Personal saving based on rigorous self-denial is hardly a virtue in a society that bursts with surplus goods. Family solidarity has lost its meaning to the thousands of old people awaiting death in the lonely no-man's land of a nursing home. Neighborly generosity is meaningless where the poor live in ghettos and the well-to-do in exurbia twenty-five miles away. These traditional virtues need to be transferred to new channels of expression and feeling.[19]

The many facets of guaranteed income make it not only an important subject of this section on income assurance, but also one of the leading

---

[19]Elizabeth Wickenden, "Income Policy Options in Society," in Levitan et al., *Towards Freedom from Want,* p. 17.

current labor issues, which comprise the theme of the final section of this book.

Readings

Friedman, Milton. *Capitalism and Freedom.* Chicago: University of Chicago Press, 1962.

Green, Christopher, and Robert J. Lampman, "Schemes for Transferring Income to the Poor," *Industrial Relations,* 6 (February 1967), 121–137.

Green, Christopher. *Negative Taxes and the Poverty Problem.* Washington, D. C.: The Brookings Institution, 1967.

"Income Guarantees: A Spectrum of Opinion," *Monthly Labor Review,* 90 (February 1967), III–IV.

Lampman, Robert J., "Approaches to the Reduction of Poverty," *American Economic Review,* Papers and Proceeding, 55 (May 1965).

Naylor, Thomas, ed., "The Guaranteed Income in Perspective," *The Impact of the Computer on Society.* Atlanta: Southern Regional Education Board.

Theobald, Robert. *The Guaranteed Income: Next Step in Economic Evolution.* New York: Doubleday, 1966.

Tobin, James; Joseph A. Pechman; and Peter M. Mieszkowski, "Is a Negative Income Tax Practical?" *Yale Law Journal,* 77 (November 1967), 1–27.

Part Six

Issues and Policies in the 1970s

Chapter Nineteen
Technology, Work, and Leisure

Introduction: technology and human welfare

The literature on technology could fill several libraries, and a great deal of it has appeared in the past decade. References to the Industrial Revolution as a point of departure are frequent, albeit a bit strained; for the most part, however, current comments emphasize the fact that modern technology wields an enormous influence on society, and on the life of the individual. In particular, writers express concern over man's inability to adjust his institutions in such ways as to take advantage of the technology he has created —to reap the benefits of new techniques of production and enjoy the freedoms offered—without becoming the victim of some relentless and destructive process.

One similarity with earlier times should be stressed. At the time of the Industrial Revolution, economic accounts dealt extensively with the poverty and deprivation of the working masses, their crowded living conditions, their failure to share in the economic gains of new industrial techniques. In the same manner, sociological and economic tracts of our times point to the existence of poverty in the midst of affluence. Modern technology, while creating higher and higher volumes of output, nevertheless leaves unattended the economic deprivation of the lowest economic class whose relative position steadily worsens.

But in contrast to the era of the Industrial Revolution, there is an important difference in the composition of today's disadvantaged. The bulk of the fully employed workers in the current labor force are well above the poverty line. Although additional income is always desirable, their earnings do tend to reflect their growing productivity, and their living standards have risen steadily throughout the nineteenth and twentieth centuries. The problem of poverty in the United States is increasingly concentrated in that segment of the population that does not work at all, works only intermittently, or has inherited poverty. The latter process has not yet been directly confronted by society.

An even more important difference is apparent in work schedules. Whereas earlier generations of workers were on the job from dawn to dusk, with young children frequently exploited in mines and factories, and practically all teenage youths in the full-time work force, the working time of modern man has been shortened to less than a third of his day and perhaps one-half of the years in his lifespan. So while real incomes and standards of living have increased, the amount of time spent at work has declined. The gift of technology has thus been a greater output of goods, and a growth in time free to enjoy these goods.

Why, then, are contemporary writers so disenchanted with the technological revolution? And why the fright over the pace and pattern of the change it evokes? A sociologist wrote recently:

> *While we think of ourselves as people of change and progress, masters of our environment and our fate, we are no more entitled to the designation than the most superstitious savage, for our relation to change is entirely passive. We poke our noses out the door each day and wonder breathlessly what new disruptions technology has in store for us. We talk of technology as the servant of man, but it is a servant that now dominates the household, too powerful to fire, upon whom everyone is helplessly dependent.*[1]

We have not been willing, Slater continues, to ask whether the innovations contribute to human welfare, and certainly we have not been willing to refuse to introduce newly discovered techniques; since the time of the Luddites, man has "passively surrendered to every degradation, every atrocity, every enslavement" that technology brought forth.

In the view of many authors, modern technology has created not enslavement but freedom—such freedom, in fact, that identity problems are magnified. Alvin Toffler argues that the rapidity of change leads to "future shock," that is, to "an overload of the human organism's physical adaptive systems and its decision-making processes." Man has been given by technology a great many choices not formerly available to him; he is able to make and dissolve relationships easily. Yet his freedom to choose among such a wide range of options threatens his social and personal integration; "the multiplication of life style challenges our ability to hold the very self together."[2] In the same vein, Lifton's "protean man" is one who adjusts to the stresses of constant change through ". . . an interminable series of experiments and explorations . . . each of which may be readily abandoned in favor of still new psychological quests."[3]

---

[1]Philip Slater, *The Pursuit of Loneliness* (Boston: Beacon Press, 1970), p. 44.
[2]Alvin Toffler, *Future Shock* (New York: Random House, 1970), pp. 283–290.
[3]Robert Jay Lifton, "Protean Man," *Partisan Review*, 35 (Winter 1968), 17.

Economists have been mainly concerned with the role of technology in revamping jobs, in raising productivity per man-hour, in changes in the capital–labor ratio, and the labor–leisure relationship. To pursue some of the questions that arise in these broad contexts, it is necessary first to indicate the limitations of economic analysis and then to describe the meaning of technological change for input–output relationships. Finally, some economic implications of technological change—particularly for leisuretime growth and for involuntary unemployment—will be discussed.

Microeconomic theory and firm behavior

Technological change affects society in diverse ways. An advancing technology creates economic opportunities by speeding economic growth and increasing productivity. It also creates problems; inevitably, change generates the need for social and institutional restructuring. While it is a commonplace to attribute growth of output to technological change, there is no compelling empirical evidence that technological advance is responsible rather than economies of scale, learning by doing, errors of measurement, or even sunspots.[4] Further, while economic factors undoubtedly have a good deal to do with the magnitude of technological progress, they may have little to do with the direction this progress takes; in fact, it is difficult to analyze the dynamics of technological change within the existing framework of economic theory.

The adequacy of microeconomic theory to deal with technological change can be challenged on at least two bases. The first concerns the methodological adequacy of the theory itself: Can it explain what it purports to explain? How relevant are marginalist economic models in an economy that is becoming increasingly social in nature? Second, what of the pragmatic adequacy of microeconomic theory? How are the important factors of time and technological change to be handled? We need models of the technologically progressive firm. To develop such models we need to look at the characteristics that distinguish this type of firm from its nonprogressive counterpart. How are policy decisions made in the two firms? What role do firm size and industry concentration play? What is the importance of research and development?

Two concepts of the decision-making process are found in the neoclassical literature on the theory of the firm. The first treats the entrepreneur as a technician who employs optimum quantities of inputs and decides how to maximize profits by varying rates of output and prices.[5] The second concept

---

[4]See W. D. Nordhaus, "An Economic Theory of Technological Change," *American Economic Review* LIX (May 1969), 18–28.

[5]J. M. Henderson and R. E. Quandt, *Micro-economic Theory: A Mathematical Approach* (New York: McGraw-Hill Book Co., 1958), pp. 42–43.

treats the entrepreneur as a resource owner who uses rather than sells his resources, to produce a new product.[6] In this concept the entrepreneur is viewed primarily as an owner, and the technology is the knowledge the owner possesses. Entrepreneurship can be thought to perform two separate functions: that of risk-taking (wherein the risk is borne by the owner of the firm), and that of technical decision-making (in which the risk is borne by the manager of the firm).

1. technology $= f$ (total past production volume)
2. technology $= f$ (length of time in production).

The latter assumes that learning takes time in addition to activity. In the presence of technological progress, the firm necessarily operates with incomplete knowledge about future production, that is, about the goods to be produced and the techniques to be employed. Since production methods are frequently changed as new techniques are being learned, the technologically progressive firm faces not one fixed set of production possibilities, but a series of options, some only beginning to emerge. Thus, it seems necessary to change certain assumptions regarding the behavior of the individual competitive firm.[7] Neoclassical production functions, traditionally based on short-run periods, ignore the role of technological change; no long-run theory is developed. Rather, the long-run is simply assumed as an "envelope" of short-run planning periods. The envelope curve represents the minimum average variable cost to produce any quantity of output. This long-run planning function is related to output rather than to time.

New approaches to the theory of the firm must be developed if technological change is to be incorporated into a meaningful body of theory, where growth and productivity can be understood. For analysis, the economist must develop an abstract of the large modern corporation and in particular, to study the decision-making process in such corporations. Fortunately, models of economic decision making are now made possible through the use of high-speed digital computers. New developments in computer technology also allow the testing of new policies and decisions through the use of computer simulation techniques.[8] But the development of a new theory of the firm remains in its infancy.

---

[6]M. Friedman, *Price Theory: A Provisional Text* (Chicago: Aldine Publishing Company, 1962), p. 93.

[7]W. Z. Hirsch, "Technological Progress and Microeconomic Theory," *American Economic Review* (May 1969), p. 39.

[8]See T. H. Naylor, et al., *Computer Simulation Techniques* (New York: John Wiley and Sons, 1966).

Figure 19/1.   Technological progress

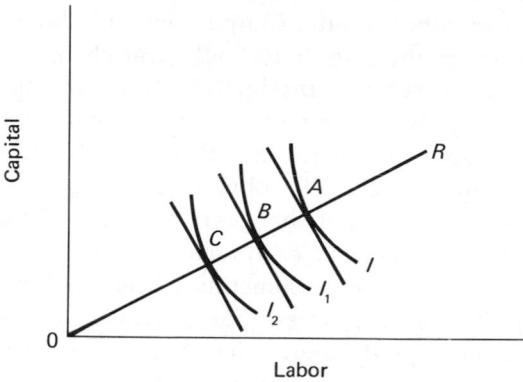

The meaning and measures of technology

What do economists mean by technological change? Basically, the term is used to refer to any change of the production function that permits the same level of output to be produced with less input, or enables the former inputs to produce a greater level of output. A production function is simply a relation between inputs and outputs. At any point in time it shows the maximum output rate that can be obtained from given amounts of the factors of production, or the minimum input quantities required to produce some given output.

In Figure 19/1, which assumes two factors of production, capital and labor, technological progress may be seen as any movement from A to B to C. I_1 and I_2 represent isoquants showing combinations of inputs capable of producing a given level of output. OR is a ray whose slope yields a constant capital–labor ratio. The points A, B, and C therefore show the points of production at the given capital–labor ratio, at various stages of technology. Technological progress may be indicated by a shift of an isoquant in the direction of the origin, since the same output can be produced with less capital and labor.[9]

Economists employ various measures of the rate of technological change. These involve the calculation of partial productivity indexes—for example, output per man-hour of labor, output per dollar of capital input, and output

---

[9]Technological progress may be capital-using, labor-using, or neutral, according as the marginal rate of technical substitution of labor for capital diminishes, increases, or remains unchanged at the prevailing capital–labor ratio. Cf. C. E. Ferguson, *Microeconomic Theory* (Homewood, Ill.: Richard D. Irwin, Inc., 1966), pp. 150–152. Thus, Figure 19/1 depicts a condition of neutral technological progress.

per unit of raw material. Such indexes are partial in the sense that output is related to only one input at a time, and the calculation assumes no changes in the quantities of other inputs. Output per man-hour is obviously an incomplete measure of the rate of technological change, yet it is of great interest; we usually expect higher productivity to be accompanied by a higher wage rate and an improved standard of living. Total productivity indexes relate changes in output to changes in both capital and labor inputs, not to changes in labor inputs alone. The obvious advantage of developing this index is that by taking account of changes over time in the amount of capital inputs, the contribution made by each factor can be isolated.

Organizational changes have sometimes been credited with being the major basis for technological progress. Some writers have tended to assume, in fact, that all technological progress has consisted of better methods and organization, which in turn improved the efficiency of capital. Examples of activities which may lead to such improved efficiency are the use of time-and-motion studies by industry, and operations research (for example, linear and nonlinear programming techniques). While technological change of this sort has been important, much of the change that has occurred is capital-embodied as well as organizational. Although we do not know precisely the extent to which recent technological advances have been capital-embodied, the available evidence seems to indicate that a great deal of the improvement has been of this kind, with common examples being found in the employment of new machinery that requires new investment, for example, the diesel locomotive in the railroad industry.

Other measures of the rate of technological change employ various assumptions regarding the production function in order to assess the extent of changes in productivity and thereby the extent of economic growth.[10] Since they have used different measures and techniques, empirical studies of the rate of technological change have led to different conclusions. Nevertheless, certain broad conclusions can be drawn: the rate of increase in output per man-hour has been greater since World War II than before; the difference appears smaller the more sophisticated the measure employed; the rate of total productivity changes has varied considerably from one industry to another, and from one nation to another.

Estimates appear to bear out the notion that technological change has been an important generator of economic growth, along with other factors, such as education, economies of scale, etc. But it is difficult to develop an adequate measure of the rate of technological change, just as it is difficult to assess the quantitative impact of that change on economic growth. Part of the measurement problem rests with the limited usefulness of production functions; other questions arise from the fact that the measures used do not isolate

---

[10]See E. Mansfield, *The Economics of Technological Change* (New York: W. W. Norton and Co., 1968).

the effects of technological change alone. Measures that supposedly show the impact of technological change actually reflect the effects of other factors, such as education, improved allocation of resources, improved worker productivity due to better health and environmental conditions, etc. Consequently, it is perhaps more useful to consider what determines technological advance than to attempt to measure its rate.

What sets the pace of technology?

To answer important questions regarding the mode and pace of technological change requires more than knowledge of economics and statistics. What determines the rate of inventions, for example? Of innovation? Of creativity itself?

The rate of change within an industry depends to a great extent on the amount of resources devoted by members of the industry and by government to the improvement of that industry's technology. A progressive industry need not be large or oligopolistic: indeed, some of the important inventions and innovative techniques that have contributed significantly to the pace of technology and to economic growth have come from individuals or smaller firms. The amount of resources devoted by the government to an industry often depends on how closely the industry is related to national defense or to the medical or other social interest for which the federal government assumes a major responsibility; on the external economies generated by the relevant research and development; and on political factors. The amount of resources devoted by private industry to research and development activity depends primarily on potential profitability.

Although a large volume of resources devoted by industry to research and development does not guarantee a diffusion of innovations, important inventions would seldom occur without substantial research support. In addition to the quantity of resources, an industry's technological progress is dependent on the effectiveness with which these resources are used, as well as the quantity of resources devoted to related research by other industries. Other factors to be considered include the environment within which research and development take place (the market structure, for example); private contributions to research and development, etc. The rate of technological change, in summary, may be considered a direct function of the effectiveness of the inventive efforts of industry itself and the extent of the spillover of technology from other industries.

The volume of industrial research and development expenditures has increased dramatically in recent years (Table 19/1). In 1941, a total of $900 million was spent on research and development in the United States. In 1970, the figure totaled $17+ billion. Much of the research and development per-

Table 19/1.   Trends in funds for industrial R&D
performance, by source, 1953-70

[Dollar amounts in millions]

Year	Total R&D		Federal		Company[a]	
	Amount	Percent change from previous year	Amount	Percent of total	Amount	Percent of total
1953	$ 3,630	....	$1,430	39	$ 2,200	61
1954[b]	4,070	12	1,750	43	2,320	57
1955[b]	4,640	14	2,180	47	2,460	53
1956	6,605	42	3,328	50	3,277	50
1957	7,731	17	4,335	56	3,396	44
1958	8,389	9	4,759	57	3,630	43
1959	9,618	15	5,635	59	3,983	41
1960	10,509	9	6,081	58	4,428	42
1961[c]	10,908	4	6,240	57	4,668	43
1962	11,464	5	6,434	56	5,029	44
1963	12,630	10	7,270	58	5,360	42
1964	13,512	7	7,720	57	5,792	43
1965	14,185	5	7,740	55	6,445	45
1966	15,548	10	8,332	54	7,216	46
1967	16,385	5	8,365	51	8,020	49
1968	17,429	6	8,560	49	8,869	51
1969	18,318	5	8,451	46	9,867	54
1970	17,858	−3	7,785	44	10,073	56

[a]Company funds include all funds for industrial research and development performed within company facilities except funds provided by the Federal Government. The data do not include company-financed research and development contracted to outside organizations such as research institutions, universities and colleges, or other nonprofit organizations. In 1970 industrial firms contracted $243 million in company-financed R&D projects to outside organizations.
[b]Estimates of funds by source were derived by interpolating data on sources of funds obtained in the 1953 and 1956 surveys of industrial research and development.
[c]Funds by source estimated by the National Science Foundation.
Source: United States National Science Foundation Review of Data on Science Resources (Industrial Research and Development); U.S. Department of Defense, 1971.

formed by one sector is financed by another sector; the federal government finances a substantial amount of the research and development conducted by private industry. In 1953, about 40 percent of the private sector's research and development was financed by the federal government and in 1963, 60 percent; for government-sponsored university research, the comparable figures are 60 percent in 1953 and 75 percent in 1963. In addition, the federal government sponsored a large portion of the research and development carried out by nonprofit organizations other than universities. Government assistance does not guarantee the infusion of new techniques into the economy, of course; but the federal government's financial contribution to the continuation of an innovative society is now clearly more than half the total. It follows that the public attitude toward the value of research, and the extent to which tax dollars are directed toward this endeavor, are major influences on the pace and direction of innovation.

Some economic effects of technological change

The interaction of technology and society produces both positive and negative effects. New industrial technology—machines, processes, etc.—strengthens the economy by increasing growth and productivity, and also by redistributing income. But the introduction of new techniques calls for structural changes within the economy, particularly those changes necessary to accommodate to the relative importance of individual supply factors.[11] New machines and techniques of production alter the inputs (materials, parts, labor skills, etc.) that each industry uses to manufacture its products. We may cite, for example, the shift from the use of coal to that of petroleum; the replacement of steel and tin by plastic, as in the container industry.

Such changes lead to dislocations of businesses and employment patterns. Society must respond by exploiting the opportunities created by technological change, while containing its negative effects. Just as there exist economies and diseconomies of scale, there also exist economies and diseconomies of technological advance. Some of the consequences of the implementation of technology are causing great public concern at present: smog, water pollution, urban sprawl, sonic booms, ecological conflict between industry and environmentalists.[12]

Increase in time free of work

By creating new opportunities for action, technology offers individuals and society many new options, and thus appears to lead to value changes either by bringing some previously unattainable goal within the realm of choice, or by making some goals easier to implement by reducing their costs.

---

[11]See A. P. Carter, *Structural Change in the American Economy*, in the series "Harvard Studies in Technology and Society" (Cambridge: Harvard University Press, 1970).

[12]C. E. Mesthene, *Technological Change and Its Impact on Man and Society*, in the series "Harvard Studies in Technology and Society" (Cambridge: Harvard Press, 1970). Chapter II is devoted to a discussion of the impact of technological change on values.

Consider, for example, how time free of work has grown; leisure time, whether defined as hours away from work or as "discretionary" time, has increased, and average weekly hours of work have declined over time (Figure 19/2). The workingman's paid vacation time is similarily increasing. Finally, as a man now enters the labor force later in life and retires earlier, the leisure available to the workingman has grown significantly as a result of the change in the pattern of worklife. Changes in labor-force size and composition, particularly changes in labor-force participation rates, shifts in worklife expectancy, etc., have accelerated since World War II, and have led to important changes in the concept of work in modern societies. The potential growth in leisure provided by technological advance reinforces this new concept of work.

Figure 19/2.   Average weekly hours in private nonagricultural establishments, manufacturing and trade, 1953 to date (seasonally adjusted)

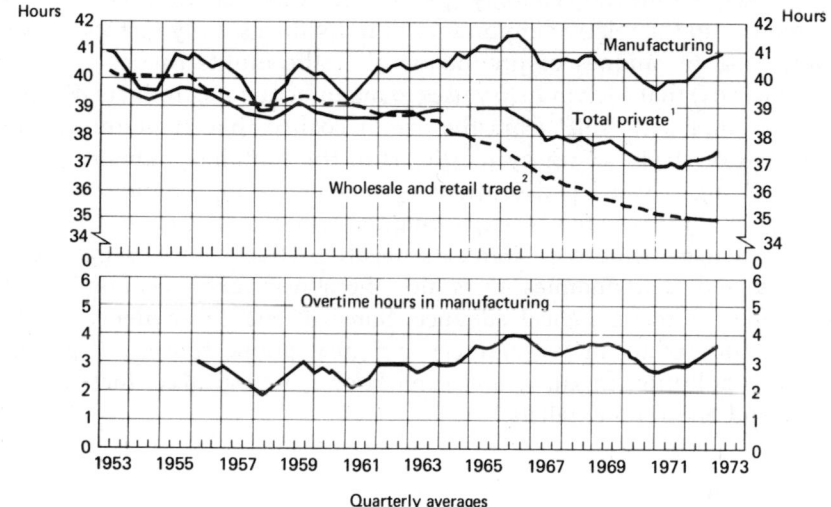

1 Annual averages prior to 1964

2 Beginning in 1964, data include eating and drinking establishments not previously available

Note: Data for 2 most recent months are preliminary

Source: Employment and Earnings, March 1973.

Alternative forms of leisure need to be considered, as time free of work continues to grow. Should society increase the level of education and training for those entering the labor force? Or lower the retirement age of labor-force participants? Or would most workers opt for longer annual vacations? The total amount of free time made available by improvements in output per man-hour may be quite large, even when allowance is made for rapid rises in real GNP. The allocation of this leisure is important, given the different degrees of utility man may associate with different forms of leisure. As with the unequal distribution of income, the distribution of leisure requires further study, which might reveal that the portion of economic growth accruing to man in the form of leisure time is being allocated less evenly than income.[13]

The demand for leisure may be viewed as the inverse of the supply of labor. Whether labor's demand for shorter hours of work is due to fear of unemployment or to a desire for increased leisure is an important question. Without better data than we now have, it is difficult to assess the elasticity of workers' demand for leisure with respect to wage increases. The question of the preferred proportions of work and leisure, which remains to be answered in the light of empirical evidence, will turn on the desire for "work"; the value of noneconomic factors in one's life, for example, kinship and other institutional factors such as church membership, community participation, etc.; the strength of desire for goods for current use, and "the effective desire to accumulate."

The conclusion that advancing technology is rapidly making possible both increased output and reduced working time is an important one for economic analysis. Attempts have been made to measure the worth of this increase in nonworking time by assuming that it could have been otherwise spent in the production of goods. In this way it is possible to estimate GNP and the rate of economic growth when an assumed value of leisure is included. The much higher national product figures that emerge from these calculations provide a somewhat broader perspective within which the long-run effects of technological change can be appraised.

While technology gives the worker more time free of work, it also demands that he be more highly (or differently) trained while he is at work. The need for improved labor-force quality, prompting nationwide retraining and relocation programs, has led to reappraisals of the Nation's education levels and goals. The investment in human capital often pays a higher return than investment in physical capital. The diversion of free time into education thus has great appeal, both as a short-run "constructive" use of time and as a long-run source of return.

The spectre of unemployment

In analyzing the relationship of technology to employment levels, economists have considered the rate at which labor-saving devices will displace workers, and the types of policies needed to counteract the job loss, as well

---

[13] J. Kreps and J. J. Spengler, "The Leisure Component of Economic Growth," in *The Employment Impact of Technological Change,* Appendix Vol. II, National Commission on Technology, Automation and Economic Progress, 1966, pp. 356–358.

as how much the infusion of new techniques into the working world will improve productivity per man-hour. The total number of jobs in an economy, at any given time, may be viewed primarily as a function of the aggregate demand for goods and services. Other things being equal, the greater the demand for goods and services, the greater is the level of employment with the given state of technology. Through time, increased productivity per man-hour has been offset by an increased demand for goods and services, and employment has therefore increased.

However, the problem lies not with increasing employment, but with increasing unemployment. The total output of goods and services must rise at a rate sufficient to offset both the productivity rise and the growth in the number of job seekers. Estimates of the latter can be projected, but, as we have seen, to estimate the rate of future productivity change is extremely difficult. The other elements that determine the strength of the labor market are also difficult to forecast: To what extent will aggregate demand grow? What will be the composition of the aggregate demand? How much labor will be required? How much labor will be offered by the population? An economy that strives to maintain high levels of employment must anticipate shifts in demand, resource-supply and use rates, an addition to the rate of productivity growth.

To attribute unemployment to technological progress is simplistic; if total needs are considered, there would seem to be no reason to fear the elimination of jobs. It is true that shortages in certain areas will appear in the course of technological change. Moreover, a shortage of labor in one sector is not necessarily eased by a surplus in another. But the unemployment problem, more broadly viewed, arises because the pace of technology and the rapidly changing size and age distribution of the labor force create structural unemployment problems with which fiscal and monetary measures cannot always deal successfully.

Query: What use of man's time?

Mr. Creech, it is said, wrote on the margin of the Lucretius which he was translating, 'Mem.—When I have finished my book, I must kill myself.' And he carried out his resolution. Life . . . is a dreary vista of monotonous toil, at the end of which there is nothing but death, natural if it so happen, but if not, voluntary, without even a preliminary interval of idleness. To live without work is not supposed to enter into our conceptions.[14]

---

[14]Leslie Stephen, "Vacations," reprinted from *Cornhill Magazine,* Vol. 20 (1869), in Eric A. Larrabee and Rolf Meyersohn, eds., *Mass Leisure* (Glencoe, Ill.: Free Press, 1958), pp. 281–290.

The contemporary intellectual revolution, generally referred to by the technical word, automation, is providing machines which . . . assuming drudgery and monotonous repetitive operations, increase productivity. Within the industrial system a relentless logic necessitates abundance. Leisure, as we experience it, becomes a function of an unseen but very real and enormously fruitful configuration of scientific concepts and theories. . . . [15]

Transition from the first of these two views—that the purpose of life being work, life itself might well end when work ends—to the second—that life is greatly enriched by a technology that reduces the amount of work necessary—has not been an orderly one, and even today there is no unanimity of opinion as to the value of leisure.

In contrast to Aristotle's belief that "the goal of war is peace, of business, leisure," the uneasy feeling that life with little work has little purpose seems to pervade much of today's thought. Contemporary writers often deplore the growing freedom from work, which provides "a great emptiness," devoid of meaning. Lacking training for leisure and having no strong interests or devotions, one author argues, persons without work lead dismal lives. The void created by leisure has thus replaced ". . . the days when unremitting toil was the lot of all but the very few and leisure was still a hopeless yearning." [16] In less extreme form, concern is frequently voiced over the idleness forced upon youth by lack of job opportunities, and upon the elderly by early and compulsory retirement from work.

Americans have traditionally believed, according to Margaret Mead, that leisure should be earned before it is enjoyed. The function of recreation is to prepare man for further work, and as soon as it appears that there will be more time available than is actually needed for this purpose,

Alarm spreads over the country. People are going to have too much leisure. . . . This means more time than is needed to relax and get back to work again—unearned time, loose time, time which, without the holding effects of fatigue before and fatigue to come, might result in almost anything. [17]

Our sense of responsibility for how other people spend their leisure time is characteristic of American life; indeed, as David Riesman says: "our bonanzas, our windfalls . . . have been interpreted by the most sensitive and respon-

---

[15]Paul F. Douglass, foreword to "Recreation in the Age of Automation," *Annals of the American Academy of Political and Social Science,* 313 (September 1957), ix.

[16]Robert M. MacIver, *The Pursuit of Happiness* (New York: Simon and Schuster, 1955).

[17]Margaret Mead, "The Pattern of Leisure in Contemporary American Culture," *The Annals of the American Academy of Political and Social Science,* 313 (1957), 13.

sible among us as problems."[18]   We are proud, in fact, of being such responsible members of society that we ourselves have no leisure. But Riesman argues that criticism of the work-oriented Puritans is probably overdone. The moral seriousness of puritanism has in fact helped to bring society to the position in which leisure *can* become a problem for a majority of the people.

The problems inherent in the acquisition and assimilation of leisure are comparable, the author continues, to problems that arise in other areas of social progress: "Every social advance is ambivalent in its consequences." Because we are at the frontier of the development of leisure, there are of course conflicts in attitudes toward its use; knowing very little about what leisure means to people—how much they read, for example, or how widespread is the interest in painting or chamber music—assumptions are made that may in fact considerably understate the nation's capacity for activities that earlier work schedules have prohibited.

Currently there are a number of areas of pioneering in leisure: music, painting, and literature; sociability and conversation; sports. While these fields are being developed for masses of people, anxieties as to the values of leisure and the merits of using it in particular ways are to be expected. But Riesman argues that only historical amnesia can blind one to the humanizing effects of reduced work (including the elimination of child labor) and increased time free of work.

Technology and the quality of life

The problems that technology generates are not altogether bound up in the *amount* of leisure time made available. In large part, they have to do with the *quality* of the leisure, or at least with the quality of the social and physical environment in which the leisure may be used. Deterioration of the physical environment is now being charged against the technology: automobiles, traffic congestion, and exhaust fumes; factories and air pollution; industrial waste and clogged bodies of water. In reality, the sheer growth in numbers of people has been a major source of these evils, although one could argue that only an advanced technology would have enabled the increased population to survive.

Increased alienation and depersonalization of life that supposedly afflicts many persons at present (particularly the young) is also being attributed to the growing mechanization of most activities. In the workplace such alienation is not necessarily occurring, according to several investigators; on the contrary, the automation of work actually reduces alienation by giving the

---

[18]David Riesman, "Some Observations on Changes in Leisure Attitudes," *The Antioch Review,* 12 (1952–1953), 417–436.

worker greater control over his job.[19] Moreover, the greater freedom to move from one work- and lifestyle to another, with several such changes in the course of a lifetime, makes possible a better meshing of individual preference and work content.

Suggestions for control of the rate of technological change—and hence the rate of job displacement, the rapidity of change in job requirements, and the effect on our physical environment—have been numerous. In total, they amount to proposals for assessing the probable impact of any proposed technological change, and a willingness to prevent the introduction of those techniques and processes found questionable. Instead of accepting all innovations, society needs to exercise some veto power in the interests of a better ecological fit, a more manageable pace, a less destructive effect on those traditional patterns thought to be desirable. The obvious question immediately occurs: Can the probable result of any new technology be accurately appraised? How much retarding of industrial technology can we afford?

These questions regarding the control of technology only now emerging will persist throughout the student's worklife. For, just as the technology in large measure dictates the nature of his work, so, too, it influences the quality of his life away from the workplace. It becomes more and more important, therefore, to "recognize the individual's right to such amenities as privacy, quiet, and clean air," where resources are "diverted from industrial gadgetry to the replanning of cities and the recreating of the environment."[20]

Readings

Carter, A. P. *Structural Change in the American Economy.* Cambridge: Harvard University Press, 1970.

Dumazedier, Joffre. *Toward a Study of Leisure.* New York: The Free Press, 1967.

Galbraith, J. K. *The New Industrial State.* Boston: Houghton Mifflin Company, 1967.

Harvard University Program on Technology and Society, *Research Reviews Nos. 2–6.* Cambridge: Harvard University Press.

Jaffe, A. J., and J. Froomkin. *Technology and Jobs: Automation in Perspective.* New York: Praeger, 1968.

---

[19]See Robert Blauner, *Alienation and Freedom: The Factory Worker and His Industry* (Chicago: University of Chicago Press, 1964); Jon M. Shepard, *The Impact of Mechanization and Automation on Alienation in the Factory and Office* (Springfield, Va.: Clearinghouse for Federal Scientific and Technical Information, 1970); and William A. Faunce, *Problems of an Industrial Society* (New York: McGraw-Hill Book Co., 1968).

[20]Harvard University Program on Technology and Society, *Technology and the Individual,* Research Review No. 6 (Cambridge: Harvard University Press, 1970), p. 10.

Kreps, Juanita, ed. *Technology, Manpower, and Retirement Policy.* Cleveland: World Publishing Company, 1966.

Mansfield, E. *The Economics of Technological Change.* New York: W. W. Norton and Co., 1968.

Chapter Twenty

Full Employment and Wage–Price Stability

A look at the record

The interrelationships between money wages, prices, and employment are best viewed in the perspective of post-World War II economic trends. In summary, the overall picture has been one of rapid economic growth. Table 20/1 shows the trend in prices, as represented by the annual percentage change in the consumer price index and the implicit GNP price index (GNP deflator).[1] The movement of money wages is shown by the annual percentage change in average hourly earnings in manufacturing.

The indexes clearly indicate that the postwar economy has been characterized by inflation. Since the beginning of 1946, the consumer price (the "cost of living") index has risen in all years except two—1949 and 1955. Over the whole period of 23 years, the consumer price index rose at an average annual rate of 3.1 percent. If consumer prices continue to rise at this average annual rate, the cost of living will double in less than three decades.

The GNP deflator has also shown an almost continuous rise in the postwar period, falling only in the year 1949. Over the two and a half decades the GNP deflator rose at an average annual rate of 3.3 percent. Since 1946 the general level of prices has more than doubled. The wage index has risen each year of the postwar era, the increase in hourly earnings averaging 4.9 percent a year. Thus, wages have increased at an average rate of 4.9 percent while the increases in the cost of living and general price level has averaged 3.1 and 3.3 percent, respectively. The difference between the increase in money wages and the increase in prices represents the increase in real wages.

Since the beginning of 1946, there have been four periods in which the unemployment rate has stayed below 4.5 percent for any length of time: the post-World War II boom, 1946 to 1948; the Korean War period, 1951 to 1953;

---

[1]The implicit GNP price deflator is a price index that covers all the varied goods and services included in the economy's GNP. It is constructed by breaking down final product as finely as possible and then adjusting each part by a price index appropriate to the goods and services included in it. Summing the adjusted parts yields GNP in constant dollars; and dividing GNP in current dollars by GNP in constant dollars yields the implicit GNP price deflator.

the years from 1955 to 1957; and from 1965 to 1969. During those same intervals, the consumer price index and the GNP deflator rose at annual average rates of 4.8 and 4.6 percent, respectively. During the other 13 years of the period (when unemployment was high) the consumer price index and the GNP deflator increased at average annual rates of about 1.4 and 1.6 percent, respectively. Therefore, prices rose approximately four times as fast during the years of low unemployment as during the years of high unemployment.

Table 20/1.   Wage, price, and employment trends, 1947–1970

Year	Percent of labor force unemployed (annual rate)	Annual percentage change in average hourly earnings in manufacturing	Annual percentage change in consumer price index	Annual percentage change in GNP deflator
		(Adjusted, 1967 = 100)		
1946	3.9%	6.9%	8.5%	11.8%
1947	3.6	14.8	14.4	11.9
1948	3.8	9.3	7.7	6.6
1949	5.9	4.5	−1.0	− .6
1950	5.3	3.1	1.0	1.3
1951	3.3	7.8	8.0	6.8
1952	3.0	5.1	2.2	2.1
1953	2.9	5.4	.7	1.0
1954	5.5	3.2	.5	1.5
1955	4.4	3.1	− .4	1.4
1956	4.1	5.2	1.5	3.4
1957	4.3	5.1	3.5	3.7
1958	6.8	4.1	2.8	2.5
1959	5.5	3.1	.8	1.7
1960	5.5	3.3	1.6	1.6
1961	6.7	2.9	1.1	1.3
1962	5.5	2.5	1.1	1.1
1963	5.7	2.4	1.2	1.3
1964	5.2	2.5	1.3	1.5
1965	4.5	2.6	1.7	1.8
1966	3.8	3.3	2.9	2.8
1967	3.8	4.7	2.8	3.2
1968	3.6	6.1	4.2	4.0
1969	3.5	5.8	5.3	4.8
1970	4.9	6.5	5.7	5.5
1971	5.9	5.6	4.3	4.7
1972	5.6	6.3	3.3	3.0

Source: Computed from data presented in Economic Report of the President, 1973.

The relationship between the money wage and the level of unemployment is similar to that between prices and unemployment. During the periods of low unemployment wages rose at an average annual rate of 6.1 percent. The average annual increase in the wage index during the years of high unemployment was 3.4 percent, or slightly more than half as large as the change during times of lower unemployment.

The wage and price trends of the postwar years can be summarized thus: first, during the period both prices and wages increased significantly; second, during the periods of low unemployment, prices have risen much more rapidly than during the high-unemployment years, except for the period since 1969–1971; and third, during the periods when prices have risen most rapidly, wages have also increased at a faster rate. It should be noted that the wage–price data do not reveal whether wage increases have helped to cause prices to rise or have merely been in response to price increases during the period.

Since price stability is a major economic goal of our economy, the problem of postwar inflation has received considerable attention. Discussions of inflation have followed two different courses. Initially, analyses centered upon the causes of inflation, some of the explanations being new and others being variants of older theories. These explanations of inflation, which can be classified into three general groups—demand-pull, cost-push, and structural theories—are discussed in a subsequent section of this chapter.

More recently, study of the theory of inflation has moved in another direction. Noting that periods of low unemployment have been associated with higher-than-average increases in prices and wages (and vice versa), economists have considered the possibility that the rate of inflation and the level of unemployment are systematically related. Most current research on inflation is directed to the question of whether there is such a systematic relationship and (when one is thought to exist) to the problem of identifying its approximate shape.

The inflation–unemployment trade-off

Our major economic goals in recent decades include those of full employment, price stability, sustained and rapid economic growth, and balance-of-payments equilibrium. When these goals can be simultaneously achieved without conflict, the problems of the policy maker are greatly simplified; when they conflict, economic policy is much more difficult to determine. When conflict arises, a decision must be made as to how far to pursue one objective at the expense of another. Some trade-off between the conflicting goals must be made. The analysis of the postwar price–employment data suggests that such a trade-off exists between price stability and full employment.

Despite some disagreement on the theoretical explanation of price and employment, or output, movements, there is general agreement on their broad relationships. It is generally conceded that at some level of employment and output prices begin to rise and, moreover, that this rise occurs at a level below what is usually defined as full employment. As employment and output move toward full employment, prices rise more rapidly. In other words, any movement closer to full employment is accomplished at the cost of some additional inflation.

The conflict between the goals of full employment and price stability can be illustrated by the trade-off curve of Figure 20/1, where the rate of unemployment is measured on the horizontal axis, and the annual percentage change in prices is measured on the vertical axis. The general shape of the trade-off curve indicates that the rate of inflation will increase more rapidly, the lower the level of unemployment.

Figure 20/1.   The shift in the trade-off between inflation and unemployment

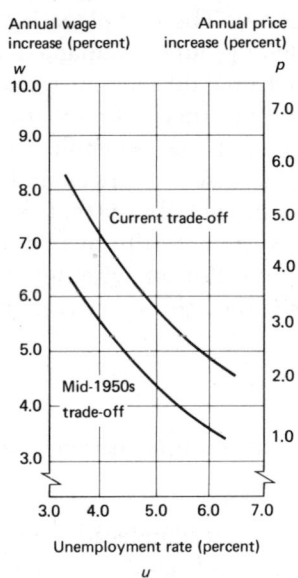

Source: U. S. Department of Labor. *Monthly Labor Review,* 94, No. 2 (February 1971), 71.

The slope and position of the trade-off curve depend upon the underlying structural elements of the economy: its resource base, the rate of technical change, the attitudes and short-term expectations of the public, institutional

arrangements (particularly labor markets and their price-setting mechanisms), and international relationships.[2] A change in any of these factors
affects the trade-off curve.

Given such an inflation–unemployment trade-off curve, consider some of
the important policy questions. If the economy is run in such a way as to keep
prices stable, what level of unemployment will ensue? Or alternatively, if the
aim is to maintain some minimum level of unemployment, what will be the
behavior of prices? Estimating the inflation–unemployment relationship requires two steps: first, to estimate an equation describing the behavior of
wage rates, or average hourly earnings; second, to relate the change in wage
rates to the changes in prices either by a simple mark-up theory or, more
ambitiously, by a price equation in which the wage, or some measure of labor
cost, is an explicit variable.

In the section immediately following, we review the pioneering work
and, briefly, some of the subsequent studies that have dealt with wage adjustments. Crude formulations of how wage changes influence price changes
relate the two directly; the fact that a price increase occurs only after wages
rise by an amount greater than the increase in productivity, for example, is
much too simple an explanation of price behavior. However, there are plausi-
ble explanations that make price behavior roughly symmetrical with wage
behavior. Therefore, for the purpose of this discussion, wage changes may be
viewed as a proxy for price changes without any reference to ultimate causal-
ity.

The Phillips curve

The first attempt to quantify the relationship between changes in wages
and unemployment was undertaken by Professor A. W. Phillips of the London School of Economics.[3] Phillips related wage changes to the percentage
of the labor force unemployed in the United Kingdom from 1861 to 1957. The
data revealed a fairly consistent inverse relationship during the period.

In the data for England, Phillips found that an annual increase in wages
equal to the general increase in productivity, *with prices remaining stable,* was
associated with an unemployment rate of about 2.5 percent. Stated another
way, unemployment rates below 2.5 percent would cause wages to increase
faster than productivity, and presumably would be associated with rising
prices. Since the wage level is both a cause and an effect of the price level,
the Phillips curve does not indicate whether wages push up prices, or prices

---

[2]Ronald G. Bodkin; Elizabeth P. Bond; Grant L. Reuber; and J. Russell Robinson, *Price Stability and High Employment: The Options for Canadian Economic Policy* (Ottawa: Economic Council of Canada, 1966), p. 7.

[3]A. W. Phillips, "The Relationship Between Unemployment and the Rate of Change of Money Wage Rates in the United Kingdom, 1861–1957," *Economica* (November 1958), pp. 283–299.

pull up wages. To keep money wages absolutely stable, Phillips suggested that the unemployment rate would have to rise to approximately 5.5 percent.

When graphed this relationship took the form of a nonlinear, downward sloping line. Such curves relating wage changes to the rate of unemployment have come to be known as "Phillips curves." Phillips' results are illustrated in Figure 20/2.

Figure 20/2.   The Phillips curve

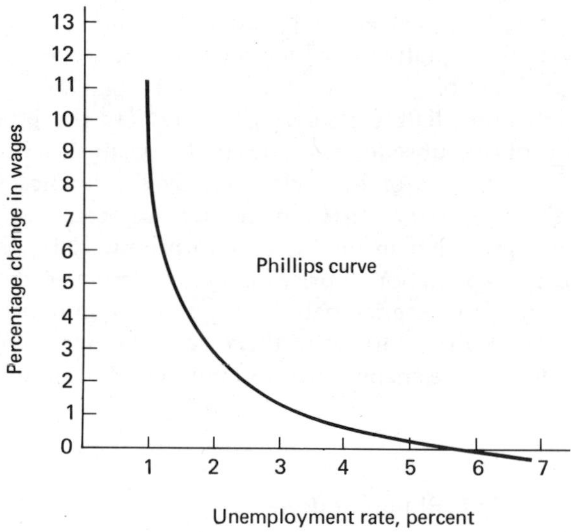

Unemployment rate, percent

The Phillips curve purports to show the rate at which wages will rise for any given level of unemployment. The downward slope of the Phillips curve indicates the inverse wage-change–unemployment relationship; that is, lower rates of unemployment are associated with faster rising wages, and vice versa. The nonlinearity of the Phillips curve indicates that a given reduction in the unemployment rate will cause a greater increase in wages the lower the initial level of unemployment. The intercept on the unemployment axis, A, indicates the rate of unemployment consistent with stable wages. Unemployment rates greater than A would cause wages to fall, and unemployment rates less than A would cause wages to rise.

The implications of a close, long-run relationship between wage changes and unemployment are many; the relationship indicated by the Phillips curve implies that movement towards a goal of full employment must be accompanied by rising wages. Thus, the Phillips curve suggests that there has to be a certain trade-off between unemployment and wage changes. In other words, to achieve a reduction in unemployment we must accept a rise in wage rates.

In summary, Phillips' conclusions concerning the wage-change–employment relationship are: (1) changes in the wage rate can be explained largely in terms of changes in the unemployment rate; (2) the relationship between wage changes and unemployment is nonlinear; and (3) the form of this relationship is quite stable over long periods of time. This study, though an important first step in the discussion of wage-change–employment relationships, suffers from being too restrictive; it pays little or no attention to variables other than the unemployment rate that may have significant independent effect on the wage change.

Following Phillips' work, a number of other analyses of the wage-adjustment mechanism have been made. These studies use the data of several countries—Britain, United States, France, West Germany, Canada, and Japan —and contain experiments with many variations in lag structure and in the choice of independent variables. Generally, the percentage change in wage rates or (as in the United States studies) the change in average hourly earnings from one quarter or year to the next is explained as a function of one or more of the following variables: the unemployment rate, the absolute or percentage rate of change of the unemployment rate; the rate of change in prices; the profit rate; and the change in the profit rate. The usual conclusion is that wages will tend to rise faster the lower the unemployment rate, the faster unemployment is falling, the faster prices are rising, the higher the profit rate, and the faster profits are rising.[4]

Studies in the mid-1960s of the situation in the United States suggested that, *if prices are held stable,* the annual wage increase associated with a 3 percent unemployment rate is between 4 and 5.5 percent. Alternatively, assuming a productivity increase of 2.5 percent a year and no change in prices, an unemployment rate of between 5.5 and 8.5 percent would be associated with an annual wage increase equal to the increase in productivity.[5] Recently the American economy has increased productivity at closer to 3 percent per annum. This improvement would tend to lower the expected rate of wage increase for any given rate of price increase and unemployment. On the other hand, rising prices (a dominant characteristic of the post-World War II economy) would tend to increase the expected rate of wage increase for any given rate of unemployment and productivity growth. Finally, the results of the studies suggest that, other things being equal, higher profits would cause wages to rise faster.

---

[4]For a summary of the literature, see Ronald G. Bodkin, *The Wage–Price Productivity Nexus* (Philadelphia: University of Pennsylvania Press, 1966), pp. 23–63; Ronald G. Bodkin et al., *Price Stability and High Employment,* pp. 31–75; and George L. Perry, *Unemployment, Money Wage Rates, and Inflation* (Cambridge: The M.I.T. Press, 1966), pp. 1–18.

[5]See R. G. Bodkin et al., *Price Stability and High Employment,* pp. 46–54 and pp. 67–75.

The conclusion widely drawn from these estimates is that low rates of unemployment are likely to be associated with wage increases that are greater than the increase in productivity. If wages increase faster than productivity, unit labor costs must rise; and sustained increases in the wage rate and labor costs are associated with a rising price level. These conclusions imply a permanent and rather discouraging trade-off between inflation and unemployment, the policy implication being that sustained inflation is necessary to the maintenance of low unemployment rates.

More recent studies emphasizing the role of price expectations in the labor market suggest that the inflation–unemployment trade-off is a short-run phenomenon; that is, that sustained inflation will not help to permanently lower unemployment rates.[6] The sharp increase in prices beginning in 1968, which was only temporarily interrupted by Phase I and Phase II controls in 1971–1972, and which in mid 1973 has approached an annual rate of 10 percent—accompanied by an unemployment rate that stubbornly refuses to fall below 5 percent—has made the conventional Phillips curve theory an unrealistic explanation of the current situation.

In modifying his earlier work, Perry argues that the rate of unemployment has become a poor proxy for a measure of labor-market tightness.[7] He notes that unemployment rates are high for women and teenagers who comprise an increasing share of the labor force and of the unemployed. These groups make a below-average contribution to total production, so that the shortfall of full-employment output at a given overall level of unemployment is less today than in the past.

Thus, with a 5 percent unemployment rate, the labor market is much tighter than at the same rate in the past and the upward pressure on wages and prices greater. In other words, the short-run Phillips curve is shifting still further to the right, a condition that makes a full-employment policy all the more unattainable.

Theories of inflation

Three of the more widely known theories of inflation are reviewed here. At one extreme is the traditional demand-pull theory, and at the other the more recent cost-push explanation. The latter is sometimes referred to as administered-price or sellers' theory of inflation. A third explanation is the structural or demand-shift theory.

---

[6]See Milton Friedman, "The Role of Monetary Policy," *American Economic Review*, LVIII (March 1968), 1–17; Robert E. Lucas, Jr., and Leonard A. Rapping, "Price Expectations and the Phillips Curve," *American Economic Review*, LIX (June 1969), 342–350; and E. S. Phelps, "Money Wage Dynamics and Labor Market Equilibrium," *Journal of Political Economy*, LXXVI (August 1968), 687–711.

[7]Perry's views are summarized in "Inflation versus Unemployment: The Worsening Trade-Off," *Monthly Labor Review*, February 1971.

Demand-pull inflation

Demand-pull inflation is characterized by an excess of aggregate demand, which in turn is explained in either of two ways: by the quantity theory of money or by Keynesian analysis.

The classical school of economists subscribed to the quantity theory of inflation; the price level is thought to be directly dependent on the quantity of money, and inflation is thought to occur when the quantity of money increases. More specifically, the crude formulation of the quantity theory of money ascribes inflation to the effect of increased money spending at the full-employment level of output. Increases in the volume of money lead to increased spending that, in a full-employment economy, can only bid up prices. A more sophisticated view of the process suggests that the increase in the quantity of money finds its way into the economy in the form of increased bank loans to finance investment. Investment then exceeds the current rate of saving, and hence, aggregate demand exceeds the full-employment supply of goods and services. The effect of the excess aggregate demand is to raise prices as buyers bid for the limited supply of goods. Inflation is halted when the supply of money ceases to expand.

The work of Keynes suggests another interpretation of the inflationary process.[8] In Keynesian analysis, as in the classical or quantity theory, inflation arises when aggregate demand exceeds the full-employment level of output. However, Keynes found that the determinants of aggregate demand emerged from a wide range of influences, not merely the quantity of money. In particular, Keynes viewed aggregate demand as the sum of the household sector's demand for consumption goods (C), the business sector's demand for investment goods (I), and the government sector's demand for goods (G). Aggregate demand $= C + I + G$. Whenever aggregate demand exceeds the full-employment level of aggregate supply, inflation occurs.

Keynesian demand-pull inflation has frequently been expressed in terms of an "inflationary gap." The "inflationary gap" concept is pictured in Figure 20/3, where aggregate demand is represented by the $C + I + G$ line and aggregate supply is represented by the 45° line. We know that equilibrium is achieved when aggregate demand equals aggregate supply, or when $Y = C + I + G$, where Y is aggregate supply. In our illustration, this occurs at the point of intersection of the aggregate demand function with the 45° line; that is, the equilibrium level of income is Y_e. But suppose the full-employment level of income (at the existing price level) is Y_f. In this case, the level of income cannot reach Y_e. At the full-employment income, Y_f, aggregate demand exceeds aggregate supply, leaving an "inflationary gap" of AB. The inflationary gap causes prices to rise. In short, prices rise because the demand for goods and services exceeds the supply available at existing prices.

---

[8]John Maynard Keynes, *The General Theory of Employment, Interest, and Money* (New York: Harcourt Brace Jovanovich, 1936).

Figure 20/3.   The inflationary gap

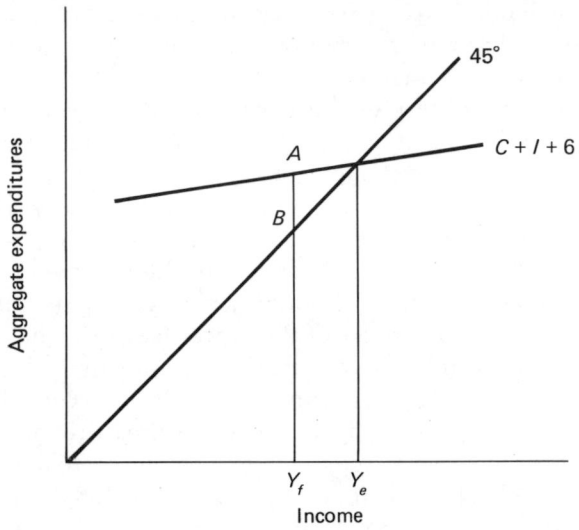

In the Keynesian theory inflation can be caused by a wide range of influences on the components of aggregate demand—consumption, investment, and government spending. Thus, the Keynesian theory breaks the direct link between the quantity of money and aggregate demand postulated by the quantity theory, and argues that the quantity indirectly affects prices through its effect on the components of aggregate demand. Despite these differences, both theories explain inflation, when it occurs, as the result of an excess aggregate demand.

In the case of demand-pull inflation, unions are thought to play a passive role. Excess demand tends to pull up prices. As prices rise, producers find themselves in a more profitable position, and attempt to expand output to meet the demand. In attempting to expand output, producers compete for the limited supply of labor, thus bidding up wages. Stated another way, the excess aggregate demand creates an excess demand for labor, and wages rise in response to the excess demand for labor. Under these conditions, wages would rise even in the absence of unions. Unions play a passive role, since the wage increases they demand are in response to the rising demand for labor. Thus, rising wages are a result of rising prices, and although unions play a part in the mechanics of inflation, they are not the cause.

It has even been suggested that the existence of unions tends to retard the rate of wage increase in periods of excess aggregate demand and rising prices,[9] because union wages are set by collective-bargaining agreements,

[9]See Albert E. Rees, "Postwar Wage Determination in the Basic Steel Industry," *American Economic Review*, XLI (June 1951), 389–404.

which extend over a period of two or three years; hence, workers cannot continuously bargain up their wages in response to rising demand. Under these conditions, unions are seen to create a lag in the response of wages to an increase in demand. They therefore may retard the rate of increase in wages.

Cost-push inflation

Demand-pull inflation can occur only when there is excess aggregate demand; cost-push inflation, however, can take place in the absence of such conditions. Simply stated, cost-push inflation occurs when *autonomous* increases in producers' costs are passed along as higher prices. If wages increase faster than productivity increases, unit labor costs rise. When such an increase in wages occurs (in the absence of excess aggregate demand) and the cost increases are passed along in the form of higher prices, cost-push inflation is said to occur. The possibility of this type of inflation turns on the ability of wages to rise, even without excess demand for labor, and the corollary ability of producers to pass cost increases along in the form of higher prices.

Cost-push inflation would not be possible in an economy of competitive labor markets; there, wages would rise only in response to changes in the demand for and supply of labor—the demand depending upon variations in the productivity of labor and aggregate demand for output. Therefore, cost-push inflation requires the existence of organized labor with sufficient strength to push up wages, even in the absence of any excess demand for labor. Where unions have such strength, wages can rise without such excess demand.

The ability of producers to pass cost increases along in the form of higher prices is also conditioned by the existing market structure. The degree to which a firm can raise price without a reduction in output and employment is dependent upon the elasticity of demand for its output: the more inelastic the demand, the greater the possibility of a price increase without a significant loss in sales. The *individual* firm faced with a perfectly elastic demand for its product (pure competition) finds it impossible to raise price in response to increasing costs. Such a price increase by a single firm loses the firm all its sales to the other firms in the industry. However, if the union secures an industrywide wage increase, cost-push inflation is at least a possibility, since all firms will raise price in response to the industrywide wage increase. Hence, no single firm need fear a substantial loss in sales to its competitors. Of course, the industry as a whole may lose sales to other industries, in the wake of its price increases.

Since the demand curves facing oligopolists or firms operating in very imperfect labor markets are less elastic than those in more competitive markets, such firms present unions with the best opportunities for securing wage increases in excess of productivity increases, with a minimum loss of jobs. It has been suggested also that in practice oligopolists set a price that is less than the profit-maximizing amount. If this is the case, oligopolists can increase their profit by increasing their price, even in the absence of an increase in demand; the possibility of cost-push inflation is thus much greater. Therefore, cost-push inflation, when it occurs, tends to be most pronounced in unionized, oligopolistic industries.

In summary, union wage increases in excess of the increase in productivity will lead producers to post higher prices. This is cost-push inflation. It requires no excess demand and can even occur when there is considerable unemployment. Obviously, the cost-push theory of inflation is based on the assumption that both unions and businesses have some significant degree of market power and therefore can increase wages and prices in the absence of any excess demand. Strong, aggressive unions are viewed by some observers as the initiators of the inflationary pressures.

Structural inflation

The structural theory of inflation holds that rising prices result from changes in the composition, not the total volume of demand.[10] Inflation arises through the effect of both demand-pull and cost-push forces; it is initiated by a shift in demand, and the price rise then is generalized through the economy by cost forces.

The structural theory reasons that due to the market power of unions and businesses, wages tend to be flexible upward but not downward. Wages and prices are therefore relatively insensitive to decreases in demand while they respond rather quickly to increases in demand. Consequently, a rapid shift in demand leads to a general rise in prices, even without a growth in the level of aggregate demand.

Suppose the level of aggregate demand remains the same, but its composition changes: an increase in the demand for the product of one particular industry and an equivalent reduction in the demand for the product of another industry. This structural change in demand will tend to bid up prices and wages in the industry experiencing an expanding demand. However, since prices are relatively inflexible downward, prices and wages in the industry experiencing a decline will remain the same, or decline only slightly. The net effect of rapidly rising prices in one industry and stable or slowly falling prices in another industry is a rise in the overall level of prices. Thus, the general level of prices and wages rises because of institutional factors that do not permit changes in relative prices and wages. It should be noted that inflation has been explained without resort to either an increase in aggregate

---

[10]Charles L. Schultze, "Recent Inflation in the United States," Study Paper no. 1 of the Joint Economic Committee's Study of Employment, Growth, and Price Levels, 86th Congress, 1st Session (Washington, D. C.: U. S. Government Printing Office, 1959).

demand or a cost-push from labor unions. It relies only on the assumption that businesses and labor unions have sufficient market power to maintain prices and wages, despite a fall in demand.

But this is not all. Secondary effects may intensify structural inflation by generalizing it to other sectors of the economy. One possibility is that workers in other industries, seeing that wages have risen in a particular sector, may also seek wage increases, even though there is no excess demand for labor in their industries. If unions are successful in obtaining wage increases in the absence of excess demand, unit labor costs rise in these industries. The firms in these industries then recover the cost of higher wages by raising product prices. Therefore, it is possible that wages and prices may rise in industries other than the one experiencing the initial increase in demand.

It is also possible that the product (for example, steel) of the industry initially experiencing the increase in demand—and rising wages and prices—is used in production in other industries. The rise in the price of this particular product raises costs in the industries using the product, and the rising costs tend to be reflected in rising prices. Again, prices and wages may rise in industries where there is no increase in demand.

A final possibility is that the initial rise in the general price level caused by the shift in demand will cause wages and prices to rise in many industries. If collective-bargaining agreements contain "escalator clauses," wages will automatically go up as the price level rises, the rising wages being reflected in an even higher price level. In summary, wage and price increases in the industries experiencing the increase in demand may spill over into other sectors of the economy, thereby strengthening the inflationary processes.

Unions play an important role in structural inflation. They do not create the inflation, but they generalize it to other sectors of the economy. The secondary effects discussed above depend almost entirely on the market power or strength of unions. Therefore, in the case of structural inflation, unions can be viewed as boosters of inflationary pressures that originated elsewhere in the economy.

These three theories of inflation are not mutually exclusive. All three forces may operate at one time: an inflationary period may be characterized by demand-pull, cost-push, and structural pressures in varying degrees. It follows that distinguishing between cost-push, demand-pull, and structural forces at the time the inflation is actually occurring is extremely difficult.

Unions and the postwar inflation

Have unions been a major cause of the postwar inflation? To this question there is something less than total agreement on the answer, which lies in the explanation of the postwar inflation: Has it been demand-pull, cost-push, structural, or some combination of the three? As we have seen, if inflation is pure demand-pull, unions play a passive role and have little or no effect on the price level. On the other hand, if the inflation is pure cost-push, unions play the dominant role in initiating the wage–price spiral. Finally, if inflation is entirely structural, unions can bolster and transmit the inflationary pressures through the economy.

Unfortunately, in the real world inflation is seldom exclusively demand-pull, cost-push, or structural; almost all inflationary periods are characterized by varying degrees of demand-pull, cost-push, and structural pressures. Thus, how major a cause unions have been of the postwar inflation can be identified only if we can isolate the inflationary pressures at work in the different years of this period. Let us see if some general conclusions can be drawn about unions and the postwar inflation, within this context.

The strongest burst of inflation occurred immediately after the end of World War II. Because of the wartime restrictions on consumption and investment, consumers and businesses had accumulated a substantial volume of savings. At the same time, the existing stock of consumers' and producers' durable goods had been greatly depleted. With the relaxation of wartime controls, effective demand exceeded supply in almost every industry. The results were high profits and rising prices and wages. It is now commonly agreed that the primary cause of the rising price level was demand-pull. If we accept this explanation, it is unlikely that the immediate postwar inflation can be attributed to union-induced wage increases. However, this does not exclude the possibility that unions played a substantial role in maintaining the existing inflationary pressures.

The next period of significant inflation coincided with the Korean War. Although there is somewhat less general agreement among economists, this era of rising prices again seems to have been the result of excess aggregate demand. With the outbreak of hostilities, consumers and businesses attempted to build up stocks of goods in expectation that wartime controls would be imposed on consumption and investment. This increase in demand for consumers' and producers' durables, combined with the increase in government military expenditures, produced an aggregate demand in excess of the existing supply. The results were rising prices and wages. Again, under these circumstances, unions could not be viewed as the primary cause of the inflation.

An interesting proposal by Albert Hart suggests that unions and businesses actually played important roles in the Korean War inflation,[11] that, anticipating wage and price controls, they tried to get their wages and prices up to a level where they would not be cramped once ceilings were imposed.

---

[11]See *Inflation: Its Causes, Consequences, and Control,* proceedings of a symposium (New York: New York University, 1968), pp. 19–20.

Therefore, he characterizes the inflation as an "expectational cost-push" process. If this indeed was true, unions and businesses played a primary role in the inflationary process. However, the Korean War inflation seems to have resulted primarily from demand-pull forces, with the possibility of additional cost-push forces. Unions can be viewed as a positive force in the inflationary process, but probably not the major force.

The next period of general inflation occurred during the three years from 1956 through 1958. This period of rising prices presented a drastically different causal pattern. In contrast to the two preceding periods, excess aggregate demand in the traditional sense was not present; unemployment was consistently above 4 percent; and there was no general shortage of goods. Price increases were largely concentrated in a few important sectors of the economy, especially in the metals (steel) and machinery industries.

The 1956–1958 inflation was characterized by an investment-goods boom, with significant cost-push elements.[12] Demand forces are thought to have been an important factor in the process. However, it was not excess demand in the traditional sense, but demand concentrated in one or two particular industries. Shifts in demand led to an overall rise in the price level, with the investment-goods industries leading the way. Consequently, this period of inflation conforms reasonably well to the structural or demand-shift theory. Thus, though it appears that the 1956–1958 inflation was initiated by a sudden shift in the composition of demand, there is little doubt that unions played a major role in fostering and transmitting these inflationary pressures through the economy.

The final period of inflation has been from 1966 to the present. During the first part of this period, unemployment was low and economic activity high. Inflation again seemed to be attributable to a number of factors: the high level of aggregate demand caused in part by the Vietnam War and expansionary monetary and fiscal policies; significant wage increases in several industries in excess of productivity growth; significant increases in demand in certain sectors; etc. It is difficult to ascribe the inflation to any single cause. However, unions can be viewed as playing an important role in the inflation, if not initiating it at least in transmitting it through the economy. In more recent years, since 1969, we have had stronger inflation with high unemployment, a pattern contrary to Phillips' curve analysis. It is still too soon to attribute causes to this phenomenon, but most observers consider unions an active participant in the group of inflationary forces.

In summary, the role played by unions has varied from one postwar inflationary period to another. Although they may have not been the primary cause of inflation, they have certainly not been an entirely passive element

---

[12]See Joint Economic Committee, U. S. Congress, *Staff Report on Employment, Growth, and Price Levels* (Washington, D. C.: U. S. Government Printing Office, 1960).

in the process. The evidence seems to indicate that unions have been a notable factor in the upward bias of wages and prices in the postwar period, especially since the mid-1950s.

The policy dilemma

Clearly, there are certain policy implications emerging from the dilemma now facing the economy. The wage-change–unemployment trade-off (the Phillips curve) and the analagous inflation–unemployment trade-off are, at least in the short run, salient features of our economy. Simultaneous full employment and wage–price stability seem unattainable, given the present tools of fiscal and monetary policy.

If, as indicated in the Employment Act of 1946, full employment is to continue to be a goal of economic policy, rising wages and prices seem to be unavoidable. Suggestions for controlling wage and price increases continue to be made, the usual basis for control being that wage and price increases on the average should be no greater than the overall increase in productivity.

Leaving aside the question of whether productivity gains are the appropriate standard for wage and price determination, several mechanisms for the implementation of such a policy have been suggested. Proposals have run the gamut—voluntary self-restraint by unions and businesses; wage and price review boards; the government, representing public interest, as a part in wage negotiations; and, in the extreme case, direct wage and price controls.

In its 1962 report the Council of Economic Advisors suggested one such mechanism, the voluntary guideposts for noninflationary wage and price behavior. However, experience has shown the guideposts to be rather ineffective in controlling inflation. With the failure of the voluntary guideposts and the continuing pressure for full employment, the possibility of some government activity in the area of wage and price setting was frequently discussed, until controls were actually imposed.

Incomes policy—the Guideposts

In Europe, where the policy was first followed, government measures that tied wage and price changes to productivity growth are called *incomes policy*. The United States, following the European pattern, set informal Guideposts, first spelled out in the 1962 Council Report, which exhorted, but did not require, firms and workers, operating mainly through their unions, to connect their price and wage behavior to the nation's average productivity growth.

While it is impossible to assign the "blame" for inflation when wages outrun productivity advances, it is true that if wages are held within the limits set by productivity increases, much of the inflationary pressure is eased. The

Guidepost formula has called for wage increases of about 3 percent, the average long-term annual productivity growth for American industry as a whole, and "appropriate price adjustments."

To conclude what is "appropriate" for price adjustment, consider a two-industry economy, one industry with a 5 percent increase in productivity, the other with only a 1 percent gain. If the first industry decreased prices by 2 percent and the second raised prices by the same percentage, the overall price level would remain stable, and wages and profits would rise by the same 3 percent in both industries.

The Guideposts suffer from two basic shortcomings. First, required price adjustments might not match market forces in the two sectors. Suppose demand is very strong in the sector with the relatively greater gain in productivity, and very weak in the other sector. Calling for price declines in the former and price increases in the latter might be just the opposite of what is needed to clear product markets in both sectors.

Second, Guideposts can only work under conditions of cost-push inflation. If demand-pull elements are operating, then workers and firms would be given the impossible task of maintaining wages and prices in a situation of excess demand. Price would not serve its market-rationing function.

Despite these weaknesses, Guideposts seemed to work for a time. From 1962 to 1965, and especially immediately following the 1964 tax cut, unemployment fell and prices remained more or less stable. But from 1966 onward, prices rose steadily and sharply, the Guideposts were discredited and discarded, and the public became disillusioned with inflation control through voluntary decisions and "jawboning." Eventually, in 1971, with prices showing no signs of abatement, the administration imposed direct controls on wages and prices.

Wage and price controls

Phase I of the control program, which put an absolute freeze on wages and prices, lasted for the three-month period August 15–November 15, 1971. Theoretically, when a freeze is established and excess demand is present, shortages should appear. But the freeze period was too short to conclude that significant demand-push forces were not behind the inflation because there was no evidence of significant shortages during the three months. Furthermore, with a 6 percent unemployment rate then, circumstantial evidence points to cost-push as an important source of inflation.

Phase II was strongly reminiscent of the Guideposts, with one crucial exception; there was much less volunteerism and Wage and Pay Boards were established to monitor changes. But the old Guidepost formula seemed to lie behind the Boards' policies. The administration set a 2 percent–2.5 percent annual price increase as its anti-inflation goal, and the Boards set 5.5 percent as the standard wage increase, which assuming a 3+ percent annual productivity growth, figures out to the Guidepost wage formula, modified to allow for a small price rise.

Early in 1973, Phase III was instituted, which in effect simply lifted the Phase II regulations and controls. Immediately, the Consumer Price Index started to rise at the sharp rate of almost one percent per month. It is still too soon to analyze the Administration's reasoning in lifting controls at that time. But one strong possibility is that it realized that demand-pull forces were very strong, considering our booming economy, and that labor and price setters were not about to be confined by Phase II limits, especially during the many collective-bargaining negotiations scheduled later in 1973.

The current alternative means to checking inflation seem to center on monetary and fiscal policies to take the steam out of the boom, or even more rigid controls, rationing, etc. The first alternative seems the most likely to be adopted.

Readings

Bodkin, Richard G. *The Wage-Price-Productivity Nexus.* Philadelphia: University of Pennsylvania Press, 1966.

Bowen, William G., and Stanley H. Masters, "Shifts in the Composition of Demand and the Inflation Problem," *American Economic Review,* 54 (December 1964), 975–984.

Bronfenbrenner, M., and F. D. Holzman, "Survey of Inflation Theory," *American Economic Review,* 53 (September 1963), 593–661.

Friedman, Milton, "What Price Guideposts?" in George P. Schultz and Robert Z. Aliber, eds. *Guideposts, Informal Controls, and the Market Place.* Chicago: University of Chicago Press, 1966.

Hansen, Bent. *A Study of the Theory of Inflation.* London: Allen & Unwin, 1951.

Keynes, J. M. *The General Theory of Employment, Interest, and Money.* New York: Harcourt Brace Jovanovich, 1936.

Kuhn, A., "Market Structures and Wage-Push Inflation," *Industrial and Labor Relations Review,* 12 (January 1959), 243–251.

Phillips, A. W., "The Relation between Unemployment and the Rate of Change of Money Wage Rates in the United Kingdom, 1861–1957," *Economica,* 25 (December 1958), 283–299.

Samuelson, Paul A., and Robert M. Solow, "Analytical Aspects of Anti-Inflation Policy," *American Economic Review,* 50 (May 1960) 177–194.

Schultze, Charles L. *Recent Inflation in the United States,* Joint Economic Committee, Study Paper No. 2., 86th Congress. Washington, D. C.: U. S. Government Printing Office, 1959.

Sheahan, John. *The Wage-Price Guideposts.* Washington, D. C.: The Brookings Institution, 1967.

Solow, Robert M., "The Case Against the Case Against Guideposts," in George P. Schultz and Z. Aliber, eds. *Guideposts, Informal Controls, and the Market Place.* Chicago: University of Chicago Press, 1966.

Introduction: Who are the minorities?

Blacks

    Labor-force participation
    Occupational levels
    Income levels

Women

    Labor force participation
    Occupational levels
    Income levels

Commonalities

Contrasts

Chapter Twenty-one

Minority Groups in the Labor Force

Introduction: Who are the minorities?

The problems of minority groups in the labor force offer challenges to the development of manpower policies that aid in the efficient use of human resources, and to improvement in the social and political status of these groups of people. Their underutilization in the labor force is merely a part of the larger question of informal and formal discrimination. The term "minority" as it applies to certain groups in the labor force does not merely denote racial or ethnic minorities or numerical minorities; it may describe any "disadvantaged" group of workers. Thus, although they comprise slightly more than half of our total population, women may be considered (and are in fact, numerically) a minority group in the labor force. Similarly, handicapped and older workers suffer disadvantages, as do racial minorities such as blacks, Spanish-Americans, and American Indians.

While only two major groups, blacks and women, will be dealt with here, all minority groups in the labor force, regardless of whether their minority status is based on race, color, sex, or age, are confronted by varying degrees of disadvantage. Inequities in hiring and promotion, a concentration in the lower levels of the occupational structure, and comparatively low wages characterize the situation of minorities in the labor force. Often the disadvantages of such groups are the result of earlier handicaps in education and training, limited occupational and geographic mobility, and particular cultural, social, and psychological factors, which may or may not be the result of discrimination.

As minority groups constitute an important segment of our human capital, their participation in the labor force warrants more detailed consideration.

Blacks

The nation's largest racial minority group, the more than 22 million blacks, is also the most obviously disadvantaged minority in the labor force. During the past decade, the civil rights movement has turned public attention to their problems, and as progress has been made in securing equal rights of citizenship to this excluded segment of our society interest has come increasingly to focus on black employment problems. The experience of blacks in the labor force illustrates the interrelationship of poverty and discrimination, two key domestic issues that are particularly important for students of labor economics.

Labor-force participation

The economic expansion of the past decade that has increased the demand for manpower has had significant effects on the employment situation of blacks. While there was a 24 percent rise in employment of white workers between 1961 and 1972, black employment increased by 26 percent, or 1.8 million. The aggregate labor-force picture for recent years is one of a relatively greater advance in the economic position of blacks, but the gains in job opportunities have not eliminated the severe discrepancies in the unemployment rates, occupational levels, and wages of black workers as compared to white workers.

To review the earlier discussion on racial differences in work activity, the labor-force participation rate of nonwhites has traditionally been higher than that of whites, but during recent years this higher rate has held only for females. When separated by sex and color, some significant differences appear. The participation rate of the white male (80 percent) is higher than that of the nonwhite male (74 percent), while the white female rate (43 percent) is much lower than that of the nonwhite female (49 percent). Further scrutiny of the figures, by age and sex, shows that the participation rate of nonwhite male teenagers is lower than that of white male teenagers; a similar pattern holds for those workers over forty-five years of age. While nonwhite teenage girls have the lowest participation rate, the percentage of nonwhite women in the labor force rises steadily and exceeds that of white females among those women above twenty-four years of age. That a greater proportion of black women work may be explained by the high incidence of poverty among black families, the large number of fatherless families, and the fact that job opportunities for blacks of low educational levels are better for women, who become household workers and fill other low-level jobs, than for males.

Unemployment rates offer another vantage point from which to assess the status of blacks in the labor force. Although the increases in black employment from 1961 to 1972 reduced the unemployment rate by nearly 19 percent (from 12.4 to 10.0 percent), the rate was still twice that of white workers. As the unemployment rate rose after 1969 the black rate remained at about twice the white rate: 10.0 to 5.0 percent. The problem for black teenagers is particularly acute; in fact, the gap between white and nonwhite teenagers' rates of unemployment is not closing. Poor quality education and higher school dropout rates offer a partial explanation for the lack of improvement, and substantiate the need for manpower programs aimed at this group.

While they offer one index of the disadvantage suffered by blacks in the labor force, comparisons of employment and unemployment rates do not reveal the entire picture. The concept of the labor force as "those employed and those unemployed" is not entirely adequate for purposes of examining the situation of blacks; it obscures the existence of "hidden unemployment," which is significant within this minority group. The distinction emphasized in Chapter 3 between the unemployed and those who are out of the labor force is particularly relevant to blacks, who are often able to work but are so apathetic or discouraged about the prospects of a job that they either have never entered or have dropped out of the labor market. Hence, they are not included as members of the work force, and not counted among the unemployed.

To the extent that there are potential workers who would enter or reenter the labor force if jobs were available, there is some concealed unemployment that is not reflected in unemployment rates. Although the size of this segment of potential workers is difficult to estimate, studies that compare the participation rates of white and nonwhite workers by age, sex, and education over time indicate that the true black rate of unemployment is about three times, rather than twice, that of white workers.[1]

In the labor market blacks also suffer from, among other things, disproportionately high representation among the ranks of the long-term unemployed, among the workers who experience several periods of unemployment during the year, and among those who must settle for part-time work. These facts have been explained by the queue theory of the labor market,[2] or the notion that the "last hired is the first fired." The queue theory holds that there is a continuum of workers, arranged in order of their desirability to employers, and that different groups of the labor force are located at various points along the continuum. Workers at the higher end of the queue are the most attractive to employers and experience little change in their employment situation as the aggregate demand for labor expands and contracts. The workers concentrated at the lower end of the continuum, however, are more sensitive to changes in the aggregate demand for labor, and thus their employment situation is much less stable. When the demand for labor expands, employers extend their choices farther down the continuum; as the demand for labor contracts, employers are able to choose those workers near the higher end.

Applying the queue theory to blacks in the labor force helps to explain why their employment gains are relatively higher than those of other workers

---

[1]See Charles C. Killingsworth, "Negroes in a Changing Labor Market," in Arthur M. Ross and Herbert Hill, eds. *Employment, Race, and Poverty* (New York: Harcourt Brace Jovanovich, 1967), p. 62.

[2]See Lester C. Thurow, *Poverty and Discrimination* (Washington, D. C.: The Brookings Institution, 1969), pp. 46–64.

Table 21/1. Employed persons, by occupation group, color, and sex, selected years, 1959–70

Occupation group	1970 White Male	1970 White Female	1970 Negro and other races Male	1970 Negro and other races Female	1969 White Male	1969 White Female	1969 Negro and other races Male	1969 Negro and other races Female	1968 White Male	1968 White Female	1968 Negro and other races Male	1968 Negro and other races Female
All occupation groups:												
Number (thousands)	44,157	26,025	4,803	3,642	44,048	25,470	4,770	3,614	43,411	24,340	4,702	3,467
Percent	100.0	100.0	100.0	100.0	100.0	100.0	100.0	100.0	100.0	100.0	100.0	100.0
Professional, technical, and kindred workers	14.6	15.0	7.8	10.8	14.6	14.3	7.0	10.0	14.1	14.6	6.6	9.5
Farmers and farm managers	3.6	.3	1.7	.1	3.8	.3	1.6	.2	4.0	.3	2.0	.2
Managers, officials, and proprietors, except farm	15.3	4.8	4.7	1.9	14.8	4.7	4.2	1.5	14.7	4.9	3.6	1.6
Clerical and kindred workers	7.1	36.4	7.4	20.8	7.0	36.3	7.6	19.9	7.1	36.0	7.1	18.3
Salesworkers	6.1	7.7	1.8	2.5	5.9	7.6	1.8	2.3	6.1	7.6	1.7	2.2
Craftsmen, foremen, and kindred workers	20.8	1.2	13.8	.8	20.8	1.2	14.2	.9	20.9	1.2	13.4	.8
Operatives and kindred workers	18.7	14.1	28.3	17.6	19.4	15.0	28.2	18.3	19.3	15.0	28.2	17.4
Private household workers	.1	3.4	.3	17.5	.1	3.5	.3	19.4	.1	3.8	.3	22.1
Service workers, except private household	6.0	15.3	12.8	25.6	5.9	14.9	13.2	24.8	6.0	14.4	14.2	25.1
Farm laborers and foremen	1.7	1.5	3.9	1.5	1.7	1.7	4.3	1.8	1.9	1.8	4.8	2.3
Laborers, except farm and mine	6.2	.4	17.5	.7	6.1	.5	17.8	.8	5.9	.4	18.1	.6

Table 21/1. (continued)

	1967				1966				1965				1959			
	White		Negro and other races		White		Negro and other races		White		Negro and other races		White		Negro and other races	
	Male	Female	Male	Female	Male	Female	Male	Female	Male	Female	Male	Female	Male	Female	Male	Female
	42,834	23,528	4,646	3,366	42,331	22,690	4,588	3,288	41,844	21,601	4,496	3,147	39,493	18,512	3,972	2,652
	100.0	100.0	100.0	100.0	100.0	100.0	100.0	100.0	100.0	100.0	100.0	100.0	100.0	100.0	100.0	100.0
	13.8	14.4	6.2	9.1	13.2	14.1	5.8	8.7	12.8	13.9	5.7	8.5	11.2	12.9	3.6	6.1
	4.1	.4	2.2	.2	4.4	.5	2.4	.5	4.7	.5	2.7	.5	6.8	.6	5.5	.6
	14.4	4.8	3.4	1.5	14.4	4.9	3.4	1.5	14.5	4.9	3.4	1.6	14.6	5.5	2.8	2.0
	7.2	35.6	7.3	16.6	7.2	35.4	6.7	13.5	7.2	34.7	5.7	11.8	7.0	33.1	5.1	7.6
	6.0	7.8	1.5	2.0	6.1	8.0	1.7	1.9	6.1	8.3	1.6	2.0	6.3	8.8	1.2	1.4
	20.9	1.1	12.8	.6	20.7	1.0	12.6	.7	20.2	1.1	11.1	.7	20.2	1.1	9.5	.5
	19.6	15.3	28.1	17.1	20.1	15.7	27.5	15.9	20.1	15.3	26.4	14.5	19.3	15.6	23.8	14.2
	.1	3.9	.2	24.5	.1	4.2	.3	27.8	.1	4.5	.4	30.1	(1)	5.2	.4	36.1
	6.1	14.5	14.7	24.8	6.1	14.1	15.3	25.7	5.9	14.1	15.1	24.7	5.4	13.4	14.1	21.7
	2.0	1.8	4.8	2.8	1.9	2.0	4.9	3.3	2.1	2.2	6.9	4.8	2.7	3.5	9.0	9.1
	5.9	.4	18.8	.8	6.0	.4	19.6	.6	6.3	.4	21.0	.7	6.4	.4	25.1	.8

[1] Less than 0.05 percent.
Source: Department of Labor: Handbook of Labor Statistics, 1971, Bulletin 1705.

during periods of economic expansion. Conversely, as the aggregate demand for labor contracts and brings an increase in unemployment, they suffer higher rates of joblessness.

Occupational levels

Although the labor force as a whole has moved rapidly toward higher level occupations during recent years, blacks continue to be concentrated in the less skilled and service jobs. In 1969, about 18 percent of nonwhites were employed as service workers—almost twice the figure for whites. Similarly, 8.5 percent of nonwhite workers were private household employees, as compared to 1.3 percent of white workers. While blacks have made encouraging gains in white-collar fields, increasing their percentage in such occupations from 13.8 in 1958 to 26.2 in 1969, the percentage of white workers in white-collar jobs remains significantly higher (49.8 percent) and the *proportionate* share of such jobs held by blacks is virtually unchanged. The percentage of blacks in blue-collar occupations has remained essentially the same during this period, but within this general category (which accounts for about 43 percent of all black workers) the number of skilled workers, craftsmen, and foremen, has increased.

Examination of Table 21/1 on the employment share of occupational groups and subclasses shows some improvement in black job status over a recent decade. The occupations more or less follow the occupational hierarchy from top to bottom. There are a few exceptions; farmers and farm managers in fact hold executive positions, and protective service workers hold positions of trust and some responsibility.

While just a glance at the table reveals the relatively low occupational status of the black, as we see his employment share rising as our eye moves down the occupational ladder, closer study shows some improvement. This trend of higher share of lower jobs is noticeably less pronounced for 1970 than for 1959.

Judged by occupational levels, the position of blacks in the labor force evidences some encouraging signs but, again, the complex factors that account for these changes in racial patterns of employment suggest that quantitative evaluations of the black's progress cannot be easily generalized; the institution of slavery left its stamp upon him and even one hundred years later its effects on his experience in the labor force can be seen. After the Civil War, regional migration of the black from the South to the North and West was accompanied in rough measure by occupational mobility; he left agricultural employment in the rural South for nonagricultural work in the urban North. While this geographic redistribution favored an occupational upgrading, blacks were severely disadvantaged in education and training and were culturally and socially deprived—factors that limited their movement up the occupational ladder. Discrimination further restricted the black's progress and strengthened the tradition of "Negro jobs," the more strenuous and dirty chores at the bottom of the occupational ladder. Spurred by a labor shortage and government activity in developing training programs and antidiscrimination policies, blacks made substantial gains during the 1940s, and these gains extended in the prosperity of the Korean War period.

While there has been clear evidence of a trend towards absolute improvement in the black's job status, there is some doubt whether there has also been a relative increase compared to the long-run upgrading of the white work force. The question is not an unimportant one; cross-sectional comparisons between races have more social significance than the improvement in the black occupational level over generations.

In a long-run comparison of the racial composition of the skilled and unskilled the black percentage has increased in both groups. This change came about because both groups moved towards the skilled occupations, away from the unskilled classifications in which the blacks were strongly represented to the jobs dominated by white participation. That relatively fewer blacks than whites rose to the better jobs explains the increase in black share in each group, but more importantly, also reflects a relative lack of improvement in black occupational status.

Although it is generally concluded that the economic status of the black has improved, at least absolutely if not relatively, during most of the period following World War II, the overriding importance of heavy unemployment among them greatly slowed the movement from about 1955 to 1965. In fact, had there not been significant occupational upgrading of blacks during the last two decades, they would probably have lost income relative to that of whites. Deterioration in the employment opportunities for black males, which has been blamed for many of the difficulties confronting black families, has been only partially offset by the higher participation rate of black females. Extremely high rates of unemployment among black youth, both male and female, indicating poor entrée for them into the labor force, have resulted in frequent withdrawals from the work force on the part of teenage blacks.

The black's low position in the occupational structure can also be attributed to certain social forces. They tend to live in predominately segregated neighborhoods and this residential pattern often produces racial job patterns. Job possibilities and work experience are often inferior in segregated neighborhoods; thus, even skilled and educated workers face added difficulty in upgrading their employment. There is little information about jobs outside the segregated neighborhood, with respect to both work in other areas and other types of jobs. Both external and internal forces encourage the black to apply for those jobs to which he has traditionally been relegated and about which he is likely to have information.

Even with improved motivation and more knowledge about employment possibilities, the black will continue to be disadvantaged in the labor market as long as his education and training are inferior. Educational and skill deficiencies are slowly being corrected, but the gap between blacks and whites remains wide. The median years of school completed by those eighteen years and older for all occupational groups is 12.4 for white workers as opposed to 11.3 for black workers. The differential is greater for black males (10.8 as opposed to 12.4 for white males) than for black females (11.9 as compared to 12.4 for white females). The progress of blacks into white-collar jobs has been a function not only of the overall expansion of employment in those fields, but also of the educational advances of blacks in recent years. The gains are most appreciable when educational attainment by age is examined. The proportion of blacks aged 25 to 29 who have completed high school is twice the proportion among those 45 to 54 years old, and four times that of those aged 55 to 64, according to 1969 data.

The gap in the number of school years completed widens at higher levels of education, so that while 6.7 percent of blacks in the labor force in 1969 had completed four years or more of college—almost triple the percentage twenty years earlier—the percentage for white workers was twice as high.

The rising educational levels of blacks have been encouraged by the patterns of migration from the South to the North and West, where the educational attainment of the population is generally higher. Yet even within the North, comparisons of the median years of education can be somewhat misleading, because of the great disparity in the quality of education for blacks and whites. Despite efforts at school integration, de facto segregation accounts for quite substantial differences in the adequacy of Negro schooling. Real inequalities of educational opportunity are reflected in studies such as the 1965 Coleman Report, which showed that the average black student in the twelfth grade scores at a ninth-grade level on achievement tests, a level three years behind that of the average white student.

To the inadequacy of the black's formal schooling must be added the deficiencies of his vocational training, which further hinders occupational progress. Vocational and apprenticeship training has to an extent reinforced racial job patterns. Training for traditional "Negro" jobs perpetuates the occupational caste system. The lack of sufficient educational credentials excludes many blacks from vocational schools and apprenticeship programs. Although the discrimination that earlier characterized apprenticeship training trades and barred blacks (who were thought to lower the status of trained craftsmen) has been reduced, racial prejudice still impedes their progress in the skilled trades. Improvement in on-the-job training and job experience is a primary need if the inequities that derive from the black's occupational status are to be corrected.

Income levels

All of these factors that militate against blacks in the labor force contribute to striking disparities in the earnings of white and black workers, although the differential has decreased substantially in recent years.

Differentials in earnings continue to raise the question of job discrimination against blacks; they also provide a rough measure of the status of this minority group in the work force. Bearing in mind the effects of unemployment, lower level jobs, and greater frequency of part-time work, income differences between whites and blacks testify to the fact that a segment of our society is not sharing proportionately in the rewards of increased national production.

The data in Table 21/2 indicate the large differences between the median incomes of white and black families. While improvement in employment opportunities and occupational advances have provided rapid percentage gains in income during the last decade—more rapid than those for white

Table 21/2. Median income in 1947 to 1970 of families, by race of head (in current dollars)

Year	Total	White	Negro and other races	Ratio of Negro and other races to white
1970	$9 867	$10 236	$6 516	0.64
1969	9 433	9 794	6 191	0.63
1968	8 632	8 937	5 590	0.63
1967	7 974	8 274	5 141	0.62
1966	7 500	7 792	4 674	0.60
1965	6 957	7 251	3 994	0.55
1964	6 569	6 858	3 839	0.56
1963	6 249	6 548	3 465	0.53
1962	5 956	6 237	3 330	0.53
1961	5 737	5 981	3 191	0.53
1960	5 620	5 835	3 233	0.55
1959	5 417	5 643	2 917	0.52
1958	5 087	5 300	2 711	0.51
1957	4 971	5 166	2 764	0.54
1956	4 783	4 993	2 628	0.53
1955	4 421	4 605	2 549	0.55
1954	4 173	4 339	2 410	0.56
1953	4 233	4 392	2 461	0.56
1952	3 890	4 114	2 338	0.57
1951	3 709	3 859	2 032	0.53
1950	3 319	3 445	1 869	0.54
1949	3 107	3 252	1 650	0.51
1948	3 187	3 310	1 768	0.53
1947	3 031	3 157	1 614	0.51

Source: Bureau of the Census, Current Population Reports, Income in 1970 of Families and Persons in the U.S., Series P-60, No. 80, p. 24.

families—there still exists a substantial dollar difference in incomes by race. Other data reveal that the differential for those in the highest income level was substantially greater than it was ten years earlier, despite the fact that the median income for blacks in this category rose by slightly more than 50 percent during the same period. While the dollar rise has been greatest for those in the highest income level, the percentage gains have been the most rapid for those in the lowest level, more than a 100 percent change from 1959 to 1968. The median family income of blacks was $6,516 in 1970, an advance of about 63 percent over the 1965 figure, but nonetheless still substantially below the corresponding figure of $10,236 for white families in 1970.

A favorable trend in the average income of blacks can also be observed in the rising number and percent of black families that have moved into the middle-income groups. The proportion of black families in metropolitan areas that had incomes of $10,000 or more tripled from 1959 to 1968, so that nearly one-fourth of the 3.3 million metropolitan black families are now in that category. But again it should be emphasized that relative income gain for blacks does not reflect on improvement in their occupational status. The income gain is due to migration to higher-income areas and the relative earnings gain of lower paid jobs.[3]

Women

The civil rights struggle for the economic and social advance of blacks during the past quarter-century was joined at the end of the 1960s by another fight, that of equality for women. While the struggle has not yet developed political support nor identified common objectives, an important (if not central) issue is the improved economic status of women, specifically their status in the labor force. Women, like blacks, suffer disadvantages in the labor market; both groups are easily identifiable since they are visible, and the factors leading to their disadvantages are equally complex. Income differentials and occupational levels suggest that the working woman has yet to enjoy full equality of employment opportunity and further, that the economy has yet to utilize fully an important human resource—womanpower. The fact that women accounted for about two-thirds of the growth in the labor force from 1940 to 1972, and that they now constitute almost two-fifths of all workers, is adequate reason for promoting the optimum allocation of this resource.

---

[3]Orley Ashenfelter, "Changes in Labor Market Discrimination Over Time," *Journal of Human Resources* (Fall 1970), found some improvement in the relative occupational status of black women, but none for black men over the period 1950–1961.

*Figure 21/1.   Labor–force participation rates of
married women by presence and age of children,
March 1960 to March 1972*

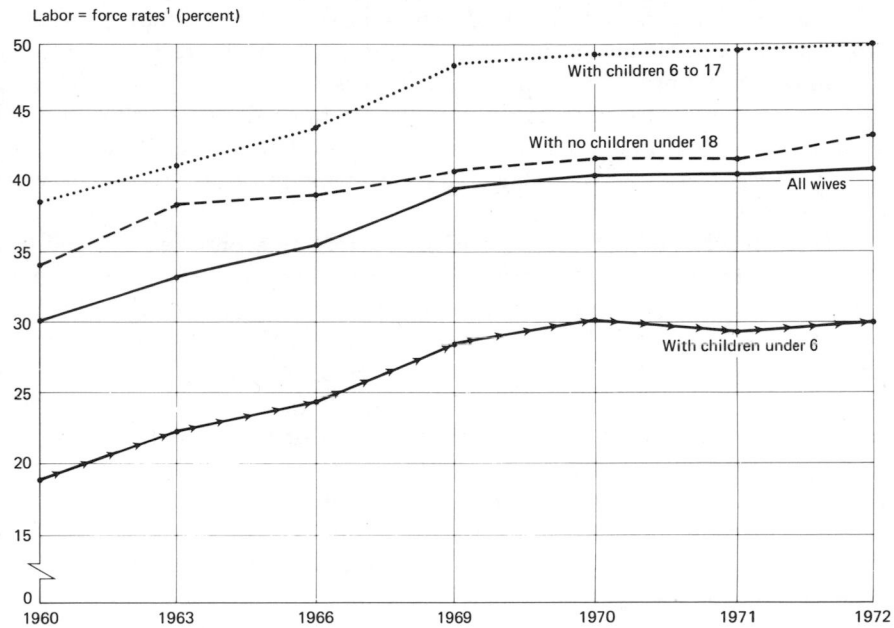

Labor = force rates¹ (percent)

¹Labor force as percent of population.
Source: Manpower Report of the President, 1973, p. 168.

Labor-force participation

The 33.2 million women workers represent 38 percent of the labor force today—a striking advance in the number and proportion of women in the work force since the turn of the century when only 18 percent (or 5 million workers) were women; and the number and proportion of married women who work outside the home has grown sharply in the past decade (See Figure 21/1). Wartime employment had caused an earlier high of 36 percent in July of 1944, when about 20 million women were in the labor force, but the proportion decreased markedly following the return of male veterans.

The growth in population and the increase in life expectancy of women, which has resulted in a changed ratio of women to men, have been important factors in this female labor-force growth. In addition to the demographic sources of the rise, there have been the following significant economic and social developments (discussed in earlier chapters): shift from an agricultural to an industrial and service-based economy and the resultant growth of employment opportunities in urban-centered activities; technological advances that have brought labor-saving devices to the home; and broadened opportunities for education and training that have improved women's job qualifications. Cultural changes have also modified the attitudes toward women workers, so that it has become socially acceptable for women to work outside the home.

These forces have led to a changing pattern in women's lives and to a dramatic shift in female employment patterns. The fact that the life expectancy of a baby girl born today is about 74 years, when in 1900 it was only 48 years, has made possible a longer worklife. Female labor-force participation varies with marital status and the presence of children; yet even a woman who marries and has children (both of which tend to happen early in a woman's life) can expect to have twenty-five to thirty years in the work force after her children have entered school. Whether they marry or not, about nine out of ten women are employed outside the home at some time during their lives. For single women, the work pattern is similar to that for men; they tend to work most of their lives. In fact, the worklife is slightly longer for the single woman than for the average man. The average worklife for married women who remain married and childless is about ten years shorter than that of a single woman. A substantial percentage of widowed, divorced, or separated women return to the labor force once they no longer have husbands; such women can expect at age 35 to average about 28 more years at work.

Much has been written regarding the social and psychological encouragements for women to join the labor force, and among a select group these factors are important. But traditionally most women have worked out of economic necessity; few women or men have had the option of working solely for personal fulfillment. Far more have needed the financial rewards of a job to keep their families or themselves out of poverty. Even when other family members contribute to income, many women feel that work outside the home is necessary to raise family living standards, or to help provide for the education of children.

Today, the typical woman worker is 40 years old and married. The median age of women workers has risen during the twentieth century and a shift toward higher labor-force participation among mature women is evident. While the general pattern for a male worker is to enter the labor force after school and remain at work until retirement, a woman's work usually occurs in two phases. After her education she takes a job, then drops out of the labor force to marry and have children, eventually returning to employment when the children have entered school. The changing worklife pattern of women is reflected in the fact that similar percentages of women 20 to 24 years old and 45 to 54 years old are in the labor force (See Figure 21/2).

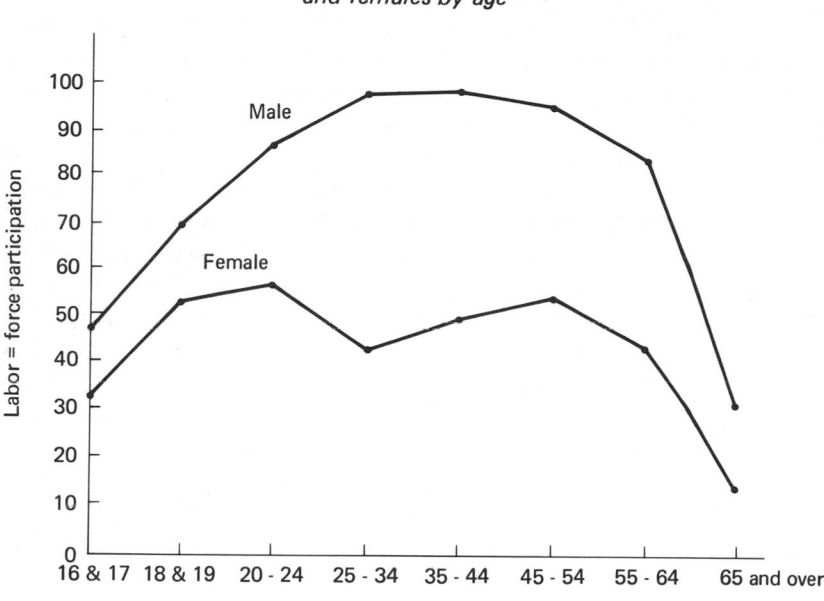

Figure 21/2.   Labor force participation rates of males and females by age

Source: U.S. Department of Labor, Manpower Report of the President, 1970, pp. 216–217.

This work pattern of married women has had a significant impact on the shape and size of the labor force. The increase in the number of married women who enter paid employment is one of the two major sources of labor-force growth during recent years. The labor-force participation rate of married women rose two and one-half times, from 15 percent in 1940 to 41 percent in 1972. While the rates for single women, married women not living with their husbands, and divorced women are considerably higher, they have not evidenced the dramatic rise characterizing the rate for married women. Nearly three out of four women in the work force (72 percent) are married.

The increase in the participation rates of married women has also affected the labor force in another important way. Working wives have increased family income, and this added buying power has contributed to the tendency to spend more on goods and services that were once produced by the housewife. The rising demand for assistance with child-care and for ready-made clothing, prepared foods, and other time-saving commodities has spurred the growth of these industries, thus increasing job opportunities for others.

Household responsibilities continue to prevent many women from working full-time, however, and others have educational obligations that prevent their working year-round. Thus, while 66 percent of all men who were employed during 1971 worked year-round, full-time, only 42 percent of the women with work experience in 1971 were similarly employed. Of the remaining women workers, about half (32 percent) worked full-time for part of the year and the remainder were employed part-time. By contrast, only 13 percent of men workers held part-time jobs.

In recent years, women have suffered a higher unemployment rate than men and the gap has been widening. While they represent 38 percent of the work force, women account for 50 percent of all unemployed persons. In 1972, the 6.6 percent unemployment rate for women 16 years of age and over was significantly higher than the 4.9 percent rate among men. The pattern of entry and reentry into the labor force accounts for some part of the higher unemployment among women.

Occupational levels

During the last two decades employment opportunities for women have expanded in almost all of the major occupation groups. Although the proportion of women employed in higher-level occupations has increased since 1940, women are still disproportionately concentrated in the less-skilled and less-rewarded occupations. The current status of women in the occupational hierarchy has caused a former director of the Women's Bureau of the Labor Department to conclude that women are relatively more disadvantaged in today's labor force than they were more than 25 years ago. As evidence, she points out that while 45 percent of all professional and technical positions were held by women in 1940, they presently hold only 40.8 percent of such jobs. At the same time, women are increasing their proportion of the less skilled and lower-paying jobs. In 1940, women comprised 40 percent of all service workers (except private household); in 1972, they held 52 percent of those jobs.[4]

The number and proportion of women in the labor force have increased in part because of the rapid growth of white-collar and service work—occupations that have traditionally attracted large numbers of women. The rise in employment opportunities in these areas has also affected the profile of women's representation in different occupations. The proportion of female clerical workers rose from 53 to 76 percent between 1940 and 1972; measured in absolute numbers, the increase was threefold. Clerical work is the largest

---

[4]Mary Dublin Keyserling, "Goals—Ways to Fuller Utilization," in *Exploding the Myths*, Report of Conference on Expanding Employment Opportunities for Career Women (Los Angeles, December 3, 1966), p. 58.

occupational group for women, followed by service workers (where the number of women has shown a similar rise since 1940), and operatives.

About one out of seven women workers is employed in a professional or technical capacity. While the 4.7 million women engaged in such work represent a substantial increase in number (a rise of almost 3.0 million since 1940), women's relative representation in that category has declined, as was noted above. Expansion of the education and health fields has rapidly increased the number of women employed in those professions. Yet within these broad categories and many occupational groups, women tend to be concentrated in the lower ranks. For instance, women are more likely to be elementary-school teachers than secondary-school or college teachers. Similarly, within the health field many more women are employed as nurses, technicians, dietitians, and therapists than as physicians and surgeons. Women are poorly represented in the higher occupational groups partly because they lack training and educational preparation, and partly because many jobs are stereotyped by sex. Just as there have traditionally been "Negro" jobs, there have also been fixed notions as to which were "women's" jobs.

The educational attainment of women directly affects their participation in the labor force and of course affects their position in the occupational hierarchy. The more education a woman has, the more likely she will seek employment. Of those women who had completed five or more years of college in 1968, 71 percent were in the labor force; and 54 percent of women who had earned a bachelor's degree, 48 percent of women high-school graduates, and 31 percent of the women with less than eight years of schooling were in the labor force.

Although there is clearly a correlation between the educational attainment of women and their occupational distribution, the data provide some evidence that womanpower is not being fully used. In 1968, nine out of ten employed women who had completed five or more years of college had professional and technical jobs, as opposed to only 30 percent of the women with one to three years of college. Almost half of the employed women with one to three years of college education and 13 percent of those with four years of college had clerical jobs.

Income levels

The disadvantage of women in the labor force is reflected in their earnings. The less rewarding types of jobs that are available to women, women's intermittent pattern of work, and the tendency of employers to offer lower rates of pay to women workers, combine to produce lower earnings.

The median income of families has been rising steadily for several decades, and the increase in the proportion of families with more than one wage earner, oftentimes a working wife, is a notable factor in this rise. More than two-fifths of the husband-wife families had a working wife in 1972, as

Table 21/3. Employment status and occupation—persons 14 years old and over by total money income in 1970, by sex (Persons 14 years old and over as of March 1971)

Total money income	Total	Employed[1] — Total	Professional, technical, and kindred workers — Total	— Self-employed[2]	— Salaried	Managers, officials, and proprietors, exc. farm — Farmers and farm managers	— Total	— Self-employed[2]	— Salaried	Clerical and kindred workers	Sales workers	Craftsmen, foremen and kindred workers	Operatives and kindred workers	Private household workers	Service workers exc. private household	Farm laborers and foremen[2]	Laborers, exc. farm and mine	Unemployed	In armed forces or not in labor force
Male																			
Number of persons thous.	70 592	48 630	6 717	731	5 985	1 541	7 235	1 798	5 437	3 242	3 108	9 299	8 878	65	4 108	915	3 521	3 080	18 882
Number of persons with income thous.	65 008	48 043	6 689	730	5 960	1 538·	7 224	1 794	5 430	3 197	3 061	9 267	8 803	58	3 985	791	3 430	2 812	14 153
Median income dollars	6 670	8 036	11 577	17 670	11 249	3 859	11 292	7 853	12 304	7 965	8 321	8 833	7 017	(B)	5 568	2 238	4 839	3 986	2 159
Mean income dollars	7 537	8 929	12 970	20 854	12 005	5 503	12 982	9 731	14 057	7 941	9 319	8 871	6 926	(B)	5 817	2 809	5 081	4 839	3 346
Year-round full-time workers																			
Percent of civilian income recipients	56.6	73.2	83.5	77.3	84.2	78.7	88.1	81.3	90.3	74.9	67.5	76.0	68.0	9.8	61.0	44.2	51.0	18.0	3.6
Median income dollars	9 184	9 225	12 477	20 209	12 144	4 476	11 937	8 410	12 806	8 931	10 243	9 417	7 786	(B)	7 234	3 631	6 731	7 487	7 344
Mean income dollars	10 312	10 373	14 105	23 127	13 091	5 716	13 583	9 976	14 655	9 217	11 590	9 601	7 906	(B)	7 643	4 044	6 777	8 055	8 098
Female																			
Number of persons thous.	77 649	30 026	4 500	218	4 282	72	1 445	378	1 067	9 956	2 081	347	3 860	1 977	5 192	309	287	2 209	45 414
Number of persons with income thous.	51 647	28 330	4 370	203	4 167	68	1 372	328	1 043	9 499	1 900	342	3 726	1 784	4 873	145	252	1 762	21 555
Median income dollars	2 237	3 844	6 675	2 463	6 830	(B)	5 523	2 910	6 224	4 646	2 279	4 276	3 885	825	2 541	1 166	3 151	2 040	1 202
Mean income dollars	3 138	4 205	6 493	4 291	6 600	(B)	6 362	4 703	6 883	4 605	2 807	4 210	3 883	1 208	2 810	1 534	3 287	2 478	1 790
Year-round full-time workers																			
Percent of civilian income recipients	30.0	51.8	62.5	26.0	64.3	38.3	74.3	66.0	76.9	60.3	32.8	58.7	54.2	15.9	38.7	22.5	46.7	12.1	2.9
Median income dollars	5 440	5 483	8 005	(B)	8 019	(B)	6 624	4 238	7 140	5 650	4 268	5 100	4 589	2 203	4 035	(B)	4 405	4 738	4 606
Mean income dollars	5 856	5 910	8 194	(B)	8 188	(B)	7 325	5 662	7 775	5 916	4 714	5 379	4 698	2 447	4 264	(B)	4 857	5 052	4 875

– Represents zero.
B Base less than 75,000.
[1] The composition of the occupation groups has changed. Therefore, they may not be strictly comparable with those of previous years.
[2] Includes a very small number of unpaid family workers.
Source: Bureau of the Census, Current Population Reports, Consumer Income, Series P-60, No. 80, Table 50, p. 110.

compared to only 30 percent fifteen years earlier. The median income for the 15 million families in which the wife was employed was 30 percent higher in 1970 than the median income for families in which the wife was not a paid worker ($12,348 as compared to $9,357—for white families only).

Families headed by women are much less prosperous than male-headed families, even when the wife in the latter family is not working. While the median income of families headed by a male year-round full-time worker whose wife is not in the paid labor force is $8,168, female-headed families have a median income of slightly less than half that, or $4,010. Disproportionate numbers of female-headed families live in poverty. About one-tenth of all families are headed by a female, yet such families account for 30 percent of all poor families. The situation of the nonwhite female family head is even more severe; 60 percent of these families live in poverty.

In addition to differentials in family incomes, depending on the sex of the family head, wage and salary data reveal how different the earnings are. Women have substantially lower earnings than men; in 1970 the median figure for women was $2,237 as contrasted with $6,670 for men. Of the wage earners in 1970, 74.5 percent of the men, but only 35.1 percent of the women, earned incomes of $5,000 or more; 15.4 percent of the women compared to only 5.6 percent of the men earned $1,000 or less. Comparisons for year-round full-time workers reduce the differential in median wage or salary incomes $5,483 compared to $9,225.

Median wage or salary incomes of workers in major occupational groups further illustrate women's earning disadvantage. Earnings of women are below those of men in every occupational category. The differences in men's and women's earnings by major occupation group are shown in Table 21/3.

The Bureau of Labor Statistics and various professional research, alumnae, and women's associations or organizations periodically make available studies that provide more detailed information on women's wages and salaries for different types of work. The median annual salaries of teaching staffs in colleges and universities, on the basis of a survey by the National Education Association, indicated sex differences in college and university faculty incomes in the mid-'60s. The median salary for all ranks was $9,275 for males and $7,732 for females. Similarly, data provided by the National Science Foundation show that mean salaries of full-time employed women scientists in each major field were from $1,189 to $3,896 a year less than the mean salaries of male scientists in the same respective fields (See Table 21/4). Data obtained from such surveys are necessary in order to assess more carefully the question of "equal pay for equal work."

Commonalities

Social scientists are quick to draw an analogy between the problems and causes of disadvantage to blacks and to other minority groups. An examination of the position of minority groups in the labor force does, in fact, reveal

Table 21/4. Mean annual salaries of professional, scientific, technical, and health personnel, by occupational field, by sex: 1969 (In dollars, as of October)

Occupational field	Total	Male	Female
Scientific personnel, total	15,277	15,462	13,166
Physical sciences	16,730	16,980	13,084
General physical	19,075	19,296	13,662
Chemistry	15,197	15,656	12,623
Physics	16,688	16,746	14,675
Biological sciences	13,243	13,295	12,106
General biological	15,099	15,829	11,233
Agricultural sciences	12,460	12,451	15,314
Animal sciences	16,219	16,384	13,638
Microbiology	14,781	15,598	12,485
Plant sciences	13,552	13,596	11,914

Occupational field	Total	Male	Female
Mathematics and statistics	16,089	16,625	13,608
Mathematics	14,475	14,873	13,082
Statistics	16,158	16,654	14,207
Social sciences	16,710	17,257	13,927
General	15,682	16,527	13,685
Economics	17,303	17,630	14,753
History	14,089	14,800	11,198
Geography and cartography	12,869	13,027	11,263
Psychology	17,600	17,452	15,234
Health personnel, total	13,469	17,378	10,499
Health officers	19,774	19,718	20,817
Nursing personnel	10,080	11,202	10,048

Source: Bureau of the Census, Statistical Abstract of the United States, 1971.

commonalities. We have already touched upon some of the interrelated and complex contributors to minority disadvantage. Examination of the labor force situation of blacks and women reveals a concentration in the less-skilled occupations, higher rates of unemployment, and a greater incidence of part-time work. Income figures reflect these factors and indicate the significant differences between white and black workers, and men and women workers. Historical, social and psychological reasons are sometimes given for black and female disadvantage in the work force. Traditionally, both groups had a "predetermined" place in society and in the world of work, although the expected roles of most women excluded them altogether from the work force. Certain psychological factors may also contribute to the economic disadvantage of blacks and women. The level of aspirations affects the type of job a worker will attempt to find and, to some degree, the extent to which his or her education is underutilized.

The literature on discrimination distinguishes seven basic types: employment, price, capital, wages, human capital, monopoly power, and occupation.[5] Discrimination in employment can be seen in the concentration of blacks and women in full-time unemployment and part-time employment statistics. Price discrimination reflects the fact that blacks and women pay higher prices for, and receive lower prices for the sales of, similar goods than the remainder of society. The gains to the selling discriminators are positive if the price elasticity of demand of the minority is less than one. Similarly, gains to the purchasing discriminator are positive if the minority supply is inelastic. Capital discrimination refers to the difficulty minorities have in borrowing capital as a result of techniques that reduce access to capital markets or make efficient use of capital difficult, if not impossible. Capital discrimination can result from or be intensified in effect by occupational discrimination and/or human capital discrimination, which reduce the entrepreneurial skill and/or knowledge available to minorities; or by price discrimination, which can increase the price of capital, that is, the interest rate, and/or restrict the quantity of loans. Wage discrimination is the most widely recognized form of discrimination and simply means that blacks and women receive smaller wages for the same work. Human capital can be taken to mean formal education judged by quantity *and* quality; job training; apprenticeships, etc.; by such discrimination smaller investments are made in blacks than in whites (women, generally, are not the recipients of this form of discrimination). Occupation, employment, or wage discrimination may be enforced by this technique. However, human capital discrimination can also conflict with wage and occupation discrimination. Monopoly power discrimination limits the employment potential of blacks and women by excluding them from job areas where wages exceed those found in (perfectly) competitive markets. Occupation discrimination limits the types of jobs blacks and women may hold, thereby increasing the minority labor supply for unre-

[5]For example, see L. Thurow, *Poverty and Discriminations*, pp. 118ff.

stricted employment. In this case, white gains result if the distribution of whites is heavily weighted in high-wage occupations. Clearly, this may conflict with the goals of employment discrimination.

Consequently, because the maximization goals of several of the forms of discrimination are not compatible, conflicts result. One should also be aware that, in the case of wage and occupation discrimination, the majority may not gain but the actual discriminator will certainly gain from the process.

Public policy has made significant gains in eliminating racial and sexual discrimination. The earlier fair employment practices measures were particularly concerned with racial discrimination, but the effect has been to reduce job discrimination, whatever its basis, in federal employment. Through the administration of the Civil Rights Act of 1964, Title VII of which forbids discriminatory practices in employment, whether based on race, color, religion, sex, or national origin, improved treatment of both women and blacks has been gained. Employers are prohibited by law from discriminating in hiring or firing; wages, terms, conditions, or privileges of employment; and in limiting, segregating or classifying employees "in any way which would deprive or tend to deprive any individual of employment opportunities or otherwise adversely affect his status as an employee, because of such individual's race, color, religion, sex or national origin." It is also unlawful for an employer to express in advertisements any specifications, limitations, or preference based on race, sex, etc.

The Civil Rights Act established the Equal Employment Opportunity Commission with the power to receive, investigate, and conciliate complaints of discriminatory employment practices against employers, employment agencies, unions, or sponsors of training and apprenticeship programs. When necessary to bring about affirmative action to end discriminatory practices, the EEOC may institute civil action in a federal district court on behalf of the complainant.

While the resort of public or legal action to eliminate an unfair employment practice may be viewed as an extreme action by an employee who is likely to fear retaliation from his employer, a substantial number of cases are brought before the Equal Employment Opportunity Commission each year. The investigations and conciliations undertaken by the EEOC have benefited disadvantaged workers directly and indirectly in eliminating unfair employment practices, whether they take the form of deliberate discrimination or a more subtle built-in form that arises from the structure of the organization involved.

Contrasts

Although there are some similarities in the labor-force status of blacks and women, there are perhaps even more points of contrast. Attempts to solve the problems of the two groups in the same manner may therefore result in more frustration than progress.

Legal guarantees against employer discrimination in the terms of employ-ment are of course important to both groups. Equally important, too, are any other steps that will help to eliminate the stereotyping of jobs by color or sex. Such stereotyping is a habit of the press, as well as some employers; witness the references to an "outstanding Negro educator" or "a widely recognized woman novelist." Flattering as these descriptive terms are intended to be, the fact that one's sex or color is mentioned at all calls attention to society's expectation that such achievements are generally those of white males.

For a woman or a black to excel professionally still causes comment, and the substitutability of black workers or women workers for white males is frequently quite limited when the job is a desirable one. But the explanation for the low rate of substitution of black for white on the job is different from that of female for male. On the average, black males have less formal educa-tion than white males. But this is not true of white women; in many occupa-tional groups, the woman is better educated. The white woman has often been paid less because she was the second earner for the family, and hence did not "need" as much money. This cannot be used as a rationale for paying black males low wages.

In accordance with the marginal productivity explanation of wages, low earnings result from low productivity which in turn is an outgrowth of low capital investment either in plant and equipment or in human capital, that is, education or training. Increased investments in education might enable blacks to move out of a marginal job into a highly productive position where his wages will reflect that higher output. But women are often already over-educated for the jobs they hold; they are underemployed, or they can find no jobs at all commensurate with their training and competence. Whereas the educational route is clearly necessary to move both male and female blacks up the occupational hierarchy, other avenues will be of more help to white women.

One of the major reasons for the lower pay of married women—either in a given job, alongside men, or in their inability to gain acceptance to higher-level jobs—is their limited geographical mobility. In almost all cases, the family locates near the husband's job, since he is considered the major breadwinner, and the wife looks for the best job available to her in that area. Once she has the job, moreover, she cannot be transferred by the firm to a different city; her opportunities for advancement are therefore limited to the work she can do in one spot. This inability to move around to seek better jobs in different locations seriously restricts her competitive position. None of these constraints apply to black males, although they are often unaware of alternative opportunities and for that reason fail to move to better jobs.

Employment problems of blacks differ from those of white women, finally, in that married women usually have the income protection afforded by their husbands, so their financial needs are not as great. Many married women have an option that blacks do not have: they can withdraw from the labor force, at least for periods of time, without permanently jeopardizing the family's welfare. This freedom of choice should not be exaggerated to argue that married women do not "need" to work; who can say whether the wife of an $8,000-a-year school teacher with two children needs to work? Nor should it be generalized to all women, including those who support themselves and their families.

Other minority groups suffer still different disadvantages. Often they tend to be concentrated in geographically depressed areas, which because of cultural ties they find difficult to leave. Or they may suffer language deficiencies, or health problems induced by the living patterns of the group. Employment solutions to these complex social problems have to be long-range, and varied to match the needs of the particular situation. Viewing "minority problems" in the aggregate tends to obscure the extent and nature of individual needs.

Readings

Becker, Gary. *Economics of Discrimination.* Chicago: University of Chicago Press, 1957.

Fernan, Louis A. *The Negro and Equal Employment Opportunities.* New York: Praeger, 1968.

Hiestand, Dale L. *Economic Growth and Employment Opportunities for Minorities.* New York: Columbia University Press, 1964.

_____. *Discrimination in Employment: An Appraisal of the Research.* Institute of Labor and Industrial Relations, University of Michigan–Wayne State University, 1970.

Killingsworth, Charles. *Jobs and Income for Negroes.* Institute of Labor and Industrial Relations, University of Michigan–Wayne State University, 1968.

Kreps, Juanita. *Sex in the Marketplace: American Women at Work.* Baltimore: Johns Hopkins Press, 1971.

Marshall, Ray. *The Negro and Organized Labor.* New York: John Wiley and Sons, 1965.

Thurow, Lester C. *Poverty and Discrimination.* Washington, D. C.: The Brookings Institution, 1969.

Tobin, James, "On Improving the Economic Status of the Negro," *Daedalus* (Fall 1965), pp. 878–898.

Investments in Human Capital

Introduction

The study of economics views men and women as consumers and as producers. As consumers we derive satisfaction from food, shelter, and entertainment; and as producers we provide the goods and services that satisfy our wants. This book has focused on the economic role of men and women as producers. And since it is a book on labor economics, it has emphasized the efficient allocation of man's productive resources and the economic well-being stemming from his role as a producer.

We have been concerned with the acquisition of productive skills and with the allocation and use of those skills to provide current and future income for the worker. The worker's income-producing skill and knowledge can be called his human capital. Just as the investment in a machine results in a future flow of output and income for the businessman, so does the investment in education and training yield knowledge, skills, and talent that provide a future flow of earnings for the worker. There are costs involved in the investment in a machine, and the businessman who sells the produce of that machine can calculate a rate of return on his investment. Similarly, there are costs of investing resources in human beings. Education, health, training, and mobility, which generate our productive contributions, are all costly investments by the individual and by society. It is possible to calculate a rate of return on the investments by relating the cost to the flow of future earnings from the productive contributions.

Human capital, like physical capital, is essentially an economic concept. It is *human* because it is an integral part of man, and human beings cannot be separated from the capital invested in them. In this sense it is closely related to the concepts of manpower, human resources, and labor discussed elsewhere in this book. Since the stress is on *capital,* however, and the economic returns to capital, it is an economic concept, compared with those that deal with the social, psychological, and political aspects of human beings.

Some have objected to the concept of human capital on the very grounds of its narrow economic base. Humanitarians of an earlier era, seeking to provide protection for workers in the marketplace, decried the tendency "to treat labor like a commodity." Similarly, some critics, motivated by the same humanitarian instincts, deplore a concept that treats labor like a machine. This view has been most forcefully stated by Neil Chamberlain:

> *As I see it, the central issue on which the validity and desirability of the human capital concept turns is how far the pecuniary calculus can be extended to embrace people in their roles as producers. Once we conceive of people as capital goods, valued economically according to their productive contributions, we presumably place them in the same category as plant and machines. . . .*

> *. . . Capital, including human capital, is integrated into a production system and controlled for purposes which lie outside of itself. We do not concern ourselves with the welfare of capital stock, except in the sense of keeping it in good running order or perhaps updating it; we do not think of capital as having wishes and needs which are independent of the production process of which it is a part. People as producers, if they are viewed as capital in a scientific and conceptual rather than an allegorical or analogical sense, must be regarded in the same light.*[1]

Economists who support the concept of human capital as a useful tool of analysis recognize that it is concerned with only one aspect of the life of a human being. It is recognized that the concept says little about social-psychological satisfactions, the joys of consumption, or questions of equity, ethics, and morality. Even the most ardent supporters of the concept would not urge that public policy be based upon human capital calculations alone. However, as noted below, it is hoped that accurate calculations of the investments and returns to investments in human capital might serve as one useful input to the decision-making process in the formulation of policies for human resources.

Actually, the concept of human capital can be used to serve important humanitarian ends. It helps to explain inequalities in the wealth of nations and in the income distribution of families in the United States. As Theodore Schultz has indicated, the investments in people turn out not to be trivial; "On the contrary, they are of a magnitude which will alter radically the usual measure of the amount of savings and capital formation. They also alter the structure of wages and salaries and the amount of earnings relative to income from property." Schultz notes that these alterations are clues to long-standing puzzles about economic growth, for the investments in human resources explain the magnitude and differences in growth rates of developing countries in a way that the former concentration on physical capital could not do. And as Gary Becker has stressed,

---

[1]Neil W. Chamberlain, "Some Further Thoughts on the Concept of Human Capital," in G. G. Somers and W. D. Wood, eds., *Cost-Benefit Analysis of Manpower Policies* (Madison, Wisc.: Center for Studies in Vocational and Technical Education, The University of Wisconsin, 1969) pp. 230, 233.

People differ substantially in their economic well-being, both among countries and among families within a given country. For awhile economists were relating these differences primarily to differences in the amount of physical capital since rich people had more physical capital than others. It has become increasingly evident, however, from studies of income groups, that factors other than physical resources play a larger role than formerly believed, thus focusing attention on less tangible resources, like the knowledge possessed. . . ."[2]

By providing greater understanding of how economies grow and how real income is distributed, human capital, as a tool of economic analysis, can contribute to the formulation of public and private policies that further the shared goals of those who take the most humanitarian view of workers and the disadvantaged in our society, policies to upgrade poor people and nations through human investment.

The theory and measurement of human capital

Like physical capital, human capital produces a flow of goods and services into the future even though the capital may have been invested in the past or the present. In order to determine the present value of the future flow of goods, services, or resultant income stemming from the investment in human beings, it is necessary to capitalize the future flow to obtain the present value. Capitalization is the process of calculating the current value of an asset that will produce an income in the future. It is a major contribution of the theory of human capital that it permits us to place labor's contribution, and the investments in skill and knowledge that constitute that contribution, in a time dimension.

The present value of human capital

Present income is more valuable than future income, for it may not only be used to satisfy consumption needs (and most of us have a time preference for the present), but it may also be invested and earn additional income. The technique for evaluating future income is to express the value of future payments in terms of the present value of the payment, as if that payment were made today. This is done by using the interest rate, which tells us what

---

[2]Schultz and Becker are widely accepted as the initiators of the current analysis of human capital, the strands of which can be found in some of the earliest economic literature, but which came to the forefront only in the decade of the 1960s. See Theodore Schultz, "Investment in Human Beings," *The Journal of Political Economy,* Supplement, Vol. LXX, No. 5, Part 2 (October 1962), especially pp. 1 and 9. See also Gary S. Becker, *Human Capital: A Theoretical and Empirical Analysis, with Special Reference to Education* (New York: National Bureau of Economic Research, 1964).

$100 today would be worth 10 years from now and, conversely, tells us how much a payment of $100 ten years from now must be discounted in order to indicate its value today. Thus, incomes in the future, discounted by the interest rate, are added together to give us the present discounted value of a capital asset, whether that asset is a machine or an embodiment of productive resources in a human being. It pays to invest in more human capital as long as the discounted present value of human capital exceeds the cost of acquiring the additional capital.

In determining capital values, an interest rate (i) is used to discount an earnings stream (E_t) over the life expectancy (n) of the asset. This provides the present capitalized value (V) of future earnings.

$$V = \frac{E_0}{(1+i)^0} + \frac{E_1}{(1+i)^1} + \frac{E_2}{(1+i)^2} + \frac{E_3}{(1+i)^3} + \ldots + \frac{E_n}{(1+i)^n}$$

$$V = \sum_{t=0}^{n} \frac{E_t}{(1+i)^t}$$

where V = capital value
E_t = net earnings in time period t
i = interest rate

If the interest rate is zero, the present value is equal to the simple sum of each income stream; the higher the rate of interest the greater the importance of early income relative to that of later income as a determinant of present value.

The concept of human capital is economically significant when related to the more traditional economic theory of the labor market. As has been noted in previous chapters, the traditional theory assumes that labor is paid its marginal product, that is, it is paid according to what it produces. If labor is not paid its marginal product and earnings do not reflect productive capacities, the concept of human capital loses much of its economic importance. For in such a case the human capital concept cannot be used to measure productive capacity, and since investments in skill and knowledge do not necessarily lead to increased earnings, neither individuals nor society would necessarily be interested in such investments in human resources. If labor is not paid according to what it produces, then the human capital concept contributes little to our understanding of the sources of economic growth or to the distribution of income among individuals and families.

As has been previously noted, there is no definitive empirical evidence that labor is paid its marginal product. However, this assumption is generally made and accepted in conventional economic theory, and its acceptance is a cornerstone of the theory of human capital. The assumption is not only required for an understanding of the inputs in productive resources but also underlies many of the policy implications derived from the analysis of the investment in human capital.

Since future streams of earnings are never certain, the factors of risk and uncertainty must be introduced into the procedures for determining present capital values. Given risk and uncertainty about future income flows, the capitalization formula must be corrected through the introduction of probabilities that future income streams will actually occur. Frequently an individual is able to make such probability estimates. However, in practice the differences in individual attitudes toward risk and uncertainty make it difficult to calculate present capital values for various subgroups of the population. However, since we use the human capital theory principally to formulate manpower policies from a social viewpoint, it is fortunate that the probability of social benefits from a particular human investment are generally higher than a probability of an individual benefit from the same investment; and for this purpose, the basic formula for capitalization can be accepted with greater reliability.

The return on human capital investments

To formulate public policy we must have a method of evaluating alternative uses of resources invested in human capital. We assume that individuals will invest in their own productive capacities to the point where the *rate of return* to investment in human capital of that particular kind is equal to the rate of return of an investment in other alternatives.

Thus, the capitalization of a rate of return must be concerned as much with the costs of the investment in human capital as with the gross value of the earnings. Cost calculations are similar to those of earnings. The stream of costs must be discounted just as the stream of future earnings must be discounted and corrections must be made in the formula for any risks and uncertainties associated with costs. Once the present value of costs has been determined through use of the discounting process, costs are simply subtracted from the present value of earnings to yield a *net* present capital value. If the net present value of acquiring a human capital asset is greater than zero, the asset should be purchased, and if the net present value is less than zero the capital asset should be bypassed in favor of an alternative. With this guide to investment in alternative human capital assets, greatest efficiency is achieved when the net present value of each type of asset is reduced to zero. At this point the market for human capital is in equilibrium.

The rate of return, often called the internal rate of return, is an alternative procedure for determining the efficient allocation of investments in human capital among alternatives. Under this procedure, the interest rate that would bring the net present value of an asset to zero can be calculated. This interest rate is called the internal rate of return. Using this procedure, investments are made in any human capital acquisition where the internal rate of return exceeds the interest rate, that is, the rate that can be earned on alternative investments. When the internal rate of return on a particular human capital investment reaches the investor's discount rate, the investment in that particular capital asset should stop.

Both rates of return and net present values are widely used in calculating human capital investments. Net present values are often preferred because assets cannot be readily compared by the use of rates of return unless the assets have the same lifespan. However, if the rates of return on human capital are known, the aggregate value of human capital in the economy can be determined. Since labor's earnings in any particular period are equal to the value of human capital multiplied by the rate of return, an estimate of the total value of human capital can be obtained by dividing labor's earnings by the rate of return.[3]

Cost-benefit analysis of manpower policies

The great advances in the theory of human capital and the use of its concepts have coincided with the revolution in manpower policy, in the 1960s. It is not surprising, then, that this confluence of events led many scholars in the manpower field to apply the analysis of human capital in the evaluation of manpower programs. The calculation of net present values and internal rates of return has been applied not only to manpower training programs, as discussed in Chapter 25, but also in the evaluation of such programs as the Neighborhood Youth Corps, the Job Corps, and vocational education and labor relocation projects.[4]

In using cost-benefit calculations to evaluate manpower policies, economists are simply plying their trade, and the theory of human capital has permitted them to go beyond the bounds of their customary labor-market analysis. The textbook definition of economics—a study of the allocation of scarce resources to satisfy human wants—is clearly applicable to the analysis of public and private expenditures designed to increase the employment and income of workers. It coincides with a growing interest of a number of government agencies in a systems evaluation of public expenditures. This has taken the form of a Planning-Programming-Budgeting (PPB) System, encouraged throughout the federal structure. A number of government officials

[3]A useful discussion of the various measures of human capital can be found in Lester C. Thurow, *Investment in Human Capital* (Belmont, Calif.: Wadsworth Publishing Company, 1970), especially pp. 15–27.

[4]The student wishing to pursue the growing literature in this field can find extensive bibliographic references in G. G. Somers and W. D. Wood, *Cost-Benefit Analysis of Manpower Policies;* W. D. Wood and H. F. Campbell, *Cost-Benefit Analysis and the Economics of Investment in Human Resources: An Annotated Bibliography* (Kingston, Ontario: Industrial Relations Centre, Queens' University, 1970); and U. S. Department of Labor, *Cost-Benefit Analysis: Theory and Application to Manpower Training Programs, A Bibliography* (Washington, D. C.: May 1971).

have insisted that rational decision-making in government planning requires a quantitative evaluation of the benefits and costs of alternative programs. With limited funds available for social-welfare programs, there is bound to be closer scrutiny of the returns to the investment in manpower policies; and, as an adjunct of human capital analysis, cost-benefit evaluation is bound to expand.

Although government officials and labor-market analysts are likely to applaud the introduction of more precise evaluation of manpower programs, it is important to remember the limitations of human-capital theory and cost-benefit analysis as applied to manpower:

First, it is a rather narrow approach, in that it deals wholly with costs and benefits and rates of return in a pecuniary sense. It has not yet been possible to integrate nonmarket factors into the formal cost-benefit evaluation formulas. It must be recognized that cost-benefit analysis, like human-capital analysis generally, cannot and should not purport to establish the goals of manpower policies. These must be determined by noneconomic as well as economic forces. It would be unfortunate, however, to scrap a promising tool of economic analysis simply because it requires the assistance of complementary tools and because the incautious fail to recognize its limitations.

Second, it must be recognized that the extension of human-capital analysis to manpower policies suffers from serious inadequacies of data and methodology. It is seldom possible to obtain the cost data in adequate detail for a sufficiently large sample of program recipients to arrive at definitive cost calculations. The present value of capital investments in manpower depend upon knowledge of income streams not only for the program recipients but also for a comparable group (control group) of similar persons who did not enroll in the manpower program. An ideal control group can seldom be obtained in the absence of an experimental research program. Such experiments are growing in number, but they are still rare, and their cost is likely to preclude rapid expansion in manpower research. Among a number of other methodological problems in cost-benefit analysis is the choice of the appropriate interest, or discount, rate. As noted above, this can be crucial in determining net present capital values, and it can make all of the difference in conclusions about the economic efficiency or inefficiency of a program as seen by the cost-benefit evaluator. A major quandary is whether the interest rate selected should be that which is applicable to certain types of private investment or that which is applicable to certain types of public or social investment. A substantial segment of economic literature has been concerned with this question, and the conclusions are by no means firmly established. Perhaps the only firm conclusion that can be reached about the extension of human-capital analysis of manpower programs is that is must be applied cautiously and its results must be interpreted as only one modest piece of information which should influence policy-makers.

Conceptual problems in estimating returns on a
college education

Critics of human-capital analysis are on firmer ground when they do not argue that it is not righteous to calculate returns on human investments, but instead question whether the measurements themselves are accurate enough to guide private and public decisions on undertaking these investments. In truth, apart from inadequacy of data, measurement of net returns faces many difficult conceptual problems, some of them insurmountable.

We study these problems with reference to one of the most important human-capital decisions of the day: investment in a college education. Only a few of the obstacles to accurate measurement are discussed; the subject is much too vast for comprehensive treatment here.

In accordance with the earlier analysis, the question of whether a college education "pays," in the narrowest economic sense, to the individual investor depends on whether discounted returns exceed costs. Consequently, we examine the conceptual difficulties in measuring costs and returns for a college education.

Costs   The cost of a four-year college education may average up to $30,000. If this figure seems high at first, it should be noted that the costs for an 18-year-old who spends the next four years in college far exceed his outlays for tuition, books, room and board above home costs, and incidentals—called his *direct* college costs. There are also the much larger—three times as large according to most studies—*indirect* costs of forgone income while attending college. These are the earnings he could have received if he had worked at a paying job instead of attending school. It does not matter that he may also work while going to college. These forgone earnings still count as investment costs in his education. If he works, he in effect holds two jobs, one in the market, the other his school work. He *defrays* his college costs with his market work but he does not reduce them, since if he were not a college student he still could have used the school time for gainful employment.

The question now arises as how to measure forgone earnings of the college student. Since he does go to school we will never know what he could have earned as a nonstudent. The earnings from the casual part-time jobs held by students are a poor guide to what they would have earned during their school years had they been serious full-time labor-force participants.

The conventional method uses the earnings of age cohorts who do not go to college as the measure of the would-have-been market earnings of college students. The use of a proxy group may be necessary, but it seriously weakens the accuracy of estimation of what college students would have earned. The two groups differ, among other things, in their ability, motivation, and family wealth and income, in a way that undoubtedly understates the forgone earnings of college students and thereby overstates the net returns to a college education.

Returns   The same problem associated with use of a proxy group to represent would-be earnings of the college group reduces the precision with which returns can be estimated. The annual returns to college, to be discounted and compared with costs, are the extra earnings *attributable* to college. A precise measurement would require not only knowledge of what the average college graduate earned in his post-college years—knowledge that is available—but also knowledge of what he would have earned during this period had he not gone to college—knowledge that is conceptually unattainable.

In this case, use of the proxy high-school graduate earnings understates the would-have-been earnings of the college graduate, for the same reasons related above for understatement of college graduate putative earnings during college years, and again thereby overstates the net returns to college.

One important imponderable, though, acts in the direction of understatement of returns to college. Many benefits other than higher earnings accrue to the college graduate: he holds a more responsible, interesting, and challenging job, he derives consumption benefits from his education in the form of widened tastes and higher prestige. But to the extent tastes change instead of widen, there may be no net gain—and there may even be a net loss—of consumption benefits. For example, television situation comedies may be more enjoyable to the high-school graduate than opera to the college graduate. Assuming leisure-time consumption pluses and minuses balance out, there remain the job-related benefits.

Thus, these are nonmeasureable, nonmonetary returns, which nevertheless can make the choice of a college education a rational one even if rough estimates that did not consider such returns showed college did not "pay," that is, if returns failed to cover costs.

All the above, and many other factors, reduce the accuracy of estimated net returns. Nevertheless, they do not deny the importance of attempting to measure the relative net returns of different human investments, made out of limited funds, even if they do suggest the need for more refined estimation procedures.

The varied investments in human capital

Even though our principal concern here is with manpower investments, it should be borne in mind that the investments in human capital go well beyond programs of primary interest to labor economists. Theodore Schultz has discussed the most important of these investments, indicating some of the questions that extensions of the human-capital analysis are required to answer:[5]

School and higher education   Although much work has been done on the returns to the investment in education, with calculations of net present values and internal rates of return to added years of schooling, further analysis is still required to determine the effects of schooling and higher education on the distribution of personal income in our society. It is especially important to know whether the inequality in the distribution of personal income stemming from ownership of nonhuman capital (income-producing property) is reduced by the returns to investments in human capital. It is especially important to distinguish between schooling (grade school and high school) and higher education in analyzing the effects of investments in education. It is likely that education in elementary schools and high schools in the United States are generally progressive in their effects on the distribution of personal income. On the other hand, there is growing evidence that higher education in this country, leaving the community college aside, is regressive in its effects upon personal income distribution.

The results of recent research provide estimates that the rate of return on elementary education is at least 35 percent and that that of high school education is about 25 percent, and that both are rising. On the other hand, the returns to college education and to graduate instruction and research appear to be stabilizing at about 15 percent, and they may be headed for a reduction. Further research in these human-capital investments is needed in the formulation of an overall national policy with regard to education.

Post-school investment in human capital   Estimates by Jacob Mincer and others indicate the economic importance of on-the-job training and other forms of post-school training for the enhancement of earnings. Schultz has estimated that, as of 1957, the stock of capital in the United States embodied in males in the labor force was $347 billion on their investment in on-the-job training as compared to the educational stock of capital in the labor force at the same time of $535 billion.[6] Given the importance of this form of human investment, much more research evaluation is clearly called for to determine the efficiency and equity of various forms of post-school training.

---

[5]"Human Capital: Policy Issues and Research Opportunities," paper presented at a Colloquium on Human Resources, May 1971, Atlanta University, under the sponsorship of the National Bureau of Economic Research.

[6]Theodore Schultz, "Human Capital: Policy Issues and Research Opportunities."

Preschool investment in human capital   The antipoverty program launched in the mid-1950s was concerned with the unequal start among children when they enter upon their regular schooling. Great hopes were placed in the Head Start programs as a method of reducing inequality. Measurement of the results of the Head Start programs, in terms of human capital analysis, has been plagued by lack of data and by methodological problems. Even so, there appears to be evidence that the returns to this investment may be higher than the relatively high returns on investment in elementary schooling. One of the costs of the investment in schooling at higher levels, that is, the opportunity cost of earnings forgone, is clearly not applicable to Head Start students. It is likely that further extensions in human-capital research will lead to policy recommendations for additional investments to overcome the labor-market disadvantages of an initial start in a setting of cultural deprivation.

Human-capital approach to migration   The human-capital approach has been applied to migration between countries as well as migration within countries. The movement of workers from areas of limited job opportunitites to other areas where they can exercise the full weight of their skills and knowledge is clearly an investment with an important labor-market return. However, this is one of the areas in which the limitations of human-capital analysis must be kept in mind. The major costs of human migration are likely to be social and psychological. Unless some monetary calculation is placed upon these costs, benefits and earnings accruing from migration are likely to result in explosive rates of return which may not be warranted in terms of human values. Extensions of human-capital theory in this area must attempt to integrate the noneconomic and economic costs and benefits.

Health as an investment   An important component of the increased productivity of the American worker in the last century can be attributed to his improved health. Thus, investments in improved health constitute important investments in human capital. However, in spite of the substantial expenditures on health research, little has been devoted to research on the economic aspects or the human-capital aspects of health. Human-capital analysis is required to answer such questions as whether expenditures on health programs should be directed to the reduction in infant mortality, terminal illness, heart transplants, prenatal care, etc. The relationship of investments in health to labor-market performance also require extensive research evaluation.

The search for information   Some have said that the best investment in manpower programs would be simply that of extending labor-market information to the work force. A knowledge of the whereabouts of jobs and their characteristics might do more, at considerably less cost, than extensive training in matching unemployed workers with job opportunities. Although improvement and expansion in the public employment services have been based upon this premise, further human capital research, of which investment in information is one aspect, is required to evaluate this manpower program in comparison with competing manpower policies.

The acquisition of children   It is not always obvious that children are human capital from which parents receive satisfactions and producer services, and that the acquisition of children can be considered an investment of the parents' own time as well as an investment of market goods and public services. Needless to say, we are now just at the frontier in the application of human-capital research to the determinants and the effects of population growth.

Conclusion

The development of human-capital theory and its application to investments in manpower policies as well as other aspects of human resources is an exciting new analytical departure. It has already demonstrated its value in the appraisal of particular manpower programs and in suggesting policy modifications that improve efficiency. Further improvements in analytical concepts as well as in the techniques of application can be anticipated.

The theory permits us to integrate many of the separate topics discussed in this volume. It helps to explain labor-market allocation, wage and income determination, investments in training and other manpower policies, and the bases and consequences of loss of income through disability or old age. A number of the puzzles that beset conventional economic theory as applied to the labor field are more readily answered within the context of human capital theory. Given the infancy of the analytical field, a bright future appears to lie ahead for the theory of human capital, and the students of labor economics would do well to explore it further.

Nonetheless, it is fitting to close this chapter with the caveats that we have expressed a number of times above. Perhaps most appropriate is a quotation from Lester Thurow, a sympathetic analyst of the investment in human capital and the author of one of the best works in the field:

A sharp distinction must be drawn between the "value" of a man and the value of a man's earnings. A man's human capital indicates the present value of his future productive capabilities. It does not indicate his worth as a human being. Personal qualities such as love, friendliness, compassion, and intrinsic worth are not included in calculations of a man's human capital. The value that he would place on himself or the value that his friends or enemies might place upon him has no relation to his human capital.[7]

Readings

Barsby, Steve L. *Cost-Benefit Analysis of Manpower Programs.* Boston: Lexington Books, 1972.

Becker, Gary S. *The Economics of Discrimination.* Chicago: University of Chicago Press, 1970.

_____. *Human Capital.* New York: Columbia University Press, 1964.

Borus, Michael E. *The Impact of Manpower Programs: An Evaluation.* Boston: Lexington Books, 1972.

_____, and William R. Tash. *Measuring the Impact of Manpower Programs: A Primer.* Ann Arbor: Institute of Labor and Industrial Relations, University of Michigan, 1970.

Caro, Francis G. *Readings in Evaluation Research.* New York: Russell Sage Foundation, 1971. "Investment in Human Beings," *The Journal of Political Economy,* Vol. LXX, Supplement (October 1962), No. 5, Part 2.

Somers, Gerald G., and Donald Wood, eds. *Cost-Benefit Analysis of Manpower Policies.* Madison, Wisc.: Industrial Relations Research Institute, University of Wisconsin, 1969.

Suchman, Edward A. *Evaluative Research.* New York: Russell Sage Foundation, 1967.

Thurow, Lester. *Investment in Human Capital.* Belmont, Ca.: Wadsworth Publishing Company, 1970.

Wykstra, Ronald A., ed. *Human Capital Formation and Manpower Development.* New York: The Free Press, 1971.

---

[7]Lester Thurow, *Investment in Human Capital,* p. 16.

Chapter Twenty-three

Investment in Education

Introduction

As noted in the preceding chapter, investment in education is one of the principal ways of developing human capital. The knowledge and skills imparted through education "pay off" in a stream of productive services that command income in the labor market. In the more conventional terms of labor economics, education makes a major contribution to the development of labor supply, thereby affecting the wages and salaries of the work force.

However, as the discussion of the preceding chapter makes clear, education is also a "consumption good," and therefore the full benefits to society go well beyond labor-market considerations. They are difficult to measure because we cannot readily place a monetary value on the widened tastes, greater social awareness, and higher prestige that is associated with more education.

From the standpoint of manpower resource development, the amount and type of education, and the appropriate government policies, are key issues of the present decade. Our discussions and analyses of these issues begin with general schooling and higher education and then proceed to vocational, technical, and career education.

Schooling and higher education

Emphasis on education in the United States

The United States has traditionally invested heavily in the education of youth and the long-run effect has been one of gradually rising levels of education, whether measured by median years of school completed, proportion of the relevant age group in college, or rate of reduction in illiteracy. Even when compared with other industrialized nations, our record of educational achievement is impressive; with about 80 percent of our youth graduating from high school, and more than 40 percent actually enrolled in colleges and universities, the proportion being educated far exceeds that in any other country in the world. Sweden, which has the next largest percentage of youth enrolled in colleges, has less than a third the proportion now pursuing higher education in the United States (see Table 23/1).

Table 23/1. Secondary school graduates, new
entrants to higher education, and total enrolment
in higher education, in relation to population of
corresponding age group, 1959 and 1970 (estimated)

Country	Secondary graduates		New entrants		Total enrolment	
	1959	1970	1959	1970	1959	1970
Switzerland	5.5	....	....	....	3.8	....
Sweden	11.0	21.7	7.6	11.7	7.1	12.2
Belgium	11.2	15.0	6.2	9.5	4.6	6.2
Denmark	5.9	11.6	4.2	8.9	3.7	5.3
Norway	11.3	21.8	5.7	5.9	4.0	4.9
Netherlands	5.8	9.2	3.9	4.4	4.7	5.0
Austria	10.0	14.1	5.0	8.9	4.2	6.4
Canada	38.0	....	15.4	23.1	10.0	15.1
United States	65.5	79.5	34.4	38.2	36.6	41.2

Source: Organization for Economic Co-operation and Development, Resources for Scientific and Technical Personnel in the OECD Area.

Comparisons of the quality of higher education are difficult to draw. It is sometimes claimed that the secondary graduate in some European systems is more nearly comparable to our college than to our high-school graduate. But this claim probably undervalues the quality of American education. It is worth noting that we have in college twice the proportion of our youth as are completing the secondary level in Sweden and Norway.

Educational attainment of the work force

The expanded education of the general population is matched by the increased educational attainment of the work force. Table 23/2 shows the steady growth in schooling.

The increase in schooling has been a relatively recent phenomenon. In fact, the age-distribution of the educational level of the work force (Table 23/3) suggests two important aspects of what might be called the "educational revolution":

1.   The growth in educational attainment will probably slacken in the years ahead. Over time, older workers leave the labor force and young people enter. The young have benefited from greater education, while the old have

Table 23/2.   Percent distribution of civilian labor
force 25 years old and over by years of school
completed, selected years

Years of school completed	March 1957–59 average	March 1964–66 average	March[2] 1972	Projected 1975
Total	100.0	100.0	100.0	100.0
Less than 4 years of high school	53.7	45.1	31.8	34.0
4 years or more of high school	46.3	54.9	68.1	66.0
Elementary: 8 years or less[1]	34.5	26.2	15.2	16.0
High school: 1 to 3 years	19.2	18.9	16.6	17.9
4 years	27.8	32.8	40.0	39.5
College: 1 to 3 years	8.4	9.6	14.0	11.1
4 years or more	10.2	12.5	14.1	15.4
Median years of school completed	11.4	12.2	12.5	12.4

[1]Includes persons with no formal education.
[2]For persons 18 years and over.
Sources: Denis F. Johnston, "Education of Adult Workers," Monthly Labor Review,
91 (April 1968), 11. Manpower Report of the President, 1973, p. 176.

relatively little schooling. The replacement pattern, of educated for lesser
educated, explains a great deal of the current steady increase in average
schooling.

Table 23/3.   Median years of school completed by
the civilian labor force 18 years and over, by age,
selected dates, 1952–70

Date	18 to 24 years	25 to 34 years	35 to 44 years	45 to 54 years	55 to 64 years	65 years and over
October 1952	12.2	12.1	11.4	8.8		8.3
March 1957	12.3	12.2	12.0	9.5		8.5
March 1959	12.3	12.3	12.1	10.8	8.9	8.6
March 1962	12.4	12.4	12.2	11.6	9.4	8.8
March 1964	12.4	12.4	12.2	12.0	10.0	8.9
March 1965	12.4	12.5	12.3	12.0	10.3	8.9
March 1966	12.5	12.5	12.3	12.1	10.4	9.1
March 1967	12.5	12.5	12.3	12.1	10.8	9.0
March 1968	12.5	12.5	12.4	12.2	11.1	9.3
March 1969	12.5	12.6	12.4	12.3	11.4	9.3
March 1970	12.6	12.6	12.4	12.3	11.8	9.6
March 1971	12.6	12.6	12.4	12.3	12.0	9.9
March 1972	12.6	12.7	12.4	12.3	12.1	10.2

Source: Manpower Report to the President, 1973.

But in a few years this trend effect will lose its force, as the future older worker group comprises those who were early participants in the educational revolution. Note in Table 23/3 the very strong growth in recent years of average schooling in the 55 to 64 and 45 to 54 age groups. Within a decade there will be little difference among age groups in years of schooling. Since there has been scarcely any growth in schooling for younger workers over the past generation, unless there is a new "educational revolution" the future average schooling of the work force will remain more or less stable.

2. The schooling data provide speculative insights into a probable source of an important modern social problem, the generation gap. Educational level differences can explain a great deal of the poor communication between old and young, to the extent education changes values, interests, and viewpoints. But happily, the same factors that will stabilize the average schooling of the work force—increased education of older workers—will also serve to remove schooling differences as a source of intergenerational misunderstanding.

Future demand and supply of college graduates

Much of the increase in schooling has been in response to increased industrial needs for highly skilled and trained manpower. The greatest work force needs are for those with a college education and beyond, to fill rapidly growing professional and technical jobs.

This trend is expected to continue. By 1975, the estimated number of persons needed in professional and technical jobs will be about 13 million—an increase of 40 percent over the 9.3 million employed in 1966. Assuming that the scientific and technological pace of recent years continues and that expenditures for research and development remain high, the Department of Labor's projections of professional manpower needs indicate the dimensions of the future job market under peacetime, full-employment conditions.

The increase in demand for professional and technical personnel calls for a rate of expansion roughly twice as high as the needed growth in all occupations. Yet even if this 40 percent increase were achieved, the nation would be far short of the "aspiration goals" set for various areas of particular need: manpower training, area redevelopment, health, housing, research and development, education, private plant and equipment, space, transportation, urban development, natural resources, national defense, international aid, and consumer expenditures. To achieve the standards set in these sectors, a total of 15.8 million professional and technical workers would be needed by 1975, or about 6.5 million more than were employed in 1966.[1] Although employment

---

[1] Leonard A. Lecht, *Goals, Priorities, and Dollars—The Next Decade* (New York: The Free Press, 1966), table F–11.

needs in all professions will grow, much faster growth is expected in some areas, such as the natural sciences and engineering, than in certain others— law and school teaching, for example.

The number of college graduates in the adult work force of 1975 will be as large as the number of workers with 8 years or fewer of school; less than a decade ago the college graduate group was only one-third the size of the less-educated component. By 1975, moreover, four out of five men in the youngest group will be high-school graduates, and one in four will have a college degree.

The numbers of new bachelor's degrees climbed even more rapidly during the second half of the 1960s than during the first half of the decade (Figure 23/1), and will continue to grow sharply during 1970–75. The number of new bachelor's and first professional degrees will increase by about two-thirds over the 1965 figure, while new master's and doctor's degrees will have doubled in number by the middle of the 1970s. In science and engineering, where the demand is particularly heavy, the supply of Ph.D.s awarded will increase somewhat faster, although still not rapidly enough to fill the gap.

Number of Ph.D's awarded

Year	Natural sciences	Engineering
1960	3,346	786
1966	5,760	2,350
1975 (projected)	11,400	6,900

In the teaching field, which has seen severe shortages during most of this decade, the demand for new elementary and secondary teachers is leveling off. A slower growth of school enrollments after 1968 will result in the creation of fewer new positions, with replacements constituting the bulk of total demand after 1970 (Figure 23/2). In colleges and universities, too, some moderation in enrollments is expected after 1969. Coupled with the current increases in numbers of Ph.D.s, the slowing of enrollments will ease the tight market for college teachers that has persisted for more than a decade. Junior college enrollments continue to grow, however, and there remains a great lag between the need for and supply of teachers in these institutions, which have until now had to staff most of their teaching posts with public-school teachers.

Employment in the health services has risen sharply in recent years, partly as a result of population growth and partly as a concomitant of higher incomes and levels of living. Health-insurance coverage, Medicare and Medicaid, and an increased general awareness of the value of health, are additional factors on the demand side. The anticipated future need for health personnel, unlike the leveling-off that will occur in the demand for teachers, is far greater than the projected supply can meet. The number of new physicians entering the work force annually is now only about 9,000; projected requirements to 1975 indicate that another 6,600 per year are needed. Of nurses, the estimates show that an additional 8,000 per year are needed. At least 15 other health occupations have been facing critical shortages, despite the fact that many of these jobs (x-ray, laboratory and dental technicians, practical nurses, for example) require relatively short training periods. According to one estimate, 1975 requirements can be met only if the annual output of dental hygienists triples, the annual number of new medical technologists and x-ray technicians doubles, and that of medical record librarians increases five times. For occupational and physical therapists, annual output must increase tenfold.

Very few of the jobs in the foregoing areas of science and engineering, primary, secondary, and college teaching, and in the health services can be performed without lengthy career preparation. The bachelor's degree has in a few decades replaced the high-school diploma as the sine qua non for a

Figure 23/1.   New college graduates, master's and
Ph.D. degrees, 1948-1975

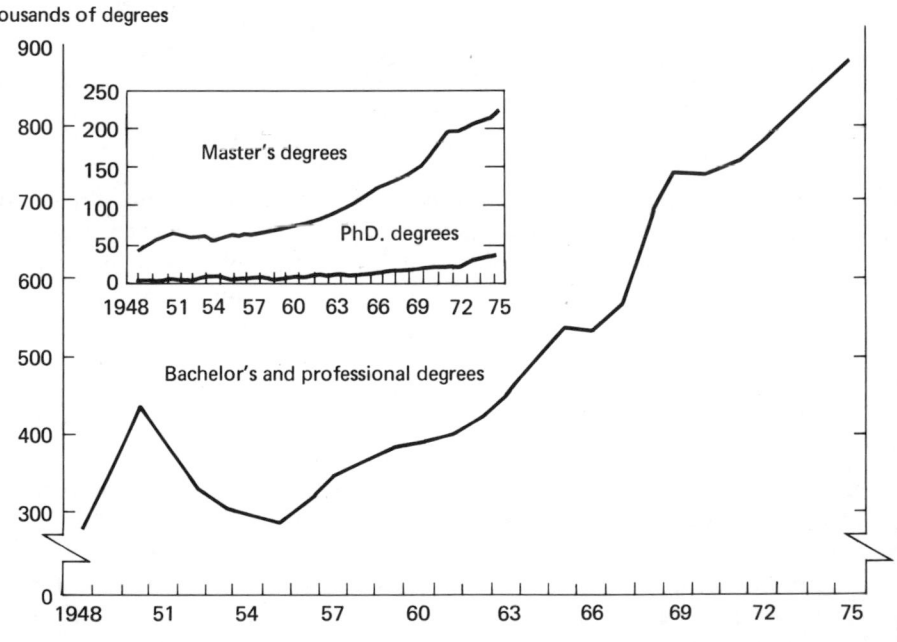

Source: U.S. Department of Labor, based on data from the U.S. Department of Health, Education, and Welfare.

successful search in the job market. For while the jobs requiring a college education are growing in number and complexity, jobs at the other end of the occupational hierarchy have declined, both absolutely and as a proportion of the total labor force. Total agricultural employment continues its long-term decline in numbers, and unskilled and semiskilled operatives are each year becoming a smaller percentage of the employed workers. For the poorly educated, this continual upgrading of the labor force not only makes labor-force entry more difficult; it also makes holding a job without interruption throughout worklife practically impossible.

Educational level of the less skilled

While there is general awareness of the growth in higher education and the concomitant increase in demand for those with a college degree and professional training, there has been a less-publicized but equally significant rise in the educational level of those holding unskilled and semiskilled jobs.

Figure 23/2. Demand for elementary and secondary school teachers, 1961-1975

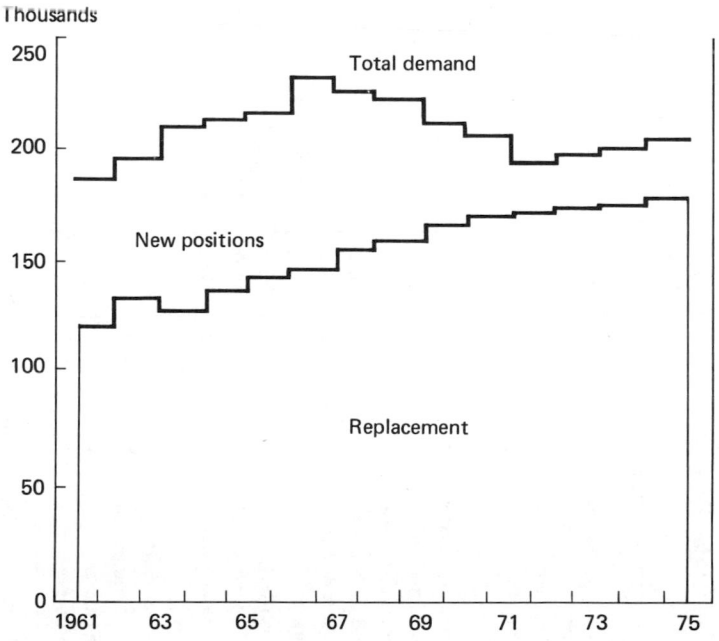

Source: U.S. Department of Labor, based on data from U.S. Department of Health, Education, and Welfare.

Table 23/4. Median years of school completed by the employed civilian labor force, 18 years and over, selected dates, 1948-72 (Persons 18 years and over for 1948-72)

Occupation group	March 1972	March 1971	March 1970	March 1969	March 1968	March 1967	March 1966	March 1964	March 1962	March 1959	March 1957	October 1952	October 1948
Total													
Both sexes													
All occupation groups	12.5	12.4	12.4	12.4	12.3	12.3	12.3	12.2	12.1	12.0	11.7	10.9	10.6
Professional and managerial workers	15.4	15.1	14.9	14.9	14.8	14.7	14.6	14.0	13.9	13.5	13.2	12.9	12.8
Professional and technical workers	16.3	16.3	16.3	16.3	16.3	16.3	16.3	16.2	16.2	16.2	16+	16+	16+
Managers and administrators	12.9	12.8	12.7	12.7	12.7	12.7	12.6	12.5	12.5	12.4	12.4	12.4	12.2
Farmers and farm laborers	9.4	10.0	9.3	9.3	9.1	8.9	8.8	8.7	8.7	8.6	8.5	8.3	8.0
Sales and clerical workers	12.6	12.6	12.6	12.6	12.6	12.5	12.5	12.5	12.5	12.5	12.4	12.4	12.4
Sales workers	12.7	12.7	12.6	12.6	12.6	12.5	12.5	12.5	12.5	12.4	12.4	12.3	
Clerical workers	12.6	12.6	12.6	12.6	12.6	12.5	12.5	12.5	12.5	12.5	12.5	12.5	
Craftsmen, operatives, and laborers	12.0	11.9	11.6	11.4	11.2	11.1	11.0	10.7	10.4	10.0	9.7	9.2	9.0
Craftsmen and kindred	12.2	12.2	12.1	12.1	12.0	12.0	11.9	11.5	11.2	11.0	10.5	10.1	9.7
Operatives	11.6	11.4	11.3	11.1	11.0	10.8	10.7	10.5	10.1	9.9	9.5	9.1	9.1
Except transport	11.6												
Transport equipment	11.7												
Nonfarm laborers	11.2	11.1	10.5	10.0	9.8	9.5	9.5	9.3	8.9	8.6	8.5	8.3	8.9
Service workers	12.0	11.9	11.7	11.3	11.1	11.0	10.9	10.5	10.2	9.7	9.0	8.8	8.7

Source: Manpower Report of the President, 1973.

Table 23/4 shows this upgrading in schooling of the industrial work force. The table presents the change in years of education for every occupational group over the past generation, but of special interest are the figures for the craftsmen and foremen and subsequent groups. The craftsmen and foremen form a group of skilled workers, and their increase in average school years from 9.7 to 12.2 years might represent a needed expansion of learning to perform the more varied and responsible duties required of skilled workers by modern technological complexities. But can the same really be said for operatives, nonfarm laborers, and service workers as a whole, those on the lower rungs of the occupational ladder?

Each of the groups increased their average schooling by more than two years, from about an eighth- or ninth-grade level to about three-plus years of high school. It is unlikely that this greater education is actually needed to perform what are still mostly routine duties. No one would suggest that these workers should have less schooling. But the data do indicate that despite the shift in labor demand towards the highly trained workers, there are still many jobs that are filled by workers who have been caught up in the "educational revolution," who could perform more challenging tasks.

There are psychological problems of possible worker uninterest at being overeducated for occupational needs. But these issues fall outside the scope of labor *economics*. The breadth of the "manpower revolution," the recent rapid change in industrial needs toward a more educated and trained work force, indicate that this problem may become less important as the number of jobs requiring little education shrinks still further.

Vocational, technical, and career education

The development of vocational-technical education

Although all education can make some contribution to productive human resources, it is clear that vocational education is especially linked to manpower development and labor-market activity. It is distinguished from general, academic education by concentrating more wholly on the employment rather than the consumption benefits to be derived from education.

Vocational-technical education has never commanded the attention or resources accorded to general, academic education. However, it has long been an area of important concern for private industry, and local, state, and federal government trade schools, business schools, and agricultural schools, linking instruction to the labor market, began to develop in the latter years of the nineteenth century. A professional group, the National Society for the Pro-

motion of Industrial Education, was formed as early as 1906; and federal
support was achieved through the Smith-Hughes Act in 1917.

In spite of these early beginnings, however, it is worthy of note that the
current flurry of government interest in vocational education coincided with
the initiation of other programs in the "manpower revolution" of the early
1960s. Because of mounting unemployment, especially among youths, and
continuing concentration of vocational education in such fields as agriculture
and home economics, a presidential task force was appointed in 1961 to
recommend new directions for federally funded vocational programs. The
panel placed principal stress on "making vocational education more available" to a broader range of students. It was found that those from relatively
disadvantaged backgrounds were generally bypassed in the vocational
schools, and such a finding was contrary to the growing philosophy in the
legislature of the 1960s. Another principal recommendation was that enrollment in vocational programs be geared more closely to the needs of the labor
market, with greater emphasis on emerging occupations and industries.[2]

The Vocational Education Act of 1963 reflected the presidential panel's
recommendations. Expenditures increased threefold from 1964 to 1967, but
little incentive was provided for reallocation of the funds from their traditional uses, and there was only minor movement toward the new directions
espoused by the rhetoric of the Act. Thus, Congress had to try once again to
achieve the 1963 goals by passage of the Vocational Education Amendments
of 1968. Authorized funds were again increased but appropriations were
delayed by presidential veto until overriding of the vetoes in the 1971 and
1972 budgets. Funds were earmarked for new programs tied to emerging
occupations, and they were to be specifically allocated to programs for students with special needs, primarily those with economically deprived backgrounds.

The extent of vocational-technical education

There has been an obvious increase in federally aided vocational-technical education in recent years and some reallocation of funds to the areas
recommended by the presidential panel's report. However, it is not clear that
these changes can be directly attributed to the 1963 and 1968 legislation, and
in any case the changes noted by the early 1970s fell short of those
anticipated under the far-reaching language of the legislation.

Total enrollment in federally aided vocational-technical programs increased from 5.4 million in 1965 to 8.8 million in 1970. As can be seen in Table
23/5, enrollment in agriculture programs declined from 16.3 percent of the

---

[2]The discussion in this section is drawn in part from Gerald G. Somers and Kenneth J. Little, eds., *Vocational
Education: Today and Tomorrow* (Madison: Center for Studies in Vocational and Technical Education, University of Wisconsin, 1971).

Table 23/5. Enrollments in federally aided
vocational-technical education, by type of
program, fiscal years 1965–70

Program	Percent distribution[1]	
	1970	1965
Total	100.0	100.0
Agriculture	9.7	16.3
Distribution	6.0	6.1
Health	2.3	1.2
Home economics	29.2	38.6
Office	24.0	13.5
Technical	3.1	4.2
Trades and industry	21.7	20.0
Other[2]	4.0[3]	——

[1]Based on unrounded data.
[2]Includes developing programs which do not fit precisely into
the occupation groups listed.
[3]Includes enrollments in exemplary, prevocational, pre-
post-secondary, and remedial programs.
Source: Department of Health, Education, and Welfare,
Office of Education.

total in 1965 to 9.7 percent in 1970; and enrollment in home economics
dropped from 38.6 percent to 29.2 percent. But the latter still had the highest
enrollment of all programs in 1970 (2.6 million). The principal increase in
enrollment occurred in office programs, moving from 13.5 to 24.0 percent of
the total between 1965 and 1970. Indeed this increase, from .7 million to 2.1
million students, accounts for much of the increase in total vocational-technical enrollment during the period. Since many of the new occupational needs
might be expected to be found under health and technical programs, it is
notable that enrollment in health increased but still represented only 2.3
percent in 1970; and the small enrollment in technical programs declined still
further, to 3.1 percent, in 1970. Although it is difficult to find data on the
extent of poverty or cultural deprivation among vocational-technical students, it has been reported that those with "special academic and socioeconomic handicaps" were only 9 percent of total enrollment in 1970, in spite of
the directive of the 1963 Act that much more emphasis be given to this group.

Vocational education, general education, and
manpower policies

Three crucial issues   Although many can agree on the
"long list" of questions concerning vocational education, there is less consensus on a short list. And yet an effort must be made to establish priorities. At

the risk of oversimplification, it is suggested that there are three key issues, closely related to each other: (1) At one end of the spectrum is the relationship of vocational and technical education to general education at the elementary, high-school, and higher educational levels. (2) At the other end of the spectrum is the relationship of vocational education to manpower programs, especially for the hardcore unemployed, the poor, and the disadvantaged. (3) In between the role of vocational education as a part of general education and its role as a device for aiding the disadvantaged is the relationship of vocational education to industrial training programs. Whereas "respectability" lies with a closer integration of vocational education and general education, especially at the higher levels, some of the pressing needs of the time lie in the direction of special programs for the disadvantaged. Since the training of workers for employment, whether they be disadvantaged or not, requires close liaison with industry, the appropriate jurisdiction between vocational education and industrial training will remain a critical issue, even as vocational educators look more fondly at their potential status in junior and technical colleges.

These issues have come to the fore in the 1970s because of the Nixon Administration's proposed Manpower Training Act. In introducing the proposed legislation, the Secretary of Labor stated, "Through this legislation we hope to lay the foundation for a comprehensive national manpower system—one that can serve the needs of the individual and afford the states and localities a major role in manpower training and program administration." Similar legislation, stressing the coordination and decategorization of manpower training and other manpower programs, as well as some decentralization of functions, has been proposed by Democratic and Republican Congressmen. As a result of these legislative proposals, a lively debate has developed between vocational educators and representatives of the Department of Labor.

Vocational educators have expressed concern over the policy objectives and implementation of the proposed legislation. The competing roles of vocational education and institutional training on the one hand and various manpower and training programs of the Department of Labor on the other have been crystallized. Arguments have arisen over the administrative relationship between the Department of Labor and the Department of Health, Education, and Welfare at the federal level, and between vocational educators, the Employment Service, and manpower agencies at the state and local levels. Although there has long been a question of coordination between institutional training at vocational schools and on-the-job training in industry, the newly proposed legislation has given an urgency to the debate; and regardless of the outcome of the legislation, a sharp light has been focused on issues which have long needed critical examination.

Under a comprehensive manpower policy, the Employment Service is given a crucial role in the planning and execution of manpower training programs. Questions arise concerning the cooperation between the Employment Service and vocational educators in assessing labor-market needs and in the placement of trainees. In spite of the strictures of the Vocational Education Acts of 1963 and 1968, there has been only limited cooperation between vocational education and those agencies of the Department of Labor that are expected to play a leading role in labor-market analysis and job placement. If the Employment Service is to be given a central role in manpower training, can this be effectively accomplished if the Employment Service and the principal vocational training institutions go their separate ways?

While many vocational educators have looked longingly toward integration with general education, especially at the higher levels, they have now been faced with the threat of an expansive system of vocational training that bypasses their institutions. Crucial to the discussion is the question of how best to help the disadvantaged. The Vocational Education Act of 1968 has ascribed a major role in this field to the vocational schools. And yet, the proposed manpower legislation advocates a comprehensive system of training, especially for the disadvantaged, which provides no specified role for vocational education institutions.

Vocational education vs. on-the-job training   The new manpower training programs have also highlighted the traditional issue of vocational education versus on-the-job training. Programs sponsored under the Manpower Development and Training Act witnessed a marked shift from institutional training at the beginning of the 1960s to on-the-job training at the end of the decade. The proposed comprehensive manpower policy would undoubtedly continue to give a critical place to on-the-job training in industry. Here, too, long-standing questions can no longer be evaded. Who should be trained in vocational schools and who should be trained on the job? Are government manpower funds being used to subsidize employers in training workers for specific, short-term jobs that cannot serve as a substitute for fundamental, long-term vocational training in community schools? Is skill training for many of the disadvantaged really necessary, or can their absorption into the labor market be equally well served by short-term counseling, job-placement programs, work orientation, or work experience?

Socioeconomic changes and legislative proposals force vocational educators to take a less leisurely look at their appropriate jurisdictional role in the spectrum of educational, training, and manpower programs. What is the comparative advantage of vocational education relative to industrial training programs and the manpower policies of the Department of Labor? This question must be answered soon, not only for the future of vocational education, but also for the achievement of the most effective social and educational policy in our society. Who can benefit more from vocational education than from on-the-job training or short-term manpower policies? What skills, what occupations, what curricula are more suited to vocational education than to the alternative, and often competing, forms of manpower development?

Evaluation of education as a labor-market investment

The discussion in the preceding chapter indicates that the rate of return is higher in elementary education than in high-school education, and that both rates are rising. On the other hand, the returns to college education are stabilizing at a lower level. Some studies have indicated that the return to graduate education in many fields may now be close to zero. The returns in these cases are determined on the basis of monetary cost and benefits. As noted earlier, the noneconomic "consumption" effects of education must also be considered in a full evaluation of the benefits of education for individuals and society. It must also be remembered that even monetary returns are high and positive for some college majors.

In vocational-technical cost-benefit calculations it has been found that vocational graduates generally can command higher earnings, at least initially, than those pursuing academic programs, especially at the post-secondary level.[3] However, the costs of vocational-technical education are also clearly above those in academic programs at equivalent school levels. The cost differentials vary with the type of program, just as the benefits do. And programs in the technical field, where earnings are highest, are also the programs in which costs are highest.[4] Unfortunately, the data on which the vocational-academic comparison are based have seldom been sufficient to hold such key factors as "ability" constant.

Therefore, no blanket conclusions can be reached on vocational-academic comparisons. However, there is reason to believe that, with rates of return to post-secondary academic education leveling off, carefully selected vocational programs may become increasingly attractive from the standpoint of an individual's monetary returns.

From the standpoint of the financial returns to society, increasing attention should be given to the possible allocation of larger amounts of financial aid to elementary and secondary education and to certain post-secondary vocational programs. The current stress on career education at all levels of the educational process would appear to be in accord with these findings on rates of return.

---

[3] See the bibliography of such studies prepared by Ernst W. Stromsdorfer, *Review and Synthesis of Cost-Effectiveness Studies of Vocational-Technical Education* (Columbus, Ohio: State University, 1972).

[4] Elchanan Cohn et al., *The Costs of Vocational and Non-Vocational Programs* (University Park: Pennsylvania State University, 1972); and Gerald G. Somers, *Cost-Effectiveness of Vocational-Technical Programs* (Madison: University of Wisconsin, 1971).

As noted previously, however, monetary rates of return should be considered in conjunction with broad social factors. The unfinished business of vocational education in extending its services to more of the disadvantaged is in keeping with such broader social views. Even in monetary cost-benefit terms, the allocation of additional vocational education dollars to welfare recipients and other persons in poverty or in a disadvantaged status may prove to be a sound investment. At the same time we should not neglect the continuing need for high-talent manpower in an era of rapidly expanding technology.

Readings

Berg, Ivar. *Education and Jobs: The Great Training Robbery.* New York: Frederick Praeger, 1970.

Blaug, Mark. *Economics of Education: A Selected Annotated Bibliography.* Elmsford, N. Y.: Pergamon Press, 1966.

_____, ed. *Economics of Education* (two volumes). London: Penguin, 1968 and 1970.

Harbison, Frederick, and Charles A. Myers, *Education, Manpower and Economic Growth.* New York: McGraw-Hill Book Co., 1964.

Teh-wei Hu; Maw Lin Lee; and Ernst W. Stromsdorfer (Jacob J. Kaufman, Project Director). *A Cost-Effectiveness Study of Vocational Education.* University Park, Pa.: Institute for Research on Human Resources, Pennsylvania State University (October 1968).

Nam, Charles B., and John K. Folger. *Education of the American Population.* Washington, D. C.: U. S. Bureau of the Census, 1967.

Perlman, Richard. *The Economics of Education: Conceptual Problems and Policy Issues.* New York: McGraw-Hill Book Co., 1973.

Ribich, Thomas J., *Education and Poverty.* Washington, D. C.: Brookings Institution, 1968.

Schultz, Theodore W. *The Economic Value of Education.* New York: Columbia University Press, 1963.

Somers, Gerald G., et al., *The Effectiveness of Vocational and Technical Programs: A National Follow-Up Survey.* Madison: Center for Studies in Vocational and Technical Education, University of Wisconsin, 1971.

Striner, Herbert E., *Continuing Education as a National Capital Investment.* Kalamazoo, Mich.: Upjohn Institute, 1972.

Weisbrod, Burton A., "Preventing High School Dropouts," in Robert Dorfman, ed. *Measuring Benefits of Government Investments.* Washington, D. C.: Brookings Institution, 1965.

Chapter Twenty-four

Manpower Training: Accomplishments and Priorities

Introduction

One of the far-reaching aspects of the manpower revolution has been the increased federal involvement in manpower training; this involvement constitutes another major investment in human capital.

As with education and vocational school programs, it is important to assess the economic implications of the occupational training programs that have been mounted in the United States since 1961. Our evaluation necessarily contains some factual data on the nature, extent, costs, and benefits (based on studies made to date); however, major emphasis is placed on conceptual and theoretical problems paving the way for the discussion of national priorities in manpower and employment policies covered in the final chapter.

Development of training programs

Large-scale publicly sponsored training programs in the United States have been put in force primarily through the Manpower Development and Training Act of 1962 (MDTA), with amendments in subsequent years. The MDTA provides institutional and on-the-job training (OJT) programs. Its institutional programs have had an impact on the vocational education system, since its courses are often held in vocational schools. They remain an important principal hope for retraining the unemployed and underemployed adult worker.

Other training efforts are carried out in the Neighborhood Youth Corps (NYC), the Job Corps, and those formerly under the Economic Opportunity Act. As is noted in the following chapter, there are a number of other manpower programs that, like NYC, contain greater elements of work experience or job creation than training. The changing enrollments in these programs are noted in Table 25/1.

There are two programs that developed late in the sixties, however, that are still important in the 1970s and that contain elements of training for the disadvantaged. In the program called Jobs in the Business Sector (JOBS), the federal government pays a subsidy to private employers to cover the costs of training and supportive services to the newly hired disadvantaged. The aid of employers in promoting the program has been achieved through a National Alliance of Businessmen. The second program, The Work Incentive Program (WIN) attempts to place welfare recipients in training programs and jobs. As is seen in Chapter 25, the JOBS program is levelling out, but WIN has just been expanded and is likely to grow further. In fact, WIN is one of the few programs receiving increased funding in 1973.

There are now over 30 different federally supported job-training programs operating simultaneously in some communities. In addition, federally supported programs for basic education, work experience, counseling, relocation, and area development policies have similar employment objectives.

In all Department of Labor funded work and training between 1964 and 1972, total new enrollments rose from 278,000 to 2.3 million. Although MDTA is not expected to grow (see Table 25/1 in following chapter), this program continues to be the major federally supported program for the unemployed that contains substantial training investments. Therefore, as a principal example of manpower policies this program is worth evaluation.

Goals and implications of MDTA

A list of program goals can be derived from the legislative mandate of training programs. Unfortunately, there is no general agreement on the proposed goals, but at the risk of oversimplification, a reasonable consensus can be summarized as follows:

1. *Goals and implications for the trainees*
    a.   *Reduction of unemployment and underemployment*
    b.   *Increased income through higher skill and productivity*

2. *Aggregate goals and implications*
    a.   *Reduction of aggregate unemployment rates*
    b.   *Effects on income distribution, poverty, and the costs arising from related social ills*
    c.   *Reduction in inflationary pressures*
    d.   *Economic growth (increased real GNP) through greater employment and productivity*
    e.   *Easing balance-of-payments problems*
    f.   *Increased revenue and reduced transfer payments*
    g.   *Expanded social and health services*

Even though some rough estimates have been made concerning the economic implications for society, it must be noted that existing empirical studies in the United States have moved little beyond evaluations of the impact on individual trainees. This is primarily because serious methodological problems besetting the studies of effects on the individual are further compounded when the evaluation is turned to the effects on society as a whole.

Methodology of evaluation

Much has been written about the conceptual problems and the methodological requirements of evaluation research in the training field. Chapter 22 provides the basic procedures, and a lengthy discussion of methodology would not be appropriate here. However, it is necessary to establish a few fundamental ground rules for the evaluation of a program such as the MDTA. To be accorded weight in a summary evaluation, a study need not include a fullblown cost-benefit or regression analysis, but the following would appear to be a bare minimum in a meaningful appraisal of the economic effects of a training program:

1. The legislative goals, that is, the hoped-for benefits, of the program must be established.

2. In attributing benefits to the program, the investigator should provide some evidence that these benefits would not have occurred in the absence of the program.

Although these evaluative criteria are basic, they are seldom met. As has been noted, even the goals of the training programs have given rise to lengthy debate in some quarters. The legislation is often couched in terms of increased employment and income for the economy as a whole, rather than for particular individuals; however, the attainment of such national benefits through retraining is difficult to establish in an analytic model and almost impossible to estimate empirically. Most of the evaluators make the sometimes questionable assumption that improved employment, income, and satisfaction for the trainee redound to a proportional benefit to society as a whole. This point is pursued further below.

Similarly, the immediate goal of retraining is to impart or increase occupational skills, and some would wish to measure the benefits of retraining by measuring skill acquisition. Evaluative studies of skill are welcome, but they are not readily forthcoming, and since employment and income gains usually reflect skill acquisition, economists, at least, are likely to use these economic variables as proxies for the aggregate of benefits to be derived from retraining.

The fact that the labor market benefits may also stem from factors other than skill acquisition—such as special counseling, job-information and placement services that may be available to trainees—reduces the sharpness of the evaluation. A complete evaluation of retraining would measure improvement in skill, employment, income, and job satisfaction; but such a full-fledged evaluation is rare indeed.

To assure that the benefits attributed to a retraining program were due to that program, some device must be found to control for improvements in general employment conditions and in other factors completely unrelated to training. The before-and-after-training status of the trainees must be compared with that of some other reference group. Ideally, this should be a control group similar to the trainees in every respect except for training. Difficulties in finding such control groups usually lead to a compromise on this approach and, frequently, to the complete abandonment of the control effort in favor of a simple before-after comparison for the trainees alone. Most government reports on operating data are generally in this form. A simple before-after comparison can provide confident evidence of program benefits only when the worker's status before training was so persistently dreary and his status after training so elevated that the change could not be attributed to chance or to the effects of nontraining variables. Moreover, the follow-up period in most of these reports is seldom long enough to warrant firm conclusions.

Even though a basic purpose of evaluation of training programs should be an assessment of the efficiency of alternative approaches to manpower goals, little has been done on comparative studies of either costs or benefits. Since there are now so many different federally supported job-training programs operating simultaneously in some communities, a comparative evaluation of training variations, alone, would appear to be timely. And going beyond training, federally supported basic-education programs, work experience, counseling, relocation policies, and area development policies in the same locality have similar employment objectives. At the present time special emphasis is being given to on-the-job training for the disadvantaged in the private sector, and to the concentration of all available manpower services (under the administrative control of a single agency) in specific "target areas" in the nation's slums.

Effects on the trainees

Characteristics of trainees

An examination of trends in enrollment data indicates that MDTA and JOBS have made some progress but still have some distance to travel in order

to reach the announced goals for training the disadvantaged.[1] This is especially true of the expanded on-the-job training. In 1966 the Manpower Administration stated that it would be the future aim of MDTA to ensure that
65 percent of the trainees were drawn from the disadvantaged. It was indicated that this goal had been reached for institutional trainees in 1970. At
the same time recognition was given to the benefits to be derived from
on-the-job training and it was announced that the little-used OJT provisions
of MDTA would be expanded so that this type of training, too, would be
increasingly available to the disadvantaged. The JOBS program had essentially taken over the functions of MDTA-OJT by 1972.

Even though progress has been made in enrolling the disadvantaged in
institutional MDTA programs since 1963, in 1971 only 12 percent of all
institutional trainees had 8 or fewer years of education, and only 9 percent
were over 44 years of age. However, 39 percent were nonwhite (See Table
24/1). The combination of these factors in the same enrollee, a more severe
test of disadvantaged status, undoubtedly represents an even smaller percentage of the total. The percentage of nonwhites has grown continuously (from
a low of 23.5 per cent in 1963), but the enrollment of older workers has shown
little increase over the years (1963: 10.4 percent), and the percentage with
only an elementary education has also failed to increase in recent years.
However, the family income of about 70 percent of the trainees has been
under $3,000 per year, and the MDTA classified most of these as "disadvan-
taged." And yet in 1971, only 16 percent of the MDTA institutional enrollees
were on public assistance and the proportion was only 12 percent for those
in JOBS or OJT.

The enrollment in MDTA's on-the-job training programs expanded
sharply in the late 1960s. Although OJT enrollees represented only 40 percent
of all MDTA trainees in 1970, this achievement is more notable when viewed
against the fact that OJT trainees represent 7 percent of the total in 1963, 10
percent in 1964, and under 30 percent in 1965.

The disturbing aspect of the OJT programs under MDTA and JOBS is not
their failure to reach higher totals, but rather failure to enroll more of the
disadvantaged. Black enrollees have increased steadily from 17 percent in
1963 to 43 percent in 1971. The latter proportion was above the percentages
of nonwhites in institutional MDTA programs for the first time. The percentage of older OJT enrollees (7 percent aged 45 and over in 1971) is close to the
average of those in institutional programs and shows little increase over
previous years. The percentage of OJT trainees with only an elementary
school education (17 percent in 1971) has increased somewhat during this

---

[1]For manpower program purposes, a disadvantaged person is a poor person who does not have suitable
employment and who is either (1) a school dropout, (2) a member of a minority group, (3) under 22 years of
age, (4) 45 years of age or over, or (5) handicapped. For purposes of this definition members of families
receiving cash welfare payments are deemed poor.

Table 24/1. Characteristics of enrollees in federally assisted work and training programs, fiscal year 1971

Percent of total enrollees

Program	Women	Negro[1]	Age		Years of school completed		On public assistance[2]
			Under 22 years	45 years and over	8 or less	9 to 11	
Institutional training under the MDTA	42%	39%	40%	9%	12%	36%	16%
JOBS (federally financed) and other OJT	29	43	41	7	17	39	12
Neighborhood Youth Corps:							
In-school and summer	45	56	100		20	76	37
Out-of-school	49	41	94		29	69	37
Operation Mainstream	27	24	5	40	45	30	20
Public Service Careers	63	44	19	20	10	31	20
Concentrated Employment Program	40	60	46	6	16	44	14
Job Corps	26	60	100	0	33	59	36
Work Incentive Program	62	40	27	5	20	43	98

[1]Substantially all the remaining enrollees were white except in Operation Mainstream, JOBS, and Job Corps. In these programs, 8 to 12 percent were American Indians, Eskimos, or Orientals.
[2]The definition of "public assistance" used for these figures varies somewhat among programs (for example, it may or may not include receipt of food stamps and "in kind" benefits). In the NYC program it may relate to enrollees' families as well as enrollees themselves.

period. Compared with institutional trainees, a smaller percentage of OJT enrollees were classified as disadvantaged (52.2 percent) and in poverty status (48.3 percent) in 1970.

Whereas MDTA and JOBS have not yet achieved their goal of reaching the disadvantaged, other manpower programs (shown in Table 24/1) enroll the disadvantaged exclusively. Most notable among these are the Job Corps; the Neighborhood Youth Corps; the Concentrated Employment Program and the public employment work and training programs—Operation Mainstream and Public Service Careers; and the Work Incentive Program to move persons on welfare into employment. When composite statistics are used for all of those programs combined, the U. S. Manpower Administration contends that 93 percent of the enrollees were poor and otherwise disadvantaged in 1971. Even so, the programs are heavily weighted toward youth, and although the relatively small public-service and rural programs have been for adults, the older worker remains seriously underrepresented in the total manpower effort.

Impact on the employment and income of trainees

The most useful evaluations of training programs have focused on institutional MDTA and similar programs established earlier by state governments and by the federal government under the ARA. Reports based on operating data of the MDTA fall short of the methodological ideal in evaluating the effectiveness of the program. A wealth of data on MDTA training has recently appeared in a report issued by a U. S. Senate Subcommittee on Employment, Manpower, and Poverty. Included are follow-up data on employment status three months after training. These benefits are cross-classified by the trainees' demographic characteristics and previous employment experience.

The data indicate that the programs are favorably affecting earnings and employment. In 1964 and 1965 the trainees had a post-training employment rate of 75 percent, and 62.5 percent were in training-related jobs. OJT trainees had an employment rate of over 90 percent. The median earnings were 21 percent higher after training than before, and through January 30, 1967, the median post-training earnings were $1.74 per hour; these results were cross-classified by trainee characteristics, and it was found that the level of post-training economic status of the disadvantaged was below average, but the improvement over their pretraining status was greater.

Although these "benefits" of retraining may be questioned because there was no comparable control group (other than national changes in general employment and income), they are supported by a study conducted for the

U. S. Labor Department by the National Opinion Research Center; studied was the post-training experience of 784 trainees and a comparable control group of 825 with significant similarities in pretraining unemployment. Those who completed training had significantly better post-training employment rates, stability of employment, and improvement in income as compared with the control group.

Although these officially sponsored evaluations are somewhat rough and ready, confidence in the findings is buttressed by an impressive number of more sophisticated cost-benefit and statistical analyses of specific MDTA and MDTA-type training programs for the unemployed.[2]

Training programs even fare well when related to other human-resource programs. It has been found that retraining may bring about greater improvements in income than will general education, especially for the disadvantaged; and when coupled with geographic mobility, retraining enhances income beyond the level reached through retraining or mobility alone.

The studies of trainee benefits from training and retraining programs are impressive. The worth of these programs as a private investment in human capital would seem to be well established. But even in the evaluations of individual trainees, there are still some nagging questions:

1.   One unanswered question is whether on-the-job training would provide even better benefit-cost ratios and whether new methods now being used to encourage on-the-job training of the disadvantaged will be successful. One of the very few research projects on this question reaches conclusions favoring on-the-job training. However, the authors admit to serious methodological deficiencies, especially with regard to data on private OJT programs. Thus, it remains to be seen whether methodological problems can be solved so as to provide a more definitive answer to this pressing question. If large government payments are required to induce employers to train disadvantaged workers on the job a significant cost factor (for society) is introduced that might significantly affect the comparative benefit-cost ratios.

2.   A second major question focuses on how the costs and benefits of training programs compare with those of job-development and work-experience programs (in which employers are simply approached by manpower representatives who try to persuade them to hire the disadvantaged). There has not yet been a sufficient comparative evaluation of these two approaches to establish benefit-cost ratios.

3.   A third question relates to time: the studies cited are constrained by a relatively short time-period of follow-up. Are the benefits of retraining, relative to control groups, sustained over longer time periods? Only two studies have used a 4 to 5

---

[2]References on evaluative studies are listed at the conclusion of this chapter.

year follow-up of the experience of trainees, and unfortunately the results go in opposite directions, which is partly attributable to the choice of different control groups. More work is clearly needed before conclusive results can be reported on the longitudinal economic effects of adult training programs for the unemployed and underemployed.

Implications for aggregate economic goals

The reduction of aggregate unemployment rates

As heartening as the results cited above may be by indicating that adult-training courses have a favorable impact on the economic welfare of the trainee, they do not necessarily say much about how well the economic objectives of society as a whole have been achieved. There are at least two schools of thought concerning the aggregate employment effects of manpower-training and retraining programs. The controversy remains primarily in the realm of theory since existing empirical studies provide only partial answers, largely on the fringes of the central question.

The pessimists   On the one hand, there are those who contend that it is very unlikely that manpower training programs have contributed significantly to the reduction in the unemployment rate that occurred between 1961 and 1967 in the United States. Moreover, some of these critics contend further that even a substantially larger training and retraining program, taken by itself, would not significantly reduce the aggregate unemployment rate. Their arguments center on the following points:

1.   Since employers hire workers in order to produce goods and services that people buy, only an increase of income and demand on the part of the purchasers of goods and services will create an increased demand for workers. Since retraining, by itself, does not bring about increased income or demand on the part of purchasers, it will not, by itself, generate more jobs and employment. The gist of this argument is that increased demand for labor comes about only through increased aggregate demand. Only expansionary monetary–fiscal policy brings about such an increase in aggregate demand. Even if large-scale government expenditures on government training programs could be construed as a major increase in aggregate demand, it is argued that the government funds spent on training programs thereby reduce roughly equivalent government expenditures that might have been made in some other sector and for some other purpose.

2.   Although training programs cannot create new jobs, it might be argued that they can reduce unemployment if the unemployment problem is substantially a structural one. If many job vacancies exist in the face of pools of unskilled, unemployed labor, then training and retraining programs to bring the unemployed workers up to the skill level required to fill the vacancies would serve to reduce the rate of unemployment in the economy as a whole. Implicit in the views of many of those who argue against the likelihood of this effect is a belief either that the unemployment problem is not substantially a structural one or that the unemployed are so unskilled, uneducated, and disadvantaged that they cannot be brought up to the level of skill required to fill the relatively high-skilled job vacancies. (The structural unemployment hypothesis was presented in greater detail in Chapter 14).

3.   Even if it could be theoretically established that government training programs could create jobs and/or reduce unemployment, the scale of the federal training and retraining programs in the United States in the 1960s, it is argued, has not been sufficiently large to bring about any such significant results. Since the inception of the training program, average annual enrollments in MDTA have never been more than 280,000, and unemployment in 1972 was over 5 million. The number of MDTA trainees available to contribute to a reduction of unemployment in any particular year is relatively small. Even when enrollment in all Department of Labor manpower programs are considered, enrollees would not represent more than one-fourth of the unemployed.

If we take a broader concept of unemployment and underemployment as well as a broader concept of manpower-training policies, the potential impact of these programs is no more significant. The committee on Administration of Training Programs concluded that "The most gross estimate indicates that less than 10 percent of persons needing the job training programs can be enrolled in them." The committee's report indicated that in individual states, cities, and neighborhoods the numbers reached are frequently much less than 10 percent.

For these reasons, the impressive showing of benefits derived from training by the trainees must not be construed as similar benefits in employment in the economy as a whole. It is possible that the trainees' improved employment status was achieved at the expense of a relative decline in the status of other unemployed workers competing for available jobs. The kinds of jobs taken by most of the trainees are probably at such a skill level that they might be fairly readily filled by nontrainees who were given the proper information and counselling.

The optimists   On the other hand there is a group of economists who adopt a more optimistic attitude toward the aggregate employment effects of government manpower training programs. They feel that the training programs to date have been sufficiently large to bring about some reduction in national unemployment, and that if the programs were greatly expanded, they could have a very significant impact on aggregate unemployment. Their arguments run as follows:

1. Unemployment is reduced because the training programs take unemployed workers off the unemployment rolls during their period of training, quite aside from any employment effects following the completion of training. By using enrollment in four manpower programs (Neighborhood Youth Corps, MDTA on-the-job training, Community Action [paid professionals], and college work study), estimates have been made that for the period 1965–67 enrollment in these programs reduced by .15 of a percentage point the overall unemployment rate in 1965, .3 of a percentage point in 1966, and .4 of a percentage point in 1967 (from 4.2 percent to 3.8 percent). While enrollment in the programs satisfied the statistical definition of employment used in U. S. household surveys, some would claim that the critical question is how successful such persons are after they leave the programs rather than their "removal" from the unemployment rolls during their training.

In somewhat similar vein, training programs can be used (as has been done in Sweden) to regulate the labor supply in the short-run as a countercyclical device. In periods of national unemployment, more trainees are enrolled in training programs and they are kept in them for a longer period of time, to help reduce aggregate unemployment. In periods of tight labor markets and inflationary wage–price pressures, training programs are reduced in both size and duration of enrollment.

It is clear that if government funds are used to establish training programs that relate training to a work situation in such a way as to be classed as "employment," the government can go far toward taking workers off the unemployment rolls and in reducing aggregate "unemployment." In these models, either the unemployed workers are given "jobs" and "employment" by being enrolled in a government-sponsored training-work program, or the unemployment rate is reduced by taking workers out of the labor force—that is, by reducing the labor supply when they are placed in a training program. If the training-work programs were based on government public works or public employment of some kind, it is conceivable that the programs could be expanded sufficiently to very substantially contribute to reduced aggregate unemployment, especially among the poor and disadvantaged. If the government were forced to rely on training-work programs in private industry, the limits would be established by the size of the incentive subsidies and by the employers' willingness to take on additional work-trainees in response to subsidy incentives. Estimates for training programs in 1965–67 could be used to project the reduction in national unemployment that might occur with a 10, 25, or 50 percent increase in enrollment in these programs.

2. Quite aside from the direct "enrollment" employment effects of training programs, these programs can be said to create jobs if the government expenditures on training facilities, instruction, and allowances augment aggregate and regional demand and do not merely replace other expenditures that would have been made in the absence of training. In depressed areas, especially, where unemployment rates are high, large-scale government expenditures on manpower-training programs would have a significant impact on total expenditures and would not be offset by a decline in other expenditures in that area. The multiplier effect of such training programs might serve to significantly increase aggregate demand and employment.

3.   Retraining programs would help to create jobs if employers were induced to establish new plants in depressed areas—which would not have been established elsewhere—because of the availability of newly retrained workers in the depressed area. Studies have indicated that lack of skilled workers in a depressed area serves as a deterrent to the entrance of new plants, and that the improvement of local skills can be an important inducement to industrialization.

4.   Training programs can create jobs if any decrease in expenditures made elsewhere (as a result of the training expenditures) is in a sector that is capital-intensive. Such a decrease in spending would not decrease employment by as much as employment would be increased through the hiring of the trained workers. Since training would reduce the real costs of labor, employers may be induced to hire more of the cheaper factor relative to capital. Furthermore, the lower cost of labor resulting from training programs might induce some shift from savings to consumption; for jobs will be created by retraining programs if employers become more willing to hire trainees because of their new skills even though the employers had no "job vacancies" before the trainees presented themselves on the scene.

5.   Aside from the job-creation effect of retraining under certain circumstances, unemployment will be reduced if structural causes are deemed to be important. Unemployed workers with new skills can fill the jobs that are vacant because qualified workers had been unavailable. If the filling of one vacant job removes a bottleneck by permitting additional workers to be hired, the training program could have a multiplier effect in reducing unemployment. This argument is based on the structural hypothesis and assumes a substantial number of job vacancies that could be filled by upgrading the skills of the unemployed. As noted above, some deny this premise, and further studies are needed to provide a factual basis for the optimism of the proponents of training on this score.

In summary, arguments can be made in support of the belief that training programs can reduce aggregate unemployment levels through direct enrollment effects as well as through post-training experience. Clearly the contribution of training can be greatest if accompanied by a vigorous expansionary monetary–fiscal policy, or public employment program. It would be empirically difficult to disentangle the employment contributions of the training programs from those of the monetary–fiscal policy or other job creation.

However, in theory it is possible to construct a model which gives a significant independent role to retraining programs in the reduction of aggregate unemployment. Up to a point, the larger the scale of the training programs, the larger the reduction in unemployment. However, where diminishing returns would begin is difficult to determine theoretically or estimate empirically.

Effects on income distribution, poverty, and costs arising from related social ills

Many of the points raised in the discussion on the aggregate employment effects of manpower-training programs also apply to the aggregate income effects. However, by concentrating on the lowest-income disadvantaged groups, the retraining programs could have an important effect in reducing poverty, regardless of their impact on the aggregate level of income in the economy. MDTA data show that 81 percent of institutional trainees and 50 percent of on-the-job trainees who were family heads and who were in training in 1966 had covered earnings of less than $3,000 or had no covered earnings for the last full year before entering training. Since a number of the training-related programs of the war on poverty, such as the Job Corps and the Neighborhood Youth Corps, are directed to more disadvantaged groups than are found among MDTA trainees, it is likely that the total national training effort has had a significant effect in raising the incomes of those in the lowest income category. As had been indicated above, most of the detailed follow-up analyses have shown a significant increase in income after training as compared to period before training. Mangum, who has made the most detailed study of this question, concludes:

> *Although its contribution to the over-all reduction of poverty is small, MDTA has made a significant contribution to the income of its poor enrollees. To have helped between 175,000 and 225,000 low income persons in a period of more than four years, half of whom were probably heads of families, to raise their incomes from just below the poverty line to a little above it is gratifying, particularly when compared with experiences of other programs. However, the dent made in the problem of the 9,000,000 poor families is hardly noticeable.*[3]

Obviously, a substantial expansion of training programs geared to the needs of the disadvantaged would help additional families to escape from poverty.

It is in this realm that the broader social benefits of retraining programs become most obvious. If, as a result of new skills, new jobs, and higher

---

[3]Garth L. Mangum, *Contributions and Costs of Manpower Development and Training* (Ann Arbor: University of Michigan, 1967).

income, the reduction in poverty is accompanied by a reduction in crime and delinquency, society gains additional benefits. (A number of studies have indicated such a relationship.) Along this line, a number of experiments have shown that training programs within correctional institutions help not only to increase employment and income after release from the correctional institution, but also to reduce recidivism.

Reduction in inflationary pressures

Some economists argue that government-subsidized retraining programs can be fully justified only in a period of tight labor markets and inflationary pressures. By this reasoning, while in a period of general labor surplus government retraining programs may merely change the composition of the unemployed, in time of labor shortages public retraining can become an important anti-inflationary force. Thus, retraining plays a major role in policies designed to bring about full employment by reducing the inflationary pressures created by expansionist monetary–fiscal policy as the economy approaches full employment.

Although this position has merit, there are caveats that must be observed. First, in a period of tight labor markets, the remaining unemployed are likely to be heavily concentrated among the hardcore disadvantaged. These are the very workers who are least likely to be trained for the critically short occupations, which usually require a higher level of general education than is customarily found among the most disadvantaged.

Second, private employers can be expected to increase their own training efforts in a period of labor shortage. Since to evaluate the economic impact of federal retraining requires the determination of what would have happened in the absence of this public activity, a period of full employment may be one in which the social net "benefits" of subsidized retraining are less than one would suppose. Finally, it should be noted that even if the benefits of retraining increase in a period of full employment, the costs of retraining may also be expected to increase in such a period. The costs of instructors and facilities will be higher, and the opportunity costs of the training will rise.

Although there are a priori grounds for believing that retraining programs can help move the economy to higher levels of aggregate employment at lower levels of inflationary pressure, the contribution of retraining to this effect depends, once more, upon the structural hypothesis: if there is a serious imbalance and mismatching between the composition of the unemployed and the composition of the additional demand for labor induced by expansionist monetary fiscal policy, the increased expenditures will result in rising prices rather than increased output in employment.

Studies are not yet available to show the extent to which retraining has helped to reduce any imbalance that might exist between the increase of job vacancies and the remaining unemployed, in a period of expansionist monetary fiscal policy. Lacking detailed information on job vacancies as well as the detailed characteristics of the unemployed, we cannot take the first step in appraising the extent of the structural imbalance, let alone appraise the contribution of retraining in resolving that imbalance. Whereas the government retraining programs have probably made some dent in the "hardcore" occupational shortages that have become almost a tradition in the labor market, there is no evidence that the impact has yet been a sizable one. In spite of the many MDTA courses in such occupations as drafting, welding, auto mechanics, secretarial work, nurses' aide work, these occupations continue to suffer national shortages.

Recent discussion of inflation in the United States has focused attention on the trade-off between inflation and unemployment—a problem analyzed in some detail earlier in the book. The structure of labor and product markets yields a relationship between the rate of inflation and the rate of unemployment. These seem to indicate that thus far it has been possible to have a lower rate of unemployment only at the cost of a higher rate of inflation. Fiscal and monetary policies alone have been incapable of attaining full employment and price stability simultaneously. Policy measures designed to influence the structure of the market, such as manpower policy, are designed to alter this relationship.

A large-scale occupational training program is an element of both manpower policy and fiscal policy. Expenditures on training or financial incentives for training affect not only market structure but also aggregate demand. To the degree there is a curve relating inflation and unemployment, it is not immediately clear, therefore, whether a large-scale training program will cause a shift of the curve or a movement along it, or both. This element of uncertainty will recur often in our examination.

Conclusion

There now appears to be fairly conclusive evidence that the large-scale retraining programs in the United States in the 1960s have resulted in increased employment and improved incomes for the trainees. Cost-benefit analyses have indicated that the expenditures on these programs have constituted a form of investment offering high and positive rates of return.

However, there are no parallel studies to show the effects of these retraining programs on aggregate levels of employment, unemployment, income, or price levels. These questions can be dealt with only in conjectural and theoretical terms while we await more definitive empirical studies. The effects of large-scale training programs on the reduction of poverty or of inflationary pressures follow directly from the conclusions drawn from their impact on employment and income. Thus, these ancillary effects must also remain largely in the realm of theory and conjecture.

However little we can say that is conclusive about the short-run, counter-cyclical effects of retraining programs, we are on much safer ground in assuming an important contribution of retraining to the long-run increase in skills, productivity, and real Gross National Product.

Readings

"The Development and Use of Manpower." *Proceedings of the 20th Annual Meeting,* December 1967. Industrial Relations Research Association, Madison, 1967.

Hardin, Einar and Michael E. Borus, *The Economic Benefits and Costs of Retraining.* Boston: D. C. Heath, 1971.

Hameresh, Daniel S. *Economic Aspects of Manpower Training Programs: Theory and Policy.* Boston: D. C. Heath, 1971.

Levitan, Sar and Garth Mangum. *Federal Training and Work Programs in the Sixties.* Ann Arbor: University of Michigan–Wayne State, 1969.

Reubens, Beatrice G. *The Hard-to-Employ: European Programs.* New York: Columbia University, 1970.

Ross, Arthur M., ed. *Employment Policy and the Labor Market.* Berkeley and Los Angeles: University of California Press, 1965.

Sewell, David O. *Critique of Cost–Benefit Analysis of Training.* Kingston, Ontario: Industrial Relations Centre, 1971.

Somers, Gerald G., ed. *Retraining the Unemployed.* Madison: University of Wisconsin Press, 1968.

Ziderman, Adrian. "Cost and Benefits of Adult Retraining in the United Kingdom," *Economica* (November 1969).

The manpower revolution of the 1960s

The need for evaluation

The evaluation of manpower policies

Some major policy considerations

Public-service employment

The need to integrate public employment with manpower, educational, and regional development policies

Role of the employment service in manpower policy

Obstacles to a manpower role

The decentralization of manpower policies

Who should be served?

Chapter Twenty-five

Manpower Policies at the Crossroads

The manpower revolution of the 1960s

Where do we go from here? The starting point in answering this question might be a brief review of how rapidly manpower policies developed, proliferated, and changed in the past decade.

In President Nixon's first message to the Congress following his State of the Union Address of 1968, he proposed a $2.1 billion manpower program, "the largest in the nation's history, to help Americans who wanted to work get a job." Anomalously, this record request for manpower programs occurred, as the President noted, after seven years of economic expansion, when the unemployment rate had been reduced from over 6 percent to 3.8 percent.

These years of economic growth had witnessed a revolution in American manpower policies. The 1968 message announced a new program for training and placing disadvantaged workers through the cooperation of government and private employers. It was simply one more addition to an unparalleled stream of similar federal legislation geared to the nation's unemployed, poor, and disadvantaged. As we entered the 1960s federal involvement in manpower programs went little beyond cooperation with the states in maintaining employment offices and promoting apprenticeship training. And the initial legislative efforts were not geared specifically to the needs of the disadvantaged. The relatively minor funds allocated for retraining programs in the Area Redevelopment Act of 1961 were designed primarily to aid depressed areas rather than depressed people. Even the Manpower Development and Training Act, passed in 1962, started at a relatively low level and was designed to give experienced workers new skills when their old skills had been outmoded by advancing technology.

The MDTA's initial programs skimmed the cream of the unemployed rather than reaching the most disadvantaged in the labor market. The retraining provisions of the Trade Expansion Act of the same year were also designed to aid in the readjustment of experienced workers displaced through the liberalization of international trade. And although the Vocational Education Act of 1963 attempted to encourage greater training efforts for the disadvantaged, it essentially strengthened a system that called for a level of education beyond their reach. Starting with this emphasis on the readjustment of the technologically and economically displaced, the federal manpower programs turned increasingly toward the disadvantaged as the decade advanced.

At the same time, the network of manpower programs for the poor was greatly expanded with the launching of the "War on Poverty" under the Economic Opportunity Act of 1964. The Job Corps (residential training centers for youth), the Neighborhood Youth Corps (work experience and training for youth), and Operation Mainstream (public service jobs and private nonprofit jobs for adults) are all directed toward the employment problems of the poor—the hard core of the nation's hard-to-place. Toward the end of 1967, the Social Security Act was amended to provide a major program of work and/or training for employable people on the rolls of the Aid to Families with Dependent Children (AFDC). This Work Incentive Program (WIN) was amended effective July 1, 1972 to increase its training emphasis. A variety of local programs were brought together in a so-called Concentrated Employment Program focused on the ghetto areas of the nation's major cities; and proposals in the late '60s urged the expansion of CEP. The Nixon Administration placed great emphasis on the JOBS (Job Opportunities in the Business Sector) program, a system of subsidies to private employers to induce them to hire, train and retrain the disadvantaged.

A highly significant manpower development in 1971 was passage of the Emergency Employment Act, which provided approximately 150,000 public service jobs for the unemployed, with an annual appropriation of approximately $1 billion. This approach to employment is likely to expand in future years. Although its initial experience was favorable when judged by numbers employed in record time in 1971, there were relatively few disadvantaged among them.

As is seen in Table 25/1, total new enrollments in these federally assisted work and training programs continued to increase in the 1970s. The expected new enrollment in 1973 is 2.9 million. However, it is also seen that there is little anticipated expansion in institutional MDTA programs and an actual decline in the JOBS program. On the other hand, the WIN program will grow.

Thus, starting from a position of near zero at the beginning of this decade, the federal government has now called upon a variety of manpower programs to help solve the problems of depressed areas, technological unemployment, foreign-trade expansion, poverty, the growing relief rolls, and inflation.

Although retraining has been accorded a principal role in this network of manpower policies, it must be noted that there has been a recent tendency to depart from retraining for a concentration on shorter-run programs. Retraining programs not only assume a greater sense of motivation on the part of the trainee, but they also call for a larger investment in time and money for both the trainee and the federal government. When fires are burning in the hearts of the great cities, there is always a temptation to put out those fires with rapid-action programs designed to place unemployed youth and adults on jobs—any jobs—and worry about their long-run productivity later. Thus, manpower programs have increasingly become a complex mixture of recruitment techniques, motivating sessions, counseling, job development, and placement, in addition to a basic emphasis on training and retraining.

To recruit, train, and place increasing numbers of the disadvantaged, attention has turned away from institutional vocational programs toward aid and cooperation from employers for on-the-job training. Just as it has been announced that two-thirds of the training under MDTA should be allocated

Table 25/1. New enrollments[1] in federally assisted
work and training programs, fiscal years
1964 and 1970–73 (thousands)

Program	Fiscal year				
	1964	1970	1971	1972 (estimated)	1973 (projected)
Total	278	1,830	2,109	2,318	2,292
Institutional training under the MDTA	69	130	156	166	166
JOBS (federally financed) and other OJT[2]	9	177	184	136	131
Neighborhood Youth Corps:					
In-school and summer		436	562	583	567
Out-of-school		46	53	49	49
Operation Mainstream		12	22	22	22
Public Service Careers		4	45	32	29
Concentrated Employment Program		110	77	69	69
Job Corps		43	50	53	55
Work Incentive Program		93	96	112	133
Public Employment Program				160	92
Veterans programs	([3])	83	86	83	83
Vocational rehabilitation	179	411	468	517	553
Other programs[4]	21	285	311	335	339

[1]Generally larger than the number of training or work opportunities programed because turnover or short-term training results in more than one individual in a given enrollment opportunity. Persons served by more than one program are counted only once.
[2]Includes the MDTA–OJT program which ended with fiscal 1970 (except for national contracts) and the JOBS Optional Program which began with fiscal 1971; also Apprenticeship Outreach, with 27,500 enrollees in fiscal 1971.
[3]Included with "other programs."
[4]Includes a wide variety of programs, some quite small—for example, Foster Grandparents and vocational training for Indians provided by the Department of the Interior. Data for some programs are estimated.
Note: Detail may not add to totals because of rounding.
Source: Office of Management and Budget, Special Analysis, Budget of the United States Government, Fiscal year 1973, pp. 140 and 142.

to the disadvantaged, it has also been indicated that a larger proportion of the training efforts will be conducted through on-the-job programs. The Nixon Administration has carried this process further than before in providing subsidies to private employers for training and placement of disadvantaged unemployed. However, the JOBS program has faltered in the recession of the early 1970s.

The need for evaluation

To those who have long looked with envy at the highly developed manpower programs of Sweden and other European countries, the rapid growth of retraining and manpower programs in the United States has been a heartening development. Although appropriations for manpower measures have not always been as generous as their most enthusiastic supporters would wish, it must generally be conceded that during the 1960s Congress showed a remarkable willingness to expand programs of training and job development for the disadvantaged. In some cases, as with the concentrated employment program for black youth in the centers of large cities, the administration and Congress moved farther and faster than even some government and academic experts deemed wise. However, the readily forthcoming amendments to the MDTA and the continuing expansion of manpower programs for the poor, as we moved through the middle of that decade, left the program administrators breathless and the academic research evaluators concerned.

Those interested in effective manpower policy raised such questions as, "Do we really know the employment and income effects of these training programs?" "Do we really know whether retraining provides greater benefits, relative to costs, than counseling, job development, or placement activities?" "Do we really know whether it is better for workers' economic security and employment satisfaction that they be trained in the vocational schools as contrasted with training by private employers, on-the-job?" Friends of the new manpower revolution urged that such questions were untimely and inopportune. They replied, "Even if we do not know the exact dimensions of the benefit-cost ratios of these training and employment programs, we are generally convinced that they are doing some good. After all, what harm can there be in attempting to give a hard-core unemployed worker some new skills or in developing the lines of communication by which he can find out about job opportunities and be placed in contact with potential employers?" Until recently, Congress was willing to go along with this point of view, expanding the network of manpower policies without raising any searching questions.

In the early 1970s, however, it is obvious that searching questions must be raised. Continuing costs of the military budget and the persistence of inflation have convinced Congress and the Administration of the need for retrenchment in social programs. The classic economic issue must finally be met in the manpower field: the allocation of scarce resources among alternative means and goals. In the euphoria of Congressional approval, it was reasonable that the stress on operations, on getting the job done, would take precedence over an evaluation of the effectiveness of those operations. But even the most enthusiastic supporters of training and employment programs must now stop and take stock. We can no longer expand in all directions. Which programs will best satisfy our goals?

The required stock-taking in the manpower field coincides with the flowering of an evaluative technique that began in the Department of Defense under Secretary McNamara and spread, on paper at least, throughout the federal government structure. This was the so-called PPBS—The Planning, Programming, and Budgeting System—which specified that before any government expenditure could be incorporated into the budget, the goals of the program had to be clearly identified, and all the alternative means to the achievement of that goal carefully studied for comparative costs and benefits. The procedures are discussed in Chapter 22 and demonstrated in Chapter 23. And only when the most favorable cost-benefit ratio is established for a particular procedure is that procedure to be translated into a budgetary item. With the spread of this systems approach throughout the federal apparatus, it is not surprising that cost-benefit analyses received central attention in the potential evaluation of training and other manpower programs.

The evaluation of manpower policies

The evaluation of the total system of federal manpower policies is similar to that indicated for training and retraining in the preceding chapter. There is evidence of economic gain for most of those enrolled in manpower programs, even though there are many participants who appear to gain nothing and there are more wide-scale failures within some particular manpower policies. As noted above, the JOBS approach to subsidized on-the-job training has not proved to be generally effective in a period of declining employment opportunities. Initial evaluations of the Work Incentive Program (WIN), designed to move welfare recipients from relief to employment, have been generally unfavorable. Relatively few enrollees in this work and training program have been able to achieve economic self-sufficiency as a result of their enrollment.[1] Experience under the Neighborhood Youth Corps and the Job Corps has been mixed.

---

[1] See the discussions of these failures in Sar Levitan and Robert Taggart, *Social Experimentation and Manpower Policy* (Baltimore, Md.: Johns Hopkins Press, 1971), pp. 47–55. See also, Olympus Research Corporation, "The Total Impact of Manpower Programs: A Four-City Case Study," September 1971. This 900-page report submitted to the U. S. Department of Labor covers research over a period of three years in Boston, Denver, San Francisco and Oakland. Its findings generally accord with those indicated in this section.

In all of these programs, success is predicated on the assumption that job opportunities will be awaiting the graduates. In an economy hovering between 5 and 6 percent unemployment, this assumption has often been unwarranted.

Even those who point to the careful studies indicating a favorable benefit-cost ratio for particular manpower policies cannot establish that these policies have had a major impact on the economy. Ten years after the passage of the MDTA, there were still millions of unemployed workers, especially among racial minorities and the disadvantaged; there were still millions in poverty, especially in depressed rural areas and in the urban ghettos. It is easy to respond that one could not expect the sums spent on manpower, so paltry compared to the mammoth national budget, to have notable national impact on unemployment, poverty, or inflation. However, proponents of manpower policies cannot prove that even a multiple expansion of manpower expenditures would have the desired effects in solving these national economic problems. A favorable benefit-cost ratio for particular programs and the participants cannot necessarily be extrapolated to a favorable benefit-cost ratio for a manpower program of ten times the size.

It is for these reasons that manpower policies in the United States are now at the crossroads. The Nixon Administration, having reallocated much of its manpower interests and funds to JOBS and WIN, only to see these programs falter, has inevitably begun to raise serious questions about the scope, direction—and even the usefulness—of the types of manpower programs that came into being in the 1960s.

Some major policy considerations

In spite of the reservations about manpower policies in some government and academic circles, it is not likely that there will be any substantial reduction in funds allocated to structural labor-market policies of the type discussed above. Indeed, given continuing unemployment, poverty, and inflation, the political and economic necessities almost require an expansion of particularized employment policies. The important questions, then, for the next decade of manpower policies center around the principal emphasis of these policies, the administration of the policies and the principal clientele to be served by newly devised manpower programs. Each of these questions is discussed briefly below.

Public-service employment

Given the limited success of the JOBS approach to assisting the disadvantaged, it is inevitable that attention has turned to government as "the employer of last resort." As an employer the public service, especially at the state and local levels, represents one of the few persistently expanding sectors of the U. S. economy. Given a persistence of high rates of unemployment in the private sector, major reliance is to be placed upon public employment if the chronically unemployed and disadvantaged are to be reabsorbed into the labor market.

The Emergency Employment Act of 1971 is a significant piece of legislation not only because of its magnitude but also because of its portent for the future. Its budget of $1 billion for fiscal 1972 meant that this program accounted for 15 percent of "manpower" expenditures in its first year, and this budget makes it by far the most significant piece of legislation since the 1930s designed for the creation of jobs in the public sector. Even its first year budget equals the combined expenditures for all other work experience and training programs for public employment, including Operation Mainstream, Work Incentive, and the Neighborhood Youth Corps. Expenditures of this size have the potential for a significant impact on the employment of the disadvantaged.[2]

The prime importance of EEA, however, is especially related to its probable future growth. It is likely to grow larger in the 1970s. There are proposals in Congress for a manifold increase in public-service employment over the 1972 budget. It is conceivable that public-service employment will play the role in the 1970s that MDTA and related manpower policies played in the 1960s as a means of attacking the problems of unemployment.

The Emergency Employment Act provides an unusual opportunity for unemployed workers in depressed areas, not only because of its current budget and probable growth, but also because it embodies features of decentralization which states and localities might utilize to give special assistance to specific areas of need. In this sense, it is the first of the "manpower" measures to embody the principles of decentralization that the Nixon Administration espoused through its proposals on revenue sharing.

Although it is not yet possible to make a full assessment of the functioning of EEA, there is reason to believe that this present act does little to reduce hardcore unemployment problems and poverty among the disadvantaged. A major increase in appropriations for public-service employment would undoubtedly improve this situation. However, unless the current approach is significantly revised, the nation's most serious unemployment and underemployment problems are not likely to be met.

The current legislation is designed to give preference to a number of conflicting groups. Although applicants must be unemployed or underemployed to qualify for EEA jobs, aid for the disadvantaged or hardcore unemployed is only one of a number of preferences listed. Most important is the fact that the Labor Department guidelines state that one-third of all participants should be Vietnam or Southeast-Asia veterans. This has resulted in the

---

[2] *The Emergency Employment Act: An Interim Assessment,* Subcommittee on Employment, Manpower and Poverty of the Committee on Labor and Public Welfare, U. S. Senate, May 1972.

fact that 30 percent of urban and 20 percent of rural participants are from this group even though Vietnam-era veterans constitute less than 7 percent of national unemployment. The official statistics indicate that the disadvantaged constitute one-third of the enrollees, and welfare recipients represent only about 10 percent of the enrollees. Since only 6 to 8 percent have had an eighth-grade education or less and since 16 to 19 percent are black, one is led to question the definition of "disadvantaged" used in the official statistics. Moreover, these proportions are roughly the same for urban and rural areas. The latter would be expected to include more of the persistently depressed areas. Because of the preference given to Vietnam veterans, there has been a tendency to bypass workers under 21 and over 55. Indeed, only 6 to 7 percent of the enrollees have been 55 and over, dependent on their urban or rural location. Whereas only 16 percent of all those the EEA hires have been under 21 or over 55, these two age groups represented 45 percent of national unemployment in 1971.

Quite aside from the limited number of jobs that might be created in the most depressed rural areas under the initial EEA approach, there is no evidence that the most needy in such areas were being assisted in proportion to their numbers in the rural population.

The initial public-service employment program was not designed primarily to aid the disadvantaged, and its tendency to bypass many of the disadvantaged affects urban as well as rural areas. However, the most persistent problems of unemployment and underemployment, especially for the relatively high proportion of older and younger workers, are most notable in rural areas. An Act that gives very high priority to such groups as Vietnam veterans and recently unemployed aerospace engineers is not likely to have a significant impact in solving the problems of hardcore unemployment in rural areas, especially where these problems have been persistent over lengthy periods of time.

The need to integrate public employment with manpower, educational, and regional development policies

There are two major lessons to be learned from the experience with manpower policies in the 1960s: first, training and other manpower programs, either institutional or private-employment, cannot be effective in the absence of suitable job opportunities; and second, isolated manpower programs are limited in furthering employment and income. Jobs must be available at the end of the lines, and manpower policies must be integrated with educational programs and other economic policies if the disadvantaged are to be materially aided in obtaining those jobs. It is here that a revised Public Service Employment measure can play its principal role.

Public-service employment can serve as the means by which manpower policy (training, relocation, employment services), basic education, vocational education, and area redevelopment can be integrated to further employment, income, and the quality of life in urban ghettos and rural depressed areas. Occupational skill training, under a variety of current programs, can be effective if it is closely integrated with the creation of new jobs in the public sector. At the same time, the skills developed through training programs and experience in public employment can serve as a major inducement to private industry to locate in areas of unemployment and underemployment. Basic literacy education, taken by itself, has done little to improve employment opportunities of functional illiterates. But when closely integrated with occupational training, on-the-job or in close connection with a job, it has proved to be a significant step forward. Not only can these integrated policies serve to further the employment and income of the disadvantaged, but, also, the skills and experience that result from them can serve to improve the infrastructure and quality of life in the areas in which they live.

It should be noted, however, that the required integration of public employment, manpower policies, educational policies, and area development will not come about without specific provisions designed to achieve such integration. The mere parallel existence of such programs does not assure their integration. More must be done than simply the present EEA stipulation of a vague preference for the graduates of manpower programs along with many other preferences. If the disadvantaged are to be absorbed, a much larger proportion of an expanded EEA budget must be earmarked for training, retraining, basic education, and other manpower services.

If EEA is to contribute significantly to the employment and income of the disadvantaged, it must provide job opportunities that are more than temporary. Career opportunities in the public service are possible only if job creation is accompanied by programs for skill development. Skill development for careers in the public service will also constitute the surest attraction for private industry in depressed areas. Upgrading through the training of present personnel to fill current shortages in public agencies should be accompanied by a specification of manpower and education services for the hard-core unemployed so that they may take their place on the beginning rung of the occupational ladder in public employment. Forestry projects and other public works can serve as a temporary haven if they are associated with skill development.

Role of the employment service in manpower policy

With the passage of the ARA, the MDTA, and the "alphabet soup" of manpower programs that have been initiated in the past ten years, the federal–state Employment Service has been called upon to play an ever-increasing role in selecting participants and in placing the graduates of manpower programs. The emphasis of these programs on the chronically unemployed, the disadvantaged, and racial minorities presented a special challenge to the traditional role of the Employment Service. The new programs called for a transformation from the traditional labor-supply and labor-matching role of USES to that of investment in human resources development for the most needy in the labor force. Authority and some resources have been allocated to the USES to enable it to assume this new role. And, in spite of serious questions about its success to date, proposed legislation by the Nixon Administration would assign even greater manpower responsibilities to the federal–state system for a decentralized manpower approach.

Obstacles to a manpower role

In their recent critique of the federal–state Employment Service, Stanley Ruttenberg and Jocelyn Gutchess reflect the earlier view of other critics in describing the major institutional barriers preventing the necessary changes required to make the Employment Service an effective national manpower administrative agency:

1.   *the basic funding process which ties the employment service to the unemployment insurance system through a tax levied on employers;*

2.   *the dichotomy that exists between the Wagner-Peyser precept of universal service and the present-day imperative to concentrate resources on those most in need of employment assistance;*

3.   *the built-in divisive contest between the unemployment insurance service and the employment service;*

4.   *the long-standing acceptance by both federal and state employment service staffs of a body of established custom, prerogative, and procedure which frustrates federal direction whether through the budgetary process or through other administrative devices;*

5.   *antiquated state civil service systems with inadequate or noncompetitive salary levels and stultified personnel policies;*

6.   *the abdication by the federal government to the states of responsibility for training of manpower staff; and*

7.   *the Interstate Conference of Employment Security Agencies, which from its unique position as a federally subsidized pressure group has presumed for itself a*

role in the operation of the national manpower program far beyond the usual concept of pressure politics in our democratic system.

It is noted that a number of these obstacles are embedded in the basic structure and historical development of the U. S. Employment Service. Others stem from the inability of staff members to adjust their attitudes and policies. Still other impediments arise from the federal–state system of government itself. Thus, some obstacles will not be easily removed, whereas others can be overcome in the near future if there is sufficient resolve to do so at the federal and state levels.

The decentralization of manpower policies

A major thrust of the Nixon Administration in the manpower field has been in the direction of decentralization of manpower policies. In keeping with his general proposal for revenue sharing with the states, it is proposed that manpower funds be allocated in a bloc procedure to the governors of the 50 states, which are to be given considerable autonomy in allocating the funds to municipalities and to various manpower programs within their jurisdiction.

Experience of the past decades indicates that some decentralization of planning and administering manpower policies would further their effectiveness. However, there are dangers of inefficiency and misdirected goals if the move to greater local control is not gradual and does not proceed on the basis of demonstrated competence and responsibility at the local level. This calls for initial programs of training for manpower planners and administrators of manpower programs at state, county, and municipal levels, and it calls for federal guidelines and careful monitoring by federal agencies.

Who should be served?

As noted above, federal manpower policies in the United States moved increasingly to a focus on the most disadvantaged workers in the labor force during the 1960s. The original MDTA thrust toward upgrading the skills of those who were in danger of displacement through technological change was redirected toward the solution of the problems of poverty and hardcore unemployment. Unlike Canada and many European countries, the United States government provides little financial aid for the training of employed workers within industry even though some assistance is provided to vocational and technical schools.

The question of appropriate target groups for federal manpower policies came to a head in late 1971 because of a sharp rise in the unemployment of "highly educated" manpower, especially scientists and engineers. It was estimated that there were approximately 75,000 unemployed scientists and engineers and approximately as many unemployed technicians. The unemployment rate of college-educated scientific and engineering workers was placed in the range of 5 percent.[3] As a result of these disturbing statistics, some urged that federal manpower expenditures be reduced in favor of aid to the "best educated" instead of to the "least educated" in American society. It was felt that the substantial investment that high-level manpower had made in themselves and that government had made in them through the educational system should be protected by further public expenditures on special programs of retraining and relocation for scientists and engineers who had been displaced by changes in technology and government defense policy.[4]

Others countered that the "most advantaged" workers in the professional ranks were still more able to help themselves, in spite of their temporary unemployment, than the least skilled and the least educated; that the scarce resources available for manpower policy should continue to be focused on the poor and the chronically unemployed.

Essentially, the decision concerning appropriate clientele for manpower programs will reflect one's value judgments and broad philosophical outlook. It is the feeling of the authors that the manpower policies of the future should continue to be oriented primarily to those who suffer most serious disadvantages in the labor market: minorities, women, the poorly educated and trained. This is in keeping with a private-enterprise economy and the notion that government should do the most for those who are least able to fend for themselves. At the same time, future manpower policy should not be unmindful of the needs of skilled, professional, and technical workers since the problems of the next decade include faltering productivity as well as poverty and unemployment. For the better-situated, more highly skilled work force, government assistance could take the form of furthering the efficient allocation of resources to meet projected needs. The use of manpower policy to mitigate inflationary pressures would call for more emphasis on upgrading employees to meet skill shortages. The policies would be so designed as to permit the most disadvantaged unemployed to fill the positions opened through the upgrading of employed workers. And efforts would be made, in turn, to ensure that the newly hired workers have an opportunity to move up the occupational ladder through further skill development.

Finally, it should be stressed once again that manpower policies in the United States can be effective only if they are integrated within their own

---

[3]See E. Wight Bakke, *Manpower Policy for Scientists and Engineers* (Washington: National Manpower Policy Task Force, March 1972), pp. 4–5.

[4]*Ibid.*, pp. 18–20.

sphere and with broader social and economic policies. The choice of training, relocation assistance, work experience, and counseling must be geared to the needs of the individual workers and the needs of society at the time the choice is made. The role of the Employment Service, area redevelopment, industrial relocation and aggregative monetary–fiscal policies must be integrally related to the choice of specific manpower policies. Public-service employment and legislation to halt discrimination based on race or sex will also be required in a total package of social and economic policies if any one of them is to be effective.

Readings

Bakke, E. W. *A Positive Labor Market Policy.* Columbus, Ohio: Charles Merrill, 1963.

Gordon, R. A., ed. *Toward a Manpower Policy.* John Wiley and Sons, 1967.

Holt, Charles C., et al., *The Unemployment-Inflation Dilemma: A Manpower Solution;* and *Manpower Programs to Reduce Inflation and Unemployment: Manpower Lyrics for Macro Music.* Chicago: The Urban Institute, 1971.

Lester, Richard A. *Manpower Planning in a Free Society.* Princeton, N. J.: Princeton University Press, 1966.

Levitan, Sar A., and Robert Taggart III. *Social Experimentation and Manpower Policy.* Baltimore, Md.: Johns Hopkins Press, 1971.

Manpower Report of the President, United States Department of Labor. Washington, D. C.: U. S. Government Printing Office, 1972.

Myers, Charles A. *The Role of the Private Sector in Manpower Development.* Baltimore, Md.: Johns Hopkins Press, 1971.

National Manpower Policy Task Force. *Manpower Policy and Programs: A Look Ahead: 1973.* Washington, D. C., December 20, 1972.

Twentieth Century Fund. *The Job Crisis for Black Youth.* New York: Praeger Publishers, 1971.

Weber, A., et al. *Public-Private Manpower Policies.* Madison, Wi.: Industrial Relations Research Association, 1969.

Weber, A., and G. Schultz. *Strategies for the Displaced Worker.* New York: Harper and Row, 1966.

Appendix Labor Laws and Glossary of Important Labor Law Terms

Laws (in chronological order)

Railway Labor Act, 1926, 1934, 1951, and 1966 This Act provides machinery for naming bargaining agents through elections conducted by the National Mediation Board. Some of its other provisions are:
a. Disputes over the application of collective-bargaining contracts in the railroad industry may be referred to the National Railroad Adjustment Board;
b. If either party (railroad or union) desires to make a change in the wages, or other bargainable conditions, it must give 30-day written notice to the other party;
c. If after all other procedures have failed and a strike is threatened, the President is authorized to appoint an emergency board to investigate and report to him concerning the dispute within 30 days. Strikes and lockouts are forbidden until the emergency board reports and for 30 days after.

Norris–LaGuardia Act 1932 This Act forbids the use of injunctions in labor disputes by federal courts except in special cases—such as when law-enforcement officials are unable to safeguard the employers' property, or when to not grant the injunction would cause greater harm to the employer than the gain derived by the union.

The "yellow dog" contract (See Glossary of important labor law terms, below) was also invalidated by this Act.

The Wagner Act (National Labor Relations Act) 1935 This Act establishes that employees' rights to organize into labor organizations and to bargain collectively concerning their wage and working conditions should be protected. This Act makes unfair labor practice the following procedures:
a. Interfering in the exercise of employees' rights to organize and bargain collectively;
b. Interfering in the formation or administration of any labor organization;
c. Encouraging or discouraging membership in any labor organization by discrimination with respect to hiring or firing;
d. Discriminating against an employee who has filed charges under this Act;
e. Refusing to bargain collectively with the majority representative of his employees.

This Act also establishes election machinery to allow employees to choose collective-bargaining representatives. To administer the Act, the National Labor Relations Board was set up.

The Fair Labor Standards Act 1938   This Act, and its various amendments, establishes minimum-wage, overtime, and child-labor standards for employers engaged in interstate commerce or producing goods destined for interstate commerce.

Byrnes Anti-strikebreaking Act of 1938   The Act forbids the interstate transportation of workers to be used to interfere with peaceful picketing or collective bargaining.

The Taft–Hartley Act, 1947   This Act was designed to correct the believed imbalance in labor–management relations by forbidding unfair labor practices of unions against employers and employees. It also attempts to protect the public against labor disputes in work stoppages that threaten the national welfare. Important provisions limiting strike activity and regulating unions are:

a. Desire to terminate or modify an agreement requires a 60-day written notice prior to the expiration date of the contract by the party desiring the change.
b. If a national emergency is deemed to exist, an injunction may be issued by the federal district court which would prohibit worker strikes for 80 days while other emergency negotiating machinery operates.
c. Officers of labor unions must file affidavits indicating that they have not been affiliated with the Communist Party and have not supported any subversive organization. (Special amendment.)

Some union activities made unlawful by provisions of the Taft–Hartley Act are:

a. Restraining employees in the exercise of their rights;
b. Restraining an employer in the selection of his bargaining representative;
c. Causing an employer to discriminate against an employee on account of his relationship with a labor organization, subject to the exception of valid union-shop relationships;
d. Refusing to bargain collectively with an employer by the designated union;
e. Inducing employees to stop working so as to force an employer or self-employed person to join a union;
f. Inducing employees to stop working so as to force the employer to bargain with the union where another union has been certified as the bargaining agent;
g. Inducing employees to stop working so as to force the reassignment of particular work from one union to a different union;
h. Charging excessive fees to become a member of the union;
i. Attempting to charge an employer to pay for services that are not performed.

Landrum–Griffen Act (Labor–Management Reporting and Disclosure Act of 1959)   This Act develops a code of conduct for unions, union officers, and employers, and introduces a set of amendments to the Taft–Hartley Act. The code of conduct includes the following provisions:

a. Each labor organization is required to have a constitution and by-laws containing minimum standards and safeguards for the rights of union members. Reports concerning policies, procedures, and financial status must be filed with the Secretary of Labor;
b. Union members' rights are to be protected within the union;
c. Standards are to be established for union trusteeships and union elections;
d. Employers and labor relations consultants are required to file reports on expenditures and arrangements that affect employees' organizing and bargaining rights.

   Amendments to the Taft–Hartley Act are as follows:
a. State courts and labor relations boards gain jurisdiction over cases rejected by the NLRB under its jurisdictional standards;
b. Permanently replaced economic strikers are given the right to vote in representative elections conducted by the NLRB within one year of the strike;
c. Employment of the secondary boycott is limited.

The Civil Rights Act of 1964   Title VII of this Act makes it unlawful for employers, labor unions, and employment agencies connected with interstate commerce to discriminate in employment or membership against an individual on the basis of his race, color, religion, sex, or national origin.

Age Discrimination in Employment Act, 1968   This Act makes it unlawful for employers, labor unions, or employment agencies to discriminate against people in the 40–65 age category in employment or membership.

Glossary of important labor law terms

Agency shop   A union–management agreement in which employees, in order to continue their employment, must either become members of the elected union or pay the union a service fee.

Ally doctrine   Ally employers—those who do farmed-out "struck work" or who are very closely identified with the struck employer—are excepted from secondary boycott prohibitions.

American Can doctrine   A rule that a craft unit cannot be carved out of an established industrial unit, if the industrial unit has a successful history of bargaining for the unit seeking to break away and has adequately represented the interests of that unit.

Arbitration   The hearing and determining of a dispute between parties by a person chosen and agreed to by both parties. The arbitrator generally has decision-making power, but his power is limited by the interpretation of the wording of the agreement.

Assumption of risk principle   A defense used by an employer to free himself from liability for injury to a worker if it could be proved that the injury was caused by risks that are common to the type of employment and were thus assumed when the person took the job.

Balkanization   A large number of small competing units of employees engaged in very similar occupations and sharing a community of interest.

Bootleg contract   A collective-bargaining agreement that is contrary to provisions of the Taft–Hartley Act.

Boulwarism   A bargaining technique developed at General Electric in which the employer makes a single offer anticipating union demands, and upon presenting the offer, maintains a take-it-or-leave-it attitude throughout bargaining.

Boycott   Organized pressure by the union against an employer in the form of a refusal to deal with that employer, in order to induce a change in a practice or practices by that employer.

Boycott, secondary   Exertion of economic pressure by the union against a third party that continues to deal with the employer who has been struck.

Boycott, tertiary   Exertion of economic power on suppliers, customers of a supplier, or a customer of an employer with whom a labor difficulty exists. This type of boycott is generally held to be illegal.

Captive audience speech   An appeal or presentation made by the employer to the employees concerning labor disputes when the employer does not allow the union an opportunity to reply under similar conditions.

Cease-and-desist order   An order issued by a labor relations board demanding that an employer or a union abstain from an unfair labor practice.

Checkoff   The employer's deduction of a certain charge, mainly dues, from the employee's wage, which charge is then turned over to the union.

Closed shop   A plant in which all employees belong to the union and in which only union workers are hired.

Collective bargaining   The entire process of negotiation by which a union and an employer come to an agreement concerning wages, working conditions, and other bargainable issues, culminating in a contract.

Common law   That law which has been handed down from English judicial decisions and the unwritten code of law.

Conciliation   An attempt by a third party to bring disputants together by persuasion and compromise. The conciliator is not vested with power to force a settlement.

Conspiracy doctrine (Hunt Decision)   The early nineteenth century doctrine that concerted employee action, even to raise wages, was subject to criminal prosecution as conspiracy, even though the means would be legal if the same action were taken by individuals.

Contract-bar rules Rules applied to determine when a current contract between the union and the management will bar a representative election sought by a rival union.

Craft union A labor organization whose membership is restricted to persons engaged in a specific type of work or occupation.

Escalator clause A clause in a union–management contract requiring wage and salary adjustments to changes in the cost of living.

Exclusive bargaining rights A situation in which no other union than the elected union can represent those employees for a specified time period and workers cannot bargain individually.

Fact-finding Investigation of a dispute by an impartial individual or panel which issues a report stating the cause of the dispute. The fact-finder may also issue recommendations for settling the dispute.

Featherbedding Receiving payment for work that is not required by the employer or performing paid tasks that are not really necessary for completion of the work.

Gissel test A set of principles used to establish bargaining rights without holding a representational election.

Good-faith bargaining Negotiation with a bona fide intent to reach an agreement if agreement is possible.

Grievance machinery The structure that exists in an agreement to settle disputes that arise out of contractual interpretation and application.

Hiring hall The hiring of union workers by the employer through a central union office. The hiring hall is most prevalent where employment is intermittent. The central office tends to spread the available work around more evenly.

Hot-cargo agreement An agreement between a union and a company in which the firm agrees not to do business with a different employer who has been struck.

Impasse The situation if no agreement has been reached due to irreconcilable differences in the parties' positions after exhaustive good faith bargaining has taken place.

Industrial union A labor organization whose membership is restricted to persons working in a plant or industry, regardless of the type of work they perform.

Initiation fee Fee charged to an individual, above and beyond the normal union dues, to become a member of the union.

Injunction A mandatory order issued by a court of equity to cause some action to take place or to prevent the action from taking place. It is generally a short-run measure until the problem can be adjudicated.

Joy–Silk doctrine   The rule that an employer may refuse to recognize a union if the employer believes in good faith that the union does not have majority status.

Local   A group of organized workers who hold a charter from an international or national union.

Lockout   An act by an employer in which employees are prevented from working at their jobs in an effort to compel the employees to accede to the terms of employment desired by management.

Make-whole orders   An order that specifies that an employee be reimbursed for wages lost because of discrimination. The level of reimbursement shall be the level of the higher paying job that person was denied because of discrimination.

Mediation   An attempt by a third party to bring disputants together by persuasion and compromise. The mediator can make proposals for settlement of the dispute and in this respect mediation differs from conciliation.

Midwest Piping doctrine   A rule that states that it is an unfair labor practice for an employer to recognize one of two or more competing unions after a representation question has been submitted to the NLRB.

Miranda–Hughes Tool doctrine   The ruling set down that the National Labor Relations Board has exclusive jurisdiction to remedy unfair labor practices.

Multi-unit bargaining   A collective bargaining arrangement that covers more than one plant.

Negotiation   The process of settling a labor dispute directly between the parties involved.

One-year rule   A rule that states that representation elections may not be held more than once a year in any given bargaining unit.

Open shop   A plant in which an employee is not required to join the union or to pay dues to the union to maintain his employment, but can remain unaffiliated.

Plant seizure   The act by which the government takes over the operation of a plant if threatened by labor–management difficulties, for the protection of the public interest.

Picketing   The patrolling of a struck establishment by union members and sympathizers carrying signs to indicate that the employer is engaged in unfair labor practices or simply to announce that a strike is in progress.

Picketing, secondary   The picketing around the place of business of a customer or supplier of the primary employer with whom the union has a dispute, to cause the object of the picketing to refrain from dealing with the primary employer.

Picketing, tertiary The unlawful picketing of a customer or supplier of an employer with whom the union has a dispute.

Racketeering Corrupt practices by union leaders, usually involving kickbacks, favors, and the misuse of funds, against either management or union members.

Runaway shops The relocation of a plant, thus causing unemployment of union members. It is an unfair labor practice if the move was designed to discourage union membership.

Scab Term, meaning "traitor," applied to a nonstriking employee by fellow employees on strike; also applied to persons (called strikebreakers) hired by the employer to replace striking workers.

Seniority Employees who have worked the longest will generally be the last ones laid-off and the first ones rehired and considered for promotions.

Shop steward The union representative, elected at the local level, who is in charge of handling labor's grievances with the representatives of management.

Slowdown A concerted slowing down of production by employees to bring economic pressure upon the employer.

Speilberg doctrine The standards set by the National Labor Relations Board for deferral to arbitration awards, that: (1) the proceedings be fair and regular; (2) all parties agree to be bound; and (3) the decision not be repugnant to the purposes and policies of the National Labor Relations Act.

State right-to-work laws Section 14(b) of Taft–Hartley Act which allowed the state to legislate so as to outlaw union security provisions.

Statute of limitations The period during which suit must be brought in response to an activity in violation or in supposed violation of the law. In most instances, state laws of limitations govern unfair labor practice cases where no federal law expressly governs the time period.

Steelworks trilogy A series of cases that establishes the function of the courts in the arbitration process and establishes certain guidelines for the arbitrators and the courts.

Strike A concerted stopping of work in order to compel an employer to agree to workers' demands or in protest against terms or conditions imposed by employment.

Strike, economic A strike not caused or prolonged by an unfair labor practice on the part of the employer.

Strike, sit-down An unlawful strike during which the strikers remain on the employer's property taking possession of the property and excluding others from entry.

Strike, unfair labor practice   A strike launched in response to an unfair labor practice committed by an employer.

Strike, wildcat   An unauthorized strike in violation of a collective-bargaining agreement for which the parent union disclaims responsibility.

Surface bargaining   The situation when one party rejects the other party's proposals, tenders his own proposal, and does not attempt to reconcile the differences.

Sweetheart contracts   A contract in which the employer agrees to pay union dues for the employees in return for certain concessions from the union.

Thayer doctrine   The standard that an employer is free to discharge economic strikers, without having to hire them back, if the economic strike activity falls outside §7 of the Wagner Act.

Union security   Collective bargaining issues, such as check-off and closed shop, in which the employer helps the union organize and maintain the work force.

Union shop   A union–management agreement in which all workers must belong to the union to keep their jobs. The employer can hire whomever he wants, but the hired workers must join the union within a specified time or lose their jobs.

Woolworth formula   A formula that requires that back pay due a worker be computed on a quarterly basis.

Work jurisdiction   The right claimed by a union in its charter that its members alone shall do certain work.

Workman's compensation   Payment of benefits to an employee injured on the job or affected by an occupational disease.

Yellow dog contract   A contract that specified that in return for employment the worker would not join a union.

Zipper clause   A clause that indicates that the parties to the bargaining had full opportunity to bargain, that the contract is complete, and that each waives his right to bargain on any subject during the term of the agreement.

Additional References

Charles J. Morris, *The Developing Labor Law,* American Bar Association, The Bureau of National Affairs, Inc. 1971, Washington, D.C.

A. Howard Myers, *Labor law and legislation,* South-Western Publishing Co., 1968, Cincinnati, Ohio.

Primer of Labor Relations, The Bureau of National Affairs, Inc., 1971, Washington, D.C.

Index